Companion to Victorian Popular Fiction

Companion to Victorian Popular Fiction

Edited by
Kevin A. Morrison

McFarland & Company, Inc., Publishers
Jefferson, North Carolina

LIBRARY OF CONGRESS CATALOGUING-IN-PUBLICATION DATA

Names: Morrison, Kevin A., 1976– editor.
Title: Companion to Victorian popular fiction / edited by Kevin A. Morrison.
Description: Jefferson, North Carolina : McFarland & Company, Inc., Publishers, 2018 | Includes bibliographical references and index.
Identifiers: LCCN 2018039531 | ISBN 9781476669038 (softcover : acid free paper) ∞
Subjects: LCSH: English fiction—19th century—History and criticism—Handbooks, manuals, etc.
Classification: LCC PR871 .C644 2018 | DDC 823/.809—dc23
LC record available at https://lccn.loc.gov/2018039531

BRITISH LIBRARY CATALOGUING DATA ARE AVAILABLE

ISBN (print) 978-1-4766-6903-8
ISBN (ebook) 978-1-4766-3359-6

© 2018 Kevin A. Morrison. All rights reserved

No part of this book may be reproduced or transmitted in any form or by any means, electronic or mechanical, including photocopying or recording, or by any information storage and retrieval system, without permission in writing from the publisher.

Front cover: James Jacques Joseph Tissot, *Hide and Seek*, oil on wood, 28⅞" × 21¼", 1877 (National Gallery of Art)

Printed in the United States of America

*McFarland & Company, Inc., Publishers
Box 611, Jefferson, North Carolina 28640
www.mcfarlandpub.com*

Table of Contents

Preface
1

The Companion
3

Works Cited
279

About the Contributors
297

Index
309

Preface

Over the course of the nineteenth century in Britain, profound and intertwined changes in the production and consumption of literature took place. Domestic and international copyright laws were harmonized and enforced. Book contracts were standardized. A system of royalties was established and, progressively, made more equitable. The professional agent emerged as an intermediary between author and publisher. Technological advances and the reduction of so-called knowledge taxes led to an explosion of print.

Through various legislative efforts that sought to establish some level of compulsory education, dramatic increases in literacy rates led to a significant expansion in the number of readers. Market trends and customer needs increasingly displaced the pricey so-called triple-decker—the dominant mode of publishing novels in three volumes for much of the period—with the comparatively affordable single-volume novel. The private circulating library—the principal means of distributing literature for much of the century—was gravely challenged by the emergence of the modern public library, supported by taxes and private donations, and also of secondhand shops. Penny weeklies and more expensive middle-class magazines featured serialized novels, and newspapers carried reprints. By the 1880s rapidly increasing literacy and an expanding market exacerbated a long-held distinction between serious and popular fiction.

With more than 300 incisive cross-referenced entries, this *Companion to Victorian Popular Fiction* provides an introduction to representative fictional works written for the mass-publishing market and read by large segments of the British public. It also includes biographical sketches of principally noncanonical writers and their publishers, the topics that concerned them, and the popular genres they helped to establish, shape, or refine. Although companions to certain aspects of popular fiction have been published, there has not been, until now, a single volume devoted to popular fiction in its entirety.

The *Companion to Victorian Popular Fiction* is organized alphabetically by authors, titles and subjects. Many entries contain references to primary and secondary sources. If a specific source is cited, the author's last name, date of publication, and page number(s) will appear parenthetically in the text. If a work has been consulted but not specifically cited, it will appear under "see also" at the end of the entry.

A complete Works Cited list appears at the end of the volume. If entries from standard reference works such as the *Oxford Dictionary of National Biography* or the *Dictionary of Nineteenth-Century Journalism in Great Britain and Ireland* have been used, these are indicated by abbreviation of the work as a whole (e.g., ODNB), rather than citation of an individual entry. A complete list of acronyms used appears at the beginning of the Works Cited list.

Names and titles that have their own entries appear in bold. If a periodical, short story or novel has its own entry, then dates of publication will be found only there; otherwise, they appear in parentheses throughout.

The Companion

Ada, the Betrayed, or the Murder at the Old Smithy (1843–44). **Penny dreadful** by **James Malcolm Rymer**. *Ada the Betrayed* opens on a stormy night when a man rushes out of a burning smithy, screaming frantically for help while holding a baby. The novel fast-forwards ten years and introduces the characters Jacob Gray and his cousin Henry. As the story unfolds it becomes clear that Henry is not only a girl, but also the same child that was saved from the fire at the smithy. Jacob Gray has disguised her as a boy and raised her in secret, so he may use her to extort money from the Squire of Learmont, who hired him and the smith Andrew Britton ten years ago to assist in the murder of his brother Mark Learmont and baby cousin Ada, who is the true heir to the Learmont estate. Gray also uses Ada and a written confession of the murder to ensure that Learmont cannot kill him to conceal his dark secret. Once Ada discovers that Gray is not her real uncle, she tries to escape. After one failed attempt, she approaches the magistrate Francis Harleton, who agrees to help her solve the mystery of her birth. Now Ada is relatively safe, the story primarily focuses on the mind games played by Gray and Learmont. The latter triumphs as he manages to locate both Gray's hideout and his confession, and has Andrew Britton murder him brutally with a cleaver. When the Squire is arrested for the murder, it is revealed that Ada is the rightful Lady Learmont. *Ada the Betrayed* has all the characteristics of a true **penny blood**; it has a wronged heroine, exciting rooftop adventures, a fair amount of violence, blood and corpses, as well as comical lower-**class** figures, such as Britton the smith and Bond the butcher.—Marjolein Platjee

Adventures of Sherlock Holmes (1892). Collection of **short stories** by **Arthur Conan Doyle**. Appearing in the *Strand Magazine* between July 1891 and December 1892, *The Adventures of Sherlock Holmes* brings together the first dozen short stories about the detective **Sherlock Holmes** and friend and assistant Dr. Watson: "A Scandal in Bohemia," "The Red-Headed League," "A Case of Identity," "The Boscombe Valley Mystery," "The Five Orange Pips," "The Man with the Twisted Lip," "The Blue Carbuncle," "The Speckled Band," "The Engineer's Thumb," "The Noble Bachelor," "The Beryl Coronet," and "The Copper Beeches." When Conan Doyle submitted the first two stories to the *Strand*, he reported that its editor "Greenhough Smith liked them from the first, and encouraged me to go ahead with them" (Lellenberg, Stashower, & Foley 2008: p. 293). Smith would reminiscence in the 1920s about his reaction in more enthusiastic terms:

> I at once realized that here was the greatest short story writer since Edgar Allan Poe. I remember rushing into Mr Newnes's room and thrusting the stories before his eyes.... Here, to an editor jaded with wading through reams of impossible stuff, comes a gift from Heaven, a godsend in the shape of

the story that brought a gleam of happiness into the despairing life of this weary editor. Here was a new and gifted story-teller: there was no mistaking the ingenuity of the plot, the limpid clearness of the style, the perfect art of telling a story [Lellenberg, Stashower, & Foley 2008: p. 293].

Holmes and Watson were first introduced toward the back of the magazine: they rapidly won their way to the front and nearly doubled the magazine's circulation.

As a test case, "A Scandal in Bohemia" offers important insights into both the character and Conan Doyle's method. The story follows **A Study in Scarlet** and **The Sign of Four**: Watson is now married and he has left Baker Street and returned to civil practice; while Holmes remained "buried among his old books, and alternating from week to week between cocaine and ambition, the drowsiness of the drug, and the fierce energy of his own keen nature" (2008: 1, p. 187). A visit from the King of Bohemia presents Holmes with a puzzle: five years ago, the King had fallen in love with Irene Adler, an adventuress, and with whom he had shared a photograph. According to the King, who is about to be married, Alder threatens to send it to his fiancée's family, which would bring his marital plans to an end. Disguised as a groom, Holmes spies on Irene and inadvertently becomes witness to her own marriage. Holmes coordinates a scene so that he—this time in the disguise of a Nonconformist clergyman—is brought into her home; Watson throws into the room a plumber's smoke-rocket and raises a cry of fire; and Irene, in her agitation, reveals the photograph's hiding place. The next day, Holmes, Watson, and the King visit her home, only to find that she had departed with her husband, and that she had left behind a photograph of herself in an evening dress and a letter revealing how she had followed Holmes and Watson back to Baker Street and promising that the King can be at peace: "The King may do what he will without hindrance from one whom he has cruelly wronged. I keep it [their photograph] only to safeguard myself, and to preserve a weapon which will always secure me from any steps which he might take in the future" (2008: 1, p. 204). As a reward, Holmes asks only for Irene's picture, "And when he speaks of Irene Adler, or when he refers to her photograph, it is always under the honourable title of *the* woman" (2008: 1, p. 205).

"Bohemia" illustrates Holmes' ability to shift shapes and makes reference to some of his prodigious talents: "It was not merely that Holmes changed his costume. His expression, his manner, his very soul seemed to vary with every fresh part that he assumed. The stage lost a fine actor, even as science lost an acute reasoner, when he became a specialist in crime" (2008: 1, p. 199). Holmes' attitude toward the King places him centrally on Irene's side. When the King laments that she is not at his level socially, Holmes' response—"she seems indeed to be on a very different level to your Majesty" (1: p. 204)—was made "coldly" (2008: 1, 204) and Holmes is visibly drawing on the register of intellect; indeed, after he receives the photograph, "He bowed, and, turning away without observing the hand which the King had stretched out to him, he set off in my company for his chambers" (2008: 1, 204). Holmes' maxims are especially revealing of his method. He explains to Watson: "You see, but you do not observe" (2008: 1, p. 189). When, in the story's early stages, Holmes shared the King's cryptic note with Watson, he reveals his reluctance to speculate: "It is a capital mistake to theorize before one has data. Insensibly one begins to twist facts to suit theories, instead of theories to suit facts" (2008: 1, p. 189). Holmes' influence is shown to be international: Watson speaks "of his summons to Odessa in the case of the Trepoff murder, of his clearing up of the singular tragedy of the Atkinson brothers at Trincomalee, and finally of the mission which he had accomplished so delicately and successfully for the reigning family of Holland" (2008: 1, p. 187). Holmes refers to others, as a means of comparison, even as he is solving this mystery: "When a woman thinks that her house is on fire, her instinct is at once to rush to the thing which she values most. It is a perfectly overpowering impulse, and I have more than once taken advantage of it. In the case of the Darlington substitution scandal it was of use to me, and also in the Arnsworth Castle business" (2008: 1, p. 201). Such allusions pepper the canon, giving it texture and substance, and they demonstrate how Watson's faith in the sleuth is developed through experience rather than implicit faith (Ue 2017).—TOM UE

See also ODNB

Ainsworth, William Harrison (1805–1882). English novelist and editor. Although his Mancunian father wanted him to pursue a legal career, Ainsworth moved to London in his early twenties and rapidly established a career as a novelist. His best-known novels of the 1830s were examples of the **Newgate novel**: the **Gothic** romance, *Rookwood* (1834), which featured Dick Turpin, and *Jack Sheppard* (1839), which was an instant hit in popular and penny theaters. Recent Ainsworth scholarship has explored how *Jack Sheppard* both exemplified and facilitated the development of a democratizing mass culture.

The criticism which *Jack Sheppard* in particular attracted encouraged Ainsworth to turn to historical romance, often focusing on important heritage sites: *The Tower of London* (1840), *Old St. Paul's* (1841) and *Windsor Castle* (1843) are his best-known works in this vein, and arguably he made an important contribution here to the preservations of historical buildings of national importance by highlighting their neglect. Ainsworth's early novels were inventively illustrated, often by George Cruikshank, with whom he worked in a notably interactive **collaboration**: these images may well explain the celebrity which he enjoyed in the 1840s, when he was even seen as a potential rival to **Charles Dickens**. Ainsworth was also an important figure in the world of the periodical: initially associated with the talented circle of writers for *Fraser's Magazine*, he edited ***Bentley's Miscellany*** after Dickens, as well as founding and editing his own periodical, *Ainsworth's Magazine* (1841–1854) and owning and editing the ***New Monthly Magazine***.

Ainsworth's career went into decline by the late 1840s, both because the historical romance was much less popular and the quality of his novels declined. *The Lancashire Witches* (1848), however, enjoyed popularity in his native county and has recently been re-issued. Most of Ainsworth's novels deal with what Peter Mandler has identified as "Olden Time"—the Tudor and Jacobean periods. They privilege exciting Gothic plots and detailed descriptions of historical settings, costumes, and ceremonies over character development to create a dramatic, dangerous, and highly sensory and evocative version of the English past. This "picturesque" approach to the past can be seen as the precursor to Hollywood historical epics and some of the interpretative techniques used in the modern heritage industry.—ROSEMARY ANN MITCHELL

See also ODNB, WI

Alcoholism. Also intemperance, intoxication, inebriety, habitual drunkenness, dipsomania, drinking monomania. In early and mid–Victorian texts, drinking is represented as a moral disease leading to moral bankruptcy and associated particularly with the working classes, with inadequate housing and contaminated water supplies sending the poor to public houses. The temperance movement, which emerged in the 1820s, sought to offer the poor alternative, improving **religious** and political activities. Realist fiction frequently introduces cautionary tales of working-class drunkenness. In Elizabeth

6 Alcoholism

Gaskell's *Mary Barton* (1848), the title character's father John and aunt Esther both drink to excess; after John commits murder and Esther falls into prostitution, both die. Stephen Blackpool's foul, drunken wife in **Charles Dickens**'s *Hard Times* (1854) offers another mid-century warning against working-class female drinking. Indeed, alcoholism—distinguished from moderate social drinking—features frequently in Dickens's work, from his earliest sketches such as "Making a Night of It" (1835), "Gin Shops" (1835) and "The Drunkard's Death" (1836) to caricatures such as the dissolute nurse Mrs. Gamp in *Martin Chuzzlewit* (1844) and Jenny Wren's infantile father Mr. Dolls in *Our Mutual Friend* (1865). Alcohol also results in spectacular deaths in Dickens's work: *Bleak House*'s (1853) Krook, whose diet consists chiefly of gin, spontaneously combusts, while Sydney Carton, the talented but alcoholic and depressed young lawyer of *A Tale of Two Cities* (1859), redeems himself by taking another man's place at the guillotine.

In female-authored fiction, alcoholism characterizes inadequate **fathers** and husbands. In Anne Brontë's *The Tenant of Wildfell Hall* (1848), Helen Huntingdon flees her abusive husband Arthur, who spends his time drinking with his rakish companions and even attempts to make his young son a drinker before dying following a drunken riding accident. Male alcoholics are particularly prominent in **sensation fiction**: in **Mrs. Henry [Ellen] Wood**'s *East Lynne*, Lady Isabel Vane is forced into a loveless **marriage** by the death of her dissolute father, leading to her subsequent adultery. In **Mary Elizabeth Braddon**'s *Lady Audley's Secret*, Helen Talboys's alcoholic father fails to provide for her and her **child** after her husband's desertion, forcing her to embark on a double life that will result in her incarceration and death. Alcoholic husbands also feature in later **New Woman** fiction, for example *The Career of Candida* (1896) by George Paston (**Emily Morse Symonds**).

The perception of inebriety as a moral flaw or a vice gave way in the late century to scientific explanations of human behavior and Darwinian notions of heredity and degeneration. Alcoholism came to be seen as a hereditary **disease**, a symptom of a wider social pathology that also included insanity, criminality, and **poverty**. Late-Victorian literary naturalism acknowledges degeneration theory in deterministic narratives in which alcoholics appear as prisoners of their heredity, which they pass to their offspring. In slum fiction such as **George Gissing**'s *The Netherworld* (1889) and **Arthur Morrison**'s *A Child of the Jago* (1896), drunkenness is the norm, parental drinking producing degenerate children. In Thomas Hardy's *The Mayor of Casterbridge* (1886), Michael Henchard takes an oath to abstain from alcohol for twenty years after selling his wife in drunken stupor, only to fall tragically and in keeping with his heredity at the conclusion of the promised period. Naturalist fiction explicitly associates alcoholism with the pressures of modernity. The title character in Hardy's *Jude the Obscure* (1895) seeks to drown his existential questionings in liquor, while in Gissing's New Woman novel *The Odd Women* (1893) Virginia Madden's inability to cope with changing gender roles drives her to drinking.

Toward the end of the century, dynamic models of psychology, including research into duality, challenged notions of stable personality by suggesting that identity, memory, and thought could be disrupted by traumatic experiences, suppressed drives, and external agents such as alcohol. With alcohol consumption peaking in the 1870s, **the law** came to recognize drunkenness as a **mental illness** and a category of diminished responsibility. The *Habitual Drunkards' Act* of 1879 defined an inebriate as "a person who, not being amenable to any jurisdiction in lunacy, is, notwithstanding, by reason of habitual intemperate drinking of intoxicating liquor, at times dangerous to himself or herself, or to others, or incapable of managing himself or herself, and his or her affairs" (42 & 43 *Vict.*, ch. 19, s. 3), providing for the voluntary commitment of alcoholics for treatment. The *Inebriates' Act* of 1898 allowed for the involuntary detention of criminal drunkards. Late-Victorian **Gothic fiction** seized upon this blurring between alcoholism and insanity, creating possession narratives in which stable personality is dramatically transformed. **Robert Louis Stevenson**'s Dr. Jekyll swallows a potion to alter himself into the uninhibited Mr. Hyde, while **Bram Stoker**'s Count **Dracula** is driven by an insatiable thirst that he transmits to his **vampiric** offspring. The symptoms of delirium tremens were dramatically depicted in the monstrous hallucinations suffered by disturbed, explicitly alcoholic characters who eventually commit **suicide**: the unnamed protagonist of Ernest G. Henham's *Tenebrae* (1898) is a hereditarily insane, alcoholic drug addict who kills his brother while suffering from terrifying visions of monstrous spiders, and in **Richard Marsh**'s *The Goddess: A Demon* (1900), alcohol-induced delusions lead Edwin Lawrence to commit fratricide.—MINNA VUOHELAINEN

See also Berridge 1999, Foxcroft 2007, Harrison 1971, Margolis 2002, McAllister 2014, McCandless 1984, North 1997, Pick 1989, Reed 2006, **Science**, Trotter 2010, Wiener 1990, Wood 2001

Alice's Adventures in Wonderland (1865). Children's novel by **Lewis Carroll**. Carroll wrote this text as a tribute to his child friend, Alice Liddell, in an attempt to immortalize her **childhood** innocence. Illustrated by John Tenniel and published in 1865, the novel follows Alice, a young British girl, who falls down a rabbit hole and enters the magical world of Wonderland. Divided into twelve chapters, each chapter depicts a different encounter in Alice's new world. Within the alterity of Wonderland, Alice encounters numerous anthropomorphic characters who guide her path: the Hatter, the Cheshire Cat, the White Hare, and the Caterpillar. The story begins with Alice sitting tirelessly on the banks of a river, readily bored of her sister's reading. She sees a curious white rabbit and follows him down a rabbit hole, falling into the peculiar world of Wonderland. There, she encounters many fantastical adventures and each character serves an existential purpose in relation to her quest. In order to proceed through the doors of Wonderland, Alice must eat and drink certain magic elements in order to find the right size of her physicality. Of course, this aspect of the text can be interpreted as a socio-normative association of feminine beauty. From there, Alice proceeds to travel through Wonderland in an attempt to find a way home. She attends a mad tea party with the Hatter, Dormouse, and March Hare, and attempts to understand the peculiar world she has found herself inhabiting. She later encounters the Red Queen and royal court, providing evidence in a court case involving the stealing of tarts. Alice later stands up against the Red Queen, and wakes up on the banks of the river Thames. Concluding that Wonderland was a curious dream, she ponders the possibilities of her imagination. Alice's stay in Wonderland embodies varying aspects of Victorian realism; the depiction of ideology and idealism is highlighted, and can be deconstructed through the theoretical lens of literary criticism. Initially, Carroll intended to self-illustrate the novel but lacked the artistic finesse. Having worked with illustrator John Tenniel at *Punch* magazine, Carroll selected him to help create the perfect Wonderland. Tenniel's **illustrations** are a pivotal aspect of Carroll's novel. Published by Macmillan and Co. in 1865, *Alice's Adventures in Wonderland* was initially poorly received. However, following the publication of its 1871 sequel *Through the Looking Glass and What Alice Found There*, the first Alice story became increasingly popular. It has recently attracted significant interest, including Robert Douglas-Fairhurst's 2015 study, *The Story of Alice: Lewis Carroll and the Secret History of Wonderland*, and various essays by Maria Nikolajeva. It is a work of **children's literature** that can be productively read in terms of gender identity, ideology, and female agency.—JADE DILLON

All Men Are Liars (1895). Novel by **Joseph Hocking**. *All Men are Liars* focuses on the gifted but impressionable Stephen Edgecumbe, whose struggles with the cynicism of the title underlie the dramatic plot as he vacillates between two main worldviews. Concepts of hypocrisy, lying, and canting are set against "truth," but applied confusingly to differing opinions and people. Stephen becomes "The Duke" in a paradoxical attempt at authenticity in which he plumbs the depths, "everywhere is lies, filth, hell" (Hocking 1895: p. 323). Reading Stephen's story dramatizes the dilemma of whom to believe and trust, and fears about hypocrisy and deception. But the message of social responsibility, including temperance, triumphs.—ANNEMARIE MCALLISTER

Allen, Grant [Charles Grant Blairfindie Allen] (1848–99). Canadian writer. Grant Allen was a Canadian-born, Oxford-educated, British-based man of letters who published prolifically in a wide variety of genres from 1877 until his untimely death at the age of 51. Of his thirty-seven novels, eight story collections, sixteen non-fiction books about **science** and nature, six travel guides, dozen other miscellaneous works, and huge body of journalism, only a handful of texts are still of interest today. But this handful reveals him as a refreshingly original thinker. An atheist, evolutionist, **socialist**, and sexual radical, Allen was wildly out of step with most of his late–Victorian contemporaries. He had made a first marriage considered unsuitable by his wealthy family and lost their support. Thereafter he wrote popular fiction voluminously to earn a living while pursuing his scientific and philosophical interests. Much of his early work consisted of potboilers. But he developed the knack of appealing to the rapidly growing popular fiction readership, most of whom were female. In 1891 his manuscript *What's Bred in the Bone*, a thriller, was chosen out of twenty thousand entries as the winner of a fiction contest sponsored by *Tit-Bits* magazine. (The £1,000 prize would be worth more than £100,000 today.) Now he was financially stable enough to write works expressing his advanced and often iconoclastic views. He is chiefly remembered today for his best-selling polemical novel ***The Woman Who Did*** (1895), which scandalized late Victorians (as it was meant to), with its account of the sufferings of a Cambridge-educated single mother at the hands of patriarchal and hypocritical Victorian society. Allen, who had absorbed evolutionary thought from both Charles Darwin and Herbert Spencer, was also a pioneer in what we would now call **science fiction**. In a letter to Allen of 1895, **H. G. Wells**, who had just published ***The Time Machine***, acknowledged that "this field of scientific romance with a philosophical element which I am trying to cultivate, properly belongs to you" (Wells p. 241). Allen's *The Great Taboo* (1890) was probably the first novel to be inspired by the anthropological ideas in J.G. Frazer's *The Golden Bough* (1890). His satirical novel *The British Barbarians* (1895) is about an anthropologist from the future who time-travels back to England to find that Victorians, notwithstanding their smug belief in their superiority over the rest of mankind, were more taboo-ridden than primitive savages. Science fiction and horror-inflected **short stories** by Allen of enduring interest include "Pausodyne: A Great Chemical Discovery" (1881), on the theme of suspended animation; "A Child of the Phalanstery" (1884), about the application of **eugenics** in utopia; "Pallinghurst Barrow" (1892; alluded to by Wells in *The Time Machine*), about how the ghosts of ancient human ancestors inhabit the present; and "The Thames Valley Catastrophe" (1897), about the destruction of London by a volcanic fissure eruption. In his use of female protagonists in his late works *Miss Cayley's Adventures* and *Hilda Wade* (1900), Allen also made important contributions to adventure and **detective fiction**.—Nicholas Ruddick

See also Morton 2005, Ruddick 1997, Wells 2001/1895

All Sorts and Conditions of Men: An Impossible Story (1882). Novel by **Walter Besant**. Serially published from January to December 1882 in **Belgravia Magazine**, a once successful but by then flailing periodical, and in a three-volume edition the same year. The novel centers on two protagonists: Angela Marsden Messenger, the wealthiest heiress in England, and Harry le Breton, an East End–born but West End–bred lad. On graduating from Newnham College, Cambridge, Angela renounces political economy, her field of study, and relocates to London's East End, where she aims to immerse herself in the living conditions of workers whose labor has generated her family's vast wealth. At a boarding house, she meets le Breton under the assumed named Harry Goslett, who, having recently discovered that he was adopted, has left the East End to learn more about "my own people" (2012/1882: p. 33). Their exchange of ideas about how best to improve life in the area is the basis of their friendship and budding romance. Believing that what many working people lack is recreation and amusement, Angela and Harry conceive of a Palace of Delight that would transform "this dismal suburb into a home for refined and cultivated people!" (2012/1882: p. 84). Through her wealth, Angela actualizes their dream, and unveils the institution to the East End residents in the novel's closing chapters. Seizing on the novel's popularity, a charitable trust enlisted Besant in their efforts, utilizing his novel to mobilize support for a People's Palace serving East London. As the *Westminster Review* put it, Besant did not simply write "the novel with a purpose," a literary form created by authors who, in fashioning themselves as reformers, sought to effect social change by acting upon their readers. Rather, he "produced something better": "the novel with a result" (Billson 1892: p. 619). A critical edition was published by Victorian Secrets in 2012.—Kevin A. Morrison

A.L.O.E. (A Lady of England) [*pseud.* of Charlotte Maria Tucker] (1821–1893). English author. Mainly an author of **children's literature**, Tucker wrote stories that were often didactic and contained strong moral messages. Her works include *Triumph over Midian* (1866), *The Giant Killer; or, The Battle Which All Must Fight* (1855), *The Crown of Success* (1863), and *Pomegranates from the Punjab* (1878). A number of her children's stories, like *The Rambles of a Rat* (1863), feature animal characters. She moved to **India** in 1875 and worked as an evangelical missionary in Amritsar and then Batala until her death.—Melissa Purdue

See also ODNB, OECL

Anarchist/Anarchism. The political belief that no individual should be subject to authority of any kind, anarchism was a very current and truly global ideology at the end of the nineteenth century. With origins dating back to Chinese Taoism of the sixth century BCE, and to the ancient Greeks, whose word αναρχια (anarchy) describes the condition of being "without leaders," it had by this point established a long-standing intellectual, literary, philosophical and political heritage (Marshall 1992: pp. 3–73). Indeed, so varied are its traditions and influences, that it can be best understood in its modern manifestation as a plurality of ideas and beliefs cohering around one central tenet: rejection of the state. Anarchism's bearing on popular literature and culture intensified at the nineteenth century's end as the human costs of imperialism and capitalism became increasingly apparent to radicals from Europe to the Philippines, and from the North America to Argentina (Anderson 2008). Recognizing its claims that all people have the right to govern themselves, according to the principle of free and voluntary agreement, radically countered the bourgeois ethic of unhindered individualism within capitalist markets, a number of authors were fascinated by this counter-cultural phenomenon.

Whereas capitalism promised to regulate markets, society and culture, anarchists swore to disrupt the existing order and bring it to an end by dissolving the state. For this reason, their beliefs became a popular topic in the literature of the late–Victorian period and were explored in the work of novelists such as Joseph Conrad, Henry James, **Arnold Bennett**, **George Griffith**, and **Grant Allen**. Some anarchists, like Helen and Olivia Rossetti, wrote fictions of their own (Meredith 1992/1903). **Oscar Wilde**, who was deeply committed to radical politics, found in anarchism, and its stress on the moral necessity of disobedience, a revolutionary set of political-aesthetic values that could guide the writer toward self-realization and liberate art from all forms of compulsion (Wilde 2007/1891). This led the anarchist journal, *The Torch*, which was edited by the Rossettis, to complain that Wilde had been convicted in 1895 for his political beliefs, just as much as he had been persecuted and prosecuted for being a sexual dissident. Sometimes, anarchist authors even fused the avant-garde ideals of the practical artist with the innovative, even shocking practices of the revolutionary, as seen in the career of the French anarchist and critic, Félix Fénéon, who was suspected of combining his literary efforts with involvement in at least one act of propaganda by deed (Cohen 1895; Halperin 1988).

The growing prosperity and influence of the middle classes characterized the mainstream political consciousness of the 1880s and 1890s along with much of the period's literary output, but bourgeois claims toward propriety and over property were challenged by the *fin de siècle* anarchists, whose alternative ideology of individualism raised the possibility of another kind of progress. Anarchism was the discourse of the other, articulating the experience of the abandoned, the dispossessed and the degraded, and it spoke to the profound alienation of the contemporary left. Its ideological motives could not be rationalized by contemporary conservatism and its demonization was given literary expression in novels such as **Robert Louis Stevenson**'s *The Dynamiter* (1885), Coulson and E. Douglas Fawcett's **Hartmann the Anarchist** (1892), all of which portray anarchists as purely destructive, always mad and deserving, in the end, of only containment and defeat.

Yet the very liminality of anarchism appealed to avant-garde writers, popular novelists and poets, and its marginalization motivated those authors who demonized it. For Wilde, it provided a rational basis for the interpretation and resolution of material problems, and did so by promising aesthetic and political fulfillment through the achievement of self-realization. For other, less sympathetic writers, and even hostile ones like Coulson Kernahan, who edited the novelization of *The Picture of Dorian Gray*, anarchism only offered the prospect of widespread political, moral and sexual breakdown. In his **shilling shockers**, *Captain Shannon* (1897) and *The Red Peril* (1908), we find those who come into contact with anarchism encountering sexual as well as political alterity in the shape of queer villains brandishing infernal machines.

Whether perceived as revolutionaries or terrorists, anarchists, with their proposals for the immediate dissolution of contemporary capitalist society, occupied a very special place in the late-Victorian political, literary, and cultural imaginaries. Their portrayal in the popular press provided conservative writers with models for villainy, political subversion, cultural dissent, and all kinds of sexual menace. Despite these hostile portrayals, anarchism had a broader appeal among a range of counter-cultural adherents who inhabited the edges and not the centers of Victorian polity. Their "no-government ethics" proposed that new models of social organization would organically—and quite rapidly—materialize through co-operative activity founded upon humanity's instinctual desire for mutual, free association and the prospect of a life lived with "no laws, no bonds" (Kropotkin 1970/1887: p. 63).—DEAGLÁN Ó DONGHAILE

Anesthesia. Prior to the mid-nineteenth century, many patients feared surgery almost as much as the disease or injury that necessitated it. Before the discovery of effective anesthesia, there was little surgeons could do to calm their patients' nerves or alleviate their pain; thus, surgery had to be quick and both patient and surgeon had to be brave enough to face the inevitably unbearable pain. Although **medical** practitioners had long felt pain necessary to life, by the late eighteenth century attitudes toward pain were changing and scientists began looking for means to prevent or alleviate pain (Snow 2009: pp. 1–27). Three effective forms of inhalation anesthesia came into use in the early nineteenth century: nitrous oxide (discovered 1772; used 1844), first used by Dr. Horace Wells; ether (1842), first used by Dr. Crawford Williamson Long; and chloroform (1847), first used by Sir James Young Simpson. Although all three drugs brought the risk of death by overdose, they helped to bring about radical changes in dentistry, surgery, and childbirth. Dentists and surgeons could undertake longer, more complicated procedures than ever before and doctors could offer women in labor effective pain management for the first time. While many patients welcomed the use of anesthetics and accepted their associated risks, some patients and doctors feared the use of these drugs would lead some surgeons to abuse their power by performing unnecessary procedures. Furthermore, even though none of the inhalation anesthetics produce instant unconsciousness, many feared that criminals would use them, particularly chloroform, to incapacitate their victims. Nineteenth-century writers worked through these complicated attitudes toward anesthesia in their fiction, with many writing **short stories** that belong to the micro-genre of anesthesia fiction. Some stories in this micro-genre are related to **medical** fiction and deal with legitimate, well-meaning doctors using anesthesia, but most are concerned with the abuse of anesthesia by corrupt doctors or by non-medical criminals.

Writers such as **L. T. Meade** and Dr. Clifford Halifax offer **medically** realistic representations of surgeons using anesthesia responsibly and for the good of their patients. For example, in "Creating a Mind" (1895) from *Stories from the Diary of a Doctor*, Dr. Halifax undertakes experimental brain surgery to create space in a small boy's prematurely fused skull to allow his brain to grow and develop normally. Both the boy's life and his inheritance depend on the success of the operation; he cannot live long with his untreated condition and his grandfather will only leave his estate to the boy if he deems him intellectually and physically fit to be his heir. Dr. Halifax's anesthetist safely sedates the boy and the surgery is a success. Meade and Halifax's inheritance plot is reminiscent of **sensation fiction**; the Victorian taste for sensational narratives, coupled with their fear of anesthetics, made stories of the abuses of anesthesia particularly popular. For example, in "Good Lady Ducayne" (1896), **Mary Elizabeth Braddon** depicts Dr. Parravicini using chloroform on Bella Rolleston so he could take her blood and give it to Lady Ducayne to prolong her life; the young doctor, Herbert Stafford, puts a stop to this practice and saves Bella. Meanwhile, Arabella Kenealy's "A Human **Vivisection**" (1896) offers a more extreme example of a doctor abusing anesthesia. In this story, the professor pays a drunken career criminal to allow him to chloroform and vivisect him in front of an audience. However, neither the professor's victim nor his audience realize he plans to bring his victim back to consciousness to observe the effect of intense pain on the workings of the human body and to test how much pain the body can endure before death. Stories such as Braddon's and Kenealy's clearly demonstrate the fear of inhumane surgeons.

Victorian fears of the abuses of anesthesia went well beyond unscrupulous doctors using it to perform unnecessary or dangerous procedures; they were also concerned it could be used to gain power over unwitting victims or for **self-harm**. In "My Folly" (1854), Edmund Saul Dixon tells the story of a Dr. Lemaire who uses both ether and chloroform, a common practice, on a patient who has dislocated his hip. The doctor explains that he usually tries to avoid listening to his patients' rambling speech as they become unconscious, but he listens to Boisson's confession of concealing his ward's true identity and fortune; Dr. Lemaire and the narrator use this information to force him to put right the wrong. While in this case a criminal is made to reform, the story raises the possibility that anesthesia could be used against the innocent, as it is in **Braddon**'s "Dr. Carrick" (1878). Dr. Carrick uses **mesmerism** to force his patient, Squire Tregonnell, to sign a new will benefitting the doctor, and then attempts to use chloroform to murder his victim and hasten his inheritance. A similarly murderous use of chloroform is depicted in **Sir Arthur Conan Doyle**'s "The Disappearance of Lady Frances Carfax" (1911), in which Holmes saves the chloroformed Lady Carfax from being buried alive. An example of the other chief fear of chloroform, suicide, can be found in M. F. Baly's "The Mystery of the Dover Express" (1896); in this story a young woman commits **suicide** by chloroform on a train rather than face exposure as a fallen woman on the birth of her illegitimate child.

The stories mentioned here are just a few examples of the range of texts that feature the (mis)use of anesthesia. The plethora of fictional works that focus on the anxieties surrounding the use of anesthetics (including **Mrs. Henry [Ellen] Wood**'s *Oswald Cray* (1864) and **Charles Reade**'s *Hard Cash* (1863) are a peculiarly Victorian phenomenon, the obverse—as Cleere [2014] argues—of a contemporary concern with aesthetics; the number of stories and **serial**ized novels catalogued in ProQuest's *British Periodicals* database that mention chloroform drops from 145 in the 1890s to only five in the 1930s. Although anesthesia was relatively dangerous until the mid-twentieth century, as the unconscious self was more thoroughly explored, anesthesia began to lose its potent connection with Victorian **Gothic**.—Jennifer Diann Jones

See also Cleere 2014, **Medicine**, **Serialization**, Snow 2009

An Angel of Pity (1898). Novel by **Florence Marryat**. Part of the genre of antivivisection fiction, which appeared in the 1880s and 1890s in response to debates over **vivisection** (scientific experiments on living **animals**) that unfolded during the last three decades of the nineteenth century. *An Angel of Pity* tells the story of Rose Gordon, a nurse with a medical degree from Edinburgh who marries the brilliant but sinister doctor Quentin Lesquard. Rose believes that their union will achieve what she considers the true purpose of marriage: benefitting the greater good of humanity because her abilities will allow her to help advance her husband's research; the novel emphasizes Rose's talent and knowledge but also stresses that women's gifts should be put in the service of men's endeavors. When Rose discovers that Lesquard is a vivisector, she persuades him through moral influence and the threat of separation to give up the practice. With Lesquard transformed and the couple reconciled, the novel's ending reads as an allegory of separate spheres ideology, as female morality guides masculine knowledge; in this, it echoes arguments made by Victorian critics of vivisection, particularly the journalist, author, and social reformer Frances Power Cobbe.—ANNE DEWITT

See also DeWitt 2013

Anglo-Indian Novel. Combining several traditional genres, including the **domestic novel**, **romance**, and **imperial adventure**, Anglo-Indian novels concern the trials and travails of British men and women in **India** and usually leads to the marriage of the hero or heroine by the end of the narrative. In his survey of Anglo-Indian fiction, Bhupal Singh notes that the "typical novel generally begins with a voyage, bringing the hero, more often the heroine, to the shores of India" (1975: p. 2). There are "shooting-parties (generally tiger hunts), picnics, visits to places of historical interest, balls and dances" (p. 2). The hero is typically a member of the British Army or Civil Service, and the heroine is usually young and beautiful. The latter's behavior as a new member of the local Anglo-Indian community or "station" generally sparks gossip among the other British "sahibs" and "memsahibs" at the local club or government house. Indians are rarely the protagonists in these novels and are representative of prevailing racial stereotypes of the period. They are portrayed as backward, superstitious, and untrustworthy, or as loyal servants to the British. Other stock characters in Anglo-Indian fiction include overbearing aunts and well-meaning but usually inept missionaries.

The existence of this body of fiction is a direct result of the British colonization of the Indian subcontinent from the eighteenth century—when India was controlled by the East India Company—until Indian independence was declared in 1947. These novels typically explore the often troubled nature of Indo-British relations, in both personal and professional settings. Philip Meadows Taylor, one of the earliest and most influential Anglo-Indian writers, helped to establish the genre through the popular reception of several novels, including *Confessions of a Thug* (1839), *Ralph Darnell* (1865), *Seeta* (1872), *Tara* (1863), and *Tippoo Sultan* (1840). Toward the end of the nineteenth century, **Rudyard Kipling** established himself as the foremost voice of Anglo-Indian fiction with works such as the collection *Plain Tales from the Hills* (1888) and the novel *Kim* (1901). The greatest period of popularity for Anglo-Indian novels coincided with the height of British power in India. This period, known as the British Raj, began after the Indian Uprising of 1857, which resulted in British direct rule and Queen Victoria's proclamation as Empress of India in 1876. The violence of the Indian Uprising resulted in increased tensions between Indians and the British and inspired the publication of several "Indian Mutiny Novels" throughout the remainder of the Victorian period, the most famous being Taylor's *Seeta* (1872) and **Flora Annie Steel**'s *On the Face of the Waters* (1896). The violence committed against British women and children in cities such as Lucknow and Delhi during the rebellion also resulted in the creation of the Anglo-Indian rape narrative, which frequently dehumanized Indian characters and reflected British concerns over the safety of women and children in the region. For this reason, Anglo-Indian fiction written prior to 1857 tends to be more sympathetic toward Indo-British relations.

Anglo-Indian fiction is generally written by women, with some of the most well-known authors being Bithia Mary Croker, Alice Perrin, Sydney C. Grier, Fanny Emily Penny, Maud Diver, and Ethel Winifred Savi. Many Anglo-Indian women started writing fiction because of their years spent in India as the wives of men in the British Army or Indian Civil Service. Left alone for long periods of time in areas with few other Europeans, they often began writing to alleviate boredom. Because these authors were intimately connected to the workings of the British Empire, many have been criticized for being imperial apologists who created one-dimensional characters set within predictable romance narratives. Yet, while racist portrayals of Indians certainly do exist in these novels, these women also created sympathetic characters (both Indian and British) and plots that reflected the potential for increased understanding between colonizer and colonized. For instance, Fanny Penny's *Caste and Creed* (1890) and Alice Perrin's *The Stronger Claim* (1903) complicate prevailing negative stereotypes about the mixed-race, "Eurasian" community, while Maud Diver in *Lilamani* (1911) presents readers with the happy marriage of an Indian woman and an Englishman.

These Anglo-Indian novels, the majority of which were written by men and women who had firsthand knowledge of India, give readers varied depictions and unique glimpses of British colonial life. Though the narratives are often formulaic and frequently rely on stereotypical images of both Indians and the British, these novels remain important cultural works that trace the development of imperial attitudes throughout the Victorian and Edwardian periods and beyond.—Melissa Edmundson

Animals. Non-human animals play a significant role in popular fiction in the nineteenth century, mirroring the transformations occurring in human-animal relations in England. Industrialization, imperialism, and scientific progress, which caused great upheaval for English citizens and their imperial/colonial subjects, equally affected the lives of animals, for better and for worse. Certainly, the Victorian period saw the reformation of England from what had been called "the hell of dumb animals" (qtd. in Ritvo 1987: p. 126)—with bull-baiting, cock-fighting, and other violent pastimes common parts of English life—to, by the end of the century, an assumption that England led the world in its care for and protection of animals. The period also witnessed, however, the emergence of **vivisection** as a common practice in scientific circles, of big-game hunting as emblematic of imperialist **masculinity** and dominance, and of animal objectification in zoos (Ito 2014) and as taxidermied décor for the Victorian home (Amato 2015, Poliquin 2012). Non-human animals as representations were important throughout the Victorian period, and popular fiction provides us with clear examples of such representation at work.

Harriet Ritvo observes that "By the middle of the nineteenth century what has been called the Victorian cult of pets was firmly established" (p. 86), with the pet occupying a central role in the Victorian home (Flegel 2015, Kete 1994, Pearson 2011). In Victorian popular fiction, therefore, pets often model familial relationships for the reader. **Children's literature** such as **Juliana Horatia Ewing**'s *A Flatiron for a Farthing* (1872) and *Six to Sixteen: A Story for Girls* (1875), both feature children who negotiate friendship and sibling relationships through pets, while **Ouida**'s *A Dog of Flanders* (1872) and **L. T. Meade**'s *Scamp and I: A Story of City By-ways* (1872) focus on poor and isolated children who find comfort in their animal companions. Children's texts also used animal characters to teach children about adult relationships, as in Madame de Chatelain's *Pussy's Road to Ruin* (1845) and Hesba Stretton's *Only a Dog* (1888). But such uses of pet characters were not restricted to children's literature: Gyp in George Eliot's *Adam Bede* (1859), Jip in **Charles Dickens's** *David Copperfield* (1850), Diogenes in *Dombey and Son* (1848), Snap in Anne Brontë's *Agnes Grey* (1847), and the various dogs of Eliot's *Middlemarch* (1871–2) all play important roles either in teaching the human characters to care for dependent and/or significant others, or in actively helping them negotiate their interpersonal relationships. Sometimes, pets stand in as family and friends for characters, as seen with Grip in *Barnaby Rudge* (1841), the many cats of **Wilkie Collins's** Miss Dunross in *The Two Destinies* (1876), and the cat and, arguably, cow of the widows and spinsters in Elizabeth Gaskell's *Cranford* (1853). Pets in Victorian popular fiction were also used to demonstrate a character's misanthropy, as with Pilot in Charlotte Brontë's *Jane Eyre* (1847), Lady Jane in *Bleak House* (1853), Bulls-eye in *Oliver Twist* (1837–39), Vixen in *Adam Bede*, and Hugh's dog in *Barnaby Rudge*. Finally, pets might be used to show violence in the home (Surridge 1994), as in Emily Brontë's *Wuthering Heights* (1847), Dickens's *Oliver Twist*, and Anne Brontë's *The Tenant of Wildfell Hall* (1848).

Charlotte Brontë's *Shirley* (1848) also includes a scene of violence involving an animal, but in this case, the titular character believes she has been infected with rabies. Rabies as a trope in the Victorian period (Howell 2015) speaks to the anxieties of a world newly shaped by **science** and Darwinism, and to the role animal characters played in helping writers negotiate animal/human boundary crossings. The recognition that humans and animals shared greater kinship than earlier conceptions of humanity had allowed (Turner 1980: pp. 60–78) opened the door for the exploration of vexed animal/human kinship, particularly in early **science fiction** and **Gothic fiction** (McKechnie 2010), in which "Darwinian theory is the master narrative that gives birth to narratives focused on the fragility of distinctions between human and animal" (Mangum 2007: p. 170). Novels such as **Charles Kingsley's** *The Water-Babies* (1863), **Edward Bulwer-Lytton's** *The Coming Race*, **H. G. Wells's** *The Island of Doctor Moreau*, and **Bram Stoker's** *Dracula* all imagine animal/human hybrids that "were part of the century's search for human origins, but [which] also came to exemplify the limits of the human" (McKechnie 2010: p. 16). Science was certainly associated with progress in the Victorian period, but such explorations reveal fear about the increased dominance of science, with the practice of vivisection, in particular, eliciting wide controversy from the publication of Claude Bernard's *An Introduction to the Study of Experimental Medicine* in 1865 to the end of the century. This conflict is captured in Wilkie Collins's **Heart and Science** (1883), in which the odious Dr. Benjulia, a vivisector, seems to be unable to distinguish between the animals on which he experiments and the human children with whom he engages, vividly capturing the fear that vivisection deadened the heart and the morality of the "man of science."

It is therefore not surprising that the threat of vivisection appears in the late nineteenth-century novel, **Gordon Stables's** *Sable and White: The Autobiography of a Show Collie* (1893). If "heart" was the opposite of "science," then no genre sought more to make audiences feel for non-human animals than the autobiography. Developing out of the eighteenth-century's so-called "it" narrative, animal autobiographies were very much about the animal as *subject*, rather than *object*—through the animal narrators, audiences were exposed to the hardship and cruelty of human society, as well as to the depth of animal relationships and interiority. Such texts reflect the Victorian revolution in regards to the treatment of animals, as seen in the passage of the first anti-cruelty laws (1822, 1835, 1849, 1876) and the foundation of the Royal Society for the Prevention of Cruelty to Animals in 1824. Animal autobiographies were popular throughout the century, and include such texts as Harrison Weir's *Memoirs of Bob, the Spotted Terrier* (1848), Charlotte Tucker's *Rambles of a Rat* (1857), E. Burrows's *Neptune: or the Autobiography of a Newfoundland Dog* (1869), Edis Searle's *Mrs. Mouser, or, Tales of a Grandmother* (1875), Ouida's *Puck* (1878), France Power Cobbe's *Confessions of a Lost Dog* (1883), and the most well-known of all, Anna Sewell's **Black Beauty**. While these autobiographies are, of course, fantastical fictions, employing anthropomorphism to create sympathy for the animal other (Cosslett pp. 65–73), Teresa Mangum notes that *Black Beauty* "challenges the tendency to read against the narrator's animalness by insisting on the distinctiveness of the animal body" (2007: p. 159). Nevertheless, as Tess Cosslett notes, such texts also rely on "various analogies between animals and types or **class**es of humans: children, women, slaves, servants" (2006: p. 73). Such texts, that is, demonstrate the intersectionality of animal subjectivity—animal autobiographies may grant the animal narrator interiority and depth, but they also, through their recourse to "lesser" humans, participate in classed and raced divisions between humans.

This is probably most clear in popular fiction that dealt with animals via narratives of imperialism. The conquering and collecting of exotic animals, both live and dead, played a key role in representing English dominance over its empire to the English at home, via spectacle such as zoos and taxidermied wild animals. The wild animal, distinguished from the domestic pet, offered opportunities for displays of dominance and control, ones that focused less on questions of cruelty than on the need for violence in repressing "savagery." Perhaps no novel reads more as imperial allegory than **Rudyard Kipling**'s *The Jungle Books*, in which Mowgli's liminal status between boy and man, jungle and village, and human and animal, captures the complexities of colonizer/colonized subjectivity. **Imperial adventure** stories for boys, found in publications like *The Boy's Own Paper*, and in novels by writers such as **G. A. Henty, R. M. Ballantyne, H. Rider Haggard**, and Jack London (1876–1916), sought to define robust, active **masculinity** in relation to the wild, but as Teresa Mangum notes, they also revealed anxieties about the limits of human power and control: "The imperialists' arrogance gives way in Haggard's novels not only to fear that human might become prey, but to the possibility that uncharted wilderness signals a world of unimaginable power, struggle, fury, and shocking death" (2007: p. 166).

As charted here, the animal in Victorian popular fiction represented, throughout the period, primarily human fears and anxieties othered onto, or worked out, through animal characters. Certainly, such texts allow for the possibility of animal subjectivity, and in the best of them, as Mangum argues, "animal alterity bites back, ripping at the human flesh of genres" (2007: p. 157). But in a period in which non-human animals served, as they do now, as objects of material culture (Amato 2015: p. 10), their circulation within Victorian popular fiction did not guarantee them a position as subjects in their own right.—Monica Flegel

Anna Lombard (1901). Novel by **Victoria Cross**. Described variously on first publication as "disgusting," "impure," "brilliant," and "powerful," *Anna Lombard* sold six million copies, ran through over thirty editions, and remained in print until 1930. The novel's narrator, Gerald, becomes engaged to Anna but discovers that she has secretly married her servant Gaida, a Pathan whose "beauty was like a sort of magic" (2003: p. 65). Despite loving Gerald, she continues her sexual relationship with Gaida. After his death from cholera it is discovered that Anna is carrying his child. Gerald marries Anna to save her reputation, both of them agreeing that the baby must be taken away before their marriage can be consummated. This potential solution is thwarted by the awakening of Anna's maternal instinct, until, hopelessly torn between her irreconcilable loves for baby and husband, she kills the child and begins marital relations with Gerald. Deliberately courting notoriety, Cross produced in *Anna Lombard* a work that inverted conventional gender roles, treated sexuality, both male and female, with unprecedented frankness, and directly challenged contemporary assumptions about race. Its **India**n setting provides a highly eroticized background, and its conclusion retains an ability to surprise and shock a hardened twenty-first century readership.—Gail Cunningham

Anna Marsden's Experiment (1899). Novel by Ellen Williams (birth–death dates unknown). Anna Marsden is a **New Woman** who becomes increasingly dissatisfied with her lonely life in a boardinghouse and so decides to leave and return as her fictional male cousin, Richard Ward. Part of her change from Anna to Richard is inspired by her failed infatuation with another boarder in her house, Rupert Deane. After befriending Anna, Rupert falls in love with Lottie, a more feminine woman in the boardinghouse. This makes Anna realize that she has no romantic or professional future as a woman and that her future might be more hopeful if she were a man. The inhabitants of the boardinghouse do not recognize Anna in her disguise, and she becomes a success both socially and professionally as Richard. In both of her identities, Anna works as a writer; however, she demeans and dismisses the so-called women's writing that she is assigned as Anna and is fulfilled by the more masculine writing that she is able to do as Richard. Rupert and Richard become close friends and move into a house and begin writing a play together. Anna falls more in love with Richard, and must watch as he in turn falls more in love Lottie who has fallen in love with Richard. The novel culminates with Rupert proposing to Lottie who refuses him due to her feelings for Richard. Rupert wanders the rainy streets of London in his disappointment, and becomes fatally ill. Anna reveals her secret to Lottie in hopes that Lottie will accept Richard and that this event will save him. It does not; however, Anna is unable to continue life as Richard once her secret is known. The novel ends with Anna on Richard's grave mourning both Rupert and her life as Richard. —Laura Chilcoat

Anti-Semitism. Currently the most common word used to denote hostility to Jews and Jewish culture, anti–Semitism actually dates from 1879, the coinage of Wilhelm Marr, a German political journalist who sought to undermine newly won Jewish civic and legal rights. In Victorian Britain the term was first adopted when referring to anti–Jewish prejudice in Europe, but by 1885 such sentiments were increasingly seen as an English problem too. This brief genealogy raises important questions. Was anti–Semitism merely a new name for an age-old phenomenon? And what does its rapid diffusion across a wide variety of oral and written linguistic forms or genres, including idioms of class, sexuality, and race, reveal about the changing nature of Victorian society?

Controversies about the figure of "the Jew" in modern life reached growing numbers of readers during the long nineteenth century because the massive expansion of print culture brought a more varied array of images and arguments into the public domain than ever before. The work of **Charles Dickens** shows how complicated this process could be. With the creation of Fagin in his **serial** *Oliver Twist* (1837–39), Dickens invented a character to rival Shylock in Shakespeare's *The Merchant of Venice*. While his entry marked a partial break with timeworn caricatures of Jews as moneylenders, Fagin is always an outsider, a career criminal who is the enemy of society. Even before Dickens had brought his story to a close, *Oliver Twist* was widely imitated, a prey to opportunistic stage adaptations and penny plagiarisms that catered to a larger working-class readership. There was now not one Fagin but several. In *The Life and Adventures of Oliver Twiss, Edited by "Bos"* (1838–39), for example, Fagin was renamed "Solomons," transformed into a vicious murderer, and, in this cliffhanger, he could be a curiously vocal champion of the rights of the poor. Nevertheless, in both the original and its copy, Fagin/Solomons is constantly referred to as "the Jew," a blunt reminder of his essential otherness. And his acquisitiveness continued to align him with older forms of Judaeophobia.

By mid-century depictions of Jews started to take on a more elusive quality linked to the abstract, systemic properties of industrial capitalism, an association heightened by the rise of movements for economic and political change, like Chartism. In G. W. M. Reynolds's novel *The Seamstress: or, The White Slave of England* (1853) archaic and contemporary anti–Jewish representations operate in tandem. Reynolds was an active Chartist and in this text the Jews live off the major groups in society, including a debauched aristocracy, a rising industrial middle class, and a deeply impoverished proletariat. Early in the book an affable Mr. Solomon is shown collecting the debts of dukes and duchesses on behalf of an unscrupulous lawyer, but more significant is the huge luxurious emporium of Messrs. Aaron and Sons with its plate glass windows and dazzling lights whom Reynolds holds responsible for the malnutrition, ill-**health**, and ultimately the deaths of those who make the goods on sale there. The name Messrs. Aaron and Sons alluded to a much-criticized London firm of Jewish storeowners and would easily have been recognized by Reynolds's metropolitan readers. The business itself is a kind of character in the novel and the tragic heroine, needlewoman Virginia Mordaunt, never encounters the Aaron family because her work comes to the store via a series of middlewomen. For Reynolds the emporium is a symbol of the tyrannical power of capital, but the racialized opposition between the wealthy Jew and the "white slave" gives this structure of exploitation a more sinister underlying meaning.

Even when treated more charitably elsewhere in Reynolds's work, Jews were emphatically "a financial nation" (Reynolds 1847: p. 172). By the 1840s the words "nation" and "race" were often used as synonyms when identifying social groups defined by a shared history and a common lineage, properties that were widely believed to be open to scientific analysis. In practice, physiological and cultural attributes were regularly confused in these studies, as in Robert Knox's claim in *The Races of Men* (1850) that the Jews were a nomadic people who knew no frontiers. Like the capital they were rumored to attract, Jews were regarded as constantly in motion, rootless cosmopolitans who belonged nowhere. These footloose stereotypes certainly circulated between high and popular fiction, so that the devious financier Augustus Melmotte in Anthony Trollope's *The Way We Live Now* (1874–5) is suspected of being Jewish, not merely because his wife looks Jewish, but because he behaves as Jews were thought to do. Fast-forward to 1903 and Israel Herstein in John A. Steuart's *The Hebrew: A Story of the Time* has exchanged a foreign ghetto for a directorship in a solid English bank. He too is not what he seems and the exposure of his shady secrets ensures his downfall.

But Herstein differs from Melmotte because in Steuart's novel the cosmopolitan plutocrat's other face is that of the migrant, reflecting the arrival of unprecedented numbers of poor Jews in the late nineteenth century fleeing persecution in Eastern Europe. From the 1880s the figure of the alien immigrant became a disturbing phenomenon in Victorian popular fiction, usually centered on London's East End. Thus in **Margaret Harkness**'s *Captain Lobe* [**In Darkest London**], a visit to Spitalfields uncovers a former slaughterhouse man, a gentile sheltered by local Jews, whose shocking deathbed confession seems to rework the infamous legend that the infamous **Jack the Ripper** had a Jewish background. Annie Fields's 1891 **short story** "Sturdy British Stock" tells how the shoemaker Steve Marshland loses his job to cheaper, more productive Jewish workers, leading to his wife's death and the murder of his daughter so that the family "made room for the pauper alien" (1891: p. 1). The mesmeric, manipulative Svengali in **George du Maurier's** *Trilby* is an alien successor to Fagin and in **M. P. Shiel**'s futuristic *The Lord of the Sea* (1901) Jewish immigrants have taken over the country, as if the long-feared phantasmatic "alien invasion" of Britain had become a reality.—David Glover

Arkwright, Richard (1835–1918). English writer. Descendant of an illustrious family of the industrial revolution, Arkwright graduated from Cambridge in 1857. He was called to the bar in 1859 and practiced as a barrister. He married Lady Mary Caroline Charlotte Byng (1838–1933) in 1862 and served as a Conservative Member of Parliament for Leominster 1866–1875. In 1886 Arkwright published ***Driven Home: A Tale of Destiny*** under the pseudonym Evelyn Owen. It is a **melodrama**tic tale of crime with a supernatural element. In 1889 came ***The Queen Anne's Gate Mystery***, a detective story. No other fiction has been attributed to him.—Emma Kareno

At Heart a Rake (1895). Novel by **Florence Marryat**. Lady Phyllis Macnaughten is a self-proclaimed **New Woman**. Although she made a love match, she becomes stifled by the lack of freedom in marriage and begins undermining her husband's wishes by befriending unsuitable women. Cissy Bernard introduces Lady Phyllis to the women's Pushahead Club, and Lady Phyllis is accepted as their vice president, despite her husband's protests. Cissy and her brutish husband run into one another while having dinner with other partners. Although Cissy's relationship with Captain Austin is innocent, her husband, Colonel Bernard, denounces her and she leaves him in disgrace. When Lady Phyllis defends Cissy's actions and suggests that Captain Austin is partially culpable for the scandal, Lord Macnaughten proposes a separation, even though he still loves his wife. Lady Phyllis gladly accepts and visits her family in the country in order to smooth the transition and begin the search for new accommodation. When the Pushahead Club returns from their hiatus, they unanimously vote Cissy out, much to Lady Phyllis's consternation because she thought that the club was intended to protect and help women. After a passionate speech, she resigns from her position as vice-president. Meanwhile, her husband unexpectedly becomes her new neighbor. Lady Phyllis, feeling isolated and disappointed by her new lifestyle, attempts to maintain a friendship with Lord Macnaughten, but he is resistant because he still loves his wife and believes her to be indifferent. The novel ends with couple reuniting over their son's sickbed.—Sarah Kniesler

A Babe in Bohemia (1889). Novel by **Julia Frankau**. Penned under the pseudonym Frank Danby, *A Babe in Bohemia* followed Frankau's debut, ***Dr. Phillips: A Maida Vale Idyll*** (1887), a highly successful but much reviled **anti-Semitic** tale of a Jewish neighborhood in London. Frankau's second novel chronicles the life of Lucilla Lewisham, who is born and dies in "Bohemia," a moniker for the city of London, which Frankau describes as having "Palaces and pig-sties." Lucilla is raised by her father after her mother dies in childbirth, "ruined, degraded ... [and] murdered" by her husband, whom, it is suggested, has given her syphilis. Her father, the editor of *Footlights*, an entertainment review newspaper, marries Nettie, an aging burlesque actress, and their home in the affluent neighborhood of Bloomsbury routinely hosts a range of bohemian degenerates and also serves as a place of confinement. In early **childhood**, Lucilla must live in the attic with her epileptic twin brother, Marius, who is described as a "poor, slow-speeched, idiot." Marius's epilepsy is also the consequence of her sexually promiscuous father. After his death around the age of eight, Lucilla is exposed to a parade of characters, friends of her father and stepmother, who smoke, drink, carry on extramarital affairs, and tell scandalous tales of their activities. As Lucilla matures into womanhood, her father and stepmother take pleasure in exposing her to their male friends. Although Lucilla falls in love with a much older man, a married journalist named Mordaunt who is a friend of her father's, she is relentlessly pursued by an array of lecherous suitors who are also visitors to the Bloomsbury house. This leads her to run away from home. While on the streets she is "saved" by the Salvation Army. Lucilla eventually reunites with the still-married Mordaunt and the two take up living together. Although Lucilla is initially happy she struggles with the boredom and isolation that characterize her existence with him. After an epileptic fit, she realizes that she possess the same disease as Marius, and slits her wrists.

A Babe in Bohemia critically engages with the sensationalist slum fiction and investigative reporting of the 1880s. Frankau draws on many of the tropes common in depictions of London's East End, which asserted connections between **poverty** and immorality. By locating her story in the West End instead, Frankau asks readers to acknowledge the wantonness of their own neighborhoods. The novel was inevitably blacklisted by **Mudie** upon its release. Little read today, it would be of interest to scholars working in disability studies and on Anglo-Jewish writing, *fin-de-siècle* fiction, and social investigation narratives.—Audrey L. Morrison

Ballantyne, R. M. [Robert Michael Ballantyne] (1825–1894). Scottish children's novelist. Ballantyne wrote over one hundred juvenile novels, the best remembered of which is *The Coral Island* (1858). Born in Edinburgh to a family of publishers and newspaper editors, Ballantyne was the nephew of James Ballantyne (1772–1833), Sir Walter Scott's publisher. R. M. Ballantyne was known for his prolific travels which began when his early attempts at economic success took him to fur-trading outposts in Canada. Later in his life, he travelled for research purposes and endeavored to visit and experience the locations that were the settings for his novels. Choosing exotic, colonial settings for novels with titles like *The Gorilla Hunters* (1861), *The Cannibal Islands* (1869), and *Six Months at the Cape* (1879), Ballantyne wrote **imperial adventures** that evoked expansionist themes and ideologies while focusing on self-reliant and morally upright protagonists. **Robert Louis Stevenson**, in a poem contained within ***Treasure Island***'s introduction, names Ballantyne as one of his influences. Like many of his contemporary novelists writing for juvenile audiences, Ballantyne focused on the formation of **masculinity** and presented a sense of **childhood** that was not limited to domestic spaces. Though his novels have not maintained mainstream popularity, at least ten of them are currently in print in conjunction with American evangelical home-schooling curricula.—Adam Kozaczka

See also ODNB

Baring-Gould, Sabine (1834–1924). English priest, translator, antiquarian, novelist, folklorist, architect, archaeologist, hagiographer, and prolific scholar. His bibliography totals over 1200 publications, and his eclectic research includes *Iceland, Its Scenes and Its Sagas* (1853), *The Book of **Were-wolves*** (1865), the biography of Robert Stephen Hawker (1876), and *The Lives of the Saints* in sixteen volumes (1872 and 1877). His novels have been described as **melodrama**tic, romantic, and **Gothic**. *Mehalah, A Story of the Salt Marshes* (1880) is arguably his most popular novel, compared by Swinburne to *Wuthering Heights* (1847). It is set along the marshland of East Mersea, where Baring-Gould was rector from 1871 to 1881. *Mehalah* was followed by, among others, *Kitty Alone: A Story of Three Fires* (1894), *Red Spider* (1887), *Bladys of Stewponey* (1897), *Eve: A Novel* (1888), *The Broom-Squire* (1896), *Guavas the Tinner* (1896), *Domitia* (1898), and *Pabo, the Priest* (1899). Many of his novels have a West Country flavor, and were inspired by his antiquarian research into local life in Devon and Cornwall. J. E. Thomas states that Baring-Gould found novels distasteful, although he admitted to reading Thomas Hardy. Despite this, he was "first and foremost a novel writer," and the reception of his novels "can broadly be placed in three categories: adoration, moderate approval, and utter contempt" (Thomas 2015: p. 165). Baring-Gould's novels have been largely forgotten, and he is most remembered for writing the lyrics to the hymn "Onward Christian Soldiers."—Joan Passey

See also ODNB

Barrie, J. M. [**Sir James Matthew Barrie, Bart**] (1860–1937). Scottish playwright and children's novelist. Commercially successful during his lifetime, Barrie is primarily remembered for his character, Peter Pan, who first appeared in the play, *Peter Pan* (1904), which later became the novel, *Peter and Wendy* (1911). Based on the infant son of Barrie's friend, Peter Davies, Peter Pan was a mischievous boy with magical powers whose desire to remain a child forever led him and his compatriots to a mystical land later visited by Wendy Darling, Peter's love interest. The character's fame—encouraged by Barrie's sequel titled *Peter Pan in Kensington Gardens* (1906)—came to define Barrie's literary output, though he wrote many plays and novels and did not always restrict himself to writing about **childhood**.

Born in Kirriemuir in Angus, Scotland, Barrie was the son of a weaver. His biographers tend to emphasize the formative effects of this modest upbringing together with the shock occasioned by his brother's death when Barrie was six years old. After studying at the University of Edinburgh, Barrie moved to London where he published his first two successful works, the collections *Auld Licht Idylls* (1888) and *A Window in Thurms* (1889). Although these early works emphasized child-characters, they were equally about Scottish culture and tradition and became very popular with a tourism-inclined English audience. Some of Barrie's work has thus been considered part of the sometimes disparaged Kailyard tradition in Victorian Scottish literature: a sort of Scottish popular pastoral genre espousing rural simplicity as an ideal. Barrie was also an avid commentator on what he saw as the constructed distinctions of British socio-economic **class**, and mocked upper class ideologies in many of his texts. He devoted his play, *The Admirable Crichton* (1902), to critiquing the class system with a plot involving a liberal lord and a brilliant butler shipwrecked on an island, resulting in a reversal of the social roles they played in Britain.

Married in 1894 to actress Mary Ansell, whom he would divorce in 1910, Barrie never had any children of his own, but was described by his contemporaries as possessing the mannerisms and attitudes of childhood well into his adult life and even old age. Soon after his divorce, the death of his personal friends Arthur and Sylvia Davies brought about Barrie's cooperation with other friends of the family in the unofficial adoption of the Davies children, who were the real-life models for the characters in the Peter Pan stories. Barrie's private investment in the welfare of children also translated into a philanthropic devotion to children's causes that culminated when in 1929 he donated the rights and all future proceeds from *Peter Pan* to the advancement of children's **medicine** at London's Great Ormond Street Hospital for Children. Not only a popular author, Barrie was also a public figure who was awarded the ceremonial post of Rector of St. Andrews University from 1919 to 1922 before becoming chancellor of the University of Edinburgh from 1930 until his death. He was given a baronetcy in recognition of his literary achievement by King George V in 1913, and his works continue to be in print into the twenty-first century. There have been many animated and live action film adaptations of *Peter Pan*, and Barrie's life has been the subject of many biographical movies famously including *The Lost Boys* (1987) and *Finding Neverland* (2004).—ADAM KOZACZKA

See also ODNB

The Battle of Dorking (1871). Novel by **George Tomkyns Chesney**. *The Battle of Dorking* is an early example of the **invasion literature** genre popular during the late nineteenth century. Initially published anonymously in *Blackwood's Edinburgh Magazine* in May 1871, *Dorking* drew on British fears of German invasion following the Franco-Prussian War. *Dorking* prompted an invasion controversy in the press during the 1870s drawing in figures as prominent as William Vernon Harcourt, future Chancellor of the Exchequer, and then Prime Minister William Gladstone, who publicly denounced the tale as damaging to British Foreign Policy. At the time of writing, **Chesney** was Principal of the Royal Indian Civil Engineering College outside London.—PATRICK M. KIRKWOOD

See also ODNB

Belgravia, a London Magazine (1866–1899). Monthly launched by John Maxwell in 1867 and edited by his soon-to-be wife **Mary Elizabeth Braddon** between 1867 and 1876, before being sold to **Chatto and Windus**. The magazine promoted Braddon's fiction—with up to four different titles serialized in one issue—but also other genres such as **illustrated** poems, journalism on **science**, urban space, contemporary fashions, the early history of industrialization, and imperialism. The magazine was a self-reflexive medium of mass communication, which offered some of the earliest theorizations of modernity and its "shock value." John Maxwell established a global distribution network for the magazine in eleven countries, adopting the transnational practices of the continental book trade pioneered by the Leipzig book industry, to reflect the new geopolitical reality of the British empire and its transnational cultural project.

The attention-grabbing rhetorical techniques that are a trade-mark of sensationalism migrated from the suspense-ridden installments of **serialized fiction** in the magazine to become a more widespread narrative strategy that was employed also in articles on science, modern **technology**, finance, in text-based advertising, and in historical accounts of contemporary events, such as the Parisian Commune. Sensationalism, therefore, became a pervasive trope of the emerging language of mass culture. By using the name of a sophisticated neighborhood of London to market **sensation fiction**, the editors employed a branding technique that provided a recognizable symbol to the miscellaneous contents of the magazine. *Belgravia* gave a sense of unity and ideological stability to the contents of the magazine, which otherwise cast doubts on the assumed moral superiority of the upper classes living there and on a blind faith in progress. In problematizing, at least temporarily, the narratives of family fortunes, and the rituals of class, periodical literature defamiliarized readers from accepted social conventions.—ALBERTO GABRIELE

See also Gabriele 2009

Beneath the Wave (1878). **Sensation novel** by **Dora Russell**. Originally **serial**ized in the provincial papers by **Tillotson's Fiction Bureau** and subsequently published in volume form by John and Robert Maxwell. The novel contrasts the experiences of two very different women: the morally upstanding but impoverished Hilda Marston and the reckless and defiant Isabel Trevor, a character reminiscent of the heroines of **Mary Elizabeth Braddon**. Key themes include the difficulties faced by gentlewomen forced to seek paid employment and the position of women within marriage. Typical sensational elements include clandestine marriages, contested wills, murder, adultery, false heirs, and **suicide**.—JANICE M. ALLAN

Bennett, Arnold (1867–1931). English novelist, essayist and editor. Bennett began his literary career editing the journal *Woman* in 1893. Early short fiction appeared in 1895 in the *Yellow Book*, while John Buchan's positive influence with his publisher helped bring out Bennett's first novel, *A Man from the North*, in 1898. Bennett would produce around twenty-five works of fiction between then and the outbreak of World War I, alongside an additional twelve works of non-fiction and four works of drama. The novel *Anna of the Five Towns* (1902) would help cement his reputation and establish for him a series of works based in Staffordshire—whether in the form of collections like *Tales of the Five Towns* (1905) or the loose trilogy begun with *Clayhanger* (1910). Humorous non-fiction like *Literary Taste: How to Form It* (1909) and *How to Live on 24 Hours a Day* (1910) would further cement him as an essayist and public commentator. The heyday of Bennett's career coincided with the advent of World War I, but he is no longer much remembered as an important figure in the period except as a target of Virginia Woolf, standing instead as a champion of the kind of literature that lost the battle against the whimsical realism of the modernists and the brutal candor of the war authors. He spent the war as an increasingly powerful figure in the British War Propaganda Bureau, and his two war novels—*The Pretty Lady* (1918) and *Lord Raingo* (1926)—reflect this experience.—NICK MILNE

See also ODNB

Benson, Edward Frederic (1867–1940). English novelist, memoirist, biographer, and archaeologist. Benson wrote prolifically, both fiction and non-fiction, with his first book, a series of observations from his time at college titled *Sketches from Marlborough*, released while he was still a student (1888). His first novel was the successful and controversial *Dodo: A Detail of the Day* (1893), a comedy celebrating the decadence of the *fin-de-siècle*, and supposedly an expose of the **New Woman**. In addition to his biting social satire, Benson was celebrated for his ghost stories, or so-called spook stories, collected by his principal publisher, Walter Hutchinson, though initially published in such magazines and *Hutchinson's Magazine* and ***Pearson's Magazine***. Notable examples include "The Bus-Conductor" (1906), and "The Room in the Tower" (1912). Benson penned **children's literature**, including *David Blaize and the Blue Door* (1918), memoirs, such as *Charlotte Brontë* (1932), and non-fiction works, such as *English Figure Skating* (1908), a sport in which he represented England. Benson followed the success of *Dodo* with novels including *The Rubicon* (1894), an eerie portrait of a quiet British village, *Vintage* (1898), and its sequel *Capsina* (1899), both set during the Greek Wars of Independence.—JOAN PASSEY

See also ODNB

Bentley's Miscellany (1837–1868). English periodical. *The Miscellany* was an illustrated monthly literary magazine published by Richard Bentley. Its editorial aim was to publish apolitical content targeting an educated middle- and upper-middle-class readership. *Bentley's* was a trendsetter because it featured **illustration**s, including those by George Cruikshank and John Leech, that accompanied original fiction in **serialization**. *Bentley's* promoted popular fiction by serializing, among others, *Oliver Twist* and *Jack Sheppard*, two **Newgate novels** written by the periodical's consecutive editor-novelists: **Charles Dickens** and **William Harrison Ainsworth**. *Bentley's* published other original literature, as well as literary criticism and general interest articles, and it introduced American authors to the British public. Dickens and his successor, Ainsworth, left the *Miscellany* due to creative differences with Richard Bentley, who exerted editorial control from 1841 until he sold it to Chapman and Hall in 1854. Under Bentley's editorship, the quality of the periodical declined. In 1854, Ainsworth returned as editor. Bentley purchased it back in 1868 and merged it with ***Temple Bar***.—SUMAN SIGROHA

See also ODNB, WD, WI

Besant, Walter (1836–1901). English novelist and historian. Born in the parish of Portsea, Portsmouth, Besant was a Victorian polymath. He studied mathematics at Cambridge University, where he graduated from Christ's College in 1859. Soon thereafter he obtained a professorial appointment at the Royal College in Mauritius. During his six years in East Africa, between 1861 and 1867, Besant developed an interest in early French poetry. Besant published his first book, *Early French Poetry*, a year after his return to England. Having determined that a scholarly career in his field of interest would be inordinately time-consuming and poorly paid, he sought other employment. From 1868 to 1886, he was secretary of the Palestinian Exploration Fund, which conducted topographical and ethnographical studies of Ottoman Palestine. His abiding interest in geography likely stems from this period. In his final years, he oversaw and contributed to the multi-volume *Survey of London*, which continues today. However, Besant is best known as a writer of popular fiction. His **collaboration** with **James Rice** on a number of novels—first **serial**ized and, between 1872 and 1882, subsequently published in three volumes—was highly successful. Their first effort, *Ready-Money Mortiboy*, was well received but they achieved greater acclaim with *The Golden Butterfly* (1876). After Rice's death, Besant established a solo authorial career. Critics have tended to concentrate on his novels about London's East End, including ***All Sorts and Conditions of Men: An Impossible Story*** (1882) and ***Children of Gibeon*** (1886). But he also wrote dystopic fiction, such as ***The Revolt of Man*** (1882), and historical **romance**s, such as *Dorothy Forster* (1884), which remain underanalyzed. An advocate of the professionalization of letters, Besant founded the **Society of Authors** in 1883. Examining the mutually constitutive interplay in Besant's career between philanthropy and the professionalization of authorship, the forthcoming *Walter Besant: The Business of Literature and the Pleasures of Reform* is the first collection highlighting their fundamental interconnectedness in his life and work. It has been contracted by Liverpool University Press for publication in 2019.—KEVIN A. MORRISON

The Beth Book (1898). Novel by **Sarah Grand**. Subtitled "A Woman of Genius," the novel follows the life of passionate, imaginative Beth Caldwell from her **childhood** in genteel **poverty**, through school and marriage, to public service for the woman's cause. Grand sets the novel twelve to thirty years before its publication, when "no one thought of the waste of women" (p. 1) and "womanliness consisted in knowing nothing" (p. 44), so that the Contagious Diseases Act (passed 1864, repealed 1886) can form its symptomatic issue. Beth discovers that her husband works in a Lock Hospital where women, found through forced examination to have venereal disease, are incarcerated for treatment. Her struggles to develop her intelligence and creativity, to preserve personal integrity in a marriage that isolates her from the community, and the realization that her husband is an unprincipled, manipulative bully, are given a wider context within women's movements by characters from Grand's earlier work, ***The Heavenly Twins***. Through them, Beth is introduced to public speaking, and at the end of the novel is acclaimed as "one of the first swallows of the woman's summer," "a great teacher … a woman of genius" (1897: p. 572).—Gail Cunningham

A Bid for Fortune; or, Dr. Nikola's Vendetta (1895). Novel by **Guy Boothby**. The first novel of a five-book series centered on criminal mastermind Dr. Nikola, created by the Australian-born popular fiction writer. The story is narrated by "Dick" Hatteras, an Australian middle-class man of English lineage who falls in love with Phyllis, the daughter of the Colonial Secretary of Australia. The latter has stolen a mysterious Tibetan stick from Dr. Nikola who, in order to induce him to return it, abducts his daughter. After various misfortunes, Hatteras manages to rescue Phyllis and Dr. Nikola retrieves his artifact.—Emilio Zampieri

The Big Bow Mystery (s. 1891). First **serial**ized in the radical newspaper *The Star* in 1891, **Israel Zangwill**'s *The Big Bow Mystery* responds to the media sensation surrounding the Whitechapel Murders of 1888. Zangwill claimed that the work was "written in a fortnight, day-by-day," and at its peak, the serial drew in more than 250,000 readers (Clarke 2014: p. 104). It was subsequently published in book form, and rapidly ran into multiple editions. While the novel is definitely popular fiction, it is also a highly intertextual work, containing references to **Dickens**'s *Bleak House*, Balzac's *Old Goriot* and the stories of Eugène Sue, as well as the memoirs of the criminal-turned-detective, Eugène François Vidocq. The novel is a locked room mystery and its plot surrounds the discovery of Arthur Constant, a promising young man, whose throat has been cut. Much of its mystery centers on the fact that Constant appears to have been murdered in a room locked both inside and out, although the story's sensational denouement reveals that in fact he is not dead when his landlady discovers his body. The widespread public and media speculation depicted by Zangwill mirrors the frenzy surrounding the **Jack the Ripper** case, particularly in its parodies of letters from the public, believing they might shed light on the perpetrator's motives. Its fictional inquest offers clear parallels to the inquiry into the slaying of Elizabeth Stride, a prostitute believed to have been one of the Ripper's victims. Furthermore, Zangwill captures the climate of suspicion and fear surrounding a corrupt police force in the 1880s.—Grace Moore

Bigamy. Bigamy provides the narrative engine for hundreds of Victorian novels. While nineteenth-century French fiction features plots of adultery, British fiction of the period is far more likely to turn on the question of bigamy. From Jane Eyre's narrowly averted marriage to the already married Rochester in Charlotte Brontë's *Jane Eyre* (1848) to Arabella's second, illegitimate marriage in Thomas Hardy's *Jude the Obscure* (1901), bigamy figures prominently in both canonical and popular British fiction. Bigamy was a favorite device of **Mary Elizabeth Braddon, Wilkie Collins,** Thomas Hardy, **Florence Marryat, Ouida, Charles Reade,** and **Mrs. Henry [Ellen] Wood,** among many others. As Henry Mansel wrote in a review of "Sensation Novels":

> so popular has this crime become, as to give rise to an entire sub-class in this branch of literature, which may now be distinguished as Bigamy Novels.... Of the tales on our list, no less than eight are bigamy stories:—"Lady Audley's Secret," "Aurora Floyd," "Clinton Maynyard," "Recommended to Mercy," "The Law of Divorce," "The Daily Governess," "Only a Woman," "The Woman of Spirit," all hang their narrative, wholly or in part, on bigamy in act, or bigamy in intention, on the existence or supposed existence of two wives to same husband, or two husbands to the same wife [2001/1863: p. 490].

The first two novels Mansel cites, **Lady Audley's Secret** (1862) and *Aurora Floyd* (1863), both by Mary Elizabeth Braddon, were often either credited with, or blamed for, the plot's popularity. **Margaret Oliphant**, for instance, claimed that Braddon "brought in the reign of bigamy as an interesting and fashionable crime" (1867: p. 263). (Oliphant herself had written a bigamy novel, 1863's *Salem Chapel*, in the immediate wake of Braddon's works.)

Braddon's twin bestsellers demonstrate the flexibility of the plot of bigamy, which is characterized by a productive tension: a bigamist can be either a villainous criminal or an innocent victim. In *Lady Audley's Secret*, the penniless but beautiful Helen Maldon marries a dashing dragoon who abandons her and their child to seek a fortune in Australia. She begins life again as a governess under an assumed name. Her subsequent marriage to a baronet is bigamous, and when her first husband returns from the gold fields, she pushes him down a well rather than admit to her crime. Lady Audley is severely punished for her attempted murder and accomplished bigamy—she ends the novel accused of madness and imprisoned in a sanatorium, where she soon dies. In *Aurora Floyd*, by contrast, Aurora is impetuous but good. She elopes with her father's groom, it is true, but she believes him to be dead before she remarries an honest squire. When her first husband turns up murdered, she is falsely suspected of the crime, but she is as guilty of bigamy as Lady Audley. Nonetheless, *Aurora Floyd* ends happily, with Aurora and her husband remarried and expecting an heir. One bigamist is guilty and is punished as a pariah, the other is innocent and is held up as a paragon of domesticity.

Popular bigamy novels tend to emphasize four motifs: (1) resistance to the courtship plot's enforcement of a single spouse; (2) enjoyment of the frisson created when bigamous spouses share a single home (what I call elsewhere the "Spouse in the House" plot); (3) anxiety about travel to and from the colonies (what I call the "Plot of Colonial Return"); and (4) uncertainty about the written evidence of marriage, including registers, certificates, and letters.

These motifs, rampant in Braddon's novels, are well exemplified in a lesser-known novel also identified by Henry Mansel in his list of popular "Bigamy Novels," Captain Lascelles Wraxall's *Only a Woman: A Story in Neutral Tint* (1860). *Only a Woman* begins when Sir Norton Folgate allows an attractive young tutor, Herbert Leigh, to live among his three daughters. Herbert flirts with the eldest, Blanche, makes an enemy of the second, Harriette, and wins the life-long love of the third, Alice. Meanwhile, the girls' beautiful but scheming maid Jessie exacts a written promise of marriage from him. Once this document is exposed, Herbert unwillingly marries Jessie, Blanche marries a wealthy fool, and Alice becomes a pensionaire in a convent. As Herbert is about to depart for Australia with Jessie, he discovers that he has inherited a fortune. Temporarily separated from his wife, he hears that her ship has been wrecked, whereupon he takes the name of his wealthy relative and is known as a single man. After an adulterous flirtation with Blanche, Herbert marries the loyal and good Alice. Meanwhile, Jessie, who survived shipwreck, has returned in disguise and also under an alias. She spitefully allows his bigamous marriage to occur, and takes a position as Alice's maid. When Herbert attempts to destroy the evidence of his first marriage, Jessie instead shows the register to Alice, precipitating her death, the final turn of the screw that converts both Hebert and Jessie into Catholic missionaries. As an indignant reviewer wrote in 1860, "If this story be in neutral tint ... we would like to know what is meant by vivid coloring!" ("New Novels" 1860: p. 15).

I. Multiple spouses. The novel's baroque twists and turns follow out the logic of imagining multiple erotic attachments. In a courtship novel, Herbert's task would be to choose among the sisters, but in a bigamy plot flirtations are crystallized into marriage, adultery, and bigamy.

II. The spouse in the house. Herbert shares a home with his sequential wives twice, first as a single man, and then after he has married them both. Bigamy novels often include lurking spouses, either in hidden rooms like Bertha Mason in *Jane Eyre* [see also, for instance, **Amelia Edwards**'s *Barbara's History* (1864); George Gifford's *King's Baynard* (1866); **Sheridan Le Fanu**'s *The Wyvern Mystery* (1869); and Arabella Kenealy's *A Semi-Detached Marriage* (1898)], or disguised as a servant or governess in the house, as Jessie is in *Only a Woman* [or as Isabel Vane famously is, in **Mrs. Henry [Ellen] Wood**'s *East Lynne*].

III. The plot of colonial return. Falsely reported deaths in the colonies proliferate in bigamy fiction. Misinformation, violence, and the dangers of sea travel combine in bigamy fiction to produce unexpected colonial returns like that of Jessie's in *Only a Woman* and George Talboy's in *Lady Audley's Secret* [see also **Harrison Ainsworth**'s *Myddleton Pomfret* (1868); Charles Reade's *A Simpleton* (1873); and **Edmund Yates**'s *A Righted Wrong* (1873), among others].

IV. Uncertain marital proof. The instability of written evidence of marriage and the degree to which a promise counts as a betrothal is also a motif of bigamy fiction, much of which turns on legal vagaries [like the differences between Scottish and English marriage law in Wilkie Collins's *Man and Wife* (1870)] or criminal trials [like those in Anthony Trollope's *John Caldigate* (1879) and *Castle Richmond* (1860)].

In spite of its formulaic nature, bigamy fiction continuously surprises. For one thing, it flouts many of the gender expectations familiar in Victorian culture by allowing the bigamist to be either a man (like Wraxall's Herbert Leigh) or a woman (like Braddon's Lady Audley). The plot's popularity among Victorian readers would be enough to justify its close study, but the rapid plot twists, disguises, and hidden identities characteristic of the plot make for enjoyable pleasure reading as well. Critics, including Karen Chase and Michael Levenson, Jeanne Fahnestock, Kelly Hager, Barbara Leckie, Maia McAleavey, and Lyn Pykett, have begun detailing the relationship between bigamy and divorce, and exploring the historical resonance of the plot, but as more and more of these novels become digitized, there is immense scope for future analysis.—MAIA MCALEAVEY

Black, Clementina (27 July 1854–19 December 1922). Black was born into a middle-class family, but after the untimely death of her mother, was forced to care for her invalid father and seven siblings. Over the course of her lifetime she published seven novels, many combining labor issues with more popular romantic or domestic themes. Her first novel, *A Sussex Idyll* (1877), presents readers with a modern pastoral romance between a city gentleman and a farmer's daughter, as if to suggest that class inequality can be solved by love. This work was followed by *Orlando* (1879), *An Agitator* (1895), *The Princess Desirée* (1896), *The Pursuit of Camilla* (1899), *Caroline* (1908), and *The Linleys of Bath* (1911). Black is perhaps best known for *An Agitator* (1895), the polemical story of union leader Christopher ("Kit") Bland. A renowned "agitator," Bland is courted by both the Conservative and Liberal parties who are desperate to win the working-class vote, but he instead aligns himself with the Labour Party and is later elected Member of Parliament (though the election results are undermined by scandal). Black also published several works of nonfiction and social journalism on contemporary labor issues. *Makers of Our Clothes: a Case for Trade Boards* (1909), co-authored with Adele Myer (met through the Anti-Sweating League) focuses on women working in the textile industry. This report was supported by the Women's Industrial Council (formerly the Women's Trade Union Association), of which Black was a founding member and editor of the council's journal, *Women's Industrial News*. Black's other non-fiction work on similar subjects include *Sweated Industry and the Minimum Wage* (1907) and *Married Women's Work (1915)*. She spent her later years fighting for women's right to vote; she was a member of the National Union of Women's Suffrage Society and editor of the organization's journal, *Common Cause*.—S. Brooke Cameron

Black Beauty (1877). Novel by Anna Sewell (1820–1878). One of the most significant works of late-Victorian fiction to address questions of **animal** cruelty, *Black Beauty* has become a classic in the field of children's literature. Framed explicitly as "The Autobiography of a Horse," a designation included in the novel's original subtitle, the novel follows the career of its eponymous hero. Tracing his descent from prized riding horse to abused cart horse, Sewell dramatizes the experience of horses in Victorian society, drawing attention to the effects of human acts of kindness and cruelty. Through a first-person narrative voiced by a horse, Sewell addresses specific issues of animal cruelty, such as questions about the cruel use of bearing reins to hold horses' heads artificially high. By recounting matters of human behavior, moreover, she takes up questions of moral and religious character that reflect her lifelong philanthropic commitments, first as a member of the Society of Friends (Quakers) and later as an Anglican.

As a work of anti-cruelty literature, *Black Beauty* proved influential in its own time. In the United States, founder of the American Humane Education Society George Angell circulated more than one million copies of the novel by 1891. The novel's central conceit—of having the animal hero speak for himself—places it in a popular tradition of fictional animal autobiography and "it" narratives (stories focusing on the circulation of objects in human society) dating from the eighteenth century. Sewell significantly advances these subgenres by making use of the sentimental mode, an approach that links *Black Beauty* to Harriet Beecher Stowe's *Uncle Tom's Cabin* (1852). Clearly indebted to *Black Beauty*, Margaret Marshall Saunders's 1893 novel *Beautiful Joe* adopts a similar approach to tell the story of an abused dog.

Black Beauty scholarship has shifted focus in recent years. Still a surprisingly understudied text, commentators have linked it to human experiences of oppression such as race, class, and gender. More recently it has become a central text in the emerging field of animal studies. This aspect of Sewell's text offers rich possibilities for further study insofar as it touches on questions that were being raised through the last third of the nineteenth century by scientists such as Charles Darwin and George Romanes, a Darwin disciple whose work extended the latter's late-career concern with questions about animal emotion and intelligence.—KRISTEN GUEST

Blaze de Bury, Marie Pauline Rose (c. 1813–1894). British writer and political activist. Reportedly born in Scotland to army officer William Stuart and his wife (née Campbell [Voisine 1955: p. 10]), this little-known author is also rumored to be the illegitimate daughter of Lord Henry Brougham (Sutherland 1989: p. 71). In 1844 she married the French musicologist Henri Blaze de Bury in the Catholic chapel at the French embassy in London. Henri Blaze de Bury had produced a French translation of Johann Wolfgang von Goethe's *Faust*. Out of gratitude, the Grand Duke of Saxe-Weimar-Eisenach bestowed a baronial title on Henri Blaze de Bury (*Staatshandbuch* 1843: p. 19). Thus, the already inveterate traveler and cosmopolitan Rose Stuart—as she was known to her friends—became a baroness upon her marriage. She had two daughters: Yetta (b. 1845) and Fernande (b. 1854), who were also writers.

Rose Blaze de Bury published some **short stories** (e.g., "The Two Bouquets" [1846] and "The Black Ring" [1850] in ***Bentley's Miscellany***) under her own name as well as under the pseudonym Arthur Dudley. Her novels were released under the pseudonyms Hamilton Murray and A.A.A. (Egloff 2017: p. 9). They include *Mildred Vernon: A Tale of Parisian Life in the Last Days of the Monarchy* (1848), *Leonie Vermont: A Story of the Present Time* (1849), *Falkenburg: A Tale of the Rhine* (1851), *All for Greed* (1867–1868), and *Love the Avenger* (1869). *Mildred Vernon* was particularly widely discussed in the British press (Egloff 2017: p. 11–12) and *All for Greed* was **serial**ized in Anthony Trollope's new *St. Paul's Monthly Magazine* alongside his own *Phineas Finn, the Irish Member*.

She was a regular contributor on literary matters to the *Revue de deux mondes* and, to a lesser degree, the *Revue de Paris*. In Britain, she made critical literary and political contributions to *Blackwood's Magazine*, the *Edinburgh Review*, the *North British Review*, and the *Quarterly Review* among others. Further non-fiction works such as *Memoirs of the Princess, Palatine Princess of Bohemia* (1853) or her widely read and well received travel volumes titled *Germania: its Courts, Camps and People* (1850) complete her extensive and varied oeuvre.

Alongside her literary contribution to fiction and non-fiction, Blaze de Bury was heavily involved in inter-European politics and diplomacy. William Blackwood described her as "a sort of masculine female political *intrigante* (an awfully clever woman)" (Gerald Porter 1898: p. 121) and, according to her contemporary Julius Fröbel, in 1862, she "turned up in Vienna as a secret agent of Lord John Russell" (1891: p. 205). Most of her writing is infused with political commentary in pursuit of her self-proclaimed aim of combatting "our ignorance, and our utter indifference to whatever may happen to our neighbors" (Blaze de Bury 1850: p. ix) and of furthering transcultural understanding within Europe.
—RACHEL MARGARET EGLOFF

The Book of the Thousand Nights and a Night (1885–88). English translation by Richard Francis Burton (1821–1890). Richard Burton privately published—in order to avoid Victorian censors—ten volumes of his version of the story collection *The 1001 Nights* (a.k.a. *Arabian Nights*, hereafter referred to as the "*Nights*") in 1885–86. Six additional volumes titled *Supplemental Nights* were published from 1886 to 1888. Sales to a 1,000-member subscriber list made Burton and his wife Isabel extremely wealthy for the first time in their lives. The story collection has often been used as evidence of the Victorian explorer's talents as a translator and anthropologist.

What is unique about Burton's version is that he painstakingly went to great lengths to include any story and poetry associated with the *Nights*, but also the comprehensive footnotes and endnotes and related essays that he added. These were necessary, in Burton's opinion, to show what the *Nights* "really is" (n.d.: xiii). These additions by Burton were met with controversy because they focused on sexualizing the *Nights*, adding details about sexuality in the East and highlighting racialist and misogynistic details and, in his "Terminal Essay," suggesting that there was a geographic cause of homosexuality (which he called "Le Vice")—entire regions of the world, the Middle East included, were prone to this due to their climate—that Burton called the "Sotatic Zone."

Victorian readers were subsequently intrigued and appalled by Burton's *Nights*. In 1885 the *Morning Advertiser* called the work "priceless" and vital in "marking an era in the annals of Oriental translation" ("Opinions" 1885: p. 359) and the *Bat*, in 1885, wrote that the work was a "gigantic service to all students of literature who are not profound Orientalists" (*Supplemental* n.d.: 6, n. p.). In 1886 the *Edinburgh Review*, however, called Burton's *Nights* "a jumble of the vulgarest slang of all nations" ("The Arabian" 1886: p. 174), "an appalling collection of degrading customs and statistics of vice" (p. 183), a "disgrace and a shame to printed literature" (p. 183), and "an ocean of filth" (p. 185) meant for the "sewers" (p. 184).

In addition, Burton has been accused of plagiarizing from a version of the *Nights* written by a colleague, John Payne. Scholarship on the association between the *Nights* of Burton and Payne has suggested that the two texts share an awkward, even literal at times, similarity to one another. Payne's version was published first and he shared sample early proofs with Burton. Burton's volumes were produced in a brief amount of time after Payne's (three years) and correspond with Payne's contents (and prose in many places) almost exactly to a large degree. Studies by Paul McMichael Nurse and Robert Irwin in particular have illuminated this controversy.

Despite this and other questions, Burton's *Nights* and its problematic textual history have been overshadowed by the reputation of its author and by Burton's additional notes and essays. Burton was an extremely controversial Victorian figure and well known throughout the world as an African explorer (most famously exploring for the source of the Nile with John Speke), as the Westerner who journeyed to Mecca and Medina masquerading as a Muslim pilgrim, and as the author of numerous books about the world: on places he had traveled to and worked in including Africa, **India**, the United States and South America. His larger-than-life persona and the risqué nature of his *Nights* have continued to ensure that it remains one of the most well-known and read versions of the story collection.—MICHAEL JAMES LUNDELL

Boothby, Guy Newell (1867–1905). Australian writer. Born in Adelaide, Boothby settled in England in 1894 after several failed attempts to become a professional playwright in his homeland. There he turned to popular fiction and soon became one of the most prolific and successful writers of his day. Between 1894 and 1907, Boothby published fifty-one books, mostly adventure novels, many of which were first **serial**ized in magazines. His plots are predictable in the main, the action generally centering on the vicissitudes of a middle-class enterprising young man who finally attains the status of a respectable Victorian gentleman. A manufacturer of best sellers, Boothby daily dictated thousands of words into a wax-cylinder phonograph and had secretaries transcribe them. Admittedly, he did not aspire to become a great writer, his only intention being to afford the lifestyle of a country gentleman. Contemporary critics conceded that he knew how to keep the reader's interest alive, but they heavily criticized his commonplace style and lack of literary ambition. His most famous character was Dr. Nikola, an international criminal mastermind starring in a series of five novels published between 1895 and 1901. The initial Dr. Nikola adventure, ***A Bid for Fortune; or, Dr. Nikola's Vendetta***, was first serialized in the conservative monthly the **Windsor Magazine** and, along with **Arthur Morrison**'s *Chronicles of Martin Hewitt, Investigator*, greatly contributed to the success of the magazine. Boothby died in his Boscombe house from acute pneumonia and is buried in Wimborne Road Cemetery in Bournemouth.—Emilio Zampieri

See also ADB, Depasquale 1985

Braddon, Mary Elizabeth (1835–1915). English author. Braddon was a nineteenth-century theatrical and literary sensation who shocked Victorians with scandals in both her writing and personal life. During her career, she penned around eighty novels, 150 **short stories**, nine plays, and a volume of poetry. Her fiction broached supernatural, detective and historical subject matter, as well as works for children, but her most renowned genre is the mid–Victorian phenomenon of **sensation fiction**—novels full of **bigamy**, kidnap and murder that set readers' pulses racing.

Braddon's writing career had an auspicious start with assistance from both of her literary mentors, the famous author **Edward Bulwer-Lytton**, and John Gilby. Gilby advised her on what exhibitions to see, sent her books to read, proof read her work, and paid her to write her first poetry collection *Garibaldi and Other Poems* (1861). Simultaneously, the printer C. R. Empson commissioned Braddon to write *Three Times Dead* (1860). Now deemed one of the first detective novels, it depicts a case of wrongful imprisonment, with a mute detective solving the mystery. While Braddon's first publications were not financially successful, they gave her invaluable practical knowledge of the publishing industry before she moved to London to launch her literary career.

In 1860s London she began her writing career in earnest by adopting the pen-name we know her by today, M. E. Braddon, and achieved lasting fame for her pair of bigamy novels: ***Lady Audley's Secret*** and *Aurora Floyd* (1863). These novels cemented her reputation as a scandalous author who probed the darker side of the upper classes, leading one critic to argue that Braddon "succeeded in making the literature of the Kitchen the favorite reading of the Drawing room" (Rae 1865: p. 204). From this point on Braddon's (in)famous reputation was secured, and she was nicknamed the "Queen of Sensation" because her plots revolved around scheming heroines who committed dangerous acts. Sensation Fiction quickly became a literary phenomenon, propounded by other authors such as **Wilkie Collins** and **Mrs. Henry [Ellen] Wood**, and together they challenged the hypocrisy of middle-class life. Overall, the 1860s saw Braddon financially secure, although she continued to write two novels a year for around the next forty years. Her work was translated into at least five different languages to be read worldwide, as well as by the most influential people in Britain, including Prime Minister William Gladstone and Queen Victoria.

Braddon's personal life was just as sensational as her novels. She was born in Soho, London, on 4 October 1835, although to make herself appear younger, she frequently stated she was born in 1837. Braddon was the third child born to Fanny and Henry Braddon, Junior. When Braddon was four Fanny left Henry because of his infidelities (Maxwell 1937: p. 273), meaning Fanny brought up Braddon alone, striving to maintain respectability as a single mother in Victorian England. Fanny offered her daughter a strong female role model and Braddon grew up independent, hardworking and well educated.

Over her lifetime Braddon revealed her creative abilities, not only as a writer, but as an editor and actress. In 1852, she began her acting career at seventeen—a daring choice for a middle-class woman due to its associations with prostitution. To maintain respectability, Braddon adopted the stage name Mary Seyton and took her mother to all performances. Braddon's aim was to be self-sufficient to support her ageing mother and she succeeded in this endeavor. Braddon's acting career lasted around eight years, during which time she toured the provinces, performed in Scotland, and débuted in the capital. She went from playing extras in crowd scenes, to having small speaking parts, eventually rising to major supporting roles and finally becoming a leading lady. Braddon worked hard, had a talent for acting and enjoyed her career. She mainly acted in comedies and farces, but also performed in burlesques, pantomimes, and Shakespearean productions, including histories and tragedies (Hatter 2013: p. 34). This experience demonstrates her comprehensive working knowledge of the theater and literature—all of which prepared her for her future career as a novelist.

Braddon next flirted with scandal in 1861 by moving in with her publisher, John Maxwell, having met him a year earlier. They lived together unmarried because Maxwell's first wife, Mary Ann Crowley, was still alive, although living with her family in Ireland due to **mental illness**. Braddon became stepmother to Maxwell's five children, while having six of her own: Gerald, Fanny, Francis (who died aged three), William Babington, Rosie, and Ted. Their unconventional relationship led to critics associating Braddon's private life with the unruly heroines of her novels, although this did not harm her popularity. Braddon continued to host garden parties with the literary and theatrical elite, boasting friendships as diverse as **Bram Stoker**, Henry Irving, George Augustus Sala, **Oscar Wilde**, **Charles Reade**, and **Rhoda Broughton**, along with the politician Henry Labouchère and the painter William Frith.

Building on her writing success, Braddon started to edit her own periodicals—*Belgravia* and the *Belgravia Annual*—giving herself more security as an author. *Belgravia* was a monthly magazine which cost one shilling and was aimed at a genteel readership. After Maxwell sold these ventures in 1876 to **Chatto and Windus**, Braddon began editing the *Mistletoe Bough*, a Christmas fiction annual. By producing a specifically Christmas annual Braddon tapped into an already established yet expanding market, indicating her strong business acumen.

Later in life Braddon suffered poor **health**, but maintained decidedly modern habits, including purchasing a car and attending the cinematic release of *Aurora Floyd*. Braddon had earned a respectable reputation by her death in 1915, but never lost her "sensational" label. At the end of the nineteenth century, E. A. B. wrote that "Miss Braddon is a part of England; she has woven herself into it; without her it would be different. This is no mere fanciful conceit. She is in the encyclopaedias; she ought to be in the dictionaries" (1899: p. 431).—Janine Hatter

Brooke, Emma Frances (*pseud.* of E. Fairfax Byrrne [1844–1926]). English writer. Brooke was born into a wealthy cotton mill family in the northern town of Bollington in Macclesfield, Cheshire. She came from a large family; she had three sisters and four brothers and she outlived them all. She never married or had children. Little is known about her educational upbringing, but after her father died in 1872 she inherited enough money to attend Newnham College, Cambridge. She joined a pioneering group of eight women and studied from 1872 to 1874, taking papers in 1873 in English Language and Literature and in 1874 in Moral Sciences: Logic, Psychology, and Political Economy. She moved to London in 1879 and began supporting herself as a writer. She adopted an interesting pseudonym, E. Fairfax Byrrne, to publish some of her work, yet other works were published anonymously, and still others, much later in her career, were written under two variations of her given name: E. F. Brooke or Emma Brooke.

In her early years in London, she worked with the Female Middle Class Emigration Society as their secretary for two years (1882–1884). This organization helped educated, middle-class women find employment as governesses and teachers in the Colonies. In 1884 a fellow Newnham College student, Mrs. Charlotte Wilson, invited Brooke to become a member of the Hampstead Historic Club to study issues concerning socialism. She joined and became the Club's secretary for four years (1884–1888). In this group, she met and became friends with Sidney Webb and George Bernard Shaw. Brooke maintained a close friendship with both of these men when she became involved with the Fabian Society, which formed in January of 1884; she did not join at the inception of this group, but became a member on 2 October 2 1885. She was an active member in the Society and in 1893 she was elected to the Executive Committee, keeping that position for three years (1893–1896). Brooke was one of the co-founders of the Fabian Women's Group, created in 1908. In this group, she wrote about and campaigned for women's economic positions in society, focusing special attention on mothers and **motherhood**.

As a self-supporting writer in London she published her first major work, a poem in blank verse called *Milicent*, in 1881 and under her pseudonym. Five novels followed, two of which she published anonymously for the Religious Tract Society: *God's Gift to Two* (1883) and *Reaping the Whirlwind* (1885, with a reprint in 1904); she wrote two novels under her pseudonym during this time. These were *A Fair Country Maid* (1883), and *Entangled* (1885). A final 1880s novel was anonymous: *The Heir Without a Heritage* (1887). Her early works dealt mostly with religious themes, though she was already beginning to develop her interests in social questions, women's and workers' rights, and issues concerning economics and socialism.

In 1888 Brooke published her most famous political essay, "Women and Their Sphere," in Annie Besant's socialist journal, "Our Corner." In this essay, she explored the roles and economic positions of women in British society, especially mothers, arguing that motherhood subjugated a woman's sexuality and her economic strength as an independent wage earner.

In January 1894 her most famous novel, **A Superfluous Woman**, was published and this event changed her life and her writing career. Brooke went from being a fairly unknown writer, except to a small circle of friends and Fabian associates, to being a well-known and extraordinarily popular writer. *A Superfluous Woman* became so famous that in Brooke's obituary the writer named this work "her first book."

In 1895, Sidney Webb, George Bernard Shaw, and Graham Wallace cofounded the London School of Economics (LSE), and as a Fabian member Brooke took courses part time at the LSE. While there, she published "A Tabulation of the Factory Laws of European Countries in so far as they relate to the Hours of Labour, and to Special Legislation for Women, Young Persons, and Children" (1898). This was an ambitious endeavor for Brooke, but one that reflected her continuing interests in women's rights and labor issues.

In 1895, the same year as the opening of the LSE, an anonymous, but overtly socialist novel was published called *Transition* (1895). The main character, Paul Sheridan, was based on Sidney Webb and his work in the Fabian Society. The first novel to be published under Brooke's given name (Emma Brooke) was *Life the Accuser* (1896). This book explored female sexuality from three women's perspectives, and the dangerous consequences of male adultery. Two more novels were published in the 1890s: *The Confessions of Stephen Whapshare* (1898) and *The Engrafted Rose* (1899). In the twentieth-century she published six novels: *The Poet's Child* (1903), *The Twins of Skirlaugh Hall, A Mystery* (1903), *Susan Wooed and Susan Won* (1905), *Sir Elyot of the Woods* (1907), *The Story of Hauksgarth Farm* (1909), and her final novel, *The House of Robershaye* (1912). In 1912, she stopped writing entirely; she was 68. Brooke died on 28 November 1926 at the age of 81 from "old age" and "cardiac degeneration" at the Heath Nursing Home in Weybridge, Surrey.—BARBARA TILLEY

See also Death Certificate 1926, "Miss Emma" 1926

Broughton, Rhoda (1840–1920). English author. Broughton was a highly popular writer who published twenty-five novels and some **short stories**, including a collection of supernatural tales, over a career spanning from the late 1860s to the posthumous appearance of her final book in 1920. Notorious for her daring portrayal of female desire, Broughton depicted women's social and sexual frustrations in narratives which anticipate **New Woman** and modernist fiction.

Descended from an aristocratic line, Broughton was born in Wales and moved in her girlhood to the family seat, Broughton Hall, where her father, a clergyman, held the parish living. Following her parents' deaths in the early 1860s, Broughton, who never married herself, lived with a sister in Denbyshire, and, subsequently, in Oxford and Richmond Hill in London. Broughton's career commenced in the mid–1860s when her uncle by marriage, the Anglo-Irish writer **Joseph Sheridan Le Fanu, serial**ized her first two novels, **Not Wisely, but Too Well** and **Cometh Up as a Flower**, in his journal *The Dublin University Magazine*. When Le Fanu secured the young author a contract for *Not Wisely* with the London publisher Richard Bentley, Broughton encountered the first of numerous negative responses from the literary establishment: Bentley's reader, Geraldine Jewsbury, was so shocked by the "thoroughly sensual" manuscript (quoted in Broughton 2013: p. 378) that she urged Bentley to void the contract. Persuaded by Le Fanu and Bentley to substitute her second story, *Cometh Up as a Flower*, for *Not Wisely*, Broughton was only able to publish the latter after extensive revision. Even so, *Not Wisely* and *Cometh Up* (both published in 1867) attracted critical outrage, with **Margaret Oliphant** singling out *Cometh Up* for incarnating the "abomination" of women's portrayal of female desire in the **sensation novel** (p. 268). Toning down the depiction of such topics as adultery in her work of the 1870s and 1880s, Broughton became associated with the genre of romantic fiction rather than sensationalism. Yet, in continuing to feature unconventional heroines dubbed by Alfred Austin "very outrageous young ladies indeed" (quoted in Broughton 2013: p. 442), her novels both reflected and popularized changing sexual mores.

By the *fin-de-siècle*, however, Broughton's fiction no longer seemed shocking, and could even be reactionary, as in her satire on the New Woman in *Dear Faustina* (1897). Nonetheless, a posthumously published essay, "Girls Past and Present" (1920), celebrates women's liberation from "the nuptial yoke" and restrictive Victorian ideologies (Broughton 1920: p. 141), and many of the innovative single-volume works Broughton wrote following the demise of the triple-decker conclude with ambiguous endings suggestive of new options for women outside heterosexual romance. Two metafictional single-volume works, *A Beginner* (1894) and the posthumously published *A Fool in Her Folly* (1920), self-reflexively depict obstacles faced by women writing about sexuality. Although the elderly Broughton was amused by how staid the younger generation found her once-controversial fiction, it indisputably contributed to the development of new ways of writing about female sexuality and experience.—TAMAR HELLER

Bulwer-Lytton, Edward (1803–1873). Writer and politician. It is difficult to overstate Bulwer-Lytton's influence on the development of popular fiction in the nineteenth century. As a writer, he was both a popularizer and an innovator; he wrote poetry, **short stories**, drama, and nonfiction, although he remains best-known for his genre-bending novels. His *Pelham* (1828) became the most widely read of the **silver fork novels** while also laying the foundation for English **detective fiction** (Sussex 2007: p. 12). He inaugurated the **Newgate novel** with *Paul Clifford* (1830) and *Eugene Aram* (1832), and his *Lucretia* (1847) is an important evolutionary link between **Gothic** and **sensation fiction**. A **childhood** devotion to historical fiction found expression in the bestselling *The Last Days of Pompeii* (1834). His *The Caxtons, A Family Picture* (1849) lent commercial heft to the domestic novel and stands in striking thematic contrast to his **occult** or metaphysical novels, *Zanoni* (1842) and *A Strange Story* (1862). **The Coming Race** (1871) is one of the first **science fiction** novels written in England. Although he enjoyed a cultural ascendancy matched only by **Charles Dickens**, Bulwer-Lytton struggled to weather the critical opprobrium with which his work was received. The earnest intellectualism, strident moralizing, and rhetorical excess of his writing provoked a journalistic backlash so vitriolic that biographer Michael Sadleir christened the practice "Bulwer-baiting" (1993: p. 255). Thus, Bulwer-Lytton's literary legacy is complex. In the words of an anonymous contemporary, "Such is Bulwer; a great author, but not the greatest we have had" ("Sir Edward": 1854: p. 266).—FIONA COLL

See also ODNB, Mulvey-Roberts 2001, Sutherland 2009

Caine, Hall [Sir Thomas Henry Hall Caine] (1853–1931). English novelist and playwright. Although he made much of his family roots in Cumbria and the Isle of Man, Caine grew up in Liverpool. On leaving elementary school he initially worked as a draughtsman, but through assiduous networking began to build a literary career. His first novel, *The Shadow of a Crime* (1885), set in Cumbria, attracted some favorable notice. His breakthrough came, however, when he chose the Isle of Man as the setting for his third novel, *The Deemster: A Romance* (1887), and began working with the actor-manager Wilson Barrett. *The Deemster* was staged as *Ben-my-Chree* in 1888, and thereafter many of Caine's **melodrama**tic novels were followed by popular dramatizations on stage, and later screen. Two more Manx novels, *The Bondman* (1890) and *The Manxman* (1894), helped to establish him as one of the most commercially successful and high-profile novelists of the 1890s. He went on to achieve even more spectacular international sales with *The Christian* (1897) and *The Eternal City* (1901), set in London and Rome. But his relentless self-promotion and public moralizing increasingly alienated critics and fellow-writers. In *Punch* he was lampooned as "the Boomster"; while **Joseph Conrad** dismissed him as "a kind of male **Marie Corelli**" (Hammond 2006: p. 131). During his lifetime Hall Caine's fame was vastly greater than that of his loyal friend and admirer **Bram Stoker**, but today he is remembered chiefly as the "dear friend Hommy-Beg" to whom Stoker's *Dracula* is dedicated.—RICHARD STORER

See also Allen 1997, Storer 2016

Caird, Mona (1854–1932). Scottish writer. One of the most prominent figures of the **New Woman** movement, Caird (née Alice Mona Alison) was born on 24 May 1854 to wealthy parents. She married James Alexander Henryson-Caird in 1877 and their only child, Alister James, was born in 1884. Caird spent little time at her marital home in Creetown, Scotland, instead preferring to immerse herself in the literary world of London and travel abroad. Despite the current absence of a full-length biography, scholarly work by Ann Heilmann (1996), which includes interviews with Caird's descendants, has revealed previously unknown aspects of Caird's life and positioned her as an important feminist writer.

After the limited success of her first two novels, *Whom Nature Leadeth* (1883) and *One That Wins* (1887), Caird gained prominence in 1888 when she attacked the patriarchal institution of marriage in her essay, "Marriage," published in the *Westminster Review*. Citing modern marriage to be a "vexatious failure" (1888: p. 197) founded on the subjugation of women as private and public property, Caird argues that marriage is little more than a legalized form of prostitution. She contends that the emancipation of women can only be achieved when the "obvious right of the woman to possess herself body and soul, to give or withhold herself ... exactly as she wills" (1888: p. 198) is acknowledged through the "free" (1888: p. 197) union of men and women. Capturing the public buzz surrounding Caird's controversial article, the *Daily Telegraph* drew on the morally sensitive subject to pose the question "Is Marriage a Failure?" By the end of September they had received twenty-seven thousand responses from the general public, many of which expressed a similar dissatisfaction with marriage and lamented the stringent attitudes toward opposite-sex friendship and divorce.

The majority of Caird's novels dramatize the repressive patriarchal institution of marriage depicted in her essay: ***Wing of Azrael*** vividly portrays a woman's experience of marital violence; the **short story** "A Romance of the Moors" (1891) demonstrates the importance of self-sufficiency prior to, and instead of, marriage; and *Daughters of Danaus* (1894) represents marriage as suffocating to a woman's intellect and independence. Caird's critique of marriage is far removed from the standpoint of many other **New Woman** writers including **Sarah Grand** (1854–1943) who repeatedly defended the "sacred institution" (1896: p. 169) in her writings. In many ways, as also evidenced by her approach to **eugenics**, birth control, free love, **motherhood**, and female self-sacrifice, Caird was a more radical figure than many of her contemporaries.

From the mid-1890s, as Caird became progressively more involved in the campaign for women's suffrage and president of the Independent Anti-Vivisection League, her writing became increasingly politicized. In addition to *The Stones of Sacrifice* (1915), Caird produced numerous non-fictional articles including "The Sanctuary of Mercy" (1895), which contained graphic depictions of animal experimentation to protest against **vivisection**. Despite a reinvigoration of scholarly interest in Caird, this latter half of her career stretching into the twentieth century is largely still to be critically assessed.—KATHERINE MANSFIELD

See also ODNB, Orlando Project

Cameron, Mrs. H. Lovett [Caroline Emily Cameron (*née* Sharp)] (1844–1921). English author. Publishing under her husband's name, Mrs. Lovett Cameron wrote over forty novels between 1876 and 1905, among them fourteen three-volume novels, which include her first work, *Juliette's Garden*, originally published in **Belgravia** magazine (1876), *Pure Gold* (1884), *A Bachelor's Bridal* (1895), and *The Craze of Christina* (1899). Early in her life, alongside two of her brothers, Cameron helped develop the short-lived six-month publication *City Advertiser*. Although she had a penchant for writing over needlepoint, Cameron's family discouraged and dismissed such work. Cameron's husband was to later embolden her to take pen to paper. Known for working on a strict daily schedule, she used the same pen to write all of her works. The majority of her titles went on to be published in several editions, among them the novel for which she was most widely known, *In a Grass Country* (1885), which went through nine editions. Widely considered a writer of romantic fiction, Cameron addressed many societal and cultural issues within her works, such as the plight of unmarried pregnant women in *A Sister's Sin* (1893) and in the contemporary debate on the **New Woman** with her work *The Man Who Didn't* (1895). Considered anti-feminist, Cameron nevertheless called for marriage reform. —AMBERYL MALKOVICH

Carey, Rosa Nouchette (1840–1909) English domestic novelist. The first of Carey's forty-one acknowledged novels, *Nellie's Memories*, was published in 1868 and the last, *The Key of the Unknown*, in 1909. Six were initially **serial**ized in the Religious Tract Society periodical the *Girl's Own Paper*. Many of the later novels were issued simultaneously in England and America. The British Library additionally attributes to her four **sensation**al novels, published under the pseudonym *Le Voleur*, although this attribution is contested.

Carey's novels reflect the concerns of middle-class women like herself. Detailing equally the challenges and the joys of marriage, home-making and family relationships, she validates the undervalued real world domestic work expected of women, single or married. Yet she also represents working women positively. Marriage is deemed a woman's natural career but Carey acknowledges that not all women can marry. She herself remained single. She also emphasizes that a woman is better not marrying at all than marrying a man who is unstable or unable to maintain a family.

Didactic, although in unexpected ways, the novels dispense with abstract intellectual debates, instead offering practical and emotional survival strategies for women. Thus, they are more than the repositories of trivia that some reviewers suggest. For example, a review in the *Academy* says of characters in *For Lilias* (1885) that their "paradise is ... an eternity of afternoon tea" ([Rev.] 1885: *For Lilias*: p. 200). Afternoon tea is ubiquitous in Carey's novels but this particular reviewer is oblivious to the validatory mode in which this tea is represented and glossed.—ELAINE HARTNELL

See also Black 1906, Crisp 1989, Hartnell 2000

Carmilla (1872). **Gothic** novella by **Joseph Sheridan Le Fanu**, **serial**ized in the *Dark Blue* (December 1871–March 1872) and presented in Le Fanu's *In a Glass Darkly* (1872) as part of the casebook of Dr. Martin Hesselius, a **medical** man with **occult** interests.

This ambiguously framed story is narrated by the subsequently deceased Laura, a motherless girl living with her English **father** in an isolated Styrian *Schloss* in circumstances that echo the precarious position of the Anglo-Irish elite to which Le Fanu belonged. The arrival of the eponymous Carmilla initiates a close bond between the two girls, who recognize one another from a shared dream that represents one of the novella's many instances of the uncanny. While Carmilla's interest in Laura appears erotic, Laura's response oscillates between attraction and repulsion. Laura begins to grow weak following nightmares in which Carmilla blends into her dead mother and a monstrous black cat that punctures Laura's breast in a subversion of the nurturing relationship between mother and child. Carmilla is eventually identified as Mircalla, the undead, succubus-like Countess Karnstein, and staked and decapitated in her tomb. In introducing the first noteworthy fictional female **vampire**, the novella shaped vampire fiction significantly by anticipating the gender anxieties of **Bram Stoker**'s *Dracula*. However, Le Fanu's treatment of non-normative sexualities is notably ambivalent: not only does lesbian vampirism represent a form of resistance to patriarchal expectations of marriage and **motherhood** but Laura remains haunted by Carmilla's memory after her supposed diagnosis and destruction by patriarchal figures.—Minna Vuohelainen

See also Auerbach 1995, **Childhood**, Gelder 1994, Sage 2000, Sage 2004, Signoretti 1996

Carroll, Lewis [*pseud.* of Charles Lutwidge Dodgson] (1832–1898). English author, photographer, mathematician, and inventor. Best known for ***Alice's Adventures in Wonderland*** and *Through the Looking-Glass and What Alice Found There*. Born 27 January 1832 in Daresbury, Cheshire, England, Dodgson was the oldest son of Frances Lutwidge and Rector Charles Dodgson, later Archdeacon of Richmond. Dodgson was a precocious learner with an active imagination. As a child, he built a marionette theater that was later housed at the Creswell Brigham's Museum for Children in Darlington. He was described as possessing "a very uncommon share of genius. Gentle and cheerful ... playful and ready in conversation" (Lennon 1945: p. 28).

Dodgson was educated at home, until age twelve, then sent to Richmond Grammar School followed by Rugby School. He matriculated at Christ Church, Oxford University, in May 1850, and became a resident January 1851. He received a BA, an MA, and honors in mathematics, classical moderations, history, and philosophy. He became mathematics teaching staff and a deacon. His career path required celibacy and allowed him relative solitude, until his literary success brought a certain popularity. He taught until 1881 but lived at Christ Church until his death. He also travelled, including a trip to Russia and visits with Lord Alfred Tennyson and Queen Victoria.

Dodgson was purportedly left handed, considered a disability at the time. He suffered a fever in **childhood** that left him deaf in one ear. Additionally, he suffered from insomnia, severe migraines with aura, possible epilepsy, and a stammer that has become part of the Carroll myth—he is said to have stammered only in adult company, but there is no proof this is true.

He began writing at a young age, including his family magazine *Mischmasch* and published literary works in *The Comic Times*, *The Train*, the *Whitby Gazette*, and the *Oxford Critic*. He wrote topical pamphlets and works on mathematics and logic under his own name. Additionally, numerous works were published by Lewis Carroll from 1856 to 1895.

On a chaperoned boating trip Dodgson reportedly entertained Alice, Lorina, and Edith Liddell, children of the Dean of Christ Church, with the first version of *Alice's Adventures*. Eventually, he fleshed out the story and John Tenniel added **illustrations** for the published version. *Alice's Adventures in Wonderland*, with its neologisms and nonce verse, was an immediate success and brought Carroll enduring fame.

Carroll's mythology as child-doting scholar-saint existed prior to Dodgson's death but was solidified by his nephew's 1898 hagiography and aggravated by his family suppressing evidence of adult female relationships. Dodgson's photographs, a collection of roughly 3,000, containing roughly thirty nude or nearly nude children, coupled with his friendships with young girls, including Alice Liddell, has led critics to suggest pedophilia. However, an aesthetic interest in the physical form of young girls was a common attribute of Victorian London's popular culture, even appearing on Christmas cards. Also, bachelors often became essentially uncles to friends' children. This controversy does not negate the enduring place in popular culture held by Carroll and his creations.—VALERIE L. GUYANT

See also ODNB, Brooker 2004, Collingwood 1898, Phillips 1971, Woolf 2010

Cassell's Illustrated Family Paper (1853–1867), ***Cassell's (Family) Magazine*** (1867–1932). Illustrated **penny fiction weekly**; from 1858, 6d; from 1867, 7d monthly. Started as a lavishly illustrated 8-page folio by the publisher John Cassell and edited at first by John Tillotson, the *Paper* immediately distinguished itself from its rivals the ***London Journal***, the ***Family Herald***, and ***Reynolds's Miscellany*** by its size, the ambition of its **illustrations** (many taken from the French *L'Illustration*) and its carefully moral tales. It was never as popular as those, managing a circulation of around 150,000 at best. Cassell himself took over the editorship in 1855 when he was declared bankrupt and his publishing house was taken over by Petter and Galpin. He lured away J. F. Smith from the ***London Journal*** with higher remuneration, and Smith's **serial**s, combined with the success of Crimean War illustrations, helped restore his fortunes. In 1858 he ceded the editorship to Petter (who raised the price to 6d). *Cassell's* was redesigned and renamed in 1867 to boost falling circulation, but it was **Wilkie Collins**'s serial *Man and Wife* (1870) which succeeded, raising the circulation to 70,000. In 1874, H. G. Bonavia Hunt was made editor and added "Family" to the title. More material was now directed toward women, especially concerning their employment. In 1894, *Cassell's* was forced to lower its price to 6d to compete with new rival the ***Strand***, and two years later Max Pemberton replaced Bonavia Hunt. Pemberton brought in Kipling, **L. T. Meade, William Le Queux, E. W. Hornung, J. M. Barrie, Arnold Bennett**, Baroness Orczy, Joseph Conrad, and many others. Nonetheless, circulation was never very high, and Pemberton resigned in 1906. *Cassell's* limped on for another three decades.—ANDREW KING

Source: Nowell-Smith 1958, Thomas 1987

Catnach Broadsides. James Catnach (pronounced *kat-nak,* according to Charles Hindley) was born in Berwick-upon-Tweed in 1794, but moved to London c. 1813, and set up a publishing business using a printing press from his father's defunct publishing business. Catnach's firm proved to be successful, and had in its employ six printers. The firm published "folk" ballads and chapbooks which sold for a penny or less. The chapbooks that they printed were usually short histories of noted medieval figures and events, such as *Guy of Warwick* and *The Wise Men of Gotham*. Many of the ballads which flowed from Catnach press were reprints of older, seventeenth-century broadsides, including *The Bold Pedlar and Robin Hood* and *Barbara Allen*. Alternatively, the stories of contemporary prose works such as Pierce Egan's *Life in London* (1821) were adapted into song, as in *The Life in London Songster; or, The Sprees of Tom and Jerry* (c. 1820). The Catnach firm often reused eighteenth-century woodblocks for the accompanying **illustrations**, and rarely did the images on their publications relate to the subject at hand. A significant factor in the firm's success, furthermore, was the ability to quickly capitalize upon news of the latest sensational crimes by churning out broadsides about them. Hence a significant portion of the Catnach press's output included "Last Dying Speeches" broadsides which were immensely popular. Some of the crime broadsides, for instance, sold upwards of 250,000 copies. Catnach retired in 1838, and died in 1841.—STEPHEN E. BASDEO

See also Hindley 1887, Neuberg 1977, Shepherd 1973

Chatto and Windus (1855–). English publisher. Now an imprint of Random House Group Ltd., the firm was founded by John Camden Hotten. Andrew Chatto bought it in 1873 upon Hotten's death and was joined by the poet W. E. Windus as a partner. Percy Spalding joined as a partner in 1876. Chatto and Windus published the work of a number of popular writers, whether new or reissued, including **Wilkie Collins**, **Arnold Bennett**, **Ouida**, **Walter Besant** and **James Rice**, and **H. G. Wells**. In 1876, it bought *Belgravia*, the magazine edited by **Mary Elizabeth Braddon**.—SUMAN SIGROHA

See also Warner 1973

Chesney, George Tomkyns (1830–1895). British novelist. Chesney was born into a prominent but impoverished Anglo-Irish family in Tiverton, Devon. He was educated at Blundell's School and then the East India Company Military College at Addiscombe. During the so-called Indian Mutiny of 1857 he was badly wounded in the assault to recapture Delhi. He later became the founding Principal of the Royal Indian Civil Engineering College outside London (1871–1880). Returning to **India** he served in a number of roles culminating in that of military member of the Viceroy's Executive Council. After being knighted he was elected as a Conservative Member of Parliament for Oxford in 1892. He served as chairman of the Committee of Service Members in the Commons until his death in 1895. His best known work was ***The Battle of Dorking***, a piece of speculative fiction highlighting the unpreparedness of Great Britain for war. Other major publications included *Indian Polity* (1868), *A True Reformer* (1872), and several novels. He also contributed articles to a number of major periodicals including *The Nineteenth Century*. In 1899 the highest award of the Royal United Services Institute, the Chesney Gold Medal, was established in memory of Chesney and the impact of his writings.—PATRICK M. KIRKWOOD

See also ODNB

Child Abuse. While the romantic conception of **childhood** as an ideal, innocent state gained widespread acceptance over the course of the nineteenth century, at the same time the realities of child neglect, exploitation, physical and sexual abuse were well known and frequently represented in the era's popular fiction across a range of genres from social realism to **Gothic**. Across the century, legislation was enacted to address child abuses, such as limiting the number of hours children could work; improving working conditions; ensuring primary education for those aged 5–12; raising the age of consent for girls from

12 to 16; and culminating in the Prevention of Cruelty to, and Protection of, Children Act, or Children's Charter, in 1889. All of these efforts recognized the manifold difficulties faced by children. Exposing what he saw as the "curse of neglected children" in the poorest haunts of London in 1868, investigative journalist James Greenwood recounts the horrors of discovering children "so hideously dirty that every rib-bone in their poor wasted little bodies showed plain, and in color like mahogany" (1868: p. 7). Neglect was not the only crime witnessed, for he had earlier encountered a mother with "a baby tucked under one arm, while she was using the other ... in inflicting a tremendous beating on a howling young gentleman of about eleven years old" (1868: p. 6). Politician G. C. T. Bartley, a contemporary of Greenwood, was among many who declared that the only option for such children was to "steal or starve in the streets," otherwise "the State must take charge of them" (1868–69: p. 188). Yet the bleak and bitter irony was that state-controlled institutions such as schools, reformatories, and **orphan**ages became increasingly notorious for the perpetration of physical, mental, and sexual abuses on the children under their care (Pavlakis 2014). While many voluntary organizations, such as Barnardo's (founded 1866) and later the National Society for the Prevention of Cruelty to Children (founded 1884), attempted to protect children, their methods of taking the children into care, raising money, and their depictions of the poor, were not free from censure either (Ash 2005).

Beaten, neglected, and exploited children are featured throughout the many fictive works that aligned themselves with reformist campaigns. Social realists such as Frances Trollope, **Charles Dickens**, Elizabeth Gaskell, George Eliot, **Arthur Morrison**, and journalists such as Greenwood and William T. Stead produced sentimental and often sensationalized portraits of the maltreated child. In Elizabeth Barrett Browning's poem "The Cry of the Children" (1843), influenced by the work of the Royal Commission for the Employment of Children in Mines and Factories in 1842, the abuses the children endure are written on their "pale and sunken faces," because "man's hoary anguish draws and presses / Down the cheeks of infancy" (2009: p. 151). The children of the poem are aware that they, like many abused child-characters such as Helen Burns in Charlotte Brontë's *Jane Eyre* (1847), Jo in Dickens's *Bleak House* (1853) and Tom in **Charles Kingsley**'s fantastical story *The Water-Babies* (1863), would "die before our time"; an awareness which, in itself, contravened the prevailing ideal of a blissfully ignorant childhood. The degradation of the children of the poor undoubtedly received the most attention in public and fictional narratives. However, popular fiction offered realist representations, such as the emotional neglect and physical assault of the teenage Florence Dombey by her enraged and wealthy father in *Dombey and Son* (1848); the manslaughter of Nell Gordon junior by his drunken, resentful, disinherited father in Maggie Symington's *Bessie Gordon's Story* (1874); the poison of a stepson for money in Pen Oliver's *All But: A Chronicle of Laxenford Life* (1886), which corresponded with court cases suggesting that the children of wealthier strata were also under threat. Similarly, issues of abuse, money and inheritance preoccupied British ghost stories in which the trope of the child ghost was used to uncover and reprimand wrongs. In Elizabeth Gaskell's short tale "The Old Nurse's Story" (1852), for instance, the increasingly malevolent young female phantom seeks (and achieves) retribution for the violence perpetrated on her by her maternal aristocratic grandfather, which had resulted in her freezing to death within sight of the manor house. In some stories a more peaceful justice can be achieved, as in "Walnut Tree House" (1882) by **Charlotte Riddell**, in which protagonist Edgar Stainton is being driven insane by the presence of a melancholy boy specter who is searching for something. It is only by finding the will that proves the boy's uncle murdered the child for his inheritance that the child's spirit is laid to rest.

The issue of child sexual abuse was particularly difficult to broach. Even in factual discourse it tended to be referred to euphemistically and framed as a lower-class issue of public morality, as in Stead's notorious journalistic exposé of child prostitution, "The Maiden Tribute of Modern Babylon," in 1885. However, the numbers of incest cases heard in nineteenth-century England signal that intrafamilial sexual abuse was also a known and prevalent problem (Jackson). If it was difficult to face the realities of child sexual abuse in the factual sphere, the cultural arena provided even less scope for engaging with non-normative, abusive sexuality. However, allusions can be discerned in the popular genre of Gothic literature, long-theorized as a vehicle for covertly discussing taboo topics, in the prevalent Gothic trope of the threatened, murdered and even ritually sacrificed child. The incident in **Robert Louis Stevenson**'s *Strange Case of Dr. Jekyll and Mr. Hyde* in which a young girl is trampled on a nighttime street has been read as hinting at child prostitution (Campbell 2014: pp. 311–12). The dark secret surrounding the doomed boy Miles in Henry James's *The Turn of the Screw* (1898) has been interpreted as sexual abuse (Scofield 2003: pp. 98–9). The recurrent consumption of child victims by the highly sexualized female **vampires** of **Bram Stoker**'s *Dracula* may also be read in this light. Given the Gothic's predilection for monstrous outsiders, it seems likely that it was replicating the social disavowal of intrafamilial child sexual abuse by pushing the threat onto external sources.—Jen Baker, Ailise Bulfin

Childhood. For the Victorians, childhood was not simply the period of life between birth and maturity, but a conceptual realm that they imbued with great significance. Building on the philosophical and aesthetic representations configured by the Romantics, childhood became more than simply a cultural idea, but an *ideal*; a utopian vision of innocence and beauty, a time of life that should be characterized by freedom from responsibility, by play, and by happiness. It is not an exaggeration to say that childhood became a cultural obsession, and, in its most glorified state, infiltrated all aspects of life. There was a proliferation of **children's literature** in the period, but childhood was also a dominant concern of literature for adults. In part, this was a means of educating adults *about* children, and reflected the concerns of social and legal institutions that the child was indeed father to the increasingly degenerate man. Yet, as well as aiding a didactic agenda, the nostalgic reconnection with the past offered by these representations also played to the taste for the sentimental. This convergence was particularly reflected in the popular genre of *Bildungsroman*, in which the psychological, physical, and moral maturation of individual character played a central role. **Charles Dickens** was a key author of the genre, exploring the psychological influences of the experiences of childhood on their future development in examples such as *David Copperfield* (1850) and *Great Expectations* (1861): the decisions and reactions of the adult Pip in the latter novel, for instance, are never free from the specters of his sensational childhood encounter with Magwitch in the graveyard, and by the equally morbid but aspirational sensibilities he derived from his youthful visits with Miss Havisham and Estella. Charlotte Brontë's *Jane Eyre* and Emily Brontë's *Wuthering Heights* (1847), similarly explored the darkness in and of childhood, and how this can positively or detrimentally carry through to adulthood and, in the case of Emily's novel, affect the next generation. In adult Victorian Popular Fiction, childhood was consistently presented as a tumultuous yet imperative period for the positive development of the child that consistently enforced the ideal of what childhood *should* and could be.

Those who wrote for both adults and children often sought to represent and encourage a reconnection between the adult and child psyche by drawing from the new forms and styles of literature for children. For instance, Jennifer Sattaur identifies George MacDonald's dark and didactic adult-fantasy *Lilith* (1895), as a novel about the spiritual ideal of rebirth, which uses "child and childhood as a locus for necessary suffering and growth, and the potential for an enlightened future" (2011: p. 11). Yet, as scholars such as Adrienne Gavin have noted, the realities of this suffering (whether necessary or not) tended to overshadow the wider cultural idealization: "childhood in Victorian texts for adults ... was a vulnerable, often painful, powerless state, frequently lonely, with the child portrayed as a victim of adult power, emotional or physical brutality, social neglect, illness, and early death" (2012: p. 9). The textual idealization also stood in stark contrast to **child abuse** of the period—particularly for those from the working classes. Many writers portrayed the child's miseries in order to provoke reform but often through a less psychologically complex depiction. Frances Trollope's industrial novel *The Life and Adventures of Michael Armstrong: Factory Boy* (1840), for instance, employed the trope of the romantic, noble, impoverished but rather flat child-character, who is abused, beaten, or killed owing to the greed and neglect of society. Like Dickens's Oliver and Tiny Tim, the eponymous Michael is contrasted against selfish, spoilt, or grotesque child-figures who present the antithesis of what the child *should* be, and is saved and socially elevated by the generosity of a few reformed upper-class characters. Depictions of the child whose living environment furthers his corruption as opposed to offering redemption became more prevalent in later texts such as **Arthur Morrison**'s *A Child of the Jago* (1896), which controversially focused the hellish topographies of a London slum through the tragic childhood of the increasingly depraved figure of Dickie. Like many other child-characters and their real counterparts, Dickie, does not survive his childhood and his death is depicted as particularly cruel and violent. Not all child deaths were so bleak, however. Some of the most famous literary depictions, such as that of little Nell in Dickens's *The Old Curiosity Shop* (1841), glorified the child's passing as a superior form of sleep, as salvation from the miseries of life, and in doing so mirrored the attitude of bereavement manuals, elegies, sculptures and other forms of memorialization of the period (Jalland 1996). Like many other such romanticized child figures, Nell's status in death was a translation of her patience, beauty and innocence in life—a burdened figure of hope and light in a world of grime and vice.—Jen Baker

Children of Gibeon (1886). Novel by **Walter Besant**. Serially published from January to December 1886 in *Longman's Magazine*, a periodical that catered to middle-class families, and in a three-volume edition in 1886. The plot resembles that of Besant's highly successful **All Sorts and Conditions of Men**. A wealthy widow adopts one of the many children born to a single mother who struggles to keep her family intact by working as a washerwoman. Lady Mildred raises the toddler alongside her own daughter, coincidentally of the same age, in order to prove that "there are, in every condition of life, children who may be trained and educated to have the manners and the instincts of the most well-bred and the most cultured" (2015/1886: p. 354). When they are both twenty, Lady Mildred reveals to her daughters, whom she has renamed Valentine and Violet, that one of them is from the West End and the other from the East End. Convinced that she is from the washerwoman's family, Valentine relocates to the East End to get to know them. There she is exposed to the cruelties of the sweated trades by witnessing the unrelenting labor of her "sister" Melenda and her roommates, who sew buttonholes. Valentine discovers that she is, in fact, Lady Mildred's biological daughter but resolves to stay in the East End and to encourage other women of her class to take an interest in the plight of the seamstress and to help effect change. A critical edition of the novel (revised first edition) was published by Cognella in 2015.—Kevin A. Morrison

Children of the Ghetto: A Study of a Peculiar People (1892). Novel by **Israel Zangwill**. Considered "the first Anglo-Jewish best-seller" (Winehouse 1973: p. 93), the novel prompted comparisons to **Charles Dickens**. Commissioned by the new Jewish Publication Society of America, it was published by the JPSA in the United States and by **Heinemann** in Britain, and translated into many languages for publication worldwide. Zangwill's first full-length novel, *Children of the Ghetto* presented a panoramic view of Jewish life in London during the 1880s and 1890s, the era of the great wave of Jewish immigration from the Russian empire. The first part of the novel, "Children of the Ghetto," focuses on the lives of immigrants in the East End, most of the adults impoverished and Yiddish-speaking, while their children adapt to the English language and English ways. In an episodic but compelling narrative, Zangwill interweaves multiple plots of love, aspiration, and generational conflict with accounts of lifecycle events, festivals of the Jewish year, Jewish communal clubs and activities, folklore, and jokes.

The second part of the novel, "Grandchildren of the Ghetto," returns to major characters of Book One ten years later, in particular the Ansell and Jacobs families, and continues their storylines, in sometimes surprising ways. It also introduces new characters, including a wealthy West End Jewish milieu. While Zangwill treats many in this group satirically, he also presents with seriousness members of the educated younger generation who ponder the future of Jewish life. Both parts of the novel combine humor and pathos characteristic of Zangwill, but the discussions and debates among characters in Book Two echo real concerns of turn-of-the-twentieth-century Jews. In 1899 Zangwill created a play of *Children of the Ghetto*, but the drama covered only the action in Book One and it received mixed reviews. It ran for just seven performances in London, and was more successful in the United States, where it was produced in Washington, Baltimore, Philadelphia, and New York.—Meri-Jane Rochelson

Children's Literature. When Alice asks, at the beginning of ***Alice's Adventures in Wonderland***, what is the use of a book with no pictures or conversations, **Lewis Carroll** presents us with a child reader who is both a shrewd critic and a demanding consumer. He accommodates his reader's penchant not only for enduring child preferences like pictures and conversations, but also for newer literary fare like nonsense and play. Nineteenth-century children's literature aimed to please its imagined readers, alongside its traditional mission of educating them. Indeed, the popularity of the so-called "Golden Age" of children's literature was the result of a robust publishing industry that catered to a variety of child tastes and was constituted by a multiplicity of child-centered genres.

The life of a nineteenth-century child protagonist was rarely dull. Whether set at home or abroad, children's literature dispensed with staler versions of the moral tale to emphasize "character," and having good character could make one a hero. Nowhere is this move more obvious than in adventure fiction's adoption of the ethos of imperialism.

Popular tales like **R. M. Ballantyne**'s *The Coral Island* (1858) and **G. A. Henty**'s *Out on the Pampas* (1871) present plucky, patriotic youths who overcome entanglements with native "others" by exercising characteristically British flair. While much adventure fiction (especially Henty's catalogue) was transparently jingoistic and formulaic, late-century works like **Robert Louis Stevenson**'s *Treasure Island* and **Rudyard Kipling**'s ***The Jungle Book*** refuse to rehearse any predictable nationalistic code of honor; rather they interrogate the very nature of honor and of loyalty. Stevenson's Jim Hawkins and Kipling's Mowgli enjoy both physical adventure and psychological introspection, where the conflict between British and other is ultimately less critical than the friction between boyhood and manhood. Seeking to minimize this tension between generations at least among its own readers, the school story appealed to both the child's desire for adventure closer to home and the adult's nostalgia for the carelessness and camaraderie of youth. Thomas Hughes's *Tom Brown's Schooldays* (1857), the standard bearer of the genre, recalls the halcyon days of the all-boys boarding school, where the chapel and the sports field unite to inculcate students with the twin values of duty and sacrifice. The adventure tale and the school story offered lessons in good citizenship, gift-wrapped for the still boisterous boy.

Victorian children's literature aimed at girls tended toward the domestic and, in the first half of the period, religious. **Mary Martha Sherwood** perfected the evangelical tale with *The History of the Fairchild Family* (1818–1847); Mr. and Mrs. Fairchild turn every lapse in their children's behavior into opportunities for religious instruction, and the lessons—like being forced to look at the hanged body of a murderer—do not flinch. Most Victorian favorites were gentler. Hesba Stretton's *Jessica's First Prayer* (1867) tells of the transformation of a ragged London waif into a proper Christian, capable of redeeming others less fortunate in turn. Because evangelicalism waned at the end of the century and because actual girls' reading preferences always included their brothers' books anyway, later Victorian women writers successfully combined and updated well-worn genres. Regendering the school story with twists of the **imperial adventure** and the fairy tale, Frances Hodgson Burnett's *A Little Princess* (first published as *Sara Crewe* in 1887) features a student at a girls' school who befriends a beggar-girl, makes up stories about being royalty, and covertly communicates with a mysterious **India**n neighbor. Likewise, **Edith Nesbit**'s chronicles of the Bastable family—beginning with *The Story of the Treasure Seekers* (1899)—allow domestic settings to blur, almost imperceptibly, into scenes of adventure and intrigue. The child's necessary subservience to her parents and unwavering devotion to God, pronounced by early-century children's fiction, gave way to the fictional siblings' reliance on each other and the power of quick wit and imagination to overcome the dangers facing them.

This veneration for imagination is the hallmark of the Golden Age. Despite the popularity of adventure and domestic fiction, the school story and religious tale, the genre most associated with Victorian children's literature is fantasy. The Grimm Brothers' fairy tales were first translated into English, by Edgar Taylor, in 1823. The success of this volume inspired a host of celebrated British writers—William Makepeace Thackeray and Charles Dickens among them—to pen original works of magic and make-believe. Magic, however, did not oust morality; many Victorian **fairy tales** delivered deceptively didactic lessons in a whirl of supernatural exhilaration and aesthetic delight. John Ruskin's "The King of the Golden River" (1841) and **Oscar Wilde**'s "The Selfish Giant" (1888) illustrate the destructive power of greed and the beauty inherent in acts of generosity. **Juliana Horatia Ewing**'s "The Brownies" (1865) enlists a fairy order to send a traditional message about being useful and solicitous, while Lucy Clifford's "The New Mother" (1882) augments the familiar lesson about obedience to one's parents with an element of horror fit to rival any of the Grimms' tales. Other fairy tales manipulated the elasticity of the genre to rethink the nature of **childhood**. **Charles Kingsley**'s *The Water-Babies* (1863) allegorizes the theory of evolution via a metamorphosing chimney sweep; drawing on contemporary scientific theories about the child's fundamental animality, Kingsley's tale imagines its hero's recapitulating the species' progress to humanity. George MacDonald's *At the Back of the North Wind* (1868) envisions the child as a religious pilgrim: not the end-recipient of codified religious instruction like the early Victorian child reader, but the generator of true religious knowledge. As his protagonist, Diamond, joins the North Wind on her global trek, he confronts the interdependence of good and evil. The fantastic turn in children's literature also offered almost unbounded creative license to talented illustrators: Richard Doyle, Eleanor Vere Boyle, Arthur Hughes, Walter Crane, and Arthur Rackham, to name only a few.

These flights of fancy have suggested to some children's literature critics that the Golden Age pedaled in escapes from social realities and attempts to preserve the supposed purity and innocence of childhood. The nonsense of Carroll's *Alice* books seems to revel in the wholesale rejection of the child's aboveground life of rules, lessons, and even common sense. Kate Greenaway's **illustrations** depicting playful gaggles of blue-eyed, curly haired, and rosy-cheeked cherubs reinforce this definition of the Victorian cult of childhood as an echo of Romantic veneration of the perfect childhood that social interaction, sexual knowledge, and textual sophistication ineradicably corrupts. But, in fact, moral lessons and real world applications were never far from the minds of Victorian writers for children; fairy tale readers were not asked to abandon their ethical instruction at the door, and *Wonderland* offers the most intricate and elaborate education in logic and language of any work of English literature to date. The moral ambiguity that developed in the adventure tale, the gender dynamics at work through the school story, the emergent skepticism that entered religious literature, the joyous naughtiness that crept into domestic fiction, and the evolutionary reconstructions of childhood that shaped fantasy all suggest that Victorian writers for children never sought to shelter their readers in a manufactured, idealized innocence. Rather, as recent scholars are convincingly arguing, children's literature enticed its intended audience with often unorthodox and irreverent opportunities for self-determination, play-acting, and textual agency.

Increasingly, scholarly engagement with nineteenth-century works for children is eroding the boundaries of the category. Limned on one side with the didactic literature, school books, religious parables, geography primers, and **science** readers that constituted the Victorian child's literary diet and on the other side with contemporary *Bildungsroman* like Charlotte Brontë's *Jane Eyre* (1847) and Dickens's *Great Expectations* (1861) that represent child experience en route to adulthood, children's literature is a permeable taxonomic class. Nor was its practice confined to the bounded, self-contained books now construed as classics. Children's periodicals flourished in the second half of the century: *Chatterbox* (est. 1866), *Little Folks* (est. 1871), *Aunt Judy's Magazine* (est. 1873), *The Boy's Own Paper* (est. 1879), *The Girl's Own Paper* (est. 1880), and many more children's journals provided subscribers with monthly or, in some cases, weekly literary diversions. And some of what we consider children's fiction was published in adult periodicals: Kingsley's *The Water-Babies* first appeared in *Macmillan's Magazine*, which printed fiction and nonfiction for a mature audience, and Kipling introduced Mowgli in a story collection for older readers. Because works branded as "for children" appeared in adult venues, catered to adult nostalgia, echoed and anticipated Victorian novels for adults, incorporated so-called adult concerns about religion and science, and yet simultaneously aimed to become the favorites of children, children's fiction was the product of a tangled intersection of audiences, contexts, and purposes. Though Carroll's Alice offers some vital requisites for appealing to young readers, both the immediate and sustained popularity of nineteenth-century children's fiction depended on much more than simply pictures and conversation.—JESSICA STRALEY

Cholmondeley, Mary (1859–1925). English author. Born in Hodnet, Shropshire, Cholmondeley was the third child and eldest daughter of the upper-class Richard Cholmondeley (nephew of the hymnist Reginald Heber) and Emily Beaumont (granddaughter of the aviator Sir George Cayley). Often incapacitated by severe asthma from her **childhood** onwards, she began publishing fiction in the 1880s. Her first novel *The Danvers Jewels* was published by the Bentley firm in 1887 and clearly shows the influence of **Wilkie Collins**. A sequel *Sir Charles Danvers* appeared in 1889, but her first notable success came with the proto-**New Woman** novel *Diana Tempest* in 1893. The 1897 *A Devotee* proved less successful, although it includes characters who would become famous in the 1899 bestseller *Red Pottage*. The character of the invalid author Hester in *Red Pottage* is based in part on Hester Cholmondeley, who had herself had ambitions to become a writer but who had died of congestion of the lungs in 1892. Cholmondeley included a selection of her unpublished writings in a postwar memoir *Under One Roof* (1918). Cholmondeley's twentieth-century novels failed to achieve the status of *Red Pottage*, although she produced two collections of **short stories** that continue to challenge received gender roles.
—CAROLYN OULTON

Circulating Libraries. During the eighteenth century, circulating libraries (also called subscription libraries) developed and proliferated rapidly in British cities to fulfill the growing demand for the reading of books, periodicals, newspapers, and other print media. These were lent to their subscribers at a monthly or annual fee depending on the income of the subscriber and the quantity of books desired to be borrowed. The lending period varied between two and six days for new publications, with delays in returning the material resulting in heavy fines for the subscribers. The subscription books or lending registers were used to keep track of the subscribers; however, the majority of these registers have not survived to this day. Usually, the copies available in circulating libraries were cheap one-volume editions; especially whole print runs of first edition fiction novels. The reasons for these cheap editions were the new technologies in printing that resulted in lower production costs and, additionally, increased the novels' initial publicity. Lending books provided booksellers with an opportunity to make money on books that they were not able to sell immediately. Subscription libraries developed out of newsrooms and coffee houses. However, in contrast to coffee houses, circulating libraries also admitted women and people from the lower classes as their members. According to Paul Kaufmann, the first use of the term *circulating library* in the *OED* was in 1742, although the concept already existed before this time (1967: p. 10). Circulating libraries were private businesses that made the reading of books affordable for people from most social classes. In addition to serving as sites of intellectual liberation, especially for women, they also provided various forms of entertainment. The majority of works available in a circulating library were novels. This was one of the reasons why they became so popular. At the same time, many criticized novels as vulgar precisely because they were so widely available.—CAROLINE BACHMANN

See also Erickson 1990, Gemmel and Vogt 2013, Hamilton and Wilson 1797, Jacobs 1995, Jacobs 2003, John 2016, McKillop 1934, **Mudie's Circulating Library**

A City Girl: A Realistic Story (1887). Novel by **Margaret Harkness**. *A City Girl* was published under the pseudonym "John Law" by Vizetelly & Company, the publisher infamous for issuing the naturalist fiction of George Moore and Emile Zola. The novel traces the experiences of Nelly Ambrose, a young seamstress living in an East End tenement whose middle-class aspirations lead to her downfall when she is seduced and abandoned by a bourgeois radical. In this "realistic story," Harkness eschews the **melodrama**tic conventions of the fallen woman narrative: instead of death, Nelly is granted life—but it is doubtful whether this life will make her happy. The novel's unaffected style and unsentimental tone draw on Harkness's work in journalism, and her precise observations of life in East Smithfield are invigorated by the three months she spent living and working as a rent collector in the East End Dwellings Company's Katherine Buildings in 1886. On completing *A City Girl* Harkness sent a copy to **socialist** philosopher Friedrich Engels, an effort that indicates the author's political aspirations and interests. While Engels read the novel with "pleasure and avidity," he criticized Harkness's representation of the working class as "a passive mass, unable to help itself" (1973: pp. 114–5). Harkness responded to this evaluation in her second novel, **Out of Work**. A second edition of *A City Girl* was published by the Author's Cooperative Publishing Company in 1890. Two critical editions have recently been published by Victorian Secrets (2015) and Broadview (2017).—LISA C. ROBERTSON

Clara Vaughan (1864). Novel by **Richard Doddridge Blackmore**, published anonymously. Originally titled *The Purpose of a Life* when **serial**ized in *Cassell's Illustrated Family Paper*, the novel was later titled *Clara Vaughan*, published by Macmillan. Since the book was narrated by a female protagonist and originally published anonymously, "it was attributed in contemporary reviews to a lady novelist, Miss **[Mary Elizabeth] Braddon**, a follower of the school of **Wilkie Collins**" (Burris 1930: p. 35). Blackmore corrected this assumption in a later edition's preface. It is sensational novel, following a trend of daughter detective mysteries of the period. The heroine of the story is the titular Clara Vaughan, who searches for her father's murderer. After mistaken assumptions about her uncle, discoveries about mysterious cousins, and assistance from a bloodhound named Giudice, Clara solves the mystery. Confused identities caused the Corsican culprit to kill the wrong brother. In the end, "desires [are] regularized, identities clarified, and a fragmented family [is] reconsolidated" (Johnson 2000: p. 263).—JOSIANNE LEAH CAMPBELL

See also Blackmore 1889, Sutton 1979

Class. By the mid-nineteenth century, literacy was no longer a privilege confined to the upper classes. Particularly after the repeal of the stamp duty in 1855 and the paper duty in 1860, reading material became more affordable and accessible to the working classes. The latter half of the nineteenth century also saw a number of legal changes that allowed for increased opportunity across the class spectrum: the Reform Act of 1867 extended voting rights to some working-class men, and the Elementary Education Acts of 1870 and 1880 increased the availability of education.

The newly literate classes craved fiction, often in **serial** form. **Wilkie Collins** speculated that the five most popular "penny-novel-Journals" were read by about three million people, whom he described as the "unknown public" (1858: p. 218). **Mary Elizabeth Braddon** frequently published in **penny fiction periodicals**, often pseudonymously: her novel *The Octoroon* (1862), for example, initially appeared in the *Halfpenny Journal*, which billed itself as "A Magazine for All Who Can Read." In 1899, the novelist **Walter Besant** observed how "reading, which has always been the amusement of the cultivated class, has now become the principal amusement of every class: all along the line from peer to chimney sweep we are reading" (1899: p. 30).

Genre novels such as **sensation fiction** were particularly popular across the class spectrum, which proved to be a great source of anxiety for contemporary critics. Novels featuring sensational plotlines such as blackmail, **bigamy**, and murder were dismissed by the *Examiner* as "Kitchen Literature," a term meant to suggest that such books were fit only for cooks or kitchen maids to read. However, as an 1865 article observed, the popularity of genre fiction "temporarily succeeded in making the literature of the Kitchen the favorite reading of the Drawing-room" (Rae 1865: p. 105). Future prime minister William Gladstone, for example, was an avowed fan of Collins's ***The Woman in White*** and the future King Edward VII sang the praises of **Mrs. Henry [Ellen] Wood**'s *East Lynne*.

Novel reading, in fact, appeared to bridge the gap among the classes. Indeed, the same novel that the master and mistress of a grand manor might read was often being enjoyed at the same time by the butler, housekeeper, cook, or maid, only in a different print form. One review from 1867 remarked how

> Kitchen Literature … delights the imagination of a scullery maid, while it gratifies the frivolity of any Lady Aramina who, sharing the tastes of Betty the scullery maid, reads Betty's books when they are republished in three volumes octavo, and differs from her humble sister only in having had the opportunity of rising to a higher level of intelligence and not having used it ["Review" 1867: pp. 500–501].

This leveling of literary taste among the social classes caused no small amount of anxiety for Victorian critics.

Frequently, the more popular a work of literature proved to be among middle- and working-class readers, the more likely critics were to denounce it as low-quality art. Mary Elizabeth Braddon was hailed as the "Queen of the circulating libraries," a triumphant assertion of how her sheer popularity promoted her to the status of literary royalty. But in an 1864 review of Braddon's novel ***Henry Dunbar***, she was alternatively dubbed "the great chef of the kitchen maids" and described as bringing her "tainted meat … upstairs for the delectation of coarse appetites in the politer world" ("Kitchen Literature" 1864: p. 404). In effect, the author, the audience, and the art itself are all categorized as lower class.

The "literary devolution" supposedly indicated by the proliferation of genre fiction dovetails with critics' fears of social devolution or even revolution: in 1868, Francis Edward Paget saw the sensationalism and sensuality of contemporary popular novels as harbingers of "a reign of lust" that could be followed by "a reign of terror" reminiscent of the French Revolution (1868: p. 303). This fear was fueled by the contents of the novels themselves. Many popular books offered glimpses of worlds in which conventional class boundaries were blurred or the social hierarchy had been turned upside down.

Working-class characters in popular fiction often enjoyed the prospect of upward mobility, as in William Makepeace Thackeray's *Vanity Fair* (1847–1848), Charlotte Brontë's *Jane Eyre* (1847), Collins's *No Name* (1862), and Braddon's **Lady Audley's Secret**. In addition, working-class readers might delight in reading how upper-class characters were brought low or lured into the world of their former social inferiors, as in *East Lynne*, **Florence Marryat**'s *Love's Conflict* (1865) or Emma Newby's *Trodden Down* (1866). In 1886, one critic described how penny novelettes would pander to a working-class audience with plots that "thrive on the wicked baronet or nobleman and the faithless but handsome peeress, and find their chief supporter among shop-girls, seamstresses, and domestic servants" (Salmon 1886: p. 112). Indeed, while working-class women held little power in the real world, popular fiction could offer a gratifying escapist fantasy in which they might even claim the upper hand.

In 1840, a valet killed his master and claimed that his murder was inspired by reading **William Harrison Ainsworth**'s *Jack Sheppard* (Brantlinger 1998: p. 71). The popularity of stories of murder, lust, and revenge among members of the lower classes was thus a cause for concern among many contemporary critics, who feared that these readers' minds might be warped or turned to crime due to their choice of leisure reading. Tracts were written warning against the dangers of novel-reading and *Servants' Magazine* contained frequent parables describing how reading popular fiction can lead to personal ruin. In the 1859 story "Daughters from Home," for example, a woman longs to become like the heroine of a romantic novel she has been reading but is instead lured into prostitution.

While it seems unlikely that many members of the working class were led into a life of vice and crime solely due to their choice of reading material, it is worth noting that many fictional working-class characters, particularly those employed as domestic servants, are seen committing criminal acts. While today, the solution that "the butler did it" is a tired cliché, nineteenth-century literature can boast its share of servant criminals. In **Charles Dickens**'s *Bleak House* (1853), for example, Lady Dedlock is framed for murder by her lady's maid, and in **Sheridan Le Fanu**'s *Uncle Silas* (1864) the governess Madame de la Rougierre terrorizes and steals from her employing family. Blackmail is a favorite crime of domestic employees. In Braddon's *Aurora Floyd* (1863), for example, the mistress of the house is blackmailed by her housekeeper, and in *Lady Audley's Secret*, a lady's maid extorts money from her mistress in exchange for her silence. Of course, members of the gentry are not immune to being lured into crime, either. The A. J. **Raffles stories** feature a gentleman thief, and Sherlock Holmes's cases often reveal the hypocritical deceptions of members of the gentry.

Wilkie Collins frequently used servant narrators to offer alternative perspectives and commentary on the events of the novel: **The Moonstone** is narrated in part by the butler Gabriel Betteredge, and its key clue comes from the pen of the housemaid Rosanna Spearman. The voice of the working classes was also often heard in the novels of Charles Dickens. In 1867, Mary Elizabeth Braddon's magazine **Belgravia** celebrated Dickens as "the great prophet of the union of the classes—the link between rich and poor, never weary of showing to the former what virtues and endurance and what charity is found under rags and in hovels; and to the latter, that the rich are not monsters and tyrants" ("Literary Honours" 1867: p. 324). Dickens did, however, create his share of "rich tyrant" characters, and he often offered overt social commentary on what he perceived to be the greed of the wealthy and powerful in contrast to the simple decency of the working classes. The miserly Ebenezer Scrooge and the crippled but noble Tiny Tim from *A Christmas Carol* (1843) are two extreme stereotypes in this vein.

Dickens was also one of many authors whose work exposed the hypocrisies and arbitrariness of the British class system. In *Great Expectations* (1861), Pip's incredible journey from humble apprentice blacksmith to well-read gentleman is the result of a chance encounter with a convict. In other popular Victorian novels, altering one's class status is revealed to be as simple as dressing the part. *The Woman in White*, *East Lynne*, and *Henry Dunbar* all contain plot devices that rely upon characters donning clothing in order to "pass" as a member of higher or lower class status. In a more explicit and extreme example, the subjective nature of class distinctions is laid bare in Collins's *The Dead Secret* (1857) when the genteel protagonist learns that she is actually the daughter of a servant whose mistress raised her as her own. While not all authors of popular fiction had patent "missions" such as Collins's crusade for social justice, their depictions of class reflected the new possibilities and perspectives of a readership that spanned the social spectrum.—ELIZABETH STEERE

Cleeve, Lucas (1868–1908). English novelist and linguist. Adeline Georgiana Isabel Kingscote (*née* Wolff) wrote under a pseudonym, although, after her marriage to Col. Howard Kingscote, she would publish under the name Mrs. Howard Kingscote. Cleeve published over sixty works, including *Tales of the Sun; or Folklore of Southern India* (1890), *The English Baby in India and How to Rear It* (1893), *What a Woman Will Do* (1900), *Eileen* (1903), and *What Woman Wills* (1908). As a response to **Grant Allen**'s *The Woman Who Did*, Cleeve was to publish her first work under her own name, **The Woman Who Wouldn't** (1895). This work was to join the late nineteenth-century debate on marriage, **motherhood**, and the **New Woman**. Cleeve faced many financial scandals, which included running many others into financial ruin, during her time in England. After declaring bankruptcy in 1899, Cleeve fled to Switzerland where she was to become even more productive; publishing up to eight novels a year. Cleeve's last six works were not published until after she died in 1908 in Switzerland.—AMBERYL MALKOVICH

Collaboration. The February 1892 edition of *Hearth and Home* proclaimed, "[c]ollaboration is one of the literary features of our age, and at the present rate of progression there seems to be some prospect of it attaining alarming proportions in the future" (Anon 1892: p. 383). The nineteenth-century upturn in collaborative endeavor is first detectable as a notable "feature" of the print marketplace (collaboration was nothing new in writing for the stage) in magazine and **serial**ized novel production of the 1850s and 1860s as writers shared the burden of satisfying rapidly growing readerships' increasing demands for new writing. In the mid-century, **Charles Dickens** collaborated extensively with the staff writers of *Household Words*, including **Eliza Lynn Linton** and George Augustus Sala, to produce a number of stories, especially for the Christmas numbers. Dickens also collaborated extensively with **Wilkie Collins** on works including, *The Lazy Tour of Two Idle Apprentices* (1857), *The Perils of Certain English Prisoners* (1857), and *No Thoroughfare* (1867).

The appetite for collaborative writing continued with a series of popular coauthored novels appearing between 1870 and 1910 including: Walter Besant and **James Rice**'s *Ready-money Mortiboy* (1872), and *The Golden Butterfly* (1876); Andrew Lang and **Rider Haggard**'s *World's Desire* (1890); Joseph Conrad and Ford Madox Ford's *The Inheritors* (1901), *Romance* (1903), *The Nature of a Crime* (1909); Somerville and Ross's (pseudonyms of

Edith Somerville and Violet Martin) *An Irish Cousin* (1889), *The Real Charlotte* (1894), and their hugely popular series of "Irish R. M." stories beginning with *Some Experiences of an Irish R. M* (1899).

The cousins Somerville and Ross are just one example of literary collaboration arising from the context of the shared familial home. Others include the brothers Edmond and Jules de Goncourt who coauthored a series of novels throughout the 1860s; the Rossetti sisters, Helen and Olivia, who cowrote one novel entitled *A Girl among the Anarchists* (1903) under the name "Isabel Meredith"; and Emily and Dorothea Gerard, who collaborated on four novels between 1879 and 1891. According to Linda H. Peterson, in the 1850s, William and Mary Howitt mentored their daughters, Margaret and Mary Anne, through journalistic apprenticeships at home, where they edited and published *Howitt's Journal of Literature and Popular Progress* and many other literary projects (1998: p. 35).

The 1880s and 1890s witnessed a trend in experimental modes of multiple authorship known as round robin or composite novels. These were usually serialized in magazines with a different author supplying each installment or chapter. Examples include *Six of One by Half a Dozen of the Other: An Everyday Novel* (1872) by six authors including Harriet Beecher Stowe; *The Miz Maze or The Winkworth Puzzle: A Story in Letters* (1882) by nine authors including Frances Awdry, Christabel Coleridge, and **Charlotte Yonge**; *His Fleeting Ideal. A Romance of Baffled Hypnotism* (1890) by, among others, the infamous circus promoter P. T. Barnum and Ella Wheeler Wilcox; and, arguably, the finest example of the composite novel form, *The Fate of Fenella* (1892) written by 24 authors including **Bram Stoker**, **Conan Doyle**, and **Florence Marryat**, published in **Cassell's Magazine**. It is significant that these novels were often marketed as oddities, published in response to a growing interest in the occupation of detecting individual hands within a multiply-authored work, as discussed in a work of 1891 by the author, critic and American Copyright League organizer, Brander Matthews. He stated that it is "curiosity which lends interest to many a book written in collaboration, the reader being less concerned about the merits of the work than he is in guessing at the respective shares of its associate authors. To many of us a novel by two writers is merely a puzzle, and we seek to solve the enigma of its double authorship, accepting it as a nut to crack even when the kernel is little likely to be more digestible than the shell" (1891: p. 1).

The demands of the serialized popular fiction market necessitated notable instances of what could be called posthumous collaboration. For instance, **Wilkie Collins** died just days after Besant took over his serial *Blind Love* (1890), while Arthur Quiller-Couch reluctantly completed the recently deceased **Robert Louis Stevenson**'s *St. Ives: Being the Adventures of a French Prisoner in England* (1897) for *Pall Mall Magazine*.

Works of short fiction in popular magazines commented on the proliferation of collaboration across the 1890s. Henry James published "Collaboration" in 1892, while an anonymous **short story** of 1901, "The Mystery of Collaboration: A Practical Experiment," satirized the efforts of a group of literary ladies in writing a round robin novel.

All of the above confirms *Hearth and Home*'s observation that collaboration was "one of the literary features" of the age, a feature often overlooked in scholarship and current undergraduate pedagogic practice.—KIRSTY BUNTING

Collins, William Wilkie (1824–1889). English author. Published in 1860, Collins's smash-hit ***The Woman in White*** established him as one of the most successful and well-known popular authors of the nineteenth century. It is generally accepted as the first **sensation novel**, and it was as a sensation author that Collins was (and continues to be) best known. Reviews of the novel initiated what would become the dominant critical attitude toward Collins, and sensation fiction more broadly; that the "plot is in point of intricacy a masterpiece," but while this "thrills your nerves," the characters are "unnatural" and the "incidents" are "improbable" ("The Woman" 1860: p. 233). Yet the public could not get enough of the mystery and excitement that sensation fiction guaranteed.

While *The Woman in White* escaped the moral critical outrage that met **Mary Elizabeth Braddon**'s *Lady Audley's Secret*, Collins drew his share of controversy. The proto-sensation novel *Basil* (1852), which features scenes of violence and adultery, was condemned for its "faulty and unwholesome" subject matter (Maddyn 1852: p. 1323). Even at this early stage, Collins was aware that what he saw as moral frankness would provoke conservative Victorian critics, and so he penned a pre-emptive "Letter of Dedication," asserting that *Basil* was a truthful reflection of "human life," in which "examples of error and crime" were "put … to good moral use" (Collins 2005/1852: p. 5). These defensive prefaces became a recurrent feature of his work and offer useful insight into his attitudes toward the rights and responsibilities of authors and the fiction they produce. The two novels which followed *The Woman in White* were, in their own ways, as provocative as *Basil* and attracted critical censure proportional to the weight that the name of Wilkie Collins now held, and to the ongoing popularity of the sensation genre. *No Name*'s (1862) Magdalen Vanstone, who commits fraud in order to secure her inheritance, angered critics because she was presented as the novel's heroine; while the mockery aimed at *Armadale*'s (1866) alluring villainess Miss Gwilt ("whose hair," as one disdainful reviewer told its readers, "is uncompromisingly red, whose morals are abominable, whose tastes are homicidal"), reveals how uncomfortable she made critics ("Armadale" 1866: p. 680).

In fact, throughout his career, Collins created distinctive, resourceful, strong-minded female characters who challenged the gender expectations of the period, most famously *The Woman in White*'s "ugly," "masculine," heroine Marion Halcombe (1996/1860: pp. 31–2). Collins's male characters also frequently countered Victorian masculine stereotypes through their physicality or emotionality (such as *Armadale*'s sentimental, sometimes hysterical Ozias Midwinter). This tendency to defy convention is a key feature of Collins's writing that led to his critical reappraisal in the 1980s.

Another aspect of Collins's work that drew late twentieth-century critics' attention was his fascination with unusual mental states (ranging from insanity, to dream states, to unconscious cerebration). Jenny Bourne Taylor's *In the Secret Theater of Home* (2013/1988) was a groundbreaking exploration of Collins's engagement with Victorian psychology and **medicine**. In subsequent decades, Collins scholarship has broadened to explore his varied depictions of difference and otherness. These representations of non-normative types (in terms of physical and mental ability, social status and ethnicity) often avoid stereotype, caricature, and marginalization. Disability studies scholars have, for example, looked at the complex characterization of the blind Lucilla Finch, who is not the weak heroine that the title *Poor Miss Finch* (1872) implies, and of the physically disabled, extremely eccentric, Miserrimus Dexter (*The Law and the Lady*, 1875). Collins's works are also attracting the attention of post-colonial researchers as they feature mixed-race characters (such as Midwinter, and Natalie Graybrooke in *Miss or Mrs.?* (1872), or otherwise engage with the problematics of Empire. The eponymous diamond in ***The Moonstone*** is, for example, stolen from **India**.

The Moonstone, Collins's most enduring work, besides *The Woman in White*, is widely credited as being the first English **detective novel**. In fact, while he is primarily known as a sensation author, Collins was a versatile writer who produced drama (including dramatizations of his own novels), **short stories**, and non-fiction during his four-decade professional career. His first published work, in 1848, was a biography of his father, the painter William Collins, and Wilkie wrote numerous articles, sketches, travel memoirs and opinion pieces for the periodical press. His close personal and professional relationship with **Charles Dickens** has sometimes led to the overshadowing of Collins's own immense success, but was undoubtedly beneficial; they travelled together, acted together, worked in **collaboration** (on the 1856 drama *The Frozen Deep*, for example), and Collins spent several years on the staff of Dickens's periodicals *Household Words* and *All the Year Round*, in which many of his works were **serial**ized.

Throughout his career, Collins criticized the hypocrisies and injustices he perceived at work in his society and its institutions. The intricacies and tyrannies of legal systems, particularly regarding marriage, inheritance and legitimacy, are recurrent themes in his work (he had undertaken legal training before focusing on writing). *Man and Wife* (1870), for example, exposed the unfairness, and ridiculousness, of Victorian marriage laws, particularly as they disadvantaged women. An increasingly heavy-handed delivery of such social messages led to a supposed lowering in the quality of Collins's later fiction (the gout he suffered from for much of his adult life, and the laudanum addiction he developed in an attempt to manage the pain have also been blamed). Nevertheless, Collins continued to develop intriguing characters and draw on topical issues: *The New Magdalen* (1873) features a sympathetically presented prostitute, **Heart and Science** a vivisectionist, and *The Legacy of Cain* (1888) engages with the discourse of degeneration (the hereditary transmission of negative traits) that strongly influenced late-nineteenth-century medical and social practice. These later works, and indeed the full range of Collins's experiments with form and genre beyond sensation fiction, provide plenty of ground for future research, a task that has been made much easier in recent years as almost all of his works have been digitized and the majority of them are freely available online.—HELENA IFILL

The Coming Race (1871). Novel by **Edward Bulwer-Lytton**. A pioneering **science fiction** novel that delineates an alternative civilization of highly evolved, rational beings, the "Vril-ya," living within the interior of the earth. It has been admired for its prescience in envisioning both weapons of mass destruction and the corollary doctrine of mutually assured destruction through its imaginative conception of the electrical-magnetic force of "vril," a force, however, that is equally adaptable for purposes of healing and communication. As a quintessentially Victorian contribution to the genre of Utopian fiction, it satirically reflects contemporaneous cultural developments (the 1867 Reform Bill, the establishment of Girton College for women in 1869, and the 1871 publication of Darwin's *Descent of Man*), while revisiting the author's interest in **mesmerism** and **occultism**, now recast as the scientific praxis of a posthuman race.

The minimal plot presents the unnamed American protagonist's descent into the subterranean realm, his first encounter with the formidable species, his subsequent sojourn with them, and his ultimately urgent escape. The bulk of the narrative is given over to the speculative and reflexive ethnography of Utopian discourse in which the narrator becomes familiarized with the mores and social system of his hosts, and in exchange reveals the deficiencies of his own culture.

The Vril-ya live in communities of 12,000 families in a "benevolent autocracy," with "a single supreme magistrate" (Bulwer Lytton 1989: p. 27) appointed for life, having ages past advanced from the savage order of "Koom-Posh," "the government of the ignorant upon the principle of being the most numerous" (p. 54). Although property is not held in common, competition and **poverty** are unknown, and the adults of the race freely pursue the occupations most congenial to them. The equality of the sexes has been assured by the physical superiority of the females, the "Gy-ei," who have the all-important prerogative to choose and court their mates. Unfortunately for the narrator, his host's daughter Zee, a philosopher and Professor in the College of Sages, develops an infelicitous love for him and in the partly comic final section of the narrative, he fears being reduced to a cinder for the mere prospect of miscegenation.

Toward the close, the text takes an interesting meta– and anti–Utopian turn. Although the "angelic order" (p. 118) of subterranean beings has secured all the "the ideals of a Utopian future" that "various philosophers of the upper world" have projected, the narrator reflects that human begins are simply not "fitted to enjoy the very happiness … to which we aspire" (p. 115). Utopia, Bulwer-Lytton asserts, would be insufferably dull and uncongenial.

Having inferred that the Vril-ya were originally "of our human race," the narrator concludes that they have over time "developed into a distinct species" inimical to our own in the struggle for existence, and foresees the eventuality of their emergence "into sunlight [as] our inevitable destroyers" (p. 128).—Bruce Wyse

Conan Doyle, Arthur (1859–1930). Scottish writer. Conan Doyle was born in Edinburgh, the third of nine children and the eldest son of illustrator Charles Altamont Doyle and Mary Foley, the latter with whom Conan Doyle formed a close relationship and corresponded regularly until her death in 1921. Conan Doyle was educated at Hodder preparatory school (1867–69), at Stonyhurst College (1869–75), and at Feldkirch in Austria (1875–76). He entered the University of Edinburgh in 1876 to read medicine. There, he met Joseph Bell, who became an important influence to his creation of **Sherlock Holmes**. Conan Doyle's earliest **short story**, "The Mystery of Sasassa Valley," appeared in *Chambers's Journal* in October 1879. His studies were interrupted by his work as a doctor's assistant in a number of places including Birmingham and as a ship's doctor on the whaler *Hope* of Peterhead. He graduated MB CM in 1881, and from October 1881 to January 1882, he served as surgeon on the steamer *Mayumba*. In 1885, Conan Doyle received his MD, also from Edinburgh, for "An Essay Upon the Vasomotor Changes in *Tabes Dorsalis* and on the Influence Which Is Exerted by the Sympathetic Nervous System in that Disease." That year, he married Louisa Hawkins, and their children Mary and Alleyne Kingsley were born in 1889 and 1892 respectively.

Conan Doyle was prolific and he wrote in a wide variety of genres. A number of short stories and articles had emerged, and his novel *The Mystery of Cloomber* (**serial**ized in the *Pall Mall Gazette* before it was published as a book in 1888) was completed by the time the first Holmes story, ***A Study in Scarlet***, appeared in *Beeton's Christmas Annual* in 1887 and subsequently in book form, in 1888, by Ward Lock, with six **illustrations** by Charles Doyle. Its sequel ***The Sign of Four*** was published by *Lippincott's Magazine* and Ward Lock and in book form by Spencer Blackett. *Micah Clarke* was published in 1889 and both *The Captain of the 'Pole-Star' and Other Tales* and *The Firm of Girdlestone* in 1890. His favorite work, *The White Company*, a romance set in the fourteenth century, was serialized in *Cornhill* magazine and published by Smith Elder. Yet Conan Doyle was and remains best known for his short stories about the detective Holmes and his friend and sidekick Dr. John Watson: they were introduced into the **Strand** in July 1891, and nearly doubled the magazine's circulation (Edwards, ODNB). For the first six stories, Conan Doyle earned £35 each, and his fee of £50 for each story was readily accepted, as was his fee of £1,000 for a dozen stories in 1892 (Grella and Dematteis 1983).

On 11 November 1891, Conan Doyle wrote to his mother, after completing "The Blue Carbuncle," "The Speckled Band," "The Noble Bachelor," "The Engineer's Thumb," and "The Beryl Coronet": "I think of slaying Holmes in the sixth & winding him up for good & all. He takes my mind from better things" (Lellenberg, Stashower, & Foley 2008: p. 300). Conan Doyle did not carry out the plan until 1893, when Holmes confronted Professor Moriarty, his equal, at the Reichenbach Falls in Switzerland (Conan Doyle and Louise had visited the falls earlier that year). "The Final Problem," which appeared in the December issue of the *Strand*, spurred over 20,000 readers to cancel their subscriptions (Grella and Dematteis 1983). Conan Doyle followed the Holmes stories with those about Brigadier Gerard. In addition to fiction, he was also an insightful writer of nonfiction: he supported British efforts in the South African War, serving as a doctor in a volunteer British Army field hospital in South Africa in 1900 and publishing two works *The Great Boer War* (1900) and *The War in South Africa: Its Cause and Conduct* (1902). He was knighted in 1902. In 1901, Conan Doyle returned to Holmes through **The Hound of the Baskervilles**, a posthumous Sherlock Holmes adventure that predated Reichenbach. A generous offer—of $25,000 for six stories, $30,000 for eight, and $45,000 for thirteen—from the American magazine *Collier's Weekly* finally brought the return of Holmes (Lellenberg, Stashower, & Foley 2008: p. 510), and he would resurface in the pages of the *Strand* from 1903 to 1904. Contemporaries would liken Conan Doyle's relationship with his creation to that of Frankenstein and his (Ue 2015: p. 228). Conan Doyle's wife Louise died of tuberculosis in 1906, and the following year he married Jean Blyth Leckie; their three children Denis, Adrian, and Jean were born in 1909, 1910, and 1912 respectively.

Conan Doyle's idea for *The Lost World* (1912) germinated in 1889, when he wrote to his mother: "I am thinking of trying a Rider Haggardy kind of book called 'the Inca's Eye' dedicated to all the naughty boys of the Empire, by one who sympathizes with them. I think I could write a book of that sort con amore" (Lellenberg, Stashower, & Foley 2008: p. 260). The novel introduced readers to the hot-tempered Professor Challenger, Conan Doyle's second most famous creation and the principal vehicle through which he would explore the **science fiction** genre: with these characters, he will travel to South American plateaus, where dinosaurs continue to roam, and make fresh discoveries including "The Disintegration Machine" (1929). During the First World War, he served as a military correspondent and historian, writing a number of volumes. Holmes himself would have his own wartime story, "His Last Bow," which appeared in the *Strand* three years into the war, and the year America entered the war. The story is set on the night of 2 August 1914. Told in the third person, it follows how, as the cover of the *Strand* intimates, "Sherlock Holmes Outwits a German Spy," and it is subtitled "The War Service of Sherlock Holmes." In his final years, Conan Doyle championed spiritualism, something to which he was introduced in the 1880s, and embraced in 1916, through works such as *The Wanderings of a Spiritualist* (1921) and *The History of Spiritualism* (1926). Conan Doyle died in Sussex on 7 July 1930, leaving behind an extensive oeuvre and some of literature's most popular characters.—Tom Ue

See also ODNB

Concerning Isabel Carnaby (1898). Novel by Ellen Thorneycroft Fowler (1860–1929). Celebrated for her witty if essentially conservative society novels, Fowler made her name with the 1898 *Concerning Isabel Carnaby*. The novel uses drawing room humor reminiscent of **Oscar Wilde**'s comic dialogue to explore and problematize class and gender identity, themes to which Fowler would return a year later in the bestselling *A Double Thread*. In *Concerning Isabel Carnaby* the conflict between aristocratic values, religious prompting and romantic attraction is explored through the unstable relationship between the upper class Isabel and her middle class suitor the Methodist Paul Seaton. In the context of the **New Woman** debate and continued tensions with regard to the status of female authorship in the 1890s, the novel notably presents the damaging effects of an ill-advised pseudonymous novel on the career and family relationships of the jilted Paul Seaton, whose position is never fully rectified despite his subsequent publication of the symbolically titled *Some Better Thing*. Fowler's novel raises a number of questions about the implications of the domestic/public divide for authors of both sexes, and what it means to be associated with a particular school of fiction, not least whether anonymity signals consciously inferior work rather than the conventional reserve of the "modest authoress." But in a twist on the central theme that is characteristic of Fowler's fiction, it transpires that the writer of the original "vulgar" attack on faithless aristocratic women is in fact Isabel herself, rather than the promising male author whose reputation has been sullied.—CAROLYN OULTON

Connor, Marie (c. 1865–1941). English novelist and poet. Noted author of **sensation fiction** who contributed to the emerging genres of mystery and **detective fiction**. As a child, she sent out a plagiarized novel of **Mrs. Henry [Ellen] Wood**'s for publication, which earned her a home visit from the publisher. Connor fell in love with the theatre and actor Wilson Barrett, who was to serve as her poetic muse. For a time, she was to travel with him under the watchful eye of her Aunt Pollie. After realizing the stage was less than glamorous, Connor returned home proclaiming she wanted to write. She became a prolific writer and penned over sixty novels between 1884 and 1937. Her works include *Beauty's Queen* (1884), *The Harvest of Sin* (1889), *The Amazing Verdict* (1904), *Her Ladyship's Silence* (1907), *Joan Mar, Detective* (1910), *The Hand of the Unseen* (1918), and *The Silence of Dr. Duveen* (1937). Connor married the popular author Robert Leighton in 1889. She most often published under *Marie Connor Leighton*.—AMBERYL MALKOVICH

Corelli, Marie [Mary Mackay] (1855–1924). English novelist. Corelli is Stratford-upon-Avon's other literary child: neglected today, she was, in the late-nineteenth and early-twentieth centuries, more popular and more widely read than Shakespeare. Her novels are the first modern English bestselling novels: published in a single volume at 6s. after the decline of the three-decker in 1894/95, they could be purchased, rather than borrowed through a lending library, and reach hundreds of thousands of people. Corelli's readership was still homogeneous, crossed all social strata from the lowly scullery maid to Queen Victoria herself, via notables such as William Gladstone, Alfred Lord Tennyson, **Oscar Wilde**, James Joyce, William Butler Yeats, Edmund Gosse, **Arnold Bennett**, Mark Twain, **H. G. Wells**, **J. M. Barrie**, Wyndham Lewis, and Ezra Pound.

Born Mary ("Minnie") Mackay in 1855 (although Corelli liked people to believe that she was born in 1864) to poet, editor, journalist Charles Mackay and his servant and second wife, Ellen Mills, Mary invented a pseudonym and literary persona after a short career as a pianist and a number of smaller literary successes in ***Temple Bar*** after July 1885. Her 1886 novel, *A Romance of Two Worlds*, caught the public imagination by storm, with its blending of art, religion and love in a narrative marked by an "emotional drive and luxuriant vitality" that even the high-brow Queenie Leavis later granted the author in her 1832 study *Fiction and the Reading Public* (1932: p. 63). Under George Bentley's fatherly guidance—he quickly understood Corelli's talent to tap into the *zeitgeist*— Corelli published in quick succession *Vendetta* (1886), *Thelma* (1887), *Ardath* (1889), **Wormwood**, *The Soul of Lilith* (1892), *Barabbas* (1893), **The Sorrows of Satan**, **The Murder of Delicia**, **The Mighty Atom**, *Ziska, Boy* (1900), *The Master Christian* (1900), *Temporal Power* (1902), *God's Good Man* (1904), *The Treasure of Heaven* (1906), *Holy Orders* (1908), and *The Life Everlasting* (1911). Her novels usually contain love plots, comments on the contemporary crisis of faith, and on "the Woman Question." The latter contains as many contradictory statements as Corelli's narrative "solutions" to religious doubt contain originality; her discourses on contemporary aesthetics—also in her essay collections *The Silver Domino* (1893) and *Free Opinions Freely Expressed* (1905)—have not received the attention they deserve as historical documents. Corelli's popularity had declined by the time of the First World War, when Corelli turned to writing patriotic essays and speeches. Her last novels—*Innocent* (1914), *The Young Diana* (1918), and *Love and the Philosopher* (1923)—received but little attention. Her **collaboration** with painter Arthur Severn on *The Devil's Motor* (1910) and her working through their one-sided and, on his side, manipulative relationship in the posthumous *Open Confession to a Man from a Woman* (1925) have been of interest to readers and scholars who focus on Corelli's love life and sexuality (she lived with her **childhood** friend and later biographer Bertha Vyver for most of her life). Her novels were published by Tauchnitz on the continent and translated into the major European languages (Danish, French, German, Greek, Dutch, Italian, Polish, Romanian, Swedish, Spanish, Czech), and also Russian, Nigerian, Hindi, Thai, and Urdu.

During a career that spanned almost four decades, Corelli wrote a total of twenty-six novels, two non-fictional collections on the contemporary literary, social and political scene, over a hundred speeches and articles, about fifty **short stories** and multiple poems and reviews. She was regularly derided by her contemporaries because of her factual blunders (she thought Michael was Michelangelo's first name, and she called Judas Iscariot's fictitious sister Judith Iscariot), the girlish image she upheld even into her sixties (in text as well as heavily retouched photographs), her flowery style, improbable plot lines and flat characters. Eight biographies—by Kent Carr, Thomas Coates/ Warren Bell, Bertha Vvyer, George Bullock, Eileen Bigland, William Scott, Brian Masters and Teresa Ransom)—have addressed Corelli's gifts and shortcomings with more or less sympathy. Beyond this female writer's undoubtedly unique character, however, her novels are valuable documents for scholars of Victorian popular literature who pursue Corelli as a publishing and literary "phenomenon," as a *zeitgeist* critic and commentator (religion and pseudo-religions; feminism and anti-feminism; education; **technology**; the sciences; the literary marketplace), and as an important contributor to the aesthetic debates of the time (romance-realism; the nascent high-low debate; aestheticism; the **Gothic**; fantasy; **sensation**alism; **melodrama**; the **short story**). Any study that seeks to answer why Corelli became the most popular author of her day must read the novels within the context of their time but also accept the novel's undeniably energy and the "magnetism in [Corelli's] pen" that not only a fan and contemporary like Gladstone (qtd. in Bigland 1953: p. 109) but also later critics and readers like Queenie Leavis, Rebecca West, and Henry Miller acknowledged.—JULIA KUEHN

Craik, Dinah Mulock (1826–1887). English author. Best known for *John Halifax, Gentleman* (1856), Craik published 20 novels, 12 children's books, and over 150 **short stories** and essays. Extremely popular, with multiple editions and translations in a variety of languages, her works were published in multiple venues, making them available to all economic groups. They were pirated in the U.S., where they often were published in paper covers as nickel-and-dime novels. A professional writer who was self-supporting and independent, Craik did not marry until she was nearly 40 years old (1865). The theme of female self-reliance resonates throughout her works. Craik was widely respected, to the extent that the early works of George Eliot were measured against her work. Of particular interest is *John Halifax, Gentleman*, the quintessential self-made man. In print continuously since first publication, the novel spans the central years of the Industrial Revolution, 1794–1834, with Halifax participating in virtually every critical event of the age. Also of interest are her first four novels. All fall into plot lines familiar to readers of women's fiction, yet each has aspects that set it apart. Her first novel, *The Ogilvies* (1849), follows three female cousins through contrasting stories of love and marriage and is unusual for its emotional intensity. ***Olive*** (1850) is a female *Bildungsroman* in which the title character is rejected by her parents and treated harshly by society because she has a slight curvature of the spine. In *The Head of the Family* (1852) Craik presents readers with an early example of what became a popular device: a story involving various members of a large family. Her fourth novel, *Agatha's Husband* (1863), is a short novel focusing on a single crisis in a woman's life: the embezzlement of her fortune by her brother-in-law. Victorian reviewers were often critical of Craik's novels because they were not as moral in tone as was expected in works by a female author. Many critics, however saw her ability to portray ordinary, middle-**class** women and men with energy and dignity a major strength in her work.—LYNN M. ALEXANDER

See also ODNB, Mitchell 1983

Cricket. A day-long summer game played in white flannels on mown grass, cricket throve not only in Victorian educational institutions but also in town clubs which, by the 1880s and especially in the industrial north of England, had become increasingly competitive and professional, with a number of women's teams emerging (Sandiford 1983). These latter developments, however, rarely show in literature. Rather, cricket became to the schoolboy fiction of the later nineteenth century what Quidditch is to the Harry Potter series today—that is, a foreshadowing of the hero's final triumph over his enemies, and an encapsulation of the qualities and values on which victory depends.

Fictional cricketing scenes can of course be found earlier in the Victorian era, most seminally in **Charles Dickens**'s *Pickwick Papers*, where, in the seventh chapter, the hero witnesses the mock-epic defeat of the rural Dingley Dell Cricket Club at the hands of the urban All-Muggleton, to the accompaniment of Jingle's "stenographic" commentary ("Capital game—smart sport—fine exercise—very" [Dickens 1837: pp. 67–70]). But it is not until after mid-century that the sport becomes synonymous with fair play, team spirit, manliness and patriotism. This is the moment of Thomas Hughes's *Tom Brown's Schooldays*, reflecting the author's experiences at Rugby School under the reforming headship of Thomas Arnold. At the beginning, the narrator states that the Brown family represents the sterling qualities of English "yeomen" (Hughes 1857: p. 1), suggesting that the value of cricket lies in the fact that "there's a place for every man who will come and take his part" (Hughes 1857: p. 27). By the end, after many trials and tribulations, Brown is chosen not only as head boy but also as captain of the cricket eleven. After playing his last match before going up to the university, he confides to his mentor how he looks forward to serving as a leader of men on imperial battle fields. In the sequel, *Tom Brown at Oxford*, the author acknowledges the vogue term "muscular Christian" as a fitting description of his sporting hero, indicating adherence to the belief "that a man's body is given him to be trained and brought into subjection, and then used for the protection of the weak, the advancement of all righteous causes, and the subduing of the earth which God has given to the children of men" (Hughes 1861: p. 113). In this way, Hughes imbued boys' school fiction in general, and the cricket scene in particular, with an ideal of physical and moral education compatible with a new era of English Imperialism, an ideal later echoed in the refrain to Henry Newbolt's stirring lyric "Vitaï Lampada," "Play up! play up! and play the game!" (Newbolt 1897: p. 21).

The cricket match remained an inevitable component of the schoolboy story that formed a major variety of the **penny dreadful** flourishing over the last three decades of the Victorian period. Yet there the ideological content was much less clear and consistent, since, as often earlier in the era, the forms of fiction manufactured for the proletariat represented something between piracies and parodies of bourgeois models. Such juvenile fiction appeared from specialist publishers (Edwin J. Brett and George Emmett, most prominently), and principally in three ephemeral formats: in penny weekly story papers led by Brett's *Boys of England* (1866–99); as independent penny weekly numbers; and as **yellowback** volumes, compiled from existing numbers and starting at a shilling. The two seminal schoolboy **serials**, each doffing its cap ironically to Hughes in its title and dating from 1871, were *Tom Wildrake's Schooldays*, issued in numbers by Emmett who wrote the story himself, and *Jack Harkaway's Schooldays*, a rival story commissioned from Bracebridge Hemyng for *Boys of England*. Both regularly refer to cricket practice and prowess, although in each case the stories are set in institutions far less respectable than Arnold's Rugby, the hero's purpose is as often to impress a sweetheart as the headmaster, while the bats, balls and stumps just as often serve as impromptu weapons. In the former, the long-awaited cricket match at the Rev. Thrashley's academy is aborted when the equipment is purloined by a group of scholars from a rival school, the prelude to riotous scenes of revenge. In the latter, on his first day at Pomona House, run by the fruitless but avaricious Lewis Crawcour, Jack establishes supremacy over his "chum" by first threatening to thrash him and then bowling him first ball at cricket. The popularity of both stories led to sequels, not all confirming to the schooldays formula; the rest are **imperial adventure** stories in exotic and colonial locations, where again animal spirits are celebrated as much as patriotic zeal. *Tom Wildrake's Schooldays* itself extended to 329 chapters, with only the first 90 in the original school setting, most of the remainder being devoted to the hero's exploits in London, **India**, Australia, and other locales; however, in 1874 the school formula was reprised in *Young Tom's Schooldays*, featuring the son of the original hero. Hemyng's Harkaway series eventually ran to over a dozen works, most tales of adventure in exotic places like *Jack Harkaway Among the Malay Pirates*, though the college framework recurred in *Jack Harkaway at Oxford*, while *Jack Harkaway's Journal for Boys* began in 1893, with "Our Dear Old Schoolboy Stories" a regular feature.

The richest surviving collection of penny dreadfuls is that of the variety performer

Barry Ono, now housed at the British Library and available in digital form (James & Smith 1998). There we find a cornucopia of school novels in numbers, from Emmett's earliest college serial *The Boys of Bircham School*, to the late Dickens pastiche *Young Pickwick's Schooldays* from Brett, as well as many other story papers, from high-spirited sheets like Brett's *Boy's Comic Journal* (1883–96) to solemnly jingoistic offerings such as H. J. Brandon's short-lived *Young Britannia* (1885). Thus, as Banham argues (2006: pp. 282–4), the schoolboy serials of the later Victorian era, with their lively variations on the cricket scene, tend as often to subvert as to uphold the ethos of Newbolt's refrain.—GRAHAM LAW

Crockett, Samuel Rutherford (1859–1914). Scottish author. His reputation now rests largely on his **short-story** collection *The Stickit Minister* (1893) and on his historical romance *The Raiders* (1894). This narrowness of reputation overlooks the fact that Crockett published more than fifty books in his short writing career, ranging from the verse collection *Dulce Cor* (1886), published under the pseudonym of Ford Berêton, to his travel narrative *The Adventurer in Spain* (1903). Raised in a strict Presbyterian tradition, Crockett studied at Edinburgh University before entering into the ministry of the Free Church of Scotland. After the great commercial success of *The Raiders*, Crockett left the ministry in 1895 to devote himself entirely to his writing. Nonetheless, his experience as a minister and his strictly religious upbringing continued to inform his fiction, which often concerns itself with the daily realities of life in small rural parishes. Much of his writing is deeply rooted in the landscape, people and traditions of Galloway, where Crockett was born and raised. Crockett has historically been seen as a key writer of the Kailyard school, but recent scholarship has questioned the extent to which Crockett's writing conforms to the style (e.g., Nash 2007: p. 92). While the rural settings, couthy humor and frequent sentimentality of Crockett's best known fiction do recall the works of Ian Maclaren and **J. M. Barrie**, there is likewise a moral seriousness in Crockett's continual critiques of hypocrisy in religious and small-town life often absent from Scottish popular fiction of their time.—DUNCAN MILNE

See also ODNB

Cross, Victoria [*pseud.* of Anne Sophie Cory] (1868–1952). English novelist. Victoria Cross (before 1901, Crosse) was the pseudonym of Annie Sophie Cory, also sometimes known as Vivian, or Vivien, Cory Griffin. The third daughter of Arthur and Elizabeth Cory, Cross was born in **India** into an unusually literary family, her father a poet and journalist and her sister Adela (Laurence Hope) becoming a popular Edwardian poet. Best known for her novels *The Woman Who Didn't* (1895) and **Anna Lombard**, Cross's work was associated with sexual **sensation**alism, the marriage question, and *fin-de-siècle* decadence. Although she never married, Cross lived from 1916 to 1939 with her uncle, Heneage Mackenzie Griffin. His will left Cross his fortune, and she was ultimately buried beside him. Cross's reputation for "poisoning the purity of British homes with her sordid writings" (Stokes 1928: p. 142) naturally declined, but her transgressive treatment of gender and race has provoked revived interest in her work.—GAIL CUNNINGHAM

Crowe, Catherine (1790–1872). English author. Best known now for her collection of supposedly real ghost tales, **The Night Side of Nature**. This text made her famous and secured her place as one of spiritualism's leading voices. Crowe was also a bestselling author, writing five novels between 1842 and 1854: *Susan Hopley: The Adventures of a Maidservant, Men and Women: or Manorial Rights*, **The Story of Lilly Dawson**, *The Adventures of a Beauty*, and *Linny Lockwood*. Two of her novels, *Susan Hopley* and *The Story of Lilly Dawson*, were adapted into successful stage plays. Crowe wrote many **short stories**, two volumes of supernatural tales, two plays and some short fiction for children. Her work was a familiar feature in magazines and journals including *Chambers's Edinburgh Journal, Household Words*, and *The Ladies Cabinet of Fashion*. Crowe was part of the literary establishment and knew Charles Dickens, Ralph Waldo Emerson, William Thackeray, and Harriet Martineau. She visited Thomas Carlyle and dined with **Wilkie Collins**, George Eliot, and Charlotte Brontë (Heholt 2015: p. 6). Crowe was quite a controversial figure and her work carries critiques of various aspects of Victorian culture and society. In *The Night Side of Nature* she lambasts the scientific community for its narrow mindedness and refusal to investigate paranormal phenomena. In her novels she frequently interrogates women's position in both the home and the workplace and some of her strongest writing comes from her depiction of the crushing **poverty** endured by the lower classes. In 1853 she published an anti-slavery essay, "Amicable Intervention in the Question of Slavery," in *The Ladies' Cabinet of Fashion*. She also spoke up for animal rights. In 1854 Crowe suffered a breakdown and she was allegedly found naked, walking the streets of Edinburgh with a card case in one hand and a handkerchief in the other, believing herself to be invisible. The story was widely and publicly reported in humiliating detail and **Charles Dickens** wrote to a friend:

> There is a certain Mrs. Crowe, usually resident in Edinburgh, who wrote a book called the Night Side of Nature, and rather a clever story called Susan Hopley. She was a Medium and an Ass, and I don't know what else. The other day she was discovered walking down her own street in Edinburgh, not only stark mad but stark naked too…. She is now under restraint of course [Storey, Tillotson and Easson 1993: p. 288].

Crowe's reputation suffered terribly under such attacks and although she recovered her **health** quite quickly, she never managed to recoup her former success as an author. Crowe's work is due a re-evaluation and a revival. Her work was pioneering and not only did it precede the Spiritualist movement, but she has also been hailed as introducing the first female detective figure in *Susan Hopley* (Sussex 2003). *The Blackburn Standard* (1845) hailed Crowe as one of the six "most popular and of course best paid" female novelists of the time and she is a neglected figure who was nevertheless at the heart of the Victorian popular fiction movement.—Ruth Heholt

The Curse Upon Mitre Square. **Shilling shocker** by J. F. Brewer (1864–1921). The novella was one of the most immediate and glaringly sensational responses to the Whitechapel Murders. It appeared only six weeks after the body—that of a forty-three year-old prostitute, Mary Ann Nichols—was found about 150 yards from the London Hospital. A number of Ripper-related novels appeared in the years following the serial murderer's killing spree, with such fiction often attempting to expose living conditions in the East End of London or to solve a crime which had baffled the police force. Brewer's story is notable for its attempts to impose closure upon the troubled interval in London's history. As its title suggests, Brewer's work is interested in place, and Mitre Square was the site at which the body of Catherine Eddowes, **Jack the Ripper**'s second victim, was found. The story—published in 1888 by the respectable publishing house Simpkin, Marshall & Co.—swiftly abandons its connections to the real, however, becoming instead a peculiar **Gothic** tale, involving a mad monk, a restless ghosts and manipulative politicians. The plots moves at an extraordinarily rapid pace, beginning in 1530 and racing through a sequence of unfortunate slayings on the cursed square, before ending with a brief examination of the squalor of East End slums. The novella's closing pages sit strangely alongside its Gothic **melodrama**, marking a generic shift from the excesses of the historical plot to a narrative that is more akin to the brutally realist slum novels which appeared at this time. This movement to the real heightens the impact of the real-life murders, while the omniscient narrator's voice becomes increasingly troubled in tone.—GRACE MOORE

The Detections of Miss Cusack (1899–1901). A series of six stories written by prolific author **L. T. Meade** and one of her regular collaborators, doctor and writer **Robert Eustace**, who provided scientific and medical advice on the plots and may have helped devise them. The stories were published at irregular intervals between April 1899 and June 1901 in the *Harmsworth Magazine* although the series seems to be incomplete (Adrian). Significant in being one of the earliest fictional professional female detectives, series protagonist Miss Florence Cusack investigates cases which are recounted by the stories' narrator and "Watson" Dr. Lonsdale who greatly admires her. She has become a detective, she tells Lonsdale, because she has no choice as she is "under a promise which [she] must fulfil," but she is passionate about her profession. Describing her on the cusp of a solution, Lonsdale writes: "An extraordinary exaltation seemed to possess her. The pupils of her eyes were largely dilated, and glowed as if some light were behind them." Attractive, clever, and highly secretive about her methods of detection, Florence Cusack is respected by Scotland Yard detectives and describes herself as "the most acute and, I believe, successful lady detective in the whole of London." The crimes she solves often use ingenious methods: "The Arrest of Captain Vandaleur," for example, concerns a gambling scam based on communication through various scents. The stories are an important late–Victorian contribution to the history of female detection.—ADRIENNE E. GAVIN

See also **Collaboration**, Greene 1998, Adrian 1998

Detective Fiction. Victorian detective fiction finds itself in the curious position of predating the concept of the official police detective: the detective department of London's Metropolitan Police was only founded in 1842, thirteen years after the establishment of the Met itself. The year before the detective force came into being, Edgar Allan Poe had written the first detective story (narrowly defined), "The Murders in the Rue Morgue" (1841), featuring C. Auguste Dupin, albeit without using the term *detective*. Poe wrote two more Dupin mysteries, "The Mystery of Marie Rogêt" (1842), and "The Purloined Letter" (1844), establishing many of the tropes of detective fiction that by the end of the century would become familiar: the eccentric unofficial consulting detective; the perplexing and often paradoxical mystery; the narratorial voice who acts as the detective's foil. Each of Poe's stories inaugurates a different strand of detective fiction: "Morgue" offers a locked room mystery (in which the crime takes place in an impossible situation, typically a room locked from the inside with no other occupant but the victim); "Rogêt" a fictionalization of an existing murder case that anticipates postmodern "true crime"; and "Letter" the metaphysical detective story that turns on a paradox illuminating an epistemological principle.

Poe's model of the ratiocinative detective did not immediately take root in British literary culture, where early nineteenth-century crime writing had been dominated by sympathetic portrayals of criminals rather than law enforcers (including the *Newgate Calendar*, a compendium of biographies of inmates of the notorious prison, and the related **Newgate novels** of **Edward Bulwer-Lytton** and **William Harrison Ainsworth**). Early nineteenth-century resistance to the establishment of a police force continued well into the century, where the figure of the detective was dangerously close to the specter of the policeman as emblematic of a state espionage more popularly associated with continental politics. The social unrest of the 1840s made the detective force slightly more sympathetic figures in the 1850s, facilitated by **Charles Dickens**'s writings on the detective force; in particular three articles for *Household Words* based on his observations of Inspector Charles Field ("A Detective Police Party" [1850], "Three Detective Anecdotes" [1850], and "On Duty with Inspector Field" [1851]). Field likewise provided the model for Inspector Bucket in *Bleak House* (1852–3), often incorrectly cited as the first fictional depiction of a detective in English literature, but nevertheless an important early portrayal of the force.

Despite Dickens's mid-century attempts to rehabilitate the police, Victorian detective fiction privileged the individualism of the private investigator, albeit as a figure of questionable social standing. In the 1860s, the development of detective fiction became entangled with that of **sensation fiction**. Novels such as **Mary Elizabeth Braddon**'s ***The Trail of the Serpent*** and ***Lady Audley's Secret*** and **Wilkie Collins**'s ***The Woman in White*** contain substantial elements of detection and mystery. *Lady Audley's Secret* made the liminal status of the detective clear: Robert Audley is reluctant to take on the detective role in investigating his friend's disappearance both because of his supposedly lymphatic nature and the ambiguous class position of the detective. Collins's ***The Moonstone*** offers an uneasy compromise: it features an official police detective, Sergeant Cuff, but his powers are limited and the mystery is resolved by amateurs. The frequently made claim that *The Moonstone* was the first English detective novel overlooks ***The Notting Hill Mystery*** (1862–3) by Charles Felix (Charles Warren Adams), which like *The Moonstone* focused on altered and mesmeric states of mind, but with fewer of the trappings of sensation fiction. *The Moonstone*, while still concerned with bodily sensation, mediated between feeling and knowledge, sensation and epistemology, with later sensation-detection blends such as Collins's *The Law and the Lady* (1875) moving gradually in the direction of epistemology. In the last quarter of the nineteenth century, however, detective fiction would become increasingly concerned with rational deduction over bodily sensation, though it would always retain a bodily, materialist element, particularly in the context of late-Victorian discourses of degeneration and the biological determinism of Cesare Lombroso's criminal anthropology, although the genre never fully endorsed Lombroso's work, not least because the idea of criminality being legible on the body was at odds with the genre's investment in mystery.

One might identify 1887 as the starting point of *fin-de-siècle* detective fiction on the basis of two parallel events, one well known at the time but largely forgotten now, the other having minimal contemporary impact but retrospectively gaining significance. The first was the U.K. publication of **Fergus Hume**'s ***The Mystery of a Hansom Cab***; the second, the appearance of **Sherlock Holmes** in **Arthur Conan Doyle**'s *A Study in Scarlet*. Both texts had a certain belatedness; Hume's novel had first appeared in Australia (its setting) in 1886, the same year that Doyle wrote *Scarlet* and sold it to Ward, Lock and

Company, who kept it back for a year on the basis of a crowded popular fiction market. The significance of *Hansom Cab* lay in its inversion and updating of the sensation novel (in which Australia had largely figured as a convenient "offstage"), combined with elements of the New Journalism (the Melbourne slum chapters echoing London excursions by Andrew Mearns, **George Sims**, and W. T. Stead). *Hansom Cab* was also notable for its phenomenal sales and innovative marketing. By contrast, *A Study in Scarlet* received a muted reception from both publishers—only finding a publisher at the fourth attempt—and readers when it eventually appeared in *Beeton's Christmas Annual*. **The Sign of Four**, a second Holmes novel, commissioned by *Lippincott's Magazine*, fared similarly. *Sign*, focusing on the murderous consequences of bringing **India**n colonial treasure to England, owed much to *The Moonstone*; indeed, much detective fiction from the late 1860s onwards thematized problems of empire and of the invading foreign body. Dickens's unfinished *The Mystery of Edwin Drood* (1870) brings Sri Lanka to provincial England; **Guy Boothby**'s *Dr. Nikola* novel sequence (1895–1901) formed the template for later Orientalist master criminals, most famously Sax Rohmer's Fu Manchu (1915).

A major factor in Hume's decline and Doyle's rise was the popularity of **short stories**. Detective fiction of the 1890s was significantly influenced by the ***Strand Magazine***, a sixpenny illustrated monthly launched by George Newnes to capture an emergent middlebrow, middle-class readership. The *Strand*'s focus on well-illustrated short features and stories, imitated by competitors including the *Idler*, the **Windsor**, and the **Ludgate Monthly**, came to be dominated by the growing field of detective fiction. While Hume prolifically published over a hundred novels, he wrote relatively few short stories; by contrast, Doyle made it the pre-eminent mode for his detective fiction. Holmes's success dates from the detective's first appearance in short story form in ***The Adventures of Sherlock Holmes***, after which the first two novels were re-evaluated. Doyle only returned to the Holmesian novel when bringing the detective back from the dead in the retrospective adventure **The Hound of the Baskervilles**, the most successful of the four novels (the fourth being *The Valley of Fear* [1915]), but Holmes won his public largely through the 56 short stories published up to 1927. Holmes's success derived from three factors. Firstly, Doyle's innovative blending of the emphasis on rationality and the importance of imagination in deduction. Secondly, his skill in presenting a deductive method that seemed plausible and imitable by readers (Holmes's displays of reasoning are indebted to Poe, but whereas Dupin follows a chain of literary and philosophical references, Holmes extrapolates from the recognizable details of everyday life). Finally, Doyle understood better than most of his contemporaries that detective fiction is essentially a genre of the absurd. The popular image of the ascetic Holmes downplays the humor of the stories (especially "The Red-Headed League" and "The Blue Carbuncle").

Yet it would be reductive to consider 1890s detective fiction solely in relation to Doyle. **Arthur Morrison**'s ***Martin Hewitt, Investigator***, for instance, is often read solely as a response to Doyle, but Morrison's detective fiction (in texts such as *The Dorrington Deed Box* [1896–7]) is distinctive enough to stand in its own right. Likewise, the *Strand*'s first detective story had been provided not by Doyle, but his friend **Grant Allen**. "Jerry Stokes" (1891) offered a liberal critique of the death penalty, with further **serials** exploring similarly critical territory; *An African Millionaire* (1896–7) compared late-Victorian capitalism to confidence tricks, while **Miss Cayley's Adventures** and *Hilda Wade* (1899–1900) centered on female detectives. The **New Woman** detective would become a fixture of 1890s crime writing: the *Strand* had to compete with female detectives including C. L.

Pirkis's *The Experiences of Loveday Brooke* (1892–3), two series of George R. Sims's ***Dorcas Dene, Detective*** and M. McDonnell Bodkin's *Dora Myrl* (1900). The New Woman also became a master criminal, in series such as **L. T. Meade** and **Robert Eustace**'s *The Brotherhood of the Seven Kings* (1898) and *The Sorceress of the Strand* (1902–3). Meade's detectives were frequently medical doctors or scientists—the culmination of the late-Victorian period in which crime was increasingly discussed in the language of medico-scientific positivism.—CHRISTOPHER PITTARD

See also **Mesmerism**

Dickens, Charles (1812–70). English novelist. Charles Dickens was the most widely read novelist of the Victorian age. He is generally regarded as one of the greatest writers in the English language, and many of his fictional creations have entered popular culture. Dickens's idyllic early **childhood** abruptly came to an end when his father, John Dickens, was imprisoned for debt in 1824, and Charles, at twelve years old, had to work at Warren's Blacking Warehouse, pasting labels on pots of boot blacking. A fortuitous inheritance freed John Dickens, although Charles's mother, Elizabeth, was at first reluctant to remove Charles from the factory, a reluctance that he never forgave her. This time was a formative experience about which Dickens never spoke, although he worked his first-hand knowledge of social inequality into several of his fictional pieces. Debtors' prisons feature in the *Pickwick Papers* (1836–7), *David Copperfield* (1849–50), and as the main character's childhood home in *Little Dorrit* (1855–7). Having briefly returned to school, Dickens first worked as a clerk before becoming a law reporter. His keen observations of the legal system inform scenes set in law courts in several of his works, in particular *Bleak House* (1852–3), which satirizes the bureaucracy of the legal system within a larger indictment of social irresponsibility. In 1836, Dickens married Georgina Hogarth, with whom he had ten children before separating in 1858 when he had an affair with the actress Ellen Turnan.

Dickens's first pieces of writing were humorous sketches of daily life, published under his pseudonym "Boz" and collected in book form in 1836 as *Sketches by Boz*. The *Pickwick Papers* maps out the shift from short sketches to the **serial**ized triple-decker, or three-volume novel. While Dickens was first hired to provide episodic tales to complement Robert Seymour's engravings, after Seymour's **suicide**, the young illustrator Hablot Knight Browne, or "Phiz," replaced him. The power dynamic had changed, and so Dickens was able to develop a connected narrative. *The Pickwick Papers* fascinatingly becomes a fully fledged novel when Mr. Pickwick enters a debtors' prison. In addition, Pickwick's Cockney manservant Sam Weller is one of Dickens's most enduring comical creations or Dickensian figures. At that time, Dickens also began writing the first installments of *Oliver Twist* (1837–39), a foundling narrative inspired by recent changes to the Poor Laws. Both texts exhibit a unique interweaving of comedy and social criticism, and a similar mix recurs throughout Dickens's work. In *Nicholas Nickleby* (1838–9), he produced farcical scenes involving the evil schoolmaster Squeers in order to criticize "Yorkshire schools," where unwanted children were scandalously mistreated. In *The Old Curiosity Shop* (1840–1), Dickens created the much-beloved, idealized child character Little Nell. At the same time, he also worked on *Barnaby Rudge*, his first historical novel. In 1842, Dickens embarked on his first visit to the United States and Canada. The tour inspired both his travelogue, *American Notes for General Circulation* (1842), and *Martin Chuzzlewit* (1843–4), in which he criticized emigration propaganda and exposed land speculators in America. The novel's focus on different forms of fraud reflects Dickens's chagrin over the absence of international copyright laws at the time.

The 1840s saw a new phenomenon that Dickens was instrumental in establishing: annual Christmas publications. The first of his Christmas books, *A Christmas Carol* (1843), is one of Dickens's best known as well as most often retold and adapted narratives. It was followed by *The Chimes* (1844), *The Cricket on the Hearth* (1845), *The Battle of Life* (1846), and *The Haunted Man* (1848). Dickens continued to edit and contribute to collections of interconnected stories by multiple authors that were likewise published specially for a holiday season that was beginning to be actively commercialized at the time. Dickens's middle works also include *Dombey and Son* (1846–8), best remembered for its depiction of sentimentalized child death, and his most autobiographical novel, *David Copperfield* (1849–50), which he considered his "favourite child." Both an important *Bildungsroman*, or novel of personal growth, and a panoramic novel, *David Copperfield* vividly evokes the child protagonist's point of view and the retrospective narrator's recollection of early childhood memories. The novel also contains some of the most famous Dickensian characters, including the feckless Mr. Micawber and the villainous Uriah Heep. Dickens's subsequent novels are sometimes considered his "dark" novels. *Bleak House* (1852–3) is Dickens's most complex experiment in narrative form, juxtaposing a *Bildungsroman* told in retrospect by a young female protagonist, the illegitimate Esther Summerson, with a first-person omniscient narrative in the present tense. *Hard Times* (1854), by contrast, is Dickens's most straightforward contribution to the social-problem novels of the time, criticizing utilitarianism and dramatizing the effects of industrialization. In *Little Dorrit* (1855–7), Dickens creates the heavily satirized Circumlocution Office to expose bureaucracy. *A Tale of Two Cities* (1859) is a historical novel set during the French Revolution. *Great Expectations* (1860–1), a first-person narrative that can be considered a rewriting of the more straightforwardly autobiographical *David Copperfield*, reworks and thereby transforms traditional inheritance and courtship plots. Miss Havisham, who stops all clocks at the moment when her intended bridegroom deserts her, is both a memorable Dickensian creation and a figure of pathos. *Our Mutual Friend* (1864–5) is a sensational narrative of double identities that revolves around two main symbols of regeneration, the river and a landscape of dust mounds. *The Mystery of Edwin Drood* (1869–70) was left unfinished at Dickens's death in 1870.

Best remembered as a novelist, Dickens was also the editor of the journals *Household Words* (1850–9) and *All The Year Round* (1858–70). He contributed countless non-fictional pieces of social criticism, co-wrote several plays with **Wilkie Collins**, acted in numerous plays, and conducted enormously successful reading tours of his novels. Dickens was also actively involved in different charity projects and exposed hypocritical philanthropists in his writing. His fiction has remained intensely popular and has formed the basis of repeated film and television adaptations, theatrical productions, and intertextual rewritings.—Tamara S. Wagner

Dickens, Mary Angela (1862–1948). English novelist and journalist. The eldest grandchild of **Charles Dickens**, Mary Angela Dickens wrote several articles about her memories of her grandfather before publishing her first fiction in the form of **short stories** in the journals *Household Words* and *All The Year Round* (which were, at the time, edited by her father, Charles Dickens, Jr.). Much of the short fiction was collected in the volume *Some Women's Ways* (1896). She produced *Children's Stories from Dickens* (1893), and

Dickens's Dream Children (1926), a work of **children's literature** that rewrote Dickens's characters for a younger audience. After "A Mist of Error," a sixty-page story that appeared as the summer number of *All The Year Round* in 1890, Mary Angela Dickens published several successful novels that were heavily influenced by **sensation fiction** and sentimental literature. In 1893, she was described as "one of the most promising of the young novelists of to-day," ("Miss Mary" 1893: p. 11) following her first two novels, *Cross Currents* (1891) and *A Mere Cypher* (1893). *Cross Currents* is her best-known work; other novels include *A Valiant Ignorance* (1894), *Prisoners of Silence* (1895), *Against the Tide* (1897), *On the Edge of a Precipice* (1899), *The Wastrel* (1901), *Unveiled* (1907), and *The Debtor* (1912). The changing tastes of the twentieth century led to her retirement from writing: her final book, *Sanctuary*, was published in 1916, and reflects the author's conversion to Catholicism (as does *The Debtor*). She died on the 136th anniversary of her grandfather's birth.—Emily Bell

See also Sutherland 1989

Diehl, Alice Mangold (1844–1912). English author. Diehl's career as a music teacher was supplemented by writing in multiple genres, and she eventually became a full-time novelist. She believed passionately in improved opportunities for women's training and professionalization and worked as a tutor at the North London Collegiate School for Ladies. Diehl wrote poetry, journalism, nonfiction, biography, **short stories**, and more than forty novels. From the 1880s onward, her fiction treated social and romantic themes and emphasized the social, sexual, and particularly educational differences which women confronted. Her writing subtly rather than radically questioned contemporary gender and class inequalities.—Erin Louttit

See also Diehl 1897, 1908

Disease. From the incurable to the irritating, the indeterminate to the specific, sickness has long been a feature of British art and literature. With the rising authority of medical professionals, advancements in scientific **medicine**, and the influx of popular healthcare manuals and medical treatises during the nineteenth century, new methods of diagnosis and ideas about transmission and prevention emerged, even as outmoded attitudes still held sway. Disease functions as social critique and shapes narrative technique, providing writers with material for the stories they tell and how they tell them. George Eliot's realism, **Charles Dickens**'s sentimentality, and all the Brontës' feminist **Gothic**ism rely on a confluence of mental and physiological conditions that were deemed—though not always accurately—hereditary, contagious, environmental, or some combination of all three.

The diseases most commonly represented in fiction fall into two categories—(1) individual and (2) epidemic—and they are depicted with varying degrees of specificity. Charlotte Brontë never refers to the disease that kills Helen Burns in *Jane Eyre* as consumption (also known as tuberculosis and phthisis), but the intermittent coughing, symbolic surname, and serene death make it clear that Helen's sickness is both familiar and fitting, an individual disease that symbolizes her uniqueness and isolation. The typhus epidemic at Lowood, on the other hand, is identified as such, and its impact is quantifiable, killing just over half of the school's pupils. The type and specificity of the disease underwrites Brontë's indictment of institutionalized negligence and hypocrisy. While maintaining the distinction between individual diseases and public **health** crises allows writers to target a particular social issue, typically involving gender and class, more often than not these categories overlap, blurring the personal and the public, as Dickens famously does in *Bleak House*. When Jo the crossing sweep brings an unnamed disease (most critics diagnose it as smallpox) from the city slums to the country estate, Dickens depicts the resulting sickness as a great equalizer, aligning the impoverished masses with a genteel, young heroine. Not only do Brontë's and Dickens's representations of disease reflect contemporary conditions and contribute to public health policy debates, but they follow a recognizable trajectory that moves from crisis through diagnosis to cure or death. Disease provides these authors with politically charged and metaphorically rich ways to advance their plots, define their characters, and tap into readers' anxieties about their own and the nation's physical and moral health.

1. Individual. As the example of Helen Burns suggests, consumption, which is among the most well-represented of the individual diseases, typically functions as a sign of feminized innocence and purity as well as passion that cannot survive in an indifferent or outright hostile world. Dickens repeatedly uses a consumptive aesthetic to align his dying darlings with starvation, abuse, indifference, industrialization, or greed. Little Dick in *Oliver Twist* and Paul Dombey in *Dombey and Son* suffer on opposite ends of this spectrum. Bessy Higgins in Elizabeth Gaskell's *North and South* reads as a "working-class version of the disease" (Byrne 2011: p. 68), as she explains to Margaret Hale how her lungs have been poisoned by the fluff from her factory work. While Dickens and Gaskell do not refer specifically to consumption, **Mrs. Henry [Ellen] Wood**'s *East Lynne* does, as when a disguised Lady Isabel returns home and learns that the son she abandoned is consumptive. The son's sickliness acts as a moral retribution for bad mothering.

Like consumption, "brain fever" (phrensy or inflammation of the brain) appears in a number of novels as an isolated and isolating disease. But because it is associated primarily with shock, overwork, emotional trauma, and guilt, it gives writers a convenient way to pull characters temporarily and abruptly out of the action, and to return them at will. Pip's fever in *Great Expectations*, for example, not only allows Dickens to slow the action down by incapacitating the first-person narrator, but it makes way for Joe Gargery to reemerge as Pip's caretaker and redeemer. Gaskell's use of brain fever works in the reverse, as it occurs during the first half of *Ruth* in order to remove the heroine's seducer and the father of her child from her plot so she may properly repent. When Mr. Bellingham (now Donne) returns and Ruth gets exposed as a fallen woman, Gaskell turns to another form of disease—typhus—to achieve final closure and total redemption through (Ruth's, not Bellingham's) death.

2. Epidemics. Typhus and cholera are among the most common epidemic diseases featured in fiction, particularly in Condition of England novels of the 1840s–50s. Not only do readers recall past epidemics and become anxious about future ones, but diseases of this sort comment on contemporary debates about public health. By 1829, typhus had been distinguished from typhoid fever, a point George Eliot makes in *Middlemarch*, and while both were different from cholera, all three share an association with **poverty**, industrialization, and sanitary reform. Until the causes of these diseases were more fully understood and accepted, miasma (the putrid emanations from filthy environments), overcrowding, poor ventilation, and starvation were largely blamed for fostering epidemics. **Charles Kingsley** sets his novel *Two Years Ago* amidst a cholera outbreak in order to demonstrate, as Dickens does with his novels and speeches, the medical and moral imperatives of sanitary reform. Harriet Martineau's *Deerbrook* offers a detailed

scene of hygienic nursing that, similar to *Ruth*, invokes female fortitude and duty as the community's saving grace. But while Ruth must become diseased and die in order to earn her metaphorical cleansing, *Deerbrook*'s Margaret enters the infected area unsullied and immune, her utility functioning, in part, as a "moral vaccine" (Sparks 2009: p. 36). Epidemics provide writers with the ideal setting for characters, particularly doctors and women, to demonstrate their trustworthiness, foresight (or lack thereof), professionalism, and humanity. In *The Daisy Chain*, **Charlotte Yonge** highlights the physical and emotional toll a cholera outbreak takes on the physician, while in *Deerbrook*, the newly arrived doctor's cutting-edge knowledge and superior care counteract the town's concerns about his rumored cadaver usage.

As the above examples demonstrate, writers use disease in a number of ways, drawing on the interplay between the individual and the epidemic, and between strategic specificity and purposeful ambiguity. Not only do these depictions appeal to readers who want to play doctor, but they demonstrate the aesthetic value of diagnostic uncertainty and the limits of metaphorical disease.—ERIKA WRIGHT

See also Gilbert 2008, Ward 1999

Dixon, Ella Hepworth (1857–1932). English author, editor, and journalist. Best known today for her only novel, ***The Story of a Modern Woman***, Dixon contributed human interest stories, art critiques, "at home" essays, and short fiction to various London periodicals in the late-nineteenth and early twentieth centuries. The youngest child of William Hepworth Dixon, editor of the influential *Athenaeum*, she received a solid formal education as a child, including studies abroad in Germany and France, and in her youth at home she came into frequent contact with many of London's most renowned writers and their work. She contributed for decades to such periodicals as *Lady's Pictorial*, *Woman*, *Ladies' Field*, *Pall Mall Magazine*, and **Oscar Wilde**'s *Woman's World*. Each of these magazines became for Dixon a proving ground for what she called a "kind of moral and social trades-unionism among women" (Stead 1894: p. 71). Dixon never married, and in her work, both as a journalist and novelist, she used her writing to advocate for women's rights to higher education and enfranchisement. In her memoirs, published two years before her death, she expressed an appreciation for the social progress she had lived to see, writing, "I feel at home in the modern world, with its absence of hypocrisy, it broader outlook, its deeper sympathy, its collective conscience. The revolution effected by the higher education of women, their admittance to citizenship along with men, is a change such as the world has not yet seen" (Dixon 1930: p. 281).—STEVE FARMER

Dr. Phillips: A Maida Vale Idyll (1887). Novel by **Julia Frankau**. *Dr. Phillips* was an inflammatory novel published by Vizetelly under the pen name "Frank Danby." The title refers to a brilliant but unprincipled surgeon, Benjamin Phillips, and the Jewish neighborhood where he lives. The novel garnered immediate attention for its unflattering, even vicious portrayal of London Jews, who Frankau represents as shallow and materialistic. At the center of the novel is Phillips and his Christian mistress, Mary Cameron, also the mother of his young daughter. Desperate to marry her, Phillips subjects his wife to an ovariotomy, and uses the occasion to kill her with a morphine overdose. But Mary proves to have her own interests at hand, and Phillips redirects his attentions, chillingly, to his surgical pursuits as a "lady's doctor." As well as its offensive picture of Jewish culture, the novel sparked attention for its unsubstantiated link to Dr. Ernest Hart, a

physician and the first Jewish editor of the *British Medical Journal*, whose wife had died under mysterious circumstances. While it is not widely known, *Dr. Phillips* can be slated into a late-century category of "Medical Gothic" novels—along with **Robert Louis Stevenson**'s *Strange Case of Dr. Jekyll and Mr. Hyde*, **Bram Stoker**'s *Dracula*, and the novels of **H. G. Wells**—which similarly explore the power and danger of medical experimentation. Along with examinations of medical and scientific themes and Jewish integration into England, critics have extended a range of explanations for the novel's **anti-Semitism**, including authorial self-hatred, rebellion against Anglo-Jewish culture, and parody.
—Tabitha Sparks

Dora Thorne (s. 1871). Novel by Charlotte M. Brame. Named for its heroine, the lodge-keeper's daughter, the novel concerns *mésalliance* in successive generations of a titled family. **Serial**ized in the ***Family Herald*** from 1871, it is the best-known of over 100 "English" romances by Brame (1836–84), Catholic author from Hinckley, Leicestershire; many appeared in the *Herald* and elsewhere as "By the Author of *Dora Thorne*." Without copyright protection before the U.S. Chace Act of 1891, her romances were widely pirated there, often under the fabricated identity "Bertha M. Clay." Brame's career represents a fascinating case from the perspectives of both gender studies and book history.—Graham Law

See also ODNB, Law 2012

Dorcas Dene, Detective: Her Adventures (1897–1898). **George R. Sims**'s stories chronicling the adventures of the female detective Dorcas Dene were published in two series, by F. V. White, in 1897 and 1898. Dorcas is an actress who abandons the profession in order to marry an artist, Paul Dene. The pair settle in suburbia, but Paul contracts an illness which leaves him blind. Forced to find a new source of income, her neighbor, the private inquiry agent Mr. Johnson, employs her as an investigator in a case of blackmail. Working under cover, Dorcas solves the mystery and she and Johnson become partners in his inquiry business, with Dorcas continuing solo after Johnson's retirement. Sims was a successful dramatist and the cases are narrated by Saxon, a playwright who accompanies Dorcas on her adventures.

Dorcas's profession allows her greater autonomy beyond the domestic sphere than her gender might be expected to afford. Moreover, her skills as an actress allow her to insert herself back into that sphere performatively, in a plethora of submissive "roles" (nurse, parlor-maid, etc.) in order to spy on suspect households. At the same time, she remains a "womanly woman" (Sims 1897: p. 22), whose cases deal with delicate matters of familial and marital relationships and whose "exposure to the world of crime is protected by the fact that the cases are introduced, discussed, and often solved in her suburban living room, in the company of her husband, her pet dog, and Saxon" (Kayman 2003: p. 53).—Dewi Evans

Dracula (1897). **Gothic novel** by **Bram Stoker**. Published by Archibald Constable and Company, the novel tells of the evil machinations of the eponymous Transylvanian aristocrat and his foiled attempt to spread his vampiric curse to Britain. Its opening section takes the form of the diary of a young English lawyer, Jonathan Harker, dispatched to Castle Dracula in the Carpathian Mountains to facilitate the sale of English property to Count Dracula. After a series of horrific experiences, Harker discovers that he has become the Count's prisoner and that Dracula is a **vampire** who feeds on the blood of the local peasantry.

The action shifts to the town of Whitby, on England's northeast coast, where Lucy Westenra tells Harker's fiancée, Mina, about her three suitors—the psychiatrist John Seward, the rich American Quincey Morris, and the young aristocrat Lord Arthur Holmwood. After Lucy accepts Holmwood's proposal, their happiness is disturbed by a series of strange events. First, a ship crashes into Whitby harbor, the only survivor a massive black dog. Second, Lucy succumbs to a mysterious wasting illness and takes to sleepwalking on the cliffs. Unable to determine the cause of the illness, Seward calls in his old tutor, the Dutch physician Abraham Van Helsing, who adopts a highly unorthodox course of treatment, including blood transfusions and instructions that the sickroom be covered in garlic. Suspecting the doctor to be a charlatan, Lucy's mother removes the garlic, and her daughter dies. After the funeral, a series of attacks on children by a strange woman who wanders nocturnally on Hampstead Heath leads Van Helsing to reveal that this mysterious figure is none other than Lucy. Now one of the undead, she can only be laid to rest by means of a stake through the heart. Initially skeptical, Seward, Quincey, and Holmwood are finally convinced by an encounter with Lucy, who attempts to embrace Holmwood. Saved by his colleagues, Holmwood allows Van Helsing's plan to be carried out. The four men dispatch the vampiric Lucy as she lies in her coffin.

Meanwhile, Jonathan, having escaped Dracula's castle, is reunited with Mina. They marry and return to England, where Jonathan is horrified to glimpse the count in the heart of London. Worse still, Dracula appears to have grown younger and more vigorous. Van Helsing is in no doubt that Dracula was responsible for Lucy's death. The "band of light" (as they style themselves) resolve to track Dracula to his lair. This quest becomes all the more urgent because Mina has been visited by the Count, who, forcing her to drink his blood, has begun transforming her into one of his own. Finally, the crew follow Dracula to Transylvania, where Quincey destroys him, dying in the struggle.

Stoker's novel uses the vampire as a vehicle for a catalogue of social and cultural anxieties characteristic of the Victorian *fin de siècle*. It is highly representative of the thematic and stylistic devices in Gothic fiction of the period. As with **Robert Louis Stevenson**'s *Strange Case of Dr. Jekyll and Mr. Hyde* and **Arthur Machen**'s *The Three Imposters* (1895) and "The Great God Pan" (1890), the story is told in a series of firsthand accounts (diaries, letters, wax cylinder recordings) gathered after the event—in this case by Mina Harker. Indeed, Mina's typewriting skills and talent for mustering her material become key tools in the fight against Dracula, allowing the crew of light to piece together the count's movements. Thus, the vampire's defeat is achieved not only through Van Helsing's expertise as a folklorist but through modern scientific techniques of recording and analysis. Thus the battle is figured, in a manner typical of the Gothic, as a pitched fight between the forces of modernity and superstition—between the enlightened present and the savage past.

Mina's capabilities, along with the gender role-reversal of Harker's imprisonment in the Gothic castle, a role traditionally associated with the heroines of eighteenth-century Gothic romances, signal recognition of a new autonomy for women in the age of the independent **New Woman**. The novel is more conservative, however, in its treatment of female sexual autonomy, which is depicted as latent voluptuousness, awakened by the vampire's bite and violently subdued by the disturbingly phallic image of a stake through the heart, delivered by the male characters. Written in the aftermath of **Oscar Wilde**'s trial for homosexual acts, Dracula's insatiable hunger to penetrate both men and women with his vampiric bite has been read by critics as a Gothicization of same-sex desire.

The novel's depiction of sexuality as a base, even monstrous, instinct also exemplifies anxious preoccupation with the idea that bestial savagery may not be external to the human psyche but rather a latent but repressed element within the so-called civilized mind. This reflects the Victorian belief that Darwinian evolution could cause organisms to regress to less-developed forms as well as to evolve into more complex ones—a degeneration that the blood-drinking Dracula epitomizes. Such fears were acute at a time when Britain's imperial dominance was legitimated by its belief in its own cultural and racial superiority. Despite being defeated in the end, Dracula, a regressive monster representing the power of superstition and folklore over modern **science** and the supposed racial superiority of the crew of light, can be read as the nightmarish embodiment of a *fin-de-siècle* ambivalence about the future prospects of Britain's racial, cultural, and political domination.—Dewi Evans

Driven Home: A Tale of Destiny (1886). Novel by **Richard Arkwright** published under the pseudonym Evelyn Owen by J. W. Arrowsmith, Bristol. In the California gold fields, first-person narrator George Wardour receives the dying words of a mysterious Englishman and witnesses the lynching of a friend. George develops brain fever and loses all memory of these events. Years later, George's mind is invaded by a supernatural power that drives him back to England. In the seaside town of Shelterbourne, he befriends Mrs. Blythswood and is compelled to pursue the mystery of her past and her links to villainous Doctor Erbach. The novel is tightly plotted, and while George experiences terrifying, inexplicable events which give the narrative excitement and **melodrama**, they can all be linked to the original cause of his brain fever. Ultimately, there is no actual evidence to support George's supernatural story; he may be an unreliable narrator.—Emma Kareno

Dudeney, Mrs. Henry [Alice Dudeney] (1866–1945). English author. Writer of novels, **short stories**, and inventor of mathematical puzzles and games, Dudeney published over fifty volumes between 1897 and 1937, including *A Man with a Maid* (1897), *The Maternity of Harriott Wicken* (1899), and *Folly Corner* (1899). Dudeney's *The Peep Show* (1929) was adapted by Elsie Schauffler into a Broadway show. As Arthur St. John Adcock noted of Dudeney in 1928, "no other woman novelist today writes more objectively or with a stronger imaginative realism in the creation of character and the designing of story" (p. 169). Her work was also to regularly appear in *Harper's* magazine. Often considered an early Victorian feminist writer, Dudeney wrote of many social issues facing women, as well as the middle and working classes. Dudeney's "marriage problem" novels illustrate female protagonists negotiating issues within their marriages and the domestic sphere. Likewise, she tackles other social and cultural issues facing unmarried women such as illegitimate pregnancy in *The Third Floor* (1901). The American Society of Arts and Sciences, then known for excluding non–American authors, gave her honorable mention in 1920. Published posthumously, a collection of her diaries, edited by Diana Crook, *A Lewes Diary, 1916–1944* (1998), helped bring many of her works back into circulation.—Amberyl Malkovich
See also Adcock 1928

Du Maurier, George (1834–1896). English novelist and cartoonist. Born into a family of French ancestry, du Maurier studied art and enjoyed a successful career as a cartoonist and illustrator, working mainly for *Punch*, for whom he produced caricatures satirizing Victorian mores. Only after his eyesight began to deteriorate in his fifties did he embark on a literary career, publishing his first novel, *Peter Ibbetson*, in 1891. His second novel, ***Trilby***, published three years later, would be a huge success and, though du Maurier's literary career would be a short-lived one, he would have an influence that went far beyond the book's original audience. A **Gothic** romance set in the world of theater, the book would bestow on the English language the word *svengali*, named after the sinister manager who turns the titular Trilby into a star diva by **hypnosis**. The novel would also, indirectly, give the language the name of a hat, named after a narrow-brimmed model worn in the first stage adaptation. Du Maurier died soon after, in 1896, and his third novel, *The Martian*, was published posthumously. His grandchildren, born to his daughter Sylvia Llewelyn Davies, would provide the inspiration for **J. M. Barrie** to write *Peter Pan*, while another granddaughter, Daphne, would herself be a successful novelist, authoring, among other novels, *Jamaica Inn* (1936) and *Rebecca* (1938).—Tammy Lai-Ming Ho

East Lynne (1861). Novel by **Mrs. Henry [Ellen] Wood**. One of the most influential Victorian **sensation novels**, *East Lynne* is also an important **marriage novel** and a **governess novel**. Much of its narrative interest arises from its ambiguous representation of the transgressive anti-heroine. The main plot concerns Lady Isabel Vane's marriage to and divorce from Archibald Carlyle, a class-climbing member of the professional classes who has purchased her impoverished father's great house, the titular East Lynne. First introduced as a comic figure, Carlyle's eccentric elder sister systematically ruins their married life. When Francis Levison, a stereotyped wicked aristocrat, seduces Isabel, Carlyle divorces her. The narrative lingers over Isabel's growing remorse and longing for the children she has abandoned. After the death of her illegitimate infant in a railway carriage that also disfigures her beyond recognition, Isabel returns in disguise to work as her own children's governess. Meanwhile, believing Isabel dead, Carlyle marries Isabel's erstwhile rival, Barbara Hare. A second plot involves Barbara's brother Richard, who is falsely accused of a murder committed by Levison in disguise. Isabel dies forgiven by her husband, while he feels like a bigamist, showing how confused prevailing attitudes to divorce were at the time. Controversially generating sympathy for the adulterous anti-heroine, the novel simultaneously expresses fears of intrusion within the home and dramatizes the rivaling duties of mothers and servants in childrearing. The scene featuring Isabel bewailing that she cannot tell her dying son that she is his mother—one of the most notorious deathbed scenes in Victorian literature—was intensely popular. It was repeatedly performed on stage and set to music. An intricately plotted novel that anticipates elements of **detective fiction** in the subplot, *East Lynne* engages with several pressing social issues, including child custody laws and social mobility.—Tamara S. Wagner

Edwards, Amelia Ann Blandford (1831–1892). English novelist, journalist, travel writer, and **Egypt**ologist. After abandoning a burgeoning career as a musician, Edwards began writing for the periodical press in 1851. Throughout that decade, she published stories and articles in a range of popular magazines, including *Chamber's Edinburgh Journal*, *Household Words*, *Eliza Cook's Journal*, *Literary World*, the *Ladies' Companion*, and the *Illustrated London News*. Edwards also worked briefly on the staff of the *Saturday Review* and the *Morning Post*. Her first novel, *My Brother's Wife*, a sensational tale of murder and betrayal, was published in 1855 and received largely positive reviews. Edwards followed up this success with the equally sensational *The Ladder of Life* (1857) and *Hand and Glove* (1858). Her first three novels have received little or no critical attention, but deserve recognition for their contribution to early women's crime writing and as prototypes of 1860s **sensation fiction**. It was *Barbara's History* (1864), however, which established her as an important contemporary novelist and it was her most significant critical success. *A Million of Money* followed in 1864 and two collections of **short stories** in the same decade. Edwards's shorter fiction continues to be anthologized in modern collections, particularly of supernatural tales. "The Phantom Coach" is perhaps the best known of these shorter works. Although her fiction was characterized by sensational themes and tropes, critics persistently dissociated her from the current controversy raging over the Sensation Novel, identifying Edwards as a talented and superior novelist, "far above the Miss **Braddon** school" ("Review" 1866: p. 6). In addition to fiction, Edwards also wrote various non-fictional works that reflected her varied interests. These include *A Summary of English History* (1856), *A History of France* (1858), and a biographical study of Cervantes. She also published translations and original musical and lyrical compositions. Two more novels appeared in the 1870s and her final work of fiction, *Lord Brackenbury*, was published in 1880. By this time, Edwards's main energies were focused on archaeology and conservation. A trip to Egypt in 1873–74 had proved to be revelatory and instilled in Edwards a passion for ancient Egyptian archaeology that would inform her activities for the remainder of her life. In 1877 she published an account of the Egypt trip as *A Thousand Miles Up the Nile* to enthusiastic reviews and it remains her most enduring success. The interest in Egypt was not confined to travel writing. Edwards studied hieroglyphics and corresponded with the leading specialists of the day. She was later awarded honorary doctoral degrees from Columbia College, New York and Smith College, Massachusetts in recognition of her contribution to scholarship. A successful lecture tour of America near the end of her life culminated in her final publication, *Pharaohs, Fellahs and Explorers* (1891), a collection of her essays and lectures on ancient Egypt. Edwards's indefatigable work to conserve Egypt's ancient monuments led to the founding of the Egypt Exploration Fund in 1882, which was later renamed the Egypt Exploration Society (Beller 2011: p. 352).—ANNE-MARIE BELLER

Egerton, George [Mary Chavelita Bright (née Dunne)] (1859–1945). Irish writer. Born in Melbourne, Australia, to an Irish father and Welsh mother, Egerton spent parts of her **childhood** living in New Zealand, Chile, Germany, Wales, and Ireland. Her "cultural hybridity" enabled her to produce "some of the most daringly innovative and transgressive fiction of the fin de siècle" (Ledger 2006: p. ix). After working as an office clerk in New York and London, she eloped with Henry Higginson to Norway in 1887. Ledger pins the development of Egerton's "aesthetic sensibility" to her arrival there, where she read work by the masters of the "new school" of Scandinavian literature, including Henrik Ibsen, Knut Hamsun, and August Strindberg (2006: p. x). Egerton returned to Ireland in 1891 and moved to England three years later. She married twice: in 1891 and 1901. Egerton is best known for her first collection of **short stories**, *Keynotes*, published by John Lane and Elkin Mathews's firm, the Bodley Head, in 1893. The stories explored themes of sexual freedom, desire, and creativity, particularly in relation to female identity. *Keynotes* enjoyed considerable success in Britain, Europe, and North America, earning Egerton many admirers in literary circles and the Bodley Head a profit of around £500 from British sales in the first year. Lane named a series of books after the collection: the

Keynotes series included nineteen volumes of short stories and fourteen novels, including works by **Grant Allen** and Ella D'Arcy. In 1894 Egerton wrote a short story, "A Lost Masterpiece," for the inaugural volume of Lane's periodical, the *Yellow Book*, and a further collection of short stories, *Discords*. In following years, she published five more works: three collections of short stories, *Symphonies* (1897), *Fantasias* (1898), *Flies in Amber* (1905), and two novels, *The Wheel of God* (1898) and *Rosa Amorosa* (1901). She also produced translations of Ola Hansson's *Young Ofeg's Ditties* (1895), and Hamsun's *Hunger* (1899). Although these works explored similar themes to *Keynotes*, none were as commercially successful. Standlee (2010) has argued that this is likely due to their thematic links to Decadence and its fall from favor after **Oscar Wilde**'s conviction in 1895. Egerton and her work are often examined in the context of the **New Woman**, which emerged in 1894 as a key focus of *fin de siècle* discourse. Although Egerton opposed hegemonic structures that subordinated women, she rejected notions of gender equality, believing women to be superior to men, and also opposed female suffrage. Scholarly interest in Egerton's work has grown since the 1990s, but a thorough examination of her oeuvre has been hampered by early critics' dismissal of her later works. The main avenues of enquiry in contemporary scholarship include **eugenics** and essentialism, imperialism, Irish national identity, literary impressionism, feminism, and the influence of Scandinavian Modernism.—Jennifer Nicol

Egypt. Egypt is frequently the site of supernatural occurrences in fiction, although its presence also speaks to contemporary imperialism, Britain having occupied Egypt in 1882 (Fleischhack 2015). *The White Prophet* (1909) by **Hall Caine** is one text which addresses British colonial designs on Egypt. Politics has been identified as a driving force for tales in which Egypt encroaches upon British soil (Bulfin 2011). In particular, stories involving **mummies** or other mysterious Egyptian antagonists have been held to comprise a subset of **invasion literature**. These texts proliferated at the *fin de siècle*, and included **Richard Marsh**'s *The Beetle* (1897), **Guy Boothby**'s ***Pharos the Egyptian***, and **Bram Stoker**'s ***The Jewel of Seven Stars***. Concurrently, much of this literature responded to developments in archaeological practice, which was unearthing ever more relics from Egypt's past, influenced by the formation of the Egypt Exploration Fund founded by Reginald Stuart Poole and the novelist **Amelia B. Edwards**.

Egypt is often connected to **occultism** and notions of reincarnation in literature, encouraged not only by the Theosophical movement and the late Victorian magical revival, but by the earlier works of **Edward Bulwer-Lytton**, who had depicted priests of the Egyptian goddess Isis in *The Last Days of Pompeii* (1834). This supernatural strain can be read in a number of popular novels later in the century, including ***The Jewel of Seven Stars***, **H. Rider Haggard**'s *She* (1887), and **Marie Corelli**'s ***The Sorrows of Satan*** and *Ziska* (1897). As an individual with a keen amateur interest in Egyptology, Haggard, in particular, rewards study of contemporary Egyptological developments alongside his fiction. A wealth of Haggard's writings feature ancient Egypt as a setting, including *Cleopatra* (1889) and a novel co-authored with Andrew Lang, *The World's Desire* (1890). **E. F. Benson** also fostered a passion for Egypt: his novel *The Image in the Sand* (1905) reveals interests in archaeology, occultism, and romance, similar to Haggard's. Unlike Haggard, however, Benson's depictions of Egypt have thus far received little scholarly attention.

Scholars following new avenues of literary and historical investigation have produced recent studies on ancient Egypt's influence on Victorian Christianity and culture (Gange), and ancient Egypt as depicted by female writers (Youngkin 2016). There is much more to be said about female authors' engagement with Egypt; such figures include **Margaret Harkness** and **Margaret Oliphant**, who both wrote on ancient Egyptian history, and **Anna Kingsford**, a member of the Hermetic Order of the Golden Dawn, a secret society strongly influenced by ancient Egyptian religion. Other areas of interest which might produce new and interesting work include Egypt's association with sexual excesses and psychological intensity, for example, in *The Beetle* and **Robert Hichens**'s novel *An Imaginary Man* (1895). Of **Arthur Conan Doyle**'s fiction, criticism has favored his **short stories** with ancient Egyptian themes—"The Ring of Thoth" (1890) and "Lot No. 249" (1892)—at the expense of *The Tragedy of the Korosko* (1898), a novel concerning modern Egypt, Islam and imperialism.—Eleanor Dobson

Ellis, Sarah Stickney (1799–1872). English writer. A prolific and popular writer in the mid-nineteenth century, Ellis (née Stickney) published over forty books between 1830 and her death. Although she is best known for her series of conduct manuals, *The Women of England* (1839), *The Daughters of England* (1842), *The Wives of England* (1843), and *The Mothers of England* (1843), she also wrote many works of fiction, including novels and **short stories**. Sarah Stickney was the fifth child of William Stickney, a Quaker farmer, and his wife Esther. After her mother's death and her father's remarriage, Sarah helped raise her younger half-siblings. In her early thirties, an age at which she was decidedly a spinster, she turned to writing as a way to contribute to her family's floundering finances. In 1830 she published *The Negro Slave: A Tale Addressed to the Women of Great Britain*, and from then on she published a new work almost every year. Sarah Stickney first gained recognition as an author from the publications of *Pictures of Private Life* (1833–1837) and *The Poetry of Life* (1835). The first, a collection of short stories, was received as "sweet, thoughtful, agreeable, and touching" (Clapp 1844: p. 263), while the second, which discusses aesthetics in art and nature, was praised for showing "refined taste, and a well-cultured mind" (Adams 1857: p. 272). By the time she married William Ellis in 1837, Sarah was a well-established author. The marriage coincided with Sarah's conversion to Congregationalism (she was raised a Quaker, but her new husband was a Congregationalist missionary). William Ellis was apparently supportive of his wife's writing career, which continued to flourish after their marriage. Sarah Ellis's series of conduct manuals was extremely popular, gaining attention from reviewers across Great Britain and America. In addition to writing, she edited *Fisher's Juvenile Scrap-Book* (1840–1848), *Fisher's Drawing Room Scrap-Book* (1843–1845), and *The Morning Call* (1850–1852). She was also active in the community of Hoddesdon, the small brewing town where the Ellises lived. There, Sarah and a friend opened a non-denominational girls' school, Rawdon House School. Sarah and William also worked to found a local **temperance** association in Hoddesdon. In over a dozen didactic novels, multiple collections of short stories, as well as various non-fiction works, Ellis directly addressed her interests in young women's education and temperance. Her writings were primarily intended for middle-class women, whom she argues are the moral center of the household and society. However, recognizing that not all women would marry and that some women who married would not be able to rely on their husbands, Ellis advocated for women to gain an education that would allow them to be self-reliant. Thus, her educational scheme included financial literacy and practical skills that a woman could use to earn a living, along with household management skills and the usual attainments sought by middle-class women of the day. Her novels and stories often show the benefits of such an education. See also, **Family Secrets** and **Social Distinction**.—Ashley Lynn Carlson

Eugenics. The publication of Charles Darwin's *The Origin of Species* in 1859 was a momentous occasion for Victorian society and for Victorian popular literature. While the scientific community was already familiar with the concept of evolution, Darwin's book brought the concept to a much wider readership. As controversial as it was scientific, the text not only transformed the Victorian view of how humanity came to be, it also popularized an evolutionary paradigm that came to be used in a number of scientific or pseudoscientific investigations of the Victorian social order. In particular, Darwin's assertion that species evolve seemed to suggest that humankind could also degenerate under certain circumstances. This assumption gave rise to much anxiety, and had a tremendous impact on literature, during the final decades of the century.

One of Darwin's most avid readers was his half-cousin Francis Galton (1822–1911). Galton was himself an accomplished scientist and, following the publication of Darwin's seminal book, he turned his attention to the heritage of desired and undesired human faculties. In the introductory chapter to *The Origin of Species*, Darwin discusses how farmers breed **animals** to enhance certain traits. This led Galton to contemplate the possibility that the human race could be improved in a similar manner. In *Hereditary Genius*, he proposed a social scheme where citizens of particular intelligence would be encouraged to breed, where "the better sort of emigrants" (1869: p. 362) would be naturalized and where the weak would be given shelter in celibate monasteries. In *Inquiries into Human Faculty and Its Development* (1883) he gave the program the name eugenics.

Throughout his scientific career, Galton's focus was on how to encourage the improvement of those human faculties he perceived as beneficial. His disciple Carl Pearson was more interested in how to prevent those he deemed socially inept from procreating. His statistical analyses had suggested a "high degree of association between excessive fertility and undesirable traits" (ODNB). Thus, the eugenics movement became increasingly attentive to the risk that the supposedly unfit but disturbingly fertile masses would take advantage of various social welfare schemes. To ignore such a development was, the eugenics movement contended, to encourage a degeneration of the human species.

A number or related movements added to the anxieties raised by eugenics. Even before the publication of *The Origin of Species*, Herbert Spencer (1820–1903) had begun discussing the concept of social evolution. In 1864 he coined the concept of the "survival of the fittest" and worried that this mechanism would be absent in societies that helped the weak and supposedly unfit to survive through charity and social security mechanisms. Precisely who was weak and unfit was the subject of the Italian criminologist Cesare Lombroso (1835–1909). Following a line of inquiry initiated by phrenology, Lombroso linked criminal behavior to atavism, forming a school referred to as criminal anthropology. He contended that different people or races had evolved differently and that some were atavistic and therefore prone to an inherent criminal behavior. The atavistic criminal was furthermore marked by physical stigmata such as crooked noses, weak chins, protruding eyes, certain anomalies in the brain, even by tattoos. Predictably, Lombroso contended that the further south an individual came from, the more likely he or she was to have atavistic traits. Thus, the Sicilian was more primitive and criminal than the northern Italian, and the indigenous African more atavistic than the Sicilian.

This model was useful to European governments since it could be used to justify the colonial subjugation of the global East and South. If Earth's populations could be ordered according to an evolutionary, racist scale, with the white male at the top, colonization represented a natural world order. At the same time, eugenic and racial theory could be used to theorize the emergence at the *fin-de-siècle* of non-normative political movements and sexualities. Thus, the increasing presence of anti-imperialism, **anarchism**, Marxism, the **New Woman**, the suffragette movement, and homosexuality could be seen as evidence of a wide social collapse in the wake of a general degeneration of the British population. In Max Nordau's influential *Entartung*, translated into English in 1895 as *Degeneration*, social institutions, individuals, even art itself, was perceived to have degenerated so that it was incapable of directing society toward social and spiritual improvement.

Literature responded to these concerns in powerful and varied ways. Gillian Beer (1983) has influentially traced how the evolutionary narrative was employed in British writing after Darwin, and Daniel Pick (1989) has traced the relationship between degeneration and European literature. These studies show how established writers such as George Eliot, **Charles Kingsley**, and Thomas Hardy made extensive use of Darwinian concepts. As the century drew to a close and degeneration became an increasingly central notion, popular culture became progressively more interested in the subject. In **H. G. Wells**'s *The Time Machine*, the protagonist travels into the future only to find that humankind has degenerated into two different races, the effeminate Eloi that live a pleasant but politically disorganized life on the surface of the earth, and the brutal, nocturnal but technically advanced Morlocks who feed on the Eloi. In **Sarah Grand**'s novel *The Heavenly Twins*, two of the female protagonists find themselves married to men whose degeneracy manifests both in their behavior and in syphilitic infection. The more innocent of the two women fails to escape her degenerate spouse and succumbs to his illness, giving birth to a toad-like unfit baby that soon transpires with her.

The most dramatic illustration of the ubiquity of eugenic and degeneration discourse can be found in the **Gothic fiction** of the era. **Robert Louis Stevenson**'s *Strange Case of Dr. Jekyll and Mr. Hyde* tells the story of a sudden and chemically induced degeneration of both body and mind, and Mr. Hyde is frequently likened to the monkey from which, the Victorians were frequently told, they had evolved. **Bram Stoker**'s ubiquitous villain **Dracula** is equally atavistic, even to the extent that he can take animal forms. Not surprisingly, the group of white Europeans that have assembled to fight him make use of degeneration theory to explain the **vampire**. Dracula is "a criminal and of criminal type. Nordau and Lombroso would so classify him," Mina asserts in an often-quoted passage of the novel (Stoker 2011/1897: p. 317). Similarly, **Richard Marsh**'s popular *The Beetle* (1897) features an **Egypt**ian villain who embodies virtually all non-normative qualities the era found disturbing, combined with a **physiognomy** mapped on Lombroso's chart of atavistic anomalies.

Eugenic and degeneration theories were very influential during the close of the Victorian period, and continued to be so during the twentieth century when they formed the foundation of Nazism and white supremacy ideology. Even so, it should be noted that they were not universally embraced by the scientific community or by literature during the nineteenth century. Unlike *The Beetle*, Marsh's *Mrs. Musgrave—And Her Husband* (1895), constantly calls eugenic theory into question; the novel's villain is himself a eugenicist and criminal anthropologist. Similarly, in *Heart of Darkness* (1899), Joseph Conrad contends that the difference between the white colonizer and the colonized African is limited to "a different complexion or slightly flatter noses." While Conrad has been accused of racism, this particular statement does resist the racist notion that the white European is somehow born of a different and more useful human stock.—JOHAN HÖGLUND

Eustace, Robert (c. 1854–1943). Pen name of English doctor and writer Robert Eustace Barton. His often collaborative detective and mystery fiction spanned two key periods of crime writing: the late Victorian heyday of the detective **short story** and the 1930s "golden age" of **detective fiction**. His collaborators included two leading British female crime writers of those periods: **L. T. Meade** and Dorothy L. Sayers respectively. It is generally accepted that Eustace advised on and devised medical and scientific elements of plots which his collaborators wrote (Greene p. ix; Kenney p. 48). Characterized by scientific tricks and inventions, and psychic and supernatural elements, his several series with Meade include *A Master of Mysteries* (1898), about psychic detective John Bell; *The Detections of Miss Cusack*, featuring female detective Florence Cusack; *Stories of the Gold Star Line* (1899); *The Brotherhood of the Seven Kings* (1898); *Stories of the Sanctuary Club* (1899); *The Heart of a Mystery* (1901); *The Experiences of the Oracle of Maddox Street* (1902); and stories about the villainous beautician Madame Sara in *The Sorceress of the Strand* (1902–03). With Sayers he produced the crime novel *The Documents in the Case* (1930).—ADRIENNE E. GAVIN

See also **Collaboration**, Greene 1998, Kenney 1990

Evangelical Publishers. Although the oldest of the British evangelical publishers, the Anglican-based Society for Promoting Christian Knowledge (SPCK), was founded in 1698, the best known and most commercially successful was the cross-denominational Religious Tract Society (RTS), founded in 1799. These societies promoted and funded other activities but were explicitly formed to educate the populace in Christian principles through the printed word—ultimately including fiction. By comparison, the National Society (the National Society for the Promotion of the Education of the Poor in the Principles and Practices of the Church of England), established in 1811, and the ecumenical Sunday School Union (SSU), from 1803, published some fiction but were primarily dedicated to establishing and maintaining schools. In addition, independent evangelical periodicals, like their commercial equivalents, relied for their success on **serial** and short fiction. Numerous evangelical societies and presses produced fiction during the Victorian era, but only a small sample can be discussed here.

Evangelical societies differed from commercial presses in both function and organization. Their purpose was religious education rather than profit, and their initial objective was to provide the poor with wholesome alternatives to what was perceived to be the pernicious cheap commercial literature of the day (see, for example, Allen & McClure 1898: p. 192). An obvious feature of the literature the societies produced is its attempt to preserve the status quo in a world where levels of literacy among the working classes were improving steadily. Church attendance was declining throughout the century, and many in the middle and upper classes feared that an educated but irreligious working class would no longer know its place. Thus, producing religious literature for the poor was an act of self-preservation as well as piety.

Nevertheless, the religious societies fulfilled a genuine need for reading matter. For many in the working classes cheap, and often free, evangelical literature—also available through parish and religious-society lending libraries—would have been the only literature available to them. The presses of the societies were managed by middle- and upper-class committees rather than by commissioning editors and external readers, and income was derived from subscriptions as well as sales. Having subscribers (who donated a guaranteed sum annually) meant that publications could be sold at prices below those in the commercial sector; not all costs needed to be recovered from sales. The societies' subscribing members were also vital in distributing the printed material produced. Clergymen and philanthropists became subscribers because they obtained special rates for books and tracts that could be donated to schools, placed in parish libraries, given as prizes, and distributed by district visitors and clergy.

All the societies produced religious tracts, which were widely circulated. They were inexpensive to produce, printed on cheap paper without covers. For example, a twelve-page RTS tract titled *Tom Roberts, the Learned Cobbler* (c. 1850) was available at 4s per 100. Some RTS tracts cost even less. Low costs also meant that the societies could afford to make grants of tracts gratis to missions both at home and abroad, using subscription income to offset costs.

The Twelfth Report of the Religious Tract Society (1811) announced that, between 1799 and 1811, nearly nine and a half million tracts were issued. The RTS's Jubilee Memorial (1849) showed that the number of publications for that year (including tracts) was more than eighteen million; the cumulative total of items, 1799–1849, was more than four hundred million.

There is no way of knowing how many tracts were actually read, but the numbers circulated qualify them as popular literature. Moreover, though such tracts cover a variety of genres, including biography, theological debate, history, and scientific discoveries, a large number may be described as fiction, albeit intrusively didactic fiction. The plots turn on the supposed temptations and problems of the poor, such as drunkenness, love of finery, and erroneous opinions, while the realist characters and situations in the tales make them pleasurable to read. Thus, while *Tom Roberts the Learned Cobbler* is designed to ridicule free-thinking and condemn irreligion, these establishment sentiments are conveyed through the sensational story of a (fictional) man who has an alcoholic wife, a criminal son, and an inability to pay his rent. Implicitly, Tom is in this predicament because he has not run his household on religious lines. The tract contains a message for both free-thinkers and Christians, but it also contains a story.

The movement of the societies into the field of fiction came about only gradually. The National Society did not produce fiction in any quantity until the late 1880s. The SPCK envisioned producing fiction from the 1830s but did not do so until later. It was as though all the societies found the gap between tracts and didactic fiction too wide to be bridged all at once. The golden age of large-circulation, full-length fiction published by the evangelical societies began only in the late 1850s. The RTS, market leader from this point, rapidly diversified its products.

In addition to family reading, fiction series were developed for adults, young people, and children of all ages, priced to suit all budgets. The approach was very effective. Some sales figures are quoted in the back of a cheap reprint of George Eliel Sargent's *The Crooked Sixpence* (1886): a single series called "The Monthly Volume," costing 6d in paperback and 10d in cloth boards, first marketed "over thirty years ago," had had sales of more than two million. Meanwhile, "in the last four years" a series called "Cheap

Reprints," which included Hesba Stretton's popular *Jessica's First Prayer* and Mrs. O. F. Walton's *A Peep Behind the Scenes*, had sold two and a half million copies.

The marketing of *Jessica's First Prayer* shows how capable the RTS committees were in maximizing sales of any fictional text. Serialized in the RTS magazine *Sunday at Home* in 1866, it was issued in book form in 1867 and translated into numerous languages for sales overseas. More home editions followed. The author wrote a sequel and around forty other books, most for RTS publication. As with productive writers of commercial fiction, her name became a knowable brand that was marketed with great success. In fact, all the evangelical societies aimed at having marketable names, some of them brought in from the commercial world. The National Society secured works from the commercially successful high-Anglican novelist and magazine editor **Charlotte M. Yonge** while the SPCK published an authorized uniform edition of the works of **Juliana Horatia Ewing**.

Each of the evangelical societies also produced journals, though not all contained fiction. However, the SPCK experimented with various magazines for scholars and at least one for parishes. *The Child's Own Magazine*, founded in 1852 and designed for younger Sunday school scholars, did contain fiction, as did a journal called *Dawn of the Day*, founded in 1878. The latter reached a circulation of over half a million by 1898 (Allen and McClure 1898: p. 195).

Dawn of the Day, along with the commercially produced titles, demonstrated the ingenuity of the evangelical publishers in flooding whole parishes with periodicals. These were inset magazines, designed without covers for placement inside local parish magazines. Centrally produced, the high-quality pages with their national news and appealing serial and short fiction were designed to add interest to the usual four-page parish magazine detailing local parish socials, choir practices, baptisms, and funerals.

By far the most successful publisher of evangelical journals containing fiction was the Religious Tract Society. The *Child's Companion* and the *Tract Magazine* were founded in 1824, the latter issuing six million copies by 1850 (Bratton 2015: p. 40). Both outlived Queen Victoria though neither improved on the heavy didacticism of the earlier tracts. The most popular and lucrative titles were still to come. The *Leisure Hour* began its life in 1852, carrying a mixture of fiction and articles with little direct doctrinal content. At last, here was a wholesome and godly journal that could rival its nonevangelical counterparts—and it did not even bear the RTS imprint (Fyfe 2004: p.179). Its circulation soon grew to 60–70,000 weekly (Fyfe 2005: 541). By comparison, *Sunday at Home*, founded in 1854, was far more sedate and devotional, as befitted Sabbath reading. Yet an anonymous reviewer in the *Spectator* was clearly impressed, reporting that it included "miscellaneous information, history, biography, topography, even stories to fine preaching in the proportion of three to one" and concluding that "This [wa]s real progress." It, too, enjoyed a respectable circulation (Cox 1982: p. 76). The most popular and most lucrative journals ever produced by the RTS were the *Boy's Own Paper* (founded 1879) and the *Girl's Own Paper* (1880), each costing one penny for a weekly issue and sixpence for a monthly issue bound into paper covers.

The evangelical publishers produced an enormous quantity of popular fiction in the Victorian era. Much of it seems to have been directed toward the young and young in faith. It might be argued that both the publishers and the subscribers abused the trust put in them to brainwash the young and teach the poor to know their place. This would be to interpret their work too negatively, however. Committee members and subscribers were committed Christians who worked more for love than money and, in enabling the production and distribution of evangelical fictions, made affordable reading material, at the right level, available to the newly literate. Moreover, the taste for evangelical fiction seems to have grown among all classes as the century progressed. Finally, although ostensibly much of this fiction was marketed to the young, a significant proportion was sufficiently inclusive to be enjoyed across boundaries of gender, age, and class.—Elaine Hartnell

Everett-Green, Evelyn (1856–1932). English author. As a prolific writer of **children's literature**, historical tales, and romantic novels, Everett-Green published more than 350 works under the pseudonyms H. F. E., Cecil Adair, E. Ward, and Evelyn Dare. Born in London to portrait and landscape artist George Pycock Green and historian Mary Anne Everett Green, she wrote her first work when studying at Bedford College (1872–1873), but ultimately could not find a publisher. She also studied at the London Academy of Music, worked as a district visitor, Sunday school teacher, and hospital nurse. Her first novel, titled *Tom's Tempest Victory*, was published by Marr & Sons in 1880. She wrote literature for both girls and boys under the name H. F. E., but is perhaps most well known for texts such as *The Percevals; or, A Houseful of Girls* (1890), which taught genteel virtues, related pious lessons for girls, and usually ended in marriage. She also wrote historical novels and moral tales for the Religious Tract Society. In 1883, due to ill health, she moved into the country to live with a close friend, Catherine Mainwaring Sladen. The two shared homes in Somerset and Surrey, and would eventually move abroad in 1911, settling in Madeira, Portugal. Though raised Methodist, after moving abroad, Everett-Green became an active member of the Anglican community, and began to write romantic literature for adults under the name Cecil Adair. These novels, which were "remarkable for their chaste sensationalism, enjoyed a certain success" (ODNB).—Vicky Cheng

Ewing, Juliana Horatia (1841–1885). English author. The second daughter of Mrs. Margaret Gatty, she regularly contributed to her mother's monthly periodical *Aunt Judy's Magazine*, and many of her works first appeared there before book publication. In 1867 she married Major Alexander Ewing and they moved to Canada. In 1869 they returned to England and settled at Aldershot where Juliana wrote poems and such stories as *A Flat Iron for a Farthing* (1872). In 1877 they moved to Manchester and other army postings followed, but on attempting to follow her husband to Malta she fell ill and returned home. In 1883 the Ewings moved to Taunton, and the home and garden there inspired her last story *Mary's Meadow* (1886). Mrs. Ewing produced a number of quasi-fairy tales, some of them published in *Old-Fashioned Tales* (1885); and her poems, such as the gentle lament "The Burial of a Linnet," still display considerable charm. However, it is her realistic short tales, often in rural settings, which endure. Her stories about the deaths of young people, such as *Jackanapes* (1883), are probably too sentimental for modern tastes; but *Six to Sixteen* (1875) is an excellent account of Victorian girlhood and *Mary's Meadow*, with its sympathetic picture of real children, spirited dialogue and good humor, is worth reading in its own right, and points the way to such later writers as **Edith Nesbit**.—Dennis Butts

Fairy Tales. Tales about fairies permeated the Victorian era, many of them radically revamping the classic fairy tales of Charles Perrault, the Grimm Brothers, and Hans Christian Andersen. In 1823 and 1826, selections from the Brothers Grimm's fairy tales were translated into English by Edgar Taylor and illustrated by George Cruikshank. These translations marked a rising interest in fairy tales, many of which addressed a juvenile audience and participated in the development of the market of **children's literature**. This was confirmed when new translations of the Brothers Grimm's tales appeared in 1839, 1846, 1849, and 1855, and Andersen's *Wonderful Stories for Children* was translated by Mary Howitt and published in 1846. In the course of the Victorian period, moreover, numerous experiments with the fairy tale appeared: in the 1860s and 1870s, the fairy tales of **Lewis Carroll**, **Juliana Horatia Ewing**, Jean Ingelow, **Charles Kingsley**, George MacDonald, Mary de Morgan, Anne Isabella Thackeray Ritchie, Christina Rossetti, and later Mary Louisa Molesworth gradually paved the way for **J. M. Barrie**'s, **Rudyard Kipling**'s, and **Edith Nesbit**'s fairies and fairy tales at the turn of the twentieth century. The rise of folklore scholarship throughout the nineteenth century, culminating in late Victorian anthropological folklore studies, explains the popularity of fairies in the Victorian period. Ballads, tales, legends and myths were collected, leading to the development of taxonomies and indexes. Victorian collections of fairy tales climaxed in the folklorist Andrew Lang's fairy books, published from 1889 to 1910, which gathered fairy tales from all over the world.

But fairies and fairy tales were also part and parcel of the Victorians' everyday life; they were used in advertising or for home decoration, for instance, and the Victorians indulged in fairy ballets as well as fairy plays (or extravaganzas) which featured more and more technologically complex and sensational magical transformations. In nonfiction articles, fairies and fairy tales helped represent the wonders of the world of industry, as in contemporary descriptions of the Crystal Palace, compared to Fairyland in many reviews of the 1851 Great Exhibition. These modern fairies seemed miles away from the Romantic fairies of Samuel Taylor Coleridge, John Keats, and Percy Bysshe Shelley, which had been inspired by the early nineteenth-century folklore collecting.

Fairy tales also informed Victorian novels. Images of changelings, as in Emily Brontë's *Wuthering Heights* (1847) or **Dinah Mulock Craik**'s *Olive*, increasingly helped define models of femininity. By the middle of the Victorian period, the fairy metaphor had become an integral part of representations of femininity: in Charlotte Brontë's *Villette* (1853), the doll-like Paulina Home embodies the diminutive feminine ideal whose clipped wings have condemned her to an indoor life. However, the ethereal creatures did not always match the stereotype of Coventry Patmore's "angel in the house": ugly ducklings, such as the eponymous *Jane Eyre* (1847), became much more sensational in the 1860s, fairy-like heroines concealing criminal natures in the **sensation novels** by **Mary Elizabeth Braddon** and many of her fellow sensationalists. In such examples of Victorian popular fiction, the references to fairy tales or fairy-tale motifs recurrently hinted at the artificiality of the female characters who know how to handle the fashion accessories which construct the ideal woman just as much as their authors know how to use the literary clichés that define Victorian femininity.

The rise of fairy tales during the Victorian period—from collections of folk tales to mid– and late–Victorian experimental fairy tales—was also much influenced by the publication of Charles Darwin's *On the Origin of Species by Means of Natural Selection, or the Preservation of Favoured Races in the Struggle for Life* in 1859. The Victorians' world, and especially the definition of "nature," was radically altered by evolutionary theory. Hence, fairies often offered the Victorians journeys away from their own disenchanted world. In fiction, art and even popular **science** books, fairies were associated with a pristine (and endangered) natural world. They helped the Victorians voice their discontent against the mechanization of nature and the effects of industrialization and massive urbanization. Although before 1859 fairies and the rhetoric of wonder generally served to illustrate the wonders of creation and helped convey a Christian message in popular science works, in the second half of the nineteenth century fairies were linked to shifts in the understanding of natural history, and participated in the dissemination of new representations of nature. Popular science works, such as Arabella Buckley's *The Fairy-Land of Science* (1879) or Charles Kingsley's *Madam How and Lady Why* (1870) were significant examples of the way in which fairies and fairy tales strongly contributed to the mediation of knowledge about nature. They also helped raise the Victorians' awareness of environmental issues, as illustrated by Nesbit's *Five Children and It* (1902) at the close of the period, where an endangered fairy serves to educate children to the reality of extinction.—LAURENCE TALAIRACH-VIELMAS

Family Herald; or Useful Information and Amusement for the Million (1842–1940). Penny fiction weekly. The first truly mass-market periodical, the *Family Herald* was launched in the format of a four-page five-column folio to make money from new **technology** the publisher George Biggs had invested in, and from the cheap female labor employed to operate it. Women consumers were appealed to from the start with a mixture of women-centered **serial**s, but there were also general interest non-fiction articles. Circulation started at around 15,000. The reformatted, quarto, second series in May 1843 was modeled more clearly on the 1820s miscellany and set the pattern for **penny fiction periodicals** of the middle of the century. It was edited until 1857 by James Elishama Smith, and initially specialized in translations from French of the risqué but politically engaged *feuilletons* of Eugène Sue. Serializing unoriginal work continued after the Anglo-French copyright agreement of 1851, the *Herald* raiding instead American fiction, including Fanny Fern's. It also reprinted British work when it could procure the copyrights: **Mrs. [Harriet] Gordon Smythies**'s *Fitzherbert* was published in three volumes in 1838 and serialized in the *Herald* in 1857. Circulation at this time was around 250,000 a week. It dropped off to a still healthy 200,000 from around 1860. Biggs died in 1859 and the *Herald*'s clear target now became women from the respectable working- and lower-middle classes. Most of its authors now had female signatures (though genre was far more stressed than signature) and the fiction appears original. *Herald* staples, such as Charlotte Mary Brame, were clearly popular but, unlike many other women authors of the period, have not been revived.—ANDREW KING

Source: Law 2011, King 2010

Family Secrets; or, Hints to Those Who Would Make Home Happy (1842). A collection of **short stories** by **Sarah Stickney Ellis**, first published in 1842 and subsequently reprinted multiple times in England and the United States. The collection includes ten stories, each with a **temperance** theme. The stories are particularly remarkable in their depictions of **alcoholism** affecting people from different social **class**es, as well as both men and women. The first story in the collection, "The Dangers of Dining Out," which was also published as a separate book, follows a young doctor and his wife. The doctor's drinking increasingly impairs his judgment and ability to function professionally, and thus his wife is forced to economize and take in sewing work to provide for their children. The story promotes temperance, but also connects with other issues, including domestic violence (implied in several scenes) and the need for middle-class women to be able to work for pay without reproach when circumstances require it. "The Dangers of Dining Out" concludes, as do many of the stories in the collection, by suggesting that greater participation in the domestic sphere can cure men's alcoholism. In contrast, stories such as "Confessions of a Maniac" and "The Favorite Child," associate alcoholism among women with too great a confinement in the domestic sphere. As a collection, therefore, *Family Secrets* calls for men to spend more time at home, and for women to be more active and gain broader influence in the public sphere.—Ashley Lynn Carlson

See also Ellis 1848

Fane, Violet (1843–1905). English poet, novelist and ambassadress. Born as Mary Montgomerie Lamb prematurely on 24 February 1843 at Littlehampton, Sussex, Violet Fane was the eldest daughter of Charles James Savile Montgomerie Lamb and Anna Charlotte Gray. Following her father's death in 1856, she was introduced to London society by Lady Sophia Adelaide Theodosia Pelham. Here, she became rapidly well-known as a great conversationalist and a woman of considerable wit. She fell in love with Clare Vyner in the early 1860s, but their attachment did not lead to marriage. In 1864, she married Henry Sydenham Singleton, Esq., then forty-five, although her first love remained in her heart. Fane's unrequited love for Vyner inspired many of the poems she wrote in the 1860s, most of which were published in her 1872 debut *succès de scandale* poetry collection, *From Dawn to Noon* (Wilfrid). With her first collection, Fane established herself as an adulteress with poems such as "Lancelot and Guinevere," as well as an erotic poetess, who eagerly illustrated female sexual desire in a manner that reminds one of John Keats and Barry Cornwall. Such scandalous themes run throughout Fane's next publication, *Denzil Place: A Story in Verse* (1875), which offers a sympathetic depiction of adultery. *Denzil Place* illustrates Fane's admiration of one of her literary forbears, Elizabeth Barrett Browning. Fane's next publication, *The Queen of Fairies and Other Poems* (1876), combines the lyric tone of *Dawn to Noon,* the novelistic and narrative elements of *Denzil Place,* and its scandalous subject matter, as the title poem is a lyrical ballad that tells of extramarital sex and female erotic desire. Delving into prose in the latter half of the 1870s, Fane published a play, titled *Anthony Babington*, and her very popular autobiographical prose satire, *The Edwin and Angelina Papers*, which was first **serial**ized in *The World* magazine between 1877 and 1878, and then published as a one-volume book in 1878. As her first entirely prose work, *The Edwin and Angelina Papers* demonstrates the extent to which Fane utilized her own love life, or, rather, her marriage *à la mode*, as inspiration for her poetry as well as her prose. Fane's use of autobiographical content continued in the 1880s, most notably in *Sophy, or the Adventures of a Savage* (1881). Going from serialization in *Time: A Monthly Miscellany of Interesting and Amusing Literature* to several editions as a three-decker novel, *Sophy* was Fane's most popular novel. Two less successful novels followed: *Thro' Love and War* (1886) and *Helen Davenant* (1889). Turning to poetry in the 1890s, Fane published two extraordinary yet mostly overlooked poetry collections, *Under Cross and Crescent* and *Betwixt Two Seas*. Written after her marriage to Sir Philip Currie, the ambassador to the Ottoman Empire between 1894 and 1898, these collections offer orientalist views of the East with a political twist. Especially in *Betwixt Two Seas* (published by John C. Nimmo, which was later acquired by George Routledge and Sons after William **Sonnenschein** joined the firm), Fane published poems that were about the Armenian massacres that took place in Istanbul and elsewhere in the Ottoman Empire between 1894 and 1896, which she witnessed while living in the Ottoman capital. These poems transform Fane from the mostly trivialized writer of pretty verses into a marginalized figure who is situated at the intersection of class, gender, and politics. Thus, Fane becomes a prism through which our understanding of women's writing in the nineteenth century considerably alters. Looking at Fane's literary works, her later poems in particular, sheds new light on how politics, culture and women's writing entwine, and thus, it raises new questions about women writers' self-positioning with regard to self-censorship and the contextual or contingent nature of political engagement.—CEYLAN KOSKER

See also ODNB, *Wilfrid Scawen Blunt Papers*

Fathers/Fatherhood. In the essay "Four Types of Fiction" (1902), published in *The Academy and Literature*, the author bemoans the conventionality of popular fiction, writing that popular fiction can be divided into four subcategories: "The Romantic Adventurous—The Social—Murder and Sudden Death—The Amateur" (p. 525). In the first two cases, a contemporary example features a father playing a rather conventional role in the child's narrative. In the sample "Romantic Adventurous" tale, we witness the fraught transfer of the beautiful maiden from father to lover. The "Social" tale features a heroine who has to manage an inheritance and suitors after her father's death. In both cases, the father performs the function expected from the "family romance"; he is the impetus for the action of the heroine's journey. As Freud (1909) wrote, "Indeed, the whole progress of society rests upon the opposition between successive generations" (p. 236). However, Freud argues, "these works of fiction … still preserve, under a slight disguise, the child's original affection for his parents" (p. 239). In the romance, and the realist novel that springs from it, the father's moral failings add challenging, but not deadly, obstacles to the child's *Bildungsroman*. Yet, in other kinds of popular fiction—**Gothic**, sensation, religious, and **melodrama**, to name a few—the father poses a different kind of threat to the heroine and her text, and a divergence from the concept that "original affection" must be maintained.

Authors who write in both high and popular literary modes offer helpful insights into the differences between narrative modes. Elizabeth Gaskell (1810–1865), for instance, wrote novel-length industrial fictions, as well as short-form Gothic stories. In novels such as *North and South* (1855) and *Wives and Daughters* (1866), Gaskell follows the Austen model of the affectionate but ineffectual father. By contrast, in stories such as "The Old Nurse's Story" (1852), "A Dark Night's Work" (1863), "The Sin of a Father" (1858), and "The Manchester Marriage" (1858) the patriarch is murderous, bigamous, deceptive, or dangerous. Gaskell used her short form fiction to explore the darkness. In lighter pieces of short fiction, such as the sketches in *Cranford* (1853), she imagines a society in which women arranged their own affairs without husbands, fathers, and brothers.

In her **sensation fiction** *East Lynne*, **Mrs. Henry [Ellen] Wood** offers two fathers—one who models sinister seduction and abandonment, and another who models coldness and neglect. **Wilkie Collins**, who rejected a traditional marriage arrangement and lived with one woman and fathered children with another, used his popular novels, too, to offer alternatives to the family romance. The controversial *No Name* (1862), tracks the fate of two women who were born out of wedlock as they attempt to secure suitors, no matter how nefarious, as substitute for the absent father. **Rhoda Broughton**'s *Cometh up* *as a Flower* (1867) features a father-daughter relationship so intense that its protagonist, Nell LeStrange, cannot imagine life without "one "woven into the fabric of my very life" (Broughton 2010: p. 255). The relationship resembles that of Austen's Emma or Elizabeth Bennett with their attachments to their weak but loving fathers. In the case of Nell LeStrange, her father's flaws teach her skills in sending away debt collectors and sneaking away to liaise with suitors; yet, her life isn't in danger until her father dies and she is left in the hands of her jealous and conniving sister. **Margaret Oliphant**, whose prodigious production of fiction was done to compensate for the failings of the men in her life as she raised her own and her brother's children, by no surprise contained men who are "ninnies who have given up on life" or "failures in their work," as well as much "enmity between parents and children" (Terry 1983: pp. 73, 76).

A number of authors who are otherwise seen as part of the high canon included elements of sensation in their father-based fictions. Famously, **Dickens**'s *Great Expectations* (1861), centers on the mysterious benefactor of the protagonist, who ends up being the disgraced father of his love interest, Estella. It could be argued that his writing in the 1840s and 1850s—works such as *Dombey and Son* (1848), *Tale of Two Cities* (1859), and *Hard Times* (1854)—contain the most narratively consequential fathers of his age. Thomas Hardy's one sensation novel, *Desperate Remedies* (1871), follows strongly along the lines of Freud's family romance, as the thwarted love affair of the father leads to the future romantic and economic difficulties suffered by the daughter. Hardy, of course, ends his career as a novelist with the most famous fratricide in Victorian literature, within the story of the tragic father *Jude the Obscure* (1895).

Adventure tales and **detective fiction**s pose an exception to the expectation for a feminized narrative mode and female audience that is often imposed on other forms of popular fiction such as melodrama, sensation fiction, and Gothic romances. Here, as Bradley Deane (2014) writes in a study of **masculinity** in popular adventure tales, masculinity is shaped through comparison between the British male body and the "others" encountered through imperial conquest. By late century, the locus of social shaping through these tales has shifted from the adult male to the boy, thus linking the shaping power of these tales to future, rather than current, heads of households.

What is most interesting about analyzing fatherhood in particular, or masculinity in general, within popular fiction is the special status of popular fiction as a feminized kind of writing. Many of the authors, and presumably, many of the readers, were female, yet the writing presents an "'unfeminine' knowledge" and "worldliness" to its impressionable readers (Mitchell 2012: p. 123). In that manner, the texts by their very nature subvert patriarchal control. Institutions such as **Mudie's Circulating Library** played some role in keeping the naughtiest books out of the average reader's hands, by refusing to carry titles they found improper or offensive (Terry 1983: p. 11). By contrast, religious novels and popular fiction for young girls offered more didactic messages, preserving the nuclear family and obedience to the patriarch.—Melissa S. Jenkins

See also ODNB

Flames, a London Phantasy (1897). Novel by **Robert Smythe Hichens**. A supernatural fantasy, *Flames* is Hichens's fifth novel and the first of his longer works of fiction. It centers on the intimate friendship between two young but very different men: the decadent and aristocratic Julian Addison and the refined, intellectual, and ascetic Valentine Cresswell. The two admire one another. Julian credits Valentine's influence in restraining him from pursuing the coarser pleasures, although he always remains tempted. Valentine, who abstains from all indulgences, longs to know what it would be like to feel desire.

Wondering if it might be possible to switch souls, the two delve into the supernatural and begin working with the occultist Marr, whom, Julian notes, appears "Satanic." On Julian and Valentine's fourth sitting for a soul transfer, Valentine loses consciousness. Dr. Levillier, who is called to the scene, pronounces him dead and, at that moment, Julian sees a flame. However, Valentine inexplicably regains consciousness shortly afterward, although behaving somewhat oddly. Several days later, Julian learns that on the same night that Valentine lost consciousness, Marr died. Growing increasingly uneasy around Valentine, whose behavior is out of character, Julian decides to inquire into the circumstances of Marr's death. He develops a friendship, and a brief sexual relationship, with Cuckoo Bright, a garishly dressed prostitute, who serviced Marr on the night he died. He also learns from Cuckoo that Valentine frequents an area of the city where prostitutes congregate, which confirms his suspicion that his friend is different. Cuckoo confesses her belief that Valentine is wicked and reveals through her actions that she is in love with Julian. Moved by Cuckoo's unverbalized feeling for him, Julian strives to be a better man, yet he struggles to renounce his friendship with Valentine. Thus, Cuckoo takes matters into her own hands and begins prying into Valentine's life. When he learns of her actions, Valentine visits her at home and menacingly suggests that Marr, whom she feared as a client, may not yet be done with her. He then describes how sometimes a soul lives on after an individual's death through seizing "upon another home," suggesting Marr's spirit has possessed Valentine's body. Before he leaves he declares "I am Marr."

Undeterred, Cuckoo seeks help from the physician who attended Valentine. After investigating Valentine's claims and observing his actions closely, the doctor tells Cuckoo that only she can protect Julian from his friend, whose influence had now led him to throw "his life to the pleasures of the body," through her womanly love for him. The doctor then learns from Marr's ex-wife that her husband seemed to become possessed by the devil two years into their marriage, a change that resembles Valentine's. In order to protect Julian, Cuckoo stops selling herself, even though she starves as a consequence of having no income. Ultimately, Cuckoo's love prevails and she and Julian take on the spirit who has possessed Valentine. Cuckoo is able to destroy Valentine, but not before the sudden death of Julian.

Hichens would return to **occultism** a few years later in *The Prophet of Berkeley Square*, where he treats such matters with a very light touch. In *Flames*, however, spiritualism is a gateway to danger, insanity and sin.—Audrey L. Morrison

Food. Food and dining habits reveal the inconsistency of the Victorian period. It was both a time of famine—an entire decade became known as the Hungry Forties—and a time of excess, as the gains of imperial expansion were transported to feed Britain's greedy nation. However, while food acted as a symbol of power with the wealthy Great British citizen literally consuming the rewards of invasion, fears simultaneously existed over the prevalent adulteration of everyday items.

During the Victorian era, many basic foodstuffs such as bread, wine, tea, spices and confectionary were tampered with in order to affect appearance (to make bread whiter) or to increase the profit for the seller (adding water to milk). This could prove fatal, as arsenic was used to make bread whiter, a red lead dye was sometimes added to cheese, and sweets were laced with copper and lead. This practice was so frequent in breweries that "how to" guides were published for manufacturers who wished to adulterate their beer. It took until the 1875 Sale of Food and Drugs Act to bring these practices under control. The threat of adulterated food is revealed in **Charles Dickens**'s *Our Mutual Friend* (1864–5), a novel that is full of the dirt and detritus of the Victorian world, when dinner is called by the Veneering's "melancholy" retainer, the author indicates that what he is actually saying is "Come down and be poisoned, ye unhappy children of men!" (1864: p. 51).

The two worlds of food, the power of empire and the danger of contamination, collide in Henry Mayhew's novel, *1851, or the Adventures of Mr. and Mrs. Sandboys and Family, Who Came Up to London to "Enjoy Themselves," and to See the Great Exhibition* (1851). This novel, while ostensibly focused on the Great Exhibition and its magnificent and plentiful foodstuffs, also features Dr. Twaddle who advocates "nourishing food" and a diet subject to analysis to prove it free of dangerous substances. Dr. Twaddle's cautious advice serves to illuminate the attitudes to the newly discovered **science** of food in the Victorian period as well as a sense of loss of dietary control due to the prevalent practice of adulteration.

The Victorians were avid inventors and innovators and this extended to the food production industry, in particular through the innovative work of one of the first celebrity chefs, Alexis Soyer (1810–1858), head chef of the Reform Club and the first chef to cook using gas. He was responsible for numerous inventions such as a magic stove which allowed food to be cooked at the table and he demonstrated the philanthropic attitudes of the period as he set up numerous soup kitchens.

In addition to the new industrialized processes, such as canning foods, dining and cooking at home also underwent huge changes and perhaps the most notable of these is the increasing importance of the household manual. *Mrs. Beeton's Household Management* was the most famous and this huge tome included not only recipes, but also sections on how to lay the dinner table, etiquette, managing servants, and cooking for invalids. These guides were essential for the growing middle classes, as while the husband worked his way up the ranks in his world of work, his wife was expected to match their changing class and finances within the home. While eminently practical these guides could also be seen as a source of oppression for women. In one of the most notable examples in Victorian popular fiction, the hopeless Dora from Dickens's *David Copperfield* actively rejects the authority of the recipe book that David gifts her and instead lets her dog, Jip, trample it underfoot while she ignores its and her husband's instructions.

Food operated on distinct gendered lines with the expectation that men needed a masculine diet rich in red meat. The connections between roast beef and Englishness existed well before the Victorian era but it was in this period that the body of the man and the **health** of the nation came to be even more inextricably entwined. While the eighteenth century figure of John Bull and his proud consumption of meat, wealth, and power were now viewed through a more critical lens, he still remained a popular figure and was used on multiple food labels as a means to appeal to consumers' patriotic feelings. Codes of manliness were deeply embedded within the diet and harsh criticism was levied at those who failed to adhere to its rules, in literature with textual punishments for deviation directed at characters such as Jos, from W. M. Thackeray's *Vanity Fair*, who grew fat from his overindulgence in curries and is condemned for supposedly going native, or **Wilkie Collins**'s criminal Count Focso from ***The Woman in White*** who gobbles sweet treats and girlish pastries and is damned to death and exposure in the Paris Morgue.

Throughout most of the period, the need to diet was seen to be primarily a male concern, as women were assumed to naturally be in possession of small bird-like appetites. The large majority of diet books were directed at men such as William Banting's *Letter on Corpulence* (1863). This early version of the Atkins diet became so popular that people would ask each other "Do you Bant?" However, there was a strong female concern with food throughout the century that extended beyond the kitchen and into control of women's consumption. This struggle to control the female body is evident in **Lewis Carroll**'s *Alice's Adventures in Wonderland* as Alice grows or shrinks depending on her consumption, which serves to reinforce the appropriate amount of physical and metaphorical space a woman is allowed to take up in the world. The dangers of overindulging female appetites, and the connections made between food and sex, are also revealed in **Bram Stoker**'s *Dracula* where Lucy's overindulgence—both gustatory and sexual—ensures that she falls victim to Dracula's bite.

Women's romantic feelings as well as sexuality are also revealed through food. In Dickens's *Great Expectations* (1861), Miss Havisham is famous for her wasted wedding feast which stands as a decaying symbol of her broken engagement and failure as a woman. The uneaten bridecake serves as a marker of the importance of success in marriage for women and the dangers of failing to achieve this goal. However, the wedding feast was not the only way that women's emotional ties to food and love were revealed, as it was also considered a symptom of love sickness to refuse food. Isabella Linton from Emily Brontë's *Wuthering Heights* (1847) acts this out as she naively pines for Heathcliff, which stands in opposition to Cathy's anguished starvation later in the novel. Isabella's fasting is rooted in the eighteenth century's cult of sensibility whereas Cathy's is an expression of trauma. While Brontë was writing well before the first medical diagnosis of anorexia nervosa in 1873/4, links were made throughout the period between women's starvation as a mechanism to express protest, torment, and feelings of powerlessness.

Hunger, however, is rife throughout Victorian literature. While one section of the Victorian population was gorging itself, the other was forced to exist upon a highly limited diet due to **poverty** and famines. Hunger is deeply embedded in Dickens's work. In *Oliver Twist* (1837–39) the eponymous hero's fate changes when he has the audacity to ask for more. This novel is used as a vehicle for Dickens to rail against the injustices of the workhouse and the treatment of the urban poor within contemporary society. Mayhew in his *London Labour and London Poor* (1851) collected and edited the words of lowly working people to illuminate the poverty and desperate conditions of the working class in London. This piece of investigative journalism contributed to the growing philanthropic movement in Victorian England and provides a factual backdrop to some of the issues Dickens was highlighting in his social problem novels.

With regard to food, Dickens's work is also one of contrasts as he is also responsible for popularizing the Christmas feast as we imagine it today. This most notably appears in *A Christmas Carol* (1843), as Scrooge turns his back on his sour, miserly ways and "whoops" and "hallos" in his joyful embrace of the Christmas spirit as he hurries to buy the prize turkey that is twice the size of little Tim. This serves to reinforce the enduring appeal that Dickens and, by extension, the Victorians hold and the strong legacy of attitudes to food and consumption that they have left behind.—JOANNE ELLA PARSONS

Fothergill, Jessie (1851–1891). *Fin-de-siècle* English novelist. Hailing from a long line of Quakers who believed in Christian activism, Fothergill used the pen to advocate for social and political reform, especially for women's rights and vocations as well as for improved conditions and wages for factory workers. Born 7 June 1851 to Thomas and Anne Fothergill, her father was a successful co-owner of a cotton factory in Manchester. However his sudden death when she was only 15 forced her mother, sister, and herself to assume a more modest lifestyle. This change caused Fothergill to come to a better understanding of the strengths and struggles of the industrial classes which she reflected in her two factory novels *Healey* (1875) and *Probation* (1879). They are unique in their presentation of factory workers who possess intelligence, dignity, and morality. When she was in her twenties, she and her sister went to Germany to study music where she garnered information for *First Violin* (1877), which would become her most popular novel. Not only was it dramatized twice and then performed in Boston and on Broadway and then at the Crown Theater in Peckham, the novel was included in the *Library of Famous Literature* (vol. 20) in 1900. It has never been out of print. Her other novels are *Aldyth* (1877), *The Lasses of Leverhouse* (1878–79), *Kith and Kin* (1881), *Peril* (1884), *Borderland* (1886), *The Wellfields* (1899), *From Moor Isles* (1888), *A March in the Ranks* (1890) and *Oriole's Daughter* (1893). Fothergill also published several **short stories** ("Made or Marred" and "One of Three") plus several articles in *Temple Bar* ("Some American Recollections," "Wuthering Heights," and "Flowers and Fire"). Her fiction portrays strong female characters, women who suffer because their lives are governed by patriarchs, and unhappily married couples and therefore reveals much about the changing attitudes about the **New Woman** at the *fin de siècle*. Plagued with severe asthma most of her life, she planned to permanently resettle in Rome when Helen Black interviewed her to be listed in *Notable Women Authors* (1893). While in Berne, Switzerland, Fothergill succumbed on 28 July 1891.—Brenda Ayres

See also Ayres 2010a and 2010b, 2016

Four on an Island (1892). Novel by **L. T. Meade**. A castaway tale in the Robinsonade tradition, *Four on an Island* was reviewed by *The Spectator* as a "favorable specimen of its class" ([Review] 1892: p. 10), and it has been seen by scholars as remarkable for its depiction of a heroine characterized by self control, competence, and plucky good cheer. An Anglo-Brazilian colonist's children, Isabel and Ferdinand Fraser, are shipwrecked on an island with their cousins after a storm, forage for **food**, and survive until rescued. The novel shows Meade's interest in the **New Woman** movement when Ferdinand twists his ankle and Isabel assumes a leadership role in which she "shoots guns, swims with sharks, yet still sews a straight seam and finds time to stew a turtle supper for her fellow castaways" (Norcia 2004: p. 348). Isabel not only sews the flag together, but climbs the highest tree on the island to affix it, an act which ultimately ensures their rescue. Ferdinand commends her, "'You are the real leader, the real captain. You have had twice my pluck, twice my courage, from the first'" (Meade 1892: p. 201). Thus, Meade—a prolific **children's literature** author—positions Isabel as Crusoe's literary heir, showing readers that imperial survival and success are achieved through a combination of domestic and adventurous skills. Editions in the U. K. were published by W. & R. Chambers in 1892 and 1899; in the U.S. the work was published by Grosset & Dunlap, Cassell, and Stitt Publishing Company.—Megan A. Norcia

Frankau [*née* Davis], **Julia** [*pseud.* Frank Danby] (1859–1916). English novelist, journalist, and art historian. Born into a prominent Jewish (Reform) family based in London's Maida Vale, Julia Davis Frankau launched her controversial career with a bitter stereotype of insular, materialistic Jews in ***Dr. Phillips***, *A Maida Vale Idyll* (1887). The novel is about a Jewish surgeon who spurns his wife and community in pursuit of his Christian paramour, Mary Cameron, an equally amoral social climber. Thinly veiled under a Christian penname, Frank Danby, Frankau's portrayal of English Judaism and illicit sexuality enraged Jewish and Anglo readers, which only fed its popularity. *Dr. Phillips* was one of several novels at the *fin-de-siècle* that were written by, and hostile to, English Jews, such as **Amy Levy**'s *Reuben Sachs* (1888) and Leonard Merrick's *Violet Moses* (1891). Clearly influenced by Zola's naturalism, Frankau's subsequent thirteen novels target a range of identities and loyalties; *Pigs in Clover* (1903), for instance, explores the imperial politics that led to the Boer War (1899–1902) and fed English **anti–Semitism**. Her candid and apparently well-informed portrayals of life in decadent London examine topics from syphilis (***A Babe in Bohemia***), to gambling (*Baccarat* 1904) to infidelity (*Joseph in Jeopardy* 1912). Frankau was a popular London hostess to fellow writers including **Oscar Wilde**, **Arnold Bennett**, George Moore, and Marie Belloc Lowndes. In mid-life she produced three scholarly works on eighteenth-century engraving, but remains known, if modestly, for her provocative novels.—Tabitha Sparks

See also ODNB, Endelman 1994

Gerard, Dorothea (1855–1915). Scottish author. Dorothea Longard de Longgarde *née* Gerard wrote widely of Eastern Europe in works such as *Recha* (1891), *Miss Providence: A Novel* (1897), *The Supreme Crime* (1901), *The Blood-Tax* (1902), *The Austrian Officer at Work and at Play* (1913). The target audience for her works was English speakers traveling abroad. She occasionally coauthored works, such as *Beggar My Neighbour: A Novel* (1882), which appeared over three volumes, with her sister and fellow novelist, Emily Gerard (1849–1905). Gerard was also widely known as a **romance** writer. Her works explore themes of prejudice, especially in relation to **anti–Semitism**, as well as ethnic and societal borders. She married an Austro-Hungarian officer and spent the majority of her life in in Austria.—Amberyl Malkovich

Gerard; or, The World, the Flesh and the Devil (1892). Novel by **Mary Elizabeth Braddon**. Gerard, one of Braddon's later novels, is a rewriting of the Faust myth through an engagement with *fin-de-siècle* fears of moral degeneration, loss of religious belief, illegitimacy and increasing scientific knowledge. *Gerard* has two key source texts: Goethe's *Faust: A Tragedy* (1808) and Honoré de Balzac's *La Peau de Chagrin*, or *The Wild Ass's Skin* (1831). The novel introduces Gerard Hillersdon, a financially troubled writer, who must balance a two million pound inheritance with the news that he will only live a few years unless he leads a sedate life. The novel follows Gerard's intellectual and emotional development through a love triangle with Edith Champion and Hester Davenport, as well as his dubious relationship with Justin Jermyn—a fate reader. Braddon's novel critiques the rise of Atheism, and the vulnerable position it left women in when male suitors denied marriage due to their lack of belief in God. While Braddon's updating of the Faust myth relied on reducing supernatural elements in favor of pseudo-scientific advancements, a *Pall Mall Gazette* review bemoaned the "sham supernatural which is mixed up with hypnotism and thought-reading" ("Some Recent" 1892: p. 3). *Gerard* is Braddon's attempt at writing high brow literary fiction in order to distance herself from her perceived popular roots with which she won her fame, and as a result is a fascinating contrast to her better-known work.—Janine Hatter

See also **Mesmerism and Hypnosis**

Ghosts: Being the Experiences of Flaxman Low (1899). Series of **short stories** by Kate and Hesketh Prichard (1851–1935, 1876–1922). *Ghosts* chronicles the work of the **occult** investigator or psychic **detective** Flaxman Low, an athlete and "psychical student" (1899: p. 249), who is typically called upon to resolve hauntings of country houses named in the titles of the stories themselves: "The Story of the Grey House," "The Story of Sevens Hall," etc. Dependable, genial, and given to bouts of abstraction, he is also a determined hero "who finds defeat intolerable" (p. 250). Like the unnamed investigator in **Bulwer-Lytton**'s "The Haunted and the Haunters" (1859), Low's credo is that there is "no such thing as the supernatural; all is natural" (p. 193). He is a "scientist" (p. 44) and insists there are "no other laws [in psychic phenomena] but those which are … extensions of natural laws" (p. 223). Although the supposed **science** is tenuous and the overarching explanation is often "influence" ("spiritual influences" [pp. 23, 158]; "atmospheric influences" [p. 48], "abnormal influences," "evil influences" [p. 196]), Low's preference for dealing "with these mysterious affairs as far as possible on material lines" (p. 136) is warranted. The spiritual agencies often appropriate "a physical medium for action" (p. 96) so that some tales end with the destruction of this medium (whether house, Egyptian mummy, Malayan "red-blossomed creeper" vine, corpse, or painting).

Ghosts adopts **Arthur Conan Doyle**'s narrative lexicon of "data," "clues," "methods," "chains of evidence," and "theories," providing a patina of ratiocination for stories of the occult. Yet if a pastiche of Holmes is evident when Low offers his solutions to the mysteries, the solutions often involve a narrative sleight of hand. Low reconciles seemingly incongruous details of the preternatural phenomena (for example, how an apparent ghost can be an old man and a child at the same time in "The Story of 'The Spaniards'"), but side-steps fundamental ontological questions with perfunctory allusions to spiritualism ("the power of expanding and contracting … is a well-known attribute of spiritualised matter" [p. 147]). His explanations are often thin: "I lapse into the purely theoretical" (p. 23); "I cannot give you all the links in my own chain of reasoning.… Much is still obscure" (p. 71).

The Prichards play a Watson-like role, making public the activities of the psychical investigator. A letter from the authentic "Low," quoted in the introduction, recommends that his case notes be made into narratives "of a popular character" (p. viii) and his real identity be disguised. The end of the series introduces a Moriarty-like figure, Dr. Kalmarkane, a rival in the "special branch of knowledge" (p. 277) to which Low has dedicated himself. In a scene modeled on Doyle's "The Final Problem," Kalmarkane confronts and threatens Low; he subsequently deploys a "parasite intelligence to prey upon and wreck [Low's] body and mind" (p. 293). Ultimately though, Low emerges wounded but victorious from a traditional duel at Calais.

Low's social world is markedly masculine. Women appear in the background while men—military, business, estate holding, and professional—solicit Low's assistance and help confront the malign preternatural forces.—Bruce Wyse

See also **Mummies**

Ginx's Baby (1870). Novel by Edward Jenkins (1838–1910). *Ginx's Baby* is now firmly relegated to the forgotten best sellers category of mid–Victorian fiction, but it was a literary sensation in its day. The novel's author was a Canadian-born lawyer who emigrated to Britain in 1864, and pursued a career that encompassed both politics and journalism. He published many articles in popular monthlies such as *Good Words* and sought to confront comfortable middle **class** values through a detailed account of social ills. His fiction was always a servant to his reformist ambitions, and he wrote outspoken novels on issues such as the social consequences of drunkenness (*The Devil's Chain* 1876) and the ill treatment of agricultural labor (*Little Hodge* 1872). *Ginx's Baby* describes the increasingly desperate urban wanderings of a small child and his family through the supposedly charitable institutions of London toward the ominously titled final chapter—"What Ginx did with himself." Using a consistently sardonic tone and a range of inventive typographical strategies, the novel exploits the clashes between a predominantly comic mode, the pursuit of documentary naturalism, and a persistent sense of personal outrage. Two characteristics of Jenkins's fiction still make a claim on our attention—the well documented extent to which his work had a significant outcome on social policy through its success in fostering public debate, and the acute level of literary self-consciousness that he showed in his often experimental use of the narrative voice in constructing social realist fiction.—Brian Maidment

Gissing, George (1857–1903). English writer. Gissing was born in Wakefield, Yorkshire, and the eldest of five children. He was a brilliant pupil both at Lindow Grove in Cheshire (1871–72) and at Owens College (now the University of Manchester) (1872–75). Well versed in literatures both ancient and modern, Gissing participated actively in the intellectual life of both institutions, directing and performing in school productions and writing and delivering scholarly papers. His distinguished academic career terminated, on 31 May 1876, when he was caught stealing from the college's locker rooms—the funds were to be used to save Marianne Helen (Nell) Harrison, a young prostitute with whom he had fallen in love. Gissing was expelled from Owens College and sentenced to a month of hard labor. Following his imprisonment, his mother and friends arranged to send him to America, where he taught French, German, and English for a few months in Massachusetts, before ending up desperate and penniless in Chicago where the kind-hearted editor of the *Chicago Tribune* and other editors in the city published his very first **short stories**. Gissing would return imaginatively to this episode through Whelpdale's adventures in chapter 28 of *New Grub Street* (1891). Gissing returned to England in 1877, where he settled into London lodgings. Reunited with Nell, whom he married in 1879, and often working as a private tutor, Gissing produced a succession of working-class novels, including *Workers in the Dawn* (1880), *The Unclassed* (1884), *Demos* (1886), *Thyrza* (1887), and *The Nether World* (1889).

Yet Gissing was equally adept at writing about other social strata, as his middle-class novels *Isabel Clarendon* (1886) and *A Life's Morning* (1888) reveal. Some of his early admirers include George Meredith, Thomas Hardy, and the leader of English Positivists Frederic Harrison. In 1884, Gissing separated from Nell, and she died in a Lambeth slum in 1888—an event that had a profound impact on his darkest novel *The Nether World*. In an often-quoted diary entry from 1 March, he describes in minute detail the state in which he found her room, before outlining his literary mission:

> In nothing am I to blame; I did my utmost; again and again I had her back to me. Fate was too strong. But as I stood beside that bed, I felt that my life henceforth had a firmer purpose. Henceforth I never cease to bear testimony against the accursed social order that brings about things of this kind. I feel that she will help me more in her death than she balked me during her life. Poor, poor thing! [Gissing 1978: p. 23].

Gissing began writing the novel shortly thereafter on 19 March.

The 1890s was a remarkably productive period: he wrote in a wide variety of genres and responded to the dramatic changes in social and cultural life. In 1891, Gissing married Edith Underwood, another uneducated young woman, who became the mother of his children Walter and Alfred. Edith became increasingly difficult and violent as years went by and the couple separated in 1897; she was to be confined to an asylum some years later. *New Grub Street*, his masterpiece about the life of writing, relays the stories of a number of writers, including Edwin Reardon and Jasper Milvain, as they respond to contemporaneous changes in the education system and consequently the commodification of literature. Gissing followed the novel with *Born in Exile* (1892), a powerful work that dramatizes contemporary debates about religion and **science**. Novels like *The Odd Women* (1893) and *In the Year of Jubilee* (1894) explore the Woman Question, holding, in close scrutiny, both the potentials and the challenges of marriage for women. The decline of the tradition of publishing in three volumes, combined with the rise of periodicals, spurred Gissing to write a large number of stories and shorter works of fiction, including *Eve's Ransom* (1895), *Sleeping Fires* (1895), *The Paying Guest* (1895), and *The Town Traveller* (1898). In the same year, he met a Frenchwoman, Gabrielle Fleury, who sought his permission to translate *New Grub Street*; they fell in love and as his wife would not agree to a divorce and Gabrielle was single, they decided to live in France in 1899.

Gissing also cemented his reputation as a writer of non-fiction. The end of the decade found Gissing making a number of fresh departures. In 1896, he received an offer from his Owens College schoolmate John Holland Rose to write a monograph on Dickens for the publisher Blackie and Son. The completed work *Charles Dickens: A Critical Study* (1897) harmonized biography with analysis, offering sustained reflection on Dickens's art, veracity, and moral purpose; characterization; satiric portraiture; women and children; humor and pathos; style; radicalism; and comparisons. This well-received study was followed by a series of articles, an abridged and revised version of *Forster's Life of Dickens* (1902), and introductions to the Rochester and Autograph editions. Gissing's trips to the Continent in 1888, 1889, and 1897 speak to his lifelong interest in the classics, and this is brought to bear in his travel book *By the Ionian Sea* (1901). Yet *The Private Papers of Henry Ryecroft* (1903) was the work for which Gissing is best known, "for half a century putting all Gissing's non-belletristic titles in the shade" (Coustillas, ODNB). Following the untimely death of the fictitious character Ryecroft, his papers were allegedly collected by Gissing, who assumes the role of his friend and editor. *Ryecroft* was first **serial**ized in the *Fortnightly Review* as *An Author at Grass*: the work offers insights into many issues—it harkens back, for instance, to Gissing's treatment of British imperialism in *The Crown of Life* (1899)—while attending to a wide range of themes, from **food** to Shakespeare, and from physical education to nature. Gissing died of myocarditis in 1903, leaving unfinished *Veranilda* (1904) his novel about Rome in the sixth century, and an oeuvre that has exercised considerable critical attention and that inspired adaptations on the radio and on stage.—Tom Ue

See also ODNB, Coustillas 2011–1, Korg 1983

Gothic Fiction. Literary genre. The term *Gothic* derives from the Germanic Goths, who sacked Rome. In Gothic fiction, forces antithetical to contemporary ideas of modernity threaten to overturn it or entrap and corrupt its denizens. The destabilizing effect central to Gothic fiction since its emergence in the eighteenth century is tied to the notion of the survival of a savage, unenlightened past within a progressive modernity.

Modernity's enlightened values are simultaneously threatened and thrown into relief by the transgressions of Gothic antagonists. Hence, Gothic fiction "shows no respect for the wisdom of the past, and indeed tends to portray former ages as prisons of delusion" (Baldick 1992: p. xv). It is also preoccupied with transgressions of familiar boundaries and with the claustrophobic entrapment evinced by a heightened sense of such boundaries. Gothic fiction thrives on threats to the normalcy and stability of the "world" of a text's implied readership.

The first wave of Gothic fiction in eighteenth-century Britain reflected the anti-medievalist sentiments of the Protestant Enlightenment and harked back to an age of Catholic excess, political and ecclesiastical corruption, and religious extremism. The landscape, usually in mountainous Southern Europe, was populated by villainous priests, tyrannical aristocrats, and violent banditti. Set pieces occurred in decayed, often haunted buildings, typically abbeys or castles, where the heroine became entrapped. Character and setting combined to produce a "Gothic effect," combining "a fearful sense of inheritance in time with a claustrophobic sense of enclosure in space," which produces "an impression of sickening descent into disintegration" (Baldick 1992: p. xix). The first Gothic novel, Horace Walpole's *The Castle of Otranto* (1764), portended to be a transcription from a medieval Italian manuscript that chronicled the downfall of the corrupt line of Manfred, lord of Otranto. It includes supernatural elements and numerous scenes of violence or threatened sexualized violence. In novels such as those by Matthew Lewis and Charlotte Dacre—which retained the medieval European setting and brought the anti-Catholic themes of villainous monks and nuns, satanic compacts, and the horrors of the Inquisition more explicitly to the fore—sexualized violence was taken to gruesome extremes. Anne Radcliffe popularized a more genteel version of the Gothic in her romances, notably *The Mysteries of Udolpho* (1794). The last major work in this initial wave of Gothic writing was Charles Maturin's *Melmoth the Wanderer* (1820). These texts present a world antithetical to the eighteenth-century ideal of Protestant moderation, democracy, and the rule of law: a world of decay, corruption, Catholic idolatry, wanton violence, and sexual perversion.

Gothic fiction remained a popular form for cheap **serial**ized texts that took advantage of the more lurid aspects of the genre. So-called **penny dreadfuls** exploited the demand for Gothic fiction well into Victoria's reign. Texts like G. W. M. Reynolds's interminable penny serial ***The Mysteries of London*** (and its successor, *The Mysteries of the Courts of London* [1848–56]) were eagerly consumed by a new working-class urban readership that reveled in its catalogue of crime, squalor, and depravity. But while Reynolds's ***Wagner the Wehr-wolf*** retained the European setting of earlier Gothic texts and a protagonist resembling Maturin's Melmoth, *Mysteries of London* transposed the terror and claustrophobia of the Gothic castle onto the slums of the rapidly expanding English metropolis, the horrors of the Inquisition replaced by those of urban **poverty** and vice. **James Malcolm Rymer**'s ***Varney the Vampire*** and the anonymous ***The String of Pearls*** (believed to be a **collaboration** between Rymer and Thomas Peckett Prest) peopled this Gothicized London with **vampires**, cannibals, and demonic barbers—reflecting the more prosaic but no less hellish realities familiar to their working-class readers.

For all their unsophisticated style, eccentric plots, and graphic violence, the penny dreadfuls illustrate how the Catholic, Southern-European paraphernalia of the Gothic first wave had become displaced, during the first decades of the Victorian period, by a new focus on the hidden terrors of contemporary urban existence. Diffused through the mid–Victorian novel, the Gothic became less a distinct genre and more a subversive mode whose excesses could be tactically deployed to produce a "Gothic effect" within conventionally realist modes of fiction. Julia Briggs captures this mid–Victorian blend of high-minded realism with the Gothic in her analysis of *A Christmas Carol* (1843), which she sees as Dickens's attempt to use Gothic excesses to expose the "forces of poverty, greed and ruthlessness that simultaneously maintained and threatened his society" (2012: p. 180). As Briggs implies, writers like Dickens used Gothic elements—the dark cityscapes of *Oliver Twist* (1837–1839) through which its protagonist is pursued by Sykes; the corpse-like Miss Havisham, entombed in her decaying mansion in *Great Expectations* (1860–61); the arcane workings of Chancery and the fates of those caught up in its mysteries in *Bleak House* (1852–1853)—to illustrate the depths beneath society's most sacred institutions. In Dickens, the class system, urbanization and industrialization, and even the legal system have Gothic secrets to reveal. While Dickens used Gothic devices, Charlotte Brontë Gothicized the domestic sphere in *Jane Eyre* (1847). The antics of Rochester's imprisoned, insane wife complicate and undermine the dynamics of the conventional Victorian marriage plot.

The mid–Victorian appropriation of the Gothic themes and preoccupations reached its epitome in the **sensation fiction** of the 1860s: "a new domesticated version of eighteenth-century Gothic, trading in secrecy, sexuality, and violence" (Davis 2004: p. 324–5). The plots of sensation novels, in which mundane, middle-class domestic life is constantly threatened by hidden secrets and past sins, raised the troubling possibility that even the most ordinary residence could be haunted by secrets worthy of Otranto or Udolpho. They offered, as Henry James put it, "those most mysterious of mysteries, the mysteries that are at our own doors" (quoted in Davis 2004: p. 325). In **Wilkie Collins**'s *The Woman in White*, for example, the heroine Laura Fairlie is the double of the insane, domestically abused Anne Catherick, who haunts the novel. Sensation novels did for the Victorian ideal of domestic bliss what, stylistically, their sensational plots did for the realist mode. They presented a "strange undermining double to the world of realism" (Davis 2004: p. 325), intimating that the Victorian middle-class ideal of domestic happiness was only one terrible revelation away from transformation into a monstrous reflection.

Yet for much of the Victorian period Gothic fiction subsisted as the staple of unsophisticated penny dreadfuls or lent sensational elements to thrillers in which the domestic milieu was far removed from dark castles and outlandish villains. The genre staged a full return toward the end of the nineteenth century in a number of narratives by writers such as **Robert Louis Stevenson**, **Bram Stoker**, **Arthur Machen**, **Richard Marsh**, and **Oscar Wilde**. These texts used supernatural or otherwise extraordinary devices to expose the transgressive desires and savage impulses that threatened to undermine the supposedly civilized culture and society of late–Victorian England. In such works, however, the protagonists are threatened by their own sublimated savagery, which is shown to be repressed, rather than eradicated, by the civilizing influence of social boundaries and expectations. Stevenson's ***Strange Case of Dr. Jekyll and Mr. Hyde*** and Wilde's *The Picture of Dorian Gray* (1890) include protagonists who, through supernatural or pseudoscientific means, inhabit two identities at once, transgressing (and thus exposing) the separation between public façade and private or subconscious impulse.

The Freudian notion that repressed sexual desire might lead to its return in a more monstrous form is addressed in several texts—most notably in Stoker's ***Dracula***, in which virginal Victorian women are transformed by the vampire's bite into raging nymphomaniacs. Dracula's bite is also blind to sexual difference, evoking the specter of same-sex desire. The mysterious, unnamed crimes of Wilde's Dorian Gray (which cause the downfall of men and women alike) also speak to contemporary fears of sexual dissidence, while tempering it with the potentially subversive idea that hiding so-called vices behind a respectable façade ultimately transforms the soul into a monster. Even in *Dracula*, the vampire's ability to awaken voracious sexuality and bloodlust in its victims speaks to contemporary fears about the mind's capacity for barbarous regression. In this sense, the period's Gothic fiction reflects the emergent disciplines of psychology and psychoanalysis, which undermined the idea that personal identity was fixed rather than fluid, stable rather than mutable, singular rather than multitudinous. While mid–Victorian narratives had transferred the realm of the Gothic from the castles of medieval Europe to the dark streets of London's slums and then, in sensation fiction, to the heart of the middle-class home, late–Victorian Gothic represented an even narrower purview for its imagined horrors: the human subject itself.

The Gothic's insistence on the potential decay of the individual body or psyche also plays upon late–Victorian anxieties about evolutionary degeneration. These arose from a mistaken assumption that Darwinian evolution contained the possibility of an organism's reversion to baser stages in its evolution. This reversion is readable in the descriptions of Gothic monsters such Dracula and Hyde, not to mention the tendency of Machen's protagonists to disintegrate into primordial protoplasm. Such reversion was a particularly troubling concept at the height of the British Empire, whose license to conquer and rule other countries and races was founded on presumed racial and cultural superiority. Assumption of superiority is seen in the physical descriptions and non-British origins of Dracula and the creatures in Marsh's *The Beetle* (1897), **Guy Boothby**'s ***Pharos the Egyptian***, and **H. Rider Haggard**'s ***She*** (which also reflects a late–Victorian Gothicization of the increased autonomy of women, especially the figure of the **New Woman**). These invaders from overseas suggest the prospect of an empire endangered by forces construed as terrifyingly, monstrously other.

This preoccupation with racial purity and with the relativism latent in the idea that imperial dominance might be more a question of might than right had its origins in a source even more far-reaching than Darwinian evolution. Darwin's theory, which made untenable humanity's assumption of a unique place in the laws of nature, compounded a growing sense of humanity's insignificance within the vastness of time. A common belief among Victorian Christians held that Earth's creation could be traced back a mere six thousand years, but recent discoveries in geology challenged this view. The Gothic was well equipped to reflect the troubling implications of these discoveries. It imagined a human race adrift within a vast, unknowable temporal wilderness, in which all certainties were ephemeral. At the root of late–Victorian Gothic's vision of individual and national decay was a new pessimism about positivist notions of human development. The pervasive anxiety at the Gothic's heart—that human progress was not inevitable but transient and reversible—was now supported by hard scientific evidence. Consequently, even the genre of **science fiction**, which emerged at the end of the nineteenth century, seems profoundly Gothic in its implications. In ***The Time Machine***, for example, **H. G. Wells** presents a vision of a distant future in which mankind has degenerated into a two races, the animalistic Morlocks feeding on their decadent, effete neighbors, the Eloi. Later the Time Traveler journeys to the natural end of the world, where humanity has been superseded entirely by crablike monsters.

The Gothic fantasies of the late–Victorian period thus crystallize the ontological anxieties that permeated Victoria's reign. As a genre profoundly concerned with the implications of humanity's relationship with time and history, the Gothic foreshadows the more overtly nihilistic terrors of twentieth-century horror fiction and the total dissolution of old forms of being and thinking which, in the last two decades of the nineteenth century, also spurred the rise of literary modernism.—Dewi Evans

Grand, Sarah (1854–1943). Irish writer, public speaker, and suffragist. Most known for coining the term **New Woman** in 1894, Grand was born Elizabeth Bellenden Clarke, in County Down, Ireland, on 10 June 1854. Her father was a naval lieutenant working as a coastguard. When he died in 1861, her family moved to Scarborough, Yorkshire, to be closer to her mother's family. Her education was sidelined to fund her brother's education, but at the age of fifteen, she attended the Royal Naval School in Twickenham, where she was expelled for organizing a club that opposed the Contagious Diseases Acts. She was later sent to a finishing school in Kensington.

At the age of sixteen, Frances married David Chambers McFall, a 39-year-old widower who was a military surgeon to the Royal Irish Fusiliers. At the time of their marriage, he had two sons: Haldane, 10, and Albert, 8; in their first year of marriage, they had a son named David Archibald Edward. During her married life, Grand traveled widely in Asia, including China, **India**, and Japan, and these experiences later influenced her writings on women's rights. In 1873, she wrote her first book, *Two Dear Little Feet*, about the hazards of wearing tight shoes for fashion. In 1879, she and her family returned to England, where McFall worked at the Lock Hospital in Warrington, Lancashire, and participated in enacting the Contagious Diseases Acts. Grand's unhappiness at this stage of her marriage is represented in her semi-autobiographical 1897 novel, **The Beth Book**. After 20 years of marriage, she used the earnings from her first novel, *Ideala* (1888), to leave her husband and move to London, where she focused on a writing career. In 1893, she invented the persona of "Madame Grand" as a means to distance herself from her husband's name.

Grand is most known for her New Woman fiction, but she was also an activist who wrote and spoke about a range of women's issues, including women's suffrage and educational opportunities for women. She was deeply committed to realist fiction, and her novels featured stories of individual and collective female development. One of her more successful novels, *The Beth Book*, traces the development of an unhappily married woman who leaves her husband and moves to London to write and give speeches on women's rights. Written between 1895 and 1896, *The Beth Book* was published in 1897 as the third installment of a trilogy. According to Jenny Bourne Taylor, "*The Beth Book* radically reconceptualizes nineteenth-century fictions of development through Beth's own growing consciousness" (2013: p. 10).

The trilogy's first novel, *Ideala*, depicts a woman who leaves her unhappy marriage and travels to China with a group of missionaries. There she undergoes a feminist transformation as she learns from the struggles of Chinese women restricted by bound feet. After returning to England, Ideala publicly advocates on behalf of women's rights and draws parallels between the oppression of women in China and England. **The Heavenly Twins**, the second novel in the trilogy, was a transatlantic phenomenon because of its representation of syphilis in an apparently respectable family. The novel's protagonist, Edith Beale, contracts the venereal disease from her husband and later goes insane. Six editions of the novel were published in 1893, and 20,000 copies were sold in England (Heilman and Forward 2000: p. 8).

Critics have noted contradictions in Grand's perspectives on women and gender. Although her work made important claims for women's importance in public life, she also continued to valorize **marriage** and the family. Ann Heilmann and Stephanie Forward argue that Grand spoke to both traditional and progressive female audiences. They write, "She used radical feminist arguments when she located women's oppression in their sexual objection in the home; yet, by underwriting traditional assumptions about women's nature and duties, she aligned herself with the most conservative branch of social purity politics" (2000: p. 2). Because of this "conservative approach to social purity feminism," Heilmann (2004) identifies her in terms of "feminism of a transitional period" (pp. 3, 4). After her career as a writer, Grand served as the mayoress of Bath from 1922 to 1929.—JESSICA R. VALDEZ

Grave Robbing. In the nineteenth century, grave robbers, sack 'em up men, or resurrectionists all described men whose occupation it was to find anything in graves and coffins that could be stolen and sold, including bodies. Grave robbing is also an old practice associated with stealing archeological artifacts and raiding ancient tombs. Before the Anatomy Act of 1832, which required doctors to obtain licenses in order to practice anatomy on cadavers, it was extraordinarily difficult to charge grave robbers with desecrating a grave by emptying its contents. The case that helped to curb this practice and to enact the 1832 law was the suspicious death of a 14-year-old Italian immigrant boy in London. In 1831 three men presented the boy's body to the dissecting room of King's College Hospital, declaring that the boy died from natural causes. A quick-thinking porter alerted one of the doctors who examined the boy and declared his death a murder, for he appeared to be abused and his neck was broken. The sensationalism surrounding the trial of the three men who killed an innocent child for money helped to shed light on illegal activities to obtain bodies for medical men, including grave robbing practices. The three men were charged with murder (two of them were hanged and dissected), and a year later the Anatomy Act passed. Grave robbing abated after this, for it was now possible to charge people with the crime of robbing and desecrating graves for monetary gain. Grave robbers frequently appear in popular fiction.—BARBARA TILLEY

See also Nuland 2001, Quigley 1994

Gray, Maxwell [*pseud.* of Mary Gleed Tuttiett] (1846–1923). English novelist and poet. A native of the Isle of Wight, Tuttiett wrote under the nom de plume Maxwell Gray. Her first novel, *The Broken Tryst* (1879), went largely unnoticed, but her third literary effort, **The Silence of Dean Maitland**, was the novel of the season. Other well-received works include *The Reproach of Annesley* (1888), *The Last Sentence* (1893), *The House of Hidden Treasure* (1898), and *The Great Refusal* (1906). Gray also penned several volumes of poems as well as **short stories**. She contributed to *Atalanta* magazine, founded by **L. T. Meade**, which targeted young middle-class women. Despite her many successes in the Victorian and Edwardian periods, she is almost completely forgotten today.—KEVIN A. MORRISON

The Green Carnation (1894). A short novel by **Robert Hichens**, satirizing **Oscar Wilde** and 1890s' decadence. First published anonymously, it was a bestseller in the winter of 1894. Lord Reggie Hastings (a version of Lord Alfred Douglas, Wilde's lover) and the aesthete Esmé Amarinth (clearly modeled on Wilde) attend a country house party given by Mrs. Windsor. She hopes to persuade Reggie to marry her wealthy cousin, Lady Locke, but he is more interested in Lady Locke's young son, Tommy. Following Esmé's lecture on "the art of folly," Reggie proposes marriage, but Lady Locke rejects him as absurd and derivative. Unabashed, Reggie and Esmé return to London. Hichens's novel is at once a parody, a pastiche, and a backhanded celebration of Wilde, who is referenced several times. It captures perfectly his paradoxical humor (e.g. "people teach in order to conceal their ignorance," p. 167), but also suggests that his teachings may corrupt. The relationship between Reggie and Tommy is especially troubling, notably when Reggie tells the boy that "To be natural is generally to be stupid" and gives him a green carnation to wear to church (p. 130). The novel's ambivalence toward marriage (Hichens remained a confirmed bachelor) and its thinly veiled misogyny, together with its genuine wit make it difficult to regard as wholly satirical. Recognizing how it had prejudiced public opinion against Wilde, Hichens withdrew the novel from sale following Wilde's disgrace in 1895, and did not reprint it until after Douglas's death in 1947.—NICK FREEMAN

Griffith, George (1857–1906). English writer. Real name George Chetwynd Griffith-Jones. Griffith was a writer of both proto-**science fiction** and popular **science** articles, especially for the popular illustrated magazines published by C. Arthur Pearson. Griffith supplied a number of **serial** novels depicting future wars for Pearson, most notably *The Angel of the Revolution* (1893), where a group of **anarchist**, nihilist, and **socialist** rebels band together under the command of a crippled Russian Jew to take advantage of the political instability caused by an Anglo-Russian war to impose an Anglo-Saxon global government. The major advantage of "the Terror" is a fleet of superior air-ships with unsurpassable destructive power. *Angel* was a hit, and it was an important step forward in the development of the scientific romance, as it combines the Jules Verne–like invention story (*Angel*'s air-ship is explicitly compared to one from Verne), **invasion literature** (in the style of ***The Battle of Dorking***), and utopian fiction (the new government imposes drastic reforms) into a form that more closely resembles modern science fiction, with both technological and sociological extrapolation.

Griffith went on to write many novels where small groups of individuals acquired weapons of mass destruction, though the identities of those groups changes from book to book, including Tsarist sympathizers, utopian colonists, a capitalist cartel, and French pirates. Griffith's political sympathies fluctuated: *Angel* is as sympathetic to its socialists as *The Great Pirate Syndicate* (1899) is to its capitalist oligarchs. A consistent fascination was the immense destructive power of future **technologies** like air-ships and submarines, and when his novels compare state violence to terrorist violence, it's difficult to tell if it is to authorize terrorist violence or critique state violence. His utopias often feature prominent racism.

Griffith's other stories used fantastic themes such as immortality, invisibility, **mummies**, **occult**ism, and space travel. He had many imitators, especially in the genre of future-war fiction, including **M. P. Shiel** and **William Le Queux**, and **H. G. Wells**'s *The War in the Air* (1908) features a character who learned everything he knows about air warfare by reading Griffith—whom Wells mentions only to disparage.—STEVEN MOLLMANN

See also Bleiler 1990, Eggeling 2017

Griffiths, Arthur (1838–1908). English writer. Authorship was the second act in the professional life of Arthur Griffiths, whose literary production was preceded by service in the British army as well as a career in prison administration. Both of these occupations furnished Griffiths with experiences that he mined for his creative endeavors. His initial output, beginning with *The Queen's Shilling* (1873), consisted primarily of military novels. While Griffiths channeled the exposure to criminality and the carceral stemming from his prison governorship into factual and historical works like *The Chronicles of Newgate* (1884), this repository of knowledge was also a major inspiration for his fiction. In 1883, upon assuming the editorship of *Home News for India, China, and the Colonies*, a newspaper that served as a news source for expatriate English readers, Griffiths initially used the publication as a vehicle for the circulation of his fiction output from this time. *Fast and Loose* (1883–84), the novel he **serial**ized in the journal, both harked back to the large-canvas **Dickens** serial novels with its interwoven nexus of diverse characters but also reflected the emerging popularity of **detective fiction** in its tale of the exposure of corruption at a London bank involving white-collar criminals and criminal underworld figures. The course of Griffiths's career reflected the late nineteenth-century shift from the hegemony of the three-decker to the predominance of the one-volume novel. Contemporaneous to their 1884 publication of the three-volume edition of *Fast and Loose*, Chapman & Hall also published Griffiths's one-volume detective novel, *No. 99*. The latter format was arguably more attuned to Griffiths's style of writing. He achieved his greatest commercial success here with the railway murder mystery, *The Rome Express* (1896), which had reportedly sold 45,000 copies by 1910. Much of the novel is set in Paris and French popular novelists like Emile Gaboriau were a major influence on Griffiths's writing. While the majority of Griffiths's output faded into twentieth-century obscurity, *The Rome Express* has enjoyed a degree of restored contemporary visibility with its inclusion in the anthology, *The Penguin Book of Victorian Villainies* (1984), edited by Graham and Hugh Greene.—Paul Raphael Rooney

Guy Livingstone; or, "Thorough" (1857). Novel by George Alfred Lawrence (1827–76). Published anonymously in a single volume by J. W. Parker, a firm associated with the school of muscular fiction, *Guy Livingstone* launched Lawrence's literary career. His idealized conception of a gentlemanly hero "of the gladiator type" ([Rev.] 1857: p. 971) capitalized on British patriotic fervor in the immediate aftermath of the Crimean war. Guy is an officer in the Life Guards and "the perfection of muscular power" (1857: p. 356). His virile **masculinity**—he is a champion jockey and boxer—makes him irresistible to women, and it is women who bring about his fall. Guy's resolve to settle down to civilian life with (icily) chaste Constance Brandon is floored by the siren Flora Bellasys who is determined to separate them (Constance catches the pair kissing and dies of grief). Meanwhile, Guy's romantic friendship with violet-eyed silky-haired fellow officer Charlie Forrester comes to rather more a violent end. Charlie is murdered by a jealous rival after having eloped with Guy's cousin, Isabella. The novel's denouement is eminently moral. Having lost both his fiancée and best friend, Guy suffers a fatal fall from his horse, his death mourned by a repentant Flora and his betrayal of Constance forgiven by her brother Cyril. The novel would be parodied by Bret Harte as "Guy Heavystone; or, Entire" in *Sensation Novels Condensed* (1871), but Lawrence's success was emulated by **Ouida**, whose early novels owe an enormous debt to *Guy Livingstone*.—Jane Jordan

See also Jordan 2011

Haggard, H. Rider [Sir Henry Rider Haggard] (1856–1925). English writer. A prolific novelist who wrote over fifty works of fiction, Haggard was born into a well-to-do family of Danish descent, the eighth of ten children, Haggard was educated at Ipswich grammar school followed by cramming preparations for the civil service exam. His early schooling was not considered promising, however, and in his autobiography he describes himself as "more or less of a dunderhead at lessons," whom his father declared "only fit to be a greengrocer" (1926: p. 5). In 1875, at the age of nineteen, Haggard was offered a position as assistant to Sir Henry Bulwer, an old friend and neighbor of the family who had been made lieutenant-governor of Natal, and rose quickly into positions of considerable responsibility. He was inspired by the landscape of South Africa, travelling widely and hunting wild game. His right-wing political sensibilities were formed in the context of his colonial service, particularly his experience of the annexation of the Transvaal in 1877, during which Haggard was appointed special commissioner to Theophilus Shepstone. He married and returned to England, taking first to ostrich farming and later studying for the bar, at which time he also began his writing career in earnest.

His first book, *Cetywayo and His White Neighbors* (1882) was a bitterly critical account of British colonial policy in South Africa. Haggard paid Trubner and Company a subvention of £50 in order to publish 750 copies of the book but poor sales meant that he lost this sum. A second edition was published in 1888, which also seems to have sold slowly. In his autobiography Haggard claimed that a third edition sold thirty thousand copies in 1899 (1926: p. 207), though by his own admission some of these sales may have been to people who thought they were buying another one of his novels.

Haggard's reputation rests chiefly upon his novels, the majority of which fall into the category of the **imperial adventure**. His first novel, *Dawn* (1884), again did not sell well, while his second, *The Witch's Head* (1885), was deemed by Haggard himself to be inferior to the first, "except for the African part" in which he discovered the imaginative milieu that would define his literary outputs thereafter (1926: p. 218–19). Following these commercial disappointments Haggard returned to the bar to earn a living and it was not until the phenomenal success of **King Solomon's Mines** that he was able to devote himself entirely to writing. *King Solomon's Mines* and **She** are by far the most important of his novels. With them Haggard had invented the "lost world" genre that flourished between the 1880s and the First World War. Much of his subsequent output consists of sequels, prequels and crossovers of these two novels, of which the most significant are *Nada the Lily* (1892), *Ayesha: The Return of She* (1905), *Marie* (1912), *Child of the Storm* (1913), *Finished* (1917 and *She and Allan* (1920).—MERRICK BURROW

See also ODNB

Harkness, Margaret (1854–1923). English writer. A slum journalist and social problem novelist, Harkness's writings at the end of the nineteenth century helped to raise awareness about urban **poverty** and the plight of London's East End poor. She was born on 28 February 1854 in Worcestershire into a solidly middle-class family. Her father, Robert Harkness, was a Church of England clergyman and her mother, Jane Waugh Law Harkness, claimed aristocratic origins. Harkness's pseudonym "John Law" may have been taken from her mother's maiden name, or it may have been inspired by the economist, John Law of Lauriston. Harkness was second cousin to Beatrice Potter (she even introduced Potter to future husband Sidney Webb), with whom she formed a friendship during their school studies in Bournemouth and, later, through their philanthropic work in London's

East End. Indeed, Potter introduced Harkness to the Katharine Buildings, the setting for *A City Girl: A Realistic Story*. It was also during her time in London's East End, during the late 1880s, that Harkness met and befriended female reformers such as Annie Besant, fellow slum journalist known for her work on the 1888 London Matchgirls' Strike; Olive Schreiner, author of the proto–New Woman novel, *The Story of an African Farm* (1883); and Eleanor Marx, daughter of Karl Marx and an active socialist in her own right. Harkness was best known for her slum novels, which were more widely distributed than other social problem novels of the 1890s. Her best-known titles include **A City Girl**, **Out of Work**, *Captain Lobe: A Story of the Salvation Army* (1889; republished as **In Darkest London**), *A Manchester Shirtmaker* (1890), and *George Eastmont: Wanderer* (1905). Writing for a mostly middle-class audience, Harkness would often paint the East End slum as the object of pity and, at the same time, issue a call to action by readers to recognize their own responsibility toward the dejected poor.

Harkness is still remembered by many scholars of Victorian literature as the woman to whom Friedrich Engels once wrote an infamous letter complaining of the author's inaccurate representation of the urban working-class. Engels was writing in response to Harkness's first novel, *A City Girl* (1887), which details the sexual downfall of a young East End seamstress named Nelly Ambrose after she falls in love with and is impregnated by Arthur Grant, a married man and middle-class idealist who subscribes to radical socialism. Engels took greatest issue with the novel's characterization of the working-class as too "passive" in their tragic fate, a representation that he characterized as "not quite realistic" insofar as it did not fit with his own personal knowledge of the laboring class. In all of her subsequent novels, Harkness tried to address such critiques by complicating popular stereotypes of working-class and poor, but she did still persist in her call to English rich and West End readers to realize their responsibility to the poor and to work together toward reformist ends. Through a blend of realistic detail and a larger sociological narrative, Harkness not only exposed this class divide, but she also argued for a social solution that required participation from the privileged classes and those in power, as much as (if not more than) than those who are poor and out of work (the subject of her second novel, published in 1888).—S. Brooke Cameron

Harraden, Beatrice (1864–1936). English novelist and suffragist. An alumna of Cheltenham Ladies' College, Harraden continued her studies at Queen's College and Bedford College. Graduating from the University of London with first class honors, Harraden was introduced into literary circles by **Eliza Lynn Linton**, who referred to her protégé as "Little B.A." on account of the younger woman's educational attainment. Her first publication, a **short story** titled "Child Ciss: A Tale of the Stage," appeared in **Belgravia** during 1885. Further stories were published in various periodicals, including the *English Illustrated Magazine*, the *Graphic*, and *Blackwood's Magazine*.

Harraden is best known for *Ships that Pass in the Night*, a tragic romance set in a Swiss tuberculosis asylum. The work was a great success when published by Lawrence and Buller in 1893, despite its initial rejection by William Blackwood, who feared its "futile ending" would prevent it becoming "a popular novel" (Finkelstein 2002: p. 139). Translated into numerous European languages, it proved the most popular of her novels, although Harraden considered *The Fowler* (1899) to be her best work. Other novels included *Katharine Frensham* (1903), *The Scholar's Daughter* (1906), *Out of the Wreck I Rise* (1912), *Where Your Treasure Is* (1918), *Patuffa* (1923), and *Search Will Find It Out*

(1928). Harraden also published a collection of short stories, *In Varying Moods* (1894), and two books for children: *Things Will Take a Turn* (1891) and *Untold Tales of the Past* (1897). Her nonfiction work included *Two Health-Seekers in Southern California* (1897), a guide to convalescence abroad, and the preface to Linton's *My Literary Life* (1899). A keen suffragist, Harraden served as vice-president of the Women Writers' Suffrage League under **Flora Annie Steel**'s presidency. She regularly addressed audiences at the Women's Social and Political Union (WSPU) and was a contributor to the organization's journal, *Votes for Women*. Her most notable pro-suffrage publication was the short play, *Lady Geraldine's Speech* (1909). Harraden's position as a literary celebrity was marked by her inclusion in Sarah Tooley's "Some Women Novelists" (*Woman at Home*, December 1897). In 1930, she was awarded a civil list pension for her literary work.—Fiona Snailham

See also ODNB, DNCJ, Crawford 2003

Hartmann the Anarchist; Or, the Doom of the Great City (1893). Novel by E. (Edward) Douglas Fawcett (1866–1960). A poet, novelist, mountaineer, philosopher, and **occult**ist who dabbled in Theosopy, Fawcett was the older brother of Percy Fawcett, the great explorer of South America who disappeared in Brazil in 1925 on a mission to locate the lost city of Z (ODNB). *Hartmann the Anarchist*, Fawcett's first novel, was **serial**ized in *The English Illustrated Magazine* from June to September 1893 and was published in book form the same year by Edward Arnold, with **illustrations** by Fred T. Jane. It is set in 1920 but explores several preoccupations of the 1890s: socialism, anarchist violence, civil unrest, technological innovation, and flying machines. In terms of genre, it is somewhere between the "dynamite novel" that flourished in the 1880s, the future-war novels popularized by **William Le Queux** and others of that ilk, and **science fiction** in the manner of Jules Verne (Melchiori 1985: pp. 142–9; Houen 2002: p. 31).

The narrator is Stanley, a socialist who falls in with a group of **anarchists** led by Rudolph Hartmann. Hartmann is a wealthy and brilliant engineer who has been inspired with a pessimistic hatred of society: "He regarded civilization as rotten from top to foundation, and the present human race as 'only fit for fuel'" (Fawcett 1893: p. 26). Longing for a return to the noble savagery of Rousseau, and convinced that conventional anarchist bombings will achieve little, Hartmann invents a super-lightweight metal that he uses to build an "aëronef" (airship), ominously named the *Attila*. His plan is to destroy cities from the air, starting with London; an anarchist army (he claims to have twelve thousand adherents in London alone) will then "fire the streets in all directions, rouse up the populace, and let loose pandemonium" (Fawcett 1893: p. 84). Unfortunately, an early victim of the bombing of London is Hartmann's mother; a distraught Hartmann then scuttles the *Attila*. Stanley reports that order is "completely re-established" within days, and "gradually the Empire recovered from the shock" (Fawcett 1893: pp. 213–4).

In 2009 Ian Bone, founder of Class War, reissued the novel with illustrations by Stanley Dornwood.—Andrew Glazzard

See also McLean 2016, **Political Violence**

Health. While definitions of health often cite "freedom from bodily pain or sickness" as its key features (Johnson's *Dictionary of the English Language*), Victorian medical writers were more equivocal about what health meant, preferring instead to emphasize an individual's ability to function in society with the ease and equanimity befitting his or her class, age, gender, and geographic location. James Milner Fothergill suggests in *Main-*

tenance of Health (1874) that health is "the balance betwixt various parts of the organism" (1874: p. 1); William Strange recognizes that "[h]ealth is made up of a variety of ideal images which present themselves in a different guise to the mind of almost every individual" (1864: p. xvii). Rather than offering a single, quantifiable definition to which all must adhere, medical handbooks by professionals and laypersons depict health as relative and rare, most often appreciated when it is gone. Bruce Haley sums up Victorian health as "mens sana in corpore sano" (1978: p. 21), a Latin expression roughly meaning "a healthy mind in a healthy body."

And yet, as Michel Foucault and others argue, **medicine**, **science**, law, and literature framed health as a shorthand for a set of moral and physical standards designed to advance middle-class ideology and the Imperial project. Whether they were referring to public health policy or domestic medicine, these institutions emphasized the maintenance of compliant, clean, fit, (re)productive bodies became the hallmark of a healthy Victorian citizenry (Gilbert 2007); deviations signaled **disease**. Young women should bloom and bustle, but only in the most benign and pleasing ways; a gentleman should care for his estate, have an acceptable profession, and exercise. Clever, busy women who want "something to do," and foppish men who do not, were pathologized and punished. By the end of the century, **New Women** and dandyish "new men" challenged the norms that pervaded British culture, contributing to anxieties about the degeneration of the nation.

From the domestic fictions of **Charlotte Yonge** and **Dinah Mulock Craik** to the sensational stories of **Wilkie Collins,** and from late–Victorian **imperial adventure** to **Gothic** writers **Robert Louis Stevenson** and **H. Rider Haggard**, popular literature exploited this tension between fixed and variable definitions of health. In Yonge's *Clever Woman of the Family* (1865), Rachel Curtis is the picture of health. She is physically fit and attractive, but she represents the wrong kind of energy and fortitude. At twenty-five, she starts a girls' vocational school, dabbles in "homeopathic doctress[ing]," and embraces her spinsterhood. She fails on all accounts, getting conned out of financing for the school, presumably contributing to the death of a village girl, and, after succumbing to a brief illness, settling into a quiet, married life.

While being a wife and mother were the mark of ideal female health, not all "clever" women needed to shut themselves up in marriage. ***The Woman in White***'s Marian Holcombe exhibits a mannish strength and intellectual independence that helps to save her weak, sickly sister. Anthony Trollope's Miss Dunstable (*Doctor Thorne*) proves to be the most physically and financially healthy of all, refusing to sell herself on the marriage market, while managing to advise the novel's young hero. Trollope underscores her competence, as she explains that "she took a physician with her for the benefit of her health, whom she generally was forced to nurse" (1858: p. 162). These characters point to forms of healthy femininity that challenge the norms set by writers like Yonge.

Dinah Mulock Craik's bestseller, *John Halifax, Gentleman* (1856), offers a masculine ideal of the healthy hero. The titular character's physical and mental fitness allow him to transform from impoverished **orphan** to wealthy family man. Determination, hard work, perseverance, and strength prove to be among the key features that distinguish John from other characters, particularly the self-described "puny wretch," Phineas Fletcher, who narrates the story. When recounting his first meeting with John, Phineas describes his **physiognomy** and physique variously as "Saxon," "well-shaped," "rugged," "resolute," "strongly built," and "muscular" (pp. 31–32). All the ingredients of a would-be gentleman. Readers learn of John's superior work ethic, humility, sociability, and ingenuity (he administers the smallpox vaccine on his children before it was common to do so). Such qualities exemplify British progress and thus the fitness of certain individuals to govern their homes and the nation.

During the latter decades of the century, many Victorians worried that England was no longer producing healthy, virile gentleman-heroes on the model of John Halifax. To many, the nation seemed to be weakening, the overall resolve and constitution of its citizenry degrading. A prominent cause for concern was the changing economy and its effects on how and where people lived and worked. H. Rider Haggard expressed this concern succinctly, asking, "What will be the effect upon the national health and physique, and, therefore, upon the national character, of the transplanting of the sturdiest classes of our inhabitants, the dwellers in the rural districts, from their wholesome country homes to the crowded courts of sweltering cities?" (1899: p. 466). To Haggard and others, the answer was clear, and declining health was inevitable.

Concerns about health in the late–Victorian period tended to focus not on individuals, but instead on the relative health of the English race or nation as a whole—an inevitable result, perhaps, of the increasing acceptance of Darwinian thought and its emphasis on long-term changes within species. This concern for the long-term maintenance of the race found expression in the **eugenics** movement initiated in the 1880s by Francis Galton. Finding symptomatic evidence of declining national health at every level of society became something of a popular pastime even before the English translation of Max Nordau's *Degeneration* was published in 1895. The destitution of the poor, confinement of middle-class clerks, and idleness of the rich suggested national degeneration; so did women's emancipation, smoking, vegetarianism, bicycling, and any number of other things. Literature and the arts fell under close scrutiny, with Nordau singling out Wildean Aestheticism and Decadence, Pre-Raphaelite art and literature, and proto-modernist texts as particularly troubling evidence of rampant degenerationism (*Degeneration*).

In this context, late–Victorian authors of popular literature could not help but respond and contribute to the popular discourse on the presumed decline of national health. The national obsession with declining health in the form of bodily sickness, deviancy, and madness surely finds expression in the spectacle of the reversion of the upstanding gentleman, Dr. Jekyll, into the corrupt and anti-social Mr. Hyde in **Robert Louis Stevenson**'s tale (1886). **Arthur Conan Doyle**'s **Sherlock Holmes** stories contain any number of depraved villains, and their brilliant protagonist himself operates in the margins of health, flirting with cocaine addiction to alleviate his depressive ennui. Likewise, the nation, and especially its women, seem particularly open to the spread of disease in **Bram Stoker**'s *Dracula*. Each of these texts highlights not just fears of declining health, but a desperate struggle to fight off sickness and decline on the part of a few stalwart English heroes.

With their robust, virile English heroes exported to the fields of empire, the *fin-de-siècle* **romances** of empire or adventure which were tremendously popular during the last two decades of the Victorian period similarly express concerns about English health. In Haggard's exemplary **King Solomon's Mines**, Englishmen flee an emasculating, altogether too domesticated England to embark on a treasure hunting adventure in remotest Africa. They return home rejuvenated: they have proved their mettle in harrowing physical and mental ordeals, restored order to a remote tribe by dethroning a diseased and degenerate tyrant, and claimed a fortune in diamonds which allows them to settle on estates in the English countryside as robust, patriarchal squires. Haggard's novel, like many late-Victorian romances of empire and adventure, affirms popular fears about the enervating and emasculating effects of life in modern England, but offers, in its display of English bodies forcefully reclaiming control and vanquishing degeneracy, a promise that the health of England's people, nation, and empire can be restored through a reassertion of traditional hierarchies.—ERIKA WRIGHT and DANIEL P. SHEA

Heart and Science (1887). Novel by **Wilkie Collins**. In writing the didactic novel *Heart and Science,* Collins aimed to influence readers' minds on what he called "the hideous secrets of Vivisection" (1998/1887 p. 38). He consulted with several anti-**vivisection**ists, including Frances Power Cobbe, in order to portray the vivisector (pp. 38–9). The villain and furtive vivisector is Dr. Nathan Benjulia; Dr. Ovid Vere and his distant cousin, Carmina Graywell, play protagonist and victim. After the death of her father, Graywell arrives in England to live with her father's sister, Mrs. Gallilee (Ovid's mother). Graywell and Vere quickly fall in love, but Gallilee, intent on embezzling Graywell's inheritance, sends Vere to Canada to recuperate his **health**. Gallilee torments Graywell, inducing **hysteria**. Benjulia is called, but on noticing that Graywell's symptoms resemble a **disease** he has tried to cure, Benjulia allows the supposed **mental illness** to continue its course, even aiding it at times through **mesmerism**. Before Graywell's illness inflicts irreparable harm, Vere returns and provides the correct **medicine** and cure, publishing his findings, which destroys Benjulia. Robbed of his life's work, Benjulia bequeaths his estate to Zo (Gallilee's daughter) then enters his (hitherto unseen) **vivisection** laboratory and frees all of the **animals**. He sets fire to the building and himself, committing **suicide**. The novel ends with Vere and Graywell happily married. As **sensation fiction**, *Heart and Science* met with tepid reviews in both the popular and medical presses, though critics, past and present, acknowledge its anti-science stance against the rapidly changing late-nineteenth century.—THOMAS G. COLE, II

The Heavenly Twins (1893). Novel by **Sarah Grand**. Together with **George Egerton's** *Keynotes*, Grand's work initiated the so-called "New Woman fiction" movement that created immense controversy in the 1890s. It relates the interlocking stories of three young women, Evadne, Edith and Angelica, whose transitions from girlhood to marriage result, variously, in celibate co-habitation, depression, attempted suicide, cross-dressing, and syphilitic madness and death. Nineteen at the beginning of the novel, Evadne has "a mind of exceptional purity as well as exceptional strength" (1992/1893: p. 23). When on her wedding day she receives a letter detailing her husband's sexual history, her purity dictates her revulsion and her strength of mind makes her insist on a celibate marriage. Grand demonstrates the practical wisdom of this (as well as arguing its moral justice) through the example of Edith, who, accepting the conventional wisdom that a good woman will effect moral reform in a reprobate husband, is rewarded for her credulity by contracting the syphilis which infects her child and causes her own madness and death. Observing these examples with horror is the young Angelica. She and her brother Diavolo are the eponymous Heavenly Twins, ironically named for their **childhood** escapades. The twins' antics as children provide much-needed comic relief, but Angelica's growth into young womanhood complicates their relationship and generates uncertainty about woman's role. After witnessing Edith's deathbed ravings, Angelica abruptly proposes to an older family friend—"Marry me! ... *and let me do as I like*" (p. 321)—at which point the narrative apparently abandons her.

The central section of the novel, "The Tenor and the Boy—An Interlude," features a mysterious Tenor who is visited at night in his humble cottage by a Boy who introduces himself as Diavolo. Despite his yearning for the remote Angelica, the Tenor's growing intimacy with the Boy carries strong homoerotic overtones. These are, however, instantly dispelled when, after a boating accident, the "Boy" is revealed to be Angelica herself. Not only has she deceived the Tenor as to her sex, but now announces in passing that she is married. Her conduct, she explains, is a desperate bid to escape the constraints imposed on women: "I wanted to *do* as well as to *be*" and "to see the world as men see it" (p. 450f). By contrast, Evadne is sinking into apathy and depression, her sexual "self-repression" causing a "morbid state of mind" (p. 646) from which she is finally rescued by the love of the good man who narrates the novel's final section.

In spite or perhaps because of its highly controversial subject matter, *The Heavenly Twins* became an instant best-seller. Beyond the shock effect, though, Grand effectively combines polemic with psychological realism. Her descriptions of depression and madness are genuinely harrowing, and she succeeds in circumventing Victorian restrictions on writing about sex, effectively evoking both Evadne's frustrations and Angelica's sexual immaturity. Capturing the *fin-de-siècle* interest in feminist issues, Grand's Heavenly Twins are, as the Boy tells the Tenor, not "signs of the Zodiac" but "signs of the times" (p. 383).
—Gail Cunningham

Heinemann (1890–). English publisher. Founded by William Heinemann, the publishing house has, over the years, focused on contemporary popular fiction and drama, translations of European literature under the brand Heinemann's International Library, and classical Greek and Roman works as part of Loeb Classical Library. The list of popular authors includes, among others, **Hall Caine, Robert Louis Stevenson, Sarah Grand, Robert Louis Stevenson, Israel Zangwill, Robert Smythe Hichens,** and **Somerset Maugham**. It has also published works by Fyodor Dostoyevsky, Ivan Turgenev, and Henrik Ibsen, among others, in translation. By means of these translations, Heinemann was instrumental in making these contemporary and classical works of literature available to the masses for the first time and at affordable prices. Along with **Chatto and Windus**, Heinemann played a crucial role in ending the dominance of the triple-decker novel.
—Suman Sigroha

See also *EB*, Hall 1986

Henry Dunbar (1864). Novel by **Mary Elizabeth Braddon**. James Wilmot commits forgery for his master, is dismissed without a character reference, and resorts to a life of crime. When James's former master, Henry Dunbar, returns to England after a thirty-five-year absence in **India**, James murders him, usurps his identity and fortune, and testifies that the corpse found by police belongs to his former servant, James Wilmot. Hearing of her father's supposed death, James's daughter, Margaret, confronts the so-called Henry Dunbar only to discover that her father is the true murderer. Ultimately, her amateur detective work and continued filial devotion allow him to escape punishment. This understudied novel would interest scholars who examine the performativity of social **class** and gender, false identities, and crime in **sensation fiction**. It would also enhance discussions of sensation fiction's influence on **detective fiction**, as it includes both professional and amateur detectives.—Sarah L. Lennox

Henty, G. A. [**George Alfred Henty**] (1832–1902). English novelist. Henty began his writing career in his early twenties, when commissioned in the army during the Crimean War (1853–6) and the *Morning Adviser* published letters he sent to his father. After marrying and having four children, he resigned his commission and, following the premature death of this wife from tuberculosis, turned to war correspondence. He covered, among many international conflicts, the war for independence in Italy, the Spanish Civil war, the Anglo-Asante war in the Sudan, and the Franco-Prussian war, becoming increasingly disillusioned with European geopolitics and fatigued by the road. In the 1870s he turned from journalism toward the production of the **serial**ized novel. His 1872 *The Young Franc-tireurs* records the adventurous exploits of two British teenagers who join the French forces during the Franco-Prussian war. It was "the first of a new sort of boy's book" that, as Henty explains in the preface, was to give "under the guise of historical tales full and accurate accounts of all the leading events of great wars" (ODNB). In the years that followed, Henty wrote more than 80 historical adventure novels for boys, along with hundreds of **short stories**. These narratives stretch from 1200 BCE to the late nineteenth century, thus covering a vast section of mostly European history. His output was tremendous and often consisted of three or four novels per year for his main publisher Blackie & Sons of Glasgow.

Henty's books were extremely popular during the late nineteenth and early twentieth century and were instrumental in the rise of the **imperial adventure** genre to which **H. Rider Haggard**, **Rudyard Kipling**, and John Buchan also contributed. This genre was disseminated through the novel but also by publications such as *Boy's Own Paper*, *Captain*, *Young England* and *Union Jack*, the latter edited by Henty himself until it failed in 1883. Henty's heroes are typically white, brave and thoroughly Christian boys in their late teens. His most popular novels take place in the contemporary historical moment and carry titles such as *With Buller in Natal* (1901), *With Roberts in Pretoria* (1902) and *With Kitchener in the Soudan* (1902). While the historical detail, as far as the unfolding of particular battles are concerned, is generally correct, Henty's fiction describes history as taking place primarily in the violent confrontation of nations and peoples, and in the decisions of the white, male powerbrokers that engineer these clashes. Henty's oeuvre in its entirety can thus be seen as an attempt to describe first the slow rise of the British Empire out of 3000 years of European conflict, and then the continuing global spread of Anglo-Saxon hegemony during the nineteenth century. In his fiction, this rise is largely attributed to the sheer, natural pluck of the Anglo-Saxon male, always ready to lay down his life for his country and his friends.—JOHAN HÖGLUND

See also ODNB

Her Father's Name (1876). Novel by **Florence Marryat**. After her father's **suicide**, Leona Lacoste works to maintain her independence and uncover the truth about her father's past. The novel begins in Brazil where George Evans has been living under the pseudonym of George Lacoste. When a conniving neighbor threatens to reveal, unless Leona agrees to marriage, that George Evans is an Englishman wanted for the **murder** of Abraham Anson, Lacoste commits suicide. Leona discovers the truth of her father's identity in his papers and subsequently flees Brazil to avoid hearing her father's name tarnished. She is next seen aboard a ship to New York dressed as a man. Don Christobal Valera, her longtime friend who is desperately in love with her, discovers her aboard the ship and begrudgingly agrees to assist her in her aims to become an actress.

In New York, Leona achieves great success on the stage, although she is constantly haunted by references to her deceased father, George Evans. Because of her height, she is cast in traditionally male roles, professionalizing her cross-dressing. Although Leona is greatly admired by both men and women, she is careful to maintain a spotless reputation and avoid romances so as to maintain her independence. Christobal, working as a clerk, occasionally confesses his love and proposes marriage to her, but she repeatedly rebuffs him, determined to work for and maintain authority over herself. Christobal succumbs to a violent illness just before he is to be sent to England by his firm. The firm decides to postpone the work until Christobal can travel, but Leona intercepts the messages and finds that Christobal is meant to work with her uncle, Henry Evans. Incoherent Christobal is sent to the country to recuperate under the watchful eye of his mother, and Leona travels to London masquerading as her dear friend.

In London, Henry Evans invites the false Christobal to live with him during his stay. There, Leona forms a close relationship with Lucilla Evans. Lucilla is an invalid, as she suffers from **hysteria**. Leona recognizes Lucilla as a useful source of information, so she works to foster a relationship with the girl. Because Leona is impersonating Christobal, the relationship between Leona and Lucille is rife with queer potential, which is emphasized by Leona/Christobal's flirtations with other women who appear at the Evans residence.

Leona dons multiple disguises and travels throughout England to gather information about the murder of Abraham Anson. Not only does she confirm her father's innocence, but she also uncovers a signed confession from the true murderer. She also discovers that Lucilla is actually her half-sister. Leona prematurely reveals all to her uncle because she is worried that Christobal has transferred his affections to Lucilla. She details the evidence she found, and the novel ends with promises of a marriage between Leona and Christobal and Leona receiving her rightful inheritance. Containing elements of both **sensation fiction** and **detective fiction**, *Her Father's Name* has been compared by Craton (2009) to **Wilkie Collins**'s *No Name* (1862).—Sarah Kneisler

Hichens, Robert Smythe (1864–1950). English novelist. Educated privately and at Clifton College, Hichens studied music before becoming a journalist in 1889. After publishing *The Coastguard* (1886), a novel he later disparaged, Hichens wrote **short stories** for *Mistress and Maid* and the *Pall Mall* magazine. He suffered a serious illness in 1893, and in 1894 went on a recuperative voyage to **Egypt**. North Africa became a recurrent setting in his fiction, but the trip was more notable for meetings with **E. F. Benson**, Lord Alfred Douglas, and Reginald Turner. Having heard their stories of **Oscar Wilde**, Hichens wrote a satirical novel, ***The Green Carnation*** (1894), which he published anonymously. Its brilliant pastiches and parodies of Wilde, whom he knew slightly, made it a commercial success. Having admitted his authorship, he became a professional writer. Hichens combined writing fiction with a job as the music critic of the London *World*, but the position restricted his opportunities for foreign travel and was quickly abandoned. A prolific novelist, he became a significant presence in English popular fiction until the 1940s, combining **melodrama**tic romance with evocative travelogues, and occasionally writing crime and supernatural stories. Hichens's biggest successes were *The Garden of Allah* (1904), *Bella Donna* (1909), and *The Paradine Case* (1933); a number of his books were adapted for the screen. His finest ghost stories, including "How Love Came to Professor Guildea," appear in *Tongues of Conscience* (1900). His autobiography, *Yesterday* (1947), is entertaining but unreliable.—Nick Freeman

See also ODNB, DLB

Hocking, Joseph (1860–1937). Cornish novelist and United Methodist minister. At the age of sixteen, Hocking apprenticed to a land surveyor before entering the ministry of the United Free Methodist Church. Following in the footsteps of his older brother, Silas K. Hocking, Joseph became a successful writer of popular novels alongside his ministerial duties. He published almost a hundred works and sold millions of copies. His strong faith influenced his writing and he believed popular novels to be the ideal vehicle to transmit his religious views in an easily accessible format. *Jabez Easterbrook* (1891), Hocking's first commercial success, is often thought to be his first work, but his earliest novels appeared between 1887 and 1889. *Jabez Easterbrook* set the tone of religious conversion and individual reformation that defines Hocking's didactic purpose novels of the 1890s, such as **Weapons of Mystery** or *The Story of Andrew Fairfax* (1893). From the mid-1890s, he increasingly focused on integrating Cornish historical themes in his fiction, especially the period of evangelical revival in the eighteenth century. In *The Birthright* (1897), for instance, John Wesley directly appears as a character. Strong anti-Catholic sentiments determined much of his writing before the First World War. During the war, he published patriotic tales of heroic deeds before returning to historical or local Cornish settings in the last two decades of his career. Much of his work remains unexplored to this day and offers extensive material for future scholarship on religious and national, especially Cornish, identity and popular fiction.—Laura Habbe

See also ODNB, Kent 2002

Holdsworth, Annie (1860–1917). Anglo-Caribbean editor, novelist, and suffragette. Born in Jamaica to the Rev. William Holdsworth, who worked with freed slaves as a missionary, Annie—also known as Eliza Ann Holdsworth—was a feminist and often published under the pseudonym Max Beresford. In 1898, she married author Eugene Lee-Hamilton and became sister-in-law to novelist **Vernon Lee**. Lee-Hamilton and Holdsworth were to have two daughters, one of whom was to die in 1904 after only living for a year. She served as co-editor of *The Woman's Signal* and, during the 1890s, on the staff of W. T. Stead's *Review of Reviews*. Holdsworth's novels include *Joanna Traill, Spinster* (1894); *Spindles and Oars: or, Chronicles of Skyrle* (1896); *The Valley of the Great Shadow* (1899); *The Iron Gates* (1906); and *Lady Letty Brandon* (1909). She co-authored *Forest Notes* with her husband and published **short stories** such as "A Study in Oak" (1886), which appeared in **Belgravia**. Holdsworth's work often explores the challenges facing the **New Woman** and unmarried women, calling for them to develop families outside of the traditional domestic sphere through adoption and caring for other children within communities.—Amberyl Malkovich

Holmes, Sherlock. Fictional character created by **Arthur Conan Doyle**, whose private detective work is the basis of four novels, including *A Study in Scarlet*, *The Sign of Four* (appearing first in *Lippincott's Magazine*), and *The Hound of the Baskervilles* (serialized in the **Strand Magazine**), as well as several collections of **short stories**, including *The Adventures of Sherlock Holmes*. Holmes served as the inspiration for, among other characters, **Arthur Morrison**'s detective **Martin Hewitt** and **E. W. Hornung**'s jewel thief A. J. Raffles. The **Raffles stories**, Doyle once remarked, are an inversion of the Holmes series.—Kevin A. Morrison

Hornung, E. W. (1866–1921). English writer. Hornung was born in Yorkshire, and educated at Uppingham School. He spent a part of his youth, from 1884 to 1886, in Australia to improve his poor **health**, an experience that is formative to much of his writing including his first novel *A Bride from the Bush* (1890). Hornung is best known for his immensely successful stories about A. J. **Raffles** (see Ue 2015), a play on the **Sherlock Holmes** canon. Hornung married **Arthur Conan Doyle**'s sister Constance in 1893, and his first Raffles collection, *The Amateur Cracksman* (1899), was accordingly dedicated "To A. C. D. This form of flattery." An inverse on Holmes and Dr. Watson, Raffles is a **cricket**er—Hornung had a lifelong interest in the sport—and gentleman thief and Harry "Bunny" Manders, his biographer and accomplice. According to George Orwell, Raffles's death in "The Knees of the Gods" (1898) helps to cancel out his crimes; nonetheless, the mystery that shrouds this event "continues to elude, frustrate, and fascinate Bunny and ourselves as readers" (Ue 2015: pp. 226–27). Hornung's only son Oscar died in World War I, a tragedy that led him to volunteer and to write both about his son and his own experiences. Hornung and Constance went to the south of France after the war, where he died on 22 March 1921 and left behind four unfinished books: "His Brother's Blood," "The Graven Image," "Goddesses Three," and "An International Reputation." Hornung was buried a few feet away from his friend **George Gissing**.—Tom Ue

See also ODNB, Rowland 1999

Hubback, Catherine (1818–1877). English novelist. Perhaps best known as a niece of Jane Austen, Hubback was born Catherine Anne Austen at Chawton, Hampshire, where her aunt had spent her last years. She married John Hubback, a London barrister, in 1842 and had three sons (Klippert 2012: p. 12). In 1847 her husband experienced a mental breakdown. While she sought medical treatment for him, Hubback wrote books to support herself and her sons (Wheeler 2012: p. 193). By 1850 Hubback and her sons moved back into her father's house, and she published her first novel, *The Younger Sister*, based on a narrative called "The Watsons," which had been left unfinished by Jane Austen (Klippert 2012: p. 13). By the following year Hubback published two more novels. She proceeded to publish seven additional novels before 1865 for a career total of eleven books. Of her works, five novels were republished in the United States and her last novel, *Love and Duty* (1864), was printed only in the United States and not in Britain. Only one of her books, *The Rival Suitors* (1857), was popular enough to go through a second printing. She mostly wrote in the novel-of-manners genre, highlighting the experiences of a heroine struggling to negotiate the vicissitudes of middle and upper middle-class Victorian society. Within the pages of her novels, Hubback set forth an elaborate and unspoken system of social and even legal codes associated with culturally constructed womanhood. Hubback's works addressed some of the darker and more difficult circumstances connected with marriage, **motherhood**, and ideal womanhood including **bigamy**, cruelty, and infidelity. Hubback not only employed tropes and conventions popular in fiction of her day, but also dramatically represented the plight of women whose innocent ignorance, inferior legal status, and economic dependence made them vulnerable. Her painful personal experiences provided Hubback with unique insight into the legal, economic, and social hazards that could beset innocent Victorian women. In 1862 Hubback left her father's home at Portsdown Lodge and moved to Birkenhead to keep house for her eldest son, John Henry (Klippert 2012: p. 14). Around New Year's 1871 Hubback sailed to America and crossed on the transcontinental railway from New York to California where she lived with her middle son, Edward (Klippert 2012: p. 19). During her first year in California, Hubback published a short story titled "The Stewardess" in *Overland Monthly*, the first literary magazine in the west, but she never published another story or novel afterward because publishers would not meet her price (Wheeler 2013: p. 202). In 1876 Hubback crossed the country again to live in Virginia with her youngest son Charles and his family until her death from pneumonia in 1877 (Wheeler 2013: p. 217, Hunter 2009: p. 12). During her years of authorship, reviews of Hubback's novels appeared in periodicals including *The Athenaeum*, *The Literary Gazette*, and *The Saturday Review*. Aside from this contemporary notice, more commercial than cultural, Hubback and her novels received very little recognition from her contemporaries.—JACQUELYN C. WENNEKER

Hume, Fergusson Wright [Fergus] (1859–1932). English novelist. A prolific author of popular fiction, Hume was born in England on 8 July 1859, the second son of Scottish couple James Collin Hume (1823–1896) and Mary Fergusson (d. 1867). When Fergus was three years old, the family emigrated to Dunedin, in New Zealand's South Island, where James Hume found employment as Superintendent of the Otago Lunatic Asylum. Owing to this well-paid work, the Hume boys received the best education available, attending the first secondary school in Dunedin, Otago Boys' High (founded 1863), and New Zealand's first higher-education institution, the University of Otago (founded 1871). Fergus became a lawyer, serving his articling under the New Zealand attorney general. He was admitted to the Bar in 1885. Later that year, he and his sister emigrated to Melbourne, where he found work as a solicitor's clerk. By the mid–1880s, with a population approaching half a million, Melbourne was the largest metropolis in the Southern hemisphere. The London journalist George Augustus Sala visited in 1885, dubbing it "Marvellous Melbourne" (p. 7)

Fergus Hume's real passion was not the law, however, but literature and the theater. Back in Dunedin in 1882, his first novel, *Professor Brankel's Secret: A Psychological Study*, had been **serial**ized in the town newspaper, the *Saturday Advertiser*. In Melbourne, Hume placed articles on theater in *Table-Talk*, a periodical devoted to reviews and society gossip. Determined to make a name for himself as a playwright, in 1885 Hume decided to write a novel strategically designed to attract the attention of local theater-managers. As he explained: "I enquired of a leading Melbourne bookseller what style of book he sold most of. He replied that the detective stories of Gaboriau had a large sale…. The style of stories attracted me, and I determined to write a book of the same class; containing a mystery, a murder, and a description of low life" (1896: p. x).

Over the next few months, Hume constructed a novel very much in the Gaboriau mold—*The Mystery of a Hansom Cab*.

The novel had a rather inauspicious start. In the summer of 1886 it was rejected by George Robertson, the leading Melbourne publisher at the time, and Hume spent six fruitless months toting it around other publishers. As a result, in October 1886, Hume had five thousand copies of the novel published at his own expense. These sold out in seven days. A second and third printing followed until, three months later, twenty-five thousand copies had been sold, a circulation unheard of in Australian literary history. A few months after its spectacular Australian debut, Hume sold the rights to the novel for fifty pounds to a London speculator, Frederick Trischler, who immediately rebranded himself the "Hansom Cab Publishing Company" (Hume p. x). Hume would never make another penny from the novel.

The first London edition of the novel followed in November 1887, where it also enjoyed phenomenal sales the year before the publication of **Arthur Conan Doyle**'s first

Sherlock Holmes story, *A Study in Scarlet*, the novella often thought of as the first significant work of late-Victorian **detective fiction**. In October 1888, just eleven months after *Hansom Cab*'s U. K. debut, the *Illustrated London News* reported that sales now exceeded three hundred thousand copies, declaring the novel to be "the most popular book of modern times" ("The Author" 1888: p. 410). Stage versions of the novel enjoyed successful runs in New York, Melbourne, and London. So great was the novel's cultural currency, that a full-length parody, *The Mystery of a Wheelbarrow, or, Gaboriam Gaborooed*, by W. Humer Ferguson, was published in 1888.

Keen to capitalize on the success of *Hansom Cab*, Australian publishers now clamored for more of Hume's work. He had nothing new, so in 1887 he reissued his old first novel, *Professor Brankel's Secret*, with Melbourne firm Kemp & Boyce. In April 1888, Hume sailed for England, determined to commit himself to writing full-time for that larger and more established market. Within a few weeks of his arrival, he had finished *Madame Midas*, a sequel to *Hansom Cab*, which then appeared simultaneously in novel form and on the stage in July 1888. Booksellers shared Hume's hope for another success story like *Hansom Cab*; one hundred thousand copies were printed in the first run and sold quickly, but reviews were generally negative. His next book, *The Girl from Malta* (1889), would be his last for the Hansom Cab Publishing Company. After an argument with Trischler, Hume took his next novel, *The Piccadilly Puzzle* (1889), a London murder mystery influenced by the **Jack the Ripper** murders, to F. V. White, a publisher of **yellowback** fiction. His swift follow-up was *Miss Mephistopheles* (1889), a sequel to *Hansom Cab* and *Madame Midas*.

Afterwards Hume published another 140 novels—up to eight per year—most of which were mystery stories, but none came close to matching the success of *Hansom Cab*. His final novel, *The Last Straw*, appeared in 1932, a few months before his death. As Sussex notes, despite his prolific output, Hume "never consolidated his early career success into the literary reputation he craved" (2015: p. 188). He produced too many books for lowbrow publishers and, as a result, could not shake his reputation as a hack writer. He died in relative **poverty**. In the twentieth and twenty-first centuries, his work was virtually unknown outside of Australia. As a result, *Hansom Cab* was regarded by early critics of the crime genre merely as "a curiosity because of the enormous sales it inexplicably achieved" (Symons 1972: p. 62). In the past few years, several scholars (Pittard 2011; Clarke 2014; Sussex 2015; Knight 2015) have begun to argue for Hume's recuperation. Thus far, only *Hansom Cab* and *Madame Midas* have been the subject of academic study. Hopefully, as part of broader moves to argue for the importance of non-canonical writers, more work will be completed on Hume's contribution to the burgeoning nineteenth-century crime genre.—Clare Clarke

Hunt, [Isobel] Violet (1862–1942). English novelist and **short story** writer. Daughter of the painter Alfred William Hunt (1830–1896) and the novelist and translator Margaret Raine Hunt (1831–1912), Violet Hunt spent her youth among members of the Pre-Raphaelite circle. These early influences led Hunt to develop her own free spirit, which transferred itself into her later writing and social activism. Many of Hunt's novels feature rebellious, unconventional heroines who are important examples of the emergence of the **New Woman** in Victorian fiction at the turn of the twentieth century. These include *The Maiden's Progress* (1894), *A Hard Woman* (1895), *The Human Interest* (1899), and *White Rose of Weary Leaf* (1908), which is considered by many to be her best work. Hunt also established herself as a leading literary hostess in London and remained active in many feminist causes throughout her life, including an active role in the Women Writers' Suffrage League. In addition to writing novels, Hunt also published two important contributions to the supernatural/weird fiction genre, *Tales of the Uneasy* (1911) and *More Tales of the Uneasy* (1925). Her autobiographical writing provides vivid portraits of many leading literary figures of the late Victorian and Edwardian periods. These include her numerous diaries, as well as *Their Lives* (1916), *Their Hearts* (1921), and *The Flurried Years* (1926).—MELISSA EDMUNDSON

See also ODNB, Belford 1990

Hurst and Blackett (1852–1926). English publisher. Henry Blackett and Daniel Stow Hurst founded the publishing house, afterwards took over Henry Colburn's publishing business in early 1853, and succeeded him by continuing to publish and supply three-decker novels to the **circulating libraries**. It published a number of popular women writers, who mainly wrote **romance fiction**, including Geraldine Jewsbury and **Margaret Oliphant**.—SUMAN SIGROHA

See also Sutherland 1989

Hypnosis. See **Mesmerism and Hypnosis**.

Hysteria. Medical pathology. Hysteria indicates the presence of one or more of a range of bodily symptoms with no evident physical cause, such as seizures, catalepsy, paralysis, numbness, choking, stuttering, random pain, excessive sensitivity, involuntary spasms, fits, gaping, laughing and weeping. Also called hypochondria, spleen, vapors, melancholia and nerves, hysteria's causes and cures were a subject of debate throughout the Victorian era. The medical profession was increasingly invested in recording and cataloguing illness, **disease**, and pathology. Hysteria, having variable symptoms, mimicking other illnesses, and lacking evidence of underlying biological conditions, resisted categorization. Instead, hysteria became a useful catch-all diagnostic category itself, under which were filed all manner of physical symptoms whose cause eluded medical practitioners.

While hysteria had been an acknowledged medical condition for centuries, the Victorian era marked a significant shift in medical and cultural understandings of the disorder. In the early nineteenth century, doctors were largely divided into two camps over the supposed cause of hysteria: gynecological or neurological. Hysteria's link to the female reproductive organs is inherent in its very etymology; the word is derived from the ancient Greek *hystera* meaning uterus, and the illness was long thought to be triggered by the womb wandering around the body causing spasms, pains, or choking. By the end of the eighteenth century, the gynecological diagnosis stressed the presence of vapors: noxious gases produced in the uterus, polluting the rest of the body. This opinion was increasingly contested by neurologists, who asserted that instead, hysteria was caused by disturbances in the nervous system. This suggested that men, too, could be at threat from hysteria. Yet the stigma of hysteria as a female disorder endured, supported by the perception that women had weaker nerves and were predisposed to instability.

The neurological diagnosis took the lead by the end of the century, perhaps ratified by the development of nerve-staining **technology** in the 1850s. Testament to this is the *Oxford English Dictionary* (OED)'s definition of hysteria, which dates from 1899: "1. *Pathol.* A functional disturbance of the nervous system, characterized by such disorders as **anesthesia**, hyperesthesia, convulsions, etc., and usually attended with emotional disturbances and enfeeblement or perversion of the moral and intellectual faculties (also called colloquially *hysterics*)." Yet many doctors continued to insist that hysteria's cause was gynecological, most likely to emerge in unmarried, childless women whose bodies became unbalanced if they refused to fulfill their biological role. In the 1890s, the pathology was linked to the monstrously androgynous figure of the **New Woman**, who refused to conform to the domestic norms of femininity, marriage, and **motherhood**. Hysterical also became a byword for Decadence in relation to art and literature. In *Degeneration* (1892), Max Nordau attacked the aesthetic taste of the *fin-de-siècle* disposition as evidencing a convergence of degeneration and hysteria.

Inevitably, writers were drawn to the topic of hysteria. Its inherent contradictions, inconsistencies and paradoxes articulated questions about pathology and performance, the mind/body divide, **mental illness** in relation to gender and **class**, and reading the language of the body. While the pathology itself may not be directly stated, the language of hysterical symptoms and behaviors pervades nineteenth-century fiction; convulsions, swooning, catalepsy, paralysis, stuttering, prolonged nervous episodes, fits and frenzies. The protagonist of Charlotte Brontë's *Jane Eyre* (2008/1847), "shaken as my nerves were by agitation," (p. 17) and "frantic anguish and wild sobs," has a "species of fit" (p. 18) when locked in the red room by her aunt as a child. In Emily Brontë's *Wuthering Heights* (1998/1847) Cathy is similarly "struck during a tempest of passion with a kind of fit"(p. 115), also described as a "frenzy" (p. 116), a "malady," (p. 114) and "brain fever" (p. 118): "tossing about, she increased her feverish bewilderment to madness, and tore the pillow with her teeth; then raising herself up all burning, desired that I would open the window" (p. 108). The swooning heroines of **melodrama** found a muse in the performative, histrionic figure of the hysterical body. In **Wilkie Collins**'s *The Woman in White*: "she had been taken with a sudden fright, my mistress said, and master he told us she was in a fit of convulsions" (1996: p. 367). **Mary Elizabeth Braddon**'s sensation novel *Lady Audley's Secret* mentions hypochondria twice, hysterical four times, and melancholy and convulsive thirteen times apiece. In **Charles Dickens**'s *Great Expectations* (2008: 1861): "here my sister, after a fit of clappings and screamings, beat her hands upon her bosom and upon her knees, and threw her cap off, and pulled her hair down, which were the last stages on her road to frenzy" (p. 104). The word *hysterical* occurs twice in George Eliot's *Middlemarch* (1872), while "nervous" or related words occur thirty-five times, and the heroine Dorothea is compared to Saint Theresa, the patron saint of hysterics. **Lucas Malet** subverts the gendered expectations of hysterical characters with her stuttering protagonist James Colthurst in **The Wages of Sin**. Perhaps the most famous literary depiction of hysteria, Charlotte Perkins Gilman wrote *The Yellow Wallpaper* (1892) as a scathing critique of her own doctor Silas Weir Mitchell's "rest cure" for nervous disorders. It depicts a woman suffering from "temporary nervous depression—a slight hysterical tendency" (1981: p. 1), who is driven mad by the alleged cure of total bed rest and lack of mental stimulation.

In the last decade of the nineteenth century, the concept of hysteria evolved once again. In *Studies on Hysteria* (1895), Freud and Breuer asserted that hysterical symptoms were caused by a disturbance of the unconscious mind, moving from a physiological to a psychological origin. A repressed traumatic memory manifests itself in somatic expression; physical afflictions such as seizures, paralysis or pain, forming a language of the body to communicate the unspeakable psychological distress. Their talking cure promised to extract the buried memory of the original trauma, negating the purpose of the symptoms and restoring the body to normality. These studies are regarded as the starting point of psychoanalysis. Their psychological, rather than physiological, interpretation of the cause of hysteria went on to become the dominant perspective in the early twentieth century.—Louise Benson-James

See also OED, Logan 1997, Mukherjee 2007, Oppenheim 1991, Scull 2009

Illustration(s). Illustration was central to both the aesthetic and commercial identity of Victorian popular fiction. It served a range of functions beyond the widely shared assumption that illustration extended and gave shape to the imaginative purposes embodied in a text. Illustration, in alliance with typography, crucially established the brand identity of serialized fiction for both journal and part issue publications. It was a fallback method of storytelling for semi-literature consumers of fiction. Also, drawing on the widespread presence of broadside, theatrical and song sheet images across a wide range of social discourses, illustration offered readers many kinds of visual pleasure that could be either part of the reading experience or a discrete form of aesthetic consumption.

The illustration of popular fiction was established and developed by the joint pressure of two major cultural shifts in the early Victorian period—the adoption of wood engraving from the 1820s on as the dominant reprographic method for producing graphic images until the advent of photo-reprographic processes later in the century, and the exploitation of various kinds of **serialization**, especially in magazines, as the normative way of publishing lengthy fictional texts. The wood engraving, with its implicit allusion to broadsides and other forms of ephemeral popular print culture, was widespread within mass circulation serialized fiction, and is to some extent one of the key characteristics of what constitutes the "popular," standing in contradistinction to the full-page etched and engraved plates that illustrated more aesthetically ambitious (or perhaps more "middle class") serialized fiction. **Dickens,** for example, drew back from experimenting with small wood engraved images dropped into the text early in his novelistic career, and remained faithful to the full-page engravings that had characterized his work from *Sketches by Boz* on, and which gave his work an air of "respectable" and aesthetically ambitious endeavor. It would be wrong, however, to equate the wood engraving too closely with the popular and the etched and engraved image with the self-consciously literary. Many "literary" novels augmented full page plates with smaller scale wood engravings dropped into the text. Thackeray, himself an illustrator, used decorative capitals and wood engraved vignettes within the typeset page to augment full-page engraved plates. There were many deluxe editions of popular authors like Eugene Sue that used full-page portrait engravings or lithographs alongside ambitious and tonally sophisticated wood engravings. There were also relatively down-market serialized novels that gave away quite large-scale colored lithographs with early issues as a marketing device.

Nonetheless the wood engraving remained the chosen reprographic medium for most popular fiction eager to take advantage of its cheap and rapid production cycle, the durability of wood blocks and, most of all, the ease with which the wood engraving could be combined with type and printed off in a single process. Lithography remained something of a rarity within mass circulation novels, but was sometimes used to give cultural credibility to down-market murder stories. Lincoln Fortesque's re-working of *Jack Sheppard* for a less sophisticated audience than **William Harrison Ainsworth**'s celebrated novel, for example, replaced full-page George Cruikshank engravings with crudely drawn if vigorous lithographs that harked back to the broadside tradition in their style and content. Many distinguished artists, such as Sir John Gilbert, were prepared to provide drawings for down-market serial fiction, and not afraid to sign their work even when it appeared in cheap magazines aimed at the lower end of the market. Talented amateur draughtsmen, like the journalist and writer George Augustus Sala, also contributed illustrations to novels published by **Edward Lloyd**.

The idea of a popular illustrated serial issue novel predates the Victorian period. The Regency origins of illustrated serial fiction are evident in one of the first mass circulation popular novels, Pierce Egan's *Life in London* from 1823. While originally published accompanied by expensive colored aquatints by George and Robert Cruikshank, Egan's novel was transformed into a staggering range of cheap commercial imitations, many of them involving graphic or pictorial elements with the original aquatints translated into wood engravings often in the crudest broadside manner. Elsewhere within Regency print culture the wood engraving was beginning to be widely associated with serialized fiction. The numerous weekly miscellanies launched into the marketplace in the 1820s, each issue prefaced with a vignette wood engraving, quickly began to take advantage of a rapidly increasing reading public by addressing niche interests. While short fiction and even longer serialized narratives formed some of the many "miscellaneous" elements that made up these crudely assembled and derivative magazines, journals with titles like *Tales of Travellers*, *Tales of Terror* and *Tales of the Wars*, which were wholly constructed out of fictional elements, began to emerge. By the early 1830s successful journals like *The Terrific Register* or *The Penny Novelist* had made fiction, much of it translated from French or German or imported from American sources, the basis for a successful magazine. Illustration was an essential element in this success.

The commercial impetus given to illustrated fiction by the serial novels published by Dickens and his contemporaries confirmed the commercial desirability of illustration as an element in fictional publications. The shameless vulgar down-market pastiches of *Pickwick* drew jobbing comic draughtsmen like Charles Jameson Grant into the production of quickly drawn illustrations for cheap serials by T. P. Prest, **James Malcolm Rymer**, and Eugene Sue. The next generation of entrepreneurs of popular fiction such as **Edward Lloyd**, John Dicks, and G. W. M. Reynolds recognized that there was a strong appetite for more sophisticated images to accompany part issue or serialized fiction, and furnished their publications with tonally complex and often quite large-scale wood engravings that drew on the iconography of theatrical **melodrama**, figurative painting and topographical prints as well as the broadside tradition in order to provide something more elaborate than a simple translation of the text into visual terms.

The later nineteenth-century **penny dreadful**, boys' and girls' fiction magazines, and cheap re-issues published by Edwin Brett and John Dicks, continued to use wood engraved illustrations. *Dick's Standard Library of Popular Works* notably retained versions of the original illustrations for the texts reprinted in the series, although these images were hardly improved by their adaptation to Dicks's cheap printing **technology**. Increasingly, as part of the wider changes to reprographic methods that took place in the second half of the nineteenth century, process engravings derived from photographs began to be widely used for both magazine and volume publication of popular fiction.
—Brian Maidment

Imperial Adventure. The adventure narrative is intrinsically linked to the expansion of empire. Since the publication of Daniel Defoe's *Robinson Crusoe* in 1719, the adventure story has furnished entertaining but often racist stories of empire in which white male Europeans bravely resolve the many challenges that the colonial context is seen to present. These texts became increasingly popular toward the end of the Victorian period and constitute a central site for the articulation of imperialist discourses. Even the few texts that attempted to query the notion that the British had the right and the obligation to subjugate the global East and South typically failed to dismantle the racist paradigm that informed discussions on the relation between the British and the non–European world.

The early nineteenth century saw the publication of a number of texts that can be characterized as imperial adventure. Walter Scott's first novel *Waverley* (1814) is set in a Scotland that takes on the characteristics of an unruly, colonial frontier territory demanding the attention of the English crown. Similarly, early U.S. literature by Charles Brockden Brown and James Fenimore Cooper, popular in Britain, are frontier adventure stories that revolve around the armed struggle for land in the New World and the role that idealized, white, male protagonists could be imagined to play in this process. However, as the Victorian era began, British literature, following a European trend, turned increasingly toward national, political and domestic themes. While Emily Brontë, **Charles Dickens**, and **Wilkie Collins**'s fiction referenced the empire in the margins of novels like *Wuthering Heights* (1847), *Great Expectations* (1861), or **The Moonstone**, most of their output revolved, like that of William Thackeray and George Eliot, around the more mundane struggles of ordinary citizens in a transforming and transformative Britain.

This introspective trend was challenged in the early 1880s when the British had begun to realize, in the words of Lord Seeley, that they had acquired a vast empire "in a fit of absence of mind" (1883: p. 10). This discovery was engineered partly by a new form of literature produced, as Elaine Showalter has discussed, by a set of male writers who wanted to counter what they felt was "a feminization of literature" (1991: p. 77). This effort consisted of a programmatic attempt to write a clearly gendered form of fiction that can be referred to as the "male quest romance" (Showalter 1991: p. 81). It was thus designed to educate a young, male generation for the imagined challenge that the empire constituted. The first of the chief engineers of this literature were **G. A. Henty**, **Robert Louis Stevenson,** and **H. Rider Haggard**. Like many other male, Victorian authors, Henty started his writing career as a journalist and war correspondent. He used his experience from France, Russia, Africa, **India**, and Palestine as the foundation for a "new sort of boy's book that would set a pattern for future work" (ODNB). Much of his fiction was first **serial**ized in one of the many boys' magazines that appeared in the 1870s and 1880s and which became crucial outlets for the imperial adventure story. Like Henty, much of Stevenson's fiction is historical and uses the expanding British Empire as the backdrop for epic coming-of-ages tales such as **Treasure Island**.

If Henty and Stevenson re-invented the imperial adventure narrative, Haggard and Kipling arguably perfected it. Both writers spent significant time in the British colonies and could provide their stories with significant authenticity. Haggard's tremendously successful **King Solomon's Mines** and **She** are in many ways the ultimate imperial adventure stories. The plots send British males on quests into what was termed "undiscovered sections" of the African continent. These African spaces are at the same time highly sexualized and sources of atavistic and irrational forms of power capable of challenging European modes of rational thought and behavior, a combination that has earned them the epithet *Imperial Gothic* (Brantlinger 1988: p. 227). Haggard's fiction is typical also in its assumption that the white skin of the Europeans, their advanced weaponry, and their strength and prowess, once they have shaken off the stupor of civilization, will, as in *Robinson Crusoe*, elevate them into kings or even gods in the eyes of the primitive indigenous inhabitant. Kipling tells similar stories in "The Man Who Would be King" (1888) and *Kim* (1900–01), even if his portrayal of both colonizer and colonized is significantly more nuanced than Haggard's.

The Boer conflicts of the late 1890s and the rise of Germany as an imperial contender prompted the appearance of a more defensive type of imperial adventure tale. While the pursuit of fame and treasure in an often sexualized landscape dominated the first wave of adventure writing, texts published during the second turned toward themes of invasion and the need to protect the empire's geographical, ideological and sexual borders. Baden Powell used the image of the efficient boy spy and informant from *Kim* to found the Boy Scouts in Britain, an organization tasked with helping to defend the nation against European aggression. **Invasion literature**, especially the many military invasion novels written by **William Le Queux**, and Erskine Childer's ***The Riddle of the Sands***, tell adventure stories about how other European nations make war on Britain in the interest of destroying the empire. In **Bram Stoker**'s ***Dracula***, and in **Richard Marsh**'s *The Beetle* (1897), the invasive threat instead rises from a generic and colonized East. At the turn of the century, there are also texts that use the adventure paradigm to criticize the imperial discourse that saturates this genre. Joseph Conrad's *Heart of Darkness* (1899) novella is a very dark adventure narrative that reveals the predatory nature of the colonial enterprise. Yet, as later postcolonial critics such as Chinua Achebe have observed, the racist paradigm persists also in this text. The white adventurer may be revealed as a tyrant rather than a just king in this tale, but he is still a ruler and Africa remains a repository of contagious darkness and primitivism.—Johan Höglund

In Darkest London (1891). Novel by **Margaret Harkness**. First published as *Captain Lobe: A Story of the Salvation Army*, *In Darkest London* remains perhaps the best known of the "slum stories" **Harkness** published under the pseudonym "John Law" at the end of the nineteenth century ("A Slum" 1890: p. 2). Hard on the heels of ***A City Girl*** and ***Out of Work***, her quintessential slum fiction story "Captain Lobe" was **serial**ized in the *British Weekly*, a self-styled "Journal of Social and Christian Progress," in 1888. The novel follows the titular character Captain Lobe, a **Salvation Army** officer, and his fiancée Ruth, heiress to a factory in the East End of London. The narrative consists of vignettes that use the protagonists' movements through the city to illustrate social problems such as in-work **poverty** and slum housing, and the Salvation Army's efforts to combat these extremes of poverty. *Captain Lobe* was published in book form immediately after the serial concluded in December 1888, appearing in 1889 with Hodder & Stoughton, the *British Weekly*'s publisher. In 1891, radical publisher William Reeves included the novel in his progressive Bellamy Library under the new title *In Darkest London*. This deliberately echoed *In Darkest England and the Way Out*, published the year before by the founder of the Salvation Army, "General" William Booth. Booth contributed a foreword to the Reeves edition of Harkness's novel calling on readers to help the "poor and outcast" people described (in Law 1893: p. ii). Hodder & Stoughton re-issued the text under its original title in 1915 and 1925.—Flore Janssen

In Gipsy Tents (1880). Text by Francis H. Groome (1851–1902). Published by William Nimmo, *In Gipsy Tents* is a curious autobiographical, ethnographic, and philological text. Groome's title, spelled with an *i*, reflects the malleable spelling of the term ***Gypsy*** throughout the century. Covering such topics as "Welsh Gipsies," "Gipsy Music," and "Romani Folk-Tales," it owes much to *Lavengro* (1851) and *The Romany Rye* (1857) by so-called Gypsy scholar George Borrow. It is as much concerned with family as folklore, being also an account of one man's close relationships with the Lovells and their relatives, valuing their words and practices and attempting to situate what they tell him in the context of nineteenth-century research about **Romani** people in Europe. In the twenty-first century, one can critique the discourses that frame Groome's work and which his work informs, in particular the social forces that mean he confidently marshals authority for knowledge about travelling Romani people: he claims to know them better than they know themselves. However, the reader does find nineteenth-century Romani voices here, albeit edited (to what extent we cannot know), elaborated and explained by a white, comparatively wealthy, middle-class, privately educated, house-dwelling man. Throughout *In Gipsy Tents*, the reader acquires tales of **animals** bought and beloved, relatives remembered, and the mundane business of existence in the camp. *In Gipsy Tents* traces the broad arc of British Romani history while noting, from a particular and privileged perspective, details of late-nineteenth-century travelling Romani life around Britain, from Ledbury to Lancashire and into Wales and Scotland.—Jodie Matthews

See also ODNB

India. In the latter decades of the nineteenth century, the Indian subcontinent became a prominent feature of popular fiction by British authors living and working in the metropolitan center and by a growing body of Anglo-Indian writers. These texts share a number of common themes: India frequently appears in stories of mutiny, marriage, and/or mystery. Yet these narratives do not necessarily fix a hierarchical relationship between the colonial power and the native subject. Rather, as Bart Moore-Gilbert suggests, these texts demonstrate the processes of cultural negotiations between India and England, and they explore the constant contradictions and irresolutions that prevented colonial discourse from ever attaining the unity and authority to which it aspired (p. 6). Thus, although these texts often reiterate racial prejudices and imperial ideologies, they also suggest that the subcontinent could never wholly be controlled or contained. They show that Britain's presence in India left an indelible mark on both colonizers and colonized.

The First War of Indian Independence cast a very long shadow onto the Victorian cultural consciousness. Its presence is felt, in some shape or form, in almost every fictional text written about India in the second half of the nineteenth century. The most basic narratives of colonial rule, and of national and racial identities, are issued through fictionalized retellings of the major events. In particular, novels produced in the popular adventure mode, by **G. A. Henty** and James Grant (1822–1887), perpetuate a very binary image of India and England. As Patrick Brantlinger notes, these authors reduced the multifarious reasons for the Sepoy Rebellion to a Manichean narrative of good versus evil (1988: p. 222).

Grant's *First Love and Last Love: A Tale of the Indian Mutiny* (1868) and Henty's *In Times of Peril* (1881) establish the apparently inherent barbarism of the Indian people in order to contrast this with the innately moral heroics of the British male protagonists. These novels shock and thrill through their use of sensationalist rhetoric and violent images, especially those depicting violence against women and children. In this way, they justify vicious retaliations by the colonial forces and support the exclusion of women from the public sphere. Furthermore, they reassure readers of Britain's imperial might by quashing the Rebellion time and again. But, despite their bombastic bravado, these adventure narratives simultaneously reveal a sense of anxiety: the Indians may have been overpowered, but their supposedly innate savagery remains intact, a fact which points to the potential for further conflict and the fragility of the colonial order. Indeed, the vast number of mutiny novels throughout the Victorian period suggests a vehement need to replay the myth of imperial power, which seems in itself an act of reassurance. There was evidently a fear that the Indian people could and would rebel again, and this lingered in the colonial imagination throughout the rest of Britain's rule.

Occasionally, writers like **Flora Annie Steel** and Philip Meadows Taylor (1808–1876) explored the gender and racial tensions that surrounded the conflicts of 1857. They understood, to some extent, that imperial policy in the first half of the nineteenth century was partly responsible for the Indian Rebellion. Thus, in Steel's *On the Face of the Waters* (1896) and Taylor's *Seeta* (1872), military conflict plays out alongside the wider contexts of colonial life, including interracial relationships. Typically, here, the fictional affairs between white men and non-white women are temporary. The Indian ladies and their mixed-race offspring must die to make way for the restoration of order: the proper union of the English hero and heroine. Nonetheless, such narratives admit to the intimate and proximate relations between colonizer and colonized at a time when imperial ideologies sought to emphasize the distance and difference between them, both in a material and a psychological sense.

Perhaps the most notable example of interracial romance occurs in Maud Diver's *Lilamani: A Study in Possibilities* (1911). In this novel, a British man and Indian woman meet and marry in continental Europe, before moving to England. Although Lilamani faces various prejudices from her husband and his family, the mixed-race relationship is ultimately successful and produces a child that survives a trilogy of novels. This challenge to the narrative trope outlined above was made possible by the emergence of the **New Woman** in the late nineteenth century. Diver, in the context of colonial discourse, compared the seemingly selfish desires of the New Woman with the traditionally selfless domesticity of the Indian wife. And, like many other imperial writers at this time, she saw modern femininity as posing a threat to the security of the British Empire. In this way, she showed the extent to which gender and imperial politics overlapped at the turn of the century and emphasized the role that British women played in securing the future of the colony.

Until recently, Diver and her peers have received little critical attention. **Anglo-Indian** women's writing was seen to have little to offer, aesthetically or politically. This perspective emerges from a persistent bias that denigrates women's genre fiction and erroneously separates domestic and political life. In actual fact, female authors often wrote about courtship and marriage in order to negotiate women's imperial identities and colonial duties, as well as issuing a response to the changes and challenges to marriage laws in Britain. Because, as Mary Procida states, "Anglo-Indian women … were married not only to their husbands but to the Raj itself," the discourses of domesticity overlapped with the discourses of imperialism (p. 30). Thus, many so-called romance narratives actually demonstrated the extent to which the public and private spheres converged in British India. Female authors such as Bithia Mary Croker (c.1848–1920) refuted the notion that Victorian women were outside the imperial experience, an idea perpetuated by George Francklin Atkinson's *"Curry & Rice" on Forty Plates; Or the Ingredients of Social Life at "Our Station" in India* (1859) and Henry Stewart Cunningham's *The Chronicles of Dustypore* (1877).

Croker wrote approximately twenty-six novels set in India (Gupta pp. 62–64). These include *The Cat's Paw* (1902), *Babes in the Wood* (1910), and *Proper Pride* (1885) in which she suggested that British women played a part in fostering and defending the growth of the Empire. She admitted the difficulties of this role, particularly in terms of how it impacted upon female subjectivities, and she registered real anxieties about the colonial situation. Imperial ideals required Anglo-Indian women to uphold Victorian femininity and exemplify an anglicized way of life in India; however, many found this to be completely impossible in the colonial outpost. Indeed, **Florence Marryat**'s **bigamy** novel *Véronique: A Romance* (1869) goes so far as to suggest that such expectations destroy the very values upon which they are based.

Alice Perrin (1867–1934) and **Rudyard Kipling** similarly articulated concerns about the impact of the imperial situation on the British colonizers. While their writing offers little consideration of the extensive consequences for the colonized people, they do acknowledge indigenous resistance to the colonial forces. Perrin and Kipling wrote a number of **short stories** that, rather than naturalizing the imperial situation, saw the British presence in India in terms of dislocations and disruptions. This literary form, which does not require the narrative resolutions of the nineteenth-century novel, more effectively encapsulates the unresolved tensions and unsettling ambiguities of the colonial space. For example, in Perrin's story "Caulfield's Crime," from *East of Suez* (1901), the uncanny return of a ghostly jackal punishes the British protagonists for the killing of a local fakir, who disrupted their hunting trip. The indigenous **animal** intrudes upon the domestic space, which acted as a metaphor for empire more generally, and shows Britain to be vulnerable to Indian forces. Thus, Perrin reminds her readers that Britain will suffer, physically and psychologically, for its colonial aggression, and she expresses a kind of imperial guilt, an idea that features strongly in a number of Victorian crime narratives.

British crime writers frequently represented India as a locus of nefarious activity, wherein contact with racial others and proximity to great wealth corrupted imperial representatives. These individuals neglect their wider responsibilities and seek to secure their own fortunes through theft and deception. However, as seen in **Wilkie Collins**'s early detective novel, *The Moonstone*, and **Arthur Conan Doyle**'s *The Sign of Four*, Britain's rapacious attitude to its colony provokes indigenous figures who then seek revenge or retribution on English shores. Such texts do not generally question the legitimacy of imperial practices; rather, they express apprehension about the potential repercussions. In so doing, such texts collapse the difference and distance between East and West: movement back and forth between imperial outpost and metropolitan center, and criminal activity on both sides, blurs the racial and national boundaries established by colonial discourse.

At the same time, an emphasis on the illicit aspects of life in India undoubtedly authorized imperial surveillance as a means of control. Those Indian practices that appealed to the macabre Victorian imagination were particularly popular among contemporary readers. Hence, Taylor's *Confessions of a Thug* (1839) evokes obscure superstitions and bloodthirsty traditions, and, for all its claims to authenticity, it surely legitimizes a need for colonial rule. However, even in Kipling's *Kim* (1901), perhaps the most famous colonial surveillance novel, the power of imperial observation is undermined; India emerges as ultimately unknowable and its mysterious nature provokes Britain's ongoing fascination.

Evidently, then, Victorian popular fiction expresses a wider cultural interest in India. Yet, for the most part, these texts are less interested in exploring indigenous culture and society and more focused upon unpacking Britain's relationship with the subcontinent. Sitting outside official imperial discourse, they could more readily admit to the tensions, ambiguities, and ambivalences of Britain's colonial legacy.—ÉADAOIN AGNEW

Invasion Literature. Invasion literature was a paranoid body of popular fiction that engaged with widespread concerns about the possible invasion of Britain by an array of hostile foreign forces in the period between c. 1870 and c. 1914 as the geopolitical climate worsened internationally. Regardless of the fact that invasion was unlikely to occur, "invasion neurosis," as Cecil Eby puts it (1987: p. 11), became a notable societal phenomenon as escalating European imperial rivalry and mounting anti-colonial resistance in the British empire provoked fears of invasion by the armies of rival European imperial powers and even by the forces of so-called uncivilized nations. In addition to public debate and (often sensational) press coverage, popular fiction provided one of the major channels for the dissemination of invasion fears, proffering nightmare visions of armed Prussians stomping down London's Strand and hordes of Oriental barbarians sacking Europe's capitals. Considering the possible consequences of developments in military **technology** and international diplomacy, these early **science fiction** tales burgeoned in the period before 1914 as popular authors and their readers became increasingly convinced that war on an unprecedented scale was imminent. Notable invasion tales include General Sir **George Tomkyns Chesney**, *The Battle of Dorking*; Rear-Admiral Philip Colomb et al., *The Great War of 189-* (1892); **William Le Queux**, *The Great War in England in 1897* (1894) and *The Invasion of 1910*; Erskine Childers, *The Riddle of the Sands*; and **H. G. Wells**, *The War in the Air* (1908). Also relevant is the so-called yellow-peril variant of the genre depicting invading hordes from China and Japan and exemplified by **M. P. Shiel**'s virulently racist *The Yellow Danger*. The threat of invasion also figured prominently in the intersecting body of spy fiction, within which *The Riddle of the Sands* also fits, alongside works by Le Queux, E. Phillips Oppenheim, and John Buchan. The prevalence of the genre prompted P. G. Wodehouse's 1909 satiric rejoinder *The Swoop!*, in which a troop of heroic Boy Scouts liberates Britain from simultaneous occupation by nine foreign armies.

While the mid-nineteenth century had seen some invasion fears and corresponding fictions, the key impetus for the genre was the Franco-Prussian War of 1870–1 (Clarke 1992; Scully 2012). After this brief but significant event in which a newly militarized and technologically advanced Germany beat imperial France with relative ease, Britain's fears for its own position were dramatically expressed in fictional form when Chesney wrote ***The Battle of Dorking*** to warn Britain of its vulnerability by depicting a successful, durable German occupation. Chesney's text was a runaway bestseller and caused an immediate debate, helping to start a public campaign for military "preparedness." It also kicked off a school of follow-on texts, supporting and countering its assumptions, in which, over the subsequent decades, Britain was invaded by whichever European power or powers with whom relations were most hostile at the time. These gradually came to replace the factual tract or pamphlet as the principle popular means to disseminate invasion concerns (Clarke 1997). Following Chesney's success, worrying international incidents tended to produce flurries of corresponding fictional invasions, many of which sold in large numbers. And one of the most striking things about this body of fiction was the demonstrable effect it had on public opinion, provoking (often irate) coverage in newspapers, parliamentary debate and army and navy organization proceedings (Matin 2011a, Kirkwood 2012). Developments in military technology, such as airships and submarines, also informed sensational invasion scenarios, the 1880s being notable for several works which dramatized the negative side of the 1882 debate on developing an English Channel tunnel linking Britain and France. By the 1890s, as international relations deteriorated and changes in the literary marketplace led to an increased demand for sensational, topical **serial** and one-volume novels, the invasion tale had gained major momentum and it thrived in the period immediately before the outbreak of war in 1914.

The typical invasion tale depicted the initially disastrous but ultimately vanquished military invasion of Britain, though there were many plot variations and some were deeply pessimistic. The admonitory and often hysterical tone of most of this body of work is amply reflected in the following quotation from ***The Invasion of 1910***, an international bestseller by one of the genre's major exponents, Le Queux: "The repeated warnings had been disregarded, and we had, unhappily, lived in a fool's paradise, in the self-satisfied belief that England could not be successfully invaded" (1906: p. 333). Le Queux then proceeded to drive home the lesson in his portrayal of a corpse-strewn London ground beneath the heel of the German invader. The invasion genre was also notable for the participation of military men, who used it to champion their favored schemes for achieving military preparedness, whether via conscription, fortification or naval aggrandizement (Matin 2011b). Chesney's and Colomb's titles denote their military service, for instance; Childers had volunteered during the South African War (1899–1902); and the revered veteran Field-Marshall Earl Roberts endorsed both of Le Queux's works—further adding to the public controversy they caused.

While invasion fiction has traditionally been seen as arising largely from European diplomatic tensions and been confined to writing depicting the armed invasion of Britain, recent scholarship highlights its additional imperial origins (Bulfin 2015a, Matin 1999, Rieder 2008), reveals concomitant concerns with internal political threats (Hughes and Wood 2014, Taylor 2012) and draws attention to adjacent bodies of fiction such as Gothic and crime fiction which addressed the fear of invasion metaphorically via the figures of the exotic supernatural intruder and the foreign criminal (Bulfin 2015a). Scholars are also starting to push the boundaries of the genre in terms of timespan and geography, identifying the continued presence of the invasion theme in fiction published during and after the First World War and drawing comparisons with contemporary fictional accounts of invasion published across the British empire and in many Western imperial nations—e.g., France, Germany and the U.S.A.—AILISE BULFIN

See also **Invasion Network**

The Invasion Network. Research network. The Invasion Network fosters collaboration between scholars working under the broad theme of invasion, with a particular focus on British invasion fears in the late-nineteenth and early-twentieth centuries. Bringing together literary scholars, social and cultural historians, and a range of other specialists and independent researchers from around the world, the network aims to further understanding of an influential socio-cultural phenomenon that, while often considered in passing, has rarely been analyzed in great detail. The goal of the network is to examine the military, cultural and demographic parameters of invasion anxiety. Areas of interest include invasion fears as expressed in defense policy, military debate, political discourse and journalism, and related cultural phenomena such as the **invasion literature** genre of scare-mongering fiction, the series of related popular invasion plays and the school of satirical cartoons which sent up these works.

Past collaborations have seen the network focus on the key invasion-scare author (and amateur spy) **William Le Queux** and on fears of invasion across the British empire. More recently the network seeks to expand its focus geographically to consider the fear of invasion as a global phenomenon, examining invasion fears in any region in which the fear became a notable phenomenon and investigating how fears of invasion and future conflict expressed in different nations and regions informed each other. The network also seeks to expand its focus temporally to take in the period between the Franco-Prussian War (1870–1) and the rise of the German Third Reich to examine how fears of invasion and future conflict have evolved over time, while retaining consistent components such as xenophobia and sensationalism. It is envisaged that future projects will focus on Second World War and contemporary invasion fears.

Emerging out of two key workshops, "Empire in Peril: Invasion-Scares and Popular Politics in Britain, 1890–1914" (Queen Mary University of London 2013) and "Master of Misinformation: William Le Queux, Invasion Scares and Spy Fever, 1880–1930" (Trinity College Dublin 2015), the network is conceived as a forum through which to develop, promote, and publish research addressing the experience of invasion anxieties. This includes maintaining a list of scholars working in the area, offering a platform for advertising conferences and other events, providing a blogging space for discussion and debate, and running a series of related events. It is hosted online at https://invasionnetwork.wordpress.com/ and co-organized by Ailise Bulfin and Harry Wood.—Ailise Bulfin, Harry Wood

The Invasion of 1910 (1906). Best-selling invasion novel by **William Le Queux**. One of the most influential works of **invasion literature**, this novel details the efficient Prussian invasion and occupation of a gravely unprepared Britain against the backdrop of growing Anglo-German antagonism. Written expressly to frighten the British public out of what Le Queux saw as complacency about national security, the novel deploys a range of tactics to achieve this, from an inset endorsement by revered military veteran Lord Roberts, to the inclusion of detailed battle maps and proclamations, to the lurid account of the siege of London, which transforms the empire's capital into a **Gothic** necropolis "of shadow, of fire, of death" (Le Queux 1906: p. 199). Accordingly, Britain's ultimate victory is costly, dishonorable and fails to restore geo-political balance: Germany retains annexed Holland and Denmark, while "[t]he British Empire emerged from the conflict outwardly intact, but internally so weakened" that collapse seems inevitable (Le Queux 1906: p. 548). Initially **serial**ized in the sensationalist *Daily Mail*, the novel became notorious for its controversial advertising campaign (Stearn 1992: pp. 13–17), which featured "sandwichmen ... parading the streets of the West End dressed in uniforms of the Imperial German Army" and was denounced in the House of Commons ("German Uniforms" 1906). Pivotal in the cycle of early-twentieth-century invasion tales that proliferated in the worsening pre-war geo-political climate, the novel can be read as a forerunning instance of atrocity propaganda and was viewed as inflammatory and dangerous by many contemporary readers ("Literary Week" 1906: p. 245).—AILISE BULFIN

Iota [Kathleen Mannington Caffyn] (1852/3–1926). Anglo-Irish novelist and **short story** writer. Best known for her novel *A Yellow Aster*, which was associated with the **New Woman** because of the heroine Gwen Waring's radical views on marriage and disgust at sexual relations. Its success launched Caffyn's career as a popular fiction writer. She published seventeen more novels concerned with the intricacies of love, courtship and marriage. Their plots commonly involve a love triangle and the temptation and avoidance of adultery by the female protagonist. Aside from her connection to the New Woman, Caffyn is significant as both an Anglo-Irish and an expatriate Australian writer. The daughter of Irish Protest landowners, she immigrated to London in her twenties and trained as a nurse. In 1879, she moved to Australia with her husband the surgeon and oculist Stephen Mannington Caffyn. The couple hosted a salon for writers and artists from their home in Brighton, one of Melbourne's Bohemian suburbs. Both husband and wife began writing fiction. Caffyn's first published story appeared in a volume of tales by Australian ladies. In 1892, the couple returned to London, but remained part of an Australian expatriate community of writers and artists. Two of Caffyn's novels *A Comedy of Spasms* (1895) and *Dorinda and Her Daughter* (1910) have Australian settings. A number of other novels contain Irish settings and characters. According to James Murphy, *Anne Mauleverer* (1899) is "the most substantial Irish-content work" by an Irish New Woman writer (2011: p. 205).—NAOMI HETHERINGTON

The Island of Doctor Moreau (1896). Novel by **H. G. Wells**. In one of his earliest and most infamous "scientific romances," Wells exploits late-nineteenth-century anxieties over scientific advancement, **medicine**, and **vivisection** through the portrayal of a mad doctor experimenting on a menagerie of **animals**. Saved from a shipwreck, Edward Prendick arrives on the unnamed island. Prendick, horrified by the surgeries Moreau performs in his "House of Pain," believes the Beast Folk he sees are formerly humans, but the mad scientist tells of his attempts to humanize the **animals**. Fearing the House of Pain, the Beast Folk obey Moreau—they never intervene in his **vivisection** experiments. Moreau works tirelessly on a puma who is his final victim, for she breaks free and the two kill each other, which leaves an unstable Prendick among the Beast Folk. During the following months, Prendick loses his mind as he assumes the habits of the Beast Folk, who revert back to animals. Eventually rescued, Prendick withdraws to the English countryside, fearing all humans will revert back to beasts. A cautionary tale, *Moreau* easily fits into the genres of **science fiction**, **Gothic fiction**, utopia, and adventure fiction and the traditions of lost colonies and castaways. The novel implicitly relates to contemporary debates about **science**, **eugenics**, and the **New Woman**. Critics have approached *Moreau* from psychoanalytic, feminist, and post-colonial perspectives. Even a century later, *Moreau* continues to be popular, attracting new readers, and yielding three film adaptations.—THOMAS G. COLE, II

See also SARAH GRAND, MONA CAIRD

Jack the Ripper. Name attributed to the assumed lone serial killer who committed five murders in the Whitechapel district in the East End of London between 31 August 1888 and 9 November 1888. The popularized moniker Jack the Ripper originated from the signature of a handwritten letter that was sent anonymously to London's Central News Agency on 27 September 1888 claiming responsibility for several of the murders. Although the message is believed to be a journalistic stunt, the designation Jack the Ripper came into common usage in police reports and press coverage and persists to the present day. While eleven murders were committed in total in Whitechapel from 1888 to 1891, only five victims have conclusively been attributed to Jack the Ripper based on the similarity and timing of their murders: Mary Ann Nichols, Annie Chapman, Elizabeth Stride, Catherine Eddowes, and Mary Jane Kelly. These canonical five victims were all living in near-**poverty** at the time of their deaths, and most financially supported themselves through occasional prostitution. The violent nature of the murders, which involved severe bodily mutilations, together with the failure of the London Metropolitan Police to identify the criminal, generated a media storm. Journalists led the speculation into potential suspects, a list that included surgeons and medical practitioners, escaped asylum patients, and a number of Jewish butchers living in the East End.

Newspaper circulation and sales skyrocketed as a result of the immense public interest in the crimes and their unidentified perpetrator. The *Star*, a radical evening newspaper begun on 17 January 1888 by journalist and Irish nationalist T. P. O'Connor, established its readership and reputation in large part through its investigations into the homicides. The crimes also had a profound influence on late-Victorian popular fiction. A notable example is the first fictional account of Jack the Ripper, John Francis Brewer's shilling booklet, **The Curse Upon Mitre Square**, which attributed the murder of Catherine Eddowes in September 1888 to the ghost of a homicidal sixteenth-century monk and connects it to several others committed in the vicinity from 1500 onwards. Another late-Victorian text that has become inextricably linked with Jack the Ripper is **Bram Stoker**'s 1897 novel, **Dracula**. Although the novel was published nearly a decade after the murders in Whitechapel, it recalls the events through its depiction of a figure who preys on women to sustain his thirst for blood. Stoker himself alluded to the relationship between Dracula and Jack the Ripper in his 1901 preface to the Icelandic edition of *Dracula*, writing, "This series of crimes has not yet passed from the memory—a series of crimes which appear to have originated from the same source, and which at the same time created as much repugnance in people everywhere as the notorious murders of Jack the Ripper" (1986: p. 11).

Jack the Ripper was also frequently compared to popular Victorian literary characters in the popular press. The London *Times* compared Jack the Ripper to the inhuman killer of Edgar Allan Poe's popular detective story, "The Murders in the Rue Morgue" (1841), while the *East London Advertiser* emphasized the bestial brutality of the murders through references to Mr. Hyde of **Robert Louis Stevenson**'s **Gothic** novella, *The Strange Case of Dr. Jekyll and Mr. Hyde*. In 1894, when ongoing investigations into the Whitechapel murders remained a subject of interest for British and global newspaper readers alike, the American *Cincinnati Commercial Gazette* interviewed **Arthur Conan Doyle** to get the famed fictional detective **Sherlock Holmes**'s opinion of the case. According to Doyle, Holmes's approach would be to reprint the letter supposedly written by Jack the Ripper, which Doyle believed to be genuine, in leading British and American newspapers, offering a reward to anyone who could identify the handwriting.

The Whitechapel murders also prompted some Victorian writers to address the widespread poverty in East End districts of London. Among these writers was John Law (**Margaret Harkness**), whose 1889 novel, *Captain Lobe: A Story of the Salvation Army*, republished in 1891 under the title *In Darkest London*, sheds light on the daily violence of life in the East End. Although the novel does not mention Jack the Ripper by name, it includes a sympathetic depiction of a gentile slaughterman who confesses to slitting the throat of a drunken woman as a result of his brutalizing profession. He hides among the Jewish butchers in the East End to avoid detection, a detail that touches on the police inquiries into a series of East End Jewish butchers, especially John Pizer, also known as Leather Apron. Although no conclusive evidence was brought against Pizer or any other Jewish suspects, newspaper coverage appealed to rising **anti–Semitism** and widespread anxiety over the growing communities of foreign immigrants in London in order to highlight Jewish involvement in the crimes.—Oriah Amit

See also ODNB, DNCJ

The Jewel of Seven Stars (1903; 1912). Novel by **Bram Stoker**. First published in 1903, and reissued with an alternate ending in 1912. It is unclear whether this revision was Stoker's own or the work of his publishers. The plot sees an **Egypt**ologist attempt to revive the fictional Queen Tera, whose mummy is among his collection. In the original ending, Tera's body vanishes and all but the narrator are left mysteriously dead, while in the 1912 version the experiment does not appear to work. *The Jewel of Seven Stars* is one of a number of novels dealing with **mummies** and supernaturalism in this period, and one of the most frequently addressed by modern critics. Three recent editions are noteworthy for their scholarly introductions (Glover 1996; Leatherdale 1996; Hebblethwaite 2008). These studies and others (Byron 2007; Dobson 2017a) have addressed Stoker's use of contemporary physics to inform the magical **science**s he attributes to Tera. Other critics have produced Freudian readings of this text (Auerbach 1981; Smith), or connected the main female characters (Tera and her doppelganger, the Egyptologist's daughter, Margaret) to the figure of the **New Woman** (Pal-Lapinski 2005). Some of the most original work on this text focuses on place, particularly the novel's trio of settings—London, Cornwall, and Egypt—(Trower 2012), and the **Gothic** trope of the mummy's hand (Briefel 2008; Corriou 2015). Recent critical interest in **animals** in fiction suggests that an examination of the novel's animals might prove fruitful. Similarly, the evident connections between the novel and *fin-de-siècle* **occult**ism and psychical research have been relatively underexplored.—Eleanor Dobson

Joseph's Coat (1881). Novel by David Christie Murray (1847–1907). Published in three volumes by **Chatto & Windus**. *Joseph's Coat* follows the story of Old Joe and Young Joe in the case of a stolen inheritance. Old George, Young Joe's uncle, finds papers hidden in Old Joe's coat, including the marriage license of Young Joe and Dinah, Old George's caretaker. The couple is happily reunited and married alongside friends Ethel Donne and John Keen. It was hailed by the *Pall Mall Gazette*—as reprinted in *The Gentleman's Magazine* (March 1896)—as "a true work of art."—Amberyl Malkovich

Joshua Haggard's Daughter. Character novel by **Mary Elizabeth Braddon**. Published in Braddon's magazine *Belgravia* from December 1875 through December 1876. It is Braddon's thirty-first novel. In subsequent editions Braddon truncated the title to *Joshua Haggard*. The two titles reflect the novel's dual emphasis on Joshua Haggard and his daughter, Naomi. The first volume focuses on the engagement between Naomi and Oswald, the squire's eldest son, and the marriage between Joshua and Cynthia, a young, naïve, circus runaway. The second volume follows the repercussions of Oswald falling in love with Cynthia. In a jealous rage, Joshua murders Oswald and denounces Cynthia. Oswald's younger brother Arnold investigates the disappearance of Oswald, uncovering Joshua's murder and falling in love with Naomi in the process. In the final movement, Cynthia dies of a mysterious illness and Joshua, after unsuccessfully attempting to reconcile with Cynthia, dies of a stroke. Arnold forgives Joshua of his past faults and marries Naomi. Robert Lee Wolff (1979), Braddon biographer and scholar, reads the novel as a classical tragedy and marks it as the first in Braddon's peak literary decade, 1875–1885 (p. 258).—SCOTT C. THOMPSON

The Jungle Book (1894). One of the best-known collections of children's **short stories** by **Rudyard Kipling** in the tradition of **Anglo-Indian** writing. The first three stories are all set in **India** and feature the jungle adventures of Mowgli, a human boy or "man-cub," raised by a family of wolves and tutored by various memorable jungle **animals** such as the bear Baloo or the panther Bagheera. Names such as these and also Kaa (the snake) and Sher Khan (the tiger) were derived from **Indian** folk tales and linguistic traditions, reflected Kipling's Orientalist knowledge base, and *The Jungle Book* has received extensive treatment from postcolonial scholars studying Kipling's investment in **Imperial adventure** fiction. Two of the volume's later stories, "Servants of the Queen" and "Toomai of the Elephants," present directly military themes involving animals in the service of the Imperial establishment. "Rikki-Tiki-Tavi" tells the story of a young Anglo-Indian boy and his mongoose. "The White Seal," the only story in the collection that does not take place in India, is set on an island in the Bering Sea and features Arctic animals along with native hunters and elements of Eskimo culture. All seven stories are about **animals**, and all seven give them human traits and the power of speech in the effort to present moral lessons endorsing late–Victorian conservative values like industry, bravery, adaptability, and loyalty. One year after *The Jungle Book*'s success, Kipling published *The Second Jungle Book* (1895), a collection of five further stories all featuring Mowgli.—ADAM KOZACZKA
   Source: ODNB

Keynotes (1893). Collection of **short stories** by **George Egerton**. Published by the Bodley Head, this debut collection contained nine stories, each exploring the development and subordination of female sexual and social ambition. The volume's style and focus has strong connections to the Scandinavian Modernists. Egerton dedicated the volume to Knut Hamsun, and Ledger has noted Henrik Ibsen's influence on the "intense psychological penetration" her "charismatic and tormented" female protagonists (p. xviii). Because of its focus on female interiority, *Keynotes* was both praised as a book "for [women]," and maligned as "neurotic and repulsive" (Ledger 2006: p. xiii). Nonetheless, it was a commercial success: it sold over six thousand copies in the first year, was translated into seven languages, and twice reprinted in the first six months. The cover for the collection and the iconic image of a key, which adorned the spine of the volume, were designed by Aubrey Beardsley.—JENNIFER NICOL

Kidnapped (1896). Historical adventure novel by **Robert Louis Stevenson**. The first among its author's Scotland-set adventure novels with Jacobite themes, *Kidnapped* is often grouped along with its sequel, *Catriona* (1893), and *The Master of Ballantrae* (1889) as set apart by its subject matter from Stevenson's other adventure stories like ***Treasure***

Island. Following in the footsteps of Romantic novelist Sir Walter Scott's Waverley novels, *Kidnapped* tracks a young male protagonist as he brushes shoulders with famous historical figures and witnesses major historical events. The novel's assertive, athletic, but inexperienced teenage hero, Davie Balfour, has a rough **childhood** and then encounters first **Gothic** danger in the House of Shaws, then nautical adventure aboard Hoseason's smuggling vessel, before embarking on a harrowing trek across the Scottish wilderness with a Jacobite rebel as travelling companion. This Highland character, Alan Breck Stuart, is in the novel responsible for the 1752 retributive killing of government agent Colin Roy Campbell in what passed into history as the "Appin murder." The law and **political violence** are central to *Kidnapped*, since the resolution of this case has been remembered as a miscarriage of justice in which a biased court convicted and executed the killer's brother, James, despite clear proof of his innocence. Guilt and innocence are major themes in the novel, and Stevenson presents a sort of moral ambiguity that allows him to lament the oppression of the Highlanders while nevertheless presenting the Jacobites as dangerous and disingenuous. Like much of the boys' **imperial adventure** fiction of the day, *Kidnapped* celebrates military **masculinity**.—ADAM KOZACZKA

See also ODNB

Kingsford, Anna (1846–1888). Pioneering female doctor, writer, and Christian mystic. After completing her medical studies in 1880, Kingsford promoted causes such as vegetarianism, anti**vivisection**, and women's suffrage. During the 1880s, her spiritual teachings and visionary powers made her so well-known among **occult** practitioners that she became the president of the Theosophical Society from 1883 to 1884 and founder of the Hermetic Society in 1884. In writing her literary works, Kingsford often collaborated with her fellow religious advocate, Edward Maitland. Her most notable books include *The Perfect Way* (1882), *Dreams and Dream-Stories* (1888), and "*Clothed with the Sun*" (1889).—INDU OHRI

See also **Collaboration**, ODNB, Pert 2006

Kingsley, Charles (1819–1875). Novelist, social reformer, naturalist, and clergyman. The eldest child of an impoverished gentleman turned clergyman, Kingsley's **childhood** saw the family move frequently for his father's work, exposing him to landscapes which would mark his later writing. In particular he loved the shore where as a child he collected and studied sea life. Kingsley was educated at home before being sent to school in Clifton in 1831. There he witnessed the Bristol Riots, an event which resonates with his deep sympathies for poorer **class**es during the Hungry Forties. He would attend the Chartist demonstration at Kennington Common (April 1848) and contribute to Christian socialist journals. This concern is evident in his reforming novels, *Yeast* (1848), *Alton Locke* (1850), and *Two Years Ago* (1857). He attended King's College London and Magdalene College, Cambridge where he earned a first in classics before being ordained. Later he would lecture at Queen's College for Women (1848) and at Cambridge where he was appointed Regius Professor of Modern History (1860). Kingsley's qualifications for this role were somewhat dubious; as the author of the historical novels *Hypatia* (1851), *Westward Ho!* (1855), and *Hereward the Wake* (1866), his historical scholarship consisted largely of research for fiction. His first work of **children's literature** was *The Heroes* (1856), a retelling of Greek myth. *The Water-Babies* (1863) draws on his fascination with the **science** of the seashore. Kingsley was immersed in the controversies of his day: from religion to science to social reform, and his varied work reflects these rich interests. —CAMILLA CASSIDY

See also ODNB, Chitty 1974, Colloms 1975, Drabble 2000

Kingston, William Henry Giles (1814–1880). English author. The son of a businessman with interests in Portugal, he began work in Opporto, and wrote adult novels. In 1851 he published *Peter the Whaler*, a sea-story for boys, and its success encouraged him to produce many similar stories from then on. Kingston played a role in public life, contributing to the debates on Emigration and on the Volunteer Movement, and he helped establish the Mission to Seamen. He edited *Kingston's Magazine* from 1859 to 1863, and in 1880 began a magazine for boys *The Union Jack*, but his **health** broke down after the first issue and he died a few months later. Although Kingston wrote various kinds of books, his knowledge of the sea gave his maritime tales their superiority. In particular, his stories about the gradual rise of three boys, told successively in *The Three Midshipmen* (1873), *The Three Lieutenants* (1875), *The Three Commanders* (1876) and *The Three Admirals* (1877), represent his best work, full of breezy energy and humor in the tradition of Smollett and Marryat. According to J. S. Bratton, Kingston lost confidence in his work in his later years, and produced an increasing number of books marred by religious didacticism. A poll of favorite authors chosen by children in 1884 placed Kingston second only to Dickens, but today he survives mainly as a figure of historical interest.—DENNIS BUTTS

Kipling, Joseph Rudyard (1865–1936). English novelist. Kipling was born in **India** where his father was employed as professor of architectural sculpture. Only five years old, Kipling was sent with his sister to a dreary boarding school in England. In 1877, Kipling's mother Alice returned to England and in 1878, Kipling was sent to public school at the United Services College at Westward Ho!, the setting of his novel *Stalky & Co.* (1899). At this school, Kipling developed his writing skills as the editor of the school paper. Following his release from school, Kipling's father secured for him a position as sub-editor of a local newspaper in Lahore. After an absence of eleven years, Kipling returned to India. In his posthumous autobiography *Something of Myself* (1937) he describes how, during the four-day journey between Bombay and Lahore, "my English years fell away, nor ever, I think, came back in full strength."

Back in India, Kipling was furnished with his own room, office box and servant and began a furiously productive period first at the *Civil and Military Gazette*, and then at a number of other newspapers. He also began to write poetry and **short stories** that attracted international attention for their exploration of the complexity of **Anglo-Indian** life. While pro-imperial, these do not routinely evoke the racist dichotomies that much other imperial fiction relied on; "Without Benefit of Clergy" tells the story of how a blissful union between a British civil servant and a young Muslim woman is destroyed by sudden illness rather than the impropriety of the situation. Indeed, the offender of much of Kipling's fiction is not the British administrator who goes native, but the racist and culturally inept European colonial officer.

The short story collection *Plain Tales from the Hills* (1888) was an international hit and made it possible for Kipling to travel to Britain to try his luck as a full-time writer. The journey to London took him through China, Canada and the U.S. where, in New York, he met Mark Twain. Finally installed in London in 1889, he continued his hard work, struggling to meet the constantly increasing demand of newspapers and publishers.

He made friends with a number of the late-Victorian society's most important male writers, including **H. Rider Haggard**, Andrew Lang, Thomas Hardy, and the American Wolcott Balestier. During this period, his fame increased further and he sometimes collapsed under the strain of the many assignments and his growing celebrity. In 1891, he made another journey to India, but returned suddenly to Britain to marry Balestier's sister.

The couple's honeymoon was cut short in 1892, when their bank failed. The couple settled in Vermont where they started a family and Kipling wrote *The Jungle Book*, and *Captains Courageous* (1897). In 1896, a family dispute and a foreign policy quarrel made the family relocate to Britain. On a new visit to the U.S. in 1899, Kipling's daughter Josephine contracted pneumonia and died. Kipling did not return to the U.S., but he made it a habit to spend his winters in South Africa where Cecil Rhodes welcomed him. In 1900–1901, Kipling's novel *Kim* was **serial**ized in *McClure's Magazine*. It tells the story of the **orphan** Kimball O'Hara who is discovered and adopted by a host of substitute fathers; a Tibetan Lama to whom he becomes a loyal disciple or "chela," the Pashtun Mahbub Ali, and the British Army officer Colonel Creighton. It is Creighton who realizes that Kim is the son of an Irish soldier who perished with his wife a number of years ago. After Kim has received a British education, Creighton reintroduces him into Indian society so that he can work as spy in the Great Game that Britain is playing with Russia over Afghanistan. Kim is an enthusiastic participant in this game and courageously counters the Russian spies and their plans of invasion.

Like so much of Kipling's writing, *Kim* meanders through a complex ideological landscape where the British come across as competent and authoritative rulers of India, and where the Indian rebellion of 1858 is described as a "madness." At the same time, the novel also reveals a real, perhaps even insurgent, love for indigenous India. The protagonist Kim is not the plucky English public-school boy of **G. A. Henty**, but a dirt-poor, Irish, Catholic orphan who often wishes he could shed his whiteness. Kim's formal loyalties may lie firmly with the British, but Kim's heart belongs to the road through India that he walks, to its diverse cultures and peoples, and most of all to the Lama with whom he travels. At the end of the novel, just before the Lama stumbles into a muddy stream and declares that he has achieved enlightenment, Kim actually renounces his British heritage and embraces his status as native: "I am not a Sahib. I am thy chela." This statement rests comfortably beside early short stories such as "Without Benefit of Clergy," but is difficult to reconcile with "The White Man's Burden" of 1899, a poem that appears to insist that colonialism is essentially an altruistic mission on behalf of an inept and ungrateful global indigeneity. In this poem, Kipling joins the voices of many other pro-imperial British writers of the era and comes across as the patriarchal "prophet of British Imperialism" that George Orwell termed him.

In 1907, Kipling was the first English writer to receive the Nobel Prize for literature. In the years before the war, he devoted more and more of his time and energy to the preservation of a British Empire that had already begun to fray at the edges, especially in South Africa. Although he remained productive until his death in 1936, he did not publish any more novels. His output declined further after the outbreak of World War I, and in the wake of the death of his son John in 1915. While Kipling has left an indelible mark on English fiction and is still being read, his literary reputation has suffered greatly from his pro-imperial stance.—JOHAN HÖGLUND

See also ODNB

Lady Audley's Secret (1862). Novel by **Mary Elizabeth Braddon**. Serialized in September 1861 in the periodical *Robin Goodfellow*, and continued in the *Sixpenny Magazine*, Braddon's third novel appeared as a triple-decker in 1862. Included since 1862 in Tauchnitz's "Collection of British Authors," and sold on the European continent in **collaboration** with Galignani in France, Braddon's breakthrough novel after the initial lukewarm reception of her works was immediately championed by the Tasmanian bookseller and publisher Walch in Hobart who, despite the controversy it caused, built expectations on the arrival of the first shipments in Australia from the columns of his *Literary Intelligencer*. The novel's international success grew steadily in the following decades: serialized in the Austrian *Abend-Blätter* in 1876, it was adapted for the stage in Berlin the same year, and reissued in German, Italian and French translations throughout the 1870s–80s.

This novel about female and male social mobility in a strictly hierarchical society, among suspicions of wrongdoing cast on upper-class characters, double identities, and mysterious disappearances, blends elements of the marriage plot of the domestic novel, the archetypal narratives of the returning hero after a long absence (a la *Martin Guerre*), and the sociological observations of the French *roman de moeurs* in an excitingly new combination. Braddon updates the successful formulas of these narrative forms with the riveting tempo drawn from her experience as an actress in stage **melodramas.** The masterfully entangled plot lines reflect a modern, increasingly globalized world of fast communications, conspicuous consumption of luxury items, in which the fabled accumulation of fortunes in the Australian mines coexist with passing intuitions of the horrors implicit in the colonial expansion.

The heroine of the title, Lady Audley (Helen Talboys [née Maldon]), takes the identity of the governess Lucy Graham after her husband, a disinherited baronet, abandons her and their child in **poverty** to seek fortune in Australia. Through her angelic charm she captivates an older neighbor, Sir Michael Audley, who proposes an appealing transaction by asking her hand, a union opposed from the beginning by his natural daughter Alicia. When Lady Audley's first husband George Talboys returns from Australia he reads by chance her fake death notice in the newspaper and visits the grave containing a swapped corpse of another unfortunate woman. The fortuitous chain of events of the plot puts his bereavement in the care of a very devoted old friend he meets by chance, the bachelor barrister with strong literary inclinations Robert Audley, who takes him for a relaxing weekend in the countryside at his uncle's estate, Audley's Court. While Lady Audley excuses herself from meeting the guests, the mysterious disappearance of George galvanizes Robert, who obsessively imagines that Lady Audley's charm might be a spellbinding performance scripted through the dubious calculations made popular by the enticing female characters of the French popular literature he avidly consumes.

The story is as much about opening the narrow horizons of the geography of the traditional British novel to an increasingly globalized world made of accelerated travel and communication, as it is, at a metaliterary level, about deprovincializing Victorian fiction by replacing the moralizing and uplifting strain of bourgeois realism from the earlier part of the nineteenth century with a strong influx of the destabilizing worldview contained in French fiction. Robert's fervid imagination filters every move by Lady Audley through the screen of his projected reminiscences of French fiction, whereas Lady Audley learns from the same source how to be a Lady and, most importantly, how to protect the fetishized glamour of her newly acquired upper-class status from any external challenge. Lady Audley is captivated as a reader not so much by the saccharine romanticism of

French literature satirized by Flaubert, which brings Lady Audley's French provincial counterpart Madame Bovary to her much expected and climactic doom, as by the more modern stories of ruthless social mobility hidden under a charming refinement that populate French fiction, with no punitive end in sight for the heroines depicted. The mysteries of the title are solved not so much by the work of a detective investigating the scene of a crime as through a constantly updated literary game in which each antagonist double guesses the opponent through an elaborate network of possible literary reminiscences that might shape personal choices in the real ("literary") life. When the novel closes in on Lady Audley and demands that her fictional, fetishized social value be measured against the golden standard of unalloyed class identity unadulterated by foreign mixtures, it is symptomatic that Robert dispenses with his whole collection of French books that animated his juvenile musings and marries the sister of his much cherished friend and social peer George. Lady Audley, equally symptomatically, is immured far away in a Belgian sanatorium through an easily obtained certificate of **mental illness**, thus preserving the inheritance line in favor of the young Audleys. The titillating fictions of French novels are thus dispelled and the values of the dominant class reaffirmed. The only main character that is consciously uninterested in the identity-formation power of modern fiction is, ironically, George Talboys, who dismisses the overtures on the subject of "fashionable literature" by the "pale governess" on board of the *Argus* at the very beginning of the novel with the ritualized aggressiveness of rigid politeness. The only novel in his library is the one closer to home, *Tom Jones,* in which the high-born youth is only temporarily thrown off his position in society.

French, and occasionally German fiction, constitute only some of the types of print capitalism, which make, together with other forms of capitalism, the outlines and motivations of the characters—and the narrative structure of the novel—a porous membrane that incorporates suggestions coming from the sensorium of the modern capitals of colonial empires. Commodity culture infiltrates the material dissemination of popular fiction when readers are exposed to novelistic installments appearing in periodical form next to advertisements, or, when outdoors, to the increasing visual hyper-stimuli that target the eye of the urban dweller on a street flanked by shop windows, with a plethora of posters and signs on every wall. These advertisements, which are incorporated in the fabric of the novel, may be showcasing beauty products (such as hair dyes or cosmetics) that Lady Audley aptly employs to refashion her gender and class identity—while all too willing to share the tricks with her servant—or "commodities for the millions" (Gabriele 2009), the fabled universally accessible products of industrial production, that Lady Audley carefully selects to adorn the space of her home. The narrative voice points to specific British manufactures, following the early techniques of branding in Victorian advertisement that replace the general publicity given earlier in the century to specific commodities of transparent use-value with an address of a dealer: Copeland's porcelain is a distinctive product that may be available to all for a few shillings and it is, therefore, a more vulgar, dispensable commodity that can be sacrificed in a fit of long-repressed rage. The Victorian sophisticated home illustrated in the novel displays a jarring mix of crafts pointing to every corner of the British colonial or semi-colonial empire: Turkey carpets, Moroccan armchairs, japanned cases, biscuit china, Indian tea caddies shawls, and filigree work are an encyclopedia of fragmented histories that can be caught with the all-encompassing glance of a sovereign subject. Even the followers of German idealism at that time—remarks the narrator impersonating a servant to "her Lady"—may be far from lost in the dialectics of "Ego and non–Ego," and be instead all attentive to the fluctuating value and yield of "India Bonds, Spanish Certificates an **Egypt**ian Script." Lady Audley distances herself from the more available brands of commodity culture by surrounding herself with the rarer products of individual genius that may be coveted not through the networks of print advertisements but through the word of mouth and shared appreciation of connoisseurs of means: her chamber is adorned with paintings by Claude, Poussin, Wouvermans, Cuyp and Salvator. She later ponders whether she may have to sell her high-end antique furniture, including "Leroys and Benson's" clocks and "Gobelin tapestried chairs." Her drawing room displays the acquired luxury made of "all that gold can buy": "rich in satin and ormolu, buhl and inlaid cabinets, bronzes, cameos, statuettes and trinkets." As a sign of her acquired social status, Lady Audley also poses for a portrait in the modern style of the Pre-Raphaelites: the painter catches a disquieting trait not seen before, the flip-side of the traditional gender roles through which women were imagined, and a later reference to the modern style of the Pre-Raphaelite Brotherhood underscores the same new traits. This artistic and real-life project of impersonating a new image for women is left unfinished, and a curtain will fall on the portrait at the end of the novel. **Sensation fiction**, when read in installments, explores the liminal spaces of identity-formation that challenge accepted societal norms, but the overall narrative logic of the book inevitably reinstates traditional values.—ALBERTO GABRIELE

See also Gabriele 2009, Miller 1988

Lawless, Emily (1845–1913). Irish novelist and poet. During her lifetime, Lawless ranked as one of the foremost Irish writers, publishing novels, poetry, **short stories**, a biography of Maria Edgeworth, a popular history of Ireland, and naturalist works. The majority of her ten novels treat Irish themes, *Hurrish* (1886) and *Grania* (1892) being the best known. **Margaret Oliphant**, **Rhoda Broughton**, William Gladstone, and Sir Horace Plunkett numbered among her literary and political circle. Lawless took an active role in the production and promotion of her work, Hansson speculating that the writer's awareness of her multiple audiences—Irish, English, American—may have influenced in part Lawless's complex negotiation of politics in her writing (2007: pp. 21–24). Because it was deemed insufficiently nationalistic, Lawless's work was buried in the nation-building that followed the establishment of the Irish Free State in 1922. Recovery of Lawless's writing began in the 1940s when such poems as "After Aughrim," "Clare Coast," and "Dirge of the Munster Forest" were identified as celebrating Irish landscape and history. Although her Irish novels were reissued in the 1970s, identity politics continued to complicate her inclusion in Irish and feminist canons. Critical interest has grown in recent years, including the appearance of the first Lawless monograph in 2007, which has laid the foundation for further study. While many early discussions focused on *Grania*, scholars have begun to explore the range of her writing, ecocritical and feminist perspectives appearing particularly fruitful. Her complex political identity remains a rich source for investigation. —SANDRA HAGAN

See also ODNB, DIL

Lee, Vernon [Violet Paget] (1856–1935). British writer. Lee was a prolific writer across numerous platforms; **short stories**, novels, plays, art history, and travel writing, and an essayist on subjects as varied as religion, art, literature, music, social and political theory, women's equality and anti-militarism. She is best known today for her supernatural short fiction, and works of aesthetic theory. Growing up between Italy, Switzerland, France, and Germany, from her teenage years, Lee researched European history, art, music, theater, and culture. At twenty-four years old she published *Studies of the Eighteenth Century in Italy* (1880), a text which was instrumental in the revival of interest in eighteenth-century drama and music. On summer visits to England, she was welcomed into notable literary and artistic circles, and became known as a woman of letters and prominent intellectual. Lee published well-received supernatural stories throughout the 1880s and 90s. Her first full length novel was the controversial *Miss Brown* (1884), a satire of Pre-Raphaelite artistic circles and Decadence. It was badly received by both reviewers and Lee's friends and acquaintances due to its shocking impropriety and the thinly veiled fictionalization of real people. Lee described herself as an "aesthetician." From the early 1890s and into the twentieth century, Lee and painter Clementina (Kit) Anstruther-Thomson conducted experiments to record human bodily responses to art, to determine whether aesthetic responsiveness is primarily physiological or psychological. These pioneering studies introduced the concept of "empathy" to the field of aesthetics.—Louise Benson-James

See also ODNB, Maxwell and Pulham 2006

Le Fanu, Joseph Sheridan (1814–1873). Anglo-Irish writer and newspaper publisher. Known for his works in the genres of **sensation fiction** and **Gothic fiction**, Le Fanu's most influential work, the **vampire** novella ***Carmilla***, had a significant impact on **Bram Stoker** and his novel ***Dracula***. He is also known for his novels, chiefly ***Uncle Silas*** (1864), and his short fiction including his collection *In a Glass Darkly* (1872). Le Fanu was born in Dublin to a family of Anglo-Irish Huguenots and educated in law at Trinity College, where he began his first ventures in publishing, submitting to *Dublin University Magazine*, a venue his work would appear in throughout his career. Later in life Le Fanu bought interests in several Dublin based newspapers and other periodicals in which he engaged in a limited amount of political activism and as a publisher of a diverse range of fiction. While Le Fanu published his first novel *The Cock and Anchor* in 1834, his major literary successes would come in the 1860s and early 1870s and appear to be fueled (at least in part) by distress over the death of his wife in 1858, the death of his mother in 1861, and the need to provide a steady income to support his family. His position in Dublin publishing during this period of time allowed Le Fanu to make in-roads into the English marketplace, including placing novels with Richard Bentley's influential publishing house and short fiction and **serial**s with markets such as the **Charles Dickens**'s periodical *All the Year Round*. Le Fanu died on 7 February 1873 in the home he rented from his brother-in-law in Dublin. Le Fanu's fiction consistently (if subtly) engages in negotiations between different spaces and identities, featuring hybrid nationalities and liminal boundaries. This, alongside Le Fanu's connection to Ireland and political figures such as Irish statesman Isaac Butt, has led critics to examine the colonial and post-colonial dynamics of Le Fanu's works, while his supernatural subject matter has placed the works productively in the context of the **Gothic** tradition.—Jude Wright

See also ODNB, McCormack 1980

Le Queux, William Tufnell (1864–1927). English novelist. Le Queux was one of the most productive writers of his era, with more than 200 novels published during his lifetime. A household name at the turn of the century, he ventured into virtually all popular genres of his period, producing romantic **melodrama**s, crime fiction, and **imperial adventure** stories that, the advertising of one edition claimed, "put more of **Rider Haggard** into one volume than even Rider Haggard could do." However, it is as the purveyor of crime, espionage and **invasion literature** that he is best known. Le Queux's *The Great War in England* in 1897 (1894) was one of many successful military invasion novels, a genre that arguably peaked with his ***The Invasion of 1910***, produced with the aid of Field Marshall Lord Roberts and newspaper magnate Lord Northcliffe. The novel stoked Germanophobia and jingoism in Britain prior to World War I and Le Queux continued to put out fiction that demonized the German soldier during the war. Recent research into Le Queux has debunked his own claims that he was an expert on criminology and an important operative for the British Secret Service.—JOHAN HÖGLUND

See also ODNB

Linton, Eliza Lynn (1822–1898). English novelist. By the time Eliza Lynn Linton died in 1898 at the advanced age of 76, she was known throughout Great Britain as the foremost antifeminist of her age. The author of 20 novels and literally thousands of periodical essays, Linton stood stoutly against the advancing tide of women's rights despite the fact that her own life trajectory represented an unconventional, independent narrative. Her ubiquitous presence in the journals and booksellers of her day had brought her fame and fortune, and not a little obloquy and ridicule into the bargain. Yet after a sympathetic biography by George Somes Layard in 1901, her work languished virtually unread throughout most of the twentieth century. Today, however, she is read as an iconoclast, an agnostic, an evolutionist, an enigma, and a proto-lesbian.

Eliza Lynn was born the youngest of 13 children in the Lake District in 1822. Her mother and oldest sister died before she was a year old, and her vicar father showed little interest in parenting. The child grew up ill-behaved, quarrelsome, and defiant. In her peculiar 1885 autobiographical novel *The Autobiography of Christopher Kirkland* (written as a man), she describes shocking her pious father with irreligious opinions, and resenting him for failing to provide her with an education. Eventually he consented to send her to London to research and write, and her literary career began. She landed a job with the *Morning Chronicle* as the first salaried woman journalist in England, and hoped to achieve a success in fiction equal to *Jane Eyre*. But after her third novel *Realities* was panned by critics as repulsive and improper, she fled to Paris, abandoning the novel for periodical journalism. In Paris she developed the trenchant misogynistic persona that would bring her success. Upon returning to England she married William Linton, an artist and engraver, and a sympathizer of radical causes. She supported him and his children until their increasing incompatibility led to separation in the late 1860s. By this time Linton was producing her breakthrough essays, including the notorious "Girl of the Period" middle article for the *Saturday Review*. This article and its companion pieces excoriated modern British young women, whose irreverence, fancy dress, and feminism seemed to Linton's narrator to resemble the demi-monde. Linton continued writing in this tone for the rest of her journalistic life. Her novels, by contrast, seemed to elicit sympathy for some of the very sorts of women she so negatively described in the periodicals.

In her own time Linton's journalism earned her many readers, but more ridicule than admiration. Critics were often puzzled by her novels, finding it impossible to tell how the author intended readers to feel about her rebellious heroines. After the decades of obscurity following Linton's death, two of her novels, *Joshua Davidson, Christian and*

Communist (1872), and the Christopher Kirkland autobiography, were reprinted in Garland's Novels of Faith and Doubt series in the 1970s. In the 1990s and 2000s several others of her novels reappeared in print as part of the ongoing recovery project for lost Victorian women novelists. The particular books in this group had in common with each other connection to themes being explored in late-twentieth century feminist criticism: social class, sexuality, urban life, women's rights. More recent twenty-first-century criticism of Linton has focused on her journalism, examining themes and strategies in her anti-woman essays, and analyzing the choices she made in her effort to achieve success.

Never a top-rank author in her own day (her antagonism and jealousy toward George Eliot were well known), the irascible Mrs. Linton was noted and notorious for her extreme opinions far more than for the quality of her work. Today she speaks to us of the nigh-unto-unnavigable choices available to nineteenth-century Englishwomen. Her most powerful social novel earned savage reviews; her heroines—Perdita Winstanley in *The Rebel of the Family*, for example—seemed to her contemporaries both admirable and shameful; her journalistic misogyny was plainly over-the-top; her marriage could not survive her independent achievement. She, as well as characters in her fiction, bent Victorian gender in ways difficult for her culture to comprehend. We read her today as a female Quixote, tilting in vain at the forces of change in her world.—Deborah T. Meem

Lloyd, Edward (1815–1890). English publisher. Born in Thornton Heath, the youngest of three sons, Edward Lloyd had a modest upbringing. His father, a former yeoman farmer, changed profession regularly and was declared bankrupt numerous times, leaving Lloyd with a particular thirst for business. He began his career working in a solicitor's office and studying at the London Mechanics' Institute, where he was awarded a silver pen for excellence and first met **James Malcolm Rymer**. In 1833 he published a guide to shorthand, *Lloyd's Stenography*, before establishing his own cheap bookshops in London.

Lloyd soon learned not only what was popular with readers but also how to harness this readership. After selling comic valentines and story books, he began producing his own periodicals. His earliest works were collections of criminal biographies, akin to the popular Newgate Calendar or **Newgate novels**: the *Calendar of Horrors* (1835), *History of the Pirates of All Nations* (1836), and *History and Lives of the Most Notorious Highwaymen* (1836). These publications took their inspiration from the popular writers of the day—**Edward Bulwer-Lytton** and **William Harrison Ainsworth**—but lacked the novelists' clear moral framework, replacing an enquiry into the criminal's sensibilities with a glorified description of their debauched acts. This set the tone for Lloyd's own brand of salacious fiction: the **penny dreadfuls**.

By the mid-1830s one author had triumphed over the popular press like no other: **Charles Dickens**. To capitalize on this trend Lloyd began issuing penny editions of Dickens's works. These publications deliberately replicated the physical appearance of Dickens's **serial**ized novels, bore similar names—*Nickelas Nickelberry* (1838), *Barnaby Budge* (c. 1841), *Martin Guzzlewit* (c. 1842)—and followed ostensibly the same plot. Indeed, in June 1837 Lloyd was brought before the Court of Chancery, accused of "fraudulent imitation" of *The Posthumous Papers of the Pickwick Club* (with *The Penny Pickwick*), but was absolved on the basis that his publication was of inferior quality.

Crucially, though, these were not mere plagiarisms. Lloyd carefully adapted Dickens's novels to suit an audience further down the social scale, introducing more comic and criminal escapades as well as indicators of his readers' working-**class** lives, such as references to the skittle alley and penny gaff theater. He maintained his disregard for moral teaching and often succeeded in subverting Dickens's original plot: for example *The Life and Adventures of Oliver Twiss* (1838) revels more in the illicit activities of Solomon's (Fagin's) gang than Oliver's rise from the criminal underbelly. In all likelihood many readers would have gained access to Dickens's stories through Lloyd's editions, which reportedly achieved a circulation of up to fifty thousand.

In the 1840s Lloyd issued a collection of weekly periodicals, including *Lloyd's Penny Weekly Miscellany* (1842–7), **Lloyd's Penny Atlas** (1843–5), and *Lloyd's Entertaining Journal* (1844–7). These publications retailed for one penny, were prefaced with his name (a clever marketing technique that allowed Lloyd to develop a recognizable brand), and were heterogeneous in quality, incorporating serialized novels, short fiction, verse, comic interludes, and correspondence. Lloyd's output was prodigious and as the market for cheap print burgeoned, he issued works that were as eclectic as his readers' interests, from songbooks and treatises to theater round-ups.

These periodicals were the vehicle for the **penny dreadfuls**, a peculiar type of serialized fiction which borrowed motifs from **Gothic fiction** and **sensation fiction** and was characterized by a salacious and emphatic tone. Lloyd published over 200 serialized novels, and among the most popular were *Ada, the Betrayed*, a wistful tale of corruption; **Varney the Vampire**, part of a wave of supernatural fiction featuring **vampires**; and *The String of Pearls*, which introduced the character of Sweeney Todd. These stories featured recurrent motifs, such as **orphan**s, fortune tellers, and mystical happenings, and played on the dichotomies of good versus evil and rich versus poor.

The authorship of these works was not acknowledged. Many of the stories can be attributed to **James Malcolm Rymer** or Thomas Peckett Prest, Lloyd's principal writers, but he also welcomed unsolicited (and unpaid) contributions from amateur writers. Fiction was constructed in a deliberately cultivated piecemeal manner, installment by installment rather than a retrospectively truncated narrative. Lloyd even provided his writers with a special eight-page writing book in which to submit their weekly contributions. It was, however, carefully scrutinized. It was common practice for Lloyd to "place the manuscript in the hands of an illiterate person—a servant or machine-boy" for judgment (Frost 1880: p. 90). He kept abreast of literary trends, issuing timely translations of Eugene Sue's popular *The Wandering Jew* (1845) and *The Memoirs of Madame Lafarge* (1841), the account of a notorious murderer.

Lloyd was an early pioneer of the use of **illustration**. Initially he used rough woodcuts to accompany his stories, but these grew in complexity as his career developed. In 1840 he started publishing the **Penny Sunday Times**, which led with a large illustration two years before the *Illustrated London News*. In an editorial he assured readers that "we will spare neither cash nor exertion in rendering our illustrations perfect" and he was good to his word. Barely a single work was issued without a colorful woodcut, which gave him monopoly over the bookseller's stand and provided a point of reference of his sizeable illiterate audience. Illustrations were also honed to capture readers' sympathies. G. A. Sala records that Lloyd once instructed that "the eyes must be larger; and there must be more blood—much more blood!" (1895: p. 209).

But Lloyd's influence does not lie solely in the type of fiction he produced. He was also instrumental in the expansion of the field of popular publishing. Notably, in 1856 Lloyd imported Richard Hoe's revolutionary rotary printing press from America and went on to establish his own paper mill in 1861 furnished with esparto grass he cultivated from land in Algeria, followed by a second in 1877. Lloyd's series of pioneering innovations made popular fiction increasingly cheap, but he triumphed by mirroring as closely as possible his readers' interests.—SARAH LOUISE LILL

See also ODNB, Catling 1911

Lloyd's Penny Atlas and Weekly Register of Novel Entertainment (1843–45). English paper. Published by **Edward Lloyd**, the weekly, which targeted lower-middle-class readers, was one of a number that he began and closed over the years. Unlike *Lloyd's Weekly Newspaper*, this publication was not a significant and long-running success. It offered cheap **sensation fiction** in a **serialized** format and short fiction accompanied by woodcut **illustration**s.—SUMAN SIGROHA

See also DNCJ

London Journal; and Weekly Record of Literature Science and Art (1845–1928). **Penny fiction weekly**. One of the harbingers of mass media, the *London Journal* achieved regular sales in excess of half a million copies in the early 1850s when its most characteristic contributor, J. F. Smith, **serialized** six long novels. After Smith left in 1856, the *Journal* lost ground as more rivals appeared and new ownership and a new editor tried to educate its readers by running novels by Walter Scott. In the 1860s, again under new ownership, it focused on sentimental sensation novels by its new editor Pierce Egan and by American women novelists, especially E.D.E.N. Southworth and Harriet Lewis, and the Canadian May Agnes Fleming. Three novels by **Mary Elizabeth Braddon** also appeared in the 1860s: illustrated reprints of ***Lady Audley's Secret*** and *Aurora Floyd*, and an early version of ***Henry Dunbar*** titled *The Outcasts*. The *Journal* gradually ceased to address a generic family readership: by 1868 it was a women's weekly that offered clothing patterns, monthly fashion plates, and **illustrations** in addition to fiction. In 1884 it was sold yet again and started to reserialize Smith novels (with their original illustrations). From 1890 it was edited by Herbert Allingham who in 1906 relaunched a *New London Journal* as a general interest magazine with yet another rerun of Smith. It still lost money and in 1912 the *London Journal* became a supplement to *Spare Moments* (begun in 1888), in which form it remained, still reprinting stories from its glory days, until both ceased in 1928.—ANDREW KING

Source: Jones 2012, King 2004

Longman's Magazine (1882–1905). English periodical. Of general interest, it was a mainstream monthly magazine that featured authors from both sides of the Atlantic. Published by Charles J. Longman, the magazine had an anonymous editor. It promised quality literature to its readers and published high-class traditional fiction, mainly **serialized** historical **romance**, action and adventure novels, poetry, **short stories**, reviews, and general interest informative articles on diverse scientific subjects. It was also known for its section titled "At the Sign of the Ship," written by the critic Andrew Lang, in which he expressed his personal opinion on both literary and non-literary matters. The periodical tried to steer clear of major contemporary political, religious, or literary topics and to maintain a light and entertaining tone for the magazine. **Robert Louis Stevenson, Grant Allen, Rudyard Kipling, Margaret Oliphant,** and **H. Rider Haggard** were some of the authors who contributed. Since it did not carry **illustrations** or photographs, *Longman's* could not compete with magazines like *Harper's* and the *English Illustrated*, and was discontinued.—SUMAN SIGROHA

See also DNCJ, ODNB, WD, WI, Maurer 1955

The Lost Stradivarius (1895). Supernatural novel by John Meade Falkner (1858–1932). The protagonist is Sir John Maltravers, heir to the estate of Worth Maltravers, who comes under the influence of the ghost of a debauched eighteenth-century libertine, Adrian Temple, the former owner of a Stradivarius violin hidden in a secret compartment within Sir John's college rooms. Sir John's obsession with artistic pursuits, and the homoerotic undertones of Temple's influence, were topical themes following **Oscar Wilde**'s trial for "gross indecency" in April to May 1895, while the novel's preoccupation with physical and moral degeneration is typical of *fin-de-siècle* **Gothic fiction**.—DEWI EVANS

Lucy, the Factory Girl. Novel by David Pae (1828–1884). An evangelical **melodrama** about a kidnapped child, *Lucy, the Factory Girl* is set mainly in Glasgow's notorious Tontine district. One of nearly 50 **serial**s syndicated by Pae himself, an editor and novelist from southern Scotland. *Lucy* appeared anonymously in British provincial newspapers on multiple occasions, initially in 1858 in the (Edinburgh) *North Briton* and *Glasgow Times*. Among the most widely read newspaper novels, it was also issued in 1860 as a single signed volume from Thomas Grant in Edinburgh, and was reprinted in a scholarly edition from the (Hastings) Sensation Press in 2001.—GRAHAM LAW

See also DNCJ, Donaldson 1986, Law 2000, Pae 2001

The Ludgate Monthly (1891–1901). English periodical. A general interest magazine first edited by Philip William May, its name was changed to the *Ludgate Illustrated* magazine to emphasize the importance it placed on picture and then again to simply the *Ludgate* in 1895. Aimed at families, including women readers, it **serialized** novels, published **short stories** and general articles. Some of the authors published by it included C. L. Pirkis, **Walter Besant**, Rudyard Kipling, Rafael Sabatini, and Richard Dowling. It was a less successful rival to the ***Strand Magazine*** and was later assimilated in the *Universal Magazine*.—SUMAN SIGROHA

See also Bateson 1969, Sims 2011

Machen, Arthur (1863–1947). Welsh author. Born Arthur Llewellyn Jones-Machen, the son of a Monmouthshire clergyman, Machen was educated at Hereford Cathedral School before moving to London to pursue a literary career. He worked as a publisher's cataloguer, translator, and tutor, enduring considerable hardship before small legacies allowed him to write full-time. A contribution to John Lane's Keynotes series, *The Great God Pan* (1894), won him significant notoriety; its heady mix of **occultism**, sexual transgression, and relatively graphic accounts of bodily dissolution led the *Westminster Gazette* to denounce it as "an incoherent nightmare of sex." *The Three Impostors* (1895), an occult mystery influenced by **Robert Louis Stevenson**, was harshly reviewed in the wake of the **Oscar Wilde** scandal, and Machen's career stalled. Although he continued writing, his next novel, *The Hill of Dreams*, was not published until 1907, and his exquisite prose-poems of the late 1890s only surfaced as *Ornaments of Jade* in 1924. Literary marginalization was accompanied by personal distress when his first wife, Amy, died in 1899, leading to a period of depression and involvement with the Hermetic Order of the Golden Dawn. He remarried in 1903.

His legacies exhausted, Machen became an actor and then a journalist, working full-time for the London *Evening News* from 1910 until 1921. In the early twentieth century he published a literary manifesto, *Hieroglyphics* (1902), which insisted great literature was "ecstatic" (e.g., transportative), the satirical *Dr. Stiggins* (1906), and *The House of Souls* (1906), a collection of **Gothic** tales such as "The White People," which continues to influence supernatural fiction today. Increasingly interested in mysticism and the Celtic church, and close friends with the occultist A. E. Waite (1857–1942), Machen published works with a strong religious element, notably "A Fragment of Life" (1904), and stories of the Holy Grail's rediscovery, "The Great Return" (1915) and *The Secret Glory* (1922). His tale "The Bowmen," a seemingly factual account of First World War British soldiers receiving supernatural assistance from the spirits of Henry V's archers, sparked persistent belief in the "Angels of Mons" following its appearance in the *Evening News* in September 1914.

After the war, Machen was celebrated by the American writers Vincent Starrett, James Branch Cabell, Carl van Vechten, and most notably, H. P. Lovecraft, who hailed his abiding influence in *Supernatural Horror in Literature* (1927, revised 1934) as well as in his own fiction. Machen spent the early 1920s working on his autobiography (1922–24) and a rueful scrapbook of his largely negative reviews, *Precious Balms* (1924), before returning to supernatural storytelling with *The Children of the Pool* (1933) and *The Green Round* (1936), which included the visionary **short story**, "N." He continued to publish occasional fiction and essays until shortly before his death.

Alongside Algernon Blackwood and M. R. James, Machen has long been recognized as an important Gothic and fantasy writer, but unlike them, he also has important links with 1890s' decadence, and, through his work as a reader for the publisher Grant Richards, the modernist era, advising on the publication of James Joyce's *Dubliners*.—Nick Freeman

Malet, Lucas [Mary St. Leger Kingsley] (1852–1931). English novelist. In September 1901, Methuen published what would be their longest and perhaps most controversial novel, Lucas Malet's *The History of Sir Richard Calmady*. Originally contracted in 1894, the much-anticipated book, a candid treatment of the life of a disabled aristocrat, was an instant bestseller. In 1901, it was second only to **Rudyard Kipling**'s *Kim* [O'Connell 2012: pp. 108–22]). But the book, which controversially featured a (later excised) scene of genital stimulation, met with mixed reviews. One *Times* reviewer proclaimed the novel "an offence against good taste [and] manners," while William L. Alden remarked that the book would rank its author "high on the roll of living English novelists" ("Recent Novels" 1901: p. 12; Alden 1901: p. 722). And yet despite Malet's commercial and critical success in her own lifetime, she is little-known today. Born Mary St. Leger Kingsley, Lucas Malet grew up in an influential family of writers. Her father was the Anglican clergyman and author, **Charles Kingsley**; her uncle was the writer Henry Kingsley and her cousin the African travel writer, Mary Kingsley. Although Malet publicly expressed affection for her father, she appears to have found his influence stultifying. Kingsley did not, for instance, permit Malet to read novels. Indeed, Malet's conversion to Catholicism in 1902 has frequently been read as a reaction against the "muscular Christianity" espoused by Kingsley and her pseudonym interestingly aligns the writer with her *female* ancestors—her grandmother Mary Lucas and her great-great-aunt Malet. In the 1870s, Malet was enrolled at the Slade School of Fine Art, but withdrew from her studies when she became engaged to William Harrison, Kingsley's friend and assistant curate. The marriage proved an unhappy one, and Malet's literary career helped to fund the separation from her husband—a move which she managed through "therapeutic" visits to the Continent.

In a career that spanned over forty years and included sixteen popular novels, two collections of **short stories**, and a **children**'s Christmas morality, Malet demonstrated great adaptability. At the *fin de siècle* her beautifully crafted aesthetic novels attracted frequent comparison to her contemporary Henry James; in the aftermath of World War I, when her own embarrassed circumstances made writing a matter of financial urgency, she produced highly psychological Modernist prose. Although there is a perception that Malet's dwindling fortunes can be attributed to the less incendiary character of her fiction in the wake of her conversion, this claim has been countered by Patricia Lorimer Lundberg in her 2003 biography of Malet. "[H]er novels," notes Lundberg, conversely "became … more daring and disruptive of social norms" (2003: p. 7).

The project to recover Malet's writing began, in earnest, in the mid–1990s. A 1994 book chapter by Patricia Srebrnik bought much-needed attention to the writer, exploring Malet's resistance to the patriarchal culture of the Kingsley household. In articles published in 1996 Talia Schaffer highlighted the ways in which canonical male writers, such as Thomas Hardy and Henry James, appropriated ideas from Malet. The product of two decade's research, Lundberg's literary biography, *An Inward Necessity: The Writer's Life of Lucas Malet* was published in 2003 by Peter Lang; the same year a new critical edition of *Calmady*, edited by Schaffer, was published by Birmingham University Press. These early interventions were followed by a period of relative quiet. It was not until 2011, when Catherine Delyfer's monograph, *Art and Womanhood in Fin-de-Siècle Writing: The Fiction of Lucas Malet, 1880–1931* (Pickering & Chatto, now Routledge), appeared in print, that Malet scholarship really gained momentum. In the last five years *Richard Calmady* has been taken up by a number of scholars in the emerging field of disability studies (see, for example, O'Connell 2012; Miller 2012; Ehnenn 2017). To assist the recovery of Malet's oeuvre, it is now right that new critical editions of the major works are commissioned. At the time of writing, the first edited collection of essays on her work, *Lucas Malet, Dissident Pilgrim: Critical Essays* (eds. Jane Ford and Alexandra Gray) has been contracted by Routledge for publication in 2019.—Jane Ford

Marryat, Florence (1833–1899). English author. Florence Marryat, daughter of the novelist Captain Frederick Marryat (1792–1848), was born in Brighton, Sussex on 9 July 1833. One of eleven children, Marryat was educated at home using her father's extensive library after her parents legally separated when she was six. She married her first husband, Thomas Ross Church, in 1854 but after a period of separation they divorced in 1879 with Church citing his wife's adultery in the legal proceedings. Later that same year Marryat married her second husband, Francis Lean, but this similarly ended in separation in 1881.

It was during the period of separation from her first husband that Marryat began her literary career. Published in 1865, Marryat's first novel, *Love's Conflict*, was written in 1863 while she was nursing her children with scarlet fever. Despite the novel's limited success, the publication of *Too Good for Him* and *Woman Against Woman* during the same year helped make Marryat a recognizable figure in the literary world. A prolific writer for the remainder of her life, Marryat published continuously from 1865 to her death in 1899 to produce a total of 68 novels. During her lifetime Marryat's novels sold successfully not just in Britain but also in Europe and America where she negotiated contracts with foreign publishing houses. She also edited *London Society* from 1872 to

1876, recognizing like **Mrs. Henry Ellen Wood** (1814–1887) and **Charlotte Riddell** (1832–1906) the advantages of having her own magazine to promote her work. Later in life Marryat enjoyed a career as an actress after doctors suggested she stop writing for her **health**. It was during this period, in the fourteen years preceding her death, that Marryat finally found happiness with the actor Herbert McPherson.

Although Marryat distanced herself from the genre of **sensation fiction** by insisting that she wrote from experience, the inclusion of strong-willed heroines and controversial themes including portrayals of seduction, marital cruelty, extra-marital sex, murder, incest, **bigamy**, and insanity suggest otherwise. However, contrary to her assertion, Marryat acknowledged in 1869 that *The Girls of Feversham* was her first novel in "which not a line is to be found which can be called 'sensational'" (as cited in Maunder 2004: p. x). This movement away from sensationalism to a focus on the bitterness of women's lot in marriage and society in novels such as the unfortunately little-known *The Nobler Sex* (1892) points to the influence of the emerging genre of **new woman** fiction on Marryat's work (although it is arguable that Marryat included similar expressions of dissatisfaction in her earlier novels) as well as her adaptability to literary trends. Elaine Showalter argues that Marryat's 1870s novels are examples of "transitional literature" because they offer a "genuinely radical protest against marriage and women's economic oppression, although still in the framework of feminine conventions that demanded the erring heroine's destruction" (2009: p. 23). Thus, for the majority, Marryat's novels end conventionally with the female protagonists punished for their transgressions. However, in *The Prey of the Gods* (1871), which Catherine Pope identifies as Marryat's rewriting of Wood's ***East Lynne*** (1861) ("*The Prey of the Gods*" n.d.), Marryat constructs a happy ending for the rebellious heroine, suggesting her to be a more subversive writer than she is typically given credit for.

During the 1890s Marryat's novels transitioned to include commentaries on other social debates including an understudied repeated critique of **vivisection** in novels such as *The Blood of the Vampire* (1897) and ***An Angel of Pity***. Marryat's later fiction also demonstrates a preoccupation with spiritualism. After her conversion to Roman Catholicism, Marryat explored her experience with séances in *There is No Death* (1891) and its sequel, *The Spirit World* (1894), as well as fictional works, including *The Strange Transfiguration of Hannah Stubbs* (1896).

Despite her reputation and high literary production during her lifetime, as the *Times* in their obituary predicted, Marryat slipped from public consciousness after her death (Maunder 2004: p. vii). Although the scholarly revival of Marryat novels was initially slow, her work has gained in notoriety over the last few decades as critics have begun to reassess the canon and assumptions of popular fiction. Andrew Maunder's inclusion of *Love's Conflict* in his series, *Varieties of Women's Sensation Fiction, 1855–1890* (2004) has greatly helped reestablish Marryat's significance in Victorian—specifically sensation—literary history. Moreover, the recent publication of ***Her Father's Name*** (1876), *The Dead Man's Message: An Occult Romance* (1894), and *The Blood of the Vampire* by the independent publishing house Victorian Secrets has introduced her novels to new readers. However, despite an increase in the availability of Marryat's novels and a steadily growing body of scholarship, few critics have solely addressed her work and so, given the sheer volume of novels Marryat produced, there is still much to be (re)discovered about this important Victorian author.—Katherine Mansfield

See also ODNB, Pope n.d., Orlando Project

Marsh, Richard [*pseud.* of Richard Bernard Heldmann] (1857–1915). English author and journalist. Marsh was a professional author of **Gothic**, crime, romantic, **humorous**, and **detective fiction**. He began his career writing boys' school and adventure stories for **G. A. Henty**'s *Union Jack* (1880–1883) under his real name Bernard Heldmann, adopting the penname Richard Marsh in 1888 after a prison sentence for fraud. His greatest success came with *The Beetle: A Mystery* (1897), a split **invasion** narrative with many similarities to **Bram Stoker**'s near-contemporaneous *Dracula*, in which an **occult** Egyptian shapeshifter wreaks havoc in *fin-de-siècle* London. A series of Gothic novels followed, including *The House of Mystery* (1898), a tale of female duality and **mesmerism**; *The Goddess: A Demon* (1900), which brings a remarkable **India**n sacrificial idol to a foggy London; and *The Joss: A Reversion* (1901), a tale of urban **poverty, imperial adventure**, and mutilation. In the twentieth century, Marsh turned to crime thrillers and popular **romance**s, and, eventually, to war and spy fiction, producing on average three volumes per year. A prolific contributor to the popular press, Marsh also authored a substantial number of **short stories**, including the **serial** adventures of the lower-middle-class clerk Sam Briggs (1904–1915) and the lip-reading female detective Judith Lee (1911–1916), both of which appeared in the ***Strand Magazine***. While appealing to a middlebrow readership, Marsh's fictions frequently subvert hegemonic discourses of gender, **class**, race, and criminality, demonstrating an affinity with the transgressive identities commonly found in earlier **sensation** and **Newgate novels**.—Minna Vuohelainen

See also Höglund 2013, Kirkpatrick 2010, Margree 2016, Vuohelainen 2009, Vuohelainen 2013, Vuohelainen 2014, Vuohelainen 2015

Martin Hewitt, Investigator. A series of seven detective stories by **Arthur Morrison**, first published in the ***Strand Magazine*** in 1894, and in volume form by Ward, Lock & Co. The detective's first appearance in the *Strand*, with **illustrations** by Sidney Paget, led contemporary reviewers to read him as a replacement for **Doyle**'s **Sherlock Holmes**, supposedly killed off in 1893. Morrison, however, distances Hewitt from Holmes; whereas the latter embodied an abstract **science** of deduction and superhuman powers of observation, Hewitt "has no system beyond a judicious use of ordinary faculties" (p. 3). In appearance, he has "as little of the aspect of the conventional detective as may be imagined," and is more closely aligned than Holmes with legal institutions, starting his career as a solicitor's clerk. Hewitt's method is more social than theoretical, solving mysteries through his ability "to be thoroughly at home among any and every class of people, and to be able to interest himself intelligently, or to appear to do so, in their various pursuits" (p. 36). Like Doyle, spaces of empire inform the stories, comedically in a story where an exotic parrot is employed as a jewel thief, but more prominently in "The Affair of the Tortoise," which problematically contrasts western civilization with Haitian savagery—the apparent murder of a Haitian by a Frenchman further deflects any British colonial guilt. Although most episodes take place in sporting and social settings familiar from Doyle, Morrison's tales have a more realist edge—sometimes providing translations of criminal jargon—and occasionally note the limitations of Hewitt's reconstructions.
—Christopher Pittard

Masculinity. **Wilkie Collins**'s popular novel ***The Woman in White*** begins with this assertion by the narrator, Walter Hartright: "This is the story of what a Woman's patience can endure, and what a Man's resolution can achieve" (1996/1860: p. 5). Despite Collins's gender-bending characters, this is a rather traditional summary of expected gender roles in the Victorian period: that good women patiently and quietly endure, while good men must work to achieve their manhood. *The Woman in White* can in fact be read as a narrative tracing Walter's attempt to earn his status as a man, through rescuing his future wife Laura from her cruel husband and his own professional progress. Much popular Victorian fiction depicts manhood as something to be attained. As Herbert Sussman puts it, "for the Victorians manhood is not an essence but a plot, a condition whose achievement and maintenance forms a narrative over time" (1995: p. 13).

That Victorian fiction focused on the realization of manhood is in part because the status of gentleman could now be achieved rather than simply assigned at birth. New understandings of the gentleman in mid-century England emphasized the importance of moral integrity as defining a man. In *Self Help* (1859), Samuel Smiles argues that the qualities of a "True Gentleman" depend "not upon fashion or manners, but upon moral worth—not on personal possessions, but on personal qualities" (1859: p. 326). While Smiles's optimistic model of masculinity was no doubt attractive, his narrative is also a guidebook for middle-class living. In other words, the gentleman was ideally a professional man, who could provide for his wife and family. Another way in which manhood could be achieved was through physical strength. For example, writers like Thomas Hughes and **Charles Kingsley** popularized muscular Christianity in the mid–Victorian period. The term is typically attributed to an 1858 review of Hughes's *Tom Brown's Schooldays* (1857), in which the critic emphasizes "the great importance and value of animal spirits, physical strength, and hearty enjoyment of all the pursuits and accomplishments which are connected to them" (Stephen 1858: p. 190). The muscular Christian brought together Christian virtues with physical fitness, and he can be seen as an ancestor to the imperial hero of late-century adventure fiction.

Yet what happened when a man lacked in moral worth, financial independence, or physical strength? Victorian scholars have examined such outsider figures, but the depiction of working-class masculinities in particular deserves further exploration, either through examinations of the many secondary characters prevalent in popular Victorian fiction or by exploring texts read by servants and the working classes, such as **penny dreadfuls** or **sensation fiction**. That Ur-text of the Victorian gentleman, **Charles Dickens**'s *Great Expectations* (1860–61), in fact suggests that Joe the blacksmith is a gentleman. His unique combination of physical strength and compassion reminds Pip of "the steam-hammer, that can crush a man or tap an egg-shell, in his combination of strength with gentleness" (1999: p. 111). His moral worth makes him a Smilesean gentleman, even if his working status puts that into question.

Victorian popular fiction also offers an array of men who do fit into prescribed models of physical prowess. Karen Bourrier's recent *The Measure of Manliness: Disability and Masculinity in the mid–Victorian Novel* (2015), for example, traces men with disabilities in the novels of popular realist writers such as **Charlotte Yonge** and **Dinah Mulock Craik**. Writers of sensation and **Gothic fiction** also experimented with different kinds of male bodies. To return to Wilkie Collins, the sensational, legless, dandyish Miserrimus Dexter, who appears in Collins's 1875 detective novel, *The Law and the Lady*, is one such example. The narrator describes him as a "fantastic and frightful apparition, man and machinery blended in one" (Collins 1992: p. 206). Dexter is not a figure of pity but instead one of fascination. His masculinity is spectacular and performative, and seems to betray the way in which *all* masculinity is a kind of performance.

The late-Victorian period, with its anxieties over physical degeneration, took the earlier scrutiny on the male body to a new level. Fears of degeneration were linked with the emerging **science** of **eugenics**, which advocated the improvement of the race by encouraging fit reproductive pairings. One example of the kind of fit body encouraged by eugenics was that of the world's first modern celebrity bodybuilder, Eugen Sandow. A plaster cast of his form was put on display at the Natural History Museum as a representation of the ideal form. Ideas of the pure English male body (or European in the case of the Prussian-born Sandow) were also exemplified in the vision of the New Man. Many New Women writers imagined a New Man who adopted a female-inspired model of sexual virtue and rejected degenerate behavior (MacDonald 2015: p. 19). The New Man was thus opposed to both the late-Victorian rake and the decadent dandy. The dandy was often paired with the **New Woman** in the late-Victorian press since both figures challenged traditional gender constructions; however, the dandy's life of languor, in addition to mocking earlier-century ideals of duty and hard work, also opposed the New Woman's earnest socio-political aims.

While the New Man is most easily observed in New Women novels of the period, he is also found in late-century popular fiction, such as **Bram Stoker**'s *Dracula*, a text obsessed with the definitions of manliness. While Jonathan Harker begins the novel as an energetic young man, he returns from Dracula's castle with brain fever. He risks being overshadowed by the other young men in the novel, especially the American Quincey Morris who represents the growing strength of the new global power. Yet Jonathan's potential unhealthiness is always overshadowed by Dracula's corrupting, foreign body. The best future New Man may in fact be Mina and Jonathan's child. He is Jonathan's son, but Mina believes that some of Quincey's "brave … spirit has passed into him" (Stoker 2011/1897: p. 351). That the New Man might in fact be a man of the future shows how writers like Stoker saw masculinity as a plot, one that continued to develop as Victorian ideals about race, purity, and professionalism shifted and transformed.—Tara MacDonald

Maugham, William Somerset (1874–1965) English writer. One of the world's most popular writers of the early twentieth century, selling an estimated 40 million books, and also the most highly paid. Born in Paris, where he spent his formative years, he lost his parents at a young age and was subsequently raised by an emotionally distant uncle in London. After studying **medicine**, he published his first novel, *Liza of Lambeth*, in 1897, drawing on his experience of living in the south London borough. Its success prompted Maugham to abandon a nascent medical career and become a full-time writer. Maugham was prolific from early on, writing a string of hit West End plays as well as over twenty novels and eight volumes of short fiction. During World War I he served as an ambulance driver in France, during which time his semi-autobiographical novel *Of Human Bondage* was published, in 1915. The tale of a club-footed painter, Philip Carey, **orphan**ed at a young age, the book was a huge bestseller. Following his discharge from the Red Cross, Maugham entered Britain's spy services, for whom he operated as a courier in Switzerland, while continuing to earn a living as a writer. Further successes in the inter-war period included two *romans à clef*—*The Moon and Sixpence* (1919), based on Paul Gauguin, and *Cakes and Ale* (1930), that features a late-Victorian writer with a strong resemblance to Thomas Hardy.

Although he was briefly married in his forties, and fathered a daughter, Maugham lived for much of his life in same-sex relationships, first with Gerald Haxton until Haxton's death in 1944, and then with Alan Searle, until Maugham's own death in 1965. From the 1920s on, he lived in Cap Ferrat on the French Riviera, where invitations to his villa were much coveted.

The Razor's Edge (1944) is among his most enduring later works. An account of the spiritual awakening of a traumatized American World War I pilot, it drew heavily on Maugham's own travels in **India** in the previous decade. His travels would also result in a number of books, such as *On a Chinese Screen* (1922), *My South Sea Island* (1936), and the 1925 novel *The Painted Veil*, set in Hong Kong and China.

Maugham's simple, pared-down style, possibly the result from speaking English as a second language during his early **childhood**, was largely out of kilter with the literary modernism of his day, although this scarcely affected his popularity. In public at least, he was modest in his assessment of his stature, declaring himself to be a "second rater." A number of his books remain in print, such as *Of Human Bondage*, *The Painted Veil*, and *The Razor's Edge* and his legacy lives on particularly in the Somerset Maugham Award, which he inaugurated in 1947, and which is awarded to British writers under the age of 35.—Tammy Lai-Ming Ho

See also ODNB

Meade, L. T. (1844–1914). Irish writer and editor. Once a household name, Meade was one of the most prolific writers of nineteenth- and early-twentieth-century literature, having authored over 250 novels for more than thirty publishers with contemporary book sales in the multi-millions. Elizabeth Thomasina Meade was born the eldest of six children to an Irish protestant rector and raised during the country's Great Famine. Forbidden to read a novel until age fourteen, she began writing soon thereafter and later moved to London to pursue her career. In 1879 Meade married Alfred Toulmin Smith but continued to publish under "L. T. Meade" or "Mrs. L. T. Meade," the name she adopted for both public and private life. Together they raised three children and one daughter who died in infancy. The pace of Meade's writing never flagged despite her increased participation in professional activities and women's advocacy groups. From 1887 to 1893, Meade served as co-editor of *Atalanta* magazine, a middle-class girl's periodical aimed at promoting education and employment for young women. Under her direction, the magazine featured highly celebrated literary figures. Meade contributed scores of articles, essays, and **short stories** to contemporary journals, and published in myriad genres including crime and **detective fiction, sensation fiction, romances,** plays, university novels, Robinsonades, mysteries, and girls' school stories (her *A World of Girls* helped define the genre). She has further been credited with originating the medical mystery. Despite her extensive and respected contribution to literature, scholarship on Meade's work and biography remains limited.—Jacqueline H. Harris

Medicine. The nineteenth century saw the formalization of the field of medicine, and the practice of medicine even in the twenty-first century still relies on many of those nineteenth-century foundations. As recent as the eighteenth century, surgery remained the bailiwick of the "barber-surgeon" who would cut hair but also perform surgeries such as tooth extraction and blood-letting. Only in 1745 did the London Company of Surgeons become a distinct association, separate from barbers (Bynum 1994: p. 5). Thereafter, there was a slow yet deliberate hierarchizing and professionalizing of the field of medicine.

Generally, the three strata of medical practitioners were apothecaries, surgeons, and physicians. Their roles overlapped during the century, but by the *fin de siècle*, there were clear distinctions regarding credentials, associations, and colleges. Surgeons often dispensed with "external disorders" while physicians "dealt in theory, diagnosis, and prescription" (Sparks 2009: p. 12). Furthermore, a surgeon might only have a bachelor's degree, but a physician required a medical doctorate. Additionally, the practice of medicine moved away from extensive interviews of a patient to the disinterested examination of the patient's body, as Michel Foucault famously argued in *The Birth of the Clinic*— what he called the "medical gaze." In the early part of the century, there was movement away from the centuries-old humoral theory to anatomy. Anatomy and physiology heavily informed medicine, and in order to better understand the functions of the body, morbid anatomy enlightened medical professionals on healthy and diseased bodies. The public often considered anatomy museums, medical colleges, and its practitioners relatively objectionable. Members of Parliament wrote legislation aimed at carefully regulating anatomy museums as well as medical practice in general (Anatomy Act of 1832, for example, or the Contagious Disease Acts). The advent of **anesthesia** made a great impact on the practice of medicine as well.

Medicine as a noble pursuit, worthy of high esteem, was a common perspective among medical professionals. Writers such as T. H. Huxley, a trained biologist, attempted to place scientific naturalism, a contemporary but major influence on the field of medical **science**, as a moral calling. Those who studied nature would become "more moral" (DeWitt 2013: p. 26). Efforts to sanitize and moralize medicine occurred throughout the century, as medicine was still scrutinized. These attempts are not without reason, because among the credentialed or licensed doctors, there were still purveyors of pseudoscientific cures or phony medicinal drugs. Though the American Medical Association had formed in the 1840s with a code of ethics, the British Medical Association (established first as the Provincial Medical and Surgical Association in 1832) had no clearly defined code of ethics until much later. Practices could vary widely among British doctors. Therefore, the Medical Act of 1858 created the General Medical Council (GMC), the first modern registry of qualified doctors in the United Kingdom. If doctors were stricken from the registry, then they were no longer allowed to practice medicine. Prior to the formation of the GMC, there had been the Apothecaries Act of 1815, which established the apprenticeship model for apothecaries. There had also been the establishment of the Royal College of Physicians in 1518 and the Royal College of Surgeons (though under a different title) in 1540. These colleges afforded licensure for specific geographic areas, notably London. Historically however, any surgeon or physician wanting to practice medicine sought approval from the local bishop, which meant if the doctor moved or tended to patients not within his diocese then additional requests were needed from other bishops. The GMC, which still exists, was the remedy to address these issues. In turn, patients could more successfully determine legitimate doctors from quacks hawking snake-oil medicine.

Owing to the disparity in knowledge and education among medical professionals and laypeople, the public harbored a vague mistrust of doctors for much of the late nineteenth century. Several critics have pointed to the obscure knowledge doctors seemed to possess. Gone was the apothecary or surgeon who knew the patient well, and in his place was the "clinician as an expert who relied on vision and non-verbal cues to interpret the condition of the patient" (Gilbert 2013: p. 182). Because of this perceived esotericism, readers of popular fiction became fascinated with the figure of the doctor. The doctor, whether mad scientist or kindly practitioner, was a pervasive character, reaching as far back as Jane Austen (Mr. Perry in *Emma* [1815]) and as late as **Bram Stoker** (Drs. Van Helsing and Seward in ***Dracula***). Arguably, the rise of the mad doctor motif in Victorian popular fiction includes Mary Shelley's Victor Frankenstein, although himself not a doctor but a student of science. Other notable figures are the doctors of **Wilkie Collins**, **Charles Dickens**, George Eliot, and **Charles Reade** as well as *Dr. Phillips*; *Mona Maclean, Medical Student*; Dr. Moreau (see **H. G. Wells**'s *The Island of Doctor Moreau*); and Dr. Jekyll (see **Stevenson**'s ***Strange Case of Dr. Jekyll and Mr. Hyde***). One of the most common ailments patients, particularly women, suffer from in popular fiction is **hysteria**, which could easily be seen as a **mental illness** during the nineteenth century.

In the closing decades of the century, women as medical doctors, such as Sophia Jex-Blake, became possible, although still rare. Elizabeth Garrett Anderson had become a licensed apothecary in the 1860s through a loophole, which was quickly closed. Like medicine, the field of nursing became a profession during the nineteenth century and was still open to women. Many practices that had been in the hands of women, such as midwifery, dwindled because of the professionalization of medicine. Debates of whether to admit women to medical colleges occurred among doctors, with limited success for women's admission occurring as early as the 1870s in Ireland and as late as the 1890s in England. Significant numbers of applicants, however, did not happen until the twentieth century. Victorian popular fiction afforded some early female doctors, such as Margaret Todd's ***Mona Maclean*** and Arabella Kenealy's *Dr. Janet of Harley Street* (1893), although most depictions were still of men.—Thomas G. Cole, II

See also Bynum 1994, DeWitt 2013, **Disease**, Gilbert 2013, **Grave Robbing**, **Health**, Sparks 2009

Melodrama. One of the most popular literary and theatrical forms of the nineteenth century, melodrama is known particularly for its appeal to working-**class** audiences. It also exerted an extensive influence on political discourse and genres like realism and the **sensation** novel. Melodrama tends to present a simplistic opposition of good and evil, in which characters represent moral totalities. Winifred Hughes writes, "The opposing powers are always outside the self—villains, social orders, natural disasters. Strife or division is entirely projected into the exterior world, the world of action, which becomes hostile and menacing" (1981: p. 12). As a result, melodrama often relies on textual and visual legibility, wherein the moral status of characters is figured through names or physical appearance. Stock characters include the noble hero, the aristocratic villain, and the long-suffering virtuous heroine. It is also characterized by excessive and exaggerated emotion, so many contemporary critics associate melodrama with its valorization of nonverbal communication. According to Juliet John, melodrama privileges spontaneous emotions and, in doing so, publicizes the private.

Melodrama stage plays emerged in the working-lass theater of the early nineteenth century, often in unlicensed theaters in London and Paris. The first English melodrama is arguably Thomas Holcroft's *A Tale of Mystery* (1802), an adaptation of a French melodrama. Melodrama stage plays partly resulted from the Licensing Act of 1737, which restricted legitimate drama to Drury Lane and Covent Garden; any other drama was required to highlight its differences from spoken drama, pushing melodrama in the direction of pantomime and music (Williams 2012: p. 198).

Early melodrama was a combination of music, drama, pantomime, and tableaux. According to Carolyn Williams, "music and tableaux provide punctual markers of the narrative structure as well as guides for the audience's affective response" (2012: p. 193). As a result, it is marked by dramatic shifts in temporality and register. These moments interrupt the narrative and force viewers to reflect on and interpret what has happened. According to Martin Meisel, melodrama relies on serial discontinuity, or narrative dramatized in a series of frozen moments; it relies on situations rather than coherent narrative. Sub-genres included domestic and crime melodrama.

Its influence extended to the novelists of the period and spawned sub-genres like the sensation novel of the 1860s. **Wilkie Collins** and other sensation novelists were criticized for drawing upon melodramatic tactics and relocating them into the everyday sphere of the middle class. H. L. Mansel (2001/1863) famously critiqued the sensation novel for its "aims at electrifying the nerves of the reader." Although the sensation novel draws upon this melodramatic tradition, Hughes argues that it also reworks the meaning of melodrama by relocating this tension into the heroine and making her represent moral ambivalence rather than moral certainty (1981: p. 44). In doing so, the sensation novel strains **romance** and realism to their limits, flouting the categories of art. **Penny dreadfuls** also relied heavily on melodramatic tropes. **George W. M. Reynolds**, for example, drew on Eugene Sue's melodramatic *Les Mystères de Paris* (1842–1843), when he wrote ***The Mysteries of London***, one of the most popular penny-issue novels of its time.

Melodrama was largely overlooked by scholars until the 1960s, when cultural studies reinvigorated interest in popular forms and blurred distinctions between high and low art. The more widespread revival of melodrama is usually attributed to Peter Brooks's *The Melodramatic Imagination* (1976). Brooks defines melodrama as a mode rather than a genre, "as a certain fictional system for making sense of experience" (1976: p. xviii). In an increasingly secularized world, melodrama, for Brooks, seeks to create moral legibility and value. He argues that the nineteenth-century struggled to conceive of a modern world without providential order, and thus melodrama operated under the imperative of "uncovering, demonstrating, and making operative the essential moral universe in a post-sacred era" (1976: p. 15). In doing so, melodrama sought to restore a sense of moral purpose and order to the world. However, his psychoanalytical approach has since been critiqued, particularly because it locates melodrama within the mind of the individual and "out of history" (Hadley 1995: p. 9).

Many critics have argued that nineteenth-century stage melodrama reinforced middle-class norms in its focus on the family. These accounts imagine the working-class to be largely passive in their reception of middle-class ideology. More recent critics have complicated this account and have suggested the varied ways in which melodrama was a politically engaged and even radical mode. Juliet John has argued that melodrama was popular because it "offered an inclusive populist aesthetics" (2011: p. 3). Patrick Joyce and Judith Walkowitz emphasize the importance of melodrama to the construction of social narratives. Melodrama was a common trope in radical politics because of its critique of aristocracy and democratic openness to interpretation. Other scholars have highlighted its particular appeal to female audiences because of its emphasis on questions of gender and power.—Jessica R. Valdez

Mental Illness. As a scientific discipline, what we today call psychology consolidated itself only in the last quarter of the Victorian period, yet interest in the workings of the human mind had broadly taken two intersecting forms throughout the century: understanding the inner workings of the human mind through psychological self-investigation (introspective psychology) and defining mental pathology through the observation of mentally abnormal or insane individuals (alienism) (Vrettos 2002: p. 69). The definition of mental illness did not only exercise Victorian medical professionals but the general readers of newspapers, periodicals (such as **Charles Dickens**'s *Household Words* and *All the Year Round*), and the Victorian novel. Victorian popular fiction offers a particularly rich seam for representations of "abnormal" psychologies, and pathological states of mind are a central concern of the **sensation fiction** of the 1860s and 1870s as well as of the *fin-de-siècle* **Gothic**. Both **Wilkie Collins**'s *Poor Miss Finch* (1872) and **Mary Elizabeth Braddon**'s *Thou Art the Man* (1894) feature epileptic characters; monomania (the pathological fixation of the mind on one singular object) looms large in Anthony Trollope's *He Knew He Was Right* (1869), **Charles Reade**'s *Hard Cash* (1863), and Braddon's ***Lady Audley's Secret***; and **hysteria** threatens to engulf the **vampire** hunters in **Bram Stoker**'s ***Dracula*** at almost every turn. To some Victorian reviewers, popular fiction itself was positively dangerous, by not only portraying mental illness in its characters but potentially inducing it in its readers. Henry Mansel famously accused the sensation novelists of "preaching to the nerves" with their suspenseful fictions of **bigamy**, incest, and intrigue—consequently producing and feeding into "a diseased appetite" (2001/1863: p. 45).

One major field of interest for Victorian alienists was the relationship of the body and the mind, and the grounding of mental illness in physiology in particular, as signaled by the title of Henry Maudsley's collection of lectures, *Body and Mind* (1871). Maudsley, the most eminent of mid–Victorian alienists, conceptualized insanity as a degeneration of the mind that had its roots in an individual's diseased family history: "In a great many cases ... there is something in the nervous organization of the person, some native peculiarity, which however we name it, predisposes him to an outbreak of insanity" (1871: p. 43). Through the mechanisms of hereditary transmission, psychiatric patients were thought of as vulnerable to dysfunctions within their nervous systems, which, in turn, would result in mental disturbances such as nervous disorders (like hysteria and epilepsy) or forms of madness (like monomania or moral insanity). This psychological materialism was central to many studies on the etiology of mental illness, and the somatic basis of mental disease was the bedrock of Maudsley's psychopathology despite the essential invisibility of heredity's working mechanisms. The invisible "native peculiarity" that might predispose individuals to the development of mental illness offered great opportunities for Victorian novelists throughout the period, who recognized the potential for suspense, surprise and sensation in plots of family secrets and diseased inheritances. In Charlotte Brontë's *Jane Eyre* (1847), Mr. Rochester's first wife Bertha Mason is secretly kept under lock and key at Thornfield Hall after succumbing to the madness she has inherited from her Creole mother. The fate of the protagonist in **Oscar Wilde**'s *The Picture of Dorian Gray* (1891), whose immorality and cruelty can be contextualized as symptoms of moral insanity (a form of madness theorized by the English physician James Cowles Prichard in 1835), is also linked to a potentially diseased family history (Wilde 2003/1891: p. 137).

Ever since Michel Foucault's discursive history of insanity (*Madness and Civilization* 1964), the contrast between the incarceration of the insane in eighteenth-century madhouses (most notoriously in St. Mary Bethlehem's in London) and the more humane approach designated as the "moral management" of the mentally ill in asylums (such as the York Retreat founded by William Tuke in 1792) has become something of a historiographic orthodoxy. However, this progressive Victorian myth was noticeably undercut by a number of anxieties concerning the fragile and mutable boundary between mental **health** and mental illness as well as the danger of false diagnosis and the abuse of administrative power by Victorian doctors (Vrettos 2002: pp. 75–76). The fate of Wilkie Collins's heroine Laura Fairlie in *The Woman in White*—whose incarceration in a mental asylum by the wicked Sir Percival Glyde and his Italian associate Count Fosco constitutes the prerequisite for a fraudulent attack on her inheritance—can be read as a troubling reminder of the potential dangers of institutional abuse in the Victorian period. The eponymous villain in Braddon's *Lady Audley's Secret* declares herself to be mad and is locked away in a private asylum at the end of the novel, yet whether she is, in fact, insane remains ambiguous and unresolved, a narrative uncertainty highlighting the slipperiness of "the narrow boundary between reason and unreason" that makes minds "mad to-day and sane to-morrow, mad yesterday and sane to-day" (Braddon 2012/1862: p. 176). In the case of Henry James's *The Turn of the Screw* (1898), this borderline between mental illness and mental health is so elusive that two opposing camps of criticism have formed around the question whether the governess is mad or sane: How we read her state of mind determines everything else in the narrative.

The mental illness that received most popular interest in the latter part of the nineteenth century was hysteria, and the spectacular lectures of the French neurologist Jean-Martin Charcot (1825–1893) at the Salpêtrière Hospital in Paris drew large audiences of students, who wanted to experience the hysterical fits of Charcot's female patients and the doctor's suggested treatments (such as **hypnosis**) first hand (Scull 2015: p. 277). Even though Charcot believed hysteria to afflict patients of both sexes, the disorder (after all etymologically rooted in the Greek word *hystera* for "womb") was primarily associated with the female sex in the popular imagination so that it bore "the stigma of being a humiliatingly female affliction" (Showalter 1991: p. 106) when affecting men. Victorian fiction is replete with examples of male characters in danger of succumbing to this debilitating disease, from Collins's high-strung Frederick Fairlie in *The Woman in White* to **Richard Marsh**'s otherwise virile Paul Lessingham in *The Beetle* (1897), who under the influence of the novel's eponymous monster is drained of his **masculinity** and turned into a "fibreless, emasculated creature" on "the border line which divides madness from sanity" (2004/1897: pp. 245, 242).

Considering the nineteenth century's fascination with aberrant mental states and their treatment, the figure of the mad-doctor, who patrolled and enforced the boundary between sanity and insanity, became a focal figure for Victorian novels—with the lingering anxiety that these doctors might themselves be dangerous, if not downright mad. In **Robert Louis Stevenson**'s *Strange Case of Dr. Jekyll and Mr. Hyde*, the lawyer Utterson is deeply troubled by his friend's ever more reclusive behavior and fears for the doctor's mental health: "So great and unprepared a change pointed to madness" (Stevenson 2006/1886: p. 30). The medical practitioners in Wilkie Collins's *Heart and Science* (1883), **Arthur Machen**'s *The Great God Pan* (1894), and **H. G. Wells**'s *The Island of Doctor Moreau* are Faustian overreachers whose cruel **vivisection**ism can be read as a symptom of their own mental derangement. Victorian popular fiction time and again negotiates the slippery boundary between mental illness and sanity, and this discursive opposition was frequently mapped onto the doctor-patient-relationship with alarming, yet intriguing, consequences.—Stephen Karschay

Merrick, Leonard (1864–1939). English novelist and playwright. Born of Jewish heritage as Leonard Miller, Merrick was to study law at Heidelberg with the intention of becoming a solicitor. Due to financial losses suffered by his family, Merrick was forced to abandon his chosen career path. He moved to South Africa at the age of eighteen, where he was to work as an overseer for the Kimberley diamond mines, as well as in a solicitor's office. Many of his South African experiences are woven into his writing. During the 1880s he was to take to the stage and work as both an actor and actor-manager in London, and the theater had an impact on his writings as well. His many works include *Mr. Bazalgette's Agent* (1888), *The Worldlings* (1900), *Conrad in Quest of His Youth* (1903), *While Paris Laughed* (1918), and *Four Stories* (1927), as well as the plays *When the Lamps Are Lighted* and *The Elixir of Youth* and **short story** collections. Some of his works have been adapted to film, including *Conrad in Quest of His Youth* (1920). Highly regarded by fellow contemporary writers such as **J. M. Barrie**, George Orwell, G. K. Chesterton, and **H. G. Wells**, many of them worked in **collaboration** with E. P. Dutton to publish the fifteen volume *The Works of Leonard Merrick* (1918).—Amberyl Malkovich

Mesmerism and Hypnotism had a great impact on the Victorian era. While building on two very different assumptions on how the human body and psyche operate and to which outside influences they are susceptible, these practices often merged, especially in public consciousness when performed as entertainment, and when appearing in the fiction of the period. The possibility that an outside agent can use the energies of his body and mind to control, even to heal, the mind and body of a subject formed an undercurrent in the fiction of the long Victorian period. However, popular literature was most interested in mesmerism and hypnotism during the final decades of the era, when these practices were linked to supernatural and sinister types of agency in the late-Victorian **Gothic** novel.

The concept of mesmerism was coined in the late eighteenth century by Frans Anton Mesmer (1734–1815), a German physician who theorized that human life flowed as magnetic fluid through channels of the body, and that certain illnesses could be attributed to obstructions in this flow. He proposed that a mesmerist could make use of an innate "animal magnetism" to unblock these obstructed channels. Even though a French commission dismissed the notion of magnetic fluid, Mesmer's practice spread throughout Europe and reached Britain in the early nineteenth century. The physician and phrenologist John Elliotson was one of the champions of the practice and the friendships he formed with W. M. Thackerey, Charles Dickens and **Wilkie Collins** survived Elliotson's dismissal from his hospital following the revelation that Elliotson's main subjects, the Okey sisters, were frauds.

After this revelation, however, mesmerism was formally debunked as a medical practice in Britain and thus confined to a liminal territory between sensational and often sexualized entertainment on the one hand, and disreputable yet at times strangely effective medical treatment on the other. Indeed, the discourse on mesmerism and hypnosis in society and popular literature remained caught between these two extremes throughout the Victorian period, even after efforts by medical pioneer James Braid to dismiss the underlying theory of animal magnetism, and instead focus on the effect that the practice had on the patient. It was not until the work of Hippolyte Bernheim and Jean-Martin Charcot in France that the practice regained scientific currency and re-entered **medicine** as a legitimate treatment. As such, it was used in particular in the identification, and sometimes treatment, of the ubiquitous "hysterical woman" of the late–Victorian period. Hypnosis was also theorized in relation to the anxiety of degeneration. Some followers of Charcot perceived susceptibility to the hypnotic state as evidence of a degenerate mind, while others viewed the same talent as evidence of a progenerate state (Luckhurst 2000: p. 151–3).

Mesmerism informs a number of literary works from the nineteenth century and was of particular importance to the Gothic novel. As observed by Roger Luckhurst, the practice arrived in Britain when British literary culture was dominated by the Gothic novel, a genre deeply interested in the strange pliability of the human psyche, and in the instability of the subject as it wavers between reason and delirium (148–9). Indeed, the mesmerized state can be understood as one of surrender to a dominant force, but also a temporary transformation into the Other. In this way, the mesmeric trance is Gothic in the sense that it creates a longing for the stable, scientific structures of modernity, yet it also appears to disturb the foundation of Enlightenment and reason. This understanding of mesmerism as providing new ways of understanding the human being persisted during the Victorian era. Thus, **Edward Bulwer-Lytton** and Dickens, himself a practitioner of the craft, portrayed the entranced state as mystical but still potentially useful and beneficial.

The debunking of mesmerism as a legitimate medical practice did eventually produce dark accounts in the popular literature of the final decades of the Victorian period. Thus, the late–Victorian Gothic novel typically cast the mesmerist or hypnotist as a villain who uses his, or in several cases her, tremendous power to selfish, destructive ends. In many texts, the villain is a degenerate Oriental predator who uses mesmerism to infiltrate an already unstable society. **Bram Stoker**'s **vampire Dracula** and **Richard Marsh**'s Egyptian sorceress in *The Beetle* (1897) are the most often cited examples of such mesmerists. These villains use mesmeric practices to open up an **occult** rift in the fabric of modernity. To close this rift, the powers of **science** must be brought to bear on the challenge that the Oriental mesmerist constitutes. In *The Beetle*, the formidable inventor Sydney Atherton resists the Egyptian sorceress's attempts at mesmerizing him and instead treats her to "a little exhibition of electricity" (Marsh 1897: p. 131) that puts her shaking and salaaming on the ground. However, the rift produced by destructive mesmerism can also be sealed through the use of the more legitimate practice of hypnosis. Thus, when Mina Harker has been bitten and put into a trance-like state by Dracula, Van Helsing puts her into a hypnotic trance and thereby reverses the psychic flow so that the vampire can be located.

At the same time, critics have noted that the entranced state brings with it a paradoxical, liberating quality that enables a loosening of Victorian morals that is both powerful and furtively desirable. In ***Dracula*** and in J. E. Muddock's **short story** "The Crime of the Rue Auber," the mesmerized women become both sexually inhibited and capable of drastic violence against men. In **H. Rider Haggard**'s bestselling *She*, the expansive will of the ancient yet preternaturally beautiful Ayesha cannot be resisted. Similarly, the mixed-race psychic vampire Harriet Brandt of **Florence Marryat**'s ***The Blood of the Vampire***, and Kate Northcott in **Arthur Conan Doyle**'s "John Barrington Cowles," both use their mesmeric powers to gain power. In this way, accounts of mesmerism or hypnosis in Gothic fiction also reveal anxieties regarding the emergence and dissemination of the **New Woman**, the suffragette movement, and feminism.—Johan Höglund

See also ODNB

The Mighty Atom (1896). Novel by **Marie Corelli**. Published by Hutchinson in two volumes in 1896, this novel addresses Victorian idea(l)s of education, and especially the role of religion in it. The eleven-year-old Lionel Valliscourt is, following his father's instructions, subjected to a **childhood** and form of education for which he is neither physically nor psychologically fit. Like James Mill or Thomas Gradgrind in **Dickens**'s *Hard Times* (1854), Lionel's father is, as a material positivist, a proponent of facts and knowledge and a denouncer of spirituality and the imagination. In quiet Devon, Lionel—who is meant to study here without distraction—gets to know the young clergyman Reuben Dale and his six-year-old daughter Jessamine, whose Christian faith leads Lionel to query his father's atheism. Lionel realizes over the course of the novel that God must be that *Mighty Atom* at the beginning of all life, and its *raison d'être*. When the boy returns to Devon after a short journey—prescribed to him by his doctor after a nervous collapse when he heard that his unhappy mother had left his despotic father for another man—Lionel hears that Jessamine has suddenly died. In order to find out whether God really exists and whether He is life's alpha and omega, Lionel hangs himself in his study. His father remains cold and unapologetic with regard to his educational ideas but Lionel's tutor, Professor Cadman-Gore, an influential and recognized pedagogue, becomes a conduit for Corelli's questions regarding children's atheistic education in late-Victorian Britain.—Julia Kuehn

Miss Cayley's Adventures (1899). Series of **short stories** written by **Grant Allen**. Serialized in the ***Strand Magazine*** from 1898 to 1899, *Miss Cayley's Adventures* was published as a single volume in 1899. It is about a **New Woman** who travels from England to Switzerland, Italy, **Egypt**, **India**, Japan, and finally through Canada before returning to England. Miss Lois Cayley begins her journey by working as a lady's maid for an elderly woman, although she quickly departs as this position is below her social standing and Miss Cayley wishes to travel the world. While still employed as a lady's maid, Miss Cayley meets and falls in love with the woman's nephew, Harold Tillington. He proposes, but Miss Cayley refuses him explaining that she will only marry him when they are equals, specifically when he is penniless and friendless. Miss Cayley has repeated run-ins with Tillington's family across the globe and she often works as an amateur detective, mostly solving crimes that surround this family. Her role as a so-called lady detective has garnered the most academic attention. Arlene Young has listed Lois Cayley as typical of 1890s lady detectives who are "more businesslike than their predecessors" (2008: p. 24). In addition to detective work, Miss Cayley also finds employment as a bicycle saleswoman, typewriter-girl and copyist, and journalist. Joseph Kestner (2004) has noted that this novel responds to many assumptions about typical New Woman activities and employments. As yet, there is no scholarship that focuses specifically on the role of travel in the narrative.—Laura Chilcoat

Mr. Bazalgette's Agent (1888). Detective novel authored by Leonard Merrick (1864–1939). Originally published by George Routledge and Sons. Features the female detective protagonist Miriam Lea, who somewhat dubiously joins a private detective agency owned by the eponymous Mr. Bazalgette after she experiences financial difficulties and requires a new position (Kestner 2003: p. 37). Merrick famously disliked this novel and attempted to source every copy of it after publication in order to destroy them, with substantial success. Consequently, the novel remained relatively unknown except in specialist academic circles until it was republished as part of the British Library Crime Classics in 2013.—SAMUEL SAUNDERS

See also ODNB

Mona Maclean, Medical Student (1892). Novel by Margaret Todd (1859–1918), under the pseudonym Graham Travers. The narrative follows the romantic and medical adventures of its titular heroine, a student at the London School of Medicine for Women. After failing her intermediate examinations, Mona takes a break from her studies, traveling to Norway with her aristocratic relations before staying in Borrowness, Scotland with her cousin Rachel, a shopkeeper. Rachel requests that Mona conceal her identity as a medical student from the local community. Much of the narrative is concerned with Mona's female friendships and romantic entanglements, particularly with Ralph Dudley, a male medical student whom she meets in Scotland. The novel, published in three volumes, appeared after more than two decades of debates about the propriety of women studying and practicing **medicine**. Its positive treatment of a medical woman can be regarded as polemical, although its tone is light and optimistic. At the time of writing, Todd was a student at the Edinburgh School of Medicine for Women and the protégée and companion of pioneering female doctor Sophia Jex-Blake. Todd later qualified in medicine and worked as an assistant physician to the Edinburgh Hospital and Dispensary for Women and Children. She produced several further novels and a biography of Jex-Blake. Upon its publication, *Mona Maclean* was generally well-received in both the popular and medical press. It ran to fifteen editions by 1900. In recent decades it has attracted the attention of critics interested in **New Woman** writing and the Victorian medical-woman movement.—ALISON MOULDS

The Moonstone (1868). Novel by **Wilkie Collins**. *The Moonstone* is the first full-length work of **detective fiction** in English and Collin's seventh novel. While complex, the crux of the novel's plot lies in the ostensible theft of the Moonstone diamond—an imperial heirloom inherited by Rachel Verinder. Franklin Blake, with the help of others, seeks to recover the diamond. Ultimately, he discovers that he himself stole the diamond under the influence of opium secretly administered by Doctor Candy, and Rachel's cousin Godfrey Ablewhite stole the diamond away from an unconscious Blake.

The Moonstone continues Collins's techniques in **The Woman in White**. He refines the multiple, first-person narrative structure: eleven narrators offer their stories of the Moonstone diamond and its theft. Within these narratives, the novel is acutely aware of its own textuality. For example, the gardener, Gabriel Betteredge, practices a sort of **occult** fortune-telling with his copy of *Robinson Crusoe* based on quotations chosen at random from the book, and cites them by page number.

Obsession with textuality reaches its apex with Ezra Jennings, Doctor Candy's assistant, who cites pages from William Benjamin Carpenter's *Principles of Human Physiology* (1853). Through Carpenter's *Principles*, Jennings reads the delirious ramblings of a fatally ill Candy to unravel the mystery of the missing diamond. Jennings himself epitomizes the novel's obsession with both the margins of stories, and marginalized identities. Jennings suffers from an unspecified **disease** or disability, and critics often identify him with nonnormative sexuality. This marginalized position grants him an empathy that surpasses Candy's rational **medicine**.

Emphasis on marginalized voices manifests in the polyvocal form of the text itself. The evangelical Drusilla Clack's narrative centers around the distribution of religious tracts and her belief that reading those texts will save her sinful aunt, Lady Verinder. Sergeant Cuff, a Dupin-esque detective, insists he "ha[s] never met with such a thing as a trifle yet" (Collins 1868: p. 221). As D. A. Miller points out in *The Novel and the Police*, Cuff "turn[s] trifles into 'telling' details, telling—what else?—a story" (1988: p. 35). Telling stories is in part the crux of the novel itself.

Further on the margins lie stories read only secondhand. The **India**n Brahmins in pursuit of the diamond do not write as such, but divine by reading ink in a seer's hand. A household maid, Rosanna Spearman, hides Blake's incriminating clothing in the sinking sand near the manor. Later, after Cuff accuses her of taking the diamond, Spearman takes her own life in the same sands, and her letter becomes her only advocate.

In addition to critiques of **class**, gender, and imperialism, *The Moonstone* is vital for thinking about the intersection between law and **science**. Forensic detective work like Cuff and Blake attempt combines the methodologies of science with the ramifications of law. Their utter failure, which results in the **suicide** of Spearman, is a foil for Jennings's success with the science of mind. With his knowledge of psychology, Jennings fills in the missing words from Candy's narrative, and deduces the answer to the mystery.—Peter J. Katz

Morrison, Arthur (1863–1945). English writer and journalist. Born in Poplar in the East End of London. Morrison's father, an engine fitter on the docks, died from tuberculosis when Morrison was eight, leaving his wife to bring up three children. His upbringing under the harsh realities of life in the East End, informed the slum fiction for which he was later acclaimed. Early contributions to *Cycling Magazine* and other journals in 1880 illustrated a passion for cycling, evidenced in stories, including "The Affair of the Avalanche Bicycle and Tyre Co. Limited" from his collection *The Dorrington Deed Box* (1898). Entering serious journalism as a writer for the *Globe* in 1885, his thirteen sketches titled "Cockney Corners" for the *People* in 1888, signaled a talent for detailed description of life in the East End of London, with its endemic **poverty**, unemployment, and violence, recently illustrated by the Ripper murders in Whitechapel. In 1889, he joined The People's Palace, a philanthropic scheme in the East End as sub-editor of the *Palace Journal* under **Walter Besant**, completing a series of articles titled "Whitechapel," "On Blackwall Pier," and "Christmas Eve on the Streets," as Newens explains (2008: p. 21). *The Shadows Around Us*, supernatural stories first printed in the *People* in 1891, drew little attention. His story "The Street," a tale of working-class life and slum conditions in the East End, which appeared in *Macmillan*'s *Magazine* the same year, anticipated *Tales of Mean Streets* (1894), *A Child of the Jago* (1896), *To London Town*, (1899) and *The Hole in the Wall* (1902), a minor classic. His work is credited to Naturalism, a movement in literary representation animated by the scientific realism of Emile Zola.

Morrison's work for the **Strand Magazine** saw his creation of the detective Martin Hewitt as the replacement for **Sherlock Holmes** in the first series of seven stories for the magazine, later published in the collection titled **Martin Hewitt, Investigator**. A second collection of six stories, *The Chronicles of Martin Hewitt*, appeared in the **Windsor Magazine** in 1895 followed by six more titled *The Adventures of Martin Hewitt* in 1896. A later collection *The Red Triangle: Being some Further Chronicles of Martin Hewitt* appeared in *Harmsworth's London Magazine* in 1903. Countering his principled detective Hewitt with a villainous private inquiry agent, Horace Dorrington, in 1897, he published *The Dorrington Deed-Box,* a collection of six stories.

Morrison's passion for oriental art resulted in the publication of an authoritative work *Painters of Japan* in two volumes in 1911. A talented dramatist, his plays "That Brute Simmons" (1904), "A Stroke of Business" (1907), and "The Dumb Cake" present fertile ground for critical attention alongside the detective narratives. Averse to intrusion into his personal life, Morrison insisted on being judged solely on his writing and instructed his widow to burn his papers on his death, as Peter Miles informs readers in his 2012 Introduction to *A Child of the Jago* (p. xi).—Kate Morrison

Motherhood. In Victorian Britain, motherhood became elevated as a central part of the age's domestic ideologies. The experience of mothering became idealized and often romanticized, generating highly sentimentalized images. Simultaneously, medical discourse on maternity became both professionalized and increasingly circulated in popular culture, with the focus shifting from the mother's moral influence to a scientific approach to infant care. As attitudes and representations of mothering underwent ongoing changes, the nineteenth century saw influential developments in the medical, legal, emotional, and aesthetic conceptualization of motherhood. Victorian culture produced powerful and lasting images of motherhood.

In the course of the century, expectations, realities, and representations of mothering achieved an unprecedented centrality in popular culture. While social change, in particular the rise of the middling classes, underpinned the formation of a regular cult of idealized motherhood, the significance of literary portrayals demonstrates the impact of literature on intersecting social and cultural developments. The elevation of motherhood was in itself shaped by three interconnected developments: the Victorian cults of **childhood** and the literary child figure; new medical interest in early infancy and child psychology; and the concept of the domestic sphere in bourgeois ideologies. Although domestic ideologies dominated popular culture, however, they were no more reflective of the realities of childrearing than the literary child was of children's everyday lives. The experience of maternity differed vastly, depending largely on a woman's class position. The new middle-class ideal of mothering as an intimate, emotional bond between a mother and her child was largely defined—as so many middle-class ideologies were—against the delegation of childrearing duties to live-in servants in aristocratic households on the one hand and hands-off attitudes among the working classes on the other. Although rising members of the middle classes might attempt to emulate upper-class childrearing practices, they could not easily replicate the often extensive contingent of nurses and nursemaids in wealthier families. The practical question of affordability thus additionally contributed to the sanctification of a more involved parenting in the middle-class home. Hence, while "the children of upper-middle-class families lived in a separate world," "such a pattern of child care was possible only for a small segment of the middle class. ... For the majority of middle-class families, in which at most one or two servants were employed, the chief caretaker of the children was the mother herself" (Gorham 2013/1982: p. 17). Conversely, middle-class reform writers tended to vilify what has been termed the "benign neglect" (Frost 2009: p. 17) that characterized everyday childrearing among the working classes. Practically, moreover, working-class or lower-middle-class mothers "might well do more hands-on parenting than their wealthier counterparts" (Nelson 2007: p. 57), yet childrearing was frequently shared within large families. Much of the popular culture material necessarily reflects middle-class attitudes toward the lower classes rather than the realities of working-class parenting itself. The condemnation of any parenting that did not conform to the new middle-class ideal, however, was in itself perhaps the strongest evidence of the power of this ideal and how it became propagated.

The emergent ideal of middle-class motherhood, however, informed, rather than reflected, the reality. A growing proliferation of advice books on childrearing and magazines targeted at mothers is evidence of the new cultural interest in motherhood. Shifts in the focus of these publications track changes in the conceptualization of motherhood itself. Thus, the first mothers' magazines and guidebooks set the mother's moral influence in the foreground, conceptualizing "a maternal spirituality" (DNCJ: p. 429). In the course of the century, advice material on childrearing increasingly insisted on a scientific approach, focusing on physical aspects, and citing the latest medical theories.

Although popular fiction produced some of the most memorable and influential sentimental images of idealized motherhood, it also critically engaged with these developments. The new interest in early childhood as a formative phase ensured that both idealized mothers and maternal absence or **child abuse** featured centrally in the genre of the *Bildungsroman*, the novel of education or coming-of-age story. In **Charles Dickens**'s *David Copperfield* (1850), the mother is both an object of nostalgia in the first-person narrator's childhood memories and an object of criticism in a careful reassessment of a mother's practical and moral responsibilities. Although maternal death facilitates **orphan** narratives and is often central to a mystery of origins, throughout much of the century, the representation of a mother's main role moreover testifies to her continued importance throughout adulthood. In Elizabeth Gaskell's *Wives and Daughters* (1866), seventeen is tellingly described as a particularly "awkward age for a motherless girl" (1996/1886: p. 101), the age in which a girl, it is suggested, needs her mother most. A mother's duties included her active involvement in her daughters' courtships, although nineteenth-century popular fiction increasingly ridiculed and vilified the figure of the match-making mother. By contrast, the mother's significance to infants and young children became increasingly developed in and to an important extent through popular fiction. Many of the most detailed evocations of the newly emergent ideal of intensive mothering emerged from representations of substitute or adoptive mothers. **Dinah Mulock Craik**'s adoption novel *King Arthur: Not a Love Story* (1886) describes the everyday care of an infant and growing child in unprecedented detail, while romanticizing a woman's longing to parent a child as part of the novel's plea for formal adoption laws. Although the Adoption Act was not passed until 1926, the Victorian age saw numerous campaigns for laws regulating motherhood and its rights. Catherine Norton's petition for revised custody laws capitalized on the identification of a mother with her children in popular culture in order to attack patriarchal laws that rendered all legitimate offspring the property of the father. Her campaigns informed not only her own writing, including her novel *Lost and Saved* (1863), but also Anne Brontë's *The Tenant of Wildfell Hall* (1848), **Mrs. Henry [Ellen] Wood**'s *East Lynne* (1861), and **Wilkie Collins**'s *The Evil Genius* (1886). The second half of the century also saw a revised representation of working-class motherhood. George Moore's *Esther Waters* (1894) deliberately reworked George Eliot's stark evocation of infanticide in *Adam Bede* (1859), detailing how the young servant Esther successfully raises her illegitimate son. This theme is also prefigured in Gaskell's *Ruth* (1853), which dramatizes a young needlewoman's love for her illegitimate baby.

Motherhood in Victorian popular culture was not simply sentimentalized, but also sensationalized, criticized, and at the end of the century, presented in its stark realities in different strata of society. Current work on Victorian motherhood, in fact, stresses

that scholars need "to consider motherhood a 'live' issue, posing a surprising range of questions and challenges in its many incarnations" (Rosenman and Klaver 2008: p. 17).
—TAMARA S. WAGNER

Mudie's Circulating Library. Charles Edward Mudie (1818–1890) founded Mudie's Circulating Library (also known as Mudie's Select Library) in 1842 from his shop in Bloomsbury. Although **circulating libraries**, which rented books to their patrons for a subscription, had existed since the sixteenth century, it was not until the nineteenth century that they became arbiters of national taste—Mudie's perhaps most of all. Mudie's Select Library set up headquarters in New Oxford Street in 1852, and offered efficient lending services to metropolitan, provincial, and colonial readers. The basic annual subscription was a guinea, which allowed only a single volume to be borrowed at a time; the most popular subscription was two guineas which allowed borrowing four volumes simultaneously. By mid-century, Mudie's subscribers numbered over 25,000. Mudie's was selective about both the social standing of its clientele and the moral status of the books it circulated. The library is identified with the triple-decker publication format that dominated literary publishing until the beginning of 1895, when Mudie's refused to accept any further original novels in three volumes. The price of a triple-decker novel was set at a constant 31*s*.6*d*. from 1821 until 1894; this price was out of reach for most readers to meet. Mudie's depended upon the three-volume format to circulate novels to three times as many patrons as a single-volume novel could reach. The circulating library facilitated the expansion of the middle-class reading public, but was also widely criticized for censorship.—ERICA HAUGTVEDT

See also ODNB, DNCJ, Griest 1970, Law 2000, Roberts 2006

Mummies. The author credited with creating the first reanimated mummy in modern literature is Jane C. Loudon (*née* Webb), whose triple-decker novel *The Mummy!: Or a Tale of the Twenty-Second Century* was published anonymously in 1827. Set in 2126, Loudon's futuristic **science fiction** tale sees the **Egypt**ian pharaoh Cheops brought back to life by an electric spark. This trope of electrical reanimation recurs in Edgar Allan Poe's "Some Words with a Mummy" (1845), a satirical **short story** which—as a result of Poe's eminence—has received more critical attention than Loudon's novel. Other, later mummy tales have also been the focus of a number of academic studies of mummies as a literary and cultural trope, particularly as a subset of late Victorian **Gothic fiction**; primary works include **Arthur Conan Doyle**'s "Lot No. 249" (1892), Theo Douglas's *Iras: A Mystery* (1896), **Guy Boothby**'s *Pharos the Egyptian*, and **Bram Stoker**'s *The Jewel of Seven Stars*.

Academic studies of mummies in fiction often record the division of reanimated mummies into two camps: the attractive female mummy (often posited as a romantic interest for a male protagonist), and the threatening male mummy (Day 2006; Luckhurst 2012). Some alluring female mummies, such as Stoker's fictional Queen Tera, resist pigeonholing, combining sexual allure with physical threat. Mummy narratives are also frequently linked to **invasion literature**, particularly as a result of the emergence of the majority of mummy tales subsequent to the British occupation of **Egypt** in 1882 (Bulfin 2011; Deane 2008). The mummy operates within Victorian material culture, connoting Britain's imperial ownership of Egypt and its commodities (Daly 1994). Though fitting comfortably within the tradition of imperial Gothic identified by Patrick Brantlinger

(1988), mummy fiction has been shown to engage with a range of generic conventions, including those of the **fairy tale** (Dobson 2017b).

Literary criticism has focused on mummies which wield supernatural power, are reanimated, psychically active or preserved to an uncanny degree. Little work has thus far been produced on mummies which are mere objects, successfully integrated into public and private collections with no sinister or romantic repercussions. Other aspects of mummies in fiction which would benefit from scholarly attention include mummies as depicted by female authors, for example in Louisa May Alcott's "Lost in a Pyramid; or The Mummy's Curse" (1869) and **Marie Corelli**'s novel *The Sorrows of Satan*. Scholars have also tended to favor mummies appearing in fiction toward the final decades of the Victorian era, as well as ancient Egyptian mummies rather than the preserved bodies of other ancient cultures. Similarly, little work has yet been produced on **illustrations** of mummies which accompany mummy fiction; illustrations appear in certain editions of the mummy fictions of Poe, **Rider Haggard**, Doyle and Boothby, for example.—ELEANOR DOBSON

The Murder of Delicia (1896). Novel by **Marie Corelli**. Published by Skeffington in one volume in 1896, this short novel tells the story of the young, beautiful, successful author Delicia Vaughn who has been married to the former soldier and aristocrat Wilfrid de Tracy Gifford Carlyon for a few years. While she is to her husband a faithful, devoted, and caring wife whose generous income from her popular successes sustains the household, he takes advantage of her kindness and integrity to lead an extravagant and expensive life consisting of parties, gambling, and female entertainment. When Delicia learns that Wilfrid has commissioned an expensive item of jewelry for the dancer Marina—a working-class girl who is currently *en vogue* on the London stage and in the upper social circles—she realizes how trusting and foolish she has been. She leaves Wilfrid, especially after she has unintentionally overheard him say to an acquaintance that his wife Delicia is, like all writing women, "unsexed."

In a subplot, actor Paul Valdis confesses to his friend Delicia that he has for a long time admired and loved her. She thanks him for his feelings but rejects his advances in a friendly but determined manner; she remains committed to her marriage despite, and even after, her husband's betrayal. Separated from Wilfrid and with a broken heart, Delicia completes her final novel, which will become the most popular of all her works, and then dies of a heart attack. The final pages of the novel see an unapologetic Wilfrid, to whom Delicia has left in her will a small but sufficient allowance. The biggest share of her money, however, has been bequeathed to London's poor. Delicia's St. Bernard dog, Spartan, now lives with Paul Valdis who loved the authoress with a true and faithful heart, just like the dog.

The novel invokes a number of social issues, from the Matrimonial Causes Act to the Married Women's Property Act. Most prominently, Corelli invokes a battle she fought throughout her career, namely the prejudice—popularized in *Punch* cartoons and elsewhere after the emergence of the **New Woman** writers—that all female authors were "unsexed." George Eliot is famously referred to by a reviewer in this novel as "an old hen that imagined it could crow." The denunciation of society's conviction that successful women must surely be devoid of femininity is a recurring motif in Corelli's fiction. Characters like Delicia Vaughn, Mavis Clare (***The Sorrows of Satan***), the heroines of *A Romance of Two Worlds* (1886), and *The Life Everlasting* (1911), and the eponymous heroine in *Innocent* (1914), are therefore hyperfeminized, virtuous, and popular artists—barely disguised versions of how Corelli saw herself, and how she wanted to be perceived by the public. The "masculine," cigarette-smoking, cycling, and trousers-wearing Honoria Maggs in *My Wonderful Wife: A Study in Smoke* (1889) is a counter image of Corelli's feminine woman, although the text—which reads, from a modern perspective, as profeminist—shows, in combination with the other novels, Corelli's ambivalent stance toward women's independence.—Julia Kuehn

The Mysteries of London (1844–56). Novel by George W. M. Reynolds. This **serial** by novelist and journalist Reynolds was issued in weekly penny numbers from September 1844 until October 1856, initially (vols. 1–4) as *The Mysteries of London* and subsequently (vols. 5–12) as *The Mysteries of the Court of London*. The title change followed Reynolds's split from his publisher George Vickers (probably as a result of Reynolds's 1846 decision to abandon his editorship of Vickers's **London Journal** in favor of setting up his own ***Reynolds's Miscellany***), and the eight volumes of *The Mysteries of the Court …* were published under John Dicks, whose partnership with Reynolds would last until the author's death in 1879.

The *Mysteries* were rapidly and enormously successful, cementing Reynolds's position as a central figure of the early Victorian mass market press and scandalizing the middle and upper classes with their combination of radical politics (Reynolds was a prominent Chartist and a republican), sensational storylines (many of which were drawn from contemporary headlines), and softcore erotica (both written and pictorial; the later volumes in particular feature numerous **illustrations** of female characters in states of provocative undress). This subversive mix of content caused additional disquiet because Reynolds's audience was identified as largely working class and significantly female: an obituary in the *Bookseller* described his readers as "half-educated girls" ("Obituary" 1879: p. 601).

Although there is reason to believe that the serial's audience was broader than its contemporaries chose to acknowledge (some surviving copies bear the imprint of aristocratic libraries), Reynolds certainly directed his writing to a readership of the new urban poor. The *Mysteries* takes its cue (as it took its title) from Eugene Sue's *Mystères de Paris* (1842–1843) in depicting a high-low vision of London life, where a corrupt aristocracy employs and exploits an abject, sometimes criminal working class. Unlike Sue, however, who saw the solution to his city's plight in a paternalistic charity administered by a moral bourgeoisie, Reynolds was not afraid to advocate for bloody revolution. Interspersing its murders, blackmail, and betrayal with lengthy passages of political polemic, the *Mysteries* sought to enlighten and empower the increasingly literate working class.
—Janine Hatter

The Mystery of a Hansom Cab (1886). Novel by **Fergus Hume**. Set in Melbourne, Australia, this popular detective novel revolves around the murder of Oliver Whyte in a hansom cab. When Brian Fitzgerald is wrongly accused of the murder, he has to choose between saving his own neck or the good name of his fiancée Madge Frettleby, as both his alibi and the murder are connected to the scandalous Frettleby family secret. A secret which will reveal that Madge is an illegitimate child and that a poor girl from the slums is the true heiress to the Frettleby family fortune.—Marjolein Platjee

Nesbit, Edith (1858–1924). British writer. Born in London, Nesbit was the youngest child of John Collis Nesbit, an agricultural chemist, and his wife, Sarah Green. She was educated in French and German boarding schools. The difficult experience of being separated from the family at an early age is reflected in her **childhood** memoir "My School-Days" (1897). In 1876, her first poem was published in *Sunday Magazine*. In 1880, she married Hubert Bland, her lifelong companion, and the source of many joys as well as sufferings. Both helped start the Fabian Society in 1884, sharing the socialist passion with a group of friends including **H. G. Wells** and Bernard Shaw. Hubert was famous for his infidelity, and possibly as a response Nesbit had a series of affairs including her relationship with Shaw. Driven by financial troubles, Nesbit shifted from poetry to popular fiction, and the publication of the first of the Bastable books, *The Story of the Treasure-Seekers* (1899), marks this successful turning point in her career. It was followed by several works of **children's literature**, including *The Would-be-Goods* (1901), *Five Children and It* (1902), *The Phoenix and the Carpet* (1904), *The Railway Children* (1906), and *The Enchanted Castle* (1907). These titles were all characteristic of Nesbit's singular combination of vivid imagination and realism. She also wrote many **fairy tales**, collected in *The Book of Dragons* (1899), *Nine Unlikely Tales* (1901), and *The Magic World* (1912). Often considered the first modern writer for children, Nesbit was a major contributor to the golden age of children's literature.—Haejoo Kim

See also ODNB, Briggs 1987, Jones 2006, Uglow 2005

The New Monthly Magazine (1814–1884). British monthly magazine published in London by Henry Colburn, under the initial title of the *New Monthly Magazine and Universal Register*. Established in opposition to more liberal journals, especially Richard Phillips's *Monthly Magazine*, it was "virulently Tory" in outlook (Higgins 2006). When the magazine's political leanings failed to impress the reading public, Colburn appointed the poet Thomas Campbell as editor in 1821, retitling it the *New Monthly Magazine and Literary Journal*. During the 1820s it became one of the most noteworthy metropolitan magazines, eschewing politics in favor of literary miscellanea such as essays, stories, biographies, reviews, and poetry. Over the years the *New Monthly*'s contributors included Mary Shelly, Stendhal, W. M. Thackeray, William Hazlitt, with his "Table Talk" essays, and John Polidori, whose "The Vampyre"—often viewed as the progenitor of Gothic **vampire** fiction—appeared in the April 1819 issue (albeit attributed to Lord Byron). The magazine briefly regained its political edge under the editorship of **Edward Bulwer-Lytton** (1831–1833), a staunch supporter of the Reform Act, never, however, losing its literary character. As Colburn explained in 1833, the magazine's ultimate goal was to provide "not only articles connected with criticism … and belles-lettres, but whatever can amuse, instruct, and refine" (p. 2). In 1837, the publication changed its title to the *New Monthly Magazine and Humorist*, the better to compete with journals such as ***Bentley's Miscellany***, finally settling for the *New Monthly Magazine* in 1853, under which name it appeared until 1884.—Agnieszka Jasnowska

New Woman. The term *New Woman*, in the upper case, has long been attributed to **Ouida** (Marie Louise Ramé) in her response to an essay by **Sarah Grand**. Recent scholarship by William A. Davis, Jr., uncovered an earlier appearance of the term, in the lower-case: "[Mary] Jeune named the New Woman in that year [1889], Sarah Grand provided wide circulation and popularity five years later, and Ouida ensured its lasting place in culture by turning it into a label that stuck" (Davis, Jr. 2014: p. 580). Jeune's, Grand's, and Ouida's articles reveal the importance of the periodical press as the medium through which the separate spheres ideology was variously challenged or upheld. Both Jeune and Ouida argue for the importance of the private sphere for women, the former honing in on **motherhood**. By contrast, Grand argues for the moral superiority of women and how they can effect larger social changes. In "Women of To-Day, Yesterday, and Tomorrow," which appeared in the *National Review* in December 1889 and in the U.S. in the *Eclectic Review* in February 1890 (Davis, Jr. 2014: p. 578), Jeune responds, in turn, to an article by Lady Catherine Gaskell that appeared in the November number of the *Nineteenth-Century*. According to Jeune, "Education has changed the condition of women materially, and the increased freedom they enjoy has put them on a footing of something nearer an equity with men which long ago would have been impossible" (1890: p. 177). Jeune is critical of both the manner in which women are educated, finding it impossible for women to "know[] any one subject but superficially" (1890: p. 179), and the New Woman for her transgression of the separate spheres ideology by taking on more public roles: "Fortunately, our girls have hitherto escaped [by abandoning "the distinctive qualities that once were the pride and glory of Englishwoman"], and the sudden emancipation and development of the new women has not touched them; but the golden circlet and the orange blossoms break the charm, and the modest, gentle maiden soon blooms into the female propagandist" (1890: p. 182). Jeune concentrates her criticism on the physical strain caused by these developments, but she is convinced "that the life of high pressure they are striving to follow must infallibly break them down, and women will gradually accept the stern fact that, first of all, they must be wives and mothers and then they can be whatever their strength and leisure will allow" (1890: p. 185). She concludes by arguing that motherhood will spur women to return to the private sphere, where she will find greater compensation:

> The soft faces of her children, their fond kisses, and the little arms thrown lovingly round her neck will be sweeter by far to her than the theories of universal brotherhood and the equality of man and woman, which gave her such infinite satisfaction in the past; and one by one as the old opinions and convictions drop away will she find that only since she renounced what then appeared to her a creed full of the purest and highest aspirations has she really learned to live, ad that in striving to be all-powerful she was weak, but that in acknowledging her weakness she became strong [1890: p. 185].

Grand's "The New Aspect of the Woman Question" appeared in *The North American Review* in March 1894 and it addresses "the Brawling Brothers," those who criticize the women aspiring to better the world and who accuse them of trying to dis/replace men:

> That woman could ape man and desire to change places with him was conceivable to him as he stood on the hearth-rug in his lord-and-master-monarch-of-all-I-survey attitude, well inflated with his own conceit; but that she should be content to develop the good material which she finds in herself and be only dissatisfied with the poor quality of that which is being offered to her in man, her mate, must appear to him to be a thing as monstrous as it is unaccountable [1894: p. 270].

Grand, drawing on language from the domestic register, reasons that men cannot understand, and consequently abuse, "the new woman":

> Women were awaking from their long apathy, and, as they awoke, like healthy hungry children unable to articulate, they began to whimper for they knew not what. They might have been easily satisfied at that time had not society, like an ill-conditioned and ignorant nurse, instead of finding out what they lacked, shaken them and beaten them and stormed at them until what was once a little wail became convulsive shrieks and roused up the whole human household [1894: p. 271].

The blame rests partly with women, who had entrusted the social system to the management of men, not "considering whether his abilities and motives were sufficiently good to qualify him for the task" (1894: p. 271). Grand is optimistic that the current struggle will bring about positive change—"The man of the future will be better, while the woman will be stronger and wiser. To bring this about is the whole aim and object of the present struggle, and with the discovery of the means lies the solution of the Woman Question" (1894: p. 272)—and she ends with a call for action: "It is for us to set the human household in order, to see to it that all is clean and sweet and comfortable for the men who are fit to help us to make a home in it. We are bound to raise the dust while we are at work, but only those who are in it will suffer any inconvenience from it, and the self-sufficing and self-supporting are not afraid. For the rest it will all be benefits. The Woman Question is the Marriage Question, as shall be shown hereafter" (1894: p. 276).

Two months later, in the same periodical, Ouida responds to Grand in "The New Woman." Ouida describes the prevalence of the term *New Woman* in popular discourse: "The Workingman and the Woman, the New Woman, be it remembered, meet us at every page of literature written in the English tongue; and each is convinced that on its own especial W hangs the future of the world" (1894: p. 610). Ouida is strongly critical of the New Woman, who, she views, "wants to get the comforts and concessions due to feebleness, at the same time as she demands the lion's share of power due to superior force alone. It is this overweening and unreasonable grasping at both positions which will end in making her odious to man and in her being probably kicked back roughly by him into the seclusion of a harem" (p. 612). Like Jeune, Ouida proposes that women turn toward the private sphere, toward the resources that they possess rather than "concentrat[ing] on and desiring and demanding those she has not" (p. 613). She finds the New Woman harmful, "with her fierce vanity, her undigested knowledge, her over-weening estimate of her own value and her fatal want of all sense of the ridiculous" (p. 615), and argues that women are not always victims, that greater responsibility be placed on them: "The error of the New Woman (as of many an old one) lies in speaking of women as the victims of men, and entirely ignoring the frequency with which men are the victims of women. In nine cases out of ten the first to corrupt the youth is the woman. In nine cases out of ten also she becomes corrupt herself because she likes it" (p. 615). Finally, Ouida uses an agricultural metaphor to describe the New Woman's neglect of the private sphere and its consequent damage on both spheres: "The New Woman reminds me of an agriculturalist who, discarding a fine farm of his own, and leaving it to nettles, stones, thistles, and wireworms, should spend his whole time in demanding neighboring fields which are not his. The New Woman will not even look at the extent of ground indisputably her own, which she leaves unweeded and untilled" (p. 618).

The New Woman appeared in many guises in fiction and, as we have seen, the periodical press throughout the 1880s and 1890s (Ledger 1997: p. 2). Her "elusive quality," as Sally Ledger has convincingly argued, "clearly marks her as a problem, as a challenge to the apparently homogenous culture of Victorianism which could not find a consistent language by which she could be categorised and dealt with. All that was certain was that she was dangerous, a threat to the *status quo*" (1997: p. 11). As a genre, according to Kate Flint, New Woman fiction "may be said to have created and consolidated a community of woman readers, who could refer to these works as proof of their psychological, social, and ideological difference from men" (1993: p. 305). The New Woman novel is concerned with the lives of middle-class women and the elements that make it controversial "include protests against the restrictive upbringing of girls and the inadequacies of their education; the challenging of the assumptions that women's best possible future lay in marriage, that the only place to bear and bring up children was within such a marriage, and that, indeed all women possessed a 'maternal instinct'; the importance placed upon women's struggles and achievements in their working lives, whether as journalist or doctor, teacher, or musician; and the questioning of double sexual desires" (Flint 1993: p. 294). New Woman novelists developed a range of literary techniques, prefiguring those of the modernists, to reflect this "fascinating period of transition away from Victorian separate spheres" and "the stresses, anxieties, and freedoms women experienced as they rebelled against traditional roles" (Schaffer 2013). Three innovations specific to the genre—nonfiction manifestos, the allegory, and journalistic immediacy—"signal the reader that this is no longer a detailed fictional universe in which to immerse oneself, but rather, a highly constructed text that aims to argue, convince, and override the reader" (Schaffer 2013).

One of **George Gissing**'s **short stories**, "The Tyrant's Apology," appeared in the *English Illustrated Magazine* in July 1895 and it effectively dramatizes some of the issues pertaining to the genre. In it, the first-person narrator reveals his marital woes to Jamieson, who was once in love with his wife Jenny; the story, borrowing from the form of the dramatic monologue, aims both to lessen Jamieson's concern for Jenny and to challenge her version of events (Ue 2013: p. 7). Prior to their marriage, Jenny was visibly a New Woman, as the narrator recollects: "Her cigarette-smoking, her night rambling, her talk about forbidden things—pah! She wished to be thought a fast girl, and it's rather wonderful, when one comes to think of it, that the limits of the possible weren't passed. She imagined herself a light of fashion over yonder" (Gissing 2011–2012, 2: p. 259). Following her father's economic "smash" and his abandonment of his family, Jenny was left with only relatives in the country who could and would help her: "Her mother, as I daresay you know, behaved very badly; she was frightened out of her wits, I suppose, and showed the primitive selfish instinct without disguise" (2: p. 260). In the early stages of their married life, Jenny and the narrator had tried to live in modesty, she swapping her former life for no company but that of the domestic's and the narrator's, a subscription to **Mudie's**, and clothes (Ue p. 8). Jenny's promptings led the couple to add to their domestic comforts until they began to run into debt, Jenny abandoning her former ways in the meantime: "No more 'fast' doings: no cigarettes, no doubtful talk, no disreputable company. I had told her what I thought of that kind of thing, and she was careful to please me" (2: p. 265). The narrator largely absents himself from partaking in these extravagances and blames Jenny, shifting his anger from the larger society—to which they sought conformity—to her. Only in passing does he confess to Jamieson: "And the truth was I found life a good deal pleasanter than before. I had decent meals and comfortable chairs. Jenny showed a bright face when I came home, and was recovering a good deal of her old liveliness in conversation" (2: p. 264). By the end of the story, the narrator pushes for a return to modesty, and Jenny is shown to be his victim: "It may take years of steady ruling before Jenny gives up all hope of a return to the fashionable life…. Her rights as an individual? Humbug! She is *not* an individual; it's the rarest thing to meet a woman who is" (2: p. 267). The narrator threatens Jenny, should she find this life intolerable, with separation and an allowance.—Tom Ue

Newgate Novels. A subgenre of fiction popular in the 1830s and 1840s that focused on crime, criminals, the urban underworld, and prisons. While earlier British fiction had featured criminal protagonists, such as Defoe's *Moll Flanders* and Lewis's *The Monk*, the Newgate School set itself apart by treating its criminals sympathetically: its protagonists, drawn directly from publications of criminal biography such as the *Newgate Calendar* or fictionalized on a similar model, were frequently cast as merry adventurers or unfortunate victims of an unjust society. Critics reacted vehemently to these new novels, dubbing this a "gallows school of literature"; William Maginn suggested in *Fraser's Magazine* that the sympathetic representation of crime and criminals was likely to "fill many a juvenile aspirant for riot and notoriety with ideas highly conducive to the progress of so ennobling a profession as that of housebreaking" (1840: pp. 227–8). Critics' fears arose equally from the fact that Newgate novels were wildly popular: many novels were adapted immediately to the stage, some at several theaters simultaneously, making their stories accessible to a wider audience than would have read a three-volume novel. Many Newgate novels also featured **illustrations**, including images of the criminal protagonist reproduced as inexpensive prints available for purchase or simply for visual consumption in booksellers' windows. Some Newgate novels, such as **Edward Bulwer-Lytton**'s *Paul Clifford* (1830) and **William Harrison Ainsworth**'s *Rookwood* (1834) and *Jack Sheppard* (1839), included a dozen or more original songs that facilitated theatrical adaptation and spread the novels' influence still further. The Newgate School even spawned an early merchandizing phenomenon: W. M. Thackeray complained that, at one of the theaters where *Jack Sheppard* was playing, "people are waiting about the lobbies, selling Shepherd-bags [*sic*]—a bag containing a few pick-locks that is, a screw driver, and iron lever … .Such facts must greatly delight an author who aims at popularity" (1945: p. 395).

Bulwer-Lytton is credited with inaugurating the Newgate School in 1830 with *Paul Clifford*. A novel of social and political critique modeled on Godwin's *Caleb Williams* (1794), *Paul Clifford* features a brave, virtuous protagonist who turns to a life of crime only after having been imprisoned for a crime he didn't commit. The trials of the young hero exemplify the social injustices characterizing early Victorian Britain, where, the narrator contends, the poor are criminalized rather than helped, and a corrupt judicial system serves the interests of the ruling class alone. Although it set the model for many Newgate novels that followed, *Paul Clifford* is unusual to the extent that its dashing highwayman does not end up at the gallows: the novel ends with Paul escaping prison and beginning a new, prosperous life in America. Bulwer-Lytton was able to grant his hero a happy ending in part because the protagonist was fictional, rather than based on a real historical figure, and in part because the critical backlash against Newgate fiction was yet to come.

Unlike Bulwer-Lytton, Ainsworth based central characters in his novels *Rookwood* and *Jack Sheppard* on real criminals who had featured regularly in ballads and popular theater, as well as in the *Newgate Calendar*, a text found in middle-class homes in the early nineteenth-century almost as often as the Bible. *Rookwood* is largely a **Gothic** family drama played out on English soil, but it features the early eighteenth-century highwayman Dick Turpin. Capitalizing on the Turpin legend, Ainsworth embellished it by attributing to the highwayman a 320-mile ride from London to York on his horse Black Bess. With *Jack Sheppard*, Ainsworth took the romancing of crime several steps further: the novel focuses on the historical Sheppard's legendary escapes from a series of English prisons, and fictionalizes these feats as part of the plucky young criminal's showdown with the notorious eighteenth-century thieftaker, Jonathan Wild. Further, Ainsworth stages Sheppard's procession to Tyburn as the spectacle of a celebrity appearing before his adoring fans, rather than the shameful death of a convicted felon. Critics' fears about the dangerous influence of such a figure on impressionable readers and theater-goers were fueled in 1840 when a valet accused of murdering his employer suggested that he got the idea from Ainsworth's novel.

In addition to Bulwer-Lytton and Ainsworth, other popular Newgate novelists include **Charles Dickens** and Thackeray. Although both Dickens and Thackeray deplored Newgate novels and worked hard to distinguish their own fiction from what they saw as the school's lamentable romancing of crime, their novels of the 1830s and 40s were regularly associated with the Newgate School. With *Oliver Twist* (1837–9), Dickens claimed to present a realistic depiction of criminals, stripping them of the trappings of romance and showing them in the squalor and violence in which they actually lived. Thackeray, however, accused him of encouraging readers to sympathize with pickpockets and prostitutes in the figures of the charming Artful Dodger and the unfortunate Nancy. Thackeray himself admitted to finding such sympathies difficult to resist: wanting to cure the public of its seemingly insatiable appetite for crime fiction, he published *Catherine* (1839–40), a novel about a thoroughly unlikeable eighteenth-century criminal who murdered her husband. Before the **serialization** of the novel was complete, though, he confessed in his correspondence that he had grown quite fond of his heroine. Other novels associated with the Newgate School include Dickens's *Barnaby Rudge* (1841) and Thackeray's *Barry Lyndon* (1844) and *Vanity Fair* (1848).

The appetite for Newgate novels did finally wane by the mid–1840s, as readers' attention was increasingly engaged by novels focused on the trials of the working poor, rather than criminals. Later Victorian fiction influenced by the Newgate School include **sensation fiction** and boys' adventure novels.—Lauren Gillingham

Nigel Bartram's Ideal (1868). Novel by Florence Wilford (1836–1897). Little-known today, the novel is a sensational Künstlerroman that explores a woman's struggle to align her literary ambitions with social expectations of femininity. Marion, the novel's heroine, successfully publishes the **sensation** novel *Mark's Dream*, but is forced to keep her authorship a secret as she endeavors to be her husband, Nigel Bartram's, Ruskinian ideal. Nigel, a literary critic as well as Marion's husband, initially presumes *Mark's Dream* to have been written by a man. However, when Marion questions his assumption of the author's gender, his criticism reverts from assessing the literary acclaim of the novel to a judgment based on female immorality. His review is presented as the catalyst in prohibiting Marion's creative output as it forces her to realize that social expectations of femininity do not correspond to her literary ambitions. The climax of the novel, and Marion's own crisis of identity, comes when, discovering that Nigel's brother is in financial difficulties, Marion is motivated to produce another novel. However, when her authorship and intention to write a second novel are revealed, Nigel reacts with horror, banning Marion from publishing and leading her to believe he has destroyed her manuscript. The novel concludes with Marion taking Nigel's job of literary critic as he is forced to acknowledge her intellectual superiority. *Nigel Bartram's Ideal* demonstrates the importance of writing in allowing women to shape their own identity; a concept which anticipates the **New Woman**'s representation of creative industry.—Katherine Mansfield

The Night Side of Nature; or, Ghosts and Ghost Seers. Novel by **Catherine Crowe**. Published in two volumes in 1848, *The Night Side of Nature* is a study of supernatural folklore including chapters on dreams, presentiments, wraiths, apparitions, doppelgängers, and haunted houses. The work is also credited with introducing "poltergeist" into the English language. In a 26 February 1848 review in the *Examiner*, Charles Dickens called the book "one of the most extraordinary collections of 'Ghost Stories' that has ever been published" (in Slater 1996: p. 80).—MELISSA EDMUNDSON

See also ODNB, Dalby 2005

Not Wisely, but Too Well (1867). Novel by **Rhoda Broughton**. Notable for its pioneering depiction of female desire, *Not Wisely* is the first novel Broughton wrote. It was probably drafted in 1863 and **serial**ized by Broughton's uncle by marriage, **J. S. Le Fanu**, in *The Dublin University Magazine* in 1865–66. Although the London publisher Richard Bentley initially accepted ***Not Wisely*** on Le Fanu's recommendation, the horrified response of Bentley's reader, Geraldine Jewsbury, to the manuscript, which she deemed "as bad as any French novel" (in Broughton 2013: p. 379), caused Bentley and Le Fanu to persuade Broughton to void the contract for the book, and to publish in its place her tale ***Cometh Up as a Flower***. In order to render *Not Wisely* acceptable for volume publication, Broughton promised Bentley to "expunge" the serial version of "coarseness & slanginess" and to replace the murder-**suicide** of the original ending with a blander conclusion (in Broughton 2013: p. 381). After revising the manuscript, however, Broughton rejected the terms Bentley offered her and published the book with **Tinsley** instead. Despite her extensive bowdlerizations of the serial (for a detailed comparison of the novel's two versions see Broughton 2013: pp. 385–428), the triple-decker *Not Wisely* continued to shock, as well as to sell briskly. Among the story's more scandalous aspects were its portrayal of a respectably born young woman nearly entering, on two separate occasions, into an adulterous liaison with a married man, and the depiction, remarkably frank for the period, of her attraction to his muscular physique. Unsurprisingly, these risqué elements, which caused the novel to be associated with the controversial genre of **sensation fiction**, attracted critical disapproval, with *The Athenaeum* even declaring the story blasphemous. In a more sympathetic appraisal, the reviewer for the *Spectator* called Broughton "the novelist of revolt" and, referring to both *Not Wisely* and ***Cometh Up as a Flower***, compared her portrayal of discontented, unconventional heroines to those of Charlotte Brontë and George Eliot (Broughton 2013: p. 438). Charlotte Brontë's influence is evident in *Not Wisely*, which recasts *Jane Eyre*'s plot of a young woman who, upon discovering that her aristocratic lover is married, refuses to become his mistress. Unlike *Jane Eyre*, however, neither the serial nor the volume form of *Not Wisely* ends with the heroine's marriage to the now-reformed rake, suggesting a more pessimistic view of heterosexual romance than Brontë's novel. In general, Broughton's intertextuality in *Not Wisely*—her numerous echoes of, and quotations from, a variety of literary works—attests to a complex dialogue with earlier writers and narrative traditions on the subject of representing feminine experience.—TAMAR HELLER

The Notting Hill Mystery (1862–63). Novel by Charles Felix, pseudonym likely used by Charles Warren Adams (1833–1903). **Serial**ized in *Once a Week* (1862–63) and later published in book form (1865), *The Notting Hill Mystery* offers a meticulous forensic analysis of two intertwined murders and may be regarded as "the first full-length modern English-language **detective novel**" (Ashley 2012: p. xiii). The narrative is a dossier compiled by private detective Mr. R. Henderson respecting possibly fraudulent life insurance claims by Baron R for the untimely demise of his wife. The dossier includes depositions, journal entries, letters, memoranda, a marriage certificate, and a floor plan. Although he lets the documents speak for themselves, Henderson has "arranged" them "in the form in which they would be laid before counsel" (Adams 2012/1865: p. 7) if a case were ever to be brought against the Baron in court.

Gertrude and Catherine Boleton are **orphan** twins with a "wonderful [physical] sympathy" (p. 26), each sister manifesting the illnesses of the other. Catherine, younger and more resilient, is abducted and becomes the mesmerist Baron R's medium "Rosalie"; the sickly Gertrude marries Mr. Anderton. The Baron guesses at their kinship and establishes that "Rosalie" (Catherine) is third in line to a legacy of £25,000. He marries Rosalie, leaving three people between himself and the legacy: Mrs. Anderton, her husband, and Rosalie. He ingeniously poisons Mrs. Anderton by proxy, mesmerically willing his wife to administer antinomy to herself, which causes her twin sister, the constitutionally weaker Gertrude, to die. The Baron manipulates Mr. Anderton into committing **suicide** and subsequently compels his wife, in a somnambulistic state, to fatally consume acid, thus acquiring a life interest in the legacy *and* £25,000 in life insurance. The novel is an early exploration of mesmeric crime, but ironically Henderson is a determined skeptic who deprecates **mesmerism** as a delusion. Henderson frankly acknowledges his interpretative dilemma: either he must "ignore a chain of circumstantial evidence so complete … it seems almost impossible to disregard" or reach a conclusion "at variance with all the most firmly established laws of nature" and so "impossible to accept" (p. 6). Henderson solves the mystery of the two parallel deaths, but this resolution is predicated on another, irreducible mystery.—BRUCE WYSE

The Occult/Occultism. The Victorian period is frequently considered to be a period of rational thought, order, and of scientific advances. All of which are true, however, it was also a period which had a deep preoccupation with the occult. The religious feeling that marked the earlier portion of the century was followed by a crisis of faith, in part as a result of Darwin's controversial new evolutionary theories in his *On the Origin of Species* (1859), and this combined with the constant presence of death—mortality was high and cemeteries were overflowing—and the almost magical scientific advances of the age led to an increased fascination with the otherworldly, which in turn led to the rise in spiritualism.

Spiritualism is the belief that the dead wish to communicate with the living and that this is facilitated by mediums. The Fox sisters from New York had a significant impact on the creation of the spiritualist movement. In 1848 the two younger siblings (Margaret and Kate) used a system of rappings and various tricks, such as apples tied on string and bounced up and down in order to create a banging noise, to convince their mother that their house was haunted. They claimed that they were able to communicate with the spirit world and, in particular, with the ghost of a man who had been murdered in their home many years before. Their terrified mother told the neighbors about her daughters' fantastic powers which led to newspaper articles on their strange and wonderful abilities. Following this and under their older sister Leah's directions, they were able to enjoy highly successful careers as mediums until they revealed their hoax in 1888.

The spiritualist movement arrived in England in 1852, when an American woman, Maria B. Hayden (1826–1883), made the journey to England in order to act as a medium. She performed séances and received a mixed reception, in particular from the rather unkind British press. However, she was also not without her supporters and she was soon followed by many more mediums in order to meet the public's desire to commune with the spirit world. Women were generally perceived to be more sensitive and so in some ways spiritualism provided a forum full of opportunities, both a financial and with regard to influence. Although, it is important to remember that in a world where women had severely restricted legal rights this power would always have strict limitations. Séances also provided opportunities to perform, as they were theatrical events and contained many performative aspects such as music, dramatic flourishes and, clearly, acting.

Men, however, were more prominent in the art of **mesmerism** or animal magnetism as it was also known. Franz Anton Mesmer (1734–1815) theorized that energy transferred between all animate and inanimate objects and he termed this "animal magnetism." He believed that by manipulating this energy through the use of hypnotic trances it could help heal patients. And in time, these ideas developed into the practice of **hypnosis** as we understand it today. The Scottish surgeon James Braid popularized this term in 1841 and was a keen champion of hypnosis. **Charles Dickens** was fascinated by mesmerism and as well as attending lectures on the subject he also became a keen practitioner.

The developments in technology during the period also allowed a new market to emerge in so-called sprit photography. Due to the limitations in early photographic quality and equipment it was fairly easy to produce a ghostly figure as the subject merely had to move during the shot for a blurred otherworldly image to appear. Initially these photographic tricks were used to create novelty pictures and postcards for amusement. However, this technique was soon used in a fraudulent manner in order to create fake images of deceased relatives or as proof that the spirit world existed. The spirit world had indeed become a rich source of income for those who were happy to prey on the desperate and vulnerable. Partly in response to this the British Society for Psychical Research was founded in 1882 to study the use of apparitions, haunted houses, mediumship, mesmerism, Reichenbach phenomena (also known as Odic Force, an hypothetical vital life-giving energy), séances and thought-transference. The Society's intention was to provide a scientific basis for analyzing these strange phenomena and also to expose fraudulent mediums and tricks.

One of the Society's most famous members was **Arthur Conan Doyle,** the creator of the highly logical Sherlock Holmes. Despite the success of his **detective fiction,** Doyle was most proud of his work in spiritualism; he frequently lectured on the topic and wrote many books on the subject. One of his novels, *The Parasite* (1894), features a woman with psychic powers who uses them to play tricks on a scientist when he rejects her advances. Doyle was not the only author to find inspiration in the occult; for example, Henry James's *Turn of the Screw* (1898) and Elizabeth Gaskell's *The Old Nurse's Story* (1852) both draw on aspects of the supernatural. One of the most popular collections of supernatural tales was **Catherine Crowe**'s *The Night Side of Nature* (1848). These hugely popular ghost stories and anecdotes of weird phenomena are mediated with Crowe's own voice framing and directing the narrative and which presents them as truth. Crowe's work is still in print today, which perhaps reveals the undying appeal of the afterlife.—
JOANNE ELLA PARSONS

Oliphant, Margaret Oliphant Wilson (1828–1897). Scottish writer. In addition to publishing nearly 100 novels, Oliphant was the author of essays, reviews, biographies, literary criticism, and histories. Of the 11,560 authors indexed in the *Wellesley Index to*

Victorian Periodicals, only eleven women have more than fifty entries attributed to them; with 252 entries, Oliphant by far surpasses all other women contributors to Victorian periodicals (Scriven 2007: p. 34). Following the death of her husband Francis in 1859, Oliphant supported her children and extended family with her earnings as a writer. She began her career as a novelist with the 1849 publication of *Passages in the Life of Mrs. Margaret Maitland*. Her most popular novels during her lifetime were those in the "Chronicles of Carlingford" series, published between 1861 and 1876: *The Doctor's Family and Other Stories*, *Salem Chapel*, *The Perpetual Curate*, *Miss Marjoribanks*, and *Phoebe Junior*. Most recent scholarship on Oliphant examines the Chronicles of Carlingford or later novels such as *Hester* (1883) and *Kirsteen* (1890). Many of Oliphant's novels were **serial**ized in periodicals such as *Blackwood's*, *Cornhill*, and *Macmillan's*. Oliphant also served for decades as, in her words, a "general utility woman" for *Blackwood's*, contributing regular essays and reviews, as well as taking on larger projects (translations, biographies, histories) suggested by editors John and William Blackwood. Her regular book review columns in *Blackwood's*—from "Our Library Table," in the 1850s, to "The Looker-On," in the 1890s—allowed her to develop an influential critical voice.

Oliphant worked primarily within the genre of realist fiction, and many of her best-known works are domestic novels, but she also wrote historical novels and supernatural tales, including stories such as "The Open Door" and (1882), "The Library Window" (1896). Scholars have focused on Oliphant's representation of women and her role as a woman writer; her biography and her sheer productivity as a writer also feature significantly in contemporary scholarship. Despite her long career, varied oeuvre, and prominence as critic, however, Oliphant has remained at the margins of the literary canon, in part because her prolific output is seen as a sign of mediocre artistry, a perception to which Oliphant herself sometimes contributed. Another reason for her marginal position in the canon is her perceived conservatism and antifeminism. While Oliphant's views on the "condition of women" have been intensely debated by scholars, Elisabeth Jay perhaps puts it best when she concludes that Oliphant's "anti-feminist conclusions [in her essays and fiction] were predicated on a thoroughly feminist analysis" (1995: p. 292). Much work remains to be done on Oliphant's lesser-known novels and stories, as well as her innovations in form and genre—more specifically, how she reworks generic and formal conventions in ways that posit social and cultural criticism at odds with the conservative conclusions of her novels. Oliphant's prominent role as a critic and reviewer and her popularity in her own day—**Mudie's Circulating Library** still listed 89 of her titles in its 1898 catalogue—also warrant more careful consideration than they have received to date.
—Ann-Marie L. Dunbar

See also WI

Olive (1850). Novel by **Dinah Mulock Craik**. *Olive* has often been considered a response to Charlotte Brontë's *Jane Eyre*. Both *Bildungsromans*, the two novels share interests in race, nationality, disability, and womanhood. Craik's novel, her second, chronicles the life of Olive Rothesay from birth. Suffering from a spinal deformity, Olive is neglected by her parents: Sybilla Hyde, a young English woman, and Angus Rothesay, her Scottish-Celtic father. After the death of her father, Olive is thrust into the role of her mother's caretaker. Soon thereafter she becomes the family's breadwinner upon learning that her father was heavily indebted. Economic necessity emboldens Olive to pursue her passion of becoming an artist. She ultimately wins the love of widowed father and preacher Harold Gwynne, whose faith, once lost, is restored by Olive's unfaltering devoutness. Although the novel features a traditional marriage plot, Olive's transformation into wife and mother is groundbreaking because it refuses the clichéd narrative that disability must produce tragedy and pity. Although relatively unknown today, the novel can be profitably read at the intersection of race and disability. Some may argue that Olive's physical disability symbolizes apprehension over miscegenation within England. But given the anti–Celtic sentiment of the time, Craik's presentation of Olive as tremendously kind and generous affirms the potential for Britain to become a united kingdom. Instead, any anxieties about racial otherness are displaced onto Olive's half-sister. The illegitimate daughter of Olive's Scottish father and a West Indies woman, Christal Manners is characterized as violent, passionate, ill-tempered, and selfish. Olive first learns of Christal's existence when, after the death of both parents, she comes across a letter of her father's. For her part, Christal is unaware of her illegitimacy. Upon discovering it, she attempts to kill Olive before fleeing the country. Ultimately Christal returns to live near Olive in a nunnery, redeemed by her half-sister's love and forgiveness.—AUDREY L. MORRISON

Orphans. In response to the proliferation of abandoned children dominating the social landscape in Victorian Britain, the euphemistic and literal figure of the orphan, or foundling, or waif, dominated the popular fiction of the period. Overwhelming population growth, coupled with high mortality rates, meant that nineteenth-century Britain was a young society, with those under fourteen constituting from between a third to forty percent of the population throughout the period (Hopkins 1994: p. 161). Within those statistics, children bereaved of one or both parents, and neglected or abandoned children figured significantly (Peters 2000: p. 7). Luckier orphans were cared for by extended family members, while others were fostered or adopted to strangers for a fee. Many of the orphaned poor suffered in often brutal institutions such as "orphan asylums," foundling hospitals and workhouses, or scraped a living through begging, scavenging, petty crime or prostitution in the streets.

The deprivation experienced by the vast numbers of uncared for street children, was often romanticized, as in the series of emotive paintings by Augustus Mulready (1844–1903), yet the fiction of the era also represented the differing lived experiences of the orphan. From **Juliana Horatia Ewing**'s *Six to Sixteen* (1872) to Thomas Hardy's *Jude the Obscure* (1895), orphans across varied works were depicted in the care of extended family members. Like some real children, Estella, of **Charles Dickens**'s *Great Expectations* (1861), and Eppie in George Eliot's *Silas Marner* (1861), were adopted by strangers—some of whom, as in the latter novel, were kindly and protective, while others, as in the former, were manipulative and selfish. Fictional representations of the orphan offered a means by which criticisms of social injustice in general, and **child abuse** in particular, could be made by authors with a social mission. Although **short stories** such as Camilla Toulmin's "The Orphan Milliners—A Story of the West End" (1844) and Frank T. Bullen's "The Orphans" (1899) littered periodicals, it was through the form of the novel, according to Nina Auerbach, that the orphan figure was historically raised (p. 398). Orphan characters feature notably across the novels of major writers such as William Makepeace Thackeray, Anthony Trollope, and Elizabeth Gaskell, with a proliferation of moralizing waif fictions appearing mid-century, such as Hesba Stretton's *Jessica's First Prayer* (1867), Georgina Castle Smith's (pseud. Brenda) *Froggy's Little Brother* (1875), Mrs. Walton's *A Peep Behind* *the Scenes* by (1877), and Mrs. Edmund Juxon Whittaker's *Rag and Tag: Or a Plea for the Waifs and Strays of Old England* (1878).

Perhaps nowhere, however, is the orphan's presence more ubiquitous and varied than in Dickens's best-selling works: figures such as Oliver, the pitiable "parish boy" protagonist of *Oliver Twist* (1837–39), Little Nell, the angelic heroine of *The Old Curiosity Shop* (1841), and Jo, the barely human crossing-sweeper of *Bleak House* (1853)—a novel notable for its cast of orphan characters—allowed Dickens to express some of his most scathing social criticisms, as in the following direct appeal to the reader in response to Jo's preventable death: "Dead, your Majesty. Dead, my lords and gentlemen.... Dead, men and women, born with heavenly compassion in your hearts. And dying thus around us every day" (1868: p. 734). It is Estella's beauty in *Great Expectations* that makes her a desirable product for adoption, for, as social journalist James Greenwood noted in *The Seven Curses of London,* the wealthy "have grown so accustomed to associate cherubs with chubbiness, and chubbiness with high respectability and rich gravies, that they would ... scarcely be seen conversing with an angel of bony and vulgar type" (1869: p. 31). Such disparity is addressed by Dickens in *Our Mutual Friend* (1864–5), when Mrs. Boffin, unable to acquire the beautiful infant she and her husband desired for adoption, resolves to take "Sloppy," a strange creature of unknown parentage from the poorhouse, and declares, "'let it not be a pet and a plaything for me, but a creature to be helped for its own sake'" (1864: p. 186).

As well as a means of inciting reform, as a figure which stood outside the confines of everyday society, the orphan also allowed for different narrative and character development possibilities to be explored. Seemingly influenced by depictions of destitute children penned by Thackeray and Dickens, Greenwood had earlier attempted to give voice to the orphan through the medium of fiction in his work *The True History of a Little Ragamuffin* (1866), which, as with the orphan protagonists of Dickens's *David Copperfield* (1850) and *Great Expectations,* combined the narrative function of social critique with that of the *Bildungsroman* to pursue the transition of the vulnerable, marginal child character to accepted, successful middle-class citizen. The ambiguous closure that characterizes both Greenwood's novel and Dickens's latter novel—in which the behavioral growth of the protagonists and their happiness is in question—is reflected in the narratorial journeys of many such orphans in key works from the period. In Charlotte Brontë's *Jane Eyre* (1847), the eponymous first-person narrator relays the prejudices she faced in her **childhood** as an outsider in a familial household, and among mistreated orphans in an institution later on, finding happiness and acceptance in adulthood only in another form of seclusion. For Heathcliff of Emily Brontë's *Wuthering Heights* (1847), marginalized by his unseemly heritage in childhood, social standing and financial independence in adulthood never seem to rid him of such a taint.

Less sympathetic orphan characters throw into relief some of the darker cultural work carried out by the representation of the orphan. Auerbach states that the orphan "stands supreme and a little monstrous, the great artificer, the self-made man," (1975: p. 403), identifying orphans as a peripheral and indeterminate "social penumbra." Laura Peters reads the figure as an outsider scapegoat through which the validity of the middle-class nuclear family is re-asserted, whose function is both redemptive and threatening (2000: p. 27). Building on this, David Floyd interprets the orphan in its *fin-de-siècle* incarnation as an ambivalent figure whose disruptive potential is not contained by the kinds of satisfying narrative closure provided by many of the mid-century texts. Certainly, the orphan was a figure through which some of society's less palatable issues could be broached without bringing them too close to home. This is evident in the implication that the young girl Nancy in *Oliver Twist* is a prostitute, while sexual abuse has often been read as the root of the unease generated by the orphans Miles and Flora in Henry James's *The Turn of the Screw* (1898). Also problematic is the expendability of Kimball O'Hara as a pawn in the "great game" of espionage and empire-building in **Rudyard Kipling**'s *Kim* (1901) and the nihilism expressed via the orphan characters in Hardy's *Jude*.

Moralizing restrictions of piety, sensibility, and adherence to the oppressive adult world had dominated earlier representations of orphans in the **children's literature** of **Mary Martha Sherwood** and in specific works such as **Charles Kingsley**'s *The Water-Babies* (1863). Yet, by the *fin de siècle*, the autonomous child had come to be more liberally celebrated. In Kipling's ***The Jungle Book*** (1894), orphaned Mowgli is an outcast to both the animal and human worlds, but, as in works like **J. M. Barrie**'s *Peter Pan* (1904) and Frances Hodgson Burnett's *The Secret Garden* (1911), the naturalized, wild, and romanticized spaces of the Jungle, Neverland, and the secret garden also permit the abandoned or neglected child to rebel and flourish, free from the didacticism of earlier texts. Rather, the lessons to be learned from these stories about the ideals of childhood were directed at adults.—AILISE BULFIN, JEN BAKER

Ouida [*pseud.* of Marie Louise Ramé] (1839–1908). A prolific novelist, **short story** writer and essayist. Of Anglo-French parentage (she later affected a title, de la Ramée), Ouida's literary career was launched in **Bentley's Miscellany** and **William Harrison Ainsworth**'s ***New Monthly Magazine*** in the late 1850s. Her first novels were hybrid romances, combining aspects of the emerging sensation novel with the muscular fiction made popular by George A. Lawrence.

Her bestseller of this period was ***Under Two Flags***, first **serial**ized in the *British Army & Navy Gazette*, in which the life of languid aristocrat, Bertie Cecil, who has sought anonymity in the ranks of the French army in North Africa, is saved by the androgynous *vivandière*, Cigarette; the novel was immediately dramatized in Britain and America. The adoption of her genderless pseudonym led to the assumption that Ouida was in fact a gentleman (an identity cultivated by Chapman & Hall, who devised an aristocratic-looking monogram). Her sexual identity was eventually revealed by the critic Geraldine Jewsbury, and Ouida did briefly embrace celebrity by establishing a salon at the newly opened Langham Hotel where she gained a reputation for flouting convention before moving permanently to Italy in 1871. For many years she rented the picturesque Villa Scandicci outside Florence, and described her secluded life there in a rare feature, "Ouida at Home" for Edmund Yates's *World*, later reprinted in *Celebrities at Home* (1877). Careful to control her public image, Ouida only circulated two *cartes de visite* in her lifetime and resisted interviews, in particular any attempt to position her work in relation to fellow women writers.

The move to Italy prompted a decided change in the tone of her fiction and her subject matter. Ouida's writing had always been admired for its aesthetic qualities, and while the passions she described remained operatic in scale, the sympathetic verisimilitude of her accounts of Italian peasant life won the admiration of John Ruskin; moreover, the political focus of novels like *A Village Commune* (1881) led to an emergent secondary career as a social and political commentator. Ouida lived alone with her mother and never married. Her unrequited love for the Marchese della Stufa, a near-neighbor who was involved in a *ménage-à-trois* with a married English woman, led to public humiliation in Anglo-Italian circles, but Ouida revenged herself upon the pair in her brilliant *roman-à-clef*. *Friendship* (1878) is one of a series of novels in which Ouida satirized the moral code of cosmopolitan high society and thus deepened her reputation for morally outrageous fiction. The scandalous *Moths* (1880) was nearly dropped by **Mudie's Circulating Library**, but **Chatto & Windus** capitalized upon its notorious reputation by issuing the 5-shilling one-volume edition within a matter of months; the subsequent 2-shilling **yellow-back** edition features the seductive moment when the bare-footed heroine is surprised on the beach at Trouville by the fêted tenor, Corrèze. *Moths* tells the story of 16-year-old Vere Herbert who is coerced into marriage with fabulously wealthy *roué* Prince Zouroff (who was once her mother's lover), but loved from afar by Corrèze; the novel shows some ambivalence toward divorce law, but ends, significantly, with the divorced Vere's second marriage. The plot would inspire George Moore's anti-romance, *A Mummer's Wife* (1883), but numerous theatrical adaptations ensured *Moths*' sustained popularity. Furthermore, the extraordinary sales figures for this novel alone justified Chatto's efforts to poach Ouida from her former publishers, Chapman & Hall. Ouida's popularity was such that Chatto bought up her entire backlist from Chapman in the mid–1870s and thereafter became her sole publishers for the next decade, bringing out her work in a uniform 5-shilling edition in red cloth and gilt lettering.

By the mid–1880s, concern that Ouida's vogue was beginning to wane led to one last visit to London (December 1886 to May 1887) where she cultivated relationships with new editors and publishers, including the newspaper syndicator W. F. Tillotson, who circulated her new fiction to an ever wider demographic. In this sense, Ouida showed herself willing to adapt to new publishing practices, but she failed to protect her own interests: she continued to sell her copyrights for one-off payments and refused representation by the best known literary agent, A. P. Watt. Although she shared key concerns of the **New Woman** movement, including her sustained critique of matrimonial law and her espousal of **animal** rights, the ambivalence (or contrariness) of Ouida's sexual politics has affected the pace of her critical rehabilitation. Even conservative commentators regarded her essays "Female Suffrage" (1886) and "The New Woman" (1894)—the latter written as a rejoinder to **Sarah Grand**'s article, "The New Aspect of the Woman Question"—as eccentric and out-of-step with current social developments. Ouida was awarded £300 from the Royal Literary Fund in 1906, and reluctantly accepted a Civil List pension a year later; Macmillan & Co made generous advances on her last (unfinished) novel, but her final years were marred by increasing **poverty** and evictions from rented property while Chatto profited from the six-penny paperback edition of her novels. Ouida died from pneumonia at Viareggio on 25 January 1908 and is buried in the Anglo-American cemetery at Bagni di Lucca.—Jane Jordan

See also **Tillotson's Fiction Bureau**

Out of Work (1888). Novel by **Margaret Harkness**. Topical to the point of prescience, Harkness's second novel described the competition for casual labor at London's docks that contributed to the Dockworkers' Strike of 1889. *Out of Work* appeared with Swan **Sonnenschein** & Co., a popular publisher with prominent **socialists** including Friedrich Engels and Eleanor Marx. Vizetelly, who published Harkness's first novel *A City Girl*, was prosecuted in 1888 for publishing translations of Zola; this may be the reason Harkness changed her publisher.

The story charts the decline of young provincial carpenter Jos Coney under the strain of long-term unemployment and **alcoholism** after coming to London to find work. The narrative's urgency and relevance are highlighted by references to contemporary events including Victoria's Golden Jubilee and the "Bloody Sunday" riots of 13 November 1887. The riots followed a march to Trafalgar Square to protest against unemployment, and many of Harkness's activist contacts from the Fabian Society and the Social Democratic Federation were personally involved.

In *Out of Work*, Harkness responds to Engels's criticism of *A City Girl* as "not quite realistic enough." Rather than represent the working class as "a passive mass, unable to help itself," Engels affirms that realism should portray their "rebellious reaction ... against the oppressive medium which surrounds them" (1973: pp. 114–5). For Harkness, however, realism was not always realistic: *Out of Work* demonstrates that social oppression often forestalls radical energy, and concludes with Jos's supplication, "Help me, O God, for I cannot help myself!" (p. 278). Although *Out of Work* shares realism's commitment to verisimilitude, it is equally influenced by naturalism in representing how social environment constrains the characters.

While Harkness's friend Eleanor Marx positioned nineteenth-century feminism within a socialist framework in "The Woman Question" (1888), women are deliberately on the periphery of *Out of Work*, reliant on men to succeed in the "competitive system" (Law 1888: p. 59). The novel is critical of organized religion, and particularly of Methodists who, it suggests, care only that "their own souls are safe" (p. 5). *Out of Work* was reissued in 1990 in the Merlin Press Radical Fiction series.—Lisa C. Robertson, Flore Janssen

See also ODNB

Parasitology. The discipline of parasitology is traceable to multiple points of origin. Humans have been aware of parasites and parasitic **disease** since ancient times; references to diseases clearly caused by parasites appear in Ancient **Egypt**ian, **India**n, Greek, Roman, Chinese, and Arabic texts and even, some scholars argue, in the Bible. However, parasitology underwent radical development in the nineteenth century.

The name *parasite*, from the Greek *parasitos* (beside the grain), was originally given to temple assistants, who separated grain for religious ceremonies in exchange for a meal (OED). The term was later broadened to refer to those who sought free access to the table. It was employed by Middle Comedy poets and fused with the *kolax* (a hungry opportunist) to codify obsequious, sycophantic behavior; the character that resulted from this fusion was used to criticize unequal patronage relationships. The parasite thus became a figure associated with material, particularly gastronomic, exploitation. In the seventeenth century, protobotanists used the term to refer to plants. Thomas Browne's *Pseudodoxia Epidemic* asserts that "mistletoe ... living upon the stock of others are termed parasitical plants" (p. 148). However, the term fully made the transition from the cultural to the biological sphere in the nineteenth century. The terminology of *parasite* and *host* was thus from its beginnings underscored by social power dynamics, and for the public, retained a dual significance in the popular imagination.

The figure of the parasitic aristocrat or capitalist was common in mid-century novels, raising ethical concerns about social functioning. These depictions were also often accompanied by a sense of biological atavism borrowed from natural history's discussions of adaptation and degeneration. In **Charles Dickens**'s *Bleak House* (1853), for example, the parasitical capitalist Smallweed, the dandyish Turveydrop, the **vampire**-like Vholes, and the childlike Skimpole represent differing versions of societal parasites. George Eliot in *The Mill on the Floss* (1860) and *Middlemarch* (1871–2) uses the parasite to advocate social responsibility and considers parasitism in relation to co-adaptation, a framework borrowed from Charles Darwin's *On the Origin of Species* (1859) in which he consciously includes parasites within his descriptions of the "beautiful co-adaptations" that exist "everywhere and in every part of the organic world" (p. 61).

Novelists, particularly in the late century and in developing genres like **science fiction**, took to challenging Darwin's contention that "the war of nature is not incessant, that no fear is felt, that death is generally prompt, and that the vigorous, the healthy, and the happy survive and multiply" (1860/1859: p. 79). Indeed, in late century fiction, we see a hybridization of organic and social parasites to form a **Gothic** literary archetype that challenges domestic space, social hierarchies, and imperial politics. In novels like **Richard Marsh**'s *The Beetle* (1897), **Bram Stoker**'s *Dracula* (1897), and **Arthur Conan Doyle**'s *The Parasite* (1894), the antagonists transgress the boundaries of the domestic and enact somatic subjugations on upstanding members of British society. Their exploitation in each case is described as an intangible psychic power that has physical consequences—symbolically embodying both the psychological impact of sycophants and the bodily impact of organic parasitism. Notably these three works, among others, use **mesmerism** and the **occult** to amplify the parasite's societal threat. Their victims suffer from physical illness following their encounters. These narratives highlight the power of the parasite-host relationship as a framework for exploring concepts of self, other, nationhood and personhood. Such frameworks were particularly germane for burgeoning genres such as science fiction, **invasion literature,** and **detective fiction**. Internal parasites were often thought symptomatic of immorality or the result of divine disfavor—a popular fallacy that helminthologist T. Spencer Cobbold notes prevailed at least until the 1880s (1879: p. 2). This added a moral narrative to depictions of parasitism used in fiction to explore the politics of social contagion. In the nineteenth century, the lexis of blame and of disease supplemented the parasite's original function as a model for critiquing unequal patronage relationships, updating it to address the anxieties that characterized the *fin de siècle*.

As research into biologically parasitic behaviors became more prominent, the model of the parasite-host relationship entered professional and popular discourse. This model was particularly pertinent to early psychoanalytic and evolutionary theorists, who saw frameworks for thinking about somatic autonomy in the realities of organic competition. Anne-Julia Zweirlein argues that the biological parasite was increasingly psychologized at the turn of the century, with the figure in literature "transferred onto an interiorized Pre-Freudian psychological … plane, the parasite symbolizing the protagonists' own deepest anxieties" (2005: p. 169). This transferal can be read in George MacDonald's *Lilith, A Romance* (1895). The parasite-host relationship, biogenetic theory, and MacDonald's theological treatise together shed light on this unusual novel. Lilith's selfishness is represented as physical parasitism; the motif reoccurs throughout as a point of entry for discussions of the boundaries of selfhood. The abounding biogenetic anxieties in this novel are also present in works like **Robert Louis Stevenson**'s *Strange Case of Dr. Jekyll and Mr. Hyde* and **Oscar Wilde**'s *The Picture of Dorian Gray* (1890). Both Stevenson and Wilde explore the dual nature of psychic and somatic identity. For Stevenson, the separation of the human being into constituent parts reveals a largely moral, civilized self and an amoral, primitive one. The relationship between the two is presented as parasitic;

the anxieties about biological atavism common to parasitological discourses are illustrated by Hyde, who bears something "troglodytic" in his appearance. Wilde's exploration is more nuanced but retains the essential dynamic of one self-feeding off another. Such psychic splittings challenged accepted understandings of selfhood at the end of the century. Other stories with interesting uses of the parasite-host relationship include **H. G. Wells**'s *The Time Machine* and *The War of the Worlds*, which invoke the parasitic in relation to technological advancement and biological evolution.

Following the formal recognition of bacteriology in the 1870s, and some two centuries after Dutch microscopist Antonie van Leeuwenhoek discovered microorganisms, parasitology was finally institutionalized in the Liverpool (1898) and London (1899) schools of tropical **medicine**. These were the first institutions in the world dedicated to study and research in tropical and parasitic diseases. The recognition of morphological differences between parasites of the same species at different stages of development (called the alternation of generations), and the rejection of spontaneous generation as an explanation for parasitic infestation, enabled global parasitology research to flourish. Frank Cox (2002) provides a good overview of this history. So-called worm diseases like ascariasis, ankylostomiasis, and elephantiasis had long been associated with the tropics; however, as the century progressed several high-profile tropical diseases like malaria and African sleeping sickness were also connected with parasites. In 1877 Sir Patrick Manson discovered that the mosquito was the intermediate host for the parasite that causes lymphatic filariasis (elephantiasis). This bolstered support for the mosquito-malaria theory and paved the way for Sir Ronald Ross of Britain and Giovanni Battista Grassi of Italy to discover in 1898 that the *Anopheles* mosquito transmits malaria between hosts. The discovery of insect vectors and the resultant modification of understandings of colonial environments provided the popular imagination with new ways in which to explore the Other and to interrogate imperial politics.

At the *fin de siècle*, the **vampire** was being reimagined in increasingly scientific ways. Thus it became a prime motif for exploring disease transmission. Vampire stories like **Joseph Sheridan Le Fanu**'s *Carmilla*, Stoker's *Dracula*, and **Mary Elizabeth Braddon**'s "Good Lady Ducayne" (1896) formed discursive relationships with research in parasitology by portraying their antagonists as associated with fever diseases. While Braddon specifically pairs the vampire and the mosquito—"She had suffered rather severely from the mosquitoes before Christmas" and "'he has caught you on the top of a vein. What a vampire!'" (2004/1896: p. 15)—Stoker and Le Fanu blur the boundaries of the supernatural and the medical by attributing fever symptoms to the vampire's victims. The slaying of an increasingly medicalized vampire by scientifically literate protagonists (as in *Dracula*) and the entanglement of the medical profession in the preponderance of the vampire (as in "Good Lady Ducayne") demonstrate the engagements of literature with developing models of disease transmission and have perhaps more to say about the ethics of the doctor-patient relationship. Stephen Arata's (1996) "reverse colonization" and Laura Otis's (1999) membrane model have much to offer literary criticism on the figure of the parasite. Parasitic and tropical diseases functioned in varying ways in literary texts, often framing the landscape as a pathological space, catalyzing ethical questions, or interrogating the politics of imperial rule. Much fiction retained medically outdated notions of parasitic etiology for dramatic effect: even after parasitologists had highlighted the nuanced relationship between parasites, intermediate hosts, and vectors in tropical colonies, authors continued to invoke the miasmatism of early nineteenth-century medical discourse. The parasitic relationship provided writers with a framework for exploring social, domestic, and national concerns, and especially questions of gender and race. Parasitologists also engaged with the literary imagination, using literary and historical myths of nationhood, such as King Arthur and his knights, to invest their profession with cultural authority (Taylor-Brown pp. 62–79). These efforts fed back into genres like detective and adventure **romance fiction**, contributing to the archetype of the detective-scientist as a figure of imperial and empirical authority. Further research might be directed at the significant impact of agricultural and veterinary parasitology on the literary imagination.—EMILIE TAYLOR-BROWN

Parkwater (1857). Novel by **Mrs. Henry [Ellen] Wood**. First published anonymously (April–September 1857) in **William Harrison Ainsworth**'s *New Monthly Magazine*. The sensational plot of *Parkwater* depicts a socially ambitious and deceptive working-class heroine, and culminates in the murder of her illegitimate child. A revised and extended version was first **serial**ized (January–September 1875) in the *Argosy* monthly magazine (edited by Wood 1867–1887). Critical work on *Parkwater* reflects recent trends in periodical studies: Marie Riley identifies the serial as "[Wood's] contribution to the debate about the impact of mass literacy" (p. 170), whereas Janice M. Allan focuses on anxieties about deceptive femininity, and she contextualizes the *New Monthly* version within "a new commodity culture, as well as the 1857 murder trial of Madeline Smith" (p. 8). Scope exists for further work on this understudied text, and the availability of nineteenth-century digital archives have opened up possibilities of detailed research within original publishing context(s).—ANNE-LOUISE RUSSELL

Paul Ferroll (1855). Novel by Caroline Clive (1801–72). Initially published as *Paul Ferroll: A Tale* "By the Author of *IX Poems by V*," the crime novel by poet and author Clive was the British co-bestseller of 1855 (Flower 1934: p. 11). It is arguably the first **sensation** novel (Gavin 2008: vii), and it significantly extended possibilities for crime fiction and women's writing. On publication and for the rest of the nineteenth century it was regarded as both successful and notorious. Elizabeth Gaskell, for instance, described it as a work "of fiction of remarkable merit" which had "made a great sensation" in Britain. "People ... condemn the book as 'the work of a she-devil,'" she observed, "but buy it, and read it, and in six weeks a second edition had to be issued" (Gaskell 1855: 145). Clive's tale focuses on Paul Ferroll, a widely admired but enigmatic landed gentleman, who has secretly stabbed his first wife to death in her sleep in order to marry his true love, Elinor, and who publicly shoots dead a worker he has previously helped. The central tension of the plot is over how, when, and to what result Ferroll's culpability for the murder of his wife will be revealed. A respected magistrate and esteemed author, Ferroll is highly regarded by his neighbors and peers, who rely on his judgment and action in times of danger and seek his acquaintance—something he rarely grants because of his peculiar code of honor. Equally, he is reclusive, desires sensation, and indulges in high-risk behavior which is often linked to his obsessive love for and control over Elinor. When Elinor is temporarily away, for example, he gallops his horse furiously in the middle of the night, and strips off to bathe under a waterfall. During a cholera epidemic, he visits areas where others fear to go but takes perverse pleasure in observing extreme scenes of distress and dying. Ferroll is a precursor of the multi-talented, yet psychopathic and self-absorbed killer more common in modern crime fiction.

Contemporary reviewers admired the novel's originality and power but disapproved of its subject matter, all the more so when its female authorship was discovered. They found most chilling the novel's very unVictorian amorality. Despite being twice tried and convicted of murder, Ferroll ultimately escapes both legal and poetic justice and expresses no guilt or remorse for his crimes. Probably to placate critics, Clive added to the third edition a concluding chapter in which her protagonist dies, yet there is still no real moral condemnation of Ferroll. Instead, the additional chapter continues the narrative's almost documentary-like presentation of Ferroll, which ensures that judgment on his actions is not made by the text but is reserved solely to readers.—ADRIENNE E. GAVIN

Pearson's Magazine (1896–1939). English periodical. An **illustrated** magazine that targeted middle- and lower-class readership, it was published and initially edited by C. A. Pearson. A rival to the *Strand Magazine*, it was as widely read and successful as the former, and published political discussions, **serialized** literature (including poems, novels, **short stories**, popular **science fiction**, supernatural, and horror), articles with a social bent, investigative articles, and other general interest articles. Contributors included **Arthur Conan Doyle**, Jack London, **H. G. Wells**, **Rudyard Kipling**, and G. B. Shaw. It began publishing a U.S. edition in 1899 with American and British contributors. The U.S. edition was bought by J. J. Little in 1903, diverged markedly in its content from the original, and was discontinued in 1925. The U. K. magazine published its last issue in 1939. —SUMAN SIGROHA

See also Cox and Mowatt 2014, Law 2000, Sutherland 1989

Penny Bloods. See **Penny Dreadful**.

Penny Dreadful. This term generally indicates cheap **serial**ized fiction for the working class produced between the 1830s and the end of the nineteenth century. Scholars, however, have come to accept John Springhall's 1994 subdivision of this literature into penny bloods (1830–1860) and penny dreadfuls (1860–onwards). The first label marks the early phase of the genre, featuring gory, violent plots intended for a miscellaneous audience; the second label marks the genre's shift toward adventurous plots to appeal to a specifically juvenile, chiefly male public.

Stemming from such genres as the **Gothic** and **melodrama** (see James 1963: pp. 72–96, and Crone 2012: pp. 73–8), penny dreadfuls were a product of the new mass-publication market resulting from the increase in lower-class literacy combined with unprecedented technological advancements in paper production and printing techniques. Publishers such as **Edward Lloyd** and G. W. M. Reynolds started the mass-production of literature targeting specifically the new pool of semi-literate working-class readers. The result was a singularly unbecoming reading object, consisting of eight/sixteen poor-quality, densely printed pages, with a crude, sensational woodcut **illustration** on the first page. The weekly issues were sold at one penny each, hence the name. The literary quality of the content was also rather modest: the tales of adventure and murder, larger-than-life heroes, rogues, and damsels in distress consisted of repetitive plots and flat characters written in a decidedly unrefined style. The list of most famous works includes: ***Varney the Vampyre; or: The Feast of Blood***; ***The String of Pearls*** (or, *Sweeney Todd*); ***Ada the Betrayed***; and ***The Mysteries of London***.

In his 2008 edition of *Varney the Vampyre*, Curtis Herr suggests that the poor quality of the writing could be ascribed to the necessity of meeting the reading abilities of a semi-literate public or, perhaps, to the limited literacy skills of the authors (2008: p. 12). These underpaid writers produced their stories mostly anonymously and at high speed, in compliance with the relentless pace of the penny-dreadful market, which would cut unsuccessful series at any point and stretch successful ones indefinitely. Plagiarism was common practice, the most famous example being probably the ruthless piracy of Dickens at the hands of Thomas Peckett Prest, one of the most famous penny blood authors. At an international level, American series were brazenly plagiarized, and French series would be translated into English without acknowledgments (see James 1963: pp. 129–45).

Notwithstanding their aesthetic shortcomings and dubious reputation, penny dreadfuls were an immediate and tremendous success among their intended audience, and they represent a milestone in English reading history: they were the first fiction produced for the lower-class public devoted specifically to leisure reading and not to spiritual or personal improvement. Middle-class commentators strongly opposed the genre throughout the century, particularly when it started targeting a juvenile audience. Their crusade never effectively curtailed penny dreadful production, nor did it impair the genre's popularity among readers; it did, however, build a long-lasting prejudice that scholars have started to overcome only relatively recently.

Even when approached with an unbiased mind, penny dreadfuls represent challenging research objects. Anonymity constitutes one of the chief problematic points, hampering processes of authorship attribution and, therefore, corpus reconstruction. Arbitrary attributions made in such works as Montague Summers's *Gothic Bibliography* (1940) further complicate matters. E. F. Bleiler and, more recently, H. R. Smith used stylistic analysis to attempt to rectify such misattributions, although scholars are always cautious about making any conclusive statements about authorship. So far, the two authors on which researchers were able to make the most extensive work of biographical and corpus reconstruction are Thomas Peckett Prest and **James Malcolm Rymer**, although more work needs to be done on these two extremely prolific writers. Scarcity of original material constitutes another problem: penny bloods and dreadfuls were not made to last, and penny bloods especially mostly survive only in volume form. Finally, the failure of early attempts to apply literary analysis methods intended for novels to the bulky, inconsistent penny dreadful narratives contributed to excluding the genre from scholarly attention for a long time. Researchers are exploring possible alternative methods. The history- and culture-based approaches are proving themselves fruitful tools for analysis, as they rely less on plot construction and consistency than on a reading that considers aspects of the narratives within the genre's historical and political context.

The largest collection of penny dreadfuls is the Barry Ono Collection, which is hold by the British Library and is catalogued in E. James and H.R. Smith's *Penny Dreadfuls and Boy's Adventures* (1998). For an extensive catalogue of penny bloods and penny dreadfuls, publishers, authors, and journals, inclusive of current storage locations, see M. Léger-St. Jean, Price One Penny—Cheap Literature, 1837–1860, at http://www.priceonepenny.info/index.php.—Anna Gasperini

Penny Fiction Periodicals. Penny fiction periodicals were the most widely disseminated form of popular fiction in the nineteenth century. They were usually weekly and illustrated (with some notable exceptions). The format originates in the 2d illustrated miscellanies of the 1820s such as Limbird's *Mirror of Literature* (1822–47): a 16-page octavo in double columns, with a large woodcut under a blackletter title (or subtitle) on the front page, with smaller **illustrations** scattered on other pages. This format was taken up by the secular *Penny Magazine* (1832–1846; begun by the Society for the Diffusion of Useful Knowledge) and by the religious *Saturday Magazine* (1832–1844; issued by the Society for the Promotion of Christian Knowledge). Though neither ran fiction, these two, together with the slightly more expensive (1½d) *Chambers's Edinburgh Journal* (1832–1956), are often cited as starting the cheap weekly, though there were earlier examples such as the satirical *Figaro in London* (1831–9). Quickly after them in the 1830s came the *Penny Novelist* (1832–34) which comprised reprinted fiction, the *Penny Satirist* (1837–46) and many others. What the *Saturday* and *Penny* magazines showed was that the "penny" in their titles was a site of ideological conflict. Controlling elites were unsure of the effects of cheap reading: the 1789 French Revolution had been blamed on it, and the accusation was raised again in the revolutions of 1832 and 1848; similar fears in Britain had led to the extension of the Taxes on Knowledge in the early nineteenth century. But the *Penny Magazine* and its Whig backers suggested an alternative to restricting the market: flooding it with non-political "wholesome" reading. In the 1840s arose what Dalziel (1957) called the "purified penny press" whose best known members today are the **Family Herald**, the **London Journal**, and **Reynolds's Miscellany**, joined a decade later by **Cassell's Illustrated Family Paper**. There were, however numerous similar penny periodicals such as the *Family Friend* (1849–1921, usually issued monthly though in 1852 weekly) and the several issued by **Edward Lloyd**, including his **Penny Atlas** (1843–5), **Penny Weekly Miscellany**, and the *People's Periodical and Family Library* (1846, in which **The String of Pearls** first appeared). There was also continued competition with the 1½d journals such as *Eliza Cook's Journal* (1849–1854) and the 2d (most notably), *Household Words*. There were even attempts to undercut the penny by such as Hetherington's *Halfpenny Journal* (1840) and Jeremy Queen's *Farthing Journal* (1841), though at this stage these were not sustainable. With the exception of the unillustrated *Family Herald* and the first issues of *Cassell's* (whose model was the *Illustrated London News*) the penny fiction weeklies of the 1840s and 50s largely maintained the format pioneered in the 1820s, though the position and size of the internal illustrations stabilized to enable them to be used in shop windows as advertisements, and sixteen pages of triple columns became the norm. Besides single episode tales, poetry, articles on domestic, historical, biographical and scientific topics and various kinds of filler from *bon mots* and short jokes to interesting facts, quizzes and chess problems (all of which might be added by the printer to make up complete columns or issues), the main attraction of the penny fiction weekly comprised the three or four **serial**ized novels in each issue. The major authors of these tales were J. F. Smith, G. W. M. Reynolds and from the late 1850s, Pierce Egan the Younger. If in the 1840s translations from the French had been common—Dumas, Eugène Sue in particular—from the mid-1850s, women authors from north America were also widely serialized, notably E.D.E.N. Southworth, May Agnes Fleming and Fanny Fern. Although **Braddon** published in the penny fiction market in the 1860s, she was not a star compared to much loved British women authors like Charlotte Mary Brame (1836–84) and Mary Cecil Hay (1840/41–1886), who often wrote as Howard Markham and Mark Hardcastle. While the fiction metamorphosed quite dramatically from the 1840s to the 1860s, they were always sensational and morally **melodrama**tic. From the late 1840s the best were well-designed multi-plot dramas with episodes of a clear shape and direction, leading toward cliff hang-ers. In the 1840s and 50s they often had topical resonance, though this tended to blur in the woman-centered romances of later in the century which focused on women's emotional relationships to other women and to men. Often commented on at the time, as now, was a particular characteristic of the penny fiction weeklies: a page of responses to correspondents' queries on matters which ranged from legal questions to how to dye hair. From the early 1850s, the *London Journal* ran a marriage service in these pages: readers would advertise for the kind of person they wanted to meet and the *Journal* would put them in touch with replies, inviting echoes with the romantic plots of its stories. The repeal of the paper tax in 1861, allied to improved technologies of paper production and printing, dramatically changed the economic possibilities for the cheap magazine: not only did new penny fiction weeklies appear but those that existed were able to target more precise audiences. While the purified penny press had originally been aimed at the whole family via men (who controlled the purse strings), the 1860s saw it address women more directly. Penny weeklies like *Bow Bells* (1862–9), specifically targeting women, were launched: they offered music, fashion illustration and dress patterns in addition to fiction. Penny fiction weeklies addressing children also began to proliferate: *The English Girls' Journal* (1863–4) and the *Young Ladies of Great Britain* (1869–71) were among the first to target girls, though undoubtedly the most important is the Religious Tract Society's *Girl's Own Paper* (1880–1956), itself modeled on its sibling *Boy's Own Paper* (1879–1967). Both *GOP* and *BOP* continued the ideological battle begun in the 1830s by seeking to displace disreputable fiction while incorporating some of its elements (Brett's *Boys of England* (1866–99) was a particular target). The launch of *Tit-Bits* (1881–1984) by George Newnes heralded the last period of the Victorian penny press. While *Tit-Bits* is now best known for having started the fashion for short snappy articles, it serialized some fiction (e.g., by **Grant Allen**). This was typical of the New Journalism, whose influence can be perceived very clearly in women's penny weeklies published by the press barons, like Pearson's *Home Notes* (1894–1957) and Newnes's *Woman's Life* (1895–1934). These moved away from serial fiction in favor of features, **short stories** and advertising, although Harmsworth's *Home Chat* (1895–1958) did offer serials. By contrast, *Pearson's Weekly* (1890–1939) ran serials by Allen, **Rider Haggard**, Marcus Clarke, **H. G. Wells**, and many others.—Andrew King

See also Anderson 1991, James 1963, King 2004, Phegley 2010

Penny Sunday Times and People's Police Gazette (c. 1840–1849). English periodical. This popular title was started in April 1840 by the publisher and entrepreneur **Edward Lloyd**. Each four-page number was set out in newspaper format, but in fact offered a wide range of content: police reports, coverage of specific criminal cases, woodcut images, poems, songs, theater, general reference articles, and even puzzles. As many critics have noted, the incomplete and often ill-catalogued archive record for the periodical (and confusion between this and its spin-off publications *Lloyd's Companion to the Penny Sunday Times and People's Police Gazette* Sept. 1841–Jan. 1847; the *People's Police Gazette* Nov. 1841–Dec. 1841) makes precise information about the *Penny Sunday Times* difficult to find. However, its miscellaneous format and sensational tone brought undeniable popularity and boosted the Lloyd "brand," with estimates of its circulation going as high as 95,000 and at least 20,000 (James, Catling 1911).

A key critical debate has focused on the extent to which its content was fiction or non-fiction, given that Lloyd managed to avoid the Stamp Duty tax and kept his periodical at the low price of 1d. However, recent critics have tended to emphasize what they see as Lloyd's lack of interest in such distinctions and his technique of combining different types of popular culture (Lill). The woodcuts inside and on the cover set the tone: Lloyd instructed his illustrator, George Augustus Sala, "The eyes must be larger, and there must be more blood—much more blood!" Lill (2015) has suggested that the periodical was not only influenced by its immediate predecessor *Cleave's Weekly Police Gazette*, with its emphasis on sensational crime, but owed a lot to penny gaffe theater. "True" crime sat alongside **serial**ized fiction with titles such as *Angelina; or, The Mystery of St. Mark's Abbey*, *Ernnestine De Lacy; or, The Robber's Foundling* and *Gallant Tom; or, The Perils of a Sailor Ashore and Afloat*. Either way, Lloyd's increasingly characteristic blend of **melodrama**, journalism, and fiction proved as popular with its intended working-class readership as it caused alarm among middle-class commentators. Although a London-based publication, there is evidence to suggest that it reached provincial audiences in Ipswich and Preston (ODNB).—Mary L. Shannon

See also DNCJ, ODNB

Pharos the Egyptian (1899). **Gothic** novel by **Guy Boothby**. Originally **serial**ized in the ***Windsor Magazine*** (June–December 1898), the novel, as with other notable examples of *fin-de-siècle* Gothic fiction—such as **Bram Stoker**'s ***Dracula*** and **Richard Marsh**'s *The Beetle* (1897)—involves an undead being from the East enacting a reverse form of colonialism, and wreaking supernatural revenge upon Western imperial nations. The novel takes the form of a manuscript written in later life by the reclusive artist Cyril Forrester, and telling the story of Forrester's dealings with a mysterious Egyptian named Pharos. Forrester first encounters Pharos near Cleopatra's needle, where he observes the old man mocking a **suicide** who has jumped in the Thames. He encounters Pharos again at a fashionable party, where the Egyptian's ward, the violinist Valerie de Vocxqal, has been engaged to perform. When Pharos steals an Egyptian mummy, which Forrester's father took from the Valley of the Kings, Forrester tracks Pharos across Europe to Egypt. He discovers that the mummy is that of Ptahmes, Chief of the King's Magicians under Pharaoh Merenptah—the Pharaoh of the Biblical Exodus. More astounding still, Pharos and Ptahmes are one and the same person, Pharos having been resurrected in order to carry out a terrible revenge for the plague that killed the Pharaoh's first-born son. To this end, Pharos secretly infects Forrester with a new plague, which he unwittingly spreads across Europe, in his attempt to help Valerie escape Pharos's evil influence.—Dewi Evans

Physiognomy. A pseudo**science** popular in the nineteenth century that suggested there was a direct correspondence between a person's physical features and personality traits. The term *physiognomy* (sometimes shortened to "phiz") may also refer to an individual's face. The study of physiognomy dates back to the ancient civilizations of Greece, **Egypt**, China, and the Middle East. However, during the sixteenth and seventeenth centuries physiognomy's reputation suffered because it became associated with various forms of fortune-telling, including astrology, chiromancy, and metoposcopy. It was not until the late eighteenth century that physiognomy's reputation improved.

The Swiss pastor Johann Kaspar Lavater rehabilitated physiognomy for the modern era when he published his multivolume *Essays on Physiognomy* in German between 1774 and 1778. By 1810, fifty-five editions of the book, including twenty English editions "priced to suit every pocket," had been published (Cowling 1989: p. 19). John Graham observes that because the *Essays* was so widely summarized, reviewed, and pirated, "it is difficult to imagine how a literate person of the time could have failed to have some general knowledge of the man and his theories" (1961: p. 562).

Lavater presented physiognomy as a legitimate science. The *Essays* catalogs different types of facial features based on size, shape, and other physical characteristics. Lavater argues that because the human body is characterized by "harmony and homogenous beauty" (1853: p. 9) each physical feature expresses all of an individual's inner qualities while at the same time emphasizing a particular type of trait. For example, Lavater contends that while any feature can reveal a person's intelligence, the forehead and eyes communicate this information most effectively. He recommends that physiognomists focus on the "solid" (1853: p. 12) features of the face such as the forehead, eyes, nose, mouth, and chin and cautions readers that other aspects of appearance might mislead them. However, he also acknowledges that facial expressions and "figure, color, gait, voice, [and] even smell" (1853: p. 139) may reveal clues about a person's identity. Lavater also tried to legitimize physiognomy by reframing it as a Christian act of goodwill. He argues that because man is "a copy after a Divine original" (1853: p. 4), it is the physiognomist's Christian duty to find all that is divine, good, and virtuous in him. Lavater hoped that by doing so the physiognomist would foster a "greater love of and appreciation for self, fellow man, and God" (1853: pp. 7–8).

Physiognomy's cultural significance during the nineteenth century has attracted the notice of scholars from a variety of fields ranging from art, literature, and history to anthropology, science and psychology. Mary Cowling's *The Artist as Anthropologist* (1989), Lucy Hartley's *Physiognomy and the Meaning of Expression* (2001), and Sharrona Pearl's *About Faces* (2010) provide a strong foundation for those interested in studying the subject further. Scholars such as Graeme Tytler, Nicholas Dames, and Michael Hollington have examined physiognomy in the works of canonical authors including the Brontë sisters, George Eliot, and **Charles Dickens**. Far less work has been done on physiognomy in the works of popular fiction, but this promises to be an area of growing scholarly interest.
—Sarah L. Lennox

Political Violence. Violence and the threat of political violence haunted the Victorian imagination. Political riot was endemic in Britain in the later part of the nineteenth-century. A strong sense of national threat was generated by riots that occurred at the time of the 1866–67 reform bill debates. There were further political disturbances in 1886, when unemployed East End workers rampaged through the West End, and in crowd confrontations with the police and the army in Trafalgar Square in 1887. Contemporary fears about threats to the stability of the state were compounded by the presence of growing communities of émigré radicals and exiles seeking sanctuary in London in the aftermath of failed revolutions in Europe in 1848, or in exile from conservative regimes at home. Among them were some of the major figures of European radical and socialist reform movements, notably Karl Marx, Alexander Herzen, and Giussepe Mazzini. Militancy among Fenian and republican groups in Ireland also led to bombing campaigns against targets on the British mainland. In 1884–5 bombs planted at Westminster Hall, the Tower of London, and Victoria railway station by the Irish Republican Brotherhood fed anxieties about the potential threat to politicians and the public posed by Irish terrorism. By the end of the nineteenth-century many of these fears had cohered around **anarchism**. The detonation of a bomb in Greenwich Park in 1894, and an explosion on an underground train at Aldersgate in 1897 (sometimes attributed to Irish terrorists) persuaded the popular press that a dark anarchist conspiracy was at work in the heart of the capital. A distillation of existing images of the foreign émigré, and the militant or socialist radical, the anarchist in popular fiction often used the techniques and strategies of Irish terrorism in pursuit of the aim of undermining the state and fomenting riot and revolution at home. Increasingly the figure of the anarchist came to dominate the plots of much late-nineteenth-century **sensation fiction**. Not all writers were unsympathetic to the foreign refugees and exiles that made up the ranks of anarchists in popular fiction. Both **William Le Queux** and **G. A. Henty** wrote novels that were broadly receptive to the plight of Russian nihilists, tortured, hounded into exile by the Tsarist secret police, and driven to acts of extremism by a tyrannical government. William Le Queux traced the plight of one such family in his *Strange Tales of a Nihilist*, published in 1892; G. A. Henty in *Condemned as a Nihilist,* published in 1893, imagined the political journey of a nihilist militant seen through the eyes of a wrongly accused British youth. Most of the popular fiction that related to radical politics, however, accentuated the threat posed by reformers, and the malevolence of their intentions. The earliest depictions of radical reformers and socialists associated them with domestic collapse and revolution at home arising from defeat inflicted by foreign enemies. Often they worked in **collaboration** with such invaders. Here, this material had affinities with **invasion literature** and drew on images of instability abroad, especially in France. Bracebridge Hemyng's *The Commune in London or Thirty Years Hence*, published in 1871, imagined the collapse of Britain after an attempted French invasion, and the creation of a British Commune in the capital in which British radicals allied to Irish reformers attempted the creation of a workers' state on the model of the Paris Commune of 1871. Mobs and uncontrolled street protest unleashed by defeat and directed against politicians who had failed to invest in defense, fatally weakening the state and its ability to resist invasion by foreign powers, also featured in "Posterita," *The Siege of London*, published in 1884, and in Charles Gleig, *When All Men Starve*, published in 1898. Such fiction traded in images of a weak and decrepit state in which the forces of anarchy and disorder lay just beneath the surface and might be unleashed at any moment. Gleig's volume concludes with an image of the mob sacking and looting Buckingham Palace while demonstrators cavort amidst the flames. Invasion and terrorism were overtly aligned in Donald MacKay, *The Dynamite Ship*, published in 1894. A novel of Irish terrorism, the book imagined a Fenian attack on London by an advanced steam vessel outfitted with dynamite projectiles and used to hold the capital to ransom over Irish Home Rule. At the conclusion of the novel the capital is reduced to ruins and the government submits to the Fenians' demands for separatism in Ireland. The inventive uses made by anarchists of gelignite in the constructions of bombs and explosive devices meant that the anarchist became associated in the public mind with diabolical instruments of death and destruction. Such wonder weapons, "infernal engines" and a superior **technology** of destruction wielded by individuals with anarchist intent were staple elements in the arsenals of fictional militants seeking to overcome or extract concessions from the government and the state. Their uses of these weapons became the plot devices for a number of such novels. In **Arthur Griffiths**, *the Angel of the Revolution*, first published in 1894, a secretive fraternity of anarchists circle the globe in airships, using superior technology to subdue governments and eliminate war between nations, with the intent of ushering in a new era of peace and harmony in world affairs. In ***Hartmann the Anarchist***, published in 1893, an airship is again used to rain down destruction on London, destroying the Palace of Westminster, in order to further Hartmann's aim of world revolution. As such fiction developed, the aims of anarchists became more grandiose. In J. S. Fletcher's *The Three Days' Terror*, published in 1901, anarchists conspire, using advanced chemical compounds, to dissolve London into dust. Similarly in Linbach's *The Azrael of Anarchy*, published in 1894, Dunstan Gryme, a cultivated scientist, uses his skills to propagate an epidemic that causes panic and paves the way for revolution and invasion. Some of this fiction that speculated about futuristic scenarios of destruction has rightly become associated with the **science fiction** genre, rather than the political thriller. Most plots and assassinations in anarchist political fiction were incubated in lower-class drinking dens off Oxford Street and in the émigré ghetto of Soho, where foreign revolutionaries intrigued with Tsarist spies. This was the social geography of anarchism traced in H. Barton Baker's *Robert Miner: Anarchist*, published in 1902. A common thread in all anarchist fiction, however, was that of cosmopolitan individuals, strong, charismatic, intelligent and articulate, who use their talents to further their misguided ends. Anarchist leaders are often urbane, charming and utterly ruthless. Captain Shannon in Coulson Kernahan's novel of that name, published in 1896, is an amoral anarchist, whose flamboyant persona was probably modeled on that of **Oscar Wilde**. Despite his veneer of sophistication, he shows no hesitation in blowing up passengers in a railway train, and engineering assassinations. In many anarchist novels the action takes place not in the dingy meeting houses of plebeian anarchist cells, but rather in the parlors and sumptuous surroundings of the cosmopolitan elite. In Richard Henry Savage's *The Anarchist*, published in 1894, plotters seek to infiltrate a society family and claim the fortune of an heiress. The villainous nature of anarchists, their inventive use of weapons of mass destruction, and their implacable dedication to an obsessive political mission made them the perfect villains for late-nineteenth-century fiction. Their prevalence meant that they gained a significant place in mainstream fiction. Henry James's *The Princess Casamassima*, first published in 1886, draws on themes relating to the family legacy of the Paris Commune and its role in inspiring a youthful revolutionary, with tragic consequences. In mainstream fiction, anarchists were sometimes viewed as grotesques or as comic foils. In **Robert Louis Stevenson**'s collection of **short stories**, *The Dynamiter*, first published in 1885, a hapless anarchist, Zero, struggles to rid himself of his bomb before it detonates. Reception of these works and their readership are largely unresearched. In addition, there are affinities with invasion panic fiction that remain to be untangled in the scholarship relating to this area.—Antony Taylor

Poverty. Life was undoubtedly grim for the Victorian poor. The abject destitution experienced by those at the very bottom of the social ladder was represented time and again in the popular fiction of the period and accounts of poverty were eagerly consumed by readers. G. W. M. Reynolds's **The Mysteries of London** (1844–45), a cheap weekly **serial**, was particularly popular. This fiction sensationalized the miserable condition of the poor, shocking readers with the wretched degradation that existed within spitting distance of the affluent neighborhoods of the metropolis. Non-fiction writings during the period similarly fueled the public fascination with poverty; contemporary investigative journalism such as Henry Mayhew's *London Labour and the London Poor* (1851), Blanchard Jerrold and Gustave Doré's *London: A Pilgrimage* (1872), and **George R. Sims**'s *How the Poor Live* (1883) documented the overcrowded and insanitary living conditions of the poor.

Fiction was a powerful vehicle for the promotion of social and political ideologies surrounding poverty and its causes. In Harriet Martineau's series of short tales, *Poor Laws and Paupers Illustrated* (1833–34), she aimed to represent the principles behind nineteenth-century Poor Law reform. In an attempt to tackle pauperism, the 1834 New Poor Law overhauled the existing system of poor relief by seeking to make the workhouse the main form of help offered to the destitute. Prior to these changes, the poor had frequently been able to receive financial relief outside the workhouse. However, contemporary critics argued that this financial aid encouraged pauperism by rewarding improvidence, to the detriment of honest ratepayers; in Martineau's tale "The Hamlets," poverty is linked to idleness and the high poor rates, which fund outdoor relief, threaten to bankrupt the respectable residents of the community. The New Poor Law aimed to curtail outdoor relief and implement a disciplinary workhouse system, so that the poor would be compelled to alleviate their own poverty rather than relying upon the state. Martineau's propagandist fiction demonstrates the ideal working of this new system: at the end of "The Hamlets" the workhouse is empty and the poor are self-supporting.

By contrast to Martineau's fiction, **Charles Dickens**'s *Oliver Twist* (2008/1837–39) and Fanny Trollope's *Jessie Phillips* (1843) sought to illustrate the cruelties of the New Poor Law and the role of social circumstance in creating poverty. *Oliver Twist*, **serial**ized in ***Bentley's Miscellany***, occupies a particularly central position in the large body of anti–Poor Law literature that emerged in the 1830s and 40s. The text satirizes the state's approach to poverty and its treatment of the poor; in the novel, the board of guardians, responsible for overseeing the workhouse, decree that "all poor people should have the alternative (for they would compel nobody, not they,) of being starved by gradual process in the house, or by a quick one out of it" (Dickens 2008/1837–39: p. 10). In keeping with popular sentiment, the Poor Law is constructed here as a deliberate attempt to starve the poor to death. The horrible reality faced by the poor is manifest when Oliver, apprenticed to an undertaker, visits a slum to measure the body of a dead woman for burial. The conditions in this part of town are so horrific that the "very rats, which here and there lay putrefying in its rottenness, were hideous with famine" (2008: p. 38). Like the rats, the deceased woman has been left to starve to death in squalor. When her husband recounts that, "I begged for her in the streets: and they sent me to prison" (2008: p. 39), blame is firmly attributed to the inhumanity of a state that implicitly equates the poor with vermin. Indeed, many of the so-called crimes committed in the novel seem trivial when compared to the vindictive machinations of the law.

Poverty, in the world of *Oliver Twist*, is a crime; even the infants at the baby farm, where Oliver is placed prior to the workhouse, are deemed to be "culprits" and "juvenile offenders against the poor-laws" (2008: p. 4). In criminalizing the infants, the text draws attention to the absurdity of a state that holds children accountable for their economic status. Later, on his way to London, a hungry Oliver is frightened by notices threatening imprisonment to beggars. Then, in the metropolis, he narrowly escapes three months of hard labor after being wrongly accused of stealing a handkerchief. In a brief glimpse inside the police cells, the text introduces men sentenced to prison for crimes including playing the flute, begging in the streets, and selling saucepans without a license. The state, it seems, actively works to keep the poor impoverished by criminalizing the idle and the industrious alike. At the novel's close, the Artful Dodger, another child left at the mercy of society, is likely to be transported for pickpocketing. Repeatedly, the novel draws attention to draconian laws that punish the poor.

The novel had immense cultural resonance; throughout the century, discussions of the New Poor Law frequently referenced Oliver's sufferings and employed "Bumble," the name of the pompous beadle, as shorthand for inhumane officialdom. In fact, *Oliver Twist* remains intrinsically associated with the workhouse in the popular imagination today and is still mentioned by the media in discussions about welfare. However, *Oliver Twist* is just one of many works that sought to direct public attention to the condition of the poor. Elizabeth Gaskell, for instance, depicts the abject poverty experienced by the working classes in the industrial north in her novels *Mary Barton* (1848) and *North and South* (1854–55). By contrast, Thomas Hardy's *Tess of the d'Urbervilles* (1891) and *Jude the Obscure* (1895) explore the tragic consequences of poverty in the agricultural south. At the end of the century, novels by authors such as **Walter Besant**, **George Gissing**, and **Arthur Morrison** provided readers with detailed representations of poverty and wretchedness, and collectively formed a recognizable genre of slum fiction. In a nation that prided itself on progress, modernity, and scientific advance, Victorian fiction stripped away the façade to reveal the dark underside of a deeply unequal society.
—Laura Foster

The Prophet of Berkeley Square (1901). Novella by **Robert Smythe Hichens**. Acknowledged by Hichens in his autobiography to be a failure, *The Prophet of Berkeley Square* is a farce of middle-aged bachelor Hennessey Vivian's flirtation with **occultism** and prophecy. Referred to as the Prophet, Hennessey is a "man of thirty-eight, of excellent fortune, of fine connections, and of admirable disposition." He lives at No. 1000 Berkeley Square in London with his devoted butler, Mr. Ferdinand, a "bulky and veracious gentleman" and his widowed grandmother, Mrs. Merillia. The Prophet, **orphan**ed at infancy, was educated at Eton and Oxford and now socializes with the members of London's intellectual elite. Upon meeting with the dignified astronomer Sir Tiglath Butt, the Prophet becomes obsessed with studying the sky through his telescope. His study of the galaxy leads him to make two prophecies: first, about the weather, and second, that his grandmother will have an accident. His success with these two predictions leads him to conclude that he is, in fact, a prophet who can predict future events. The Prophet sets out to make the acquaintance of renowned prophet, Mr. Malkiel, who is known for his prediction almanacs. Hennessey tracks down Mr. Malkiel, and discovers that he lives in secrecy and goes by the name Mr. Sagittarius. At this same meeting, he also encounters an old family friend, Lady Enid, and learns that she is an occultist who pens a newspaper column under a pseudonym. Sagittarius, who does not believe that Hennessy is really a prophet, seeks to test him. These tests take a variety of turns that reveal both men to be phonies. After Hennessey's grandmother declares that Sagittarius is trying to murder her, Hennessy swears off prophesying for good. *The Prophet of Berkeley Square* evidences Hichens's ongoing interest in satirizing occultism but lacks the narrative power of *Flames* and may have been more effective as a **short story**.—Audrey L. Morrison

The Purple Cloud (1901). **Science fiction** novel by **M. P. Shiel**. Part of an emerging but little-known genre of late-nineteenth-century catastrophe fiction, *The Purple Cloud* is a landmark early science fiction novel. It envisions a massive volcanic eruption which produces a vast cloud of lethal hydrocyanic gas that gradually encircles the world wiping out all human life. The text follows the travails of a sole, and increasingly megalomaniacal, Arctic-explorer survivor as he travels the world burning down cities, before conveniently meeting a female survivor who convinces him of their duty to repopulate the earth. Regarded as Shiel's best work, it is memorable for its macabre excess, decadent prose style, and disturbing suggestion that human evolution has in fact been served by the mass extinction. Its reputation rests partly on H. P. Lovecraft's favorable evaluation in his seminal "Supernatural Horror in Literature" (1927: 1927): "The sensations of this lone survivor as he realizes his position, and roams through the corpse-littered and treasure-strewn cities of the world as their absolute master, are delivered with a skill and artistry falling little short of actual majesty" (n.p.). While Lovecraft was not convinced by the conventional "romantic" ending, other critics have seen it as evincing an idiosyncratic theology of "religious evolutionism" in which opposition between the text's dualist "Black and White Powers" guides human destiny (Stableford 2004). More recently the text has been interpreted as a proto-ecological novel which broaches the question of sustainability by relating the extinction-level event to ongoing human encroachment into the earth's remaining wildernesses (Bulfin 2015b).—AILISE BULFIN

The Queen Anne's Gate Mystery (1889). Novel by **Richard Arkwright**. Published in two volumes by F. V. White & Co, London, *The Queen Anne's Gate Mystery* is a detective story with a first-person narrator, George Pen Owen. When the wife of his friend Harry Collingwood is poisoned and Harry is arrested for the murder, George and his wife Lady Geraldine are determined to prove Harry's innocence. Lady Geraldine takes on the role of the detective. She examines the clues, interviews witnesses from different social classes, pursues the main suspect to New York and in the course of the novel explains her conclusions to George, who recognizes and admires her intellectual and social acumen. The mystery centers on a love interest of a servant girl and, throughout the story, character motivations are romantic and domestic. The legal process gives structure and a sense of urgency to the plot, as time is running out for Harry.—EMMA KARENO

Raffles Stories by E. W. Hornung. The stories follow the history of an amateur gentleman jewel-thief, A. J. Raffles, along with his chronicler and old public school friend, Bunny. Raffles is a master **cricket** player, particularly prized for his abilities as a slow bowler, which takes wile and craft rather than raw power. Hornung wrote the Raffles stories as a criminal inversion of his brother-in-law's, **Arthur Conan Doyle**'s, wildly popular **Sherlock Holmes** series. The first six Raffles stories were released in *Cassell's Magazine* (1898) followed by an enlarged book edition, *The Amateur Cracksman* (1899), a second and third collection of stories, *The Black Mask* (1900) and *A Thief in the Night* (1905), as well as one novel, *Mr. Justice Raffles* (1908). The Raffles stories were instantly popular in Britain, spawning plays, radio dramas, TV shows, a movie staring John Barrymore, and a play written by Graham Greene. At the core of Raffles's continuous appeal is his cosmopolitan, sportsman, aesthete, and criminal **masculinity**. The critical history on Raffles begins with George Orwell's essay, "Raffles and Miss Blandish" (*Horizon 1944*), where Orwell suggests the strange mélange of late–Victorian philosophical and cultural forces that makes up the Raffles persona: the cult of gentlemanly sporting, Fabian Socialism, the ironic aestheticism of **Oscar Wilde**, and the hyper-nationalism that surrounded Britain's entry into the Boer War. Outcast from the Edwardian cricket field and clubroom for their crimes, Raffles and Bunny enlist as irregular infantry and go to South Africa to fight the Boers. Raffles's history of sporting violence is completed by his sporting death: when trading shots with a Boer commando, he is killed and redeemed as an ideal for

British masculinity by his death in battle. Recent scholarship on Raffles concentrates on his place in the rhetoric of masculine adventure and that rhetoric's place inside the larger narratives of imperialism, masculine renewal, and national violence that mark the years before World War I. Within the narrative arc of this popular adventure hero is a larger fantasy history of late-Victorian **masculinity**—how it fetishized both masculine social transgression and national violence as a means to reimagine male wholeness inside the castrating reality of a fully industrialized society.—D. MICHAEL JONES

Railway Bookstalls. Bookstalls situated on railway station platforms specializing in the circulation of reading matter were one of the leading sites of popular literature dissemination during the mid- and late-Victorian periods. W. H. Smith & Son were the predominant player in England and initially Ireland, until a management buyout saw this Irish arm become an independent concern trading as Eason & Son. Scholars like Stephen Colclough have complicated the traditional account of the firm's acquisition of a monopoly in the railway reading trade, which had emphasized a purification narrative that stressed Smith's displacement of independent inept vendors who supposedly dealt exclusively in racy and insubstantial reading matter. Nevertheless, it is clear that the Smith network of bookstalls played an important role in providing many commuters and leisure travelers with a wide selection of books and periodicals that satisfied their light reading needs during rail travel. The impact of the railway book trade on the field of Victorian popular fiction is particularly discernible on a material level. With the rise of cheap book publishing modes, like the **yellowback** in the 1850s, and the **shilling shocker** and sixpenny paperback of the 1880s and 1890s, which were disseminated primarily via the bookstalls, passengers had access to editions of popular literature that were reasonably priced, compact, and potentially disposable. Additionally, reprints of previously published texts reissued in cheaper editions of this kind represented a major part of the railway book trade; thus, the potential for such works to sustain the popularity of particular titles and/or novelists was arguably considerable. Given that many of the selections of reading matter by bookstall consumers were made in haste prior to boarding an imminently departing train, both the import of the cover visuals of such books as well as the recommendations of the bookstall workers could prove decisive influences upon travelers' choices. Publisher's series of uniformly bound books were a mainstay of the railway book trade; the perceived reliability of specific ventures to furnish positive reading experiences coupled with minimal available purchasing time meant consumers often remained faithful to particular collections. Thus, the clustering of texts and authors such series engendered are potentially very enlightening about historical audiences' reading diets in this space. The railway book trade also arguably played a significant role in the proliferation of particular genres of popular fiction considered well suited to furnish mental escapism for passengers seeking to counteract the tedium and/or anxiety of rail travel. Moreover, there existed marked thematic and socio-cultural associations between railway reading and specific popular literature genres; both the **sensation novel** of the 1860s along with the **detective fiction** genre of the 1880s and beyond, were commonly equated with the phenomenon of rail travel. Periodicals like *Tit-Bits* and **The Strand Magazine** as well as *Answers* and **The Windsor Magazine** that included **serial** detective novels or interconnected series of short detective fiction stories by authors like **Arthur Conan Doyle** and **Arthur Morrison** were a key element of Victorian print media's efforts to cater to railway passengers who acquired reading matter at the bookstall.—PAUL RAPHAEL ROONEY

Reade, Charles (1814–84). English novelist and playwright. Although Reade debuted as a novelist with *Peg Woffington* (1853), based on the 1852 two-act comedy, *Masks and Faces*, that he had co-authored with Tom Taylor, he came to prominence with *It Is Never Too Late to Mend* (1856), the first of his topical best-sellers, advocating prison reform. In 1861 Reade published his magnum opus, *The Cloister and the Hearth*, a historical romance concerning the parents of the Renaissance humanist Erasmus of Rotterdam. Reade's next three fictional endeavors consolidated his reputation as a writer of sensational **melodramas**: *Hard Cash* (1863), an exposé of the cruelties rampant in lunatic asylums; *Griffith Gaunt; or Jealousy* (1866), a critique of Victorian sexual mores; and *Foul Play* (1868), a tale about the scuttling of ships for insurance, composed in **collaboration** with Dion Boucicault. Reade continued to address urgent issues of the day in his subsequent novels. While *Put Yourself in His Place* (1870) denounced the trade union practice of "rattening" or enforcing membership, *The Wandering Heir* (1873), of which Reade also wrote a theatrical adaptation, was inspired by the controversial Tichborne Case. His other prominent works are *A Woman Hater* (1877), a feminist novel featuring the struggles of a woman doctor, and *Drink* (1879), a sentimental play modeled on Émile Zola's *L'Assommoir* (1877). At the height of his career Reade was widely acclaimed as the natural successor of **Charles Dickens**, but his critical standing plummeted by the turn of the century, owing to changes in literary conventions.—Ramit Samaddar

The Rebel of the Family (1880). Novel by **Eliza Lynn Linton**. Serialized in *Temple Bar* (January–December 1880) and published in three volumes by **Chatto and Windus** at the end of that year, the novel demonstrates professional self-promotion in its citation of essays Linton had previously published in the *Saturday Review*: "Mesalliances" (1868), "Mature Sirens" (1869), "The Shrieking Sisterhood" (1870), and "Modern Man-Haters" (1871). Engaging with topical issues of **class** consciousness and female emancipation, *Rebel* introduces Mrs. Winstanley, an English widow who hopes to arrange her daughters' marriage in order to lift the family from impoverished gentility. While the prime marriage candidates are Thomasina, the stately eldest daughter with a strong sense of duty, and Eva, the pretty "child" whose coquetry risks endangering the family's reputation, the narrative is centralized around Perdita, the intellectual middle daughter with democratic views and a desire to work for a living. Ostracized by her family, the eponymous "rebel" meets Bell Blount, a women's rights campaigner and self-professed hater of men, whose Sapphic tendencies made her "too odious" for comment ("New Novels" 1881: p. 131). In placing Perdita's struggle for independence between her mother's traditional values and Blount's extreme feminism, the novel engages with issues later explored by **Sarah Grand** and associated with **New Woman** fiction. Although deeming *Rebel* "more successful than most of Mrs Linton's books," the *Athenaeum* felt unable to rank it above "the second class of novels" ("Novels" 1880: p. 741). Nevertheless, its popularity ensured a single volume rerelease (1886). Broadview Press reissued the novel in 2002.—Fiona Snailham

See also Belflower 1967, Meem 2002

The Revolt of Man (1882). Novella by **Walter Besant**. Originally published anonymously and attributed to either Anthony Trollope or Charles Dilke, *The Revolt of Man* was later claimed by Besant as his own. It was in the vanguard of late nineteenth-century texts that established dystopic fiction as a **science fiction** subgenre. Set in late twenty-first-century England, the novella depicts the supposed consequences of women assuming control of the government and key social and religious institutions. The antifeminist satire was an early intervention into debates about the modern woman or, as she became known in the 1890s, the **New Woman**.—Kevin A. Morrison

Reynolds's Miscellany of romance, general literature, science, and art (1846–1869). **Penny Fiction weekly**. A spinoff of the **London Journal**, of which G. W. M. Reynolds had been the first editor until a quarrel with its owner, the *Miscellany* was, from its third six-monthly volume (November 1847) published by George Dicks, one of the most successful publishers of cheap reading material and well known for his publication of cheap playscripts and reprint editions. Titled *Reynolds's Magazine* for its first few months, the periodical began as a vehicle for Reynolds's own work, though from March 1847 he was joined by Gabriel Alexander and in 1848 by Edwin J. Brett (who was to become a well-known publisher of children's literature). Circulation was not enough to sustain the *Miscellany* and by July 1848 Reynolds had declared bankruptcy, whereupon Dicks bought the periodical and employed Reynolds as editor for a new series. Both fiction and non-fiction had addressed political issues from the start, but when Reynolds became involved in Chartism, some sections became much more politically explicit. In the 1850s the tone became less strident: from 1849 Reynolds channeled his political energies in to the *Political Instructor* (which metamorphosed in to *Reynolds's Newspaper* from 1850). J. F. Smith and Piece Egan the Younger contributed a **serial** each, along with more fiction by Edwin Brett and Reynolds himself. Reynolds's literary production was severely hit by the death of his wife in 1858. **James Malcolm Rymer** became the *Miscellany's* mainstay, producing a long series of novels under the pseudonyms "Lady Clara Cavendish" and "Malcolm J. Errym." Reynolds instead edited *Bow Bells* for Dicks from 1862, into which the *Miscellany* was eventually absorbed.—Andrew King

See also Dicks 2006, King 2007

Rice, James (1844–1882). British novelist. Best known for his literary partnership with **Walter Besant**. Born in Northampton, Rice was educated at Queens' College, Cambridge, where he drifted from law into literature. In 1868, he became editor of *Once a Week*, which he ran at a financial loss until 1872. The journal brought him into contact with Besant, with whom he cowrote novels until his death. Their first work was *Ready-money Mortiboy* (1872), founded on Rice's idea. It proved a literary success if not a commercial one. The piece was subsequently dramatized by the authors and produced at the Court Theater in 1874. In addition to multiple **short stories**, Rice and Besant cowrote many novels, including *My Little Girl* (1873), *With Harp and Crown* (1874), *This Son of Vulcan* (1875), *The Monks of Thelema* (1877), *Celia's Arbour* (1879), and *The Chaplain of the Fleet* (1879). The most successful of their joint productions was *The Golden Butterfly* (1876). In 1879, Rice published *History of the British Turf*, which was a series of playful essays more than a serious contribution to history. Rice married Lillie Dickinson in 1871, with whom he had a son. He died in 1882.—Haejoo Kim

See also ODNB, Cousin 1910

Riddell, Charlotte (1832–1906). British novelist. Born in Carrickfergus (Northern Ireland), Charlotte Eliza Cowan (later Riddell) moved to London in 1855 to pursue a literary career. She became famous as the author of novels, set in the City of London, that revolve around the life stories of businessmen, accountants, manufacturers, traders, and their female companions. In *Too Much Alone* (1860), *City and Suburb* (1861), *George Geith of Fen Court* (1864), *The Race for Wealth* (1866) and *Austin Friars* (1870), Riddell narrated the hectic world of entrepreneurial capitalism in starkly realistic terms, tinged with sensational elements (adultery and **bigamy**). Both appreciated and criticized by Victorian reviewers, her choice of subject matter appeared unique. Economic preoccupations resurfaced in the ghost stories and supernatural tales Riddell wrote in the 1870s and 1880s, most of which have been reprinted in modern editions (Bleiler 1977). A prolific author, Riddell turned to the troubled history of Ireland in *Maxwell Drewitt* (1865), *The Earl's Promise* (1873), *Berna Boyle* (1884), and *The Nun's Curse* (1887), exploring the tense relationship between tradition and modernity in various Irish settings. Linked to the success of *George Geith* and to her imaginative commitment to the City of London, Riddell's popularity was not long lasting. In the late twentieth century, feminist critics (Peterson 2009; Kelleher 2000; Srebrnik 1994b) began to reassess her works, focusing on *A Struggle for Fame* (1883), a semiautobiographical artist's novel. This recovery work continues today with the reevaluation Riddell's business novels (Colella 2016; Henry 2013) in relation to the promises and disillusions of nineteenth-century capitalism.—Silvana Colella

See also ODNB

The Riddle of the Sands (1903). Best-selling espionage and invasion novel by Erskine Childers. Probably the most enduring work of **invasion literature** and a key instigator of the nascent spy genre, this novel recounts the chance discovery of secret German naval preparations for a large-scale invasion of Britain's vulnerable east coast. It memorably features the travails of two amateur British yachtsmen as they work to solve the riddle of the covert operations hidden in the dense fog and shifting sands of the isolated Frisian islands, before finally uncovering and averting the perfidious German conspiracy. Childers's tale was conceived in the aftermath of the South African War (1899–1902), which had opened with an unexpected series of British defeats, caused a full-blown invasion scare in the popular press and raised deep concerns about Britain's military capabilities (Stafford 1981: p. 495). Childers thus wrote to warn Britain of its military vulnerability, structuring his admonitory narrative around the dramatic conceit—adverted to in the novel's subtitle "A Record of Secret Service"—that he was merely an editor bringing before the public the true story of a narrowly averted invasion attempt. To this effect he loaded the text with convincing nautical and cartographical detail and worked throughout the narrative to justify his vehement call to arms in the editorial postscript: "Is it not becoming patent that the time has come for training all Englishmen systematically either for the sea or for the rifle?" (Childers 2011: p. 301).

Like many authors of invasion tales, Childers had formative experience of armed conflict in British imperial territory, having volunteered for service in a horse-drawn artillery unit in the South African War as a young man. A politically active author with a complex history of support for the contradictory causes of British imperialism and Irish nationalism, Childers's **childhood** involved strong British and Irish influences. Born in London to a father who was a British colonial administrator and a mother from a landed Irish Protestant family, he spent a key period of his childhood in Ireland. He was later educated in Haileybury College in England, a preparatory school for imperial service, and Cambridge, where he argued in college debate against the provision of home rule for Ireland, before working as a clerk in the House of Commons. While his South African War experience made him sympathetic toward the causes of small nations, he still retained a pro-imperial outlook—plainly evident in *The Riddle of the Sands*—leading to his seemingly contradictory later contributions to Britain's cause during the First World War and to armed Irish anti-colonial struggle against British rule. This latter precipitated his early death when he was executed during the Irish Civil War for the illegal possession of a firearm by the forces of the emerging Irish Free State.

A seminal instance of the early-twentieth-century invasion tales that proliferated in the worsening pre-war geo-political climate, *The Riddle of the Sands* was one of the first to envisage Germany as Britain's main enemy. Its controversial and convincing scenario brought Childers into the public spotlight and caused an outbreak of debate on defense policy, with serious attention paid by the Admiralty to Childers's scenario (Ring 1996: pp. ii–iv). The text was repeatedly re-issued before and during the First World War and in more recent years has gone on to achieve classic status.—AILISE BULFIN

See also ODNB

Robert Elsmere (1888). Novel by **Mrs. Humphry [Mary Augusta] Ward**. Largely acclaimed as one of the bestselling novels of the nineteenth century in both Britain and America, *Robert Elsmere* was **serial**ized in three volumes by Smith, Elder, and Co. in 1888. Variously known as a novel of ideas and a so-called quality novel, the text reflects the religious conflicts of faith and doubt following the Oxford Movement. Ward was the granddaughter of Thomas Arnold, an early supporter of the Broad Church. Arnold also famously incurred the irritation of Tractarian founder John Henry Newman. Another point of referential inspiration may have come from Ward's father, Tom Arnold, converting to Roman Catholicism in 1856.

Several important themes in the novel include debates over religious tolerance of dissenting ideas and persons, the skeptical intellectual and philosophical thinker, the threat of German rationalism, social reform and good works, and marriage relations between partners of differing intellectual and religious beliefs. A romantic subplot relating to the titular protagonist's sister-in-law, Rose, also appears to address the aesthetics of, and careers made available to the **New Woman**. Although Ward often promoted higher education for women, she also positioned herself against contemporary calls for female enfranchisement.

These conflicts are dramatized in the story of Robert Elsmere, a young Anglican clergyman whose interactions with his own Oxford tutor, Edward Langham, the skeptical squire Roger Wendover, and a character named Professor Grey, touches off a crisis of faith. After reading recommended works of German rationalists, Elsmere begins to doubt doctrines such as Biblical literalism, and the supernatural elements of a mythological Christianity. While he can initially justify a co-existence of natural **science**, Darwinism, and Christianity, it becomes increasingly difficult for Elsmere to dismiss criticisms against historical records of Biblical veracity. He does not become an atheist, choosing to retain belief in a Creator, but can no longer believe in miracles or the divinity of Christ. This causes a schism between himself and his orthodox wife, Catherine. After resigning his orders, Elsmere founds The New Brotherhood, an educational settlement in the East End of London, and dedicates his life to performing good works for the working-class peoples living there. Prior to his premature death from overwork and tuberculosis, Elsmere reconciles with his estranged wife. Following his decease, the New Brotherhood continues to survive, and even thrives.

Ward's novel was favorably reviewed by Walter Pater in *The Manchester Guardian*, and by William E. Gladstone in *Nineteenth Century*. The latter, titled "*Robert Elsmere* and the Battle of Belief," is often credited for sparking widespread public interest in the text. Both reviews lamented Ward's lack of ability to draw lifelike character portraits, but applauded the deft discussions of weighty material, and the sympathetic depiction of Elsmere's spiritual turmoil. Stage dramatizations were swift in production, opening in New York City and Boston. *Robert Elsmere* remains Ward's most famous and reproduced work, although the lack of an international copyright law resulted in ongoing issues with piracy.—Vicky Cheng

See also Burstein 2013, Ousby 2000

Robin Hood and Little John; or, the Merry Men of Sherwood Forest was a **penny blood**, written by Pierce Egan the Younger, and serialized between 1838 and 1840. After its **serialization**, it was then published in one volume and proved to be one of the most commercially successful Robin Hood novels published during the Victorian era, going through six editions. It was translated into French by Alexandre Dumas as *Le Prince des Voleurs* (1872) ("the Prince of Thieves") and *Robin le Proscrit* (1873) ("Robin the Outlaw"). The novel also generated an unofficial sequel by J. H. Stocqueler titled *Maid Marian, the Forest Queen* (1849). Egan's novel is clearly influenced by Walter Scott's Robin of Locksley in *Ivanhoe* (1819), as Egan depicts the outlaw as an Anglo-Saxon freedom fighter who leads a resistance movement against the tyrannical Normans. However, although the novel utilizes Scott's idea of racial conflict, these societal divisions are presented in terms of class rather than race. The novel also draws upon **Gothic** motifs: old family secrets come to light, the outlaws are hunted down through the vaults of Nottingham castle, and seemingly supernatural specters appear at certain points. Furthermore, the story contains high levels of violence, graphically described, which are often accompanied with a correspondingly graphic **illustration** (Egan himself provided the illustrations to the first edition): there are several large scale battles, as well as small skirmishes between the outlaws and the Normans, in which people receive arrows in their eyes and brains, and limbs are hacked off. The women of the novel are typical damsels-in-distress who are repeatedly rescued by the outlaws. The novel ends with Robin Hood's death by poisoning at the hands of the Prioress of Kirklees.—Stephen E. Basdeo

See also Basdeo 2016, Knight 2003

Robinson, Frederick William (1830–1901). English novelist, **short story** writer, and drama critic. The author of over fifty novels, typically in the three-volume format, Robinson also founded and edited *Home Chimes* (1884–1893), which published contributions from Jerome K. Jerome, Algernon Charles Swinburne, and **Israel Zangwill**. Robinson contributed to magazines such as ***Family Herald*** and ***Cassell's Magazine***. He enjoyed success in Britain and the USA. Much of his fiction was printed anonymously, arguably implying female authorship. For his trilogy on women's imprisonment—*Female Life in Prison* (1862), *Memoirs of Jane Cameron, Female Convict* (1863), and *Prison Characters Drawn from Life with Suggestions for Prison Government* (1866)—Robinson adopted the female anonym of "A Prison Matron." Despite "a tendency toward the sensational and sentimental" (Schwan 2014: p. 69), these important books created a "protofeminist" (2014: p. 67) platform to make visible the lives of imprisoned women, as well as the labor of prison matrons. Such concerns are shared by his later short story "Daisy March, the Prison Flower" (1881), published in *Crystal Stories* (a supplement to the *British Work-*

woman), and in *Harper's Bazar* across the Atlantic, suggesting that he reached cross-class audiences. The lives of working-**class** communities and cross-cross relations are central in much of Robinson's work, including titles such as *Owen: A Waif* (1862), and *Mattie: A Stray* (1864). He also wrote a series of novels dealing with religion, including *High Church* (1860), *Church and Chapel* (1863), and *Carry's Confession* (1865). Other Victorian writers like **Margaret Oliphant** reviewed and appreciated Robinson's work.—ANNE SCHWAN

See also ODNB, Schwan 2016

Romance Fiction. The traditional genre of English-language romance fiction underwent major changes during the Victorian era. The strain of the novel referred to as "the romance" had been a widely read literary mode since its beginnings in the eighteenth century, but over the course of the nineteenth century, it mutated into a number of newly evolving forms. In fact, by the end of the Victorian period, the term *romance* came to embrace a wide array of genres. The common denominator of these romance genres was their embodiment of the antonym to realism in fiction.

In the traditional acceptation of the term *romance*, dating back to the original Arthurian cycle of the Middle Ages—long before the emergence of the novel—this literary mode featured a narrative based in love and adventure, and entailing elements of the counter-real, such as magic, spells, enchantment, and the supernatural. By the early nineteenth century, under the influence of the **Gothic** romances of Horace Walpole and Ann Radcliffe, the domestic romances of Jane Austen, and the historical romances of Walter Scott, the mode began to branch into various subgenres, all of which came to enjoy great popularity in the hands of certain Victorian writers, many of them women.

One romance subgenre that came to the fore in popular reception during the Victorian period was the religious romance. This was often a narrative that centered on a courtship-marriage plot, and featured the moral reformation, through romantic-spiritual love, of its protagonists. Two celebrated examples of the popular religious romance were **Charlotte Yonge**'s *The Heir of Redclyffe* (1853), and **Mrs. Humphry [Mary] Ward**'s *Robert Elsmere* (1888), which is now recognized as the best-selling British novel at that point in history. Ward was only outdone in popularity by **Marie Corelli**, whose religious and supernatural romances of the 1880s and '90s culminated in her best-selling ***The Sorrows of Satan***, in which the devil is portrayed in a sympathetic, Mephistophelian light. At its heart, this single most popular British romance of the years 1837–1901 (as we now know from sales figures) supplements its mystical symbolism with a moralistic love story, in which the male protagonist learns to love the "right" woman, platonically, by the end of his tale of rags-to-riches-to-rags.

Other Victorian subgenres of the romance moved in an opposite thematic direction, toward an increasing secularization of the depicted life-world. Some of the most popular novels of the 1860s and thereafter took Walter Scott's definition of the romance plot that "turns upon marvelous and uncommon incidents" in the new direction of crime and detection. **R. D. (Richard Doddridge) Blackmore** set out to extend Scott's tradition of the historical romance with *Lorna Doone: A Romance of Exmoor* (1869), a **melodrama** set in the 1600s, involving good and evil characters who struggle to overcome the passions of a family feud. Highly popular examples of a new subgenre of romance, the **sensation novel**, set in contemporaneous Britain, include **Mary Elizabeth Braddon**'s *Lady Audley's Secret*, with a plot centering on "accidental" **bigamy**, and **Wilkie Collins**'s ***The Woman*** *in White* and *The Moonstone*. These two best-known Collins novels are now recognized as the embryonic precursors of the popular **detective fiction** made globally famous by **Arthur Conan Doyle** with his **Sherlock Holmes** novels of the later Victorian years, such as *A Study in Scarlet*, *The Sign of Four*, and *The Hound of the Baskervilles*.

A sibling genre to the emergent detective story was the **imperial adventure** romance, inspired by the action-oriented quest narratives of Walter Scott and such French writers as Alexandre Dumas and Jules Verne, but set in romanticized, "exotic" locales of the British empire of the later Victorian era. Prominent specimens in this category include **Robert Louis Stevenson**'s *Treasure Island* and *Kidnapped*, **H. Rider Haggard**'s *King Solomon's Mines*, and *She*, and **Rudyard Kipling**'s *The Man Who Would Be King* (1888) and *Kim* (1901). Few of these adventure romances, which were often consumed by boys and young men (and which later went on to inspire many film adaptations), featured love stories in their incident-filled plots; as mentioned above, it is important to keep in mind that the Victorian era had a much broader definition of the "romance" than we tend to use today.

What we today label **science fiction**, too, was originally considered a subgenre of the romance, and had its birth in the Victorian era. Inspired by Mary Shelley's *Frankenstein* (1816) and by the mid-nineteenth century tales of Jules Verne, **H. G. Wells** produced a streak of tremendously popular late Victorian sci-fi novels that have since earned him the title of "father of English science fiction": *The Time Machine*, *The Island of Dr. Moreau*, *The Invisible Man* (1897), and *The War of the Worlds*.

Another romance strain of the later Victorian era was the supernatural or fantastic romance, which had its roots in the **Gothic fiction** of a century earlier. A number of these novels and stories have since become popular touchstones of horror: **Joseph Sheridan Le Fanu**'s **vampire** novella *Carmilla*, Robert Louis Stevenson's *Dr. Jekyll and Mr. Hyde*, and **Bram Stoker**'s *Dracula*.

Finally, it was at the end of the Victorian era that what we now understand as the secular, mass-market, Mills-and-Boon or Harlequin-style romance novel began to appear: the story of love that undergoes any number of obstacles, but eventually triumphs in the union of two protagonists. This form of popular literature had its high-brow exemplars in the novels of Jane Austen and the Brontë sisters, but by 1901 had begun to democratize, in popular romance fictions that freed themselves from the shackles of moral and religious edification, celebrating an earth-bound intensity of affect. The most noteworthy example here may be the fiction of **Victoria Cross**, who offered tales of passion unencumbered by didacticism: the **short story** "Theodora" (1895), and the novels *The Woman Who Didn't* (1895) and *Anna Lombard*. Among others, Victoria Cross pioneered the emergent, secularized form of the "women's romance" that would go on in the twentieth century to become one of the most popular novel genres in history.—Martin Hipsky

Romanies/Gypsies. People who identify as Romani signal that they belong to or are descended from an historically diasporic group with roots in **India** or the Middle East (the precise locations and dates are contested). The term *Gypsy*, considered derogatory by many people today, has its origins in the labeling of Romani people as Egyptian after their initial arrival in groups in Britain. This use can be seen in draconian Elizabethan anti–Gypsy legislation, for instance. Romani scholar Ian Hancock suggests using the term *Gypsy* when referring to the stereotype found in fiction and other representational forms, recognizing Carmen and Esmeralda for what they are, and not using the term in reference to the complex picture of people and culture (2008: p. 189). Debates about terminology and representation take place in the shadow of two European genocides against the Romani people; these terms have been used to mark individuals for murder and persecution and continue to be used as slurs, but also in some cultural celebration (for instance if someone were to write "a beautiful Gypsy vardo or wagon"). Readers, scholars and writers investigating Victorian representations of Romani people and the construction of a Victorian Gypsy figure should be aware of the ways in which later politics inflect their reading.

Representations of Romani people have long suffused British, wider European, and American culture, and many of the most well-known come from the Victorian period: Mr. Rochester's cross-dressed performance in Charlotte Brontë's *Jane Eyre* (1847), Heathcliffe in *Wuthering Heights* (1847), Matthew Arnold's "The Scholar Gipsy" (1853), Maggie Tulliver's imagined subjects in *The Mill on the Floss* (1860), and the paintings of Augustus John (1878–1961). Some of these were reactions to or influenced by Romantic-period or earlier writers, poets, and visual artists. For instance, stage depictions and **illustrations** drew on Walter Scott's Meg Merrilies from *Guy Mannering* (1815), dressing Gypsy characters in an exaggerated Orientalized style. Other representations are less well known but have had a significant impact on the ways in which Romani people were figured for consumption by the rest of the population: George Borrow's work, the fiction and nonfiction of members of the Gypsy Lore Society (founded in 1888), and the illustrated reporting of Gypsy life in nineteenth-century newspapers. Some such texts exoticize and romanticize the people they represent, while others project the anxieties and desires of non–Romani people onto Gypsy characters, eliding to a greater or lesser extent the lived and documented experiences of Romanies.

Archival representations of Romanies in Britain date back to at least the sixteenth century, but the nineteenth century saw both a proliferation of Gypsy figures in art, literature, and other cultural forms and a shift in the nature of such representations with the crystallization of racist discourse at this time. For instance, one key proponent of racial **science**, Robert Knox, wrote in 1850, along with many derogatory assertions, that the Gypsies' "own feelings connect them with the *dark races*" (1862: pp. 151–9). This is not to say that nineteenth-century racial taxonomies were coherent. There was widespread use of the Gypsy figure or the term *Gypsy* as a metaphor for all manner of peripatetic or exotic traits. That broad use of the term made it harder for subscribers to racist ideology to permanently separate one racial group from another (separations which were used as the basis for moral judgment and expectations about **health**, culture, achievement, **class**, and education) because the use of the term might be a guarantor for race but might not. Indeed, many of the negative stereotypes associated with Romanies in this period (many of which have, problematically, persisted into our own century) were also attributed to other mobile populations, such as canal boat people or seasonal agricultural workers. Producers and consumers of novels, paintings, operettas, pamphlets and articles were ostensibly convinced of their ability to recognize a Gypsy, but many examples from popular fiction undermine that conviction—the secret Gypsy or the person passing as a Gypsy are familiar plot points. Examples of Gypsy characters in popular fiction include the Boswells and Lovells in Theodore Watts-Dunton's *Aylwin* (1898), Jane Lee in G. J. Whyte-Melville's *Black But Comely* (1878), those in **Edward Bulwer-Lytton**'s *The Disowned* (1829), and **Fergus Hume**'s "Romany" detective Hagar Stanley in *Hagar of the Pawn Shop* (1898). Hagar's face is described, typically, as "Oriental in its contour and hue, with arched eyebrows over large dark eyes, and a thin-lipped mouth beautifully shaped, under a delicately-curved nose" (Hume 1899: pp. 15–16). Like many other Gypsy heroines (and women are depicted far more frequently than men) "the nostalgia of the wilds, of the encampment and the open road, tortured her" (Hume 1899: p. 21). Authors of **children's literature** in particular had a fondness for using Romani people to tell a moral tale: Emma Leslie with *A Gypsy Against her Will* [1889]; M. E. Bewsher with *The Gipsy's Secret; or, Deb's Revenge and What Came of It* [1871]; Nellie Cornwall's *Twice Rescued; or, The Story of Little Tino* [1888]; and Elizabeth K. Douglas's "The Gipsy Boy" (1872) to name a few.—JODIE MATTHEWS

Russell, Dora (1830–1905). English novelist. Although now largely forgotten, Russell was a popular and prolific writer of **sensation novels** during the last decades of the nineteenth century. Writing in 1894, George Sainsbury lauded her as "the sole heir of Miss Braddon" (1894: p. 64) and she was routinely praised by critics for the intricacy of her plots, depictions of working class characters and Northumbrian regional settings. Among her most successful works are *Footprints in the Snow* (1876) and **Beneath the Wave**. Raised in middle-class surroundings, she was forced to take up her pen when her father lost his position, and irresponsible **fathers** and impoverished gentlewomen—driven, unprepared, into the world of work—dominate the plots of many of her novels. Affiliated for much of her career with the newspaper syndication agency, **Tillotson's Fiction Bureau**, the majority of Russell's work first appeared in the pages of provincial newspapers prior to being re-issued in volume form. As Tillotson's owned the copyright to Russell's work, she derived no financial benefits from their re-printing and, once she was unable to produce new work on a regular basis, was forced to live the life of genteel **poverty** and dependency despised by so many of her female characters. There is little doubt that the critical neglect suffered by Russell stemmed, in large part, from the ephemeral, commercial and grubby connotations of newspaper publishing.

Over the course of her career, Russell published over 30 novels, as well as a range of shorter narratives, incorporating a range of sensational motifs including murder, **suicide**, **bigamy**, adultery, illegitimacy, blackmail, runaway wives, false identity, and madness. In addition to issues relating to women's employment, marriage emerges a key theme within her corpus and is seldom depicted positively. Mercenary marriages, where women trade their bodies and freedom for financial security, are soundly condemned, as are the women who seek them for motives other than absolute desperation. While Russell's corpus contains a number of anti-heroines reminiscent of **Mary Elizabeth Braddon**, Russell is more interested in flawed heroines whose deviancy is tempered with womanliness and with whom the reader is encouraged to identify.—JANICE M. ALLAN

Rymer, James Malcolm (1814–84). London novelist. One of the most prolific authors of **penny bloods**, or cheap fiction serials targeting early Victorian working-class readers, Rymer is now credited with several once-famous or now-enduring titles in this genre, primarily ***The String of Pearls, or, the Barber of Fleet-street***. His work is distinguished by its interdisciplinary themes and vivid, detail-oriented portrayal of life in London in various eras.

James Malcolm Rymer was raised in London by a literary and artistic family. During the first two decades of the nineteenth century, his father Malcolm Rymer published original poetry in a magazine edited by Richard Phillips, radical publisher of Paine, Godwin, and the English Jacobin Joseph Ritson. Malcolm Rymer also wrote a novel, *The Spaniard, or the Pride of Birth* (1806), and a play, *Science and Art, A Farce* (1820), which James Malcolm Rymer published in his 1842 *Queen's Magazine* (Nesvet 2017b). Malcolm Rymer's other sons included engravers, self-described "artists," and a serial banknote-forger who practiced in London and, after his conviction and transportation, Australia (Nesvet 2017a). He initially distanced himself from his family and their pursuits. He became a civil engineer and in 1840 patented a new type of furniture castor. However, by 1842, he was editing the short-lived *Queen's Magazine* and writing penny bloods for the penny fiction magnate **Edward Lloyd**. His first famous blood, **Ada, the Betrayed**, anonymously serialized in Lloyd's *Miscellany*, earned him the pseudonym "Author of Ada." Later pseudonyms include the anagrams "M. J. Errym" and "Malcolm J. Merry." In the 1850s, when Lloyd turned away from penny fiction, Rymer wrote for the publishers John Dicks and G. W. M. Reynolds.

Besides *Ada*, Rymer's noteworthy works include **Varney**, in which the Bannerworth family is plagued by a **vampire**, Sir Francis Varney, who covets the estate left them by their late father, and his former friend. This supernatural drama is interwoven with comic scenes involving a nautical **melodrama** duo: the aging veteran Admiral Bell and his loyal sidekick, Private Jack Pringle. Roaming the country on half-pay and without a purpose, these veterans seem to have outlived their era just like vampires, but they prove the unlikely heroes of the tale, while Varney, too, finds a heroic side to himself. Rymer also wrote *Family Secrets, or a Page from Life's Volume*, which dwells on a guilty secret arguably reminiscent of Rymer's brother's conviction and transportation; *The Sepoys, or Highland Jessie*, which dramatizes the primary events of the **India**n Revolt or Sepoy Mutiny (1857–9); and *A Mystery in Scarlet*, published in the *London Miscellany* in 1866, which **Robert Louis Stevenson** greatly admired. In private correspondence, Stevenson expressed the wish that he could write heroines as well as Rymer did.

However, Rymer's most enduring innovation is the legend of the London-based homicidal barber Sweeney Todd. Temperamentally a hundred and eighty degrees away from the pacifist barber of Malcolm Rymer's *The Spaniard*, Sweeney Todd first appeared as a literary character in the penny blood *The String of Pearls, a Romance*, serialized in 1846–7 by Lloyd in his *People's Periodical*. This anonymous work was long attributed to Rymer's fellow Lloyd author Thomas Peckett Prest, but recently, the bibliographer Helen R. Smith (2002) and editor Dick Collins (2010) have persuasively reassigned it to Rymer.
—Rebecca Nesvet

See also ODNB

St. Martin's Eve (1866). **Sensation novel** by **Mrs. Henry [Ellen] Wood**. Originally published as a 16-page **short story** in the *New Monthly Magazine* (November 1853) when Wood was virtually unknown and publishing anonymously. Key elements of the plot were expanded to form the basis of a three-volume novel published at the height of her popularity by the **Tinsley Brothers**. The lasting critical importance of the novel lies in the extent to which it challenges ongoing constructions of Wood as a so-called quiet sensationalist. Its representation of a murderous mother suffering from hereditary insanity and driven mad by jealousy—one of the most destructive of female emotions within Wood's corpus—together with the ceremonial dressing and display of a female corpse, suggest that Wood could be just as sensational as **Mary Elizabeth Braddon**, to whom she was often compared. A close analysis of the textual variants between story and novel,

moreover, reveals the extent to which the explicit violence of the former was tamed as Wood embarked on an active process of self-construction in order to manipulate her reputation and critical reception. Aside from its portrait of an unregulated and passionate mother who murders her stepchild (locking him in a room to burn to death) in order to establish her own son as heir to the family fortune, the novel is most interesting in its interrogation of contemporary constructions of legal and biological inheritance as the latter is used to foreground the limits and consequences of the law of primogeniture.
—JANICE M. ALLAN

Science. While the idea of science as theoretical knowledge dates back to classical antiquity, during the nineteenth century this word gained new meaning and complexity. Science's modern definition emerged in the 1830s and built upon the tenets of natural theology, the belief that nature demonstrates the existence of God, as well the Baconian-Newtonian tradition of hypothetico-deduction, in which knowledge is produced by forming and testing hypotheses through measurable experiments.

As the Victorian era advanced science became increasingly secular and theoretical, but it was never divorced from religion and the methods of empirical reasoning. In fact, it was natural theologian William Whewell who coined the term *scientist* in an 1834 *Quarterly Review* article. Moreover, although many today credit the publication of the *Origin of Species* (1859) with ensconcing irreligion and even atheism into Western culture, Church of England clerics **Charles Kingsley** and Henry N. Hutchinson expressed greater concern with the broadening separation between science and religion than any impiety implied by Charles Darwin's theory that organisms better adapted to their environment are more likely to survive and reproduce. Nevertheless, indications of growing secularity and religious inclusiveness suggested by Oxford University's decision in 1854 to no longer require students to sign the Thirty-Nine Articles, and the popularization of Thomas Henry Huxley's doctrine of agnosticism, moved religious and scientific knowledge into separate spheres.

The increasing institutionalization and specialization of Victorian science is evidenced by the 1831 founding of the British Association for the Advancement of Science; the 1846 implementation of a Charter Committee for the Royal Society aimed at restricting membership entirely to scientists; and the proliferation of specialized organizations including the Botanical Society of London (1836), the Ethnological Society of London (1843), and the Mineralogical Society of Great Britain and Ireland (1876). Many of these learned groups published their researches in periodicals modeled on the *Philosophical Transactions of the Royal Society* (1776) and the *Transactions of the Linnean Society of London* (1791). Scientific societies used qualified peer reviewers—what the Royal Society after 1752 termed a "Committee on Papers"—to ensure that they produced and distributed only professionally vetted research. But scientific articles, debates, and reviews also appeared in popular **serial** publications such as the Whig *Edinburgh Review* and the Tory *Quarterly Review*. Periodicals devoted entirely to science including the medical journal *The Lancet* (1823) and *Nature* (1869) also emerged during the nineteenth century. But beyond these professional venues, adult education journals like the *Popular Educator* published articles intended to teach scientific concepts to the public, while, more playfully, children's books including Kingsley's *Glaucus, or the Wonders of the Shore* (1855) and Arabella Buckley's *The Fairy-land of Science* (1888) adopted fantasy elements to instruct young people. Many of these popular texts generated interest in natural history by encouraging laypersons to collect and study specimens of butterflies, beetles, ferns, and seashells.

Recent scholarship on the relation of science to popular culture has focused on the scientific method and epistemology. The invention of photography contributed to this interest in sight and objectivity, while advances in optics including the development of sophisticated microscopes and telescopes permitted the scientific community to make increasingly precise observations. Yet, the questions that interested scientists and laypersons most—those relating to astronomy, electricity, magnetism, the fossil record, and how children inherit their parents' traits—all resided to some degree outside the realm of empirical demonstration. Nineteenth-century science's dealings with less concrete inquiries seemed to open the field to metaphysical questions. For instance, it was in hopes of demonstrating spiritual phenomena that the Society for Psychical Research (1882) employed the methods of deduction to study séances. **Arthur Conan Doyle**, a committed spiritualist and trained physician, was particularly sensitive about this tension between speculative theories and empirical observation. In ***The Sign of Four***, **Sherlock Holmes** claims to deal only in facts, explaining "Detection is, or ought to be, an exact science" (Conan Doyle 2010/1890: p. 51), and yet the detective's techniques in this and other fictions as often relied upon imagination, prejudice, and theorizing.

Authors of literature were quick to respond to advances in science, both mundane and marvelous. For middle-class Victorians, science impacted everyday life through practical technologies like railroads, telegraphs, steam printing presses, as well as medical advances (**anesthesia**, vaccines) and epidemiology (pasteurization, hospital construction, sewage treatment). The realist fiction *Middlemarch* (1871) by George Eliot, for instance, examines the consequences of railroads on rural life. More fancifully, **Bram Stoker**'s ***Dracula*** thematizes the life-giving but sexualized potentialities of blood transfusions. Across the numerous fictional modes (realist, adventure, **Gothic**, metaphysical, utopian, and **science fiction**), science is frequently conflated with magic and engineering, but despite definitional ambiguity scientific ideas usually appealed to Victorians because they imagined a world where theories could be proven empirically. **Marie Corelli** used electricity to demonstrate the veracity of the New Testament in her spiritualism-infused *A Romance of Two Worlds* (1886). In William Morris's **socialist** utopia *News From Nowhere* (1890) future Britons disprove Thomas Carlyle's "dismal science" (1849: p. 672), which suggested the necessity of the capitalist economic system, through proper land management and organized labor.

Beginning with Mary Shelley's *Frankenstein* (1818), science contributed to the manner in which the nineteenth century's nightmares and anxieties were expressed. Numerous novels exposed fears about human **degeneration**, such as **Edward Bulwer-Lytton**'s ***The Coming Race***, in which the English protagonist discovers highly evolved and technologically advanced subterranean beings whose superiority suggests that they will supplant humans. Wells explores similar themes in ***The Time Machine***, when the time traveler witnesses the evolutionary consequences of class divisions for the human species in the beautiful but weak Eloi and the ugly but better adapted Morlocks. **George Tomkyns Chesney**'s ***The Battle of Dorking***, **H. Rider Haggard**'s ***She***, and **H. G. Wells**'s ***The War of the Worlds*** all depict malevolent forces equipped with superior technologies that threaten to invade England. In Chesney's fiction, it is the enemy's unnamed "fatal engines" that defeat the underprepared British navy (1871: p. 13). In these novels scientific marvels are too great to be contained, which results in apocalyptic catastrophe.—Kate Holterhoff

Science Fiction. Genre of prose fiction, either **short story** or novel, **serial**ized or single publication. Often now shortened as sci-fi or SF. The phrase was not common during the Victorian era, although the first known use of the term is by William Wilson in *A Little Earnest Book Upon a Great Subject*: "We hope it will not be long before we may have other works of science fiction, as we believe such books likely to fulfill a good purpose, and create an interest where, unhappily, science alone might fail" (1851: p.137). During the Victorian era, speculative fiction that utilized **science** was often referred to as a scientific romance. This label was so common that it was the title of Charles Hinton's 1884 collection of science fiction themed essays and short stories. Edward James notes that late–Victorian science fiction often carried subtitles such as "A Romance" or "A Romance of the Future" (1995: p. 29). **H. G. Wells** occasionally spoke of his tales as "scientific fantasies." Most scholars agree that the understanding of science fiction as its own genre began in earnest with the founding of the magazine *Amazing Stories* by Hugo Gernsback (1926). For this reason, scholarship often refers to Victorian science fiction as proto-science fiction.

John Sutherland notes that "long-established English publishers ... **Longmans** ... Macmillans ... Smith Elder ... fought shy of SF" while "progressive new English publishers, founded in the last three decades of the century, seem to have embraced it.... **Heinemann** ... Edward Arnold ... Hutchinson ... **Chatto** ... Lane" (1983: p. 124). However, the genre was not considered significantly inferior to mainstream fiction at the time.

Science fiction usually avoids fantastical elements with no basis in possible science, or unexplained magic. Science fiction also avoids supernatural or horrific elements unless there is an attempt to explain them through science. The work must include aspects of science that are speculative in nature rather than accepted and proven science. When the work includes known science, that science is explored, questioned, or extrapolated in new ways. Additionally, science fiction might include a setting of a new and unfamiliar environment (space, another planet, an alternative universe, a distant future, or our world changed due to an alternate historical event). Science fiction often postulates the existence of extraterrestrial life or alternative lifeforms on earth; and most stories consider or highlight the effects of modern issues and **technology** on mankind, the planet, or the future. While science fiction often critiques advances in science, it also initiates or forecasts innovations. For this reason, many aspects of twenty-first century culture were envisioned in Victorian science fiction prior to their materialization.

Although Aldiss (1974) argues that Mary Shelley's *Frankenstein* (1818) is the first work of science fiction, aspects of science fiction can be traced back as far as there have been advances in science, including Margaret Cavendish's *The Description of a New World, Called the Blazing World* (1666), which explored an alternate utopian kingdom accessible via the North Pole. However, the mid– and late–Victorian era saw a surge in science fiction works, with over one hundred works published each year from 1886 to 1890. This may be due in part to the emergence of evolutionary theory as championed by Charles Darwin and the industrial revolution with its rapid advances, urbanization, technological innovation, and pollution, as well as general fears as the end of the century approached.

Evolutionary theories prior to Charles Darwin's *On the Origin of Species* (1859) were primarily teleological, advocating that humanity was steadily developing toward perfection although some groundwork had been laid by earlier scientists, including Robert Chambers in *Vestiges of the Natural History of Creation* (1844). Darwin's theory observed a constant struggle for existence in which humanity was not divinely chosen but instead had evolved. Darwin's theory posited a sense of moral ambiguity and a possibility for both evolution and degeneration of our species that provoked fear, pessimism, and skepticism in believers. It also gave rise to a wave of literary works that postulated the ways in which science might improve or destroy humanity.

The industrial revolution transformed England with new inventions such at the steam engine, telegraph, photography, film, and widespread use of electricity. Such advances led writers, some of whom were also scientists, to construct new worlds and project additional advances to our own. Jules Verne, for instance, extrapolated from existing inventions to foresee the submarine in *Twenty Thousand Leagues Under the Sea* (1870) and the helicopter (as a propeller-driven airship) in *Robur the Conqueror* (1886). Robotics, space travel, time travel, and the internet were all envisioned in Victorian science fiction.

Science fiction literature explored the fears and concerns of the time. For this reason, much of Victorian science fiction has become dated. As science has evolved, much of what the Victorian reader considered science fiction no longer qualifies as such. At the time, advances in science were so rapid, popular perceptions of the natural and the supernatural sometimes blurred. For instance, the Victorian belief in the **occult** might seem fantastical to a twenty-first-century audience, but many Victorian readers considered occult happenings scientifically possible. Mid-Victorian science fiction was filled with **mesmerism**, spiritualism, and ghost stories by writers such as **Margaret Oliphant** and **Vernon Lee**. However, by the 1880s, these types of stories were often relegated to eccentric journals such as W. T. Stead's *Borderland*. Science fiction novels and short stories developed into several categories or sub-genres, although many works could fit multiple sub-genres.

Time travel: Numerous works explored the possibility of traveling to the past or the future using scientific means. Often, these works included social commentary as they compared Victorian society to other times. Examples include H. G. Wells's ***The Time Machine*** (1895), **Grant Allen**'s *The British Barbarians* (1895), and Edward Bellamy's *Looking Backward* (1887).

Future or strange worlds: Closely akin to the time travel tale, these works posit what may happen in our future or what might exist on an alien world. For instance, John Ames Mitchell's *The Last American* (1889) is a satirical short novel set in 2951 in which a Persian expedition finds the ruins of an America that collapsed due to racial, religious, and cultural intolerance. Edwin Abbott's *Flatland* (1884) discusses alternate dimensions and incorporates Euclidean geometry.

Hollow earth and lost worlds: As the titles imply, works that examined the possibility that there is another world under our feet or hidden in a wilderness. This sub-genre may have been partially influenced by colonialism. Examples of this category include Jules Verne's *Journey to the Center of the Earth* (1864) and *Twenty Thousand Leagues Under the Sea* (1870), Samuel Butler's *Erewhon* (1872), which proposes machines evolving faster than humans, **Edward Bulwer-Lytton**'s ***The Coming Race*** (1871), **H. Rider Haggard**'s ***She***, and C. J. Cutcliffe Hyne's *Beneath Your Very Boots* (1889).

World catastrophes: Several world events, including the return of Haley's Comet, natural disasters, and epidemics, led to science fiction that investigated apocalyptic events. Barely missing the Victorian period is Mary Shelley's *The Last Man* (1826). Additional examples include **George Chesney**'s ***The Battle of Dorking***: *Reminiscences of a Survivor* (1871), William Delisle Hay's *The Doom of the Great City* (1880), Alexander Bettersworth's

The Strange MS. (1883), Richard Jeffries's *After London, or Wild England* (1885), H. G. Wells's **The War of the Worlds**.

Fantastic inventions/discoveries and mad doctors: Explorations of the dangers of scientists run amok. These works often questioned the morality, ethics, and safety of scientific advancements. They also explored the ways in which science might lead to degeneration rather than evolution. Notable examples include memory removal through neural degeneration in Edward Bellamy's *Dr. Heidenhoff's Process* (1880), splitting personalities in **Robert Louis Stevenson**'s ***Strange Case of Dr. Jekyll and Mr. Hyde***, **vivisection** in H. G. Wells's **The Island of Dr. Moreau** and invisibility in *The Invisible Man* (1897).

While several works explore aspects of science fiction during the Victorian era, a complete bibliography of extant works within the genre does not exist. Suvin (1983) and Bleiler (1990) are comprehensive.—Valerie L. Guyant

See also Alkon 1994, Moskowitz 1974

Self-harm. Fictional explorations of Victorian **suicide** have been the subject of a range of monographs and scholarly articles over the past twenty years (see Higonnet [1985], Anderson [1987], and Gates [1988]). Fewer studies have considered the prevalence of non-lethal acts of self-destruction in fiction, largely because it was not until the twentieth century that self-harm began to be identified as unconnected to lunacy, mania, or suicide (Chaney 2011A: pp. 279–80). A highly visible and much studied practice in contemporary **medicine** and psychiatry, self-harm went largely undocumented by nineteenth-century physicians as a distinct category of behavior. Repetitive acts of bodily damage were thought to characterize serious mental disorder, hence in 1883 James Adam, superintendent of the Crichton Royal Infirmary, describes how "although instances of attempted self-injury are not infrequent, it will be found as a rule on inquiry that the intention in their infliction is suicidal in character—whereas instances of wilful self-mutilation, for its own sake, are much more rare" (1883: p. 213). Ranging from relatively undemonstrative or culturally sanctioned acts like self-starvation and excessive consumption of alcohol or drugs, to the most dramatic cases of self-injury, self-harm escaped the notice of professionals as a condition unrelated to suicide well into the twentieth century. Indeed, a vocabulary for framing such inexplicable acts came into currency only at the *fin de siècle* when the term *self-mutilation* began to appear in medical dictionaries (Chaney 2011B: p. 375). Self-mutilation—the most sensational and violent expression of self-harm—alone warranted entry into *A Dictionary of Psychological Medicine* (1892), which does not include an entry on self-harm in general. Nonetheless, varied fictional accounts of behaviors now recognized as forms of self-harm began to appear with increasing regularity throughout the Victorian period. Thus, a history of self-harm as a tropological concern can be traced through literary dramatizations which drew on the images and rhetoric of self-harm long before it had begun to be formally conceptualized by Victorian doctors and psychiatrists.

Although rare, self-harm did appear in mid–Victorian writing. For example, in **Charles Dickens**'s *Dombey and Son*, Edith Dombey reacts to Mr. Carker's kiss by beating her hand "on the marble chimney-shelf, so that, at one blow, it was bruised, and bled; and held it from her, near the shining fire, as if she could have thrust it in and burned it" (1848: p. 558) Self-starving female heroines feature in many of the best-known novels of the mid-nineteenth century, and there is barely a realist representation of the working classes without at least one character "sodden with drink" (Swafford 2007: p. 52). However, self-harm was fictionalized most sensationally, and most graphically, in writing by and about the **New Woman** of the Victorian *fin de siècle*. Politically aware heroines often resort to systematic self-destruction in New Woman writing, attempting to survive a male oriented world in which their bodies are commodified and their minds are devalued.

In the social purity novels of **Sarah Grand**, self-starving heroines enact the "anorexic logic" (Heywood 1996: p. 3) inscribed by a society underpropped by Cartesian mind-body dualism, vanishing into nothingness, in line with a Victorian horror of the female flesh. In Grand's infamous novel ***The Heavenly Twins*** (1893) Evadne Frayling—who attempts suicide while pregnant—starves herself as her profligate husband gains in size, and her sexual frustration and blocked material drives are transposed into deliberate self-infection, and **food** refusal. In the short stories of **George Egerton**, self-harm by excessive drinking and self-mutilation appear frequently. For example, in "Her Share" from ***Keynotes***, "Gone Under," "Wedlock," and "A Psychological Moment at Three Periods" from *Discords* (1894), and "Pan" from *Symphonies* (1897) depictions of female bodies subject to self-torture rewrite and destabilize the masculine **Gothic** tradition yet ultimately reinforce patriarchal scopic economies. In the poetry of **Amy Levy**, the rhetoric of self-harm and suicide also appears and concerns about the female body are mediated through references to blood-letting and mutilation by Levy's male poet voices (Gray pp. 218–227). In the novels of **Mona Caird** and **Victoria Cross**—who approached the Woman Question very differently—self-harm is constructed around an ideal of saintly martyrdom (see Caird's ***The Wing of Azrael*** [1889], *The Daughters of Danaus* [1894], and the *Pathway of the Gods* [1898] and Cross's ***Anna Lombard***). In the work of both these authors, the female body is subject to avoidable tortures (self-starvation, self-infection and a lack of self-care) which express the futility of women's position in late–Victorian society and protest the lack of options but to internalize their frustrations.

There remains much work to be done on the subject of self-harm in Victorian fiction, and new research in this area offers significant cross-disciplinary overlap with disability studies, medical humanities, and psychology. Little scholarly attention has been paid to instances of body-focused hyper-repetitive disorders (reflecting more masculine forms of anxiety), which appear alongside typically female expressions of self-harm in women's writing. For instance, dramatizations of compulsivity appear in the work of Victorian popular authors including Charles Dickens, Anthony Trollope, and Thomas Hardy, and gesture toward new and exciting ground to be covered. Self-harm in Victorian literature and culture is a relatively new and vibrant area of study, and Chris Millard's *A History of Self-Harm in Britain: A Genealogy of Cutting and Overdosing* (2015), Sarah Chaney's *Psyche on the Skin: A History of Self-Harm* (2017), and Alexandra Gray's *Self-Harm in New Woman Writing* (2017) represent recent interventions into this exciting field of historical and literary debate. What is clear from the depth and breadth of work ongoing in this subject area is that self-harm in popular fiction was neither a stable nor homogenous symbol in the Victorian imagination but a composite of conflicting political, social, medical, and cultural values.—Alexandra Gray

Sensation Fiction. Literary genre. The British culture industry of the 1860s coined the term *sensation fiction* to sell popular, often **serial**ized fiction dealing with controversial topics hyped by the media. Often associated with authors as diverse as **Mary Elizabeth Braddon, Wilkie Collins, Florence Marryat, Mrs. Henry [Ellen] Wood,** and **Charles**

Reade, sensation fiction, like many popular forms of cultural production, was a hybrid that capitalized on the narrative strategies and emotional impact of previous genres such as **Gothic fiction, melodrama, Newgate novels, penny dreadfuls**, and **detective fiction.** In turn it contaminated the enduring success of genres, including domestic fiction and the historical novel, with new hyphenated forms, such as the domestic-sensation novel or the historical-sensation novel, that incorporated the sensational turn. Far from being the sole province of popular fiction, the narrative strategies of sensation fiction structured the works of contemporary writers such as Charles Dickens, George Eliot, Elizabeth Gaskell, Anthony and Frances Trollope, and George Eliot. The sensation novel also became a genre of reference for authors including **Rhoda Broughton**, Pierce Egan, Percy Fitzgerald, **Sheridan Le Fanu**, Justin McCarthy, **Margaret Oliphant**, **Ouida**, **Charlotte Riddell**, George Augustus Sala, Annie Thomas, Walter Thornbury, **Edmund Yates**, and **Charlotte Yonge** (Maunder 2004). A nationalist critical strain, sometimes echoing metaliterary references to French fiction in the novels, chastised the genre as resulting from the corrupting influx of relaxed French mores. The authors of sensation fiction with more cosmopolitan horizons did absorb the lesson of French realism (Gabriele 2009). By adapting these models to the British context, sensation fiction updated the popular appeal of the previous genres of Reality Literature by evading, particularly when read in installments, the moralizing inspiration in the narrative teleology of earlier forms of bourgeois realism. The plots of sensation novels, when read at short intervals in a periodical publication, suspend any judgment on the moral constitution of the main characters, inviting the reader to reassess accepted values while navigating, at least temporarily, territory that is not charted by the ideological pull of traditional narratives upholding dominant values.

The culture of sensation cannot be extrapolated from the 1860s and read in isolation from previous traditions. The field of sensation is a vital axis in the development of British philosophy (the term *sensorium* was coined in 1650 by Henry More). Susceptibility to affects such as sentimentality developed within a wide discursive field marked since the eighteenth century by the overlapping concerns of political economists, moral philosophers, poets, and novelists (Pocock). With the rise of industrial modernity, however, sensations did not feature as the foundation of a reflection on knowledge production but rather became a contingency inflecting the accelerated tempo of unending impressions that redefined the modern sensorium, leaving little time for reflection. As a character in Elizabeth Gaskell's *North and South* remarked: "It is the town life.... Their nerves are quickened by the haste and bustle and speed of everything around them" (1855: p. 295). The positioning of a sympathetic observer, cultivating the refinement of sentimentality from a stable position of contemplative detachment from the spectacle observed, gave way to the addictive rhythms of heightened sensations consumed at every turn in the narrative of popular fiction. The reader of popular fiction was akin to the urban character of the *flâneur*, endlessly moving in the urban streets, collecting an intoxicating series of impressions multiplied by print culture and mass entertainment. In this context of constant stimulation, sensation fiction as a form of ready-made industrial literature developed, reflecting on the epochal changes that industrial modernity engendered through an equally unsystematic reshuffling of social roles, values, and practices.

The protean applications of the sensational turn, which surprised readers with uncanny revelations, developed through a system of productive exchanges with older and newer media on both sides of the English Channel, such as journalism, pre-cinematic entertainment (Gabriele 2009), and performance. They continued steadily shaping popular culture beyond the sensation craze of the 1860s. An unparalleled development of print culture capitalism from the mid-nineteenth century aided the spread and success of sensation fiction, as well as other genres. The nineteenth-century publishing industry could sell novels either in installments, fracturing the cost of a lengthy narrative, or in costly editions marketed to a different audience. The importation of cheaper paper from Africa, the repeal of taxes on paper, and the flourishing of advertising (Law 2000) were some of the measures that liberalized the publishing industry, which was also pressured to reduce prices by competition with continental publishers of pirated reprints. The steady growth of literacy, as well as the development of cultural and commercial institutions such as **circulating libraries**, public libraries, and Mechanics' Institutes in Great Britain and the colonies, further multiplied occasions for reading and made access to printed matter easier.

Sensation fiction, like many forms of popular literature, follows an often standardized plot made of repeated narrative functions that develop in canonical settings. The opening of the novel introduces characters apparently enjoying an affluent and gratifying life—the prestige of their position coupled with all the trappings of modern commodity capitalism. The sensational turn, introducing mysterious disappearances, suspicions of criminal behavior, and uncanny similarities among apparently unrelated characters, shatters the idyllic tranquility of the initial setting through the narrative function of a stranger who challenges this established order through knowledge of a compromising episode in the previous life of the main characters. The mien of social distinction and gendered propriety that the characters impersonate in the opening pages appears to be built on a shaky foundation, thus initiating the parallel peripeteias of two characters: the person whose morality is questioned and the investigating character, who tries to establish the veracity of these insinuations. While literary plots centering on a repressed misdeed that an investigator is asked to bring to light are as old as Sophocles's *Oedipus Rex*, sensation fiction does not concern itself only with the crimes of aristocratic rulers whose sphere of action is inevitably excepted from bourgeois morality. These novels do not project evil and wrongdoing on a distant past, when the abuses of power by the aristocracy could go unpunished, as some **Gothic** novels do, nor do they take the opposite perspective of demonizing the working classes as the sector of the population more prone to crime, as in the popular fiction of the earlier part of the nineteenth century. Henry James recognized the specificity of the genre by defining the sensational in the "mysteries that are at our own doors" (1865: p. 594) as opposed to a Gothic castle.

In the decades that saw the full advancement of the middle classes to political and economic power, after the age of revolution and reform had enfranchised them, the sensation novel undermined the values paraded by them as a badge of honor, i.e., honesty, frugality, and personal worth. Whereas social mobility brought the new classes to leading positions, the sensation novel cast doubt on the process of accumulating wealth (including colonial fortunes) by insinuating it was built on an original crime. Whereas the morality of the new social order required strict observance to a gendered notion of female propriety as the foundation of the social unit of the middle-class home, the sensation novel gave prominence to nonconventional female characters that had negotiated their role in society without having to abide by these rules. With sensation fiction, the rituals of class identity opened to a world of social mobility, entrepreneurial calculations and maneuvers, and reinvented and manufactured identities, exposing upwardly mobile characters to the pitfalls of "passing" in what was still a strictly hierarchical society. The mass-produced availability and ephemerality of an endless supply of sensation fiction made its master-plots easily adaptable to the pressing issues of contemporary life. These issues were debated in a public sphere shaped not only by print culture but by an equally engaged industry of modern entertainment that invited a reflective response by the audience. Writers of sensation fiction presented the fleeting and contradictory variety of contemporary society while demanding that the public assess and take part in the new dilemmas confronting modern characters. The coverage in the press of the proceedings of the divorce court, after the initial changes brought by the Divorce Act of 1857, shone a light on marital abuse and provided material for sensation fiction that exposed ongoing conflicts associated with the imbalance of power in marriage, in terms of property, child custody, and the right to divorce. The terms of the Lunatic Act, through forced hospitalization in lunatic asylums, could divest non-normative identities of any claim to inheritance. The novels with the theme of madness thus sensationalized the transmission of wealth that subtends the history of the modern novel. More than stemming from a reflective notion of realism that mirrors existing reality, the conflicts that sensation fiction dramatizes enable reflection on contemporary life that defamiliarizes readers with accepted norms and conventions. Some of the narrative techniques employed by sensation novelists, such as the multiplication of narrative voices (for instance, in Wilkie Collins's **The Moonstone**), render the reader's engagement with the mysteries more intriguing, while anticipating the innovations of high modernism.

Sensationalism constitutes a transhistorical presence characterizing the uneven development of industrial modernity in continental Europe, the United States, Britain, and the British colonies. Rather than tracking its transnational manifestations through a diffusive model radiating from the capital of the British Empire, sensationalism can be read within a more nuanced model registering the entangled relations uniting center and periphery. A recognizable genre of sensation journalism developed thanks to the short-lived initial entrepreneurial freedom of the publishers active in Australia, who pioneered many of the features later associated with New Journalism (Laube 2016). Print-culture sensationalism, which includes, besides the daily dissemination of the conventions of countless sensational narratives, the composite sequence of illustrations of tragic events of colonial and city life appearing in the periodical press, constitutes a hidden trace in the development of twentieth-century popular media. This paper trail helps reassess the emergence of cinema in the culture of the everyday of the long nineteenth century. Print-culture sensationalism shaped not only the later camera angles and viewing positions adopted by the narrative techniques of the emerging film industry. The fast-paced narrative structures that constituted a well-oiled machinery of popular fiction, as well as the controversial and riveting characters of sensation novels, had a transmedial impact on the development of silent film serials (Gabriele). Sensationalism, therefore, constitutes one of dominant tropes of industrial modernity at large, both in the lived experience of modern metropolises and in cultural forms that crystallized its fractured tempo in the various media of popular culture.—Alberto Gabriele

See also **Mental Illness**

Serials/Serialization/Series. Serials and series were key transmission modes for nineteenth-century popular culture for non-fiction and fiction, poetry and prose, words and images. The serial differs from a series in that it comprises one narrative; a series, by contrast, comprises a set of texts, each complete in itself, unified by common characters or subject matter: **Arthur Conan Doyle**'s **Sherlock Holmes** stories in the *Strand* comprise a series, whereas **Varney the Vampyre** and J. F. Smith's *Minnigrey* were both serials, though one a part-issue novel and the other serialized in a **penny weekly** periodical. For the purposes of this entry, part-issue texts such as Knight's *Pictorial Shakespeare* or Cassell's encyclopedias, both of which played a huge role in popular culture, can also be considered series. Neither series nor serials can be separated easily from volume publication or periodicals. Early series and serials were issued with the intention of their being bound together in volumes. Later, the different demands (of the market and of narrative form) required by serial- and volume-form publication meant that serials could be rewritten for volume form (e.g., **Braddon**'s **London Journal** serial, *The Outcasts*, was shortened to become the triple-decker **Henry Dunbar**, whereas **Haggard**'s serial in the *Graphic*, **She**, was lengthened for volume publication). At other times volumes might be cut into parts for a series or serial and published either separately or in a periodical (e.g., Charles Swain's long poem *The Mind* was originally published in volume form in 1831 but serialized in the **London Journal** in 8 parts in 1852). The close connection of serialization with periodicals is clearly seen in the reviews of the hybrid series/serial now often considered a watershed in publishing: **Dickens**'s *Pickwick Papers* (April 1836 to November 1837). The first review of *Pickwick Papers* appeared in the magazine columns of a newspaper as if it were a periodical, and as late as May 1837 it was still being described as a clever set of articles. Only when it was published in volume form was it regarded as a novel. There had been a good many precedents in both fiction and non-fiction but in the eighteenth-century serials tended to be reprints, often abridged, and often translated from French or German. There were original series, however, especially in the form of periodicals featuring the same character or voice, such as Roger de Coverley in the *Spectator* (Christopher North in *Blackwood's* is an early nineteenth-century example). After the 1819 Stamp Act permitted the growth of monthly periodicals, original fiction also began to be serialized in magazines such as *Blackwood's* and the *Metropolitan Magazine*. Until the 1850s and the willing dependence of publishers on **Mudie's Circulating Library**, texts were in fact rarely issued in the format we associate with books. This was for several reasons. First, while cheap cloth binding had been introduced in the early 1830s, issue in parts allowed the purchaser not only to spread the costs but also to bind the parts in various ways at varied prices. Secondly, serial issue also allowed the publisher too to spread the costs, sales of earlier issues supporting (and predicting) the production of later ones. This fundamentally economic mode of media production and consumption led to new forms of decoding texts which authors had to learn. For if initially texts had been cut up to fit the requirements of printers—sometimes in the middle of a sentence—from the 1840s novelists and publishers began to take advantage of the serial format to incite readers' desire to buy the next episode: they wanted to create "constant readers." Novelists and publishers realized that installments controlled readers' experience of texts over time, and they consequently adopted strategies to play on this, including mnemonic epithets and mannerisms connected with characters, and the organization of each episode so as to begin with plot recapitulation and end with one or more cliffhangers. This was allied with complex multi-plot, multi-location narratives that enabled suspenseful breakoffs while the scene shifted. Serials and series in periodicals would also encourage forms of intertextual connection with material published elsewhere in the same periodical: thus a novelist might mention a product or service advertised in the journal, or the lifestory of a character might allude to that of a celebrity whose biography had been given. At other times, a novelist who was writing a serial week by week or month by month might suggest or explicitly make connections to topical events. The **Sherlock Holmes** adventure "A Scandal in Bohemia" might suggest for readers recent news coverage (the Royal Baccarat scandal of 1889–91 and the Mayerling incident of 1889); G. W. M. Reynolds's part-issue *The Mysteries of London* made a point of commenting on the secret opening of letters by the post office in 1845 that had just come to light. Such topicality in turn became institutionalized. When in its 1848 serialization the *London Journal* added the phrase "which are recorded in almost every newspaper" (vol. 7, p. 154) to the words of Thomas Miller's 1839 part-issue novel *Gideon Giles the Roper*, "Let an author draw the character of a villain in the blackest colours he can use, such a one lives in the world… let those who disbelieve us sum up all the unnatural deeds," it was only rendering explicit the intertextual connections it wanted all its constituent parts to benefit from. As Turner (2014) has argued, such decoding generates both a feeling of coherent simultaneity and synchronicity, as well as confusion caused by conflicting temporalities, not least the "real time" alluded to intertextually and the time taken to narrate the event. Such instability is a key ingredient of **sensation fiction**. Finally, mention must be made of the role of **illustration** in series and serials. While the importance of illustration to serials and series as memory aids, spotlights on certain incidents as well as advertisement is very clear, much work remains to be done in this area: Leighton and Surridge (2008) think through some of the aspects of illustration for narrative, while King (2000) offers a methodology for reading serial illustration in a competitive marketplace.—ANDREW KING

Sewell, Elizabeth Missing (1815–1906). Religious writer and educator. Sewell grew up in a politically and religiously well-connected family; her siblings included Henry, the first Premier of New Zealand; William, founder of Radley College; and James Edward, warden and later Vice-Chancellor of New College, Oxford. William supposedly edited her fiction. She began writing in part after reading evangelical **Mary Martha Sherwood** and hoped to entertain as well as educate her readers with relatable heroines. Sewell, like **Charlotte Yonge**, was part of the Oxford Movement's second generation. Her pro–Oxford Movement novels emphasize the importance of education for young women (Frerichs 1974). She sought to explain how to address religious controversy in one's own belief system, and to provide examples of how parents should raise their daughters. Sewell emphasized personal responsibility no matter one's age and the importance of the role of female relationships. Sewell's early novels include: *Amy Herbert* (1844), which remained popular for decades; *Gertrude* (1845), which emphasizes the importance of female relationships and church-building; and *Margaret Percival* (1847), which presents a fairly positive view of Catholics as Margaret considers but rejects conversion to Catholicism. Sewell suggests duty to the Church of England should prevent conversion to Catholicism and assumes women have intellectual power to understand the issues. She wrote fiction and nonfiction in addition to founding a school in the 1860s. Her most important later work includes *The Experience of Life* (1853), which addresses remaining unmarried, and *Ursula* (1858).—SARAH E. MOORE

See also ODNB, Frerichs

She (1887). Novel by **H. Rider Haggard**. This bestselling **imperial** romance offers readers adventure, exoticism, titillation, and pseudo-profundity and serves as a virtual digest of late–Victorian fantasies and anxieties about empire, **masculinity**, the **New Woman**, degeneration, atavism, and immortality. At the core of the novel is the mysterious Ayesha, an imperious, all-powerful white queen ruling over an isolated people in southeastern Africa. Having once dared to stand within "the rolling Pillar of Life" (1991/1887: p. 31), Ayesha has been invested with irresistible beauty and has had her life prolonged for over two thousand years. Ayesha is an Aphrodite who radiates "ecstatic, wonderful" life (p. 189) and "a modern Circe" (p. 159) who inspires "passion and wonder and horror" (p. 249); so she is able to override the manly rectitude and self-command of the novel's two protagonists with the "power of her dread beauty" (p. 229) and her "concentrated will and passion" (p. 230). Her subjects' propitiatory epithet—*She-who-must-be-obeyed*—is abbreviated to *She* in the narrative, underscoring her archetypal nature. The introduction contains a letter from the narrator Holly to the novelist, casting the ensuing narrative as "a real African adventure … much more marvellous" (p. 3) than Haggard's ***King Solomon's Mines***. Holly—ugly, strong, an avowed misogynist—joins his handsome adopted son Leo on a quest to find the seemingly immortal queen who killed his ancestor Kallikrates in 339 BCE and to "learn the secret of Life" (p. 31). Their party is taken prisoner by the Amahagger, a matriarchal tribe where women and men seem to live "in terms of perfect equality" (p. 81) and where women are worshipped, albeit provisionally, as "the source of life" (p. 114). The prisoners are taken to the formidable She in the catacombs of the ancient civilization of Kôr. Since Leo is incapacitated by fever, She converses with Holly alone and she explains that she has been waiting for two millennia for her former lover to be "born again" (p. 150). When she subsequently lays eyes on Leo, she knows him to be Kallikrates—he is a dead ringer for the corpse she has perfectly preserved—and she affirms that "Time hath no power against Identity" (p. 237). Having captivated Leo, She declares her intent to make him and herself rulers of Britain. Although the men protest against displacing the universally esteemed Queen Victoria, Holly muses that She as empress would "speedily make ours the most glorious and prosperous empire … the world has ever seen" (p. 256), although at a terrible cost. To forestall this, the novel has Ayesha meet a catastrophic end. She steps a second time into the "Pillar of Life," finds the effects of her first exposure reversed, ages two thousand years, and dies an abject, shriveled figure. Devastated, Holly nonetheless "see[s] the finger of Providence" in her death and moralistically speculates that She "opposed herself against the eternal Law" (p. 295)—of human mortality and Christian doctrine certainly, but also gender roles and sexual relations. Yet he joins with Leo in pining for She and anticipating her return, while wishing in his heart for a polyamorous future in which two may freely love one.—BRUCE WYSE

Sherwood, Mary Martha (1775–1851). Children's author and educator. Mary Martha (Butt) Sherwood, often called Mrs. Sherwood, is best known as the author of children's and young adults' moralistic short fiction and novels, sometimes called Low Church novels, particularly during the early part of the Victorian period. In addition to a literary influence that helped to spur the development of **children's literature**, Nancy Cutt suggests "the first generation of her readers grew up to shape the Victorian period" (1974: p. ix). Sherwood's comparatively wealthy father, a Reverend in the Church of England, gave her a religious upbringing with an emphasis on education. She writes in her autobiography that before turning twelve, she translated Virgil every morning in the stocks with an iron collar on her throat. She explains she knew of no other way of being educated and thus avoided unhappiness with her parents' method. After the death of her father, she began writing and reading for a Sunday School her somewhat sensational work, including *The History of Susan Gray*. The novel warns about the dangers of military men. In 1803, she married her cousin, a military man, and moved to **India** after the birth of their first child, whom they left with Sherwood's mother. In India, Sherwood had six children, four of whom died in infancy or as young children. In addition to writing about life in India, she started regimental schools at each post during her evangelical period, which Cutt describes as ending in about 1830. Her first major work, *Little Henry and His Bearer* (1814), focuses on life in India and was republished frequently until 1883. The children's work glorifies the death of Henry, who helps to convert his Hindu Indian servant. Her most famous work, *The History of the Fairchild Family* (1818), and its 1840s sequels seek to educate middle-class children by using a fictionalized domestic setting in which parents bear a heavy responsibility to educate their children. Her evangelical fiction emphasized total depravity, the sinfulness of children, the necessity of conversion, and the problem of Catholics. After moving back to England in 1816, Sherwood wrote for varied classes and ages; her writing includes books, chapbooks and pennybooks, religious tracts, and periodicals. Cutt describes Sherwood as in her "post-evangelical period" from 1830 to 1851. During this period, Sherwood's fiction focused less on total depravity but continued to address church and cultural religious controversies. Her later work, including *The Latter Days* (1833), *The Nun* (1833), and *The Monk of Cimiés* (1834), is anti–Catholic, in part a reaction to an evangelical emphasis on the dangers of the Oxford Movement, a High Church movement that sought to align the Church of England with some of its so-called original Catholic ideals. Cutt explains that Sherwood "took up Millenarianism" (1974: p. xi). Sherwood's writing style influenced later religious authors like High Church **Elizabeth Missing Sewell** and **Charlotte Yonge**, who tried to create more complex and well-rounded characters while continuing Sherwood's aim to educate children and young people about religion.—Sarah E. Moore

See also ODNB

Shiel, M. P. (1865–1947). West-Indian novelist. Born in the British Crown Colony of Montserrat to an illegitimate father of Anglo-Irish planter origins and mother of freed-slave descent, Matthew Phipps Shiell (who dropped the second *l* of his family name when he began to publish), was educated primarily at a grammar school in Barbados before emigrating to London in 1885. Shiel's birthplace, like much of the rest of the colonial Caribbean, had a violent, repressive history, augmented by turbulent climate and topography, which made a distinctive impression on his literary work and contributed to his later cult status. As he put it about growing up in Plymouth (Montserrat) in the shadow of the massive Soufriere Hills volcano, "No one born in such a place can be quite sane" (1901: p. 630). Certainly he is notable for both the legend that his father crowned him king of the uninhabited, rocky islet of Redonda on his fifteenth birthday and the philosophic, visionary imagination of his fiction and hyperbolic, lyrical qualities of his convoluted prose. After initial failed attempts at teaching and civil service work, Shiel achieved some recognition for his literary work in the early 1890s, particularly for *Prince Zaleski* (1895), a collection of detective stories issued by the influential Decadent publisher John Lane. Following the Decadent movement's collapse, Shiel turned to the commercial "fictional serial trade," as he put it (qtd. in Billings 2010: p. 38), and began producing **invasion literature**, popular works in tune with the prevailing imperialist sentiment.

Most successful of these was the virulently racist 1898 bestseller ***The Yellow Danger***, which imagined a mass Chinese invasion of Europe and gave Shiel the dubious honor of being the first fiction writer to really popularize the so-called yellow-peril theme in Britain. Shiel's landmark contribution to early **science fiction**, the catastrophe novel ***The Purple Cloud***, followed in 1901, featuring a lethal volcanic gas cloud that all but wipes out humanity, and accompanied by other novels imaging future conflict and past wars (notably *The Lord of the Sea* (1901), which eclectically combined the theories of land nationalization and Zionism). Following a period of relative literary success in the early 1900s, Shiel's popularity began to wane and by 1913 with the shocking failure of *The Dragon*, a dated attempt to recapture *The Yellow Danger*'s success, he was in deep **poverty**. In 1914–5 Shiel was imprisoned for the sexual assault of his twelve-year-old common-law stepdaughter, his life-long interest in much younger women culminating in an act that was shocking even by the standards of his own times. This criminality remained concealed until relatively recently (MacLeod 2008: pp. 355–80) and Shiel's writing career revived in the 1920s–1930s, when he was rediscovered by the writer John Gawsworth and publisher Gollancz and his small cult following began to develop. He spent his final years working on an unpublished study of Jesus. Overall Shiel published 25 novels, as well as collections of **short stories**, essays and poems, while also working pseudonymously and in extensive **collaboration** with other writers (Squires 2001: p. 12).—Ailise Bulfin

Shilling Shockers. A term used to refer to a specific type of published fictional work. Other common terms are shilling fiction, shilling novel, and shilling volume. In the early nineteenth century, lengthy prose fiction was **serial**ized in weekly parts that were sold for a shilling. This form of novel often did not have a planned ending, instead continuing as long as there was a readership. Initially, these works involved **Gothic** elements and were designed to inspire fear and dread, such as ***Varney the Vampire*** or ***Wagner the Wehr-Wolf***. This form of shilling shocker was also known as a **penny dreadful** or a **penny blood**. These are the type of stories compiled by Peter Haining in *The Shilling Shockers: Stories of Terror from the Gothic Bluebooks* (1979). However, by mid-century, this genre was marketed primarily to a juvenile audience and had begun to include more detective stories and adventure stories with boys as main characters. These types of shilling shockers would often be compiled and sold for a second time as a novel at a higher rate.

By the 1870s, the phrase shilling shocker was more often used to refer to a novel that was bound with a paper cover and sold for a shilling rather than earlier serialized tales of earlier. These shilling shockers were often novels of crime or violence, much as the earlier penny dreadfuls had been. The price was determined by the length of the work, not the quality of the writing, so many of these works employed stilted language and borrowed, stock plots (Griffin 1955: pp. 13–14). Ordinarily, there was a title, a subtitle, and an engraving of some scene at the beginning of each novel to attract public attention, although the engraving was not always relevant to the subject matter. These works also often reflected and highlighted the city and city living. Unlike the three-decker novel, which was typically eight hundred or more pages, a shilling novel tended to run between one hundred sixty and two hundred pages, which also added to its popularity in the working and middle classes.

Many aspects of Victorian life contributed to the success of shilling shockers, including the new popularity of railway travel and **railway bookstalls**, which created a market for railway readers that were portable and light works since the rail was a smoother ride than a coach. Routledge's "Railway Library" finally ended in 1899, by which time it had produced 1,277 titles and this was only one of several publishers involved in the shilling novel market. An increase in public libraries rather than **circulating libraries** also drove the price of a novel down, as they were more likely to purchase less expensive texts that had a broad appeal. The availability of inexpensive reading materials significantly increased literacy, as did an expansion of public education options. Especially important was the 1870 Universal Education Act, which led to a young, public, educated readership. An increase in literacy rates meant that the working classes also became an important force in shaping the novel, with an estimated ninety-six percent of England's population able to read by century's end. For these reasons, the 1880s is when shilling novels saw a significant increase in popularity and sales.

In general, the genre, in all its permutations, tends to be identified with sensationalism, violence, adventure, and second-rate writing, even though this is not necessarily true of the shilling "shockers" of the latter half of the century, which included a wider variety of subject matter. However, the genre has had its defenders, including G. K. Chesterton who wrote in his essay "Fiction as Food" that "Any literature that represents our life as dangerous and startling is truer than any literature that represents it as dubious and languid. For life is a fight and is not a conversation" (1964: p. 36). While a great number of shilling shockers were written quickly and marketed inexpensively, they were also enormously popular, essentially the first mass market paperback. The juxtaposition between popular and literary can be seen in contemporary disparaging comments about "sparsely printed little shilling volume[s]" that are one of "the lowest literary forms," with critics of the time insisting it was a "class of literature familiarity with which has bred in the minds of most readers a certain measure of contempt" (qtd. in Clarke 2014: p. 14). One can read **Charles Dickens**'s opinion of the form in Volume IX of *All the Year Round*. However, Deaglán O'Donghaile (2011) uses shilling shockers, such as **Robert Louis Stevenson**'s *The Dynamiter* (1885), to make a connection between the Victorian era and early forms of Modernism. Noteworthy examples of novels sold for a shilling and marketed as shilling fiction or shilling shockers at the time are Hugh Conway's *Called Back* (1884), **Arthur Conan Doyle**'s *A Study in Scarlet*, **Fergus Hume**'s *The Mystery of the Hansom Cab*, J. M. Barrie's first novel, *Better Dead* (1887), and **Marie Corelli**'s *The Sorrows of Satan*. Perhaps the most enduring of the shilling shockers is **Robert Louis Stevenson**'s *Strange Case of Dr. Jekyll and Mr. Hyde*.—Valerie L. Guyant

Short Story/Stories. While most novelists in the Victorian period also wrote short stories, for a long time short fiction was considered an inferior literary partner to the novel. Scholars today agree that the short story emerged in the nineteenth century in relation to revolutions in publishing that included the growth of the periodical press and the expansion of literacy in the latter part of the century. Despite, or perhaps rather because of its popularity with readers, the short story seems to have suffered from an elite denigration of the massification of literature and reading. William Makepeace Thackeray, for example, urged Anthony Trollope to produce short stories for *Cornhill Magazine* (which Thackeray was then editing) on the grounds that "the public love the tarts," although he himself "prefer[ed] bread and cheese" (quoted in Liggins et al. 2011: p. 26). The idea of short stories as enticing though ultimately insubstantial literary fare contributed to an enduring critical neglect of short fiction that is, however, increasingly being rectified today. Modern scholarship describes the short story not as a lesser version of the novel but as a distinct narrative form with its own aesthetic possibilities and demands.

Edgar Allan Poe is often taken as a starting point for theorizations of the short story. In an 1842 review of Nathaniel Hawthorne's work, Poe proposed that of all prose writing the "tale" afforded "the fairest field for the loftiest talent," and went on to specify that a story must be capable of being read in one sitting, in order that "worldly interests" do not intervene to "counteract" its "impressions" (1842: p. 298). Subsequent theorists have tended to agree that the short story is characterized by a particular economy and intensity. One aspect of this economy is that, lacking the vast canvas that allowed the nineteenth-century realist novel its painstaking excavation of chains of cause-and-effect, the plots of short stories are often characterized by elisions: events occur, but readers are not permitted to understand how they have arisen, so impressions, images and emotional tones are prioritized above rational explanation. Short fiction also enjoyed a license to eschew the novel's conventional endings (marriage, death, emigration) and indeed to refuse closure: to end in ways that were shocking or unresolved.

The distinctiveness of short fiction also relates to its place within the Victorian publishing market. The speed of production of short stories in comparison to novels meant that short fiction published in magazines or newspapers (rather than in book form) could respond quickly to contemporary events and debates, giving it a topicality surpassed only by journalism. It is also likely that the minor status of short fiction meant that it escaped the level of censorship accorded to the novel: Stewart, for example, has argued that the Victorian ghost story provided women writers with a vehicle for critiquing patriarchal society precisely because its "acceptability [as] a traditional form of entertainment" meant it often bypassed the scrutiny of male editors and critics (2001: p. 112). Indeed, the short story is often believed by scholars today to have appealed particularly to authors and readers on society's margins by facilitating the expression of counter-hegemonic ideas.

This is certainly true of the **New Woman** writers of the *fin de siècle* whose short stories presented uncompromisingly frank depictions of women's intellectual, emotional, and sexual repression. These writers were crucial in developing the short story in the direction of what Hanson has called "plotless short fiction" which operated according to "a realism which is subjectively conceived," and in which priority is given to depicting psychological states over external events, often through techniques of narrative focalization or through descriptions of physical environments that reflect characters' subjective moods (1985: pp. 6–7). Experiments in short fiction in the 1890s thus helped pave the way for the emergence of literary modernism. But female authors were also using the short story to express discontent with women's lot much earlier in the century, and in seemingly formulaic popular genres. Ghost stories by **Charlotte Riddell**, **Amelia B. Edwards**, and **Mary Elizabeth Braddon** among others affirm the reality of supernatural phenomena as a way of humbling their arrogantly dismissive male protagonists and endorsing beliefs associated with women and the lower classes. Authors later in the century such as **Edith Nesbit** would exploit an increasing public appetite for violent shocks in order to pen **Gothic** tales that foregrounded the disastrous consequences of women's social inferiorization.

Victorian short story scholarship is today enjoying a particular resurgence, with the appearance of research monographs and new scholarly editions of short fiction, and with the establishment of the **Short Story Network**. Unsurprisingly, given the popularity yet ephemerality of short stories, there are large amounts of fictions that have received insufficient critical attention, by both relatively neglected authors and by writers famed for their novelistic production such as **Charles Dickens** or Elizabeth Gaskell. Critical exploration of these works promises not only to widen our appreciation of canonical writers' oeuvres—where short fiction often enabled novelists to experiment with different genres, narrative techniques and themes—but also to achieve a better understanding of the diversity of the Victorian literary landscape by extending analysis beyond the works of the canon. As Killick has recently argued, another interesting direction for scholarship is in the short fiction of the early part of the century, which has often been wrongly dismissed as a matter of "sentimental romance, simplistic allegory, and explicit moral didacticism," and hence as unworthy of critical engagement (2008: p. 6). At the other end of the period, researchers are interested in exploring a form of short fiction that became popular toward the end of the century after the enormous success of the **Sherlock Holmes** stories: the **serial**ized **short story** which features a recurrent character in otherwise discrete stories, thereby allowing readers to develop a relationship with a character while not having to read their adventures from the beginning. In general, there remains much work to be done in reckoning with the significance of short stories in relation to Victorian popular fiction and the traditional canon.—Victoria Margree

Short Story Network. Research network established in 2016 with the aim of facilitating communication and **collaboration** between researchers of short fiction from the long nineteenth- and early-twentieth centuries. Through a Facebook page, Twitter account, and regular newsletters, the Network seeks to enable scholars to share information about conferences, publications, archives, and reading groups, and through this to develop research events and publications. Researchers ranging from established academics to PhD students as well as independent scholars are invited to join. The co-organizers are Victoria Margree and Lucy Andrew, and collaboration is planned with the **Victorian Popular Fiction Association**.

Upon its launch the network had approximately thirty participants, whose expertise ranges across more than forty authors from the Victorian period, from well-known figures to relatively neglected writers whose work is now receiving renewed critical attention. Several network members are editing editions of **short stories** by popular writers, including **Arthur Conan Doyle, Charles Dickens**, and **Netta Syrett**. Participants' interests cover a range of popular genres including **detective fiction, science fiction**, ghost stories, **Gothic fiction**, humor, and romance. Topics include relatively well-established areas such as crime, gender, and the **New Woman**, as well as reflecting more recent critical developments in ecocriticism, Thing Theory, and animal studies. Many members are particularly interested in the material culture of short story publishing: in the relationship between fiction writing and journalism, and in how short fiction published in periodicals worked alongside other subject matter such as **illustrations**, advertisements, editorials, and longer serialized fiction.—Victoria Margree

The Sign of Four. Novel by **Arthur Conan Doyle**. *The Sign of Four* appeared in *Lippincott's Magazine* in 1890. When it was published in book form, by Spencer Blackett later that year, Conan Doyle wrote to tell his publisher: "I like the style and get up very much. I trust our venture will have a success" (Lellenberg, Stashower, & Foley 2008: p. 276). **Sherlock Holmes** receives a visit from Mary Morstan, a governess, who shares the mysterious circumstances behind her father's disappearance: Miss Morstan's father, an officer in a regiment in **India**, had sent her home to England as a child, where she grew up. Nearly ten years earlier, her father had obtained a twelve-month leave and she was to meet him in London. However, he had disappeared, and his only friend that they know of and who had shared his regiment, Major Sholto, professed that he had no knowledge of Morstan's return. A few years later, Miss Morstan responded to an advertisement in the *Times* requesting her address. That day, she received a cardboard box containing a pearl and, every year henceforth, she received a similar box with a similar pearl. Miss Morstan's visit to Holmes was triggered by a letter demanding a meeting and stating: "You are a wronged woman, and shall have justice" (2003/1890: 1, 107). Miss Morstan will reveal another mystery: in her father's pocketbook, she had found the plan of a building with "a curious hieroglyphic like four crosses in a line with their arms touching" (1: 110), beside which is written: "The sign of the four,—Jonathan Small, Mahomet Singh, Abdullah Khan, Dost Akbar" (1: p. 110). Holmes, Watson, and Miss Morstan are brought to the home of Thaddeus Sholto, who reveals that his father and Morstan, who suffered from a weak heart, had discovered treasure in India; that Sholto had brought it back to England; and that Morstan *had* visited him when he returned but that he had died of natural circumstances during their confrontation. Sholto had concealed the body and the treasure, with the exception of the chaplet that he had intended but did not give Miss Morstan. In his final illness, he entreated Thaddeus and his twin brother Bartholomew to make reparation to her but he was prevented from revealing the treasure's hiding place by "a bearded, hairy face, with wild cruel eyes and an expression of concentrated malevolence" (1: p. 117) pressed against the window. The man had disappeared, but Sholto had died. The brothers discovered, the following morning, that his papers had been searched and a torn sheet of paper, with the words "The sign of the four" (1: p. 117), was fixed on his chest.

Thaddeus had persuaded his reluctant brother to send a detached pearl to Miss Morstan at regular intervals: he had requested this meeting because the treasure has now been discovered and he feels that it ought to be divided. The company found Bartholomew dead at his home, a note that said "The sign of the four" (1: p. 124) at the murder scene, and a thorn stuck in Bartholomew's skin above his ear. The treasure was stolen, but there were signs of a wooden-legged man—the Sholtos' father had an aversion to men with wooden legs—and his accomplice, who has the prints of a child. Holmes correctly identifies the criminal as Jonathan Small. With the help of Toby the mongrel and the Baker Street Irregulars, Holmes catches up to Small and his accomplice in their attempted escape aboard a steam launch: the latter was killed when he had tried to shoot one of his poisonous darts from his blow-pipe, and the former had thrown the treasure into the Thames. The captured Small relates a remarkable story that culminated in the fort at Agra. Small, commanding two Sikh troopers, was in charge of guarding a small isolated door in the building's southwest side. One night, he was made an offer: a rajah had sent his trusty servant in a merchant's disguise to conceal half of his fortune, in precious stones, in Agra until peace is restored. Small and his accomplices, which include the merchant's travelling companion, murdered him, and hid the treasure, but the murder was discovered and they were arrested and sentenced to penal servitude for life. The treasure remained a secret because the rajah had been disposed and was driven away from India. Small was eventually transferred to Blair Islands in the Andamans where he met Morstan and Sholto and told them about the treasure. In exchange for a fifth of the treasure, which was to be shared by Morstan and Sholto, they promised to help Small and his three companions to freedom. However, Sholto, who was to test the story, had stolen the treasure and never returned. Small eventually escapes with the help of Tongo, an Andaman Islander whose life he had saved, but, even in England, they could neither exact their revenge on Sholto nor claim the treasure. Small and Tonga waited for the treasure's discovery. The former had no intention to kill Bartholomew when he and Tonga made the robbery. *The Sign of Four* furthers Holmes's and Watson's story—Mary becomes the latter's wife—while deepening our knowledge of the detective and his method. Holmes, we learn in the novel's early pages, resorts to drugs for lack of mental stimulus: "My mind ... rebels at stagnation. Give me problems, give me work, give me the most abstruse cryptogram, or the most intricate analysis, and I am in my own proper atmosphere. I can dispense then with artificial stimulants. But I abhor the dull routine of existence. I crave for mental exaltation" (1: p. 100) Holmes describes to Watson three qualities necessary for the ideal detective—observation, deduction, and knowledge—and realizes one of his often quoted sayings: "Eliminate all other factors, and the one which remains must be the truth."—Tom Ue

The Silence of Dean Maitland (1886). Novel by Maxwell Gray [*pseud.* of Mary Gleed Tuttiett]. Hailed on its publication as the novel of the season, *The Silence of Dean Maitland* centers on the sympathetic and kindly but ambitious and hedonistic Cyril Maitland. A newly ordained deacon in the Anglican Church, Maitland violates his duty of pastoral care by sleeping with a young working-class girl. On becoming pregnant, Alma Lee refuses to identify the responsible party. Alma's jealous, spurned suitor suggests to her father that the baby is Maitland's. A confrontation ensues, during which her father is accidentally killed, and Maitland flees the scene. Owning to a series of coincidences, his friend Henry Everard is implicated. When Maitland learns that Everard may be convicted of manslaughter, he tries but fails to introduce testimony that would free him. Following the trial, Everard is transported to Australia, where he serves out a twenty-year prison sentence. Maitland keeps a long silence while ascending the church hierarchy, ultimately being on the verge of receiving a bishopric. As he rises, his loved ones perish, including his wife and several children. When Everard returns from Australia, having fulfilled his sentence, he discovers that Maitland killed Alma's father. Having studied his friend's popular devotional works, including *The Secret Penitent* and *Verses for the Suffering*, which have won Maitland national fame, Everard determines that the torture of Maitland's soul has in itself been a sentence. He offers his forgiveness to Maitland who, plagued by a guilty conscience, confesses his sin from the pulpit before collapsing and dying. *The Silence of Dean Maitland* is one of a small number of nineteenth-century novels to be adapted across media in the twentieth century: first, as a hit play at the turn of the century; then, as a movie on three separate occasions; and, most recently, as a television miniseries. A critical edition of the novel is in production.—Kevin A. Morrison

Silver Fork Fiction. Genre of novel popular from the 1820s to the 1840s. Silver fork fiction is characterized by meticulous attention to documenting the material details of life among the aristocratic elite in the Regency era. Notable authors who wrote silver fork novels include **Edward Bulwer-Lytton**, Benjamin Disraeli, Catherine Gore, Letitia Landon, and Charlotte Bury. The majority of these novels were published by Henry Colburn, usually in three volumes. Colburn aggressively promoted these works, tantalizing his readership with implications that they contained thinly veiled references to contemporary scandals and were also sufficiently detailed and accurate to function as guides to fashionable life. This close connection between silver fork novels and the vagaries of fashion means the novels are highly specific in the trends, manners, locations, and vocabulary they reference. The desire to meticulously capture these details is often at odds with other narrative features, resulting in **melodrama**tic and often outlandish plotting, and florid style.

With the financial success of each subsequent silver fork novel, the genre became more and more attractive to writers often explicitly interested in speedy and lucrative publishing ventures. Novels were often published with subtitles indicating their focus on elite lifestyles and on capturing a precise historical instant, with examples including "a tale of fashionable life," "a tale of the day," or "a tale of the present age." By the 1840s, the genre no longer held much currency. As non-silver fork authors increasingly made the genre's conventions and stock characters the subject of satire, the silver fork novel suffered the fate it had always been most critical of: it fell out of fashion and became passé. Thomas Carlyle's *Sartor Resartus* (1836) satirized both the figure of the dandy, and the obsession with commodities, fashion, and dress that was popularly associated with the silver fork genre. Novels by William Thackeray and **Charles Dickens** likewise took aim at the fashionable world made recognizable via silver fork fiction. Once the Regency and Reform eras had ended, taking with them a specific set of cultural circumstances, a genre whose whole existence depended on that milieu could not persist either. However, some silver fork tropes were recycled into other texts and literary genres, including **sensation fiction**, Victorian domestic realism, and even **detective fiction**.

The genre takes its name from a scathing 1827 essay published by William Hazlitt in which he deplored the tendency of these novels to focus on representing material details rather than engaging with political or social concerns, lamenting that "provided a few select persons eat fish with silver forks, [authors] consider it a circumstance of no consequence if a whole country starves" (p. 332). This early critical response set the tone for discourse about the genre, which, while commercially successful, was largely maligned throughout the nineteenth and twentieth centuries for being formulaic and superficial. Critical work in the late twentieth and early twenty-first centuries has helped to highlight the ways in which these novels offer more complex interrogations of gender and class. The first wave of silver fork novels tends to take Regency dandies as their protagonists, thereby engaging with a specific and complex mode of **masculinity**. In the 1830s and 1840s, the genre shifted toward giving greater attention to how marriages were treated as economic transactions among members of the aristocracy and the nouveau riche, exploring the precarity of female agency.

Considerable critical attention has also been given to examining the potential for social and political critique latent in a genre that specialized in representing upper-class characters to a largely middle-class readership. The peak of silver fork popularity overlapped with the era immediately preceding and following the Reform Act of 1832, and two authors who worked in the genre (Disraeli and Bulwer-Lytton) went on to have significant political careers. While the material details of aristocratic lives may be presented as enviable, silver fork novels also tend to characterize those same lives as beset by betrayal, scandal, and moral vacuity. More recent readings of the genre tend to consider silver fork depictions of the wealthy as ambivalent and potentially subversive, breaking with an older tradition of seeing these texts as guides to slavish imitation. This revitalization of interest in the genre will hopefully continue to give rise to explorations of the ways in which silver fork fiction offers more sophisticated interpretive possibilities than have previously been recognized.—DANIELLE BARKLEY

Sims, George Robert (1847–1922). Novelist, playwright, poet, journalist and social reformer. Sims was born to a middle-class family in Kennington, London, in 1847. Intended by his father for a career in the family wine business, Grub Street offered a more exciting way of earning a living. Sims wrote in an age when the distinction between the novel, the newspaper and the stage was still not clear-cut. He is significant for his shape-shifting ability to move through multiple forms and genres. His prolific output commenced when he contributed to *Fun* in 1874, followed by the "Mustard and Cress" column in the *Referee*, a sporting paper. His zestful and not-too respectful style had found its home. He penned satirical verse, later collected as *The Dragonet Ballads,* the most famous of which is "In the Workhouse: Christmas Day" featuring the much-repeated opening line, "It is Christmas Day in the Workhouse."

Taking up the mantle of Henry Mayhew, Sims acquired a reputation in the 1880s as a social reforming journalist and investigator. He entered working-class dwellings in the East End of London and wrote up his observations in works such as *How the Poor Live* (1883) and *Horrible London* (1889). Sims became an authority on the housing of the poor but also an observer of all aspects of London life: his edited collection, *Living London* (1901–3), brought a range of observers together to celebrate life in the metropolis. His writings of the 1880s were notable for promoting state intervention though he later became more conservative. He also raised matters of injustice in the court system, championing the cause of Adolf Beck, wrongly imprisoned in a case of fraud. Sims helped bring about the creation of the Court of Criminal Appeal in 1907.

At the same time, he became an extremely successful playwright, writing **melodrama**s, farces, pantomimes and burlesques of all kind. The best known of these was *The Lights O'London* (1881) which toured Britain and much of the world for many years and was filmed in 1923. Sims was particularly associated with London's Adelphi Theater, known for melodrama. He would often write with other contributors and clearly never suffered from writer's block. His plays turned him into a household word. His extensive output of novels and collections of tales such as *Rogues and Vagabonds* (1886) and *In London's Heart* (1900) were essentially the equivalent of his stage melodramas. They featured crime and romance and echoed the sensation novels of the 1860s. Sims's fascination with true crime (he was obsessed with the identity of **Jack the Ripper**) explains why he began to pen detective stories. The best known of these concern the female detective Dorcas Dene. The use of a female protagonist was relatively innovative. Sims employed the wealth from his writings to subsidize his glamorous lifestyle as a *bon vivant*. Despite a prolific output, his reputation quickly declined after his death. He has been rediscovered as a campaigning journalist, a popular West End playwright, and an early contributor to **detective fiction**.—ROHAN MCWILLIAM

See also ODNB

Skene, Felicia (1821–1899). Scottish philanthropist, prison reformer, and author. Often writing under the pseudonym Erskine Moir, Felicia Mary Frances Skene was born to Sir William Forbes, sixth baronet of Pitsligo. Her father was friends with Sir Walter Scott and he was to tell her many stories, including **fairy tales**, during her **childhood**. She was to travel widely as a child to far-off lands like Constantinople and Greece, which were to later impact her work. Skene was friends with many notable figures of the period, including Florence Nightingale, Walter Savage Landor, and E. B. Pusey. In 1854, a cholera outbreak in Oxford inspired her, under the direction of Sir Henry Acland, to form a band of nurses, many of whom later traveled to Crimea. She contributed widely to periodicals, such as *Blackwood's Magazine*, including a series of articles relating her experiences visiting prisons and with prostitutes. These were eventually collected and published in *Scenes from a Silent World: Or Prisons and Their Inmates* (1889). From 1862 to 1890 she served as editor of the *Churchman's Companion*. In 1852 she published *The Divine Master*, a devotional. Skene's works include *The Isles of Greece and Other Poems* (1843), *The Inheritance of Evil: Or, the Consequence of Marrying a Deceased Wife's Sister* (1849), *The Shadow of the Holy Week* (1893), and *A Test of Truth* (1897). She sought prison reform through many of her works, including *Penitentiaries and Reformatories* (1865) and *Scenes from a Silent World*.—AMBERYL MALKOVICH

Smythies, Mrs. Gordon (1813–1883). English novelist. Harriet Maria Gordon was born in Margate, Kent. Her first novel in 1838, *Fitzherbert, or Lovers and Fortune-Hunters*, was well received, and the second one, *Cousin Geoffrey, the Old Bachelor* in 1840, established her reputation. She went on to produce over thirty novels. Her last novel, *Eva's Fortunes*, was published in 1875. Her fiction was **serial**ized in the **London Journal**. In 1842 she married Reverend William Yorick Smythies. They settled in Weeley, Essex. They had five children. Mrs. Smythies continued to publish novels anonymously. She published poems and etiquette advice under her own name. She wrote an advice column for the *Ladies' Treasury* between 1857 and 1860. She also wrote for **Cassell's Family Magazine**. Mrs. Smythies admired **Edward Bulwer-Lytton** and developed a close friendship with him. He in turn encouraged her writing, and his influence can be detected in her fiction. Her husband did not approve of this relationship and Summers (1945) has suggested that she continued to publish anonymously despite her increasing popularity, because her husband did not approve of her writing (p. 362). In the late 1850s Reverend Smythies got into financial difficulties. By the following year, 1862, Mrs. Smythies had moved to lodgings in London with their children and her mother. There she continued to support her family by her writing and became part of the London literary scene.

Mrs. Smythies was known as "the Queen of the Domestic Novel." Her novels invariably deal with matters of love and matrimony, inheritance, and family relations. These themes are reflected in the titles of her novels, including *The Marrying Man* (1841), *The Matchmaker* (1842), *Married for Love* (1857), *The Male Flirt* (1860), and *The Faithful Woman* (1865). Her novels are populated with large numbers of somewhat stereotypical characters, often introduced with short and vivid portraits in the narrative. She produces **melodrama**tic scenes to great effect and she writes with humor. Her plots are rambling and reflect conventional Victorian values and social norms.

Mrs. Smythies was often described on the title page of her novels as "the author of *Cousin Geoffrey* and *Jilt*." *Cousin Geoffrey* charts the convoluted path to matrimony of heroine Juliet St. Aubyn, aided by her sister Blanche and pursued unsuccessfully by cousin Geoffrey. *The Jilt* was Smythies's fifth novel published in 1844. It features an enterprising father and daughter both attempting to make their way into lucrative and advantageous marriages. These early novels seem to be her most popular work. H. L. Mansel (2001/1863) included *The Daily-Governess, or Self-Dependence*, published in 1861, in his review of sensation novels in the *Quarterly Review*, but that was the closest Mrs. Smythies ever came to being associated with this popular genre.

In 1866 Smythies's beloved daughter and companion died of consumption. By 1875 all her siblings and all but one child, son William Gordon Smythies born in 1849, had died. Mrs. Smythies herself died in London in 1883 after a long illness. Less than three months later Reverend Smythies remarried.—Emma Kareno

See also ODNB

Social Distinction; or, Hearts and Homes (1848–9). Didactic novel by **Sarah Stickney Ellis**. Published in two volumes, *Social Distinction* follows three generations of the Staunton family. The novel interrogates women's independence, particularly in the form of financial control, and delineates good and bad forms of selfishness and self-love. The novel also further develops Ellis's notion of women's influence, a subject that is discussed at length in her conduct manuals, such as *The Women of England*. The novel's primary villain, Mrs. Ashley, marries for money and greedily uses her husband's wealth to purchase frivolous goods. Mrs. Ashley drives the family to ruin, and also contributes to her husband's drinking habit. In this point, therefore, the novel also brings up the issue of **temperance**, as Mrs. Ashley takes advantage of her husband's **alcoholism** in order to further manipulate him and extract increasing amounts of money from his accounts. In contrast, the good women in the novel, Margaret and Kate Staunton, achieve financial independence, but do so through their own industry and through safeguarding their family wealth. They also use their influence to uphold moral principles in their households, rather than for personal gain. Ultimately, they are rewarded with an exceptional level of agency and financial control. Like many of Ellis's works, this novel of purpose went through several reprints in England and the United States.—Ashley Lynn Carlson

Socialist Fiction. British socialism at the *fin de siècle* was promoted through a variety of print materials including books, periodicals, tracts, and leaflets. It was also, as Raphael Samuel (1985) and others have noted, a deeply literary movement. Jack Mitchell states that "it was not just a matter of socialism attracting people of a literary bent … the socialist societies laid tremendous weight on the word" (1987: pp. 50–51). There were two primary media used for the distribution of socialist fiction (the book or the periodical) and three primary forms (the novel, the **short story**, or the **serialization**). In many cases serialization was followed by publication in book form.

Some socialist authors published through the mainstream press (e.g., **H. G. Wells** with Pearsons, Macmillan, and **Heinemann**) while some used radical publishers such as Henry Vizitelly (e.g., **Margaret Harkness**'s *A City Girl* and Swan **Sonnenschein** (e.g., George Bernard Shaw's *An Unsocial Socialist* and Margaret Harkness's *Out of Work*. Others published their work through presses owned by socialist groups: the Modern Press and the Nineteenth/Twentieth Century Press, associated with the Social Democratic Federation (SDF), primarily published political books and tracts; Robert Blatchford, editor of the *Clarion*, founded the Clarion Press and published work by contributors as well as his own fiction (e.g., *A Bohemian Girl* (1899); William Morris's Kelmscott Press produced handmade editions of *News from Nowhere* (1892) and *A Dream of John Ball* (1892).

Most socialist fiction was published in the socialist periodicals, as they were affordably priced (usually around 1d.) and some had a large circulation. The *Clarion* (1891–1934) accounts record average weekly sales of 45,000 in 1895, Henry Hyde Champion's

Labour Elector (1888–90, 1893–94) claimed 23,000 sales in October 1889, but the SDF's *Justice* (1884–1925) sold 3,000–4,000 per week at its peak in 1887, the Hammersmith minutes of 25 July 1886 recorded weekly sales of 2,600 copies for the Socialist League's *Commonweal* (1885–94). Although Elizabeth Carolyn Miller (2013) claims that "[f]rom a literary point of view, the *Commonweal* was the most significant socialist paper of the era" (p. 195) it ran only three long serials: William Morris's narrative poem *Pilgrims of Hope* (1885–86), and the fictions *A Dream of John Ball* (1886–87) and *News from Nowhere* (1890). The *Commonweal*'s weekly competitor, *Justice*, published only two serial fictions before 1900 (James Borlase's *Darker Than Death* [1885] and H. J. Bramsbury's *A Working Class Tragedy* [1888–89]) but the SDF's monthly publication, *To-Day* (1883–89), carried nine serials including George Bernard Shaw's novels *An Unsocial Socialist* (1884) and *Cashel Byron's Profession* (1885–86). Shaw also published *The Irrational Knot* (1885–87) and *Love Among the Artists* (1887–88) in SDF member Annie Besant's *Our Corner* (1883–88).

While the Marxist SDF and Marxist/**anarchist** Socialist League carried relatively few serializations, groups that took an ethical approach to socialism—humanizing and moralizing the scientific economics of Marxism—regularly serialized fiction. The *Clarion* carried seventeen serial fictions before 1900 (including Blatchford's *No. 66* (1893), Edward Fay's *Strictly Proper* (1893) and *With Cupid's Curse* (1898–99) by Mont Blong (Montagu Blatchford). James Keir Hardie's Independent Labour Party (ILP) periodical, the *Labour Leader* (1894–1987), published twelve serials, including Albert T. Marks's *By Shadowed Paths* (1895), S. Washington's *The Bloodstone* (1896) and Lillian Claxton's *Nigel Grey* (1896–97). ILP-founder Joseph Burgess's *Workman's Times* (1890–94) carried twenty serial fictions, including *The Blackleg* (1893) by James Sexton under the pseudonym *Citizen*, Jean Valjean's *Rebecca: A Woman's Tale* (1893–94) and Mrs. E.D.E.N. Southworth's *The Lost Lady of Lone* (1891–92). Charles Allen Clarke's periodical, *Teddy Ashton's Journal* (1896–1908), which changed its name to the *Northern Weekly* two years into its twelve-year run, published twenty-seven serial stories between its first issue of May 1896 and the end of 1900, including Will Payne's *The Rope of Gold* (1896), James Haslem's *The Mill on the Moor* (1898–99), and nine by Clarke himself, which included *A Daughter of the Factory* (1894–95) and *The Cotton Panic* (1900–01). Clarke also wrote and published, under the pseudonym Grandad Grey, a long-running series of stories for children under the cohering title *Big Bluffin and Little Barnett* (1896–1905).

The novel has been criticized as an inherently bourgeois form inappropriate as a vehicle for anti-capitalist or working-class fiction, but H. Gustav Klaus (1982) argues that "form is not the only (ideological) constituent of a text, and it is, above all, not some kind of cosmic, transhistorical category immune to change" (1982: p. 2). As Pamela Fox asserts, the use of the novel form by working-class writers demonstrates "the need to *appropriate* dominant cultural codes for the production of subversive narratives" (1994: p. 59). The problem with the book format is two-fold: the expense made regular purchase unaffordable for the working-class reader and a book publication is an autonomous work in a format that sets it apart from the socialist atmosphere of its production. This separation is exacerbated when the fiction was originally serialized in the socialist press: Morris's idyllic socialist utopia in *News from Nowhere* originally sat amid the wranglings of the Socialist League as the anarchist faction took over the group; Shaw's *The Irrational Knot*, with the issue of marriage at its center, was serialized during the spat over the Woman Question between SDF members Annie Besant and Ernest Belfort Bax; James

Sexton's *The Blackleg* tackles the limitations of trade unionism and the necessity of parliamentary representation as Burgess laid the foundations for the ILP through the *Workman's Times*. To take these serializations and strip away their context of publication cauterizes the edges that had previously enabled osmosis between the fiction and journalism and so limits the political impact of the fiction.

While some of the serials were probably syndicated fiction (Borlase and Southworth generally published in mainstream periodicals) most were written by members of the group that published the periodical. Morris published in *Justice* while a member of the SDF and when, at the end of 1884 he and ten others left to form the Socialist League, he then only published in the League's *Commonweal*. Although there is no record of an author published under the name H. J. Bramsbury there is a case for argument that *Bramsbury* is a pseudonym for Henry Mayers Hyndman, chairman of the SDF (see Mutch 2006). Blatchford did not regularly publish outside of the *Clarion* and the periodical carried fiction by all the *Clarion* board—Robert Blatchford, Fay, A. M. Thompson, and Montagu Blatchford—as well as members such as Katherine St. John Conway/Glasier and Margaret Macmillan. Clarke mainly published in the *Northern Weekly*, as did Fred Plant and James Haslem who were part of the group Paul Salveson (1987) names the Lancashire School.

Although socialist novels, in book or serial form, may appear conservative in their reliance on older literary forms, closer examination reveals a political use of multiple sub-genres. Ian Haywood has commented on the hybrid nature of socialist author Charles Allen Clarke's fiction (1997: p. 16) noting the overlap of romance, **melodrama**, and reportage among some of the forms in his work. Robert Blatchford's *No. 66*, for instance, combined realism and the melodramatic threat of the capitalist with the chivalry of romance and the popular army tale when presenting the socialist perspective. Friedrich Engels's 1888 letter to Margaret Harkness asserted the revolutionary possibilities for realism: "The rebellious reaction of the working class … their attempts … at recovering their status as human beings, belong to history and must therefore lay claim to a place in the domain of realism" (Engels 1973/1888: p. 115). By overlapping the revolutionary origins of **melodrama**, developed as a popular form during the French revolution, with the revolutionary use of realism and by connecting their narratives directly to the historical context, socialist authors presented a different perspective on contemporary society. They also suggested the possibility of change by rejecting the naturalist representation of social order as inevitable and of human beings as victims of their environment. Socialist fiction did not, though, flatten the different political perspectives of the Marxist and ethical factions as is illustrated by H. J. Bramsbury's *A Working Class Tragedy* and Charles Allen Clarke's *The Cotton Panic*.

The Bramsbury fiction was either written by Hyndman or selected for publication because of the close resemblance to "Hyndman's Marxism [which] embraced scientism and a rigid dialectic" (Bevir 2011: p. 74). In this vein, the fiction is presented as an allegory of the worker under capitalism and rejects the individualism of the realist novel as Bertolt Brecht would later do in the theater. Frank Wilson, the oppressed worker persecuted by the capitalist Cranston and his son, symbolizes the power imbalance and threat in this socialist allegory. Frank's refusal to be persuaded by socialism is the catalyst for his downfall and thus draws in the genre of tragedy. Historical events and political polemic anchor the story to the recent past and the politics of the surrounding periodical. Although the Cranstons are the primary threat, other employers, the employment system generally, the law, and insincere socialist leaders create what Jack Mitchell terms "an interlocking *system* of oppression" (1987: p. 59). The absence of back-story for any of the characters and the presentation of characters as types—the worker, the capitalist, the aristocrat, the socialist, the lover, etc.—forces the reader to both interpret and identify with Frank's experiences in a fictional, though scientific, evaluation of capitalism.

Ethical socialists, on the other hand, integrated the emotions and morality, absent in Marxist economics, into their politics and their fiction. Clarke's *The Cotton Panic* is presented as a historical novel, set during the Lancashire cotton famine of 1861–63, but is also a bricolage of genres: the romance of the working-class lovers, the melodramatic threat of the rejected Mormon suitor, the inclusion of dialect poetry and song, and war fiction. The characters' histories are described in some detail (the reader is told, for instance, of the social decline of the Milner family caused by the father's death and the cotton famine) and so flesh out and make individual the characters in ways that Bramsbury's scientific Marxism did not. Nevertheless, Clarke is not merely creating a realist fiction but, by presenting global capitalism in the introduction as a fragile balance between nations where "the activity of the machinery of the American War caused a stoppage of the machinery of manufacture in Lancashire" (Clarke 1900: p. 9), describes an "interlocking system of oppression" even wider than Bramsbury's.

The inclusion of **short stories** in the periodicals follows a similar pattern to that of the serial fiction. From the beginning of their publication to 1900, Marxist periodicals again carried many fewer short stories (*Justice*: thirty five, *Commonweal*: ten) than the ethical socialists (*Clarion*: 185, *Labour Leader*: 160, *Teddy Ashton/Northern Weekly*: 569). The content similarly follows the division of Marxist scientism and ethical morality. Dan Baxter's story "The New Shilling" (1895) published in *Justice*, sets out the Marxist theory of money fetishization through the symbol of a sentient shilling that wishes to be useful (as a button or broach) rather than a counter of fiscal exchange. The use of allegory was not restricted to the Marxist stories, though, as witnessed by Caroline E. D. Martyn's "A Mystery" (1896), published in Hardie's *Labour Leader*. Two children of nature seek "a bond that could not be broken" (Martyn 1896: p. 80) for their love but are instead offered the fetters of religion and the chains of the law. It is only after death, when their bodies are mingled in the earth and their souls are in Heaven, that they achieve the bond. Martyn uses allegory to train her focus on freeing emotional relationships from the capitalist state and suggest a better way through "a simplified life [and] a return to nature" (Bevir 2011: p. 235). British socialists designed new, hybrid forms of fiction not only to create a distinction between their political fiction and Victorian realism but also to distinguish between political ideologies within socialism.—Deborah Mutch

See also Marcoux 1992, Martin 1896, Vaninskaya 2010

The Society of Authors (1883–). In September 1883, twelve members of the Savile Club set up a working party intended to advocate for authors on matters of publishing, literary property, and copyright protection. Among them was author and historian **Walter Besant**, who in 1884 would found the Society of Authors, a professional association for writers, the first successful one of its kind. Besant was elected chairman, a position he served until 1892, and Alfred Lord Tennyson served as the first appointed president. Besant also served as editor of the society's annual journal, *The Author*, which was established in 1890. Other notable members included Thomas Hardy, George Meredith, and George Bernard Shaw, who would play a leading role in the League of Dramatists (1931), an association for playwrights. In 1896, several women authors were elected to the Society's management committee, including **Charlotte Yonge, Eliza Lynn Linton**, and **Mrs. Humphry [Mary Augusta] Ward** (Sutherland 1989: p. 593). Although contemporary issues with booksellers and publishers were many and diverse, the Society of Authors narrowed its focus to protecting the literary property of authors by copyright. By the early twentieth century, the association had successfully lobbied for international copyright agreement, and contributed to the introduction of Public Lending Right. As of 2018, the society consists of around 9,500 voting members, and several hundred more associate members. The association now advises writers, illustrators, and literary translators; it also oversees the distribution of select literary estates. Its journal, *The Author*, is distributed to members quarterly.—Vicky Cheng

The Sorrows of Satan (1895). Supernatural novel by **Marie Corelli**. The novel was one of the first modern bestsellers, reaching its fifty-fifth impression by August 1910 (Waller 2006: p. 773). Its title refers to the idea that Satan has sworn to destroy man utterly, even though man can redeem Satan by rejecting him—a tragic paradox at the root of Satan's "sorrows." The protagonist is Geoffrey Tempest, a literary hack whose **poverty** is alleviated by an unexpected bequest of five million pounds. At the same time, he receives a letter of introduction to Prince Lucio Rimânez, who encourages him to pen novels on "sexual matters," which treat "men and women simply as cattle who exist merely for breeding purposes" and which are sure to prove popular with the reading public (Corelli p. 35). Rimânez uses his influence and wealth to get Tempest's books published and to secure favorable reviews and widespread advertising—all of which (rather than genuine literary talent) underscore Tempest's newfound success as an author. As Rimânez aids and abets Tempest's literary career, the novel portrays a publishing system riven by hypocrisy and corruption, in which "merit counts for nothing" (Corelli p. 73)—a symptom of a pervasively "decadent and ephemeral age" (p. 76). Shortly after establishing his place in London society as a literary celebrity, however, Tempest receives his first hint that all is not quite as it seems—a terrifying dream in which a group of hooded figures warns of impending misery and doom. In another major plot-strand, Tempest's marriage to Lady Sibyl Elton illustrates how the corruption of the publishing world also serves to corrupt the values and morality of readers. Sibyl, a voracious reader of **New Woman** novels "that advocate almost as a sacred duty 'free love' and universal polygamy" (Corelli 1895: 201–2), has completely abandoned any sense of traditional marriage and eventually pursues an affair with Rimânez. When Rimânez rejects her advances, Sibyl kills herself, leaving a **suicide** note detailing the process of her corruption by literature. As she dies, she hears a voice entreating her to "come to your chosen lover" (Corelli 1895: p. 421), thereby linking the immoralities of modern novels to a worship of the devil. In contrast to Sibyl, the novel's other female protagonist is the writer Mavis Clare (the first recorded use of Mavis as a female forename). A thinly veiled self-portrait of Corelli, Clare's fiction is hugely popular with the book-buying public, even though her insistence on Christian themes and a strong moral sensibility is relentlessly attacked by reviewers. Eventually, it is his friendship with Clare that saves Tempest's soul. Having narrowly escaped a wraith-haunted voyage to "the world's end" (Corelli 1895: p. 470), during which Rimânez reveals his true Satanic identity, Tempest is washed ashore only to find that his fortune, and his influence over the publishing industry, have collapsed due to absconding financiers. He is left penniless with Clare as his only friend—but infinitely richer for her moral guidance.—Dewi Evans

Stables, William Gordon (1840–1910). British author. Stables was born in Scotland and qualified as a doctor in 1862. Having sailed on whaling expeditions while a student, he joined the Royal Navy as an assistant-surgeon, and, among other duties, sailed the Mozambique Coast in search of slave-traders. Poor **health** caused him to be invalided home in 1871 and he began writing. He moved to Twyford, near Reading, and his first story *The Cruise of the Snowbird* was serialized in the *Boy's Own Paper* in 1881. In 1885 Stables designed his own horse-drawn caravan, furnishing it with a harmonium and guitar, a naval sword, and revolver. Each summer Stables traveled around the country, preceded by his valet riding a tricycle, attracting considerable attention. His eccentricities were possibly the result of being a recovering drug-addict for he revealed in a magazine article that he had once taken drugs to cure insomnia.

Despite his erratic and increasingly wild behavior, Stables became a prolific author producing over one hundred and forty books. Stable wrote on **medicine** and on the treatment of animals, becoming a particular expert on dogs. He also wrote over a hundred adventure stories for boys.

These fall into three different categories: fantasy and **science fiction**, historical tales, and traditional adventure stories. *The Cruise of the Crystal Boat* (1891) is about an electrically powered airship, and Stables, possibly influenced by Jules Verne, also wrote stories about submarines and a remarkable Power Source that made both aviation and longevity possible. Among Stables' historical works, *On the Rescue* (1895) is a tale about the Indian Mutiny and *'Twixt Daydawn and Light* (1898) is set in the times of King Alfred the Great.

But Stables is more likely to be remembered, if at all, for his traditional adventure stories. His narrative style is simple and straightforward, and his narratives usually proceed chronologically, often charting a young boy-hero's progress from mischievous youth to maturity. His stories also contain humorous elements, such as the presence of comic characters, like the pompous businessman E. S. Bumbleby-Phipps (*In Regions of Perpetual Snow* [1904]), and in practical jokes.

Stables's best stories often exploit the Victorian age's obsession with exploring the polar regions. *In the Land of the Great Snow-Bear* (1887), about young Claude Alwyn who joins a scientific expedition to Greenland and winters in Baffin Bay, is a typical example. The party suffer both an attack by a polar bear and their ship being destroyed by fire, and struggle through the harshest conditions to reach civilization. Stables's polar adventures are not about battles and wars but natural disasters, such as blizzards, shipwrecks and storms, and he depicts them with some authority. But although readers of the *Boy's Own Paper* judged him their favorite writer in a poll of 1899, his work now seems dated and his popularity has not survived.—Dennis Butts

Steel, Flora Annie (1847–1929). Anglo-Indian novelist and **short story** writer. After her marriage to an engineer in the Indian Civil Service, Steel spent over twenty years in **India**, mainly in the Punjab, where she worked as a teacher and school inspector, becoming the first female Inspectress of Schools in India in 1884. In 1885, Steel was appointed vice-president of the Victoria Female **Orphan** Asylum. She developed a lifelong interest in local Indian customs, crafts, languages, and literature during this time, which led to the publication of her first work, *Wide-Awake Stories* (1884), a collection inspired by Indian folktales. This collection was followed by her first novel, *Miss Stuart's Legacy* (1893). Steel is best known today for her 1896 **Anglo-Indian novel** *On the Face of the Waters*, a work considered to be one of the best fictional depictions of the Indian Uprising of 1857. In 1894, Steel returned to India in order to conduct research for the novel, including an examination of confidential government papers relating to the Uprising. In addition to novels and story collections, Steel published her guide for Anglo-Indian women, *The Complete Indian Housekeeper and Cook* (with Grace Gardiner) in 1888 and the historical account, *India Through the Ages: A Popular and Picturesque History of Hindustan*, in 1908. After her return to England, Steel continued to be involved in social causes, particularly the women's suffrage movement. In 1913, she became president of the Women Writers' Suffrage League. Her autobiography, *The Garden of Fidelity*, was published in 1929.—MELISSA EDMUNDSON

See also ODNB, Crane and Johnston 2010

Stevenson, Robert Louis (1850–1894). Scottish author Robert Lewis Balfour Stevenson was the son of engineer Thomas Stevenson and his wife, Margaret Isabella. He studied engineering, then law, in his native Edinburgh, but abandoned both pursuits to become a professional writer. His early work consisted of essays and travel literature, the best known of which is *Travels with a Donkey in the Cévennes* (1879). Stevenson's first pieces of fiction were **short stories** for periodical publication, most notably *Latter-Day Arabian Nights* (1878) in *London* magazine, edited by Stevenson's friend, the poet W. E. Henley. In 1879 Stevenson travelled to America in pursuit of divorcée Fanny Van de Grift Osbourne, with whom he had fallen in love during a meeting at an artists' colony near Paris. They married in 1880 and returned to Scotland. Financially dependent on his parents, Stevenson wrote fiction for children's periodicals as a means of attaining much-needed income. His first attempt was the piratical adventure **Treasure Island**, serialized in *Young Folks* in 1881–1882. He went on to pen two further adventure **serials** for that magazine: *The Black Arrow* (1883) and **Kidnapped** (1886).

Residing at Bournemouth in 1886, Stevenson produced perhaps his best-known work: the **Gothic** thriller **Strange Case of Dr. Jekyll and Mr. Hyde**, which earned him something approaching financial security for the first time. He also began a long-lasting friendship with his neighbor, the writer Henry James, with whom Stevenson had corresponded after the publication of his essay "A Humble Remonstrance" (1884)—a response to James's "The Art of Fiction" (1884). Stevenson rejected James's assertion that fiction could (and should) seek to conjure a convincing illusion of reality. Instead, Stevenson argued, literature's complete separation from lived experience, of which it could only ever be a representation, meant that the fantasies of the romance writer, which offered readers a deliberate escape from "reality," were as valid a literary art form as those written in the realist tradition—a philosophy underlying Stevenson's adventure fiction and theorized extensively in his essays.

Throughout his life, Stevenson was plagued by an acute lung condition, travelling widely in order to seek a climate conducive to his **health**. After the death of his father in 1887, Stevenson, together with his wife, mother and stepchildren, left Scotland for the Adirondack Mountains of North America. There Stevenson, fresh from the success of *Jekyll and Hyde*, worked on a lucrative commission for a series of monthly articles for *Scribner's* magazine, as well as the historical adventure *The Master of Ballantrae* (1888). The family then travelled to California, chartered a yacht and embarked on an extended tour of the South Pacific, eventually settling in Samoa in 1890. Stevenson produced several stories set in the region, including the proto-modernist critique of imperialism, *The Ebb-Tide* (1894; coauthored with his stepson Lloyd Osbourne) and the posthumously published travelogue *In the South Seas* (1896). He died of a cerebral hemorrhage at the family's home at Apia, Samoa, in 1894, leaving unfinished a realist novel set in Scotland, *Weir of Hermiston*.—DEWI EVANS

Stoker, Bram (1847–1912). Anglo-Irish novelist and theater manager. Known primarily for his 1897 novel ***Dracula***, Bram Stoker was born in Dublin to Abraham and Charlotte Stoker (the former a clerk at Dublin Castle and the latter a social activist). Stoker was bed-ridden through much of his **childhood** due to an unknown illness. This experience is often credited with fueling the young Stoker's imagination. Critic David J. Skal (2016) has recently gone so far as to suggest that these childhood experiences including the possible medical use of bloodletting made a strong impression and shaped Stoker's creative output significantly. Despite these early conditions, Stoker ultimately recovered and became a formidable athlete at Trinity College where he studied science, graduating in 1871. He went on to pursue a master's degree in mathematics awarded in 1874.

In the midst of his academic career Stoker also held a position as a petty clerk at Dublin Castle, the center of Irish governance. He held this position from 1866 to 1878 and it would produce his first lengthy publication, *The Duties of Clerks of Petty Sessions in Ireland*, published in 1879. W. N. Osborough (1999) has noted some of the ways in which Stoker's experience at Dublin Castle may have shaped his later career as a writer. His diary from this period has recently been published, edited by Elizabeth Miller and Dacre Stoker (Bram Stoker's grand-nephew), and may provide further avenues for critical exploration (Stoker 2012). While not the most creatively stimulating career, the clerkship allowed the young Stoker to earn a wage and focus in his spare time on other pursuits such as athletics and especially theater.

A primary turning point in Stoker's professional life was his meeting with Henry Irving in 1876. Stoker had greatly admired Irving, one of the most famous actors of the era (and the first actor to receive a knighthood), ever since seeing him in an 1867 production of Sheridan's *The Rivals*. Stoker had been working as an unpaid theater reviewer in the *Dublin Mail* since 1871 and had seen Irving on stage as early as 1865. The partnership between Stoker and Irving would be made official in 1878 when Stoker took over as acting manager of Irving's Lyceum Theater in London. From this point until Irving's death Stoker assisted the actor in staging productions, running the front of house, and managing international tours. Stoker managed the theater until 1902 when it went into receivership.

Stoker's professional experiences in both Dublin Castle and at the Lyceum inform his most famous work, *Dracula*, in important ways. Critics have anchored the novel's assemblage of fragments drawn from different sources in the compiling of documents that were the day-to-day duties of a petty clerk. This could be further compounded by the Irish government's concern with Irish Republicanism during this period. In such a way *Dracula* might be construed as a dossier focused on an invading political adversary, as it is "To know everything about Dracula is to know how to destroy him. It is information, gathered and arranged into a collaborative and comprehensive account, that enables the group to defeat Dracula" (Richards 2009: p. 440) The novel's form also recalls the press clipping that Stoker compiled for Irving while managing the Lyceum as well as Stoker's role in handling Irving's correspondence. Irving himself has also been identified as a prime inspiration for the fictional count.

The same year that Stoker began work as manager for the Lyceum he married Florence Anne Lemon Balcombe. Balcombe, a Dublin socialite, was also being pursued by a young **Oscar Wilde**, one of the many literary figures who Stoker interacted with over the course of his life. He and Florence had one child, Irving Noel, born in 1879.

Stoker's life in London was a busy one. He worked full-time at the Lyceum while honing his craft as a writer. While Stoker had published short fiction in the 1870s and the manual *Duties of Clerks,* his first major work of creative fiction was *Under the Sunset*, a book of fairytales published in 1882. His travels on tour with the Lyceum company also provided him with material for his travelogue *A Glimpse of America* (1886). Stoker's first full-length novel was the adventure tale *The Snake's Pass*, centered on his native Ireland and the legends surrounding St. Patrick. This was followed by two other adventure novels, *The Watter's Mou* (1895) and *The Shoulder of Shasta* (1895).

Stoker began the intensive research for what would become *Dracula* in 1890. Mirroring his eventual protagonist Jonathan Harker, he spent a great deal of time in the British Library researching Central and Eastern Europe. Upon its publication the novel was certainly seen as Stoker's most important output, but its greater appreciation came in the twentieth century when the fictional count made the transition to film. Still, the novel garnered positive reviews and was published in multiple countries in English and in translation.

Stoker continued writing fiction after *Dracula's* publication, though he was never able to replicate its success. His most notable works from this period are **The Jewel of Seven Stars** and *The Lair of the White Worm* (1911). *The Jewel of Seven Stars* is one of the first works to examine the period's **Egypt**omania from a supernatural perspective (and indeed a precursor to the monstrous **mummies** of fiction and film in the early-to-mid-twentieth centuries.) *The Lair of the White Worm* is based on the folklore surrounding the "Lambton Worm," a monster said to have resided in County Durham in the north of England, stories of which had gained a certain currency during the previous century.

Stoker died of kidney failure on 20 April 1912, after several years of declining health. He was cremated and laid to rest at Golders Green cemetery in London. He was survived by Florence Stoker.—Jude Wright

See also ODNB

The Story of a Modern Woman (1894). Novel by **Ella Hepworth Dixon**. First published **serial**ly in *Lady's Pictorial* and then in a single volume by **Heinemann**, Dixon's **New Woman** novel is the story of Mary Erle's life in London following her father's death. As she struggles to support herself and her younger brother, Mary enrolls in art school but fails to flourish there. She then turns to writing but is frustrated by her editor's demands to be formulaic. Upon her betrothal to a caddish lover, Vincent Hemming, Mary feels his hands on her wrists as "links of iron" and realizes "the helplessness of woman" (p. 82). Vincent jilts Mary but later asks her to be his mistress; she refuses him. In a parallel plot, Mary's progressive friend, Alison Ives, who has ushered Mary into a world of social activism, takes up with the unfaithful doctor Dunlop Strange, from whose abandoned mistress she contracts consumption. On her deathbed, Alison proclaims: "If women only used their power in the right way! If we were only united, we could lead the world" (1894: p. 164). At the story's end, Mary trudges home from the cemetery at dusk to face the dreary world alone. Of her novel, Dixon said, "I wished to show how hardly our social laws press on women, how in fact, it is too often the woman who is made ... the moral scapegoat, and who is sent out into the wilderness to expiate the sins of man" (Stead 1894: p. 71).—Steve Farmer

The Story of Lilly Dawson (1847). Novel by **Catherine Crowe**. This is the third of Crowe's novels and the most fast-paced and rambunctious. Written as a *Bildungsroman*, we follow the kidnapped and abused Lilly as she slowly comes to self-awareness and gains freedom and agency. The story begins at the remote, isolated inn "The Black Huntsman" where Lilly is enslaved as a Cinderella figure by her cousins the sinister Littenhaus family. After a series of mishaps (including arson and murder), Lilly almost inadvertently manages to escape. What happens next is a romp through Victorian underclass society. Lilly experiences and witnesses appalling hardship and hunger, yet she comes across kindness and wisdom too, most notably in the character of the blind beggar Abel White. The novel carries some severe critiques of laissez faire capitalism, greed, and ignorance. However, Crowe's starkest criticism comes with her analysis of women's position in society, especially in relation to education and in her vitriolic assessment of men treating women "like a full-grown baby, to be flattered and spoiled on the one hand, and coerced and restricted on the other" (2015/1847: p. 202). *Lilly Dawson* is a pre-cursor to the **sensation novels** of the 1860s, but it employs realism too. A review in *The Critic* concludes that *Lilly Dawson* "is a fearful tale, wrought with extraordinary power" (Anon 1847: pp. 205–6), and this power can still be felt today. A serious piece of social commentary, *Lilly Dawson* is also a wonderful rollicking tale of pirates, murder, betrayal, lust and mistaken identity.—Ruth Heholt

Strand Magazine (1891–1950). The foremost British New Journalistic fiction paper of the 1890s, influenced by the American *Scribner's* and *Harper's*. Owned by the enterprising publisher George Newnes (1851–1910), who had made his money from the penny weekly miscellany *Tit-Bits* (1881–1984), the *Strand* was edited by Herbert Greenhough Smith (1855–1935) from its inception until 1930. The iconic light blue cover design by George Charles Haité looked east along the Strand, a central London thoroughfare, from the corner of Burleigh Street, where the editorial offices were located. A heavily illustrated 6d. monthly of 112 two-columned pages, the *Strand* offered its readers well-written, morally sound but entertaining reading, providing outstanding value for money. The first issue promised readers "cheap, healthful literature" consisting of "stories and articles by the best British writers, and special translations from the first foreign authors ... illustrated by eminent artists" (Newnes 1891: p. 3). A family paper that primarily appealed to men, the *Strand* also included material for female and child readers. Circulation soon reached 500,000, with the magazine expanding to 120 pages. This success meant that the *Strand* could offer contributors generous remuneration and access to a large audience, and the magazine was also known for its prompt editorial decisions and payments to authors. It secured signed contributions from leading popular writers, including **Grant Allen, Arthur Conan Doyle, E. W. Hornung,** W. W. Jacobs, **Rudyard Kipling, Richard Marsh, Arthur Morrison, Edith Nesbit, H. G. Wells,** and P. G. Wodehouse. The monthly revealed its New Journalistic credentials in its high human-interest content, including puzzles, brain teasers, curiosities, and features on hobbies and activities, and also contributed to the development of *fin-de-siècle* celebrity culture by printing celebrity interviews, illustrated "at-homes," portraits of celebrities at different ages, and samples of celebrities' handwriting.

Initially designed as a magazine of **short stories** complete in each issue, the *Strand* was instrumental in establishing the commercial potential of short fiction in Britain, although it also **serial**ized novels. While the first volume contained several translated stories, from its second volume the monthly pioneered the serial short story format with

Arthur Conan Doyle's **Sherlock Holmes** series, which ran in it from July 1891, with **illustration**s by Sidney Paget (1860–1908). The serial format with its recurring characters allowed readers to complete each story in one sitting, suiting the fragmented leisure patterns of urban commuters, while maintaining continuity and reader interest. So successful were the Holmes stories that Doyle would reluctantly—and to his great financial advantage—continue to produce them until 1927. **Detective fiction** came to form the backbone of the *Strand*, featuring alongside educational and investigative articles on urban problems, criminality, **medicine**, and popular **science**. While revealing a middle-class fascination with criminality, detective fiction typically concludes with the apprehension of the criminal, providing a reassuring denouement for conventional readers. However, the appearance in the *Strand* of transgressive protagonists such as Hornung's gentleman thief Raffles and Marsh's fiercely independent Judith Lee challenges the prevalent perception of the monthly as an essentially conservative venture.—MINNA VUOHELAINEN

See also DNCJ, Pound 1966, **Raffles Stories**

Strange Case of Dr. Jekyll and Mr. Hyde (1886). Novella by **Robert Louis Stevenson**.

Published on 9 January 1886 as a belated "Christmas crawler" by Longmans in two distinct formats, a cheap paper-wrapped version in the manner of the so-called **shilling shockers** that appealed to Victorian readers with affordable supernatural tales and a sturdier clothbound volume for 1s. 6d. Stevenson recounted in "A Chapter on Dreams" (1888) how key parts of the narrative supposedly emerged in his sleeping mind, after having burnt an earlier version titled *The Travelling Companion*. He then composed *Jekyll and Hyde* at a feverish pace within a mere six weeks. The novel was an immediate commercial success with forty thousand copies sold in the first six months in Britain alone.

Struggling with his baser impulses, the eminently respectable doctor Henry Jekyll devotes himself to the study of "transcendental medicine" (2006/1886: p. 50), which puts him at odds with the more orthodox practitioners of his profession such as Jekyll's erstwhile friend Hastie Lanyon. In his laboratory, Jekyll manages to compound a chemical drug that allows him to metamorphose into his "second self" (p. 58), the unspeakably misshapen but somewhat "troglodytic" (p. 16) Edward Hyde, whose depraved energies gradually take over the doctor's character, to the point that Jekyll's transformation into Hyde happens spontaneously and irreversibly. Hunted by the police and Jekyll's lawyer Gabriel Utterson for the brutal murder of the MP Sir Danvers Carew, Hyde commits **suicide** by poison in Jekyll's cabinet.

From its earliest publication, readers—among them Henry James and John Addington Symonds—commented on the novel's remarkable fusion of popular entertainment and literary sophistication. The search for Jekyll's sinister secret is woven into a complex narrative pattern, which interlaces the **melodrama**tic plot with several nested narratives (in the shape of enclosed notes, letters and Jekyll's final testament) thus producing an intricate textual network with multiple narrators. This technique, which *Jekyll and Hyde* to some extent owes to Charles Maturin's *Melmoth the Wanderer* (1820), James Hogg's *Private Memoirs and Confessions of a Justified Sinner* (1824) and the **sensation fiction** of the 1860s and 1870s, allowed its first readers to attempt their own solution of the mysterious case by following the endeavors of Stevenson's amateur detectives Utterson and Enfield. Only with the final document entrusted to Utterson's perusal ("Henry Jekyll's Full Statement of the Case") are the novel's puzzles fully resolved, and the details of Jekyll's secret revealed in retrospect.

Jekyll and Hyde participates in a reflourishing of *fin-de-siècle* **Gothic fiction**, a mode of writing that originated in the late eighteenth century and is, in its Victorian variety, noticeable for the atmospheric depiction of London's urban topography as, for instance, in **Oscar Wilde**'s *The Picture of Dorian Gray* (1891), **Arthur Machen**'s *The Great God Pan* (1894), **Marie Corelli**'s *The Sorrows of Satan*, **Bram Stoker**'s *Dracula*, and **Richard Marsh**'s *The Beetle* (1897). The Soho neighborhood of Hyde's lodgings appears to Utterson "like a district of some city in a nightmare" with its "muddy ways," its "slatternly passengers," and fog-induced darkness (2006/1886: p. 22). In this sense, the topographical map of Stevenson's London metonymically reproduces the split in Henry Jekyll's personality by contrasting the unsavory surroundings of Hyde's apartment with the more respectable area in which Jekyll's townhouse is situated (Mighall 1999: p. 151).

The genre of the Gothic also allowed Stevenson to harness the trope of the *doppelgänger* or double for his portrayal of Jekyll's fractured identity. As Jekyll's "other self" (Stevenson p. 65), Hyde is a creature who, according to the doctor, "alone in the ranks of mankind, was pure evil" (p. 55). However, Stevenson's splitting of Jekyll's identity into diverging and conflicting parts is an uneven one (Botting 2014: p. 133). While the respectable Jekyll "shared in the pleasures and adventures of Hyde" (Stevenson p. 59), Hyde seems to retain a fraction of Jekyll's sense of decorum when he attempts to appease the parents of an ill-used child by offering them a check in compensation. Rather than projecting Jekyll's baser desires onto a discreet *doppelgänger*, Stevenson's conceptualization of Jekyll and his alter ego Hyde recognizes the impossibility of distinguishing neatly between good and evil, respectability and criminality, normativity and deviance (Karschay pp. 114–115).

Jekyll and Hyde have outgrown the confines of Stevenson's novel to metamorphose into figures of almost mythical dimensions in the popular imagination, an elevated status that feeds back into endless adaptations and appropriations. Together with Mary Shelley's Victor Frankenstein and his creature, Wilde's decadent dandy Dorian Gray, and Stoker's **vampire** count Dracula, Jekyll and Hyde have recently been resurrected in the popular horror hotchpotch of John Logan's television series *Penny Dreadful* (2014–2016). Even more generally, the universal appeal of Stevenson's novel is now such that "Jekyll and Hyde" have become readily quotable signifiers for individuals with a dark secret—without any further need to reference Stevenson's tale to be comprehensible.

One of the reasons for *Jekyll and Hyde*'s enduring appeal in our post–Freudian culture is its prefiguring of psychoanalytical conceptions of identity as compounded of conscious, subconscious and social parts, with Hyde the dangerous product of Jekyll's repressed (and potentially sexual) desires. However, the ever growing literary criticism on the novel has suggested a variety of nineteenth-century contexts that can help to make sense of Henry Jekyll's relationship with Edward Hyde in less psychoanalytical but more historicist terms, ranging from theories of biological evolution and degeneration to the pseudo-scientific discipline of criminal anthropology and the related medical discourses of psychiatry and sexology. Thus Hyde can, for instance, be understood in Darwinian terms as "the animal within" (p. 62) civilized man; as an incarnation of the prototypical criminal offender, as theorized by Cesare Lombroso in *Criminal Man* (1876); and as a version of the sexual sadist, as described by Richard von Krafft-Ebing in *Psychopathia Sexualis* (1886). Harnessing these contexts allows us to read Stevenson's novel less as a generalized, quasi-Calvinistic, allegory of good and evil, and more within the historically specific framework of late–Victorian anxieties about class, sexuality, and gender.
—Stephen Karschay

The String of Pearls (1846–7). Novel likely by **James Malcolm Rymer**. Serialized in the *People's Periodical and Family Library* in 1846–7, *The String of Pearls* is best known today for including the first appearance in fiction of the character Sweeney Todd, the demon barber of Fleet Street. The novel was published by **Edward Lloyd** who specialized at that time in publishing **penny dreadfuls** but the work was anonymous. For many years it was attributed to Thomas Peckett Prest, one of Lloyd's stable of writers, but the evidence now suggests it may have been written by James Malcolm Rymer. *The String of Pearls* was dramatized on stage before it had even finished **serialization**. The reason for the story's appeal is the revelation that the barber of Fleet Street kills his clients in the acts of shaving them and then gives the bodies to his accomplice, Mrs. Lovett, who turns them into meat pies, much enjoyed by clerks and law students at the nearby Inns of Court. The idea of cannibalism at the heart of the modern city has turned Sweeney Todd and Mrs. Lovett into leading characters of stage **melodrama** and grotesque horror fiction. The characters are perhaps best known today through Stephen Sondheim's 1979 musical. The story fascinates because of the barber's chair where Todd's clients are dispatched and dropped into a cellar below.

The **Gothic** story is set in 1785 and should be viewed as a contribution to the early Victorian **Newgate novel**, comparable to works such as **William Harrison Ainsworth**'s *Jack Sheppard* (1839–40) as it contains a Hogarthian relish for the underworld of the eighteenth century. The story commences with Todd shaving and murdering Lieutenant Thornhill, who is bearing the eponymous string of pearls intended for the young Johanna Oakley from her lover Mark Ingestrie. Patriotic sailors are among the heroes while Todd is identified as a savage in the metropolis: when he first appears, the author comments that "he might have been mistaken for some **India**n warrior with a very remarkable head dress." This suggests that the immediate context for Todd was in fact the early Victorian fascination with Native Americans, fed by figures such as James Fenimore Cooper. The story involves the fate of the pearls. Johanna suspects Todd of involvement in Thornhill's disappearance and eventually disguises herself as a boy to find out the truth. There are scenes in a lunatic asylum, a thieves' den and St. Dunstan's church in Fleet Street where the smell of the bodies begins to rise from the crypt where the bodies are kept. Todd is eventually brought to justice after poisoning Mrs. Lovett and Johanna is reunited with Mark Ingestrie. After serialization, the work was published in an expanded form in 1850, although modern reprints tend to follow the 1846–7 serialization. It is probably the best-known Victorian penny dreadful today, though Todd's greatest impact was on the stage and later on film.—ROHAN MCWILLIAM

A Study in Scarlet. Novel by **Arthur Conan Doyle**. Originally titled *A Tangled Skein*, *A Study in Scarlet* is the first **Sherlock Holmes** story and it introduces readers to the fictional world of the detective and his friend and assistant Dr. Watson. Conan Doyle received £25 from Ward, Lock, & Co. for copyright: the story appeared, in 1887, in *Beeton's Christmas Annual*, and it was published in book form by Ward, Lock & Co. the following year. Both of the novel's titles are given by Holmes himself, when he confides to Watson: "I might not have gone but for you, and so have missed the finest study I ever came across: a study in scarlet, eh? Why shouldn't we use a little art jargon. There's the scarlet thread of murder running through the colourless skein of life, and our duty is to unravel it, and isolate it, and expose every inch of it" (2003: 1: p. 32). The novel is in two parts, each comprising seven chapters: "(Being a Reprint from the Reminiscences of John H.

Watson, M.D., Late of the Army Medical Department.)" and "The Country of the Saints." The start of the story finds Watson seeking less expensive living arrangements in London. Watson had recently returned to England from the second Afghan war where he was wounded in the shoulder, before being struck by enteric fever. A chance meeting with Stamford, a dresser under him at St. Bartholomew's Hospital, brought him into contact with Holmes, who is similarly looking for lodgings. Together they will occupy 221B Baker Street. Holmes describes his profession to Watson as follows:

> I'm a consulting detective, if you can understand what that is. Here in London we have lots of government detectives and lots of private ones. When these fellows are at fault, they come to me, and I manage to put them on the right scent. They lay all the evidence before me, and I am generally able, by the help of my knowledge of the history of crime, to set them straight [1: p. 18].

The adventure begins when Tobias Gregson, a Scotland Yard detective, approaches Holmes about the death of the American Enoch J. Drebber in an empty house, with no wound on his body despite marks of blood in the room. A woman's ring is revealed when the body is moved, and Gregson's detective colleague Lestrade finds the word *Rache* written with blood and scratched on the wall. Holmes identifies the physical attributes of the murderer and determines that he had arrived, with Drebber, in a four-wheeled cab, and he had long fingernails on his right hand. The murder was committed by poison, and "Rache," in German, means revenge. Having interviewed the constable who found the corpse and gathered that the murderer seeks the ring, Holmes makes a duplicate and uses it to lure him. This attempt is unsuccessful though Holmes learns that the murderer has an accomplice. A day later, the body of Drebber's secretary Joseph Stangerson, with the word *Rache* above him, is discovered. This time, however, a box containing pills is located at the crime scene: Holmes tests two pills, and learns that one of them is poisonous. With the help of "the Baker Street division of the detective police force," "half a dozen of the dirtiest and most ragged street Arabs that [Watson] clapped eyes on" (1: p. 39), Holmes and Watson apprehend Jefferson Hope, a cabdriver, who tells the remarkable story (the second half of the novel) of his love for Lucy Ferrier and how her adopted father was murdered and she was forced into marriage to Drebber. Hope had removed the ring from Lucy, who had died shortly thereafter, and had caught up and exacted revenge on Drebber and Stangerson. He had put one poison pill alongside one innocuous one in a box, and he pressured his victims into drawing a pill while he himself would take the other. While this method led to Drebber's murder, Stangerson attacked Hope and was killed. The blood came from Hope's bleeding nose. Hope himself died from an aortic aneurism before he was to appear in court.

Scarlet introduces readers to Conan Doyle's characters, fictional strategies, and some of his thematic concerns. Kyle Freeman sums up the structure of the Holmes story succinctly:

> Someone seeks out the detective at his Baker Street rooms to solve an unusual mystery. Holmes and Watson then set out to the scene of the mystery. The police are often involved, but of course they never have a clue. After an adventure or two that builds suspense, Holmes solves the case in the most dramatic way. The two investigators end up back at Baker Street, where Holmes explains any points in his chain of reasoning that might have escaped Watson's understanding, and all's once again right with the world [2003: 1: p. xxii].

Watson assumes the role of narrator for 56 of the 60 cases (commonly known as the canon). Early in the novel, Watson would find absurd a magazine article by Holmes titled

"The Book of Life." "Before turning to those moral and mental aspects of the matter which present the greatest difficulties," Holmes insists, "let the inquirer begin by mastering more elementary problems. Let him, on meeting a fellow-mortal, learn at a glance to distinguish the history of the man, and the trade or profession to which he belongs" (1: p. 17). Close and careful observation, as Holmes suggests here, comes second to the more complex moral and mental aspects of detection, all three playing powerful roles both in the Holmes stories and in Conan Doyle's imagination. By the end of *Scarlet*, Holmes retraces his thought process for the benefit of Watson (and us as readers), reasoning: "Robbery had not been the object of the murder, for nothing was taken. Was it politics, then, or was it a woman?" (1: p. 94) In the process of working out Jefferson Hope's motivation(s), Holmes identifies money, politics, and love, some of the central sources of conflict in the canon.—Tom Ue

See also ODNB

Suicide. A form of **self-harm**, suicide does not have a fixed meaning or narrative role in Victorian popular fiction. It varies in its forms and significance from the conventional narrative punishment for "fallen women" (drowning or falling from a height) or for reprobates driven by despair, guilt, or horror (***Varney the Vampyre***; Barbara Lovel in **William Harrison Ainsworth**'s *Rookwood*; the suicides, perhaps, in **Arthur Machen**'s "The Great God Pan"; Gessonex in **Marie Corelli**'s *Wormwood*), to the revenge suicide designed to frame someone else for murder, as when the Reverend Tracy in G. W. M. Reynolds's ***Mysteries of London*** implicates in his death his former mistress (who herself escapes the law by committing suicide), to the multiple forms of fake deaths—suicide of a social identity, rather than of a body (e.g., by Helen Talboys in **Mary Elizabeth Braddon**'s *Lady Audley's Secret*; Lady Isabel in **Mrs. Henry [Ellen] Woods**'s *East Lynne*; **Sherlock Holmes** in "The Reichenbach Falls"). Suicide was illegal until 1961 and, until an 1880 act allowed the burial of suicides in church ground, profoundly sacrilegious. As a concept it carried within it a double justice, earthly and divine. Through the conventions of sympathy (considered as an aspect of divine forgiveness), the divine might contradict the earthly, assisted by the medical explanations of suicide which, becoming increasingly prominent as the century progressed, suggested that suicide might be less the result of irreverent self-determination than derived from a madness which might either be natural (inherited) or caused by social pressures. This potential for contradiction allowed suicide to become a focus for the moral exploration of areas such as sexual behavior, selfishness and the acquisition of wealth, and even altruism. If sympathy for the suicide were elicited, it might be used to argue for a change in social behavior. Popular fiction itself was repeatedly blamed for causing suicide in real people (Sybil's suicide note in Corelli's ***Sorrows of Satan*** explicitly recalls this trope). The intersection of fiction and reality also worked the other way, as writers were inspired to weave stories around suicides reported in the press. Background details and hence the motivations of real suicides were often scarce: popular print culture and plays sought to provide them. The most notorious real suicide of the early part of the century was that of Margaret Moyes in 1838, who threw herself off the Monument (the highest point of London easily accessible to the public). The gory details of her death were widely reported but her motivation was uncertain: **Catnach broadsides**, aimed at the poor, offered different but equally sympathetic explanations from that of the high-status press. Later, the suicide (prussic acid and a razor) of the banker John Sadleir was to inspire both **Dickens** (Merdle) and Trollope (Melmotte).

Another kind of suicide, which technically would not be regarded as such since it was endorsed by the example of Christ, comprised willed self-sacrifice such as Cigarette's in **Ouida**'s *Under Two Flags*. Finally, sanctioned by the example of Ophelia, women's suicide might be sentimentally aestheticized, as in the case of Ouida's *Two Little Wooden Shoes*.
—Andrew King

A Sunless Heart (1894). Novel by Edith Johnstone (1866–1902). Popular enough in its time to go into three editions within a year of publication, it fell into virtually complete obscurity in the twentieth century. It is commonly classed among the **New Woman** novels of the 1890s, avowedly exploring the experience of women who have not experienced conventional romantic love. Its narrative, set chiefly in Stirling, is an apparently discontinuous one. The first part details the love of Gasparine O'Neill for her brother Gaspar and her colossal grief after his early death. In the latter part, Gasparine is a figure secondary to the lady lecturer Lotus Grace, who befriends her and reconciles her to life. Lotus is the possessor of the novel's eponymous sunless heart, as she has become incapable of love as a result of **childhood** sexual abuse by her brother-in-law. The novel's end sees Lotus restored to emotional life, but only as she dies in a railway accident. Her salvation has come not through heterosexual love: the man who once sought her affections has turned his attentions to another woman. It has not come through maternal love: she dies disavowing her own illegitimate child. Instead, the passionate dedication of another woman, the fiery Creole Mona Lefcadio, sparks her rediscovery of feeling. The novel is notable for its fascination with extremes of feeling, and its unselfconscious deviation from Victorian heteronormativity. It will be worth further consideration by scholars interested in representations of women's work, sexual trauma, and same-sex desire.
—Constance D. Harsh

A Superfluous Woman (1894). Novel by **Emma Frances Brooke**. The novel was printed by William **Heinemann** in four three-volume editions from January to May of 1894, ending in a one-volume edition in June. Published anonymously and at the height of the **New Woman** novel phenomenon (generally considered by literary critics to be 1880–1900), the story opens with the heroine, aristocratic Jessamine Halliday, wasting away from self-induced ennui. Dr. Cornerstone, a sympathetic **socialist**, restores her **health** by administering the "pill called Reality." Seeking change in her life, Jessamine disappears to the Scottish Highlands; while there, she falls in love with the handsome crofter Colin MacGillvray. As a New Woman, she offers him her body but she refuses to give her hand in marriage. After being rebuked by Colin, who desires a conventional marriage only, Jessamine returns to London and marries the physically and morally degenerate Lord Heriot. In her marriage to Lord Heriot she gives birth to two children, a crippled son and an idiot daughter; upon learning her third pregnancy she asks Dr. Cornerstone to "give me the means of dying." When he refuses, she realizes that she has the choice to end her life and the child's through her own free will. She dies after giving birth to a stillborn child, but not before she relates to Dr. Cornerstone insights about herself and her life story. The novel focuses on issues concerning the "woman question," Brooke's own socialist ideologies, and the problems of marriage and **motherhood** at the *fin-de-siècle*.—Barbara Tilley

Sutcliffe, Halliwell (1870–1932). English novelist. Sutcliffe spent most of his life living in and writing about the Yorkshire Dales, reflecting his adoration of the people and places that he encountered on a daily basis. He is most well known for his "portraits of the rough, hardy Yorkshire men and women, and … the varied incidents and scenes of the moors and fells [displayed] with picturesque force" (Unwin 1900: 194). Sutcliffe's novels are mainly categorized as historical **romance**s. His first novel was his only work in the **science fiction**/fantasy genre; *Baron Verdigris: A Romance of the Reversed Direction* (1894) was written under the pen name Jocelyn Quilp.—JOSIANNE LEAH CAMPBELL

Swan Sonnenschein, William (1855–1931). English publisher, bibliographer. Known for his classified directory of *Best Books* (1887) enlarged in 1891 and his *A Reader's Guide to Contemporary Literature* (1895). These were published combined in five parts from 1910 to 1935. After an apprenticeship at Williams & Norgate, he founded Swan Sonnenschein in partnership with J. Archibald Allen in 1878. Four years later the partnership was dissolved and the firm became a limited company. It gained a reputation for its lists in philosophy and social **science**, notably issuing the first English edition of Karl Marx's *Capital*, Sergei Stepniak's *The Russian Peasant*, Edward Carpenter's *Civilisation: Its Cause and Cure*, and Bernard Shaw's novel *The Unsocial Socialist*. Its fiction authors included **J. M. Barrie**, Henry James, **Lucas Malet**, George Meredith, George Moore, **Mary Martha Sherwood**, and **Edmund Yates**. It issued George McColl Theal's monumental *History of South Africa* and had a profitable contract to supply The Rand Club's library, Johannesburg, with books. Sonnenschein also published Kate Freiligrath-Kroeker's retellings of **Lewis Carroll**'s *Alice*, critic Harry Quilter on **Wilkie Collins** in *Preferences in Art, Life and Literature*, the **Marryat**-like adventure stories of Captain Mayne Reid, and Louise Devey's autobiography of Rosina Lytton (1887), author, notoriously confined to a mental institution by her husband **Edward Bulwer-Lytton** after a bitter divorce and released after a public outcry. In 1902 William joined the publishing house of George Routledge & Sons and the following year acquired J. C. Nimmo, publisher of **Violet Fane**. Combining Routledge's list with Kegan Paul, Trench, Trübner and Co. in 1911 gave the company a substantial backlist in literature. Under the pen name W. S. W. Anson, William edited folk tales and fables, a selection of Elizabethan lyrics and Shakespearean quotations. Under his own name he edited the works of Thomas Browne and undertook translations from German. William changed his name to Swan Sallybrass, adopting his mothers' maiden name during the First World War.—ALEXIS WEEDON

See also DLB, OCB

Symonds, Emily Morse (1860–1936). English novelist, historian, journalist, who wrote as George Paston. Born in Sprowston, Norwich, Morse was the niece of English poet and critic John Addington Symonds (1840–1893) and a friend of novelist **Arnold Bennett**. Symonds wrote six novels in the 1890s, and is best known for her last one, *A Writer of Books* (Chapman & Hall, 1898), a progressive, **New Woman** novel about a young woman, Cosima Chudleigh, who moves to London determined to become a great author. Her disillusioning experiences with the publishing world and especially its patriarchal exploitation of women recall similar portraits in **George Gissing**'s *New Grub Street* (1891) and **Grant Allen**'s *The Type-Writer Girl* (1897). In her literary technique as a "student of life," Cosima imitates the observational accuracy of the French naturalists, shunning "feminine" modes of **melodrama** and **romance**, to mixed results. Other novels by Symonds (as Paston) include *A Study in Prejudices* (1895) and *A Fair Deceiver* (1898), which also feature failed marriages and the progressive politics of the New Woman.

Symonds additionally wrote popular histories, some focused on eighteenth-century life, including *Lady Mary Montague and Her Times* (1907) and *Mr. Pope: His Life and Times* (1909), as well as several plays.—TABITHA SPARKS

Syrett, Netta (1865–1943). English author. Syrett published several **short stories** in the 1890s in such notable periodicals as ***Longman's Magazine*** and the *Yellow Book*. Her first novel, *Nobody's Fault* (1896), was the twentieth volume in John Lane's prestigious ***Keynotes*** series. Following this successful debut, Syrett wrote a new novel every few years until 1940. Syrett's novels feature women protagonists, usually from the middle class, who rebel against Victorian domesticity and pursue independent and professional lives. Her narratives affirm female sexual desire as well as the expression of that desire outside the confines of marriage. Syrett's prose style is fairly straightforward, operating in a mode of realism that made her fiction accessible to a wide audience. At the same time, her novels resist easy classification since throughout her career she experimented with the formal expectations of various narrative genres, including the feminist self-assertion found in **New Woman** fiction and the affirmation of beauty and pleasure celebrated by British aestheticism. For example, in *Anne Page* (1908) the protagonist lives alone, making an art of her life, and has a satisfying affair with an artist. In *The Victorians* (1915) Rose Cottingham is drawn to the socialist cause but ultimately finds greater satisfaction in the forms of self-expression offered by aestheticism, and she rejects a marriage proposal in favor of writing a novel. In addition to novels and short stories, Syrett wrote fairy stories, books for children, and several plays. She was able to support herself with her earnings from this prolific output.—CRESCENT RAINWATER

Technology. The intersections of technology and popular fiction in the Victorian era are intricate and multifarious. The very emergence of popular fiction as a material phenomenon owes much to the mechanization of paper-making, printing, and **illustration** techniques that begat an explosion of cheap books, magazines, and newspapers in the latter half of the nineteenth century. These innovations included the introduction to England of speedy rotary presses in the 1850s, paper made from esparto grass in the 1860s, and photographic illustration processes in the 1870s, to name just a few. Popular reading culture was also shaped by the emergence of the railway network, which provided a new environment for reading and a distribution system for printed material, and by gas and electric lighting schemes that extended available reading time. Moreover, the broad social and cultural effects of industrialization established for the middle classes what Richard Altick calls the "three great requisites of a mass reading public": "literacy, leisure, and a little pocket money" (1998: p. 306).

This new world grown thick with machines, systems, and concomitant shifts in social organization found an especially sensitive discursive register at the level of literary genre. While **science fiction** was a significant venue for fictional explorations of both utopian and dystopian visions of technology's effects on the human condition, other popular Victorian genres developed similarly exploratory perspectives on the promises and perils of technological innovation. Heroines of **sensation fiction** discovered novel vectors of flight from old identities in trains and telegraphs. **Detective fiction** propagated apart from its **Gothic** forebears on a substrate of real and imagined optical tools, visual techniques, and increasingly systematized approaches to documenting and surveilling human beings. The dynamite novel centered its depiction of anti-imperialist energies on the explosive patented by Alfred Nobel in 1867, and the evolution of militarized technologies took creative form in the airships, submarines, and weaponry that populate **invasion literature** of the late nineteenth century. In this way, genre became a first-order chronicle of "the huge imaginative energy unleashed by Victorian machines" (Pettitt 2012: p. 572). At the time, these links between technological innovation and the efflorescence of genre fiction aimed at a mass readership formed a ready avenue for critical attacks on the purpose, quality, and quantity of that fiction. H. L. Mansel, for example, famously derided the "commercial atmosphere" that surrounded the production of sensation fiction, finding it "redolent of the manufactory and the shop" (2001/1863: p. 483). However, the factory and the shop stand in synecdochal relation to techno-modernity, and it is the effects of that modernity on human experience with which many of the works targeted by Mansel were thematically concerned.

The machines and contrivances that inhabit the pages of Victorian popular fiction functioned as a means for writers and readers alike to recalibrate the relationship of the human to new technologies that threatened to expand, reduce, or replace human bodies, minds, energies, and subjectivities. The microscope and the telescope, for instance, extended the reach of the human sensorium, often to imaginative ends in fiction, as did more fantastic inventions such as Morris Monk's aerophone in **H. Rider Haggard**'s *Stella Fregelius*, a machine designed to capture sound from the realm of the dead. The workings of the human mind were regularly represented in mechanical terms: John Watson introduces **Sherlock Holmes** as "the most perfect reasoning and observing machine that the world has seen" (Doyle 1891: p. 61), while Una, the protagonist of **Grant Allen**'s *Recalled to Life*, describes the sole mental image that survives her traumatic amnesia as a photograph, "wholly unrelated in time and space, lighted up by a single spark, without rational connection before or after it" (p. 2). Indeed, shock and enervation often accompany encounters with technology in Victorian popular fiction, whether as a result of railway travel's fatiguing effects or of more nefarious possibilities wrought by modern instrumentation. Take the role played by electrical light and optical lens technology in **L. T. Meade** and Clifford Halifax's "The Horror of Studley Grange." One of the "Stories from the Diary of a Doctor" series that ran in the **Strand Magazine** in 1894, the tale's mystery features a haunting nighttime apparition: an enormous, disembodied eye that undoes the **health** and mind of Sir Henry Studley. The source of this seemingly supernatural phenomenon proves to be the terminally consumptive Lady Studley, who confesses to devising the magnified-eye illusion using "a small electric light and a strong refractor" in order to terrify her husband into dying with her (Meade 1894: p. 16).

If the coherence of the individual mind and body became destabilized in popular depictions of human-machine imbrications, so, too, were traditional supra-individual structures such as class, gender and race challenged in fictional accounts of how technology might abet new social arrangements. The Lorimer sisters turn the scopic economics of photography to their pecuniary advantage in Amy Levy's *The Romance of a Shop*, for example, confronting gendered norms about creativity and work in the process. The very constitution of the human comes under scrutiny in technologically inflected encounters with alternative versions of the species, as in **Edward Bulwer-Lytton**'s *The Coming Race*, or in similarly machine-generated encounters with other species, as in **H. G. Wells**'s *The War of the Worlds*. In Victorian popular fiction, technology alters spatial, temporal, social, and embodied experiences of the world while also enabling new ways of navigating those alterations. The saddle of a bicycle in Alice Meynell's "A Woman in

Grey" and the saddle of a time-traveling invention in Wells's *The Time Machine* comprise twinned emblems of these new modes of being: Meynell's **New Woman** cyclist revels in seating herself "suddenly upon a place of detachment between earth and air, freed from the principle detentions, weights, and embarrassments of the usual life of fear," while Wells's Traveller reports feeling "a strange sense of freedom and adventure" upon experiencing the future through his machine (2005/1896: p. 180; 1895: p. 68). Popular fictional depictions of technology made intelligible the strange senses that accompanied the progression of Victorian modernity, documenting the world that was and the world that could be.—Fiona Coll

See also Allen 1891, Altick 1998, Doyle 1891, Ketabgian 2011, Martin 2008, Meade and Halifax 1894, Menke 2008, Otis 2001, Otter 2008, Pettitt 2012, Stiles 2012

Temperance Fiction. Stories seeking to persuade readers of the evils of alcohol undoubtedly form one of the most popular genres of Victorian fiction, as revealed by circulation figures, numbers of editions, and contemporary references. Many stories, complete or **serialized**, appeared in temperance periodicals which achieved considerable circulations. For example, in the year 1860–61, the three main weekly temperance newspapers had a combined circulation of 250,000 copies, and the leading children's title had the same circulation, alone (Harrison 1971: p. 308). Even more widely distributed were tracts, pamphlets which often featured serial fiction of a heavily moralizing or improving nature, which presented themselves as true stories. They were made available in reading rooms and sold door-to-door, as well as being distributed to those in need, often inside or outside licensed premises. Although they rarely credited a named writer and are sometimes dismissed as ephemera, they were produced in huge numbers and sold cheaply or were freely available, and thus were certainly extremely influential in the cultural life of the working and middle classes. For example, in the early years of the movement in 1845, one group alone had circulated two and a quarter million copies in eighteen months (*Temperance Recorder* p. 256).

Novels achieved smaller sales, but those with a temperance theme were among the most popular; Silas Hocking's *Her Benny* (1879), with a strong temperance element, was claimed to be the first novel to sell a million copies, for example, and many temperance organizations produced or sponsored fiction, thus ensuring that it was printed in large runs and distributed widely (Kent 2002: p. 7). Many societies had access to extra production and distribution channels, and indeed had initiated composition by competitions in the 1860s for "prize novels," a tactic which provided publicity as well as spurring many writers to enter this field. One of the earliest winners was **Mrs. Henry [Ellen] Wood**, who had been attempting to publish longer works of fiction unsuccessfully until she won a prize of £100 from the Scottish Temperance Society with her first novel *Danesbury House* in 1860. This set her on the path to a successful career, and the various societies continued the strategy. In 1895 the Reverend T. Keyworth's *The Naresborough Victory* won a prize of £70, plus publication and promotion, given by the Band of Hope Union (an organization which claimed nearly three million members, in this year). Another thirty-one novels had entered the contest, thirty years after the first flush of excitement about such prizes. Novels on temperance themes were not only published by temperance organizations but bought by them, in their thousands, to be distributed as prizes in other competitions for adults and children, ensuring not only success but also author recognition for associated titles. Soon certain established writers were sufficiently attractive to join "mainstream publishers" such as Ward, Lock, & Co. or Hodder & Stoughton who, between them, published most of **Joseph Hocking**'s work.

Many popular Victorian novelists, ranging from Wood to Anne Brontë, included temperance-inspired themes in their fiction. But the most prolific writers of novels and **short stories** advocating abstinence from alcohol were usually activists who published fiction as part of their commitment to the cause. The Hocking siblings, Silas (1850–1935) Joseph, (1860–1937), and Salome (1859–1927), all became noted popular novelists employing temperance themes. Joseph became the best known writer of the three, producing nearly a hundred novels over fifty years, but the three siblings produced about two hundred publications between them (Kent p. 12). The productivity of temperance workers, often writing in addition to their main commitments of lecturing and administration, is impressive. Clara Lucas Balfour (1808–1878) produced forty-eight major publications and many more stories in periodicals or tracts, most advocating temperance. Some lesser-known writers who published fewer novels, such as Alfred J. Glasspool (1849–1928), devoted most of their writing to advice for those working with young people in the temperance cause, and shorter fiction in periodicals. Many also specialized in fiction for children, such as Mary Anna Paull (1838–1891).

Abstention from alcohol was usually presented as a positive factor in life in such stories, although the excesses of drink lent themselves to lurid and sensational depictions. By the later decades of the nineteenth century, temperance novels had adapted to suit the market, and the earlier trope of drink being the main, or only, source of personal and social problems, for example as in *Danesbury House,* must have seemed very unsophisticated. Even by the time of *Her Benny* in 1879, drink was being presented as one exacerbating factor, albeit one of the most significant, in complex social situations. By 1895 in **All Men Are Liars**, the advocating of temperance is seen as a key part of wider social reform, and characteristic tropes are presented more subtly.

Amanda Claybaugh, who has examined temperance as a key aspect of social reform in the nineteenth century novel, terms the common "road to ruin" trope a cautionary temperance tale, and Carol Mattingley, writing on U.S. novels, interestingly identifies two main tropes in temperance fiction written by men and women: women in such fiction written by men, she argues, are nearly always presented as victims, but in temperance narratives written by women, female characters are depicted as strong, resourceful, and possessing the power to intervene and either change men's behavior or remove themselves from a doomed situation. In this case the trajectory of the road to ruin is interrupted and frustrated, not only giving the reader a happy ending but offering the temperance movement optimism about its power to intervene.

The neglect of temperance fiction, apart from studies by these two writers, is surprising, and the field is ripe for further investigation, especially into the more widely circulated tract and periodical fiction. As more material becomes available digitally, this will become more practicable. The writers of temperance fiction were almost always writing from conviction and attempting to influence attitudes, and this, perhaps, does not accord with many current approaches to fiction. But the influence, reach, and centrality of temperance fiction is impossible to ignore, and its questions and concepts are still relevant today.—ANNEMARIE MCALLISTER

See also Annual Report United Kingdom Band of Hope Union 1895, Temperance Recorder 1845

Tillotson's Fiction Bureau, operating from the mid–1870s to the mid–1930s, was long the market leader in the business of fiction syndication, that is, the distribution to several independent journals of the same stories at (around) the same time, a mode of **serial** publication originating on a smaller scale in the mid-nineteenth century (Law 2000: pp. 44–63). W. F. Tillotson (1844–89) was the enterprising young proprietor of the *Bolton Weekly Journal* (1871-1976), and an associated chain of "Lancashire Journals" serving neighboring cotton towns. Tillotson's *Journals* were cheap weekly miscellanies that, in addition to a summary of the week's news, included a wealth of entertainment material, with popular fiction the key attraction. In 1873, beginning with **Mary Braddon**, the popular **sensation novelist,** Tillotson began making contracts with metropolitan authors to provide new stories not only for his own papers but also for those of "coteries" of other proprietors, many fellow members of the recently founded Press Association (DNCJ). The first such syndicate concerned Braddon's *Taken at the Flood,* which appeared simultaneously in seven news miscellanies nationwide, plus five of Tillotson's own weeklies, thus reaching a potential audience of over 250,000 subscribers, and earning the author £450 (Law 2000: pp. 41–2). Among star London authors later signing up with Tillotson were **Margaret Oliphant**, **Hall Caine**, **H. Rider Haggard** and Thomas Hardy, whose *Tess of the D'Urbervilles* was famously rejected by the Bolton firm because of its frankness on sexual matters. However, Tillotson considered **Wilkie Collins** his biggest catch, paying as much as £1300 for serial rights to *The Evil Genius* in 1886.

By then, Tillotson's business was international. The Fiction Bureau began actively to acquire serial rights for the Australian and other colonies in the late 1870s and for the U.S. from the early 1880s. In both cases regional agents were employed to generate syndicates of local subscribing newspapers as in the domestic market. Shortly before his untimely death from pneumonia, the Bolton man not only entered into a partnership with S.S. McClure's Associated Literary Press agency in New York, but also opened an office in Berlin to expand his business in continental Europe, where the policy was to sell rights to a single nationwide journal in each major language area.

Yet there was also plenty of enterprise at the local level. The Bureau had begun early to offer a weekly "London Letter" and "Ladies Column," as well other entertainment features such as children's puzzles and cartoons. Moreover, regular British clients soon included smaller country journals that could not afford the latest novel from stars like Braddon or Collins. For such papers Tillotson began to maintain a substantial backlist of old material by lesser writers at knockdown prices. Moreover, many of these papers were located in the north, and preferred stories with a general northern flavor. From the 1880s the Fiction Bureau thus began to contract with a number of reliable regional authors of limited fame, including **Dora Russell**, a Northumbrian sensationalist, and J. Monk Foster, a former miner from Lancashire writing local industrial serials (Law 2000: pp. 80–84). As an alternative to the serial novel, it also began to provide complete tales, especially for the holiday seasons, while by the final decade of the century, with the triple-decker novel in decline, it marketed in quarterly or half-yearly sets not only "short stories" of around five thousand words but also "storyettes" of half that length (Turner 1968: p. 94).

Indeed, even before the turn of the century, the Bureau was forced increasingly to rely for its profits on these petty modes of business. One reason was competition at the high end of the market from metropolitan bureaus like A. P. Watt's "Literary Agency" (Law 2000: pp. 100–13). More important in the long run, though, was that, in the home market at least, mass-market fiction magazines available nationwide were becoming a more attractive economic option to best-selling authors than even the most carefully constructive syndicate of newspapers. The moment of the later nineteenth-century fiction syndicates, with Tillotson's agency the key example, thus represented a brief phase of transition between the crafting of fiction as a petty commodity for a limited bourgeois readership and its manufacture as a mass good for popular consumption.—GRAHAM LAW

See also ODNB, DNCJ

The Time Machine. Novel by **H. G. Wells**. Published in 1895, *The Time Machine* was Wells's first novel. It initially appeared in **serial** form in *The New Review* in early 1895. It came out in two editions later the same year, published by Henry Holt and **Heinemann**, the latter being the more commonly reprinted. An early example of time travel in fiction, it would also give the world the expression "time machine," which soon entered the vernacular and remains colloquial to this day. The plot features an unnamed Victorian scientist who uses a machine he has invented to embark on a journey into the future. He travels to 802,701 CE, where he discovers inhabiting the Earth a gentle, insouciant fruit-eating people called the Eloi. His efforts to communicate with them fail and he then discovers another people, the Morlocks, ape-like, who live in darkness underground and who come out only at night. They subsist by eating the Eloi, who appear not to have adapted to the threat that lives beneath them. Time travel in the novel is more a vehicle than the theme itself. The novel is rather a pessimistic meditation on the evolutionary fate of humanity, in which the cossetted middle and upper classes have degenerated into an apotheosis of Nietzsche's last men, vulnerable to hostile predators, such as the feral, murderous Morlocks, whom the time traveller views as the descendants of a repressed underclass. *The Time Machine* continues to be one of Wells's most popular works and has been adapted for the cinema several times.—TAMMY LAI-MING HO

Tinsley Brothers (1858–1887). English publishers. William and Edward Tinsley founded the Tinsley Brothers publishing firm in 1858. While raised with little formal education, both brothers shared a passion for books and decided to establish their own publishing firm. Their publishing house was not an instant success, but after four years the brothers achieved a hit with ***Lady Audley's Secret*** by **Mary Elizabeth Braddon**. The brothers also found a niche for themselves with the popularity of sensation novels. Unfortunately, in 1866 Edward died of a stroke, leaving William as the sole proprietor. However, William continued the firm's modest success with Thomas Hardy's earlier works. In 1867 shilling magazines were intensely popular, so William formed *Tinsley's Magazine*, which ran until 1884. Hardy's first publication, *Desperate Remedies,* was not a sweeping success, but his 1873 novel, *A Pair of Blue Eyes,* established the **serialization** of a story with a "cliffhanger" (Hardy's protagonist literally hangs from a cliff). *Tinsley's Magazine* published *A Pair of Blue Eyes* from September 1872 to July 1873. Unfortunately, William did not publish Hardy's breakout success *Far From the Madding Crowd* because Leslie Stephen, of *Cornhill Magazine*, directly commissioned Hardy to write the story.

While Tinsley published Hardy's works, Tinsley required Hardy to pay £75 toward any possible losses if his works failed to sell. The theory behind "payment against profit" schemes was that the publisher should not suffer losses, so the author invested money into the text and could only be reimbursed if his text made a profit. Hardy put down £75 for *Desperate Remedies* and £30 for *A Pair of Blue Eyes*; he did not recoup his losses.

Tinsley also published **G. A. Henty**'s earlier works, which include: *A Search for a Secret* (1867), *The March to Magdala* (1868), and *The March to Coomassie* (1874). Henty became well known for his young adult novels detailing adventures in foreign lands. Henty used several publishers, but settled on Blackie and Son for most of his works, due to the firm's success in publishing and distributing school books. Many of Henty's works were written for juveniles, and Blackie and Son had already cornered that market.

William's daughter Lily published several of her works through *Tinsley's Magazine*. She serialized *In the Ring* in 1886 and *The Darrel Girls: A Story of Today* in 1887. However, in 1887 William could no longer keep his business open, suffering from a crippling £1,000 deficit, so Lily's work gained a minimal fan base.

Though William was not a successful businessman, he did author *Random Recollections of an Old Publisher*, which was published three years after his death in 1905. In this memoir, William details the many quasi-famous actors and authors that he befriended during his time as publisher. Through his account, William makes it clear that he enjoyed the social circle he established in London, and greatly appreciated the theater. However, in his memoir, William rarely addresses his business dealings, illustrating that he was more interested in his personal relationships than his ability to make a profit.—ALISON S. WALLACE

The Trail of the Serpent. Novel by **Mary Elizabeth Braddon**. Originally published in 1860 as *Three Times Dead; or the Secret of the Heath* by C. R. Empson of Beverly, Yorkshire. Republished in 1861 as *The Trail of the Serpent*, it sold one thousand copies in the first week (Wolff 1979: p. 99). The story is about the innocent Richard Marwood's struggle to exonerate himself of his uncle's murder, actually committed by Jabez North, a villainous and greedy social climber. Marwood is assisted by the mute Scotland Yard detective, Mr. Peters, whose observation, patience, and knowledge of the criminal class allow him to outwit the cunning North in the end. The novel is one of the earliest works of **sensation fiction**, which includes themes of doubling, mistaken identity, and crimes committed in the domestic setting, and of **detective fiction**, in which the detective uses logic to follow clues in order to unravel a mystery. Braddon's first novel is also notable for its depiction of the ways Mr. Peters uses his disability to his advantage.—SCOTT C. THOMPSON

Treasure Island (1883). Adventure novel by **Robert Louis Stevenson**, originally **serialized** in the children's periodical *Young Folks* between October 1881 and January 1882. Begun as a holiday amusement for Stevenson's stepson, its romanticized depiction of pirates had an enormous influence on nautical adventure fiction. The novel is set in the eighteenth century and its protagonist (and primary narrator) is young Jim Hawkins, who helps his widowed mother run the Admiral Benbow Inn on England's southwest coast. When a mysterious guest, the old sailor Ben Bones, dies at the inn, Jim finds an old treasure map among the dead man's belongings. After narrowly escaping the clutches of the villainous Blind Pew, Jim is accompanied to Bristol by Squire Trelawney and Doctor Livesey, where they charter a ship and sail off in search of the treasure. However, the ship's cook Long John Silver, and his piratical adherents, plan to mutiny and take the treasure for themselves. Jim manages to warn Trelawney and Livesey of Silver's plans and they escape ashore, along with a number of loyal men. After a pitched battle, Jim is forced to form an uneasy alliance with Silver and accompanies him on a treasure hunt, only to find that the loot has already been dug up by the castaway Ben Gunn. Eventually, the pirates are marooned on the island while our heroes depart with Silver as their prisoner. Silver escapes, however, taking a portion of the treasure with him.—Dewi Evans

Trilby (1894). Novel by *Punch* cartoonist **George Du Maurier**. Tone-deaf artist's model Trilby O'Ferrall is transformed into an opera singer when mesmerized by mysterious Jewish musician Svengali. First **serial**ized in *Harper's Magazine* in 1894, the three-volume British edition was published by Osgood, McIlvaine & Co the following year accompanied by 121 **illustrations** by Du Maurier and was a phenomenal success. Set in the Bohemian Paris of Du Maurier's youth, the novel offers a sophisticated commentary on *fin-de-siècle* literary censorship and British sexual morality more broadly. Although Svengali is the ostensible villain of the piece (like Dracula, he hails from the "poisonous East" [p. 282]), the concerted efforts of three British artists to Anglicize Trilby suggest powerfully that, like Hardy's Tess, she is "actually a victim of Puritanism" (Showalter 1998: p. xvii). At the start of the novel, the outsized, androgynous model poses naked and is unequivocally fallen ("With her it was lightly come and lightly go" [1998/1894: p. 37]). Under the influence of her new friends she quickly becomes domesticated, renouncing both cigarettes and modeling. Yet despite the hero Little Billie's passionate denunciation of the sexual double standard, Trilby's moral character continues to be interrogated and her premature demise is inevitable. When Svengali drops dead from a heart attack, Trilby wastes away (pointedly, she's at her most feminine when on her death-bed); on being shown a photograph of her late husband she goes into a trance and dies with his name on her lips.
—Jane Jordan

Tytler, Sarah (1827–1914). Scottish novelist. Prolific writer of conduct books for girls, Tytler, the pseudonym for author Henrietta Keddle, was well known for scenes of domestic realism. Her first published work for which she was paid, "Meg of Elibank" (1856), came out in *Fraser's Magazine*. Other publications were to appear in popular magazines of the day, such as *Blackwood's Magazine* and *Good Words*. Through these efforts she was to befriend authors Dr. John Brown, **Margaret Oliphant**, and **Mrs. Henry [Ellen] Wood**. Tytler's conduct books, such as *Papers for Thoughtful Girls* (1862) and *Sweet Counsel, A Book for Girls* (1866), were immensely popular. They focused on topics such as fashion, intellect, and self-sacrifice, with a keen focus on domesticity. She was likewise known for her educational texts, including *Musical Composers and Their Works* (1875) and *The Old Masters and their Pictures for the Use of Schools and Learners in Art* (1880). Tytler wrote a biography, *Jane Austen and Her Works* (1880). Tytler wrote over 140 works, but is probably best known for *Citoyenne Jacqueline* (1865), *Girlhood and Womanhood: The Story of some Fortunes and Misfortunes* (1883), *Beauty and the Beast* (1894), *Logie Town* (1887), and *Three Generations: The Story of a Middle-Class Scottish Family* (1911).
—Amberyl Malkovich

Uncle Silas (1864). Novel by Anglo-Irish author **Joseph Sheridan Le Fanu**. The work follows Maud, a young heiress who upon the death of her father is sent to live with her scheming uncle Silas and his degenerate son Dudley. With the help of a deranged French governess Silas seeks to claim Maud's inheritance. While Le Fanu rejected the descriptor it bears many of the hallmarks of **sensation fiction**. The novel is based upon Le Fanu's story "A Passage in the Secret History of an Irish Countess" (1839). This connection to Ireland (and Le Fanu's Anglo-Irish identity) has caused a number of critics to focus on

the novel's presentation of the colonial relationship, despite its setting in Northern England. Noted Anglo-Irish author Elizabeth Bowen identified Silas's estate with the Irish "big house" of the landed ascendancy class and specifically described it as "an Irish story transposed to an English setting" (1950: p. 4). Multiple critics such as McCormack (1980), Howes (1994), and Wright (2014) have connected the novel to Le Fanu's colonial and post-colonial concerns, while Sage has sought to present the novel as part of Le Fanu's **Gothic** layering of text. It also contains references to the influential Swedish mystic Emmanuel Swedenborg and the religion loosely based on his work. This mysticism is also connected to the novel's appropriation of images of magic drawn from Shakespeare's *The Tempest*. The Gothic spaces of the novel could benefit from further examination.
—JUDE WRIGHT

Under Two Flags (1867). English novel. Considered one of **Ouida**'s best novels, *Under Two Flags* was a popular bestseller that remained in print until the mid-twentieth century. The novel incorporates elements of **sensation fiction**, adventure fiction, and popular **romance fiction.** Originally **serial**ized in the *British Army and Navy Review* from 1865 to 1866, it remained unfinished when the magazine folded. It was then published as a three-volume novel in 1867. While contemporary reviews suggest that elements of the novel scandalized readers, Ouida writes in the preface that the serialized version received "much commendation" from military men and that the novel was issued "for them." Thus, unlike many sensation novels of the era, the intended audience for *Under Two Flags* was men.

The novel traces the transformation of the Hon. Bertie Cecil from an indolent dandy to a disciplined soldier. Bertie finds himself in financial distress and falsely accused of forging a check in the name of his dearest friend, the Seraph. Unwilling to implicate his brother, Bertie fakes his own death and exiles himself to Algiers where he joins the Chasseurs d'Afrique, a fictional regiment resembling the French Foreign Legion. The novel's exotic setting and **imperial adventure** serve as a proving ground for Bertie's **masculinity** and honor. In Algiers, Bertie fights alongside Cigarette, a smoking, cross-dressing, multiracial female soldier, who ultimately facilitates his return to England. For example, Cigarette rejects a military honor and insists that it belongs to Bertie, causing him to become a decorated war hero. She also meets Bertie's younger brother and shames him into confessing to the forgery, then facilitates a reunion between Bertie and his best friend, the Seraph, who is traveling with his younger sister, Venetia, in Algiers. Finally, when Bertie strikes his superior officer for insulting Venetia and is sentenced to death, Cigarette rides across the desert and throws herself in front of the firing squad, sacrificing her life for Bertie's. The novel ends with Bertie, no longer an effeminate dandy, now a stoic, long-suffering war hero, returning home to England and his life as an aristocrat with his wealthy new wife, Venetia, and his best friend, the Seraph.

The novel is remarkable for its bending of gender norms and its foregrounding of homoerotic love. Due to Cigarette's cross-dressing, smoking, and sexual promiscuity, she is often touted as a **New Woman** *avant la lettre*, despite the fact that Ouida claimed to be opposed to late–Victorian feminism. However, as Pamela Gilbert demonstrates, despite Ouida's protestations and the "contradictory messages [of] Ouida's work," Cigarette is a clear precursor to the New Woman of the 1890s (1999: pp. 170–172). Perhaps more significantly, Ouida makes the overtly homoerotic relationship between Bertie and the Seraph a central plotline. Ouida describes a "forbidden longing" (2006/1867: p. 390) that

Bertie feels for "the friend whose love he feared" (p. 475). Scholars agree that Bertie's transformation from effeminate dandy to war hero and his heterosexual marriage to Venetia seem designed to mitigate the danger of an inappropriate relationship between the two men.—Jacqueline Amorim

Vampires. The vampire made its entrance into prose during the early Victorian era. Although the number of Victorian vampire stories is limited, the drastic transformation which the character of the vampire underwent in them is remarkable. John William Polidori was the first to introduce the vampire into prose in his **short story** "The Vampyre" published in 1819. Like all vampires in Victorian fiction, Lord Ruthven's character has its roots in Victorian folklore. He, for example, exerts a strange power over mortals, which not only renders him exceedingly attractive, but also allows him to curse Aubrey, preventing him from denouncing Lord Ruthven as a vampire. Moreover, like the vampires in folklore, Lord Ruthven gains his strength from the moon, which heals him when he is injured.

The vampire in **James Malcolm Rymer**'s *Varney the Vampire* is also healed by the moon upon several occasions, and therefore prefers to embark on his more dangerous adventures during a full moon. This, however, seems to be the extent of the special powers that Varney is endowed with. Contrary to Polidori's vampire, Varney is neither charming, with his "horrible, protruding, white face," nor able to mesmerize (Rymer 2015: p. 3). Indeed, Varney often has to rely on his wit alone to get himself out of testy situations. Yet, what really sets Varney apart from other Victorian vampires is that he is the only one to repent his actions and to commit **suicide** at the end of the novel.

Sheridan Le Fanu's title character **Carmilla** has more in common with Lord Ruthven than with Varney. Like the former, she is attractive and seems to possess mesmeric powers. Although Carmilla is languid during the day and therefore mostly active during the late afternoon and night-time, Le Fanu never explicitly states that she gains power from the moon. Unlike, her predecessors Carmilla can shapeshift into a black cat at night, the purpose of which Le Fanu unfortunately does not disclose. Carmilla is eventually killed by her pursuers who drive a stake through her heart, cut off her head and burn it. This vampire killing method derived from folklore is also mentioned in *Varney the Vampire*, and used in **Bram Stoker**'s *Dracula*.

Stoker's Dracula exhibits many of the characteristics of his predecessors. Like Carmilla and Lord Ruthven, he can mesmerize his victims. Yet, where the former are described as alluring, Dracula, like Varney, never is. Moreover, Dracula can shapeshift like Carmilla, though he is not limited to one shape as he can change into a bat and a dog, as well as mist and snow. Notably, Dracula diverges from Victorian vampires in both fiction and folklore, by being the only one who becomes younger by drinking blood, who is entirely nocturnal and able to control **animals** such as wolves and rats. A difference that some scholars attribute to Stoker's decision to combine British and Transylvanian folklore.—Marjolein Platjee

Varney the Vampyre; or: the Feast of Blood (1845–1847). **Penny blood** published in weekly numbers by **Edward Lloyd** between 1845 and 1847 (Law & Patten 2009: p. 153). Extremely successful in its own time, Varney is still one of the most famous specimens of the genre. It was traditionally ascribed to Thomas Peckett Prest; however, later stylistic analyses, an early one performed by E. F. Bleiler and published in the 1973 Dover edition of Varney (1973: pp. xvii–xviii), and a more recent one performed by Helen R. Smith in 2002 ruled out Prest and indicated **James Malcolm Rymer** as a more likely author. Although some features of the text suggest that Varney may have been written by multiple hands (Herr 2008: p. 16), Rymer is by general consensus attributed main authorship.

The second work of fiction about a **vampire** in English literature, after John Polidori's *The Vampyre* (1819), Varney's episodes revolve around the adventures of the vampire baronet Sir Francis Varney. His exploits lasted for 237 numbers that Lloyd subsequently reprinted in volume form, a testament to the series' popularity. The story abruptly ends with Varney's fatal jump into Mount Vesuvius, which marks the appearance of the first suicidal vampire of English fiction. Indeed, one of the noteworthy features of Varney is Varney's complexity when compared to the typical penny blood rogue. While such characters tended to be flat, Varney is a mixture of viciousness and revenge, but also sympathy and remorse, to the point that he opts for self-destruction.

Varney clearly shows the **Gothic** roots of the genre and, conforming to penny blood style, its plot is lengthy, convoluted, and inconsistent. Innumerable side-narratives interrupt the story, which counts at least three different versions of the circumstances in which Varney became a vampire across its two years of publication. These features originated what Curtis Herr, in his 2008 edition of Varney, individuates as the chief problem with early criticism on this work: scholars evaluated it on the basis of criteria for the analysis of novels, from which perspective the work appeared as a singularly faulty and valueless piece of literature (2008: p. 17). Indeed, although Nina Auerbach, William Patrick Day, and others acknowledge Varney's importance in vampire literature, this work is still known mostly for its alleged unreadability and poor literary qualities. As Herr suggests, by contrast, Varney should not be treated as a novel because "it was never intended to be [one]" (2008: p. 17), and should be instead considered within the context of its own genre, both from an editorial and from a social and political perspective. An example of this approach is Sarah Hackenberg's 2009 reading of the characters of Varney and *The Mysteries of London*'s Resurrection Man within the mid-nineteenth-century political context.—Anna Gasperini

Victorian Popular Fiction Association. The VPFA was founded in London in 2009 in order to offer a regular forum for the dissemination of new research into nineteenth- and early-twentieth-century popular literature. It aims to foster the scholarly re-examination of non-canonical novelists and their publishers in order to recover the ways in which popular fiction was circulated and experienced by different constituencies of readers, but also to re-think the relationship between high- and low-brow literature and test out cultural definitions of the popular. The VPFA (www.victorianpopularfiction.org) hosts an annual conference and in 2018 launches its new journal, *Nineteenth-Century Popular Fiction*, with Edinburgh University Press (www.euppublishing.com/loi/ncpf). —Jane Jordan

Vivisection. The debates surrounding vivisection during the Victorian period show the complex relationship between **science** and popular culture during this period. Yet until the mid-nineteenth century, vivisection was seen as immoral, mainly undertaken by continental scientists. British scientists refuted the need to perform vivisection preferring to gain information from close observation. Waddington states that the standard themes of antivivisection narratives were "the heartless foreign vivisectionist, or the heroine's defiance of male authority to protect suffering animals" (2013: p. 247). However, as the century continued, the lack of vivisection was considered to be hindering scientific progress, thereby affecting the reputation of Britain's scientific community. In reaction to this, vivisection became part of scientific experimentation.

In 1876, the report by the Royal Commission on the Practice of Subjecting Live Animals to Experiments for Scientific Purposes was released. It was concluded that the British public found the practice of vivisection unethical and that following the discovery of anesthetic, it was possible to minimize suffering for the animal. Following the Royal Commission's report, the Cruelty to Animals Act (1876) was enacted. This Act was intended to prevent the unnecessary suffering of **animals** during vivisection. In particular it banned the use of curare, a substance which prevented movement in test subjects but still allowed them to feel the pain. However, scientists specializing in neurology argued that the use of anesthetic prevented them from observing the reactions of the brain accurately and that the animal needed to be conscious. Thus an addendum was added allowing scientists to be exempt from the Act if it could be proved that an unconscious subject would adversely affect their results.

In 1881, during the International Medical Congress, David Ferrier (1843–1928) was accused of contravening the act by testing on monkeys while they were conscious. Ultimately, Ferrier was found not guilty; his defense argued that it was his colleague who had undertaken the experiments on his behalf. According to French, writing in *Antivivisection and Medical Science* (1975), this case proved that the 1876 Act was insufficient and that scientists would continue to harm animals in the name of research (pp. 200–204).

Key anti-vivisectionists during the Victorian period were **Lewis Carroll**, author of *Alice's Adventures in Wonderland*, who wrote "Some Popular Fallacies about Vivisection," published in the *Fortnightly Review* in 1875; Marie Louise Ramé, who wrote her anti-vivisection polemic "The New Priesthood: A Protest Against Vivisection" (1894) under her pseudonym **Ouida**; and Frances Power Cobbe (1822–1904), a prominent social reformer and campaigner for female suffrage, who published *The Nine Circles of the Hell of the Innocent* (1892). Despite the apparent schism between anti-vivisectionists and scientists, attitudes toward vivisection were not absolute. Charles Darwin (1809–1882), whose theory of evolution challenged the divide between human and animal, wrote, in *The Descent of Man* (1871), "every one has heard of the dog suffering under vivisection, who licked the hand of the operator; this man, unless he had a heart of stone, must have felt remorse to the last hour of his life" (p. 40). His comments regarding "a heart of stone" expose the fear that vivisection would lead to a loss of empathy in humans.

The relationship between empathy and vivisection was consolidated in the use of fictional narratives to express the concerns of anti-vivisectionists. There was increasing concern about the use of domestic animals, such as cats and dogs, as test subjects. In reaction to the perceived objectification of animals during vivisection, activists used anthropomorphism in order to engage readers' sympathies. Waddington states that "anti-vivisectionists ... believed in the power of literature, especially stories with a sensational quality, to reveal the horrors of vivisection and reach a wider audience" (2013: p. 253). Novels such as Leonard Graham's *The Professor's Wife* (1881) and Marie Daal's *Anna, the Professor's Daughter* (1885) reflected the belief that women were more sympathetic to the plight of animals. Famous for his **detective** and **sensation fiction**, **Wilkie Collins** wrote ***Heart and Science*** with help from Cobbe. The novel featured a sinister vivisector, Benjulia, whose name and swarthy appearance suggested he was foreign, extending the illness of a young woman in order to perceive its effects on the brain. In "Heart, Science and Regulation" (2016), Murphy states that though "Collins does not explicitly mention the Cruelty to Animals Act in his novel, we might nonetheless contend that subtending the narrative is the "loss of faith" in law that characterizes post–Ferrier antivivisection discourse" (p. 383). In contrast, Edward Berdoe's *St. Bernard's: The Romance of a Medical Student* (1887), written under the pseudonym Æsculapius Scalpel, was set in a medical school in London. During the Victorian period, a rise in philanthropy helped to fund and support free hospitals. Research and teaching also took place in these hospitals and medical students gained a reputation for drinking, disorderly behavior, and questionable practices; ideas which were used in Berdoe's novel. Acknowledging the power of literature in promoting anti-vivisection ideology, Cobbe helped to fund the publication of *St. Bernard's*. The novel draws on **Gothic fiction** and Bedoe describes "ghosts of giant physiologists and vampire surgeons" (1888: p. 258).

H. G. Wells's *The Island of Doctor Moreau* continues the late-nineteenth century trend of medical Gothic. The novel depicts an unethical scientist's experiments on animals which create hybrid monsters. Wells's novel drew on the fear of vivisection, degeneration (the reversal of evolution), and the dehumanizing effects of scientific testing, representing an extreme manifestation of this behavior. The fear of evil or misguided vivisection can be found in key late Victorian Gothic texts such as **Robert Louis Stevenson's** *Strange Case of Dr. Jekyll and Mr. Hyde* and **Arthur Machen's** *The Great God Pan* (1894).—Kaja Franck

See also French 1975, Darwin 1871, Murphy 2016

The Wages of Sin (1891). Novel by **Lucas Malet** (Mary St. Leger Harrison). **Serial**ized in the *Universal Review* (1889–1890), the novel was published by **Sonnenschein** in three volumes in 1891. It was popular and somewhat controversial: "everyone read, argued over, condemned, or applauded *The Wages of Sin*" (Dickens 1899: p. 522). **Violet Hunt** called it "the first sex novel" (quoted in Schaffer 2000: p. 219). The plot follows James Colthurst, an artist with a pronounced stammer, and socialite and aspiring artist Mary Crookenden. Their violent attraction to one another is obstructed by Colthurst's mistress, Jenny Parris. With a host of eccentric peripheral characters, the story moves between Devon and London, and navigates themes of **class** and social status, **poverty**, marriage as "a sort of grave," art and aesthetics, nervous afflictions, death and **suicide**, and "the mystery, the glory, the cruel riddle and tragedy of sex" (Malet 1895: pp. 159, 22). A scientific narrative voice performs a psychological study of the characters, yet also indulges in a markedly **Gothic** style and language. Excessive, iterative, histrionic, and full of extended metaphors, this led reviewers to denounce Malet as "morbid," a label echoing Malet's description of her protagonist: "Colthurst revelled in incongruities. There was unquestionably a sinister vein in him, a rather morbid enjoyment of all that is strange, jarring, unexpected, abnormal" (1895: p. 33). Malet, like Colthurst, intended "to show that, if intelligently looked at, poverty, **disease**, sorrow, decay, death, sin … are ideally beautiful too, paintable too, intrinsically and enduringly poetic" (1895: p. 134).—Louise Benson-James

Wagner, the Wehr-Wolf (1846–1847). **Penny dreadful** by G. W. M. Reynolds. *Wagner, the Wehr-Wolf* was published **serial**ly in *Reynold's Miscellany*. The narrative is set in 1516 and follows the misadventures of Wagner who is transformed into the titular **werewolf**. Wagner starts as an old man living in **poverty** in the Black Forest, Germany. To appease his suffering, he makes a deal with John Faust who returns his youth as well as social standing and money. In exchange, Wagner must transform into a werewolf on the last day of each month. Like **Varney the Vampire**, the action takes place over an extended period of time and follows the protagonist's journeys throughout continental Europe. By the end of the novel, Wagner is able to regain his soul but loses his youth, dying of old age. The text is an example of the **penny dreadful**. It includes elements that can traditionally be found in **Gothic** and **sensation fiction**. Wagner's often gory and lewd battle for his soul is relayed in emotionally heightened language. The historical European setting and use of pathetic fallacy draw on early Gothic traditions seen in the works of Ann Radcliffe (1764–1823) and Horace Walpole (1717–1797). According to Clive Bloom, Wagner's characterization influenced **Bram Stoker**'s descriptions of **Dracula** (2010: p. 101). While Reynolds's depiction of lycanthropy, and its relationship to the devil, resembles accounts of **werewolves** from the 1500s and 1600s, Wagner's monthly transformations can be seen in twentieth and twenty-first-century werewolves.—KAJA FRANCK

See also Bloom 2010

The War of the Worlds (1898). Novel by **H. G. Wells**. An example of the immensely popular **invasion literature** genre that flourished from the 1870s to 1914, Wells's novel imagines the behavior and fate of humanity when London is invaded not by foreign forces but by aliens from Mars. Its opening compares human beings to the microbes in a drop of water, scrutinized by a man with a microscope just as the Martians have long been watching the life forms on earth. As the Martian "cylinders" rain down and the Martians deploy their weaponry, Wells shows that humanity is as helpless in the face of these superior beings as the microbes beneath the microscope. Initial disdain for the invaders—"no doubt they are mad with terror … perhaps they expected to find … no intelligent living things" (2005/1898: p. 34)—turns rapidly to panic as human firepower proves helpless against Martian **technology**. The horror is compounded by the physical repulsiveness of the Martians. Quivering, drooling, pulsating, endowed with tentacles and staring eyes, they are "at once vital, intense, inhuman, crippled and monstrous … unspeakably nasty" (p. 22). They display evolution of the brain—"they were heads—merely heads"—and devolution of the body (p. 127).

The Martians' interest in Earth is purely pragmatic: resources on Mars are becoming exhausted and human beings closely mimic Martian nutrients. They will farm people for **food**, thus reducing humanity to the condition of cattle. Wells shows that the world's most powerful nation is neither militarily nor politically capable of resistance. Its weaponry is useless, its government flees. Yet the Martians are finally defeated. Toward the end of the novel the narrator, alone in a deserted and ruined London and resigned to death, hears "dismal howling" and sees dogs gnawing on Martian flesh. The alien invaders are dying, defeated by "the humblest things … upon this earth"—bacteria. Coming from a bacteria-free planet, the Martians have no immunity; they were doomed from the moment they arrived and "our microscopic allies began to work their overthrow" (p. 168).

First serialized in the year of Queen Victoria's Diamond Jubilee, Wells's novel was read against a background of imperialist celebration and national self-congratulation. The Martian invasion dramatically punctures the second, and ironically inverts the first: it is the Martians who colonize earth, and exploit its population with the ruthlessness of imperialism at its worst. Homo sapiens, which had appeared the pinnacle of evolutionary progress, is to the Martians merely a lower species, of use but not of interest. Although Wells suggests that there have been some benefits—the invasion has taught humility, shown the interdependence of humanity and the humble bacteria, brought scientific knowledge through study of Martian anatomy and technology—such progress is ultimately unstable. The narrator is left with "an abiding sense of doubt and insecurity," and planet Earth can no longer be regarded as "a secure abiding-place for Man" (p. 179). The certainties of human life, Wells suggests, have been destroyed.—GAIL CUNNINGHAM

Ward, Mrs. Humphry [Mary Arnold] (1851–1920). English novelist. Mary Ward gained international fame with her third novel, **Robert Elsmere** (1888); the resulting career made her the bestselling novelist in English around the turn of the twentieth century. A long story of **religious** doubt and seeking, *Elsmere* caught the temper of late-Victorian society in transition and was a huge hit in both the English market, which repaid her handsomely, and the American market, which in the absence of copyright paid her nothing. She was an astute businesswoman and a religious progressive, a pioneer in women's education and the Urban Settlement Movement; she was also ambitious for aristocratic notice, a defender of Empire, and eventually a committed anti-suffragist. A complex figure, her anxieties and expostulations became a convenient target for Modernists like Virginia Woolf and Aldous Huxley, from whose attacks her reputation has never quite recovered.

But Mary Ward came by her anxieties honestly, and wrote them into her novels—27 between 1881 and 1920—as well as into her essays, war journalism, and memoir, *A Writer's Recollections* (1919). She was born in Tasmania to Tom Arnold, brother of Matthew Arnold. Quixotic and unfocused, Mary's father began work as an educator there but converted to Catholicism when Mary was four, throwing the household into emotional and financial chaos. He came to Ireland to teach at John Henry Newman's new Catholic University, taking his sons but leaving his daughter with the Arnold family in Westmoreland for nearly ten **orphan**ed years. In 1866 Tom Arnold returned to Anglicanism and tutoring at Oxford, a career cut short a decade later by his reconversion to Catholicism. This exposure to religious struggle, its impact on family and relationships and consequences for English political and cultural life, was central to her life and her novels.

Bitterly regretting the desultory education that was the inevitable portion of a half-forgotten girl in the 1850s, Mary seized hold of every opportunity Oxford offered, wangled a pass to the stacks at the Bodleian Library, and eagerly set to work reading and, in the Arnold style, writing, stories and articles. She married the tutor Humphry Ward in 1872, and became strongly influenced by the Christian social theorist J. R. Green and the liberal Anglican theologian T. H. Green. By 1878 the ambitious and now publishing young matron was also raising funds for Somerville College, the first non-denominational college for women at Oxford, and when in 1881 friends arranged a job on the *Times* for Humphry, she moved with alacrity to London, wrote pieces for magazines, gained entrance into intellectual circles, and began to plan novels.

Miss Bretherton (1884) was a **romance** plot with an underlying argument for women to professionalize themselves, and a mediocre seller, but *Robert Elsmere* four years later was a bid for international attention and got it. A review from no less a figure than W. E. Gladstone defending Christian orthodoxy against the novel's presentation of ascendant heterodoxy and agnosticism produced many dueling commentaries. In *Mrs. Humphry Ward: Eminent Victorian, Pre-Eminent Edwardian* (1990) John Sutherland suggests a provocative comparison with the previous generation's two-continent best seller, *Uncle Tom's Cabin* (1852): both novels dramatized a "violent ideological tearing apart" which intoxicated readers (1990: p. 128).

After *Elsmere*, Mary Ward wrote novels steadily, even desperately, to the end of her life, to support her large country estate and her less-than-successful husband and son, and to raise money for the Passmore Edwards Settlement houses for the working poor of London and their children which she helped to found. She saw herself as heir to the legacy of George Eliot in expressing the connection between individual personhood and the "epic" life of national history, and of Charlotte Brontë as a student of that intense inner life of asceticisms and extremities that temper the soul. Many of her novels repeated her familiar themes and emphasized the conservative side of her thought, but several besides *Elsmere* well repay reading.

Marcella (1894), perhaps the last important "condition of England" novel, stages a lively debate between **socialist** and liberal-paternalist ideals amid the stark realities of late century rural and urban **poverty**. *Helbeck of Bannisdale* (1898) brings a Hardyesque combination of natural beauty and tragic inevitability to the love story of an intellectually ambitious half-educated atheist girl and a passionately religious male, echoes of Charlotte Brontë's St. John Rivers and Paul Emmanuel. And several late-career novels written during World War I generate considerable interest, I have argued in *Behind Her Times*, as they assess changes in English culture while they continue to depict, through the lens of patriotism, that hunger for a "spiritual force" worthy of "voluntary submission" that Ward dramatized in both her male and female characters (2005: p. 208).

Some scholarship still sees Mary Ward simply as a would-be **New Woman** who betrayed the cause, and abandoned the novel of ideas for mere romances. More promising directions of inquiry probably lie in a nuanced view of the interaction of conservative and progressive tendencies in women writers of the time (Sutton-Ramspeck 2004), and in the placement of Ward in the continuing critical argument about the cultural impact of the genre of popular romance (Hipsky 2011).—Judith Wilt

W. B. Horner and Son (c.1870–c.1940). English publisher. Founded by W. B. Horner, and later carried on by one of his sons, Milton Horner, it was based successively in Dublin and London. It was a publisher of popular fiction, **penny** stories in periodicals like *Horner's Penny Stories for the People*, **romance**s, **short stories**, and content with religious and moral overtones. Cox and Mowatt mention that Harmsworths, later named Amalgamated Press Ltd., bought major shares in this established business in 1898 for its emphasis on Christian fiction (pp. 32–33), although publications continue as W. B. Horner and Son until 1940. Targeting the lower classes, mainly women, with its cheap literature, through these religious stories, it offered a different vision to its readers than that offered by other publishers and periodicals that focused their attention on tales of horror and crime. Many times its stories would be used as "services of songs" "popular in some Nonconformist chapels …reading of an edifying story… interspersed with … hymns and solos" (Neuburg 1977: p. 228). Its authors included Fanny Eden (a pen name assumed by W. B. Horner's daughter), Emily Searchfield, Dr. Rossvally, Grace Pettman, and Sydney Watson.—Suman Sigroha

Weapons of Mystery (1890). Novel by **Joseph Hocking**. The novel is told as first-person narrative from writer Justin Blake's viewpoint. At a Christmas party, Blake falls in love with Gertrude Forrest and soon contends for her hand against the charismatic Herod Voltaire, another guest at the party. Voltaire is an adept at **occult** practices and a powerful mesmerist. When it becomes clear that Gertrude prefers Blake, Voltaire puts Blake under his spell and attempts to frame him for murder. In order to save Blake from certain arrest, Gertrude agrees to marry Voltaire. She only requests a year for Blake to prove his innocence before the wedding takes place. Still under Voltaire's full control, Blake is forced to let months pass without being able to take any action. Only when he finds new faith in God after reading an instructive novel—George MacDonald's *David Elginbrod* (1863)—can he shake off Voltaire's mesmeric influence. Blake is able to prove his innocence, marry Gertrude, and settle down, supported by his newly found faith. The novel exploits acute *fin-de-siècle* anxieties about the practice of **mesmerism**, national identity, and imperial power in order to posit true Christian faith as the only weapon to overcome these threats. For the Methodist minister Hocking, the novel format represented an ideal vehicle to address a broad audience and convey his religious views. *Weapons of Mystery* is one of his earliest attempts at producing didactic novels and displays a strong focus on the theme of individual faith.—Laura Habbe

Wells, Herbert George (1866–1946). English writer. One of the earliest popularizers of the **science fiction** genre, he was a prolific writer, commentator and activist, publishing more than 120 books, 51 of them novels. After training as a biologist, studying under T. H. Huxley, he first worked as a journalist and wrote a number of scientific text books. His debut novel, **The Time Machine**, was published in 1895 and enjoyed immediate success. This was followed by a number of speculative works now considered canonical, including **The Island of Doctor Moreau**, *The Invisible Man* (1897) and **The War of the Worlds**. Wells's works, both fiction and non-fiction, throughout his career bear the imprint of his own **socialist** views; the alienating effect of industrial life on humanity was also a recurrent preoccupation. In the early years of the twentieth century, his fiction took a more naturalist turn, with a series of comic novels of lower-middle-class life, such as *Love and Mr. Lewisham* (1900) and *Kipps* (1905). Despite their ostensible levity, these works were no less socially concerned than his earlier science fiction novels. His realist novel, *Tono-Bungay* (1909), gave an account of the rise and fall of a fraudulent entrepreneur peddling a **medicine** (the Tono-Bungay of the title), based loosely on the Edwardian swindler Whitaker Wright. Wells joined the socialist Fabian Society in 1903, though later fell out with some of its key figures, George Bernard Shaw and Sidney and Beatrice Webb. He also stood unsuccessfully for election to Westminster for the Labour Party in 1922 and 1923. He turned increasingly to non-fiction from the 1910s on, writing, among other works, a bestselling two-volume popular history, *An Outline of History* (1920), which made him a rich man. While much of his later fictional output would be of debatable quality, Wells himself was unperturbed, telling Henry James in 1915, "I had rather be called a journalist than an artist" (Wells did indeed at times declare on official documents his profession to be "journalist"). A much greater concern for him was the propagation of his views on social progress, or, as became more common, the regression of the same. He paid two visits to the Soviet Union, in 1920 and 1934, during the second of which he interviewed Josef Stalin. Wells's 1933 novel *The Shape of Things to Come* (adapted three years later by Alexander Korda as a classic science fiction film) was prophetic of the world's coming turmoil—his prediction of a war breaking out in January 1940 was off by only four months. Later in life Wells was better known for his political

stances than his publications, despite maintaining an impressively high output. These days, his literary reputation rests more on the early novels, with these constituting the bulk of his work in print. Two of his sons were writers, the zoologist G. P. Wells, with whom he co-authored, along with Julian Huxley, *The Science of Life*, and Anthony West (fathered out of wedlock with Rebecca West), who would later be his biographer.
—Tammy Lai-Ming Ho

See also ODNB

Weyman, Stanley (1855–1928). English novelist. Born to solicitor Thomas Weyman and his wife, Mary Black, in Shropshire, Weyman was the second of three sons. In 1877, Weyman graduated from Christ Church, Oxford, taking his degree in modern history. He was to practice as a barrister from 1881 to 1889 with the family law firm, Weyman, Weyman, and Weyman, at the Inner Temple, Oxford. He married Charlotte Kate Eliza Painting in 1894. His first novel, *The House of the Wolf* (1889), initially **serial**ized in the *English Illustrated Magazine* (1888–89), set the tone for the publication of over thirty novels within the following decades. Due to ill **health** and the growth of his authorial career, Weyman was to give up the Bar in 1889. Weyman became known as the "Prince of Romance" due to his historical **romance** novels set against the societal and cultural turmoils of sixteenth- and seventeenth-century France. Among his works are *The King's Stratagem* (1891), *A Gentleman of France* (1893), *Under the Robe* (1884), *The Castle Inn* (1898), *The Long Night* (1903), and *Ovington's Bank* (1922). In 1911, Weyman had decided to retire from a life of letters, but in 1919, under the pseudonym Jefferson Carter, he published *Madam Constantia* to see if his work might still be popular. Thereafter, he was to publish under his own name once again.—Amberyl Malkovich

The Were-Wolf (1896). Novella by Clemence Housman (1861–1955). This werewolf novella was first published in 1890 in *Atalanta* (1887–1898), a periodical with a mainly young female readership. It was released as novella with **illustrations** by the author's brother, Laurence Housman (1865–1959) in 1896. The narrative is set in an unspecified Scandinavian country; the description of the longhouse in the opening paragraph suggests that this novel is set in the medieval period. During the course of the evening, the community's activities are interrupted by the arrival of mysterious woman, White Fell, who is seeking shelter from a storm. Her strange, "half masculine" (Housman p. 214) beauty is appreciated by Sweyn. His brother, Christian, is made uncomfortable by the effect that she has on their dog, Tyr. Rol, a young boy, and Trella, an elderly woman, are also enamored by the beautiful stranger and each are kissed by White Fell. Over the next few days, Rol and Trella disappear, leading to Christian becoming increasingly suspicious. When he sees Sweyn kissing White Fell, he is convinced that Sweyn will become her next victim. Christian chases her into the night in order to kill her. In the morning Sweyn discovers his brother's body frozen in the shape of a cross lying beside a great white wolf. The novella has been read as Christian allegory and, as such, builds on the negative image of the wolf in medieval European Christianity. During this period, the wolf became synonymous with the Devil. However, due to Housman's political interests, she was a member of the Women's Social and Political Union and fought for women's suffrage. The narrative has also been read as a metaphor for the dangers of the **New Woman**. As a female werewolf, White Fell is rare (Priest 2015: p. 3). Notably, as her name suggests, White Fell has a white pelt, a trope of the female werewolf in the Victorian period. White female **were-**

wolves also appear in "The White Wolf of the Hartz Mountains" (1839) by Frederick Marryat (1792–1848), father of **Florence Marryat,** and Gilbert Campbell's (1838–1899) "The White Wolf of Kostopchin" (1889).—Kaja Franck

Werewolves. Victorian fiction, so frequently drawing upon the folklore of the folkloric and antiquarian revival, turned to the legend of the werewolf. Chantal Bourgault du Coudray states that "in the nineteenth century, new accounts of lycanthropy were developed by antiquarians, folklorists, mythologists, historians and other social commentators" (2006: p. 14), as the werewolf was recreated in response to contemporary anxieties, such as those surrounding modernity, empire, evolution, and femininity. Rosemary Guiley defines a werewolf as "a human being who turns into a wolf and later resumes human form," and this hybrid figure recurs in horror, supernatural, and **Gothic fiction.** Guiley goes on to emphasize that "legends and myths of human transformation into wolves—one of the most feared of all animals—are thousands of years old" (2004: p. 316). Examples include Sutherland Menzies' *Hughes the Wer-Wolf: A Kentish Legend of the Middle Ages* (1838), Leitch Ritchie's "The Man-Wolf" (1831), and **Catherine Crowe**'s "A Story of a Weir-Wolf" (1845). These were followed by G. W. M. Reynolds' **serial**ization of *Wagner, the Wehr-Wolf* in *Reynold's Miscellany* (1846–1847), Dudley Costello's "Lycanthropy in London; or, The Wehr-Wolf of Wilton-Crescent" (1855), Alexandre Dumas's *The Wolf Leader* (1857), George MacDonald's "The Gray-Wolf" (1871), and F. Scarlett Potter's "The Were-wolf of the Grendelwold" (1882). Other examples include Sir Gilbert Campbell's "The White Wolf of Kostopchin" (1889), **Arthur Conan Doyle**'s "A Pastoral Horror" (1890), **Rudyard Kipling**'s "The Mark of the Beast" (1891), and Ambrose Bierce's "The Eyes of the Panther" (1891). The *fin-de-siècle* saw Rosamund Marriott Watson's poem "A Ballad of the Were-wolf" (1891), and the **short stories** "Morraha" (1894) by Joseph Jacobs, "Where There is Nothing, There is God" (1896) by William Butler Yeats, and "The Werwolves" (1898) by Honoré Beaugrand. Alongside a proliferation of novels and short stories, **Sabine Baring-Gould**'s popular *The Book of Werewolves* (1865) contains a detailed account of representations of the werewolf in folklore and mythology throughout history around the world. **Bram Stoker** notes Baring-Gould's text as an inspiration for his description of the **vampire Dracula**. The werewolf appears as a femme fatale in Clemence Housman's *The Were-wolf* (1896), one of few tales featuring female werewolves. The image of the woman as wolf or beast figures as a response to anxieties surrounding the wildness of the **New Woman**. Anxiety over the animalism and monstrosity of the werewolf frequently has imperial connotations, and is associated with the exotic as both attractive and repulsive. This becomes apparent in Kipling's "The Mark of the Beast," as the supernatural curse of lycanthropy derives from the desecration of an Indian temple. Beaugrand's Native American skinwalkers too fall into this tradition of the Victorian preoccupation with exotic cultures. Werewolves were associated with degeneration, and atavistic anxieties surrounding devolution, spurred by the popular fascination with evolution. More generally, the recurrence of werewolf narratives as based in folklore and ancient tradition is a manifestation of the collision of the ancient past with modernity, the fear of a revenant history, and the buried primitiveness of humans.—Joan Passey

Wilde, Oscar (1854–1900). Irish novelist, dramatist, and poet. Born in Dublin and raised by politically active Irish nationalist parents, Wilde would come to define a decadent and highly stylized form of late-nineteenth/early-twentieth-century British literature. Affected, sumptuously dressed, and always at the *avante garde* of anything daring, Wilde (often consciously) posed a stark challenge to the Victorian propriety and reserve for which the era has, with whatever justice, become known.

Wilde's **childhood** was spent in his parents' bookish surroundings, and a series of prizes and scholarships saw him eventually take up the study of classics at Oxford's Magdalen College in 1874. This new environment exposed him to the influence and tutelage of John Ruskin and Walter Pater, with the latter's aesthetic theories in particular germinating Wilde's developing ideas about history, art, and politics. It was during this time that his first published experiments with poetry began to appear in periodicals like the *Irish Monthly* and the *Dublin University Magazine*, and his first collection, *Poems*, would be published in 1881—at his own expense, initially, but selling out four editions in swift succession.

For an author of such enduring influence and fame, Wilde's career as a man of public letters was decidedly short. His arrival on the London literary scene in 1881 would see him embark on several years' worth of travels between England, France, and the United States, his star of fame burning brighter and brighter with each passing season. By 1895 he would be in prison, the star snuffed out. While he would continue to write while incarcerated, and publish works sporadically in the few years following his release, he would never again attain the position he once enjoyed.

His boom period was one indeed, however. A lecture tour in the United States, commenced in 1882, lasted almost a year—and introduced both Wilde and his luxuriantly affected manner to a nation far less used to such things than the drawing rooms of London or the *salons* of Paris. Wilde's first play, *Vera; or, The Nihilists* (1880), would be performed for the first time in New York City; subsequent plays like *Lady Windermere's Fan* (1882), *Salomé* (1893), and eventually the hugely successful *The Importance of Being Earnest* (1895) would earn Wilde an significant and profitable place in the modern theater.

Wilde spent the late 1880s experimenting with prose. To further poetical output were added short fiction anthologies like *The Happy Prince* (1888) and *Lord Arthur Saville's Crime* (1891), and the publication of his lengthy 1891 essay, "The Soul of Man Under Socialism," heralded a shifting in Wilde's political thought toward ideas somewhat similar to Christian **anarchism**. From 1887 to 1889 Wilde served as the editor of *Woman's World*, a fashion and lifestyle periodical that he was determined to make serious and challenging to its readers.

In 1891, Wilde published *The Picture of Dorian Gray* in book form, revised and expanded from its initial **serial** run in the pages of *Lippincott's Monthly Magazine* the previous year. It also saw Wilde's introduction to Lord Alfred Douglas, a young Oxford student who immediately captured Wilde's personal and professional interest. Just as the conflicted and debauched relationship between Dorian Gray and Lord Henry Wotton eventually leads to disaster, so too would Wilde's dalliance with Douglas: Wilde's failed pursuit of a libel case against Douglas's father for having publically declared him a homosexual would leave the author bankrupt, and criminal proceedings against him for "gross indecency" ended with his conviction in 1895. He would spend the next two years in a series of prisons, performing hard manual labor.

The last of those prisons, Reading Gaol, would inspire the final writing of his career. While Wilde spent the years between his release and his 1900 death in Paris, some of his incarceration had been spent on a meditative book-length letter to Douglas that would be published posthumously as *De Profundis* (1905). His other expression of the toll taken by his imprisonment was *The Ballad of Reading Gaol* (1898), a long poem detailing the psycho-spiritual state of the prisoner and the impact of another prisoner's execution.

Wilde's early death in Paris, in November of 1900, can be attributed to a mixture of depression, exhaustion, and lingering meningitis. His remains are now interred at the Père Lachaise Cemetery in Paris, and have become something of a pilgrimage for those who admire Wilde, his works, or the spirit of *fin-de-siècle* alterity he embodied.—NICK MILNE

See also ODNB

Williamson, Mrs. Harcourt [*pseud.* of Alice Muriel Livingston] (1869–1933). American-British novelist. Also wrote under the pseudonyms Alice Stuyvesant and Mrs. C. N. Williamson. She was born in Virginia and came to London as a young girl. She is the author of numerous novels, over twenty written jointly with her husband Charles Norris Williamson. After her husband's death, Williamson travelled extensively visiting Hollywood, New York, Paris, and North Africa. Her works include *The Diamond Code* (1932), *The House by the Lock* (1906), *The Love Pirate* (1913), and a sensation novel, ***A Woman in Grey***, which received enthusiastic reviews from the *Westminster Gazette*, *Daily Chronicle*, and *Illustrated London News*. After her death, her friend and fellow novelist **Sarah Grand** described her as a "most charming" woman and an "exceptionally talented" novelist.—MELISSA PURDUE

See also "Births, Deaths..." 1933

Windsor Magazine (1895–1939). Sometimes *The Windsor*. This extensively illustrated, sixpennyworth, 116/120 pages, monthly magazine was launched by publishers Ward, Lock under editor Stanhope Sprigg after the style of popular, illustrated, fiction-and-general-interest magazines like the ***Strand Magazine***, aiming to differentiate itself from such publications through a more overt, morally didactic tone inspired by midcentury Christian magazines. The *Windsor* aimed at both male and female middle-class readers with aspirations of social mobility, mixing escapist fiction (both **short stories** and **serialized** novels), current event articles, conservative editorializing, and domestic advice, with a fixation for British royalty and aristocracy that endured until the end of its run (indeed, until 1917 the magazine cover was a sketch of Windsor Castle). Though its editorials initially disparaged the **detective fiction** fad, the *Windsor* found its first success in luring **Arthur Morrison** and his detective character Martin Hewitt away from the *Strand*. This, and the success of **Guy Boothby**'s proto-supervillain character **Dr. Nikola** (followed by the serialization of his ***Pharos the Egyptian***), shifted the focus of the magazine away from moral didacticism and toward a more dynamic tone in its articles and fiction that favored male readers. David Williamson was hired as editor in 1896, expanding the magazine's fiction to include more mystery, ghost stories, humor, and even westerns, while articles covered **technology**, exploration, and the ever-present aristocracy. Arthur Hutchinson became editor in 1898 and remained in the position for the next thirty years, continuing his predecessor's policies of exciting fiction and articles that exemplified Victorian values while also opening the magazine up to **science fiction**. The *Windsor* featured many writers of note during the Victorian and Edwardian periods, including **Arthur Conan Doyle** (the first **Sherlock Holmes** novel, *A Study in Scarlet*, was reprinted in full for the *Windsor*'s first Christmas issue), **Rudyard Kipling** (including several of the "Just

So" stories and the serialization of *Stalky & Co.*), **H. Rider Haggard** (serializing *Ayesha*, the highly anticipated sequel to *She*), Cutcliffe Hyne, **L. T. Meade, Edith Nesbit**, Robert Barr, **George Griffith**, Camille Flammarion, **Arnold Bennett**, and work reprinted from the American magazines, including Jack London.—STEVE ASSELIN

The Wing of Azrael (1889). Novel by **Mona Caird**. Published in three-volumes, *The Wing of Azrael* was the first of Caird's novels to be published under her own name. Because of Caird's notoriety following the "Is Marriage a Failure?" debate the previous year, the novel received widespread attention. Caird argues in the preface that the work is not a fictional version of her beliefs about marriage, yet many ideas found in her essays appear in the novel. The heroine, Viola Sedley, can be seen as a proto–**New Woman**, although the book is not a New Woman novel. Caird does use Viola to explore the ways in which women are emotionally pressured to conform to social conventions and suppress their individual desires. However, Viola never attempts to live according to her independent beliefs within a hostile society, as many literary examples of new women do (including the protagonist of Caird's 1894 novel, *The Daughters of Danaus*, and **Grant Allen**'s *The Woman Who Did*). The novel contains an unmistakable New Woman character, Sibella Lincoln, whose speeches reflect Caird's own frustrations with late-nineteenth-century marriage.

The novel's first volume is a *Bildungsroman* in which Caird depicts Viola's **childhood** and her struggle for independence, as well as the pressure she faces to rebuild the family fortune (squandered by her brothers) by marrying for money. By depicting Viola's full life rather than focusing on courtship and marriage, "Caird refuses to pinpoint marriage as the single element that defines her" (Rosenberg 2010: p. xv). Caird also uses Viola's childhood to foreshadow the tensions of her marriage to Philip Dendraith. The prime illustration occurs when Philip, perched on the edge of a ruined Norman stronghold, not only toys emotionally with the young Viola, but restrains her until she agrees to kiss him. Instead, she pushes him away, causing him to fall. Philip's insistence on controlling Viola, and his mistaken assumption that she will respond in a feminine and futile manner, leads to his death at the end of the novel. When Viola plans to flee with her lover, Philip threatens to keep her captive as a madwoman. He interprets her anger as proof that she is incapable of accepting her place in society, whereas Caird acknowledges the justifiable rage of trapped women. Viola kills Philip, but although she gains her freedom, there can be no place in society for a woman who murders her husband. The only ending Caird can offer her is **suicide**.

Caird, a noted anti-**vivisection**ist, uses animal cruelty as a metaphor throughout the novel. Philip torments the young Viola's beloved dog, and during their betrothal he savagely whips his horse (Viola's lover proves his worth by stopping him). When Viola attempts to end the engagement, her mother claims such behavior doesn't affect a husband's ability to care for his wife; Caird rejects this belief by depicting Philip's brutal treatment of Viola's devoted cat, emphasizing the sexual violence within their marriage. The inability of married women to escape cruelty at the hands of their husbands is, to Caird, a stain on modern society.—TRACEY S. ROSENBERG

A Woman in Grey (1898). Novel by Alice Muriel Williamson, writing as Mrs. C. N. Williamson (1869–1933). Not to be confused with the essay of the same name by Alice Meynell (1896), published in the *Pall Mall Gazette*, the novel originally sold for six sterling and was 327 pages in length. A work of **sensation fiction** published by George Routledge and Sons, it was advertised as "A capital Story of the strongly sensational type." Some reviewers compared it to **Wilkie Collins**'s writing, especially *The Woman in White*. Set at Lorn Abbey, an ancient family seat in disrepair, the tale centers on the aftermath of a murder and the wrongful conviction of Florence Haynes. Told in the first person by Terence Darkmore, the hero of the tale, the novel mixes mystery, suspense, ghosts, and treasure. The plot includes mistaken identity, body snatchers, ghoulish medical experiments, and the revelation of the true murderer. Translated and adapted into Japanese by Kuroiwa Ruiko as *Yureito* (*Ghost Tower*) in 1901, and as *The Haunted Tower* by Edogawa Rampo in 1937. Also used by Hayao Miyazaki for his first anime film *Lupin the Third: The Castle of Cagliostro* (1979). The story was rewritten for the fifteen-part American film **serial** *A Woman in Grey* (1920), possibly the first time a literary work by a noted author was transferred to the screen in serial form. It was considered "a decided step toward the advancement of this particular form of screen entertainment" ("Arline" 1919). Williamson's writing style worked well for this form since nearly every chapter of the novel includes some form of cliffhanger or terror.—Valerie L. Guyant

The Woman in White (1860). Novel by **Wilkie Collins**. One of the founding novels of the **sensation fiction** genre and the fourth by Collins. On 26 November 1859, **Charles Dickens**'s *All the Year Round* announces that Collins's *The Woman in White* will follow *A Tale of Two Cities* in the journal's endeavor to "produce … some sustained works of imagination that may become a part of English literature" (Collins 1859: p. 95). As part of a new project in literature, Collins's "Preamble" sets out rather explicitly to teach its readers the value of such works of imagination. The law is insufficient to provide justice in every case, the Preamble posits in a gesture typical of **detective fiction**. The Preamble thus invites readers to join the novel's protagonist, Walter Hartright, in his endeavor to solve the mystery at the heart of the family. Typical of sensation fiction, the plot and relationship between the characters is complex. Walter Hartright falls in love with Laura Fairlie, who is betrothed to Sir Percival Glyde. Laura discovers a secret about Sir Percival from her cousin, Anne Catherick. With the guidance of the Italian Count Fosco, Sir Percival commits Laura to an asylum under Anne's name to preserve his secret. Hartright, with the help of Laura's half-sister, Marian Halcombe, unravels the influence Count Fosco exerts over Sir Percival, uncovers the secret, and frees the family from the tyranny of the patriarch.

While on the surface, the plot is typical of crime or **Gothic fiction**, Collins's narrative execution of the story challenges these tropes. In the Preamble, he writes as though he is Walter Hartright, and announces that he will give up his place as narrator "when his experience fails" to let persons who can speak more accurately to the circumstances take over (p. 95). This bizarre shifting of first-person narrator—which would become one of Collins's trademarks—mimics the court of law, where multiple witnesses relate the same story in an attempt "to present the truth always in its most direct and most intelligible aspect." *The Woman in White* invites the reader to join Hartright in separating the truth out of its fictions.

Collins derives this relationship with his reader in part from his experience writing crime novels in *Basil* (1852). In *The Woman in White*, Collins mixes those tropes with the trappings of the Gothic novel—with Victorian twists. The Italian villain, Count Fosco, acknowledges Anne Radcliffe's Gothic novels of the late eighteenth century. And yet, though he is the mastermind of the plots that Hartright must unpack, he thinks more than he acts, and wields words and surveillance rather than violence. While a secret bloodline forms the crux of the intrigue, it is the ill-fated Sir Percival Glyde who has a secret bloodline; instead of revealing connections upward, his secret is that he was illegitimate and unable to inherit his title and fortune. Rather than typify family structures, these men embody Victorian state institutions.

These institutions splinter the typical Gothic heroine across the female characters of the novel. Anne Catherick is buried under the name of her half-sister, Laura Fairlie. Laura, meanwhile, is committed to an asylum under Anne's name, where she is later rescued by Marian Halcombe. The women's constant shifting of roles, along with repeated cases of false identity, muddles the women's identities for the reader as well as the characters. Their stable selves are undone by their collision with institutions: inheritance, marriage, the asylum for **mental illness**.

The **serialization** of the novel, while not unique to the sensation novel or to *All the Year Round*, sensationalized the world of the reader where these institutions existed, and caused the novel to bleed into the reader's world in ways the Gothic specifically did not. The novel's immediately relevant subject matter bleeds into the text around it: the article that follows the first installment details the mistrust and political conflict in Italy—a struggle crucial to Fosco's fall at the end of the novel, for he is killed by a group of political radicals ("Italian Distrust" 1860: pp. 104–106). This relationship can also move in the other direction, so that the world feels sensational or fictional. Leading up to Laura's descent into a kind of madness, which will eventually provide Sir Percival with the grounds to commit her to an asylum, the 21 January 1860 installment is followed by a letter to the editor allegedly from a former patient of Bethlehem (Bedlam) Hospital ("Without a Name" 1861: pp. 291–292). The letter is ostensibly a heartfelt thanks to the physicians of Bethlehem, but its first-person narrative—with anticipation of "some fearful torture" that gives way to a beautiful, caring woman, and a decided awareness of its own textuality, including self-interruptions—is unsettlingly akin to the sensation novel above and across the page.

In this way, the novel lives up to the Victorian understanding of the sensation novel that would arise in the decade to follow. Where the Gothic took place in a far away place and time, and often contained at least a suspicion of the **occult**, in her analysis of *The Woman in White*, **Margaret Oliphant** notes that "[n]ot so much as a single occult agency is employed in the structure of his tale" (1862: p. 566). Instead, the novel's sensational "effects are produced by common human acts, performed by recognizable human agents, whose motives are never inscrutable" (p. 566). Collins's sensations happen at home, and their causes are equally domestic.

The Woman in White has garnered an impressive amount of scholarly attention. In addition to the novel's centrality to the formation of the sensation genre, Dallas Liddle identifies five categories of identity that scholars have investigated—namely, "age, gender/sexuality class, nationality, and profession"—but calls for a less fragmented approach to the novel's theoretical stakes (2009: p. 38). Attention to the novel's original serialization and its awareness of its own textuality might well bring together these investments in identity with the novel's questions regarding law and other Victorian institutions.—Peter J. Katz

The Woman Who Did (1895). Novel by **Grant Allen**. A best-selling novel of purpose originally published by John Lane in his notorious Keynotes series, and still in print today, *The Woman Who Did* is by far the best-known work by this prolific popular novelist of the later nineteenth century. Allen's main intention was to detail the unjust fate of women, no matter how privileged their background or how idealistic their motive, who transgressed the sexual taboos of late–Victorian England. The novel's protagonist is a **New Woman** named Herminia Barton, the beautiful, intellectual daughter of a senior Anglican clergyman. She was one of the first generation of women to receive a university-level education at Girton, the pioneering all-female college of Cambridge University. But impatient with what she deems the irrelevance of Girton's classically focused curriculum, Herminia drops out, seeking to assail the sexual double standard of her time and help the cause of women's freedom. She falls in love with a young lawyer, Alan Merrick. The marriage oath then required a woman to swear to *obey* her husband, but not vice versa, thereby enshrining wifely subordination in law. So Herminia offers herself to Alan sexually but absolutely refuses to marry him. She then becomes pregnant, and Alan insists that they leave England to avoid the scandal of a birth outside wedlock. But Alan dies of typhoid in Perugia, Italy, and now Herminia must face **motherhood** alone. Back in London she struggles for years against familial and social disapproval to raise her daughter Dolores singlehandedly, hoping that through her dogged example, life will be freer for the next generation of women. But Dolores, thoroughly conventional, eventually turns against her mother, believing (correctly) that her illegitimacy damages her own marriage prospects. The novel ends with Herminia committing **suicide**, thereby removing herself as the obstruction in her daughter's path. Though Allen intended Herminia's fate to be tragic, the novel was not always read this way. Many traditionalists believed that Herminia's rejection by her daughter and her self-inflicted death by prussic acid were suitable punishments for her flagrant moral transgressions. In 1895 the critical reception of the novel was heated and unpredictable. Progressives such as **H. G. Wells** and the leading feminist Millicent Garrett Fawcett wrote scathing reviews; the conservative *Spectator* gave it qualified praise; it was parodied in *Punch* and the *Idler*, and it generated two response-novels, *The Woman Who Didn't* by **Victoria Cross** and ***The Woman Who Wouldn't*** by **Lucas Cleeve** (both 1895). In just the first year after publication Allen's novel sold more than 35,000 copies, made its author at least £1,000, and helped put John Lane's publishing house, the Bodley Head, on a firm financial footing. Though *The Woman Who Did* is far from a great novel, it is readable, dramatic, and provocative. Even today, critics and readers are often divided about its meaning, suggesting that some of the issues it raises remain surprisingly vital.—Nick Freeman

The Woman Who Wouldn't (1895). **Lucas Cleeve** wrote this novel in response to **Grant Allen**'s *The Woman Who Did* (1895). Opalia Woodgate will marry Alan D'Arcy on the condition he "be content if I were your sister only" (1895: p. 14), as she is terrified of the physical indecencies women endure in both lovemaking and childbirth. Opalia's friends and family predict her experiment's failure: "your baby ... will have to be exhibited at the Aquarium as the child of the 'Woman who Wouldn't.' It will be quite phenomenal" (p. 128). Alan is skeptical, but he agrees to the terms, offering Opalia a pearl necklace as a wedding gift. The necklace signifies how women are culturally allowed to verbalize "no" to sex but not "yes." Eventually, Alan's frustrated **masculinity** mounts, and Opalia returns the pearl necklace after seeing him and Lady Morris—Opalia's foil—in a compromising position. Opalia ultimately recalls Alan to her side, as **motherhood**'s "compensating joy" (p. 225) will allegedly enable them to live happily ever after. In the preface,

Mrs. Howard Kingscote states, "when women cease to care for men and for children, God help the men!" (v); yet after Kingscote went bankrupt in 1899 (the scandal included several men other than her legal spouse), she lived apart from her husband and children until her death. Although this **New Woman** novel focuses on conjugal repression, scandalized reviews of its frank discussion of sexuality increased sales.—KATE FABER OESTREICH

See also ODNB

Wood, Mrs. Henry [Ellen] (1814–1887). English novelist. Born Ellen Price, Wood was a prolific author of popular fiction who published primarily as "Mrs. Henry Wood." Having started writing fiction due to financial reasons to support her family, Wood produced over thirty novels and **short stories**. In 1867, Wood purchased the family magazine *The Argosy*, for which she produced much of the material, while actively shaping the magazine's content. Wood's first full-scale novel was *Danesbury House*, written for a prize-winning contest set by the Scottish Temperance Society in 1860. In this comparatively short novel Wood first experimented with a newly popular domestic **Gothic** to convey the narrative's intended message about alcohol consumption. Throughout her writing, Wood maintained this simultaneity of sensationalism, sentimentality, and moral messages. Similarly, she advocated an emphatically middle-class ideology of domesticity and class climbing, while simultaneously supplying her predominantly female readership with details of highlife, including the minutely itemized attire of her often upper-class main protagonists. While her narratives tend to be set in fashionable society, Wood argues for the moral superiority of middle-class characters or characters associated with bourgeois values. Her breakthrough novel, ***East Lynne*** (1861), combines titillating descriptions of the aristocratic anti-heroine's transgressions and an equally lurid account of her punishment. Wood is best known for her sensation novels of the 1860s, including *The Shadow of Ashlydyat* (1863), which conveys the uncertainties of a rising finance capitalism, and ***St. Martin's Eve*** (1866), which explores the theme of hereditary insanity. She continued to write sensational narratives throughout the 1870s and 1880s, often reusing popular plots. *Court Netherleigh* (1881), for example, rewrites the divorce and remorse plot of *East Lynne* to produce a more detailed, seemingly more realist marriage novel that, however, introduces an unexpected happy ending. Simultaneously, Wood aired heavily religious discourse on everyday moral practices in the non-fictional *Our Children* (1876) and *About Ourselves* (1883). Yet Wood excelled most when she worked elements of mystery and crime into domestic narratives, such as a double murder in *The Foggy Night at Offord: A Christmas Gift for the Lancashire Fund* (1863). Similarly, the family chronicle and school story, *The Channings* (1862), intended for a younger audience, not only contains a mysterious appearance and a case of false accusations, but the novel's sequel, *Roland Yorke* (1869), is a sensation novel of concealed crime and false clues that takes the earlier narrative's villain as its main character. In her "Johnny Ludlow" narratives, which were compiled in three volumes after their initial **serialization**—*Johnny Ludlow* (1874), *Johnny Ludlow, Second Series* (1880), *Johnny Ludlow, Third Series* (1885), and posthumously, *Featherston's Story: A Tale by Johnny Ludlow* (1889) and *Johnny Ludlow, Sixth Series* (1899)—Wood further developed elements of the emergent genre of **detective fiction**. Wood is now commonly considered one of "the big three" (Phegley 2010: p. 91) sensation novelists, side by side with **Wilkie Collins** and **Mary Elizabeth Braddon**.—TAMARA S. WAGNER

A World of Girls (1886). Novel by **L. T. Meade**. Recognized as the genre-defining girls' school story, *A World of Girls: The Story of a School* was penned by one of the most prolific writers of the era. A bestselling novel which had a lasting impact upon its successors, it tells the story of twelve-year-old Hester Thornton who is sent to boarding school after the death of her mother. Instructed to be a "good girl," Hester quickly finds herself at odds with Lavender House's beloved rule-breaker, Annie Forest, whom she feels embodies the fun and freedom a proper Victorian young woman must leave behind. The focus of the novel soon centers on Annie, who befriends Hester's little sister and whose antics are mistakenly blamed for the girl's kidnapping by gypsies, prompting her to set off on a heroic rescue journey to reclaim her innocence. The novel's great success led to the release of its sequel, *Red Rose and Tiger Lily; or, In a Wider World* (1894), wherein Hester and Annie are confronted with the restrictive dictates of young womanhood amid the arrival of Hester's new stepmother and stepsister and Annie's determination to help a poor neighboring family prevent the impending sale of their ancestral home. While Meade's children's novels were popular for their trademark heroines clashing with the mischievous yet innocent antics of a rival, the frequently underestimated stories actually reveal conflicted attitudes toward the Victorian female coming-of-age experience and the author's impact upon children's literature begs further investigation.—JACQUELINE H. HARRIS

Wormwood (1890). Novel by **Marie Corelli**. Published by Bentley in three volumes in 1890, the novel addresses the problem of **alcoholism** and its consequences. The wormwood plant, *Artemisia absinthium*, has been the downfall of the novel's narrator, Gaston Beauvais, who retrospectively tells the story of his life in Paris, and his love for Pauline de Charmilles: while they were still engaged to be married, Gaston's fiancée fell in love with the young priest Silvion Guidèl who returned her love. Once Gaston had tasted absinthe—which, he is told by the Toulouse-Lautrec inspired French painter André Gessonex, is "a cure for all human ills"—his initial will to forgive Pauline and set her free turns into revenge: he cancels the wedding with Pauline and kills his rival Silvion. Pauline—ashamed of having disgraced her family—ends up in the most vice-ridden quarters of Paris, although she remains unswerving in her love for Silvion. When Gaston, who has at this point and through his drinking habit lost all decency and morality, tells her that he has murdered Silvion, Pauline jumps off the Pont-Neuf bridge and to her death. His father having banished him (a fate Gaston laments but prefers to renouncing absinthe) and also having lost his job as a banker, Gaston leads the lonely and miserable life of an alcoholic. The death of Héloïse St. Cyr—a woman who truly loved Gaston, compared to Pauline whose attachment was superficial and playful—means that Gaston's final chance for a sober and better life has disappeared. Gaston will find neither God nor forgiveness, as the novel concludes in its final chapter: "And what am I? My dear friends, I have told you—an *absintheur*! *Absintheur, pur et simple! voilà tout!*"

With this **melodra**matic and dark story of love, drugs, and murder, Corelli taps skillfully into the *fin-de-siècle*'s fascination with sin, Paris, and moral licentiousness. While parallels can be drawn to **Oscar Wilde**'s *Dorian Gray*, the **Gothic** atmospheres of **Robert Louis Stevenson**'s ***Strange Case of Dr. Jekyll and Mr. Hyde*** and Bram Stoker's ***Dracula***, and many specifically absinthe-inspired and absinthe-themed contemporary representations in paint and print, *Wormwood* is not only of the period but also forward-looking in its skillful use of interiority, psychologizing, and its anticipation of modernist stream-of-consciousness techniques. The reviewers made—as was not uncommon for Corelli—fun of the author's gratuitous and occasionally incorrect use of the French language and the insertion of some favorite rants into Gaston's confused absinthe dreams and deliberations, for instance, on dishonest journalists and reviewers. Corelli felt throughout her career that she was the victim of a corrupt press, to the point where she refused to have her books sent out for reviewing. However, the novel is not only evidence of Corelli's having a finger on the pulse of time and being able to tap into genres and themes the British public was interested in at any given time, but it is also an important document for Britain's *fin-de-siècle* anxiety about, and discourse of, degeneration, as well as the late-Victorian literary experimentation with realism.—JULIA KUEHN

Woulfe, Isabella Letitia (1817–1870). English novelist. Best known for her sensational work, *Guy Vernon* (1870), the Hon. Isabella Letitia Woulfe *née* Graves was born to Lord Thomas North Graves, 2nd. Baron Graves, and his wife, Lady Margaret Paget, and was one of twelve children. In 1844 Woulfe converted to Roman Catholicism and in 1853 wed Stephen Roland Woulfe, an Irish magistrate and high sheriff of Co. Clare. Woulfe was to die the same year that *Guy Vernon*, which became known for its depictions of travelers and two bigamist relationships, was published.—AMBERYL MALKOVICH

Yates, Edmund Hodgson (1831–94) English author. As editor of *Temple Bar*, Edmund Yates wrote a successful **serial** story, *Broken To Harness* (1865), when a need arose. He continued to write **sensation fiction** until the 1870s. **Margaret Oliphant** recognized him for the quality of his writing, "greatly above the sensational average" (1867: p. 271), but condemned him for female protagonists such as Margaret Dacre in *Land At Last* (1866), "picked up in the street by the artist hero" (1867: p. 271) and "with no intention of adapting to the dullness of a respectable life" (1867: p. 270). Yates's novels received positive reviews. *Black Sheep* (1867) is described as "a good example of the more worthy sensational art" ("Black Sheep" 1867: p. 190). Yates, himself is described as belonging to "a school of novelists of which he is becoming a very conspicuous member and representative" (p. 190). Although an established sensation writer of his time, Yates is rarely mentioned in modern criticism.

"Critical indifference" (Gilbert 2011: p. 321) are the words used to sum up the modern attitude to Yates. Sensation fiction, a controversial and popular genre in the mid-nineteenth century, has been useful as a source of feminist resistance and challenge, often through the actions of transgressive heroines who feature in such novels. Although Yates's novels feature some determined, brave and strong female characters, his narrative structure has been less useful to a feminist project. In his own time, he was referred to as "the compassionate defender of unhappy wives" ("Kissing" 1866: p. 828). He does this through a critique of masculinities exposing ethical/moral faults in his male protagonists. He stops short of a demand for radical change in women's status and rights thus allowing one reviewer, commenting on *Running The Gauntlet*, to say that "though its author more than once crosses dangerous ground, he has written nothing against good morals and correct taste" ("Running the Gauntlet" 1865: p. 595). Nevertheless, Yates's novels, in their exposure of flawed **masculinity** made almost invisible by patriarchy's ingenious resistance to interrogation, are ready for critical reassessment in terms of the ideological work of the sensation genre.—DAVID HALLIWELL

A Yellow Aster (1894). Novel by **Iota** [*pseud*. of Kathleen Mannington Caffyn]. It was widely associated with the **New Woman** because of the heroine Gwen Waring's acceptance of a proposal of marriage as a scientific experiment and her disgust when she realizes what sexual relations entail. Notorious in its day, *A Yellow Aster* has received comparatively little attention in critical studies of the New Woman on account of its conservative ending which recuperates Gwen for marriage and **motherhood**. In her study of *The Irish New Woman*, Tina O'Toole dismisses Caffyn from serious consideration because her novel fails to suggest "a radical shift in heterosocial mores" and reduces her heroine to "an essentialist mother-figure" (2013: p. 170). However, *A Yellow Aster* is of interest in understanding the range of novels associated with the New Woman and the less savory aspects of New Woman discourse including **eugenics** and biological determinism.

The novel is also significant in tracing the colonial dimensions of the New Woman and her relation to other literary and artistic movements, particularly aestheticism and decadence. Caffyn wrote most of *A Yellow Aster* while living in Australia where she and her husband ran a salon for bohemian writers and artists. Visitors included the post-impressionist painter Charles Conder, who is thought to have been the model for the decadent artist Charles Brydon, who paints Gwen's portrait in *A Yellow Aster* (Galbally 2005: pp. 40–41). Completed after the couple returned to England, the novel was published by Hutchinson, one of a number of new companies producing cheap editions of popular fiction. It went into fifteen editions in little over a year. Its original yellow cover was embossed with a flower design. Presumably intended to illustrate the novel's title, it took the form of a stylized sunflower, one of the central symbols of the aesthetic movement.

The novel appropriates decadent symbols and images, while taking a moral stand against the values they represent in elevating artifice over nature and challenging contemporary gender roles. The title flower represents Gwen's unnatural disposition as a result of her failure to develop feminine feelings. This is accounted for by her unusual upbringing. The daughter of two scientists, who locked themselves away in their study to pore over mathematical problems during her **childhood**, Gwen is incapable of love. The novel voices contemporary concerns about new educational opportunities for women and their effect on women's familial and reproductive roles. In an interview for the *Woman's Signal*, Caffyn claimed that she thought "it was quite possible to be intellectual and yet an all-round woman at the same time. But women should not allow their intellect to injure the maternal instinct" (Parker 1894: p. 155). In the eventual awakening of Gwen's womanly nature, and that of her mother, through Gwen's experience of motherhood, the novel aligns women's social and moral duty to reproduce with a biological imperative. In keeping with current scientific arguments about the immutability of gender roles, it suggests that the responsibility of motherhood cannot be evaded through modern familial arrangements.—Naomi Hetherington

The Yellow Danger (1898). Sinophobic invasion novel by **M. P. Shiel**. This virulently racist take on the **invasion literature** genre earns Shiel the dubious honor of being the first fiction writer to really popularize the "yellow peril" myth in Britain. In the novel Sino-Japanese mastermind Dr. Yen How, "embodiment" of the "antagonistic races" of the East, grants a series of advantageous Chinese territorial concessions to Britain's European colonial rivals in order to provoke a massive inter–European war (1898: p. 4). The resulting carnage allows the combined forces of China and Japan to devastate war-torn continental Europe, before being soundly rebuffed at the eleventh hour by Britain, which becomes "empress of the earth." Though Shiel's calumniation of the Chinese as cruel and revengeful in the novel is excessive even by nineteenth-century standards, he does concede that Britain will have to mend its imperialist ways in order to be worthy of this new found supremacy. The plot was inspired by a colonial crisis caused by intense European competition for strategic Chinese territory. As Shiel later explained, when the "trouble broke out in China" in November 1897, the editor of the successful Pearson publishing group quickly commissioned him to write a "war-serial" to exploit it, and Shiel incorporated aspects of the ongoing situation into the first installments of the serial as he wrote it (1929: p. 673). The public response to these installments was so enthusiastic that Pearson requested Shiel to extend the novel to twice its intended word count (Squires 2001: p. 12), making it the most successful of Shiel's three lurid yellow-peril novels. Further signaling *The Yellow Danger*'s topicality, new editions of both the serial and book version were issued in 1900 after the outbreak of the Boxer Rebellion in China.—AILISE BULFIN

See also Shiel 1898, Shiel 1929

Yellowbacks. Inexpensive, popular novels that flooded the marketplace in the second half of the nineteenth century. With the decreasing cost of print and the expansion of a literate public, publishers at mid-century realized they could rapidly expand their reading audience, and often sold yellowbacks (named for the cheap boards they were usually covered in) at train stations as cheap entertainment; sometimes they are referred to as "railway novels." Early publishers include W. H. Smith, who first set up **railway bookstalls**, Simms and McIntyre (*The Parlour Library* series, 1846–1856), George Routledge & Sons, with series including the *Railway Library*, the *Popular Library*, *Everybody's Library*, and *Sixpenny Novels* (1849–1905), as well as Ward & Lock, **Chatto & Windus**, and Chapman & Hall. The popularity of the yellowback market helped to unseat the "three-decker," or three-volume novel, and the magazine **serial** as the *de facto* medium for fiction by the later century.

"Yellowback" can be a misleading description as it refers to a mode of printing (cheap) for a target audience (popular), and not to content. Some canonical and "respectable" literature was reprinted in yellowback form, including the works of Shakespeare, **Dickens**, and the classics in translation. But the term commonly refers to formulaic novels featuring crime, suspense, and **romance**. Yellowback plots frequently feature unequivocal moral categories (*Faith and Unfaith*, Mrs. Hungerford, 1883), tests of character (*Did She Love Him?*, James Grant, 1876), or public ordeals (*Barbara Heathcote's Trial*, **Rosa Nouchette Carey**, 1877), as well as crude stereotypes (*A Bad Beginning: A Story of a French Marriage*, Katherine S. MacQuoid, 1862), and feats of daring (*Ran Away from Home*, by "Cannibal Jack" [William S. Hayward, 1866]). Toward the latter half of the century, yellowback novels were associated primarily with women writers and readers, often focusing on tests of female virtue, as we see in titles like *Beyond Atonement* (Bertha M. Clay, n.d.), *The Fickle Heart* (Fortuné Du Boisgobey, 1888) and *That Other Woman* (Annie Thomas, 1889). These novels can be unfamiliar in their **melodrama**, piety, or zeal, and were likely valued for the reading experience they provided rather than for their information or ideas. Yellowback authors are generally unknown today, but copyright laws did not prevent the works of many popular novelists, such as **Mary Braddon**, **Wilkie Collins**, and **Robert Louis Stevenson**, from being printed and sold in yellowback form, without the author's consent or remuneration.

Literary scholarship largely focuses on the exceptionality of specific texts and authors, a metric of assessment that makes it difficult to appreciate novels directed to a less educated, apolitical, and/or female readership. Their sheer number and disposability has further limited yellowbacks' scholarly appraisal, and while digitization makes these once ephemeral books widely accessible today, scholars are still uncertain of how to categorize and assess such a broad and indeterminate body of works. Significant collections of yellowbacks (both codex and digital) can be found at the British Library, the Sadleir Collection at the University of California, Los Angeles, The New York Public Library, Project Gutenberg, and the Hathi Trust.—Tabitha Sparks

Yonge, Charlotte Mary (1823–1900). English novelist and author. Under the influence of her father, a Tory ex-army officer and magistrate and Tractarian clergyman, John Keble, Yonge became the author of many well-known domestic novels, generally featuring large families who appeared in successive novels. Her novels expressed her Tractarian religious views, but are distinguished from many contemporary religious novels by the restraint and sophistication with which she dealt with religious, social and personal dilemmas: she relied on character and plot development rather than authorial commentary to make her point. Particularly influential early works included *The Heir of Redclyffe* (1853)—which had a deep impact on William Morris and D. G. Rossetti through its advocacy of a form of domesticized chivalry for young men—and *The Daisy Chain* (1856), in which the lively and attractive May family lose a mother and build a church for a neglected community.

While Yonge's political, social, and gender values were essentially conservative, she was far more responsive to, and thoughtful about, the changing world around her than has often been acknowledged. The central character of *Hopes and Fears* (1860) is a middle-aged spinster, and the novel chronicles her experience of adopting two children; Yonge herself never married, and many of her novels include sympathetic portrayals of unmarried women (and men). While *Magnum Bonum* (1879) sternly rebukes overly ambitious female intellectual aspirations, and *Nuttie's Father* (1885) advocated submission to a frankly undeserving husband and father, Yonge increasingly accepted expanding opportunities for women of her class: this is reflected in later novels such as *Beechcroft at Rockstone* (1888). More than forty years editing the *Monthly Packet*, a magazine designed for the daughters of the middle classes and the gentry, meant that she had considerable contact with and influence on younger women, including the future **Mrs. Humphry Ward**.

Recent research has also highlighted the extent to which Yonge features sympathetic characters with disabilities—including, for instance, the artist, Cherry Underwood, in *The Pillars of the House* (1873). Her interest in missionary work meant that—despite her reluctance to leave her native Hampshire—she had a global perspective: she donated the profits from *The Heir* to fund a missionary schooner in the Melanesian Islands, and wrote a biography of this region's first bishop, John Coleridge Patteson (1874). She was also capable of experimentation with emerging literary trends—*Lady Hester, or Ursula's Narrative* (1874) is a **sensation novel**, while *Chantry House* (1886) is a ghost story—and writing for a range of audiences.

An area of Yonge's output which has been neglected until recently is her history-writing, both fictional and non-fictional. Among her best-known historical tales are *The Little Duke* (1854), *The Lances of Lynwood* (1855), and *The Dove in the Eagle's Nest* (1866), all intended for a juvenile audience. *The Chaplet of Pearls* (1868), set during the French

Wars of Religion, was the first of an innovative series of novels dealing with Anglo-French religious conflicts and developments. But Yonge also wrote many history textbooks, and can be seen as a key contributor to Victorian historical cultures.—ROSEMARY ANN MITCHELL
    See also ODNB

Zangwill, Israel (1864–1926). Anglo-Jewish writer. Born in London to immigrant parents, Zangwill got his start as a writer and editor for Jewish periodicals in English, and as a humorist in Jerome K. Jerome's periodical *The Idler*. He is best known as an interpreter of the Jewish immigrant experience in Britain and America, as the novel **Children of the Ghetto** and the play *The Melting-Pot* (1908). However, throughout the 1890s and into the early twentieth century, he published fiction on a wide variety of topics, both Jewish and more general, which he compiled in collections such as *The Bachelors' Club* (1891), *The King of Schnorrers: Grotesques and Fantasies* (1894), *"They That Walk in Darkness": Ghetto Tragedies* (1899), and *Ghetto Comedies* (1907). He is also known for the novels **The Big Bow Mystery**, *The Master* (1895), and *The Mantle of Elijah* (1900). A collection of stories about failed idealists, Jewish and Christian, titled *Dreamers of the Ghetto*, appeared in 1898. **Children of the Ghetto**, a bestseller, made Zangwill a literary celebrity on both sides of the Atlantic, and he had successful tours of the United States in 1898 and 1908. His work was also widely translated. In the twentieth century Zangwill focused his literary attention on playwriting and essays, becoming active in several social movements. He wrote articles and gave speeches supporting women's suffrage, allied with groups opposing Britain's entry into World War I, and was an early English Zionist. Later, concerned about prospects for a Jewish state in Palestine, he formed the Jewish Territorial Organization (called the ITO) in 1905, to seek a homeland for the Jewish people wherever one might be found. Zangwill's reputation waned after a controversial speech in New York in 1923. He has recently been rediscovered.—MERI-JANE ROCHELSON

Works Cited

Reference Works

ADB: *Australian Dictionary of Biography.*
DIL: *Dictionary of Irish Literature.* 1996. R. Hogan (Ed.). Westport, CT: Greenwood.
DLB: *Dictionary of Literary Biography.*
DNCJ: *Dictionary of Nineteenth-Century Journalism in Great Britain and Ireland.* 2009. L. Brake and M. Demoor (Eds.). Gent: Academia.
EB: *Encyclopædia Britannica.*
OCB: *The Oxford Companion to the Book.* 2010. M. F. Suarez and H. R. Woudhuysen. (Eds.). Oxford: Oxford University Press.
ODNB: *Oxford Dictionary of National Biography.*
OECL: *Oxford Encyclopedia of Children's Literature.* 2006. J. Zipes (Ed.). Oxford: Oxford University Press.
OED: *Oxford English Dictionary.*
WI: *Wellesley Index to Victorian Periodicals, 1824–1900.*
WD: *Waterloo Directory of English Newspapers and Periodicals, 1800–1900.*

Other Works

Adam, J. 1883. "Cases of Self-Mutilation by the Insane." *The Journal of Mental Science,* 29(126), 213–18.
Adams, C. W. (pseud. C. Felix). 2012. [1865]. *The Notting Hill Mystery.* Intro. M. Ashley. London: Saunders, Otley, & Co. British Library Reprint.
Adams, H. G. 1857. "Ellis, Sarah Stickney." *A Cyclopaedia of Female Biography* (pp. 270–72). London: Groombridge & Sons.
Adcock, A. St. J. 1928. *The Glory that Was Grub Street: Impressions of Contemporary Authors.* New York: Stokes.
Adrian, J. 1998. Afterword. *The Detections of Miss Cusack* (pp. 107–10). By L.T. Meade & R. Eustace. Ed. D. G. Greene & J. Adrian. Shelburne, ON: Battered Silicon Dispatch Box.
"Advertisement." 1898, April 23. *The Athenaeum Journal of Literature, Science, the Fine Arts, Music, and the Drama.* London: Athenaeum Press.
Alden, W. L. 1901, 5 October. "London Letter." *The New York Times Saturday Review,* 722.
Aldis, B. 1974. *Billion Year Spree: The History of Science Fiction.* New York: Doubleday.
Alkon, P. 1994. *Science Fiction before 1900: Imagination Discovers Technology.* New York: Twayne.
Allen, G. 1891. *Recalled to Life.* New York: Henry Holt & Company.
Allen, V. 1997. *Hall Caine: Portrait of a Victorian Romancer.* Sheffield: Sheffield Academic.
Allen, W. O. B., and McClure, E. 1898. *Two Hundred Years: The History of the Society for Promoting Christian Knowledge, 1698–1898.* London: Society for Promoting Christian Knowledge.
Altick, R. D. 1998. *The English Common Reader: A Social History of the Mass Reading Public, 1800–1900* (2nd ed.). Chicago: University of Chicago Press.
Amato, S. 2015. *Beastly Possessions: Animals in Victorian Consumer Culture.* Toronto: University of Toronto Press.
Anderson, B. 2008. *Under Three Flags: Anarchism and the Anticolonial Imagination.* London: Verso.
Anderson, O. 1987. *Suicide in Victorian and Edwardian England.* Oxford: Clarendon Press.
Anderson, P. 1991. *The Printed Image and the Transformation of Popular Culture, 1790–1860.* Oxford: Clarendon Press.
Annual Report. 1895. London: United Kingdom Band of Hope Union.

Anon. 1847, 13 March. *The Critic*, 205–206.
Anon. 1892, 11 February. *Hearth and Home* 39, 383.
"The Arabian Nights." 1886. *The Edinburgh Review*, 166–69.
Arata, S. "The Occidental Tourist: *Dracula* and Reverse Colonisation." In *Fictions of Loss in the Victorian Fin de siècle* (pp. 107–32). Cambridge: Cambridge University Press, 1996.
"Arline Pretty Serial Completed." 1919, December 6. *Motion Picture News*.
"Armadale." 1866. *London Review of Politics, Society, Literature, Art, and Science*, 12(311), 680–681.
Ash, Susan. 2005. The Barnardo's Babies: Performativity, Shame and the Photograph. *Continuum: Journal of Media & Cultural Studies*, 19(4), 507–21.
Ashley, Mike. 2012. Introduction. In C. W. Adams, *The Notting Hill Mystery*. London: Saunders, Otley, and Co. British Library Reprint.
Auerbach, N. 1975. "Incarnations of the Orphan." *ELH*, 42(3), 359–419.
Auerbach, N. 1981. "Magi and Maidens: The Romance of the Victorian Freud." *Critical Inquiry*, 8(2), 281–300.
Auerbach, N. 1995. *Our Vampires, Ourselves*. Chicago: University of Chicago Press.
"The Author of Madame Midas." 1888, October 6. *Illustrated London News*, 410.
Avery, G. 1961. *Mrs. Ewing*. London: Bodley.
Ayres, B. 2010. "Jessie Fothergill." *The Literary Encyclopedia*. Retrieved from http://www.litencyc.com/php/speople.php?rec=true&UID=12806.
Ayres, B. 2010 & 2016. Introduction. *Kith and Kin*, by Jessie Fothergill (1881). In Carolyn W. de la L. Oulton (Series Ed.), *New Woman Fiction, 1881–1899* (vol. 1, xxiii–xlii). London: Pickering & Chatto, 2010. Republished *Routledge Historical Resources: History of Feminism*. Academic Ed. Ann Heilmann. London: Routledge, 2016.
Baldick, C. 1992. Introduction. In Chris Baldick (Ed.). *The Oxford Book of Gothic Tales* (pp. xi–xxiii). Oxford: Oxford University Press.
Banham, Christopher M. 2006. "*Boys of England* and Edwin J. Brett, 1866–99." Unpublished Ph.D. Diss., University of Leeds.
Barrett Browning, Elizabeth. 2009. *Selected Poems*, M. Stone & B. Taylor (Eds.). Peterborough, ON: Broadview.
Bartley, G. C. T. 1868–1869. "Training and Education of Pauper Children." *Journal of the Society of the Arts* 17, 188–94.
Basdeo, S. 2016. "Radical Medievalism: Pierce Egan the Younger's Robin Hood, Wat Tyler, and Adam Bell." In S. Basdeo & L. Padgett (Eds.), *Leeds Working Papers in Victorian Studies, Volume 15: Imagining the Victorians* (pp. 48–64). Leeds: LCVS.
Bateson, F. W. (Ed.) 1969. *Cambridge Bibliography of English Literature, Vol. III, 1800–1900*. London: Cambridge University Press.
Baxter, D. 1895, March 23. "The New Shilling." *Justice*.
Beer, G. 1983. *Darwin's Plots: Evolutionary Narrative in Darwin, George Eliot and Nineteenth Century Fiction*. London: Routledge.
Belflower, J. R. 1967. *The Life and Career of Elizabeth Lynn Linton (1822–1898)*. Unpublished Ph.D. thesis. Duke University.
Belford, B. 1990. *Violet: The Story of the Irrepressible Violet Hunt and Her Circle of Lovers and Friends—Ford Madox Ford, H. G. Wells, Somerset Maugham, and Henry James*. New York: Simon & Schuster.
Beller, A. 2011. "Amelia B. Edwards." In Pamela K. Gilbert (Ed.), *A Companion to Sensation Fiction* (pp. 349–60). Oxford: Wiley-Blackwell.
Berridge, V. 1999. *Opium and the People: Opiate Use and Drug Control Policy in Nineteenth and Early Twentieth Century England*. London & New York: Free Association.
Besant, W. 1899. *The Pen and the Book*. London: Thomas Burleigh.
Besant, W. 2012. *All Sorts and Conditions of Men: An Impossible Story*. K. A. Morrison (Ed). Brighton: Victorian Secrets.
Besant, W. 2015. *Children of Gibeon*. Rev. first edition. K. A. Morrison (Ed). San Diego: Cognella.
Bevir, M. 2011. *The Making of British Socialism*. Woodstock: Princeton University Press.
Bigland, E. 1953. *Marie Corelli: The Woman and the Legend*. London: Jarrolds.
Billings, H. 2010. *M. Press. Shiel: The Middle Years, 1897–1923*. Austin, TX: Roger Beacham.
Billson, C. J. 1892. "The English Novel." *Westminster Review* 138, 602–20.
"Births, Deaths, Marriages and Obituaries." 1933, 25 September. *Citizen*. p. 7.
Black, H. C. 1906. *Notable Women Authors of the Day*. London: Maclaren & Co.
"Black Sheep." 1867, 10 August. *Saturday Review of Politics, Literature, Science and Art*, 24(615), 190.
The Blackburn Standard. 1845, 24 December. Issue 571.
Blackmore, R. D. 1889. "Preface." *Clara Vaughan*. London: Sampson Low, Marston, Searle, & Rivington.
Blaze de Bury, R. 1850. *Germania: Its Courts, Camps and People*. London: Colburn.
Bleiler, E. F. 1977. *The Collected Ghost Stories of Mrs. J. H. Riddell*. New York: Dover.
Bleiler, E. F. 1990. *Science Fiction: The Early Years. A Full Description of More Than 3,000 Science-Fiction Stories from Earliest Times to the Appearance of the Genre Magazines in 1930*. Bowling Green: Kent State University Press.

Bloom, C. 2010. *Gothic Histories: The Taste for Terror, 1764 to the Present.* London: Continuum.
Botting, F. 2014. *Gothic.* 2nd ed. London: Routledge.
Bourrier, K. 2015. *The Measure of Manliness: Disability and Masculinity in the Mid-Victorian Novel.* Ann Arbor: University of Michigan Press.
Bowen, E. 1950. "Uncle Silas." In *Collected Impressions* (pp. 3–17). New York: Knopf.
Braddon, M. E. 1892. *Gerard; or The World, the Flesh and the Devil.* London: Simpkin & Marshall.
Braddon, M. E. 2004. [1896]. "Good Lady Ducayne." Whitefish: Kessinger.
Braddon, M. E. 2012. [1862]. *Lady Audley's Secret.* L. Pykett (Ed.). Oxford: Oxford University Press.
Brantlinger, P. 1988. *Rule of Darkness: British Literature and Imperialism, 1830–1914.* Ithaca: Cornell University Press.
Brantlinger, P. 1998. *The Reading Lesson: The Threat of Mass Literacy in Nineteenth-Century British Fiction.* Bloomington and Indianapolis: Indiana University Press.
Bratton, J. S. 2015. *The Impact of Victorian Children's Fiction* (2nd ed.). London: Routledge.
Brewer, J. F. 1888. *The Curse upon Mitre Square.* London: J.W. Lovell Company.
Briefel, A. 2008. "Hands of Beauty, Hands of Horror: Fear and Egyptian Art at the Fin de Siècle." *Victorian Studies, 50*(2): pp. 263–71.
Briggs, J. 1987. *A Woman of Passion: The Life of E. Nesbit 1858–1924.* New York: New Amsterdam.
Briggs, J. 2012. "The Ghost Story." In David Punter (Ed.). *The New Companion to the Gothic* (pp. 176–85). Oxford: Blackwell.
Brontë, C. 2008. *Jane Eyre.* Oxford: Oxford University Press.
Brontë, E. 1998. *Wuthering Heights.* Oxford: Oxford University Press.
[Brooke, Emma]. Death Certificate for Emma Frances Brooke, 30 November 1926. Chertsey, Surrey. Certified copy in possession of the author (Barbara Tilley).
[Brooke, Emma]. "Miss Emma Brooke Obituary." *Manchester Guardian Weekly.* 2 December 1926, p. 4.
Brooker, W. 2004. *Alice's Adventures: Lewis Carroll in Popular Culture.* New York: Continuum.
Brooks, P. 1976. *The Melodramatic Imagination.* New Haven: Yale University Press.
Broughton, R. 1920, Sept. "Girls Past and Present." *Ladies Home Journal, 38,* 141.
Broughton, R. 2010. *Cometh Up as a Flower.* P. K. Gilbert (Ed.). Peterborough, ON: Broadview.
Broughton, R. 2013. *Not Wisely, but Too Well.* T. Heller (Ed.). Brighton: Victorian Secrets.
Bulfin, A. 2011. "The Fiction of Gothic Egypt and British Imperial Paranoia: The Curse of the Suez Canal." *English Literature in Transition, 1880–1920, 54*(4), 411–43.
Bulfin, A. 2015a. "'To Arms!' Invasion Narratives and Late-Victorian Literature." *Literature Compass, 12*(9), 482–96.
Bulfin, A. 2015b. "The Natural Catastrophe in Late-Victorian Popular Fiction: 'How Will the World End?'" *Critical Survey, 27*(2), 81–100.
Bulwer-Lytton, E. 1859. "The Haunted and the Haunters; or, The House and the Brain." *Blackwood's Edinburgh Magazine, 86,* 224–45.
Bulwer-Lytton, E. 1989. *The Coming Race.* Santa Barbara: Woodbridge.
Burris, Q. G. 1930. *Richard Doddridge Blackmore: His Life and Novels.* University of Illinois Press.
Burrows, E. 1869. *Neptune: or the Autobiography of a Newfoundland Dog.* London: Griffith & Farran.
Burstein, M. E. 2013. Introduction. In M. Ward, *Robert Elsmere* (pp. 5–11). Brighton: Victorian Secrets.
Bynum, W. F. 1994. *Science and the Practice of Medicine in the Nineteenth Century.* New York: Cambridge University Press.
Byrne, K. 2011. *Tuberculosis and the Victorian Literary Imagination.* Cambridge: Cambridge University Press.
Byron, G. 2007. "Bram Stoker's Gothic and the Resources of Science." *Critical Survey, 19*(2), 48–62.
Caird, M. 1888. "Marriage." *Westminster Review, 130*(1), 186–201.
Campbell, C. 2014. Women and Sadism in *Strange Case of Dr. Jekyll and Mr. Hyde*: "City in a Nightmare." *English Literature in Transition, 1880–1920, 57*(3), 309–22.
Carlyle, T. 1849. "Occasional Discourse on the Negro Question." *Fraser's Magazine,* 670–79.
Catling, T. 1911. *My Life's Pilgrimage.* London: John Murray.
Chaney, S. 2011a. "'A Hideous Torture on Himself': Madness and Self-Mutilation in Victorian Literature." *The Journal of Medical Humanities, 32*(4), 279–89.
Chaney, S. 2011b. "Self-Control, Selfishness and Mutilation: How 'Medical' Is Self-Injury Anyway?" *Journal of Medical History, 55*(3), 375–82.
Chaney, S. 2017. *Psyche on the Skin: A History of Self-Harm.* Chicago: Reaktion.
Chatelain, Madame de. 1850. *Pussy's Road to Ruin, or, Do as You Are Bid.* Translated freely from the German. London: Joseph, Myers & Co.
Chesney, G. T. 1871. *The Battle of Dorking.* Edinburgh: Blackwood.
Chesterton, G. K. 1964. "Fiction as Food." *The Spice of Life and Other Essays.* Dorothy E. Collins (Ed.). Beaconsfield: Darwen Finlayson.
Childers, Erskine. 2011. *The Riddle of the Sands.* London: Penguin.
Chitty, S. 1974. *The Beast and the Monk: A Life of Charles Kingsley.* London: Hodder & Stoughton.

Clapp, M., Simms, W. G., Thornwell, J. H., and Whitaker, D. K. (Eds.). 1844. "Pictures of Private Life." *Southern Quarterly Review* 5, 263.
Clarion Accounts. 1895, 22 January. Clarion Archives, 7407, MS070 8 C1. Manchester Libraries, Information and Archives, Central Library, Manchester. 11 June 2015.
Clarke, A. 1900, 6 October. "The Cotton Panic." *Teddy Ashton's Northern Weekly*.
Clarke, C. 2014. *Late Victorian Crime Fiction in the Shadows of Sherlock*. New York: Palgrave Macmillan.
Clarke, I. F. 1992. *Voices Prophesying War: Future Wars, 1763–3749*. 2nd ed. Oxford: Oxford University Press.
Clarke, I. F. 1997. "Before and After *The Battle of Dorking*." *Science Fiction Studies*, 24(71), n. pag. Retrieved from www.depauw.edu/sfs/backissues/71/clarke71art.htm.
Clarke, W.K.L. 1919. *A Short History of S.P.C.K.* London: Society for Promoting Christian Knowledge; New York: Macmillan.
Cleere, E. 2014. *The Sanitary Arts: Aesthetic Culture and the Victorian Cleanliness Campaigns*. Columbus: Ohio State University Press.
Cleeve, L. 1895. *The Woman Who Wouldn't* (4th ed.). London: Simpkin, Marshall, Hamilton, Kent.
Cobbe, F. P. 1867. *The Confessions of a Lost Dog*. London: Griffith & Farran.
Cobbold, T. S. 1879. *Parasites: A Treatise on the Entozoa of Man and Animals Including Some Account of the Ectozoa*. London: J & A Churchill.
Cohen, A. 1895, June 18. [Untitled, 6] *The Torch*, 2(1).
Colburn, H. 1833. "A Few Words from the Proprietor." *The New Monthly Magazine and Literary Journal, Part 3*, 2.
Colella, S. 2016. *Charlotte Riddell's City Novels and Victorian Business: Narrating Capitalism*. London & New York: Routledge.
Collingwood, S. D. 1898. *The Life and Letters of Lewis Carroll*. New York: Century Co.
Collins, D. (Ed.) 2010. *The String of Pearls*. Ware: Wordsworth.
Collins, W. 1858, 21 August. "The Unknown Public." *Household Words*, 217–22.
Collins, W. 1859, January. "Daughters from Home." *Servants' Magazine*, 3–9.
Collins, W. 1860, 26 November. "Preamble to *The Woman in White*." *All the Year Round* 31, 95.
Collins, W. 1868. *The Moonstone: A Romance*. London: Tinsley Brothers.
Collins, W. 1992. *The Law and the Lady*. Oxford: Oxford University Press.
Collins, W. 1996. *The Woman in White*. J. Sutherland (Ed.). Oxford: Oxford University Press.
Collins, W. 1997. *Heart and Science*. Steve Farmer (Ed.). Peterborough, ON: Broadview.
Collins, W. 2005. *Basil*. Oxford: Oxford University Press.
Colloms, B. 1975. *Charles Kingsley*. London: Constable.
Conan Doyle, A. 1891. "A Scandal in Bohemia." *The Strand Magazine*, 2(7), 61–75.
Conan Doyle, A. 1893; 1986. "The Final Problem." In *Sherlock Holmes: The Complete Novels and Stories* (vol. 1, 736–55). New York: Bantam.
Conan Doyle, A. 2003. *The Complete Sherlock Holmes*. 2 vols. K. Freeman (Ed.). New York: Barnes & Noble.
Conan Doyle, A. 2010. [1890]. *The Sign of the Four*. Ed. Shafquat Towheed. Peterborough, ON: Broadview.
Corelli, M. 1895. *The Sorrows of Satan*. London: Methuen.
Corriou, N. 2015. "'A Woman Is a Woman, if She Had Been Dead Five Thousand Centuries!' Mummy Fiction, Imperialism and the Politics of Gender." *Miranda*, 11.
Cosslett, T. 2006. *Talking Animals in British Children's Fiction, 1786–1914*. Aldershot: Ashgate.
Cousin, J. W. 1910. *A Short Biographical Dictionary of English Literature*. London: J. M. Dent & Sons.
Coustillas, P. 2004-16. "Gissing, George Robert (1857–1903)." *Oxford Dictionary of National Biography*. Web.
Coustillas, P. 2011-12. *The Heroic Life of George Gissing*. 3 vols. London: Pickering & Chatto.
Cowling, M. 1989. *The Artist as Anthropologist: The Representation of Type and Character in Victorian Art*. Cambridge: Cambridge University Press.
Cox, F.E.G. 2002. "History of Human Parasitology." *Clinical Microbiological Reviews*, 15(4), 595–612.
Cox, H., and Mowatt, S. 2014. *Revolutions from Grub Street: A History of Magazine Publishing in Britain*. Oxford: Oxford University Press.
Cox, J. 1982. *Take a Cold Tub, Sir!* Guildford: Lutterworth.
Craik, D. M. 2005. [1856]. *John Halifax, Gentleman*. L. Alexander (Ed.). Peterborough, ON: Broadview.
Crane, R., and Johnston, A. (Eds.). 2010. Introduction. *The Complete Indian Housekeeper and Cook*. Oxford: Oxford University Press.
Craton, L. 2009. *The Victorian Freak Show: The Significance of Disability and Physical Differences in 19th Century Fiction*. Amherst, NY: Cambria.
Crawford, E. 2003. *The Women's Suffrage Movement: A Reference Guide, 1866–1928*. London: Routledge.
Crisp, J. 1989. *Rosa Nouchette Carey*. Victorian Fiction Research Guides 16. St. Lucia: University of Queensland.
Crone, R. 2012. *Violent Victorians*. Manchester: Manchester University Press.
Cross, V. 2003. *Anna Lombard*. Gail Cunningham (Ed.). London: Continuum.
Cunningham. H. S. 1877. *Chronicles of Dustypore: A Tale of Modern Anglo-Indian Society*. London: Smith, Elder, & Co.

Cutt, M. 1974. *Mrs. Sherwood and Her Books for Children*. Oxford: Oxford University Press.
Dalby, R. (Ed.). 2005. Introduction. *Ghosts and Family Legends*. Wales, UK: Sarob.
Daly, N. 1994. "That Obscure Object of Desire: Victorian Commodity Culture and Fictions of the Mummy." *NOVEL: A Forum on Fiction*, 28(1), 24–51.
Dalziel, M. 1957. *Popular Fiction 100 Years Ago*. London: Cohen and West.
Darwin, C. 1860. [1859]. *On the Origin of Species by Means of Natural Selection*. London: John Murray.
Davis, P. 2004. *The Oxford English Literary History, Volume 8. 1830–1880: The Victorians*. Oxford and New York: Oxford University Press.
Davis, W. A., Jr. 2014. "A New Date for the Victorian New Woman." *Notes and Queries*, 61(4), 577–80.
Day, J. 2006. *The Mummy's Curse: Mummymania in the English-Speaking World*. London: Routledge.
Deane, B. 2008. "Mummy Fiction and the Occupation of Egypt: Imperial Striptease." *English Literature in Transition, 1880–1920*, 51(4), 381–410.
Deane, B. 2014. *Masculinity and the New Imperialism: Rewriting Manhood in British Popular Literature, 1870–1914*. Cambridge: Cambridge University Press.
Death Certificate for Emma Frances Brooke, 30 November 1926. Chertsey, Surrey. Certified copy in possession of the author (Barbara Tilley).
Depasquale, P. 1985. *Guy Boothby: His Life and Work*. Seacombe Gardens, Australia: Pioneer.
DeWitt, A. 2013. *Moral Authority, Men of Science, and the Victorian Novel*. New York: Cambridge University Press.
Dickens, C. 1837. *Posthumous Papers of the Pickwick Club*. London: Chapman & Hall.
Dickens, C. 1864. *Our Mutual Friend* (vols. 1–4). New York: John Bradburn.
Dickens, C. 1868. *Bleak House*. London. Chapman & Hall.
Dickens, C. 1999. *Great Expectations*. New York: W.W. Norton.
Dickens, C. 2008. *Dombey and Son*. Oxford: Oxford University Press.
Dickens, C. 2008. *Great Expectations*. Oxford: Oxford University Press.
Dickens, C. 2008. *Oliver Twist*. Oxford: Oxford University Press.
Dickens, M. A. 1899. "A Talk with Lucas Malet." *The Windsor Magazine*, 522–24.
Dicks, G. *The John Dicks Press*. London: Lulu.com, 2006.
Diehl, A. M. 1897. *Musical Memories*. London: Richard Bentley.
Diehl, A. M. 1908. *The True Story of My Life: An Autobiography*. London: John Lane.
Diver, M. 1911. *Lilamani: A Study in Possibilities*. London: Hutchinson.
Dixon, E. H. 1930. *As I Knew Them: Sketches of People I Have Met on the Way*. London: Hutchinson.
Dixon, E. H. 2004. *The Story of a Modern Woman*. Ed. Steve Farmer. Peterborough, ON: Broadview.
Dobson. E. 2017a. "Gods and Ghost-Light: Ancient Egypt, Electricity and X-Rays." *Victorian Literature and Culture*, 45(1), 119–35.
Dobson, E. 2017b. "Sleeping Beauties: Mummies and the Fairy-Tale Genre at the *Fin de Siècle*." *Journal of International Women's Studies*, 18(3), 19–34.
Donaldson, W. 1986. *Popular Literature in Victorian Scotland*. Aberdeen: Aberdeen University Press.
Drabble, M. 2000. *The Oxford Companion to English Literature*. Oxford: Oxford University Press
Du Coudray, C. B. 2006. *The Curse of the Werewolf: Fantasy, Horror and the Beast Within*. New York City: I.B. Tauris.
E.A.B. 1899. "Miss Braddon." *The Academy*, 1432, 431–23.
Eby, C. D. 1987. *The Road to Armageddon: The Martial Spirit in English Popular Literature, 1870–1914*. Durham: Duke University Press.
Egerton, G. 1897. *Symphonies*. London: The Bodley Head.
Egerton, G. 2006. *Keynotes and Discords*. London: Continuum.
Eggeling, J. 2017. In *The Encyclopedia of Science Fiction*. Retrieved from http://www.sf-encyclopedia.com/entry/griffith_george.
Egloff, R. 2017. "Rose Blaze de Bury and the Nineteenth-Century World of Publishing." *MESH: The Journal for Undergraduate Work Across English Studies*, 1(1), 1–18.
Ehnenn, J. 2017. "Reorienting the Bildungsroman: Progress Narratives, Queerness, and Disability in *The History of Sir Richard Calmady* and *Jude the Obscure*." *Journal of Literary & Cultural Disability Studies*, 11(2), 151–168.
Endelman, T. M. 1994. "The Frankaus of London." *Jewish History* 8(12), 117–54.
Engels, F., to Harkness, M. 1973. Letter. In L. Baxandall & S. Morawski (Eds.), *Marx and Engels on Literature and Art* (pp. 114–16). St. Louis: Telos.
Erickson, L. 1990. "The Economy of Novel Reading: Jane Austen and the Circulating Library." *Studies in English Literature, 1500–1900*, 30(4), 573–90.
Evans, H. & D. 1976. *Beyond the Gaslight: Science in Popular Fiction 1895–1905*. London: Frederick Muller.
Ewing, J. H. 1873. *A Flatiron for a Farthing or, Some Passages in the Life of an Only Son*. London: Bell & Daldy.
Ewing, J. H. 1885. *Six to Sixteen: A Story for Girls*. London: George Bell & Sons.
Fawcett, E. [Edward] Douglas. 1893. *Hartmann the Anarchist; Or, the Doom of the Great City*. London: Edward Arnold.

Fields, A. 1891, 4 July. "Sturdy British Stock: How Steve Marshland and his Daughter Met the Alien Invasion." The *Evening News and Post*.
Finkelstein, D. 2002. *The House of Blackwood: Author-Publisher Relations in the Victorian Era*. University Park: Penn State University Press.
Flanders, J. 2011. *The Invention of Murder: How the Victorians Revelled in Death and Detection and Created Modern Crime*. London: HarperCollins.
Flegel, M. 2015. *Pets and Domesticity in Victorian Literature and Culture*. New York: Routledge.
Fleischhack, M. 2015. *The Representation of Ancient Egypt in Nineteenth-Century and Early-Twentieth-Century Fantastic Fiction*. Frankfurt: Peter Lang.
Flint, K. 1993. *The Woman Reader, 1837–1914*. Oxford: Clarendon Press.
Flower, D. 1934. *A Century of Best Sellers, 1830–1930*. London: National Book Council.
Floyd, D. 2014. *Street Urchins, Sociopaths, and Degenerates*. Cardiff: University of Wales Press.
Forrester, W. 1980. *Great-Grandmama's Weekly*. Guildford & London: Lutterworth.
Fothergill, J. M. 1874. *The Maintenance of Health*. Smith, Elder & Co.
"Four Types of Fiction." *The Academy and Literature*, 1593 (15 November 1902), 525–26.
Fox, P. 1994. *Class Fictions: Shame and Resistance in the British Working-Class Novel, 1890–1945*. Durham: Duke University Press.
Foxcroft, L. 2007. *Making of Addiction: The Use and Abuse of Opium in Nineteenth-Century Britain*. Aldershot: Ashgate.
Freeman, K. 2003. Introduction to Volume I. *The Complete Sherlock Holmes*, 2 vols. (pp. xxi–xxxiii). By A. C. Doyle. New York: Barnes & Noble.
Frerichs, S. C. 1974. *Elizabeth Missing Sewell: A Minor Novelist's Search for the Via Media in the Education of Women in the Victorian Era*. Doctoral Dissertation. Retrieved from VictorianWeb.org.
Freud, S. 1909. "Family Romances." *The Standard Edition of the Complete Psychological Works of Sigmund Freud, Volume IX (1906–1908)*, 235–42.
Freud, S., and Breuer, J. 2004. *Studies in Hysteria*. New ed., translated by Nicola Luckhurst. London: Penguin.
Fröbel, J. 1891. *Ein Lebenslauf: Aufzeichnungen, Erinnerungen und Bekenntnisse*, vol. 2. Stuttgart: J. G. Gottaschen Buchandlung.
Frost, G. 2009. *Victorian Childhoods*. Westport, CT: Praeger.
"From Elizabeth Gaskell to Louis Hachette." 2000. [1855, 29 October] In J. Chapple & A. Shelston (Eds.), *Further Letters of Mrs. Gaskell*. Manchester: Manchester University Press.
Fyfe, A. 2004. *Science and Salvation: Evangelical Popular Science Publishing in Victorian Britain*. Chicago: University of Chicago.
Fyfe, A. 2005. "A Short History of the Religious Tract Society." In D. Butts & P. Garrett (Eds.), *From the Dairyman's Daughter to Worrals of the WAAF: The Religious Tract Society, Lutterworth Press and Children's Literature* (pp. 13–35). Cambridge: Lutterworth.
Gabriele, A. 2009. *Reading Popular Culture in Victorian Print: Belgravia and Sensationalism*. New York: Palgrave Macmillan.
Galbally, Ann. 2005. *Charles Conder: The Last Bohemian*. Melbourne: Melbourne University Publishing.
Galton. F. 1869. *Hereditary Genius*. London: Macmillan.
Gaskell, E. 1855. *North and South*. Leipzig: Tauchnitz.
Gaskell, E. 1996. *Wives and Daughters*. London: Penguin.
Gates, B. T. 1988. *Victorian Suicide: Mad Crimes and Sad Histories*. Princeton: Princeton University Press.
Gatty, H. K. F. 1885. *Juliana Horatia Ewing and Her Books*. London: Society for Promoting Christian Knowledge.
Gavin, A. E. 2008. Introduction. *Paul Ferroll* by Caroline Clive (pp. vii–xxxii). A. E. Gavin (Ed.). Kansas City, MO: Valancourt.
Gavin, A. 2012. *The Child in British Literature: Literary Constructions of Childhood, Medieval to Contemporary*. New York: Palgrave.
Gelder, K. 1994. *Reading the Vampire*. London: Routledge.
Gemmel, M., and Vogt, M. (Eds.). 2013. *Wissensräume—Bibliotheken in der Literatur*. [*Areas of Knowledge—Libraries in Literature*.] Berlin: Ripperger & Kremers Verlag.
"German Uniforms and Street Advertisements." 1906, 14 May. Hansard HC Deb, vol. 157 cols. 187–88. Retrieved from http://hansard.millbanksystems.com/commons/1906/may/14/german-uniforms-and-street-advertise.
Gilbert, P. K. 1997. *Disease, Desire and the Body in Victorian Women's Popular Novels*. Cambridge: Cambridge University Press.
Gilbert, P. K. 2007. *The Citizen's Body: Desire, Health, and the Social in Victorian England*. Columbus: Ohio State University Press.
Gilbert, P. K. 2008. *Cholera and Nation: Doctoring the Social Body*. Albany: SUNY Press.
Gilbert, P. K. 2011. *A Companion to Sensation Fiction*. Malden: Wiley-Blackwell.
Gilbert, P. K. 2013. "The Medical Context." In A. Mangham (Ed.), *The Cambridge Companion to Sensation Fiction* (pp. 182–95). New York: Cambridge University Press.

Gilman, C. P. *The Yellow Wallpaper*. London: Virago, 1981.
Gilman, S. L., et al. 1993. *Hysteria Beyond Freud*. Oxford: University of California Press.
Gissing, G. 1978. *London and the Life of Literature in Late Victorian England: The Diary of George Gissing, Novelist*. Ed. Pierre Coustillas. Hassocks: Harvester.
Gissing, G. 2011–2012. *Collected Short Stories*. 3 vols. Ed. Pierre Coustillas with the assistance of Barbara Rawlinson and Hélène Coustillas. Grayswood: Grayswood.
Glover, D. 1996. Introduction. *The Jewel of Seven Stars* by Bram Stoker. Oxford: Oxford University Press.
Gorham, D. 2013. *The Victorian Girl and the Feminine Ideal*. London and New York: Routledge.
Graham, J. 1961. "Lavater's Physiognomy in England." *Journal of the History of Ideas, 22*, 561–72.
Grand, S. 1893. *The Heavenly Twins*. New York: Cassell Publishing Company.
Grand, S. 1894, March. "The New Aspect of the Woman Question." *The North American Review 158*(448), 270–76.
Grand, S. 1896. "The Woman's Question: An Interview with Madame Sarah Grand." *Humanitarian, 8*, 161–69.
Grand, S. 1897. *The Beth Book*. New York: Appleton.
Grand, S. 1992. *The Heavenly Twins*. Ann Arbor: University of Michigan Press.
Grant, J. 1868. *First Love and Last Love: A Tale of the Indian Mutiny*, 3 vols. London: Routledge & Sons.
Gray, A. 2017. *Self-Harm in New Woman Writing*. Edinburgh: Edinburgh University Press.
Greene, D. G. 1998. Introduction. *The Detections of Miss Cusack* (pp. vii–xiii). By L.T. Meade & Robert Eustace. Ed. D. G. Greene & J. Adrian. Shelburne, Ontario: Battered Silicon Dispatch Box.
Greenwood, J. 1869. *The Seven Curses of London*. Boston: Fields, Osgood, & Co.
Grella, G., and Dematteis, P. 1983. "Arthur Conan Doyle." *Victorian Novelists After 1885*. Ed. I. B. Nadel & W. E. Fredeman. *Dictionary of Literary Biography* 18. Detroit: Gale.
Griest, G. L. 1970. *Mudie's Circulating Library and the Victorian Novel*. Bloomington: Indiana University Press.
Griffin, L. 1955. "Shilling Shockers of the Nineteenth Century." *Manuscripts*, vol. 23 (pp. 13–15). Retrieved from digitalcommons.butler.edu/cgi/viewcontent.cgi?article=2300&context=manuscripts.
Guiley, R. 2004. *The Encyclopedia of Vampires, Werewolves, and Other Monsters*. New York: Infobase.
Gupta, B. K. 1973. *India in English Fiction, 1800–1970: An Annotated Bibliography*. Metuchen, NJ: Scarecrow.
Habitual Drunkards' Act. 1879.
Hackenberg, S. 2009. "Vampires and Resurrection Men: The Perils and Pleasures of the Embodied Past in 1840s Sensational Fiction." *Victorian Studies 52*(1), 63–75. http://doi.org/10.2979/VIC.2009.52.1.63.
Hadley, E. 1995. *Melodramatic Tactics: Theatricalized Dissent in the Marketplace, 1800–1885*. Stanford: Stanford University Press.
Haggard, H. R. 1899. *A Farmer's Year*. Longman, Green, & Co.
Haggard, H. R. 1926. *The Days of My Life: An Autobiography*. London, New York and Toronto: Longmans, Green.
Haggard, H. R. 1991. *She*. Ed. Daniel Karlin. Oxford: Oxford University Press.
Haley, B. 1978. *The Healthy Body in Victorian Culture*. Cambridge: Harvard University Press.
Hall, M. 1986. *Harvard University Press: A History*. Cambridge: Harvard University Press.
Halperin, U. 1988. *Félix Fénéon: Aesthete and Anarchist in Fin-de-Siècle Paris*. New Haven: Yale University Press.
Hamilton, J., and Wilson, T. (Eds.). 1797. *The Use of Circulating Libraries Considered; with Instructions for Opening and Conducting a Library, Either Upon a Large or Small Plan*. Bromley: J. Hamilton and T. Wilson.
Hammond, M. 2006. *Reading, Publishing and the Formation of Literary Taste in England, 1880–1914*. Aldershot: Ashgate.
Hancock, I. 2008. "The 'Gypsy' Stereotype and the Sexualization of Romani Women." In V. Glajar & D. Radulescu, D. (Eds.), *"Gypsies" in European Literature and Culture*. New York: Palgrave Macmillan.
Hanson, C. 1985. *Short Stories and Short Fiction, 1880–1980*. New York: St. Martin's Press.
Hansson, H. 2007. *Emily Lawless, 1845–1913: Writing the Interspace*. Cork: Cork University Press.
Harrison, B. 1971. *Drink and the Victorians: The Temperance Question in England, 1815–1872*. London: Faber & Faber.
Hartnell, E. M. 2000. *Gender, Religion and Domesticity in the Novels of Rosa Nouchette Carey*. Aldershot: Ashgate.
Hatter, J. 2013. "The Parade of Identity: M. E. Braddon, the Travelling Circus Performer and the (Re)Construction of Self." *St. John's Humanities Review 10*(1), 26–38.
Haywood, I. 1997. *Working-Class Fiction: From Chartism to Trainspotting*. London: Northcote House.
Hebblethwaite, K. 2008. Introduction. *The Jewel of Seven Stars* by Bram Stoker. Ed. K. Hebblethwaite. London: Penguin.
Heholt, R. (Ed.). 2015. *The Story of Lilly Dawson*. Brighton: Victorian Secrets.
Heilmann, A. 1996. "Mona Caird (1854–1932): Wild Woman, New Woman, and Early Radical Feminist Critic of Marriage and Motherhood." *Women's History Review, 5*(1), 67–95.
Heilmann, A. 2004. *New Woman Strategies: Sarah Grand, Olive Schreiner, Mona Caird*. Manchester: Manchester University Press.

Heilmann, A., and Forward, S. (Eds.). 2000. *Sex, Social Purity and Sarah Grand*. London: Routledge.
Henry, N. 2013. "Charlotte Riddell: Novelist of the City." In L. Dalley & J. Rappoport (Eds.), *Economic Women: Essays on Desire and Dispossession in Nineteenth-Century British Culture* (pp. 193–205). Columbus: Ohio State University Press.
Henty, G. A. 1881. *In Times of Peril*. London: Griffith & Farran.
Herr, C. 2008. Introduction. *Varney the Vampyre; or: The Feast of Blood* (pp. 9–26). By J. M. Rymer. Crestline, CA: Zittaw.
Hetherington, N. 2015. "Caffyn, Kathleen Mannington." In D. F. Felluga, P. K. Gilbert & L. K. Hughes (Eds.), *The Encyclopedia of Victorian Literature*.
Heywood, L. 1996. *Dedication to Hunger: The Anorexic Aesthetic in Modern Culture*. London: University of California Press.
Higgins, D. 2006. *The New Monthly Magazine: The Literary Encyclopedia*. Retrieved from http://www.litencyc.com/php/stopics.php?rec=true&UID=1682.
Higonnet, M. 1985. "Suicide: Representations of the Feminine in the Nineteenth Century." *Poetics Today*, 6(1), 103–18.
Hindley, C. 1887. *The History of the Catnach Press*. London: Hindley.
Hipsky. M. 2011. *Modernism and the Women's Popular Romance in Britain, 1885–1925*. Athens: Ohio University Press.
Hocking, J. 1895. *All Men Are Liars*. London: Ward, Lock & Bowden, Ltd.
Höglund, J. 2013. "Black Englishness and Concurrent Voices in Richard Marsh's *The Surprising Husband*." *English Literature in Transition, 1880–1920*, 56, 275–91.
Hopkins, E. 1994. *Childhood Transformed: Working-Class Children in Nineteenth-Century England*. Manchester: Manchester University Press.
Houen, A. 2002. *Terrorism and Modern Literature from Joseph Conrad to Ciaran Carson*. Oxford: Oxford University Press.
Housman, C. 2013. "The Were-Wolf." In A. Easley & S. Scott (Eds.), *Terrifying Transformations: An Anthology of Victorian Werewolf Fiction* (pp. 205–51). Kansas City, MO: Valancourt.
Howell, P. 2015. *At Home and Astray: The Domestic Dog in Victorian Britain*. Charlottesville: University of Virginia Press.
Howes, M. 1994. "Misalliance and Anglo-Irish Tradition in Le Fanu's *Uncle Silas*." *Nineteenth-Century Literature*, 47, 164–86.
Hughes, L. K., and Lund, M. 1991. *The Victorian Serial*. Charlottesville: University of Virginia Press.
Hughes, M., and Wood, H. 2014. "Crimson Nightmares: Tales of Invasion and Fears of Revolution in Early Twentieth-Century Britain." *Contemporary British History*, 28(3), 2–24.
Hughes, T. 1857. *Tom Brown's Schooldays*. London: Macmillan.
Hughes, T. 1861. *Tom Brown at Oxford*. London: Macmillan.
Hughes, W. 1981. *The Maniac in the Cellar: Sensation Novels of the 1860s*. Princeton: Princeton University Press.
Hume, F. 1896. "Preface." *The Mystery of a Hansom Cab* (rev. ed.). London: Jarrold.
Hume, F. 1899. *Hagar of the Pawn-Shop*. New York: Buckles.
Hunter, S. A. 2009. "Biography of Catherin Anne Hubback." *Catherine Hubback's Malvern; or the Three Marriages: A Critical Edition*. Thesis. University of Virginia. pp. 2–26.
"Italian Distrust." 1860, 26 November. *All the Year Round* 31, 104–106.
Ito, T. 2014. *London Zoo and the Victorians, 1828–1859*. Woodbridge: Boydell.
Jackson, L. 2000. *Child Sexual Abuse in Victorian England*. London: Routledge.
Jacobs, E. 1995. "Anonymous Signatures: Circulating Libraries, Conventionality, and the Production of Gothic Romances." *ELH*, 62(3), 603–29.
Jacobs, E. H. 2003. "Eighteenth-Century British Circulating Libraries and Cultural Book History." *Book History*, 6, 1–22.
Jalland, P. 1996. *Death in the Victorian Family*. Oxford: Oxford University Press.
James, E. 1995. "Science Fiction by Gaslight: An Introduction to English Language Science Fiction in the Nineteenth Century." In D. Seed (Ed.) *Anticipations: Essays on Early Science Fiction and Its Precursors*. Liverpool: Liverpool University Press.
James, E., and Smith, H. R. 1998. *Penny Dreadfuls and Boys' Adventures: The Barry Ono Collection of Victorian Popular Literature in the British Library*. London: British Library.
James, H. 1865, 9 Nov. "Miss Braddon." *The Nation*, 593–94.
James, L. 1963. *Fiction for the Working Man, 1830–50*. Oxford: Oxford University Press.
Jay, E. 1995. *Mrs. Oliphant: A Fiction To Herself—A Literary Life*. Oxford: Clarendon.
Jeune, M. 1890. "Women of To-Day, Yesterday, and To-Morrow." *The Eclectic Magazine of Foreign Literature, Science, and Art*, New Series 51 (January–June 1890), 177–85. Google Books.
John, J. 2011. "Melodrama." *Oxford Bibliographies*, 2.
John, J. (Ed.). 2016. *The Oxford Handbook of Victorian Literary Culture*. Oxford: Oxford University Press.
Johnson, H. 2000. "Electra-fying the Female Sleuth: Detecting the Father in *Eleanor's Victory* and *Thou Art the Man*." *Beyond Sensation: Mary Elizabeth Braddon in Context*. Albany: SUNY Press.

Johnstone, E. 2008. *A Sunless Heart*. C. D. Harsh (Ed.). Peterborough, ON: Broadview.
Jones, J. 2012 *Fifty Years in the Fiction Factory: The Working Life of Herbert Allingham*. Pleshey: Golden Duck.
Jones, R. E. (Ed.). 2006. *E. Nesbit's Psammead Trilogy: A Children's Classic at 100*. Lanham, MD: Scarecrow.
Jones, W. 1850. *The Jubilee Memorial of the Religious Tract Society: Containing a Record of Its Origin, Proceedings, and Results, A.D. 1799 to A.D. 1849*. (Incorporating the *Twelfth Annual Report of the Religious Tract Society*.) London: Religious Tract Society.
Jordan, J. 2011. "Ouida." In P. K. Gilbert (Ed.). *A Companion to Sensation Fiction* (pp. 220–231). Chichester: Wiley-Blackwell.
Jordan, J., and King, A. (Eds.). 2013. *Ouida and Victorian Popular Culture*. Farnham: Ashgate.
Karschay, S. 2015. *Degeneration, Normativity and the Gothic at the Fin de Siècle*. Basingstoke: Palgrave Macmillan.
Kaufman, P. 1967. "The Community Library: A Chapter in English Social History." *Transactions of the American Philosophical Society*, 57(7), 1–67.
Kayman, M. A. 2003. "The Short Story from Poe to Chesterton." In M. Priestman (Ed.). *The Cambridge Companion to Crime Fiction* (pp. 41–58). Cambridge: Cambridge University Press.
Kelleher, M. 2000. "Charlotte Riddell's *A Struggle for Fame*: The Field of Women's Literary Production." *Colby Quarterly* 36, 116–31.
Kenney, C. 1990. *The Remarkable Case of Dorothy L. Sayers*. Kent, OH: Kent State University Press.
Kent, A. M. 2002. *Pulp Methodism: The Lives and Literature of Silas, Joseph and Salome Hocking, Three Cornish Novelists*. St. Austell, UK: Cornish Hillside.
Kestner, J. 2003. *Sherlock's Sisters: The British Female Detective, 1864–1913*. Surrey: Ashgate.
Kestner, J. A. 2004. "The New Woman and the Female Detective: Grant Allen's *Miss Cayley's Adventures* (1899)." In W. Baker & I. B. Nadel (Eds.), *Redefining the Modern: Essays on Literature and Society in Honor of Joseph Wiesenfarth* (pp. 148–64). Cranbury, NJ: Associated University Press.
Ketabgian, T. 2011. *The Lives of Machines: The Industrial Imaginary in Victorian Literature and Culture*. Ann Arbor: University of Michigan Press and University of Michigan Library.
Kete, K. 1994. *The Beast in the Boudoir: Petkeeping in Nineteenth-Century Paris*. Berkeley: University of California Press.
Killick, T. 2008. *British Short Fiction in the Early Nineteenth Century*. Aldershot & Burlington: Ashgate.
King, A. 2000. "Defining Positions: A Pragmatic Approach to Periodical Illustrations." In B. Bell, L. Brake, & D. Finkelstein (Eds.), *Nineteenth-Century Media and the Construction of Identity* (pp. 77–92). Basingstoke, Hampshire/New York: Palgrave.
King, A. 2004. *The London Journal, 1845–83: Periodicals, Production, and Gender*. Aldershot: Ashgate.
King, A. 2008. "Reynolds's Miscellany, 1846–49: Advertising Networks and Politics." In A. Humpherys & L. James (Eds.), *G. W. M. Reynolds: Nineteenth Century Fiction, Politics, and the Press* (pp. 53–74). Aldershot: Ashgate.
King, A. 2010. "'Killing Time,' or Mrs. Braby's Peppermints: The Double Economy of the *Family Herald* and the *Family Herald Supplements*." *Victorian Periodicals Review*, 43(2), 149–73.
King, A. 2015, 14 October. "Ouida (Marie Louise Ramé)." In D. F. Felluga, P. K. Gilbert & L. K. Hughes (Eds.), *The Encyclopedia of Victorian Literature*. Blackwell Reference Online.
Kingsford, M. R. 1947. *The Life of W.H.G. Kingston*.
Kingsley, C. 1895. *The Water-Babies: A Fairy Tale for a Land-Baby*. London: Macmillan & Co.
Kipling, R. 2008. *The Jungle Books*. Oxford: Oxford World Classics.
Kirkpatrick, R. 2010. *The Three Lives of Bernard Heldmann*. London: Children's Books History Society.
Kirkwood, P. M. 2012. "The Impact of Fiction on Public Debate in Late Victorian Britain: *The Battle of Dorking* and the 'Lost Career' of Sir George Tomkyns Chesney." *Graduate History Review*, 4(1), 1–16.
"Kissing the Rod: A Novel by Edmund Yates, 3 vols. (Tinsley Brothers)." *Athenaeum*, 2017 (23 June 1866): 828.
"Kitchen Literature." 1864, 25 June. [Review of *Henry Dunbar* by Mary Elizabeth Braddon]. *Examiner*, 404–06.
Klaus, H. G. 1982. *The Socialist Novel in Britain*. Brighton: Harvester.
Klippert, Zoe (Ed.). 2012. *An Englishwoman in California: The Letters of Catherine Hubback, 1871–76*. Oxford: Bodleian Library.
Knight, S. 2003. *Robin Hood: A Mythic Biography*. Ithaca: Cornell University Press.
Knight, S. 2015. *Secrets of Crime Fiction Classics: Detecting the Delights of 21 Enduring Stories*. Jefferson, NC: McFarland.
Knox, R. 1862. *The Races of Men: A Philosophical Enquiry into the Influence of Race over the Destinies of Nations*, 2nd ed. London: Renshaw.
Korg, J. 1983. "George (Robert) Gissing." *Victorian Novelists After 1885*. I. B. Nadel & W. E. Fredeman (Eds.). *Dictionary of Literary Biography* 18. Detroit: Gale.
Kropotkin, P. 1970. [1887]. "Anarchist Communism." *Nineteenth Century*, repr. in *Anarchism: A Collection of Revolutionary Writings*. Mineola, NY: Dover, 46–78.
Lavater, J. 1853. *Essays on Physiognomy; Designed to Promote the Knowledge and the Love of Mankind*, 8th ed. T. Holcroft, Trans. London: William Tegg. (Original work published 1774–78.) Archive.org.
Law, G. 2000. *Serializing Fiction in the Victorian Press*. Basingstoke: Palgrave.

Law, G., with Drozdz, G., and McNally, D. 2011. *Charlotte M. Brame (1836–1884): Towards a Primary Bibliography*. Victorian Fiction Research Guides 36. Brighton: Victorian Secrets, 2011. http://victorianfictionresearchguides.org/charlotte-may-brame/.
Law, G., and Patten, R. L. 2009. "The Serial Revolution." In D. McKitterick (Ed.), *The Cambridge History of the Book in Britain* (pp. 144–71). Cambridge: Cambridge University Press.
Law, J. [Margaret Harkness]. 1888. *Out of Work*. London: Swan Sonnenschein & Co.
Law, J. [Margaret Harkness]. 1889. *Captain Lobe: A Story of the Salvation Army*. London: Hodder & Stoughton.
Law, J. [Margaret Harkness]. 1893. *In Darkest London: A New and Popular Edition of Captain Lobe: A Story of the Salvation Army*. London: Reeves.
Lawrence, G. A. 1857. *Guy Livingstone; or, Thorough*. London: John W. Parker & Son.
Leatherdale, C. 1996. Introduction. *The Jewel of Seven Stars* by Bram Stoker. Ed. C. Leatherdale. Westcliffe-on-Sea: Desert Island.
Leavis, Q. D. 1932. *Fiction and the Reading Public*. London: Chatto & Windus.
Ledger, S. 1997. *The New Woman: Fiction and Feminism at the Fin de Siècle*. Manchester: Manchester University Press.
Ledger, S. 2006. *Keynotes and Discords*. London: Continuum.
Leighton, M. E., and Surridge, L. 2008. "The Plot Thickens: Toward a Narratological Analysis of Illustrated Serial Fiction in the 1860s." *Victorian Studies*, 51(1), 65–101.
Lellenberg, J., Stashower, D., and Foley, C. 2008. *Arthur Conan Doyle: A Life in Letters*. London: Harper Perennial-HarperCollins.
Lennon, F. B. 1945. *Victoria Through the Looking Glass: The Life of Lewis Carroll*. New York: Simon & Schuster.
Le Queux, W. 1906. *The Invasion of 1910: With a Full Account of the Siege of London; Naval Chapters by H. W. Wilson, Introductory Letter by Field-Marshal Earl Roberts*. London: Eveleigh Nash.
Liddle, D. 2009. "*The Woman in White* (review)." *Victorian Review*, 35 (1), 37–41.
Liggins, E., Maunder, A., and Robbins, R. (Eds.). 2011. *The British Short Story*. Basingstoke & New York: Palgrave Macmillan.
Lill, S. L. "'The Father of the Cheap Press': Edward Lloyd and the Mass-Market Periodical, 1830–1855." Unpublished Ph.D. thesis, University of Northumbria, 2015.
"Literary Honours." 1867, May. *Belgravia*, 320–24.
"The Literary Week." 1906, 17 March. *Academy*, 1767, 254.
Logan, P. M. 1997. *Nerves and Narratives: A Cultural History of Hysteria in Nineteenth-Century British Prose*. Berkeley: University of California Press.
Lovecraft, H. P. 1927. "Supernatural Horror in Literature." *The Recluse*, 1, 23–59. Retrieved from http://www.hplovecraft.com/writings/texts/essays/shil.aspx.
Luckhurst, R. 2000. "Trance-Gothic 1882–97." In *Victorian Gothic Literary and Cultural Manifestations in the Nineteenth Century*. Basingstoke: Palgrave.
Luckhurst, R. 2012. *The Mummy's Curse: A True History of a Dark Fantasy*. Oxford: Oxford University Press.
Lundberg, P. L. 2003. *An Inward Necessity: The Writer's Life of Lucas Malet*. New York: Peter Lang.
MacDonald, T. 2015. *The New Man, Masculinity and Marriage in the Victorian Novel*. London: Routledge.
Mack, R. 2007. *The Wonderful and Surprising History of Sweeney Todd: The Life and Times of an Urban Legend*. London: Continuum.
MacLeod, K. 2008. "M. P. Shiel and the Love of Pubescent Girls: The Other 'Love That Dare Not Speak Its Name.'" *English Literature in Transition, 1880–1920*, 51(4), 355–80.
Maddyn, D. O. 1852. *Basil: A Story of Modern Life*. *Athenaeum*, 1310, 1322–23.
Maginn, W. 1840. "William Ainsworth and *Jack Sheppard*." *Fraser's Magazine for Town and Country*, 21, 227–45.
Malet, L. 1895. *The Wages of Sin*. London: Swan Sonnenschein.
Mangum, T. 2007. "Narrative Dominion or The Animals Write Back? Animal Genres in Literature and the Arts." In Kathleen Kete (Ed.), *A Cultural History of Animals in the Age of Empire* (pp. 153–73). Oxford: Berg.
Mansel, H. 2001. "Sensation Novels." In S. Regan (Ed.), *The Nineteenth-Century Novel: A Critical Reader* (pp. 44–47). London: Routledge.
Marcoux, P. J. 1992. *Guilbert De Pixérécourt: French Melodrama in the Early Nineteenth Century*: New York: Peter Lang.
Margolis, S. 2002. "Addiction and the Ends of Desire." In J. F. Brodie & M. Redfield (Eds.), *High Anxieties: Cultural Studies in Addiction* (pp. 19–37). Berkeley: University of California Press.
Margree, V. 2016. "Metanarratives of Authorship in Fin-de-Siècle Popular Fiction: 'Is that all you do, write stories?'" *English Literature in Transition, 1880–1920*, 59, 362–89.
Marryat, F. 1869. *Véronique: A Romance*. Leipzig: Bernhard Tauchnitz.
Marsh, R. 1897. *The Beetle*. London: Skeffington & Son.
Marsh, R. 2004. *The Beetle*. J. Wolfreys (Ed.). Peterborough, ON: Broadview.
Marshall, P. 1992. *Demanding the Impossible: A History of Anarchism*. London: Fontana.

Martin, D. 2008. "Railway Fatigue and the Coming-of-Age Narrative in *Lady Audley's Secret*." *Victorian Review*, *34*(1), 131–53.
Martyn, C.E.D. 1896, March 7. "A Mystery." *Labour Leader*.
Matin, A. M. 1999. "'The Hun is at the gate!': Historicizing Kipling's Militaristic Rhetoric, from the Imperial Periphery to the National Center; Part One: The Russian Threat to British India." *Studies in the Novel*, *31*(3), 317–56.
Matin, A. M. 2011a. "Scrutinizing the Battle of Dorking: The Royal United Service Institution and the Mid-Victorian Invasion Controversy." *Victorian Literature and Culture*, 39, 385–407.
Matin, A. M. 2011b. "The Creativity of War Planners: Armed Forces Professionals and the Pre-1914 British Invasion-Scare Genre." *English Literary History*, *78*(4), 801–31.
Matthews, B. "The Art and Mystery of Collaboration." *With My Friends: Tales Told in Partnership*. London: Longmans, Green & Co., 1891.
Maudsley, H. 1871. *Body and Mind: An Inquiry into Their Connection and Mutual Influence, Specially in Reference to Mental Disorders*. New York: D. Appleton.
Maunder, A. 2004. *Varieties of Women's Sensation Fiction: 1855–1890*, vol. 2. A. Maunder (Ed.). London: Pickering & Chatto.
Maurer, O. 1955. "Andrew Lang and *Longman's Magazine*, 1882–1905." *The University of Texas Studies in English*, 34, 152–78.
Maxwell, C., and Pulham, P. (Eds.). 2006. *Vernon Lee: Decadence, Ethics, Aesthetics*. Basingstoke: Palgrave Macmillan.
Maxwell, W. B. 1937. *Time Gathered*. London: Hutchinson.
McAllister, A. 2014. *Demon Drink? Temperance and the Working Class*. Kindle Edition.
McCandless, P. 1984. "'Curses of civilization': Insanity and Drunkenness in Victorian Britain." *British Journal of Addiction*, 79, 49–58.
McCormack, W. J. 1980. *Sheridan Le Fanu and Victorian Ireland*. New York: Oxford.
McKechnie, C. C. 2010, September. *The Human and the Animal in Victorian Gothic Scientific Literature*. Unpublished doctoral dissertation. University of Edinburgh: Edinburgh.
McKillop, A. D. 1934. "English Circulating Libraries, 1725–50." *The Library*, *14*(4), 477–85.
McLean, S. 2016. "The Conquest of the Air: Aeronautics and Social Revolution in Edward Douglas Fawcett's *Hartmann the Anarchist* and W. Graham Moffat and John White's *What's the World Coming To?*" *Literature and History* 25 (1) 3–21.
Meade, L. T. 1872. *Scamp and I: A Story of City By-ways*. London: John F. Shaw & Co.
Meade, L. T. 1892. *Four on an Island: A Story of Adventure*. London: Chambers.
Meade, L. T., and C. Halifax. 1894. "The Horror of Studley Grange." *The Strand Magazine*, *7*(37), 3–16.
Meem, D. 2002. Introduction. In E. L. Linton, *The Rebel of the Family*. D. Meem (Ed.). Peterborough, ON: Broadview.
Melchiori, B. A. 1985. *Terrorism in the Late Victorian Novel*. London: Croom Helm.
Menke, R. 2008. *Telegraphic Realism: Victorian Fiction and Other Information Systems*. Stanford: Stanford University Press.
Meredith, I. [Christina and Olivia Rossetti]. 1992/1903 *A Girl Among the Anarchists*. Lincoln: University of Nebraska Press.
Meynell, A. 2005 [1896]. "A Woman in Grey." In A. Richardson (Ed.), *Women Who Did: Stories by Men and Women 1890–1914* (pp. 177–80). London: Penguin.
Meynell, A. 1896 [1947]. "A Woman in Grey." In *Alice Meynell: Prose and Poetry*, 208–12. London: Jonathan Cape.
Mighall, R. 1999. *A Geography of Victorian Gothic Fiction: Mapping History's Nightmares*. Oxford: Oxford University Press.
Miles, P. 2012. Introduction. In A. Morrison, *A Child of the Jago*. Oxford: Oxford University Press.
Millard, C. 2015. *A History of Self-Harm in Britain: A Genealogy of Cutting and Overdosing*. Aldershot: Palgrave Macmillan.
Miller, D. A. 1988. *The Novel and the Police*. Berkeley: University of California Press.
Miller, E. C. 2013. *Slow Print, Literary Radicalism and Late Victorian Print Culture*. Stanford: Stanford University Press.
Miller, K. A. 2012. "'Your loving is unlike any other': Romance and the Disabled Body in the Gothic Fiction of Edith Nesbit and Lucas Malet." In A. E. Gavin & C. Oulton (Eds.), *Writing Women of the Fin de Siècle: Authors of Change* (pp. 193–203). New York: Palgrave Macmillan.
"Miss Braddon's Latest Novel—*The Day Will Come*." 1890, 19 July. *Athenaeum*, 3273, 109.
"Miss Emma Brooke Obituary." *Manchester Guardian Weekly*. 2 December 1926, p. 4.
"Miss Mary Angela Dickens." 1893. *The Bookman*, *4*(19). Retrieved from https://search.proquest.com/docview/3168055?accountid=15181.
Mitchell, J. 1987. "Tendencies in Narrative Fiction in the London-Based Socialist Press of the 1880s and 1890s." In H. G. Klaus (Ed.), *The Rise of Socialist Fiction* (pp. 59–74). Brighton: Harvester.
Mitchell, K. "Gender and Sexuality in Popular Fiction." In D. Glover & S. McCracken (Eds.), *The Cambridge Companion to Popular Fiction* (pp. 122–40). Cambridge University Press, 2012.

Mitchell, S. 1983. *Dinah Mulock Craik*. Boston: Twayne Publishers.
Moore, G. 2016. "'The Floodgates of Inkland Were Opened': Aestheticising the Whitechapel Murders." In K. Gelder (Ed.), *New Directions in Popular Fiction: Genre, Distribution, Reproduction*. London: Palgrave.
Moore-Gilbert, B. 1996. Introduction. In *Writing India: 1757–1990: The Literature of British India*. Manchester: Manchester University Press.
Morrison, A. 1907. *Martin Hewitt, Investigator*. New York: Harper & Brothers.
Morton, P. 2005. *"The Busiest Man in England": Grant Allen and the Writing Trade, 1875–1900*. New York: Palgrave Macmillan.
Moskowitz, S. 1974. *Science Fiction by Gaslight: A History and Anthology of Science Fiction in the Popular Magazines, 1891–1911*. New York: Hyperion.
Mukherjee, A. 2007. *Aesthetic Hysteria: The Great Neurosis in Victorian Melodrama and Contemporary Fiction*. London: Routledge.
Mulvey-Roberts, M. 2001. "Fame, Notoriety, and Madness: Edward Bulwer-Lytton Paying the Price of Greatness." *Critical Survey*, 13(2), 115–134.
Mumby, F. A, and Swan Stallybrass, F. H. 1955. *From Swan Sonnenschein to George Allen & Unwin Ltd.* London: Allen & Unwin.
Murphy, J. 2011. *Irish Novelists and the Victorian Age*. Oxford: Oxford University Press.
Mutch, D. 2006. "*A Working Class Tragedy*: The Fiction of Henry Mayers Hyndman." *Nineteenth Century Studies 20*, 99–112.
Nash, A. 2007. *Kailyard and Scottish Literature*. Amsterdam: Rodopi.
Nelson, C. 2007. *Family Ties in Victorian England*. Westport, CT: Praeger.
Nesvet, R. 2017a. "Blood Relations: Sweeney Todd and the Rymers of London," *Notes and Queries*, n.s. 64(1), 112–16.
Nesvet, R. (Ed.) 2017b. "*Science and Art: A Farce in Two Acts*, by Malcolm Rymer." *Scholarly Editing: The Journal of the Association for Documentary Editing, 38* (2017). www.scholarlyediting.org.
Neuberg, V. 1977. *Popular Literature: A History and Guide*. London: Woburn.
Newbolt, Henry. 1897. *Admirals All, and Other Verses*. London: Elkin Matthews.
Newens, S. 2008. *Arthur Morrison*. Essex, England: Alderton.
Newnes, G. 1891, January. Introduction. *Strand Magazine*, 1(3). "New Novels" *Athenaeum, 1706* (7 July 1860): 15.
Nicoletti, L. J. 2004, March. "Downward Mobility: Victorian Women, Suicide, and London's 'Bridge of Sighs.'" *Literary London: Interdisciplinary Studies in the Representation of London*, 2(1). http://www.literarylondon.org/london-journal/march2004/nicoletti.html.
Norcia, M. 2004. "Angel of the Island: L.T. Meade's New Girl as the Heir of a Nation-Making Robinson Crusoe." *The Lion and the Unicorn, 28*, 345–62.
North, J. 1997. "Ordinary Pleasures? Recreational Drug Use in the Literature of the 1880s and 1890s." In T. Hill (Ed.), *Decadence and Danger: Writing, History, and the Fin de Siècle* (pp. 150–161). Bath: Sulis.
"Novels of the Week." 1880, 4 December. *Athenaeum*, 741–43.
Nowell-Smith, S. *The House of Cassell, 1848–1958*. London: Cassell, 1958.
Nuland, S. B. Spring 2001. "The Uncertain Art: Grave Robbing." *The American Scholar, 70*(2), 125–28.
"Obituary for G. W. M. Reynolds." 1879. *The Bookseller, 260*, 600–01.
O'Connell, R. 2012. "'That Cruel Spectacle': The Extraordinary Body Eroticised in Lucas Malet's *The History of Sir Richard Calmady*." In R. McRuer & A. Mollow (Eds.), *Sex and Disability* (pp. 108–22). Durham: Duke University Press.
O'Donghaile, D. 2011. *Blasted Literature: Victorian Political Fiction and the Shock of Modernism*. Oxford: Oxford University Press.
Oliphant, M. 1867, September. "Novels." *Blackwood's Edinburgh Magazine, 102*(623), 257–80.
Oliphant, M. 1862, May. *Blackwood's Edinburgh Magazine, 91*, 564–580.
"Opinions of the Press." 1885. *Morning Advertiser*, 359.
Oppenheim, J. 1991. *"Shattered Nerves": Doctors, Patients, and Depression in Victorian England*. Oxford: Oxford University Press
Osborough, W. N. 1999. "The Dublin Castle Career (1866–78) of Bram Stoker." *Gothic Studies, 1*(2), 220–240.
Otis, L. 1999. *Membranes: Metaphors of Invasion in Nineteenth-Century Literature, Culture and Politics*. Baltimore: Johns Hopkins University Press.
Otis, L. 2001. *Networking: Communicating with Bodies and Machines in the Nineteenth Century*. Ann Arbor: University of Michigan Press.
O'Toole, T. 2013. *The Irish New Woman*. Basingstoke: Palgrave Macmillan.
Otter, C. 2008. *The Victorian Eye: A Political History of Light and Vision in Britain, 1800–1910*. Chicago: University of Chicago Press.
Ouida. 1894, May. "The New Woman." *The North American Review, 158*(450), 610–19.
Ouida. 1906. *A Dog of Flanders: Being a Story of Friendship Closer than Brotherhood*. Elbert Hubbard.
Ousby, I. 2000. "Robert Elsmere." *The Cambridge Guide to Literature in English*. 2nd ed. Cambridge, UK: Cambridge University Press.
Pae, D. 2001. *Lucy, the Factory Girl*. Graham Law (Ed.). Hastings, Sussex: Sensation.

Paget, F. E. 1868. *Lucretia: Or, the Heroine of the Nineteenth Century*. London: Joseph Masters.
Pal-Lapinski, P. 2005. *The Exotic Woman in Nineteenth-Century British Fiction and Culture: A Reconsideration*. Hanover: University of New Hampshire Press.
Parker, P. 1894, 8 March. "A Yellow Aster." The Author At Home. *Woman's Signal*, 155.
Parry, A. 1991. "Swan Sonnenschein Limited; Swan Sonnenschein and Allen; Swan Sonnenschein, Lowrey and Company; Swan Sonnenschein and Company." In P. Anderson & J. Rose (Eds.), *British Literary Publishing Houses, 1820–1880. Dictionary of Literary Biography*, vol. 106. Detroit: Gale.
Pavlakis, D. 2014. Reputation and the Sexual Abuse of Boys. *Men and Masculinities*, 17(3), 325–46.
Pearson, S. J. 2011. *The Rights of the Defenseless: Protecting Animals and Children in Gilded Age America*. Chicago: University of Chicago Press.
"Penn Portrait No. 22." 1906. *Yorkshire Notes and Queries: Being the Antiquarian History of Yorkshire*, vol. II. Bradford: Henry Casaubon Derwent.
Pert, A. 2006. *Red Cactus: The Life of Anna Kingsford*. Watsons Bay, NSW, Australia: Books & Writers.
Peters, L. 2000. *Orphan Texts: Victorian Orphans, Culture and Empire*. Manchester: Manchester University Press.
Peterson, L. 2009. *Becoming a Woman of Letters: Myths of Authorship and Facts of the Victorian Market*. Princeton: Princeton University Press.
Peterson, L. H. 1998. "Mother Daughter Productions: Mary Howitt and Anna Mary Howitt in 'Howitt's Journal,' 'Household Words' and Other Mid-Victorian Publications." *Victorian Periodicals Review*, 31(1), 31–54.
Pettitt, C. 2012. "'The Annihilation of Space and Time': Literature and Technology." In K. Flint (Ed.), *The Cambridge History of Victorian Literature* (pp. 550–72). Cambridge: Cambridge University Press.
Phegley, J. "Teaching Genre: The Sensation Novel." In A. Maunder & J. Phegley (Eds.), *Teaching Nineteenth-Century Fiction* (pp. 91–108). Basingstoke: Palgrave Macmillan, 2010.
Phillips, R. (Ed.) 1971. *Aspects of Alice: Lewis Carroll's Dreamchild as Seen through the Critics' Looking-Glass*. Toronto: Vanguard.
Pick, D. 1989. *Faces of Degeneration: A European Disorder, c. 1848–c. 1918*. Cambridge: Cambridge University Press.
Pittard, C. 2011. *Purity and Contamination in Late Victorian Detective Fiction*. Farnham: Ashgate.
Pocock, J.G.A. 1985. *Virtue, Commerce and History: Essays on Political Thought and History, Chiefly in the Eighteenth Century*. Cambridge: Cambridge University Press.
Poe, E. A. 1841. "The Murders in the Rue Morgue." *Graham's Magazine*, 18(4), 166–79.
Poe, E. A. 1842, May. "Review of Twice-Told Tales." *Graham's Magazine*, 298–300. Retrieved from http://www.eapoe.org/works/criticsm/gm542hn1.htm
Poliquin, R. 2012. *The Breathless Zoo: Taxidermy and the Cultures of Longing*. University Park: Pennsylvania State University Press.
Pope, C. n.d. *Florence Marryat*. Retrieved from http://www.florencemarryat.org/.
Porter, M. B. (Ed.). 1898. "William Blackwood to his Wife." In *Annals of a Publishing House*, vol. 3, (p. 121). Edinburgh: William Blackwood & Sons.
Pound, R. 1966. *The Strand Magazine, 1891–1950*. London: Heinemann.
Prichard, K., & Prichard, H. [pseud. E. and H. Heron]. 1899. *Ghosts: Being the Experiences of Flaxman Low*. London: C. Arthur Pearson.
Priest, H. (Ed.). 2015. "Introduction: A History of Female Werewolves." In *She-Wolf: A Cultural History of Female Werewolves* (pp. 1–23). Manchester: Manchester University Press.
Quigley, C. 1994 *Death Dictionary: Over 5,500 Clinical, Legal, Literary, and Vernacular Terms*. Jefferson: McFarland.
Rae, W. F. 1865. "Sensation Novelists: Miss Braddon." *North British Review*, 43, 92–105.
Rae, W. F. 1865. "Sensation Novelists: Miss Braddon." *North British Review*, 43, 180–204.
"Recent Novels." 1901, 16 September. *The Times*, 12.
Reed, T. L., Jr. 2006. *The Transforming Draught: Jekyll and Hyde, Robert Louis Stevenson and the Victorian Alcohol Debate*. Jefferson, NC: McFarland.
Review of *Half a Million of Money*. 1866, 4 April. *The Standard*, 6.
Review of *Leslie Tyrrell* by Georgiana M. Craik. 1867, 10 August. *Examiner*, 500–03.
[Review notice.] 1892. "L.T. Meade's Four on an Island." *The Spectator* (Special Literary Supplement, No. 3358).
[Rev. of *For Lilias*, by R. N. Carey.] 1885, 26 September. *Academy*, 699, 200.
[Rev. of *Guy Livingstone; or, Thorough*, by G. A. Lawrence.] 1857. *Athenaeum*, 1553, 971.
Reynolds, G. W. M. 1847. *The Mysteries of London*, vol. III. London: G. Vickers.
[Reynolds, G. W. M.] "Obituary for G. W. M. Reynolds." 1879. *The Bookseller*, 260, 600–01.
Richards, L. 2009. "Mass Production and the Spread of Information in *Dracula*: 'Proofs of so wild a story.'" *English Literature in Transition*, 52(4), 440–457.
Rieder, J. 2008. *Colonialism and the Emergence of Science Fiction*. Middletown, CT: Wesleyan University Press.
Ring, J. 1996. *Erskine Childers: A Biography*. London: John Murray.
Ritvo, H. 1987. *The Animal Estate: The English and Other Creatures in the Victorian Age*. Cambridge: Harvard University Press.

Roberts, L. 2006. "Trafficking in Literary Authority: Mudie's Select Library and the Commodification of the Victorian Novel." *Victorian Literature and Culture*, 34(1), 1–25.
Rosenberg, T. S. 2010. Introduction. In M. Caird, *The Wing of Azrael* (pp. vii–xxii). Kansas City, MO: Valancourt.
Rosenman, E., & Klaver, C. 2008. Introduction. *Other Mothers: Beyond the Maternal Ideal*. Ed. E. Rosenman & C. Klaver (pp. 1–22). Columbus: Ohio State University Press.
Rowland, P. 1999. *Raffles and His Creator*. London: Nekta.
Ruddick, N. 1997. "Grant Allen." In *DLB 178: British Fantasy and Science-Fiction Writers Before World War I* (pp. 7–16). Detroit: Gale Research.
"Running the Gauntlet. A Novel. By Edmund Yates, Author of 'Broken to Harness.'" In Three Vols. (London: Tinsley Brothers.) *The Reader*, 6(152) (25 November 1865): 595.
Rymer, J. M. 2008. *Varney the Vampyre; or: The Feast of Blood*. C. Herr (Ed.). Crestline, CA: Zittaw.
Rhymer, J. M. 2015. *Varney the Vampire: or, The Feast of Blood*. (Part 1). New York: Courier Dover.
Rymer, J. M., and Peckett Prest, T. 1973. *Varney the Vampyre or The Feast of Blood*. E. F. Bleiler (Ed.). New York: Dover.
Sadleir, M. 1933. *Bulwer and his Wife: A Panorama, 1803–1836*. (2nd ed.). London: Constable.
Sage, V. 2000. "Irish Gothic: C. R. Maturin and J. S. Le Fanu." In D. Punter (Ed.), *A Companion to the Gothic* (pp. 81–93). Oxford: Blackwell.
Sage, V. 2004. *Le Fanu's Gothic: The Rhetoric of Darkness*. Houndmills: Palgrave Macmillan.
Sainsbury, G. 1894. "New Novels." Rev. of *Betrayed* by Dora Russell. *The Academy*, 1160 (28 July 1894): 63–64.
Sala, G. A. 1885, August 31. "The Land of the Golden Fleece. IX—Melbourne to Adelaide." *The Argus*, 7.
Sala, G. A. 1895. *The Life and Adventures of George Augustus Sala*. Vol. 1. London: Cassell.
Salmon, E. G. 1886, July. "What the Working Classes Read." *The Nineteenth Century*, 20(113), 108–17.
Salveson, P. 1987. "Allen Clarke and the Lancashire School of Working-Class Novelists." In H. Gustav Klaus (Ed.), *The Rise of Socialist Fiction* (pp. 172–202). Brighton: Harvester.
Samuel, R. 1985. "Theatre and Socialism in Britain (1880–1935)." In R. Samuel, E. MacColl and S. Cosgrove (Eds.), *Theatres of the Left, 1880–1935: Workers' Theatre Movements in Britain and America* (pp. 3–76). London: Routledge & Kegan Paul.
Sandiford, K. A. P. 1983. "Cricket and the Victorian Society." *Journal of Social History*, 17(2), 303–17.
Sargent, G. E. 1886. *The Crooked Sixpence*. London: Religious Tract Society.
Sattaur, J. 2011. *Perceptions of Childhood in the Victorian Fin-de-Siècle*. Newcastle-on-Tyne: Cambridge Scholars.
Schaffer, T. 2000. *The Forgotten Female Aesthetes: Literary Culture in Late-Victorian England*. Charlottesville: University Press of Virginia.
Schaffer, T. 2013. "The Victorian Novel and the New Woman." *The Oxford Handbook of the Victorian Novel*. L. Rodensky (Ed.). Oxford: Oxford University Press.
Schroeder, N., and Holt, S. Hodges. 2008. *Ouida the Phenomenon: Evolving Social, Political and Gender Concerns in Her Fiction*. Newark: University of Delaware Press.
Schwan, A. 2014. *Convict Voices: Women, Class, and Writing about Prison in Nineteenth-Century England*. Durham: University of New Hampshire Press.
Schwan, A. 2016. "Frederick William Robinson, Charles Dickens, and the Literary Tradition of 'Low Life.'" In J. Bristow & J. McDonagh (Eds.), *Nineteenth-Century Radical Traditions* (pp. 63–84). New York: Palgrave Macmillan.
Scofield, M. 2003. "Implied Stories: Implication, Moral Panic and *The Turn of the Screw*." *Journal of the Short Story in English*, 40, 97–107.
Scriven, A. 2007. Margaret Oliphant's "Marriage" to Maga. *Scottish Studies Review*, 8(1), 27–36.
Scull, A. 2009. *Hysteria: The Disturbing History*. Oxford: Oxford University Press.
Scull, A. 2015. *Madness in Civilization: A Cultural History of Insanity from the Bible to Freud, from the Madhouse to Modern Medicine*. Princeton: Princeton University Press.
Scully, R. 2012. *British Images of Germany: Admiration, Antagonism, Ambivalence, 1860–1914*. Basingstoke: Palgrave Macmillan.
Seeley, J. R. 1883. *Expansion of England: Two Courses of Lectures*. London: Macmillan.
Shepherd, L. 1973. *The History of Street Literature*. Newton Abbot: David Charles.
Shiel, M. P. 1979. [1901]. "About Myself." Repr. in A. Reynolds Morse (Ed.), *The Works of M. P. Shiel*. Vol. 3 (pp. 667–68). Cleveland, OH: Reynolds Morse Foundation.
Shiel, M. P. 2004. *The Purple Cloud*. Leyburn, North Yorkshire: Tartarus.
Showalter, E. 1991. *Sexual Anarchy: Gender and Culture at the Fin de Siècle*. London: Virago.
Showalter, E. 1998. Introduction. *Trilby*. By George Du Maurier. Oxford: Oxford University Press.
Showalter, E. 2009. *A Literature of their Own: British Women Writers, from Charlotte Brontë to Doris Lessing*. London: Virago.
Signoretti, E. 1996. "Repossessing the Body: Transgressive Desire in *Carmilla* and *Dracula*." *Criticism*, 38, 607–32.

Sims, G. R. 1897. *Dorcas Dene, Detective: Her Adventures*. London: F. V. White.
Sims, M. (Ed.). 2011. *The Penguin Book of Victorian Women in Crime*. New York: Penguin.
Singh, B. 1975. [1934]. *A Survey of Anglo-Indian Fiction*. London: Curzon.
"Sir Edward Bulwer Lytton, M. Press. 1854." *The Illustrated Magazine of Art*, 4(23), 265–66.
Skal, D. J. 2016. *Something in the Blood: The Untold Story of Bram Stoker, the Man Who Wrote Dracula*. New York: Norton.
Slater, M. 1996. *Dickens' Journalism: The Amusements of the People and Other Papers: Reports, Essays and Reviews, 1834–1851*. Vol. 2. London: Dent.
"A Slum Story Writer." 1890, April 17. *Evening News and Post*, 2.
Smiles, S. 1859. *Self Help*. London: John Murray.
Smith, A. 2004. "Love, Freud, and the Female Gothic: Bram Stoker's *The Jewel of Seven Stars*." *Gothic Studies*, 6(1), 80–89.
Smith, H. R. 2002. "New Light on Sweeney Todd, Thomas Peckett Prest, James Malcolm Rymer & Elizabeth Caroline Grey." Essay. Bloomsbury: Jarndyce.
Snow, S. J. 2009. *The Blessed Days of Anaesthesia: How Anaesthetics Changed the World*. Oxford: Oxford University Press.
"Some Recent Novels." 1892, March 1. *Pall Mall Gazette*, 8407. p. 3.
Sparks, T. 2009. *The Doctor in the Victorian Novel*. Farnham, UK: Ashgate.
Squires, J. D. 2001. "Rediscovering M. Press. Shiel (1865–1947)." *New York Review of Science Fiction*, 13(9), 12–15.
Srebrnik, P. 1994. "The Re-subjection of "Lucas Malet": Charles Kingsley's Daughter and the Response to Muscular Christianity." In *Muscular Christianity: Embodying the Victorian Age*, Donald E. Hall (Ed.). Cambridge: Cambridge University Press, pp. 194–214.
Srebrnik, P. T. 1994. "Mrs. Riddell and the Reviewers: A Case Study in Victorian Popular Fiction." *Women's Studies*, 23(1), 69–84.
Staatshandbuch für das Grossherzogtum Sachsen: 1843. 1843. Weimar: Hofbuchdruckerei.
Stableford, B. 2004. "The Black-and-White Mystery of *The Purple Cloud*." Introduction to Cousin, J. W. 1910. *A Short Biographical Dictionary of English Literature*. London: J. M. Dent.
Stafford, D. 1981. "Spies and Gentlemen: The Birth of the British Spy Novel, 1893–1914." *Victorian Studies*, 24: 491–509.
Standlee, W. 2010. "George Egerton, James Joyce, and the Irish Künstlerroman." *Irish Studies Review*, 4, 439–52.
Stead, W. T. 1894. "The Novels of the Modern Woman." *Review of Reviews*, 10, 64–74.
Stearn, R. T. 1992. "The Mysterious Mr. Le Queux: War Novelist, Defence Publicist and Counterspy." *Soldiers of the Queen*, 70, pp. 6–27.
Stephen, F. 1858. Review of *Tom Brown's Schooldays* by T. Hughes. *Edinburgh Review*, 107, 172–93.
Stevenson, R. L. 1886. *Strange Case of Dr. Jekyll and Mr. Hyde*. London: Longman.
Stevenson, R. L. 2006. [1886]. *Strange Case of Dr. Jekyll and Mr. Hyde and Other Tales*. R. Luckhurst (Ed.). Oxford: Oxford University Press.
Stewart, C. 2001. "'Weird Fascination': The Response to Victorian Women's Ghost Stories." In E. Liggins & D. Duffy (Eds.), *Feminist Readings of Victorian Popular Texts* (pp. 108–25). Aldershot: Ashgate.
Stoker, B. 1986. Preface. In Richard Dalby (Ed.), *Dracula and the Lair of the White Worm* (pp. 11–12). Marlow: W. Foulsham.
Stoker, B. *Dracula*. 2011. R. Luckhurst (Ed.). Oxford: Oxford University Press.
Stoker, B. 2012. *The Lost Journals of Bram Stoker: The Dublin Years*. E. Miller and D. Stoker (eds.) London: Robson.
Stokes, S. 1928. *Pilloried!* London: Richards.
Storer, R. 2016. "Beyond 'Hommy-Beg': Hall Caine's Place in *Dracula*." In C. Wynne (Ed.), *Bram Stoker and the Gothic: Formations to Transformations* (pp. 172–84). Basingstoke: Palgrave.
Storey, G., Tillotson, K., and Easson, A. 1993. *The Letters of Charles Dickens*. Vol. 7. Oxford: Clarendon.
Strange. W. 1864. *The Seven Sources of Health*. London: Savill & Edwards.
Summers, M. 1945. "Mrs. Gordon Smythies." *Modern Language Notes*, 60(6), 359–64.
Supplemental Nights to the Book of the Thousand and One Nights with Notes Anthropological and Explanatory. No date [1886–88]. Vols. 1–6. R. F. Burton (Trans.). United States: The Burton Club.
Surridge, Lisa. 1994. "Dogs'/Bodies, Women's Bodies: Wives as Pets in Mid-Nineteenth Century Narratives of Domestic Violence." *Victorian Review*, 20 (1), 1–34.
Sussex, L. 2003. "The Detective Maidservant: Catherine Crowe's Susan Hopley." In B. Ayres (Ed.), *Silent Voices: Forgotten Novels by Victorian Women Writers*. Westport, CT: Praeger.
Sussex, L. 2007. "Edward Bulwer Lytton and the Development of the English Crime Novel." *Clues*, 26(1), 8–21.
Sussex, L. 2015. *Blockbuster! Fergus Hume and the Mystery of a Hansom Cab*. Melbourne: Text.
Sussman, H. 1995. *Victorian Masculinities: Manhood and Masculine Poetics in Early Victorian Literature and Art*. Cambridge: Cambridge University Press.
Sutherland, J. 1983. "Nineteenth-Century SF and the Book Trade." *Victorian Science Fiction in the UK: The Discourses of Knowledge and Power*. Boston: G. K. Hall.

Sutherland, J. 1989. *The Stanford Companion to Victorian Fiction*. Stanford: Stanford University Press.
Sutherland, J. 1990. *Mrs. Humphry Ward: Eminent Victorian, Pre-Eminent Edwardian*. Oxford: Oxford University Press.
Sutton, M.K. 1979. *R. D. Blackmore*. Boston: Twayne.
Sutton-Ramspeck, B. 2004. *Raising the Dust: The Literary Housekeeping of Mary Ward, Sarah Grand, and Charlotte Perkins Gilman*. Athens: Ohio University Press.
Suvin, D. 1983. *Victorian Science Fiction in the UK: The Discourses of Knowledge and Power*. Boston: G. K. Hall.
Swafford, K. 2007. *Class in Victorian Britain: The Narrative Concern with Social Hierarchy and Its Representation*. Youngstown, NY: Cambria.
Symons, J. 1972. *Bloody Murder: From the Detective Story to the Crime Novel: A History*. London: Penguin.
Taylor, A. 2012. *London's Burning: Pulp Fiction, the Politics of Terrorism and the Destruction of the Capital in British Popular Culture, 1840–2005*. London: Bloomsbury.
Taylor, J. B. 2013. Introduction. *The Beth Book*. Brighton: Victorian Secrets.
Taylor-Brown, E. 2014. "(Re)Constructing the Knights of Science: Parasitologists and their Literary Imaginations." *Journal of Literature and Science*, 7(2), 62–79.
The Temperance Recorder for Domestic and Foreign Intelligence. 1845, April.
Terry, R. C. *Victorian Popular Fiction, 1860–80*. Atlantic Highlands, NJ: Humanities, 1983.
Thackeray, W. M. 1945. *The Letters and Private Papers of William Makepeace Thackeray*. Gordon Ray (Ed.). Cambridge, MA: Harvard University Press. Vol. 1. "The Woman in White." *Critic*, *21* (529), 233–234.
Thirtieth Annual Report of the National Society for Promoting the Education of the Poor in the Principles of the Established Church Throughout England and Wales. 1841. Supplementary Paper. London: The National Society.
Thomas, J. E. 2015. *Sabine Baring-Gould: The Life and Work of a Complete Victorian*. Stroud: Fonthill.
Thomas, S. 1987. *Cassell's (Family) Magazine (1874–1910)—Indexes to Fiction*. Victorian Fiction Research Guide 12. http://victorianfictionresearchguides.org/cassells-family-magazine/.
Trollope, Anthony. 2014. *Doctor Thorne*. Oxford: Oxford University Press.
Trotter, D. 2010. *The Uses of Phobia: Essays on Literature and Film*. Chichester: Wiley Blackwell.
Trower, S. 2012. "On the Cliff Edge of England: Tourism and Imperial Gothic in Cornwall." *Victorian Literature and Culture*, 40(1), 199–214.
Turner, J. 1980. *Reckoning with the Beast: Animals, Pain and Humanity in the Victorian Mind*. Baltimore: The Johns Hopkins University Press.
Turner, M. L. 1968. "The Syndication of Fiction in Provincial Newspapers, 1870–1939: The Example of the Tillotson 'Fiction Bureau.'" B.Litt. Dissertation: Oxford University.
Turner, M. W. 2014. "The Unruliness of Serials in the Nineteenth-Century and the Digital Age." In R. Allen and T. Berg (Eds.) *Serialization in Popular Culture* (pp. 11–32). London: Routledge.
Ue, T. 2013, January. "Irony, Narrative Hybrids, and Genre Theory: The Dramatic Monologue and Gissing's Short Fiction." *The Gissing Journal*, 49(1), 1–23.
Ue, T. 2015, November. "Holmes and Raffles in Arms: Death, Endings, and Narration." *Victoriographies*, 5(3), 219–33.
Ue, T. 2017, July. "The Truth Will Set You Free: Implicit Faith in *Sherlock* and *London Spy*." *Imagining Sherlock Holmes*. Ed. Tom Ue. Special issue of *Journal of Popular Film and Television*, 45(2), 90–100.
Unwin, T. F. 1900. "Short Notices." *The Bookseller: A Newspaper of British and Foreign Literature*. Vol. 1900. London.
Vaninskaya, A. 2010. *William Morris and the Idea of Community: Romance, History and Propaganda, 1880–1914*. Edinburgh: Edinburgh University Press.
Voisine, J. 1955. *La Baronne Blaze de Bury (1813(?)—1894) Et Son Rôle Littéraire*. Doctoral dissertation. Faculté des Letters de Paris, Paris.
Vrettos, A. 2002. "Victorian Psychology." In P. Brantlinger & W. B. Thesing (Eds.), *A Companion to the Victorian Novel* (pp. 67–83). Malden, MA: Blackwell.
Vuohelainen, M. 2009. *Richard Marsh: Victorian Fiction Research Guide*, 35. Retrieved from http://victorianfictionresearchguides.org/richard-marsh/.
Vuohelainen, M. 2013. "'Contributing to most things': Richard Marsh, Literary Production, and the Fin de siècle Periodicals Market." *Victorian Periodicals Review*, 46, 401–22.
Vuohelainen, M. 2014. "Bernard Heldmann and the *Union Jack*, 1880–83: The Making of a Professional Author." *Victorian Periodicals Review*, 47, 105–142.
Vuohelainen, M. 2015. *Richard Marsh*. Cardiff: University of Wales Press.
Waddington, K. 2013. "Death at St. Bernard's: Anti-Vivisection, Medicine and the Gothic." *Journal of Victorian Culture*, 18(2), 246–262.
Waller, P. 2006. *Writers, Readers & Reputations: Literary Life in Britain 1870–1918*. Oxford: Oxford University Press.
Ward, Mrs. H. 1999. *East Lynne*. Andrew Maunder. (Ed.). Peterborough, ON: Broadview.
Warner, O. 1973. *Chatto & Windus: A Brief Account of the Firm's Origin, History and Development*. London: Chatto & Windus.

Wells, H. G. 2001. *The Time Machine: An Invention.* N. Ruddick (Ed.). Peterborough, ON: Broadview.
Wells, H. G. 2005. *The War of the Worlds.* P. Parrinder (Ed.). London: Penguin.
Wheeler, S. 2013. "No There There: Catherine Hubback Goes to California." *O My America! Second Acts in a New World,* pp. 191–217. London: Jonathan Cape.
Wiener, M. J. 1990. *Reconstructing the Criminal: Culture, Law, and Policy in England, 1830–1914.* Cambridge: Cambridge University Press.
Wilde, O. 2003. [1891]. *The Picture of Dorian Gray.* R. Mighall (Ed.). London: Penguin.
Wilde, O. 2007. [1891]. "The Soul of Man Under Socialism." In *The Complete Works of Oscar Wilde: Vol. 4: Criticism* (pp. 231–68). Oxford: Oxford University Press.
Wilfrid Scawen Blunt Papers, MS 43-1975, *Alms to Oblivion 4.* Cambridge: Fitzwilliam Museum.
Williams, C. 2012. "Melodrama." *New Cambridge History of Victorian Literature.* Kate Flint (Ed.). Cambridge: Cambridge University Press.
Williamson, A. M. 1901. *A Bid for a Coronet.* London: George Routledge & Sons.
Wilt, J. 2005. *Behind Her Times: Transition England in the Novels of Mary Arnold Ward.* Charlottesville: University of Virginia Press.
Winehouse, B. 1973. "Israel Zangwill's *Children of the Ghetto*: A Literary History of the First Anglo-Jewish Best-Seller." *English Literature in Transition, 1880–1920,* 16(2), 93–117.
"Without a Name." 1861, January 21. *All the Year Round,* 39, 291–292.
Wlaschin, K. 2009. *Silent Mystery and Detective Movies: A Comprehensive Filmography.* Jefferson, NC: McFarland.
Woolf, J. 2010. *The Mystery of Lewis Carroll.* New York: St. Martin's.
Wolff, R. L. 1979. *Sensational Victorian: The Life and Fiction of Mary Elizabeth Braddon.* New York: Garland.
Wood, J. 2001. *Passion and Pathology in Victorian Fiction.* Oxford: Oxford University Press.
Wright, J. 2014. "'I Had Peopled Else This Isle with Dudleys': *The Tempest* in *Uncle Silas.*" *Victorians Institute Journal,* 42, 98–117.
Young, A. 2008. "'Petticoated police': Propriety and the Lady Detective in Victorian Fiction." *Clues: A Journal of Detection,* 26(3), 15–28.
Youngkin, M. 2016. *British Women Writers and the Reception of Ancient Egypt, 1840–1910: Imperialist Representations of Egyptian Women.* Basingstoke: Palgrave Macmillan.
Zwierlein, A.-J. 2005. "From Parasitology to Parapsychology: Parasites in Nineteenth-Century Science and Literature." In *Unmapped Countries: Biological Visions in Nineteenth Century Literature and Culture,* A.-J. Zwierlein (Ed.) (pp. 155–72). London: Anthem.

About the Contributors

Éadaoin **Agnew** is a senior lecturer at Kingston University, London. She is the author of *Imperial Women Writers in Victorian India: Representing Colonial Life, 1850–1910* and has published articles on Victorian women's writing about India. She is working on a new edition of Julia Maitland and Mrs. A. Deane's travel writing.

Lynn M. **Alexander** is dean of the College of Humanities and Fine Arts and a professor of English at the University of Tennessee at Martin. Her work generally focuses on Victorian fiction and includes *Women, Work, and Representation: Needlewomen in Victorian Art and Literature*, editing Dinah Mulock Craik's *John Halifax, Gentleman* and coediting *The Slaughter-House of Mammon*. She is working on articles about representations of working-class men.

Janice M. **Allan** is an associate dean in the School of Arts and Media at the University of Salford. Her research interests are focused on nineteenth-century popular fiction as well as constructions of gender, deviance and literary value. Recent publications have explored the use of false hair in the Victorian period and the representation of private investigators in the fiction of Mary Braddon. She is coediting *The Cambridge Companion to Sherlock Holmes* and is executive editor of *Clues: A Journal of Detection*.

Oriah **Amit** is a graduate student at the University of California, Los Angeles. Her research focuses on Victorian crime journalism, detective fiction, and the popular press. She is on fellowship researching the development of the term "suspect" as a category of identification in mid- to late-nineteenth century journalism and fiction, especially in relation to Victorian anxieties over foreign immigration.

Jacqueline **Amorim** is an instructor in the Department of English at Florida International University. Her dissertation examined Latin American and Caribbean commodities in Victorian literature and culture, such as tobacco and chocolate, to better trace how the Victorians used these goods to make sense of their relationship to the Americas. Her research interests include empire, colonialism, adventure fiction, commodity culture, and industrialism.

Steve **Asselin** teaches at the University of Alberta's Augustana campus. Research interests include ecocriticism, travel literature, speculative fiction, and utopianism. He has received SSHRC funding to pursue research projects into polar fiction in the nineteenth century, and ecological catastrophism in the *fin-de-siècle*. He is also the author of over a dozen science fiction short stories with many small presses.

Brenda **Ayres** teaches nineteenth-century English literature at Liberty University. Besides a scholarly edition of Jesse Fothergill's *Kith and Kin*, her publications include 26 books and over 170 articles in literary scholarship. She presented on Fothergill at two conferences, with the last being "Against the Flow and Dared to Say So: Jessie Fothergill's Challenge to the Marriage Plot Novel."

Caroline **Bachmann** is a doctoral candidate at Philipps-Universität Marburg in Germany. Her dissertation focuses on the education of women as depicted in British literature from 1700 to 1900. She holds a diploma in English and American literature from the University of Kent at Canterbury, a B.A. in Anglophone studies from the University of Marburg and an MSc in literature and society from the University of Edinburgh.

Jen **Baker** defended her doctoral thesis at the University of Bristol on the monstrous revenant child in literature and culture, 1830–1914. She is a tutor at University of Bristol, and cofounder and chief editor of *HARTS & Minds*, a journal for postgraduates and ECRs of the arts and humanities, and has published on topics such as the pedophile in Gothic literature, ghost children, and childhood in the films of Steven Spielberg.

Danielle **Barkley** holds a Ph.D. from McGill University, where her dissertation focused on narrative practices in the silver fork novel. She has published on a range of Romantic and Victorian literature and research interests include the study of genre and popular fiction in the nineteenth century.

Stephen E. **Basdeo** researches eighteenth- and nineteenth-century medievalism. His Ph.D. thesis examines literary representations of Robin Hood between 1700 and 1900, and his most recent book, *The Life and Legend of a Rebel Leader: Wat Tyler*, analyzes depictions of the eponymous leader of the Peasants' Revolt in medieval and post-medieval literature.

About the Contributors

Emily **Bell** specializes in Charles Dickens, literary families, circles of influence, and nineteenth- and twentieth-century life writing. In 2017 she published in the *Wilkie Collins Journal* on her discovery of a lost autobiographical sketch written by Collins, and she has forthcoming work in the *Dickensian* on ways of commemorating Dickens in the early twentieth century.

Anne-Marie **Beller** is a lecturer in Victorian literature at Loughborough University, UK. She is the author of books on Mary Elizabeth Braddon and has published numerous articles and chapters on sensation fiction and Victorian women's popular fiction. She contributed chapters on Braddon and Amelia Edwards to Blackwell's *A Companion to Sensation Fiction* and is working on a critical edition of Geraldine Jewsbury's *Athenaeum* reviews and editing two special issues of *Women's Writing*.

Louise **Benson-James** is a doctoral researcher at the University of Bristol, looking at hysteria and the gothic in women's fiction. Her thesis examines medical hysteria and Gothic language, focusing on literature and culture, medicine, body politics, and gender, in a series of case studies on female authors spanning 1850 to 1930.

Ailise **Bulfin,** a scholar of nineteenth-century literature, lectures in the Department of English at Maynooth University, and her work focuses on representations of empire, war and trauma. She is the author of *Gothic Invasions: Imperialism, War and Fin-de-Siècle Popular Fiction*, and her critical essays examine topics such as invasion fiction, the "yellow peril," natural catastrophe and climate change.

Kirsty **Bunting** is senior lecturer in English literature at Manchester Metropolitan University and has published extensively on the topic of literary collaborations. Her most recent research focuses on Ada Nield Chew and radical suffrage networks.

Merrick **Burrow** is principal lecturer and head of English and creative writing at the University of Huddersfield. He has published numerous articles and book chapters on late–Victorian and Edwardian popular fiction, particularly with reference to masculinity and material culture. He is researching the travel writing of Robert Louis Stevenson and writing a monograph on Sir Arthur Conan Doyle.

Dennis **Butts**, a former chairman of the Children's Book History Society, taught children's literature in the MA course at Reading University. He has a lifelong interest in the relationship among politics, society, and literature and has written on many aspects of children's books, including work on Barbara Hofland and R. L. Stevenson. His most recent publication is *Children's Literature and Social Change*.

S. Brooke **Cameron** is an assistant professor of English at Queen's University in Kingston, Ontario. She has published and forthcoming articles in journals such as *Victorian Review, Victorian Literature and Culture, Victorian Poetry, English Literature in Transition,* and *Studies in the Novel*. She is completing her first book, *Critical Alliances: Economics and Feminism in English Women's Writing, 1880–1938*.

Josianne Leah **Campbell** is an instructor of English in South Carolina. She has enjoyed a long career as a professional educator and has research and teaching expertise in folklore, fairy tales, and children's literature.

Ashley Lynn **Carlson** is an associate professor of English at the University of Montana Western. She earned her Ph.D. in English from the University of New Mexico, where her dissertation focused on Victorian writer Sarah Stickney Ellis. Since then, her publications include work on nineteenth-century women writers as well as contemporary popular culture and media.

Camilla **Cassidy** is a tutor in nineteenth century literature on Middlebury College's Oxford Humanities Programme associated with Keble College, Oxford. She has published a number of peer-reviewed articles on Charles Dickens, W. M. Thackeray, Elizabeth Gaskell, Walter Scott and George Eliot, and is a regular reviewer for academic journals and the *Times Literary Supplement*. She is working on a book based on her DPhil thesis, *Twilight Histories in the Victorian Novel*.

Vicky **Cheng** is a Ph.D. student in English at Syracuse University, where she studies nineteenth-century British literature and culture. Her dissertation will investigate Victorian novels for alternate forms of female (re)production and regeneration. Other scholarly interests include mediations between textual description and visualization, structures of power surrounding the interplay of nonnormative bodies and disruptive desires, and the complexities of embodied sexualities.

Laura **Chilcoat** is working on her Ph.D. at the University of Florida. Her specialty is in Victorian literature and gender studies. Her dissertation is titled *The New Women's Queer Agenda: The Rejection of Heteronormativity in New Woman Fiction of the 1890s* and focuses on the role of queer narratives in New Women fiction.

Clare **Clarke** is an assistant professor of nineteenth-century literature and co-director of the MPhil in popular literature at Trinity College Dublin, Ireland. She has published widely on crime and detective fiction. Her first monograph, *Late Victorian Crime Fiction in the Shadows of Sherlock*, was awarded the HRF Keating Prize in 2015. She is working on a book titled *The Rivals of Sherlock Holmes*.

Thomas G. **Cole**, II, is finishing a Ph.D. in the Department of English at the University of Florida. His research focuses on women's and gender studies issues in late–Victorian fiction and medicine.

About the Contributors

Silvana **Colella** is professor of English literature at the University of Macerata and president of the European Consortium for Humanities Institutes and Centres. Her publications include books and articles on nineteenth-century literature, popular fiction and the cultures of the market. Her most recent book is *Charlotte Riddell's City Novels and Victorian Business: Narrating Capitalism*. She is working on credit crunch fiction.

Fiona **Coll** is an assistant professor of literature and technology at SUNY Oswego. Her research focuses on the entanglement of machines and human subjectivity in Victorian-era discourse. Her current book project explores how the automaton gave material form to fantasies about human exceptionalism in nineteenth-century accounts of human agency. Her writing can be found in *Victorian Review*, *University of Toronto Quarterly*, and at *The Floating Academy*. She is the editor of the *Morgan Robertson Digital Archive*.

Gail **Cunningham** is an emeritus professor of English literature at Kingston University, London. The author of *The New Woman and the Victorian Novel* in 1978, she has subsequently published widely on women in nineteenth- and twentieth-century fiction. Her more recent interests are in the history and cultural representation of the English suburb.

Anne **DeWitt** is a clinical assistant professor at New York University's Gallatin School for Individualized Study. She is the author of *Moral Authority, Men of Science, and the Victorian Novel* and is working on a project about the reception of best-selling religious novels in the 1880s.

Jade **Dillon** is a Ph.D. research student and departmental assistant within the Department of English Language and Literature in Mary Immaculate College, University of Limerick, Ireland. Jade's Ph.D. is titled *Voicing Gender: Gender Identity, Ideology, and Intertextuality Associated with Victorian Children's Literature*, and focuses primarily on Lewis Carroll's *Alice's Adventures in Wonderland* and *Through the Looking Glass* alongside *Peter Pan* by J. M. Barrie.

Eleanor **Dobson** is lecturer in nineteenth-century literature at the University of Birmingham. There, she completed her doctoral thesis on literature, culture and Egyptology across the late-nineteenth and early-twentieth centuries. Her research interests extend to science, magic and technology, classical reception, book history, and material culture, and authors including Bram Stoker, H. Rider Haggard, Marie Corelli, and Oscar Wilde.

Ann-Marie L. **Dunbar** is an associate professor of English at Winona State University, where she teaches courses on nineteenth-century British and American literature and multicultural American literature. Her research interests include Victorian literature and culture, the history of the novel, and narrative and genre theory. Her work has appeared in *Victorian Review*, the *Victorians Institute Journal*, and *CEA Forum*. Her essay on Japanese novelist Natsume Soseki in late Victorian London is forthcoming in *Victorian Literature and Culture*.

Melissa **Edmundson** specializes in nineteenth and early twentieth-century British women writers, with particular interest in women's ghost stories, the Gothic, and Anglo-Indian fiction. She is editor of a critical edition of Alice Perrin's *East of Suez* and author of *Women's Ghost Literature in Nineteenth-Century Britain* and *Women's Colonial Gothic, 1860–1930: Haunted Empire*. Her latest project is a critical edition of Dinah Mulock Craik's *The Half-Caste*.

Rachel Margaret **Egloff** is studying toward a Ph.D. in English literature at Oxford Brookes University. Her research aims to present evidence of female participation in nineteenth-century discourses on (trans)national identity in the context of European international politics, focusing on the little known and underresearched writer Rose Blaze de Bury (1813–1894).

Dewi **Evans** studied English literature at Brasenose College, Oxford, and Cardiff University. He has taught at Cardiff and Brunel Universities and published articles on Oscar Wilde and Robert Louis Stevenson. He is working on a history of the antiquarian ghost story in Victorian and Edwardian literature.

Steve **Farmer** is a senior lecturer in the department of English at Arizona State University. His area of academic interest is late-nineteenth-century British fiction. He has edited critical editions of Wilkie Collins's *The Moonstone* (1868) and *Heart and Science* (1882) and Ella Hepworth Dixon's *The Story of a Modern Woman* (1894).

Monica **Flegel** is an associate professor of English at Lakehead University. Her research is in cultural studies, particularly child studies and animal studies in the Victorian period. She specializes in analyzing representations of intimacy and familial relations, and on the overlapping representations of children and pets. She is the author of *Conceptualizing Cruelty in Nineteenth-Century England* and *Pets and Domesticity in Victorian Literature and Culture* and co-editor of *Cruel Children in Popular Texts and Cultures*.

Jane **Ford** is a visiting lecturer at Edge Hill University and the University of Chester. She is co-editor of *Economies of Desire at the Victorian Fin de Siècle: Libidinal Lives*. She is working on a monograph which explores metaphors of economic exploitation and domination in *fin-de-siècle* writing and a co-edited collection of essays on Lucas Malet (Mary St. Leger Harrison), an important but marginalized nineteenth- and twentieth-century writer.

Laura **Foster** is an early career researcher specializing in the representation of the workhouse in nineteenth-century literature and culture. Her research interests include criminality, poverty, and philanthropy. Her publications include an essay on *All the Year Round*'s workhouse narratives, and an article about the workhouse in relation to ideas of dirt and cleanliness.

About the Contributors

Kaja **Franck** recently passed the viva for her Ph.D. which she undertook at the University of Hertfordshire. Her thesis looked at the literary werewolf as an eco-Gothic monster, concentrating on the relationship between wilderness, wolves, and werewolves, and how language is used to demarcate animal alterity. She is part of the "Open Graves, Open Minds" research project.

Nick **Freeman** is reader in Late Victorian Literature at Loughborough University. He has published widely on the fiction and culture of the *fin-de-siècle*. He is the author of two longer studies, *Conceiving the City: London, Literature and Art 1870–1914* (2007) and *1895: Drama, Disaster and Disgrace in Late Victorian Britain* (2013). He has also edited Arthur Symons's *Spiritual Adventures* (2017).

Alberto **Gabriele** is the author of *Reading Popular Culture in Victorian Print: Belgravia and Sensationalism*, *The Emergence of Precinema: Print Culture and the Optical Toy of the Literary Imagination*, and the forthcoming *The Question of Nineteenth Century Mimesis: Fragmentation, Movement and the Modern Episteme* and the editor of *Sensationalism and the Genealogy of Modernity: A Global Long Nineteenth Century Perspective* (2016). His current project investigates the global dissemination of Victorian print culture through a network of dealers in ten countries.

Anna **Gasperini** earned her Ph.D. at the National University of Ireland, Galway, with a thesis on discourses of ethics, monstrosity, and medicine in the Victorian penny blood. She co-edited *Media and Print Culture Consumption in Nineteenth-Century Britain: The Victorian Reading Experience*. Her research interests include Victorian popular culture and popular fiction, Victorian medicine, and adaptation, and she is membership secretary of the Victorian Popular Fiction Association.

Adrienne E. **Gavin** is an emeritus professor of English literature and co-founder and honorary director of the International Centre for Victorian Women Writers (ICVWW), Canterbury Christ Church University, UK. She is also an honorary academic at the University of Auckland, New Zealand, where she teaches law and literature. Her publications include *Dark Horse: A Life of Anna Sewell*, critical editions of *Paul Ferroll*, *The Blue Lagoon*, *Black Beauty*, and *The Experiences of Loveday Brooke, Lady Detective* and a range of edited collections.

Lauren **Gillingham** is an associate professor of English and director of graduate studies at the University of Ottawa. She has published on Newgate and silver-fork fiction in *SEL*, *Women's Writing*, *Victorian Review*, and the Blackwell *Companion to Crime Fiction*, and is completing a manuscript titled *Being Novel: Fashion, History, and the Currency of Nineteenth-Century British Fiction*.

Andrew **Glazzard** is the author of *Conrad's Popular Fictions: Secret Histories and Sensational Novels* and *The Case of Sherlock Holmes: Secrets and Lies in Conan Doyle's Detective Fiction*. He has written widely on late–Victorian and Edwardian fiction, and is one of the general editors of *The Edinburgh Edition of the Works of Arthur Conan Doyle*, for which he will be editing *The Adventures of Sherlock Holmes* and *The Tragedy of the Korosko*.

David **Glover** is an emeritus professor of English at the University of Southampton. His publications include *Vampires, Mummies, and Liberals: Bram Stoker and the Politics of Popular Fiction*, *Genders* coauthored with Cora Kaplan, and *Literature, Immigration, and Diaspora in Fin-de-Siècle England: A Cultural History of the 1905 Aliens Act*. He co-edited *The Cambridge Companion to Popular Fiction* with Scott McCracken.

Alexandra **Gray** is a sessional lecturer in English literature at the University of Portsmouth, UK. She is the author of *Self-Harm in New Woman Writing* and a number of essays and articles on the New Woman, nineteenth-century medical history, and Victorian popular fiction. She is the coeditor of two forthcoming essay collections on Victorian and twentieth-century fiction and the cofounder of a new web-based resource on the life and work of the Victorian and early–Modernist author Lucas Malet.

Kristen **Guest** is an associate professor of English at the University of Northern British Columbia where she teaches Victorian literature. Her research, which focuses on a range of popular Victorian forms including theatrical melodrama, sentimental fiction, and detective fiction, has appeared in such venues as *Victorian Studies* and *Victorian Literature and Culture*. Her critical edition of Anna Sewell's *Black Beauty* was published in 2016.

Valerie L. **Guyant** is an assistant professor in English at Montana State University, where her areas of research include multicultural literature, Renaissance-era women's literature, fairy tales and folklore, and speculative fiction. She received her Ph.D. from Northern Illinois University. Her dissertation involved representations of female sexuality in vampire literature across millennia in Western culture.

Laura **Habbe** completed her Ph.D. in the School of English at Trinity College Dublin. Her research interests include Victorian studies, nineteenth-century popular and Gothic writing, the medical humanities and the history of science. Her thesis focuses on the representation of science in late-Victorian popular fiction and its subversion of scientific naturalism. She also holds degrees in Latin and comparative literature.

Sandra **Hagan** is a professor in the English Department at Vancouver Island University in British Columbia, Canada. She coedited *The Brontës in the World of the Arts* and contributed a chapter to that volume on an illustrated edition of Charlotte Brontë's *Villette*. She has written on Victorian hymnist Frances Ridley Havergal and presented on Amy Levy and Emily Lawless. Her teaching interests include the sensation novel and espionage fiction.

David **Halliwell** is a retired teacher. After retirement followed an academic path culminating in a completed Ph.D. in 2014. His thesis on sensation fiction was titled "'Nothing against good morals and correct taste': Subversion, Containment and the Masculine Boundaries of Victorian Sensation Fiction." He is in the second year of a postgraduate diploma in creative writing.

Jacqueline H. **Harris** is a visiting faculty member in English at Brigham Young University-Idaho. She earned her Ph.D. from the University of Nebraska–Lincoln in 2015 where she studied nineteenth-century British literature with specializations in women's studies and interdisciplinary studies. Her dissertation, "The Buried Life of the Facts of Life: Female Physical Development in Nineteenth-Century British Literature," argues that despite social dictates of propriety, euphemistic treatment of the female adolescent body pervaded literature of the era.

Constance D. **Harsh** is professor of English at Colgate University. She is the author of *Subversive Heroines*, a study of the English industrial novel, and the editor of Edith Johnstone's *A Sunless Heart*. She has also published numerous essays on Victorian fiction. Her most recent work has focused on the novels of George Gissing. Recently she served for two years as interim dean of the faculty and provost at Colgate.

Elaine **Hartnell** gained her Ph.D. from the University of Leicester and lectured in English literature in Liverpool for more than fifteen years. She has published a monograph on the domestic novelist Rosa Nouchette Carey and a range of papers on British and American popular fiction, including the Gothic. She is writing about representations of the "new werewolf" in women's romantic fiction.

Janine **Hatter** researches nineteenth-century literature, art, and culture, with particular emphasis on popular fiction. She has published on Mary Braddon, Bram Stoker, the theatre and identity, short stories as a genre, and Victorian women's life writing, as well as on her wider research interests of science fiction and the Gothic. She is coeditor of two series: *New Paths in Victorian Fiction and Culture* and *Key Popular Women Writers*.

Erica **Haugtvedt** received her Ph.D. in English from Ohio State University in 2015 and is an assistant professor in humanities at South Dakota School of Mines & Technology. Recent publications include "The Victorian Serial Novel and Transfictional Character" and "*Sweeney Todd* as Victorian Transmedial Storyworld," in *Victorian Studies* and *Victorian Periodicals Review*, respectively. Her current manuscript is on the nineteenth-century serialized narrative and expansive adaptations across media, focusing on the reception of transfictional serial characters

Ruth **Heholt** is a senior lecturer in English at Falmouth University. Her research concentrates on the supernatural, crime fiction, masculinity, the Gothic and sensation fiction. She has edited a scholarly edition of Catherine Crowe's 1847 novel *The Story of Lilly Dawson* and has coedited *Haunted Landscapes: Super-Nature and the Environment*. She is editor of an e-journal, Revenant: Critical and Creative Studies of the Supernatural: www.revenantjournal.com.

Tamar **Heller** is an associate professor of English and comparative literature at the University of Cincinnati. She is the author of *Dead Secrets: Wilkie Collins and the Female Gothic* and has coedited several essay collections in addition to editing Rhoda Broughton's two earliest novels, *Cometh Up as a Flower* and *Not Wisely, but Too Well*. She is completing a book titled *A Plot of Her Own: Rhoda Broughton and English Fiction*.

Naomi **Hetherington** is a university tutor in English and humanities in the Department for Lifelong Learning, University of Sheffield, UK. She has research interests in Victorian popular fiction; the history of feminism; gender, sexuality and religion in Victorian literature and culture and the New Woman. She is completing an article-length study of Kathleen Mannington Caffyn and the recovery of women writers of the 1890s and a monograph on the literary figure of the freethinking New Woman.

Martin **Hipsky** is professor of English at Ohio Wesleyan University in Delaware, Ohio. He teaches Victorian literature and British modernism, as well as literary theory and the history of film and cinema. His most recent book is *Modernism and the Women's Popular Romance in Britain, 1885–1925*.

Tammy Lai-Ming **Ho** is an assistant professor in the Department of English at Hong Kong Baptist University, where she teaches fiction, poetics and modern drama. She is a founding co-editor of *Asian Cha*, an editor of *Hong Kong Studies*, and has edited or coedited several volumes of poetry and fiction published in Hong Kong. Her first poetry collection is *Hula Hooping* and she is the recipient of the 2015 Hong Kong Arts Development Council Young Artist Award in Literary Arts.

Johan **Höglund** is an associate professor at Linnaeus University and director of the Linnaeus University Centre for Concurrences in Colonial and Postcolonial Studies. He has published extensively on the relationship between popular culture and imperialism in *English Literature in Transition*, *Game Studies*, *Continuum*, and *The European Journal of American Studies*. He is the author of *The American Imperial Gothic: Popular Culture, Empire, Violence* and coeditor of *Animal Horror Cinema: Genre, History and Criticism* and *Transnational and Postcolonial Vampires*.

Kate **Holterhoff** is a Marion L. Brittain postdoctoral fellow at the Georgia Institute of Technology. Her research areas include nineteenth- and early-twentieth-century British literature, visual culture, digital humanities, and the history of science. She has published articles in *Digital Humanities Quarterly*, *English Literature in Transition, 1880–1920*, *The Journal of Victorian Culture*, *The Journal of the History of Biology*, and *Victorian Network*. She directs and edits the digital archive VisualHaggard.org, a literary and art historical resource indexed by NINES, which centralizes and improves access to the illustrations of Victorian novelist H. Rider Haggard.

Helena **Ifill** of the University of Sheffield specializes in Victorian popular literature, particularly sensation fiction and the Gothic, as well as Victorian science and medicine. She is a coorganizer of the Victorian Popular Fiction

Association and co-series editor for *Key Popular Women Writers* and *New Paths in Victorian Literature and Culture*. She is the author of *Creating Character: Theories of Nature and Nurture in Victorian Sensation Fiction*.

Flore **Janssen** is a research student at Birkbeck, University of London. Her thesis examines women's work, writing, and activism from 1880 to 1920 through the work of Margaret Harkness and Clementina Black. With Lisa C. Robertson she is editing a forthcoming collection of essays on Harkness.

Agnieszka **Jasnowska** received her Ph.D. from the School of Fine Art, History of Art and Cultural Studies at the University of Leeds. Her research interests include nineteenth century literature and culture, detective fiction, Sherlock Holmes, Bakhtin, language theory, literary criticism and identity politics. She has worked as a researcher, translator and teacher and is the reviews editor of *parallax* journal.

Melissa S. **Jenkins** is the author of *Fatherhood, Authority, and British Reading Culture*. She is an associate professor of English and women's, gender, and sexuality studies at Wake Forest University. Her research interests include the history of the novel, gender studies, and transatlantic race studies.

D. Michael **Jones** teaches at East Tennessee State University. His work cuts across Romanticism, the long nineteenth century, genre fiction, American twentieth century popular culture, working-class literature and masculinity studies. He is the author of *The Byronic Hero and the Rhetoric of Masculinity in the Nineteenth-Century Novel* (McFarland).

Jennifer Diann **Jones** is a lecturer and researcher at the University of Portsmouth. Her research interests include nineteenth-century literature, culture, and medicine; narrative theory; and aesthetic theory. She is working on a book-length study on anesthesia in Victorian literature and culture and is coediting a volume on literary orphans with Diane Warren and Alexandra Gray. She has work published or forthcoming in *Studies in the Novel*, *Victoriographies*, *The George Eliot Review*, and *Peer English*.

Jane **Jordan** is a senior lecturer in English literature at Kingston University, London, and cofounder of the Victorian Popular Fiction Association. She has published widely on Ouida, including *Ouida and Victorian Popular Culture* with Andrew King.

Emma **Kareno** is an independent researcher and writer with an M.A. from the University of Tampere, Finland, and a Ph.D. from Stirling University, Scotland. Her doctoral thesis is titled *Sherlock's Pharmacy: Victorian Detective Fiction and Drugs*. She blogs on sensation fiction at perilsofsensation.blogspot.com/ and on Nordic crime fiction at palmuandcompany.blogspot.com/. Her reviews have appeared in the *TLS*.

Stephan **Karschay** is an associate professor (*Junior professor*) of British literature and cultural studies at the University of Hamburg, Germany. His main research interests are the relationship between literature and science in the nineteenth century, Gothic fiction, film and media from the eighteenth to the twenty-first centuries, and representations of the human body. His publications include articles on a variety of topics and a book, *Degeneration, Normativity and the Gothic at the Fin de Siècle*.

Peter J. **Katz** is an assistant professor of English at Pacific Union College in Angwin, California. He earned his Ph.D. from Syracuse University in 2015. His work centers on embodiment and empathy, sensation fiction, history of the book, and Victorian science of mind, and has appeared in *Critical Survey, Victorian Literature and Culture,* and the *Journal of Victorian Culture*.

Haejoo **Kim**, a Ph.D. candidate in English literature at Syracuse University, specializes in nineteenth-century British literature and culture. As an interdisciplinary scholar, she is interested in how the modern self and body are negotiated at medical and moral discourses, particularly in relation to the concepts of sympathy, health, temperance, and vegetarianism.

Andrew **King** is a professor of English at the University of Greenwich, UK. His many publications on nineteenth-century popular print culture include *The London Journal 1845–1883*, *Victorian Print Media* (edited with John Plunkett), *Ouida and Victorian Popular Culture* (edited with Jane Jordan), the Colby prize-winning *Routledge Handbook to Nineteenth-Century Periodicals and Newspapers* (edited with Alexis Easley and John Morton), and *Researching the Nineteenth-Century Press: Case Studies*.

Patrick M. **Kirkwood** is a history instructor at Metropolitan Community College–Blue River in Independence, Missouri. He graduated with a Ph.D. in transnational and comparative history from Central Michigan University in May 2016. His research is concerned primarily with British and American imperialism during the late nineteenth and early twentieth centuries. His work has appeared in the *Graduate History Review*, the *Michigan Historical Review*, *Civil War History*, and the *Journal of World History*.

Sarah **Kniesler** has an MLitt from the University of St. Andrews and is working on her Ph.D. at the University of Florida. She specializes in Victorian literature, detective fiction, and women's studies. Her dissertation focuses on female desire and the family and considers how this desire relates to genre distinctions in popular nineteenth-century novels by women writers.

Ceylan **Kosker** is a visiting instructor at the Department of English Language and Literature at Bilkent University in Ankara, Turkey. Her area of expertise is nineteenth-century women's writing, with an emphasis on the liminal nature of women's writing within the cultural and economic milieu of the period. She is preparing a literary biography of the Victorian poet, novelist, and ambassadress Violet Fane.

Adam **Kozaczka** is completing his Ph.D. at Syracuse University, from which he also holds an MA in English literature. His dissertation is about the romance of violent, Celtic masculinity in the late-eighteenth and early-nineteenth centuries and on the relationship between the historical novel's sense of character and the criminal law's sense of character evidence. His work has appeared in *Journal of the Fantastic in the Arts* and is forthcoming in the *Burney Journal* and in multiple critical anthologies.

Julia **Kuehn** is a professor of English at the University of Hong Kong, where she teaches courses on nineteenth-century literature and culture. She has published on women's, popular and Empire fiction, as well as on (China-related) travel writing in the Victorian era and beyond.

Graham **Law** is a professor in media history at Waseda University, Tokyo, specializing in the print culture of the later nineteenth century. His books include *Serializing Fiction in the Victorian Press* and *Charlotte M. Brame (1836-1884): Towards a Primary Bibliography*. He has also edited a number of works of Victorian popular fiction, including David Pae's *Lucy, the Factory Girl* and Dora Russell's *Beneath the Wave*.

Sarah L. **Lennox** teaches part-time at Eastern Connecticut State University. She earned her Ph.D. with a specialization in Victorian literature from the University of Florida. Her research interests include fictional representations of the body, nineteenth-century science and pseudoscience, and genre studies. Her work has appeared in the *Victorian Institute Journal*'s Digital Annex, *Victorian Review*, and the *Journal of Commonwealth Literature*.

Sarah Louise **Lill** was awarded her Ph.D. from Northumbria University in 2015 for a thesis titled "'The Father of the Cheap Press': Edward Lloyd and the Mass-Market Periodical, 1830–1855." She divides her time between conducting research in the field of Victorian periodicals and working as a freelance journalist and arts editor for a lifestyle magazine. She is currently co-editing a volume of essays on Edward Lloyd with Rohan McWilliam.

Erin **Louttit** is an independent scholar. Her doctorate was conferred by the University of St. Andrews and her research interests include the literature and culture of the long nineteenth century, faith, gender, and the supernatural. She has published on Rudyard Kipling, reincarnation in Victorian fiction, Alice Mangold Diehl, and epic poetry about Buddhism.

Michael James **Lundell** is an assistant professor of English at Palomar College in San Marcos, California. He received his Ph.D. in literature from UCSD. He. His teaching and research interests include *The 1001 Nights*, late 18th–early 20th century English literature (particularly the Victorian Period in a transnational context), Arabic literature, film studies and orientalism. His monograph, *The 1001 Nights: Paratexts of Empire*, explores the postcolonial nature of the genesis and reception of the *Nights*.

Tara **MacDonald** is an assistant professor of English at the University of Idaho. She has published widely on Victorian masculinity, sensation fiction, and neo-Victorian fiction. She is author of *The New Man, Masculinity, and Marriage in the Victorian Novel* and coeditor of *Rediscovering Victorian Women Sensation Writers*.

Brian **Maidment** is a professor of the history of print at Liverpool John Moores University and president of the Research Society for Victorian Periodicals. His research centers on down-market print culture, especially illustrated periodicals, in the Regency and early Victorian period. His most recent book is *Comedy, Caricature, and the Social Order, 1820–1850*.

Amberyl **Malkovich** is an associate professor of British nineteenth-through-contemporary literature and culture, children's and young adult literature and culture, women's and gender studies, multiethnic literature, digital humanities, and popular literature and culture at Concord University. She is the author of *Charles Dickens and the Victorian Child: Romanticizing and Socializing the Imperfect Child*.

Katherine **Mansfield** is a doctoral candidate in English literature at Cardiff University. Her thesis, "Sensationalising the New Woman: Crossing the Boundaries between Sensation and New Woman Literature, 1859-1901," explores the relationship between sensation and New Woman fiction to investigate the extent to which sensation literature is a forerunner to the early development of the New Woman novel, and consequently how the two genres blur, or cross, temporal and conceptual boundaries.

Victoria **Margree** is a principal lecturer at the University of Brighton. With Daniel Orrells and Minna Vuohelainen, she is coeditor of an essay collection on *fin-de-siècle* author Richard Marsh. She is cofounder (with Lucy Andrew) of the Short Story Network, has published articles on the ghost stories of Charlotte Riddell and Edith Nesbit, and is developing a monograph on the uncanny short fiction of women writers from 1860 to 1930.

Jodie **Matthews** is a senior lecturer in English literature at the University of Huddersfield in West Yorkshire. Her work examines the representation of people who moved around Britain in the nineteenth century, in particular Romani people, canal boat people, seasonal agricultural workers and showpeople.

Maia **McAleavey** is an associate professor at Boston College. She is the author of *The Bigamy Plot: Sensation and Convention in the Victorian Novel* as well as articles that have appeared in *Victorian Studies, Representations, Dickens Studies Annual*, and *Victorian Review*. She is working on a project on the family chronicle.

About the Contributors

Annemarie **McAllister** is a senior research fellow in history at the University of Central Lancashire, specializing in UK temperance history. She has published many articles in journals and collections, curated three exhibitions including the virtual site at www.demondrink.co.uk, and is author of *Demon Drink? Temperance and the Working Class*. Relevant to her article here is "Onward: How a Regional Temperance Magazine for Children Survived and Flourished in the Victorian Marketplace," *Victorian Periodicals Review* (Spring 2015).

Rohan **McWilliam** is professor of modern British history at Anglia Ruskin University, Cambridge, UK. He is the author of *The Tichborne Claimant: A Victorian Sensation* (2007). He has written articles on melodrama, radicalism and popular fiction. He is writing a history of the West End of London since 1800.

Deborah T. **Meem** is a professor of English literature and women's, gender, and sexuality studies at the University of Cincinnati. She has written about Eliza Lynn Linton in *Journal of the History of Sexuality* and elsewhere, and has edited critical editions of four of her novels: *The Rebel of the Family*, *Realities*, *The Autobiography of Christopher Kirkland* (with Kate Holterhoff), and *Sowing the Wind* (with Holterhoff).

Duncan **Milne** is a Ph.D. candidate and a member of the Centre for Literature and Writing at Edinburgh Napier University. He is completing a thesis on Scottish literary tradition and the mediation and development of Robert Louis Stevenson's critical reception. His work as a research assistant at Edinburgh Napier University involves working on the Robert Louis Stevenson website and in keeping the Ernest and Joyce Mehew Stevenson Collection.

Nick **Milne** is a part-time professor in the University of Ottawa's Department of English. His research focuses on British print culture from 1870 to 1939, with a particular emphasis upon popular and establishment First World War literature. His work has appeared in *Canadian Literature*, *The British Journal of Canadian Studies*, *Mythlore*, and *Christianity & Literature*, among other venues.

Rosemary Ann **Mitchell** is professor of Victorian studies and deputy director of the Leeds Centre for Victorian Studies at Leeds Trinity University, West Yorkshire. She is also associate editor for the *Journal of Victorian Culture*, and a committee member of the British Association of Victorian Studies. Her publications include *Picturing the Past: English History in Text and Image, 1830–1870*, articles in *Nineteenth-Century Contexts*, *Clio*, and *Women's History Review*, and over 150 entries for *The Oxford Dictionary of National Biography* (2004–).

Steven **Mollmann** is an assistant professor of English and writing at the University of Tampa. He has published on science and literature in works by Elizabeth Gaskell, George Griffith, Manjula Padmanabhan, and H. G. Wells, in journals including *English Literature in Transition*, the *Gaskell Journal*, and *Science Fiction Studies*. He is at work on a study of British novels from 1818 to 1910 that feature scientists as characters.

Grace **Moore** is a senior lecturer in literary studies at the University of Melbourne, Australia, where she is also a senior research fellow at the Australian Research Council's Centre of Excellence for the History of Emotions. Grace's research interests encompass ecocriticism, fire, Australian ecology, Charles Dickens, Anthony Trollope, the history of emotions, and neo–Victorianism. She is the author of *The Victorian Novel in Context* and *Dickens and Empire*, as well as many essays on Victorian literature and culture.

Sarah E. **Moore** is an assistant clinical professor of business communication at the University of Texas at Dallas. Her research includes women's fictional writing about religious controversy, business communication pedagogy, and gendered communication in work settings. Her recently completed dissertation analyzed representations of lived religion in Victorian Anglican women's High Church novels.

Audrey L. **Morrison** is a graduate of the S. I. Newhouse School of Public Communications with expertise in print media and gender studies. Her work on feminism and popular culture has appeared in *Ramona Magazine*. She is working on representations of spiritualism and occultism in Victorian periodicals.

Kate **Morrison** recently completed her Ph.D. thesis at Anglia Ruskin University, Cambridge. Her area of research concerns illegality in Victorian and Edwardian detective and spy fiction between 1880 and the First World War.

Kevin A. **Morrison** is the author *of Victorian Liberalism and Material Culture: Synergies of Thought and Place* and *A Micro-History of Victorian Liberal Parenting: John Morley's "Discreet Indifference"*; editor of two popular Victorian-era novels by Walter Besant, *All Sorts and Conditions of Men* and *Children of Gibeon*; and of the forthcoming essay collection, *Walter Besant: The Business of Literature and the Pleasures of Reform*.

Alison **Moulds** is a third-year D.Phil candidate in English literature at St. Anne's College, University of Oxford. Her thesis looks at the construction of professional identities in nineteenth-century medical writing and fiction. She is part of the Arts and Humanities Research Council–funded project Constructing Scientific Communities and is working with the Royal College of Surgeons of England.

Deborah **Mutch** is a senior lecturer at De Montfort University, Leicester, UK. Her research focuses on the fiction written and published by the members of the British socialist movement between 1880 and 1914. She has published articles in journals such as *Victorian Periodicals Review*, *Victorian Studies*, and *Nineteenth Century Studies* and her most recent book was an edition of Margaret Harkness's *A City Girl*.

Rebecca **Nesvet** is assistant professor of English at University of Wisconsin, Green Bay. Her most recent essay publications include "Penny Bloods and Dreadfuls" in *Teaching Victorian Literature in the 21st Century*, edited by Jen Cadwallader and Laurence Mazzeno.

About the Contributors

Jennifer **Nicol** is an early-career researcher based in Nottingham, UK. She completed her Ph.D. at Loughborough University in 2016. Her doctoral thesis examined the solitary or lonely woman in *fin-de-siècle* literature and urban culture, with a particular focus on the life and works of Amy Levy, George Egerton, and Sarah Grand.

Megan A. **Norcia** is an associate professor at SUNY Brockport whose research and teaching interests focus on empire and nineteenth-century children's literary and material culture. Her research topics include imperial geography, mapping London in children's books, and castaway tales. She has analyzed imperial geography in *X Marks the Spot: Women Writers Map the Empire for British Children, 1790–1895*, and her work has appeared in journals such as *Victorian Literature and Culture* and *Children's Literature Annual*.

Deaglán **Ó Donghaile** is a senior lecturer in English literature at Liverpool John Moores University. His is the author of *Blasted Literature: Victorian Political Fiction and the Shock of Modernism* and is writing monograph titled *Oscar Wilde and the Radical Politics of the Fin de Siècle*. His research interests lie in the relationship between revolutionary politics and literary writing at the end of the nineteenth and beginning of the twentieth centuries.

Kate Faber **Oestreich** is an associate professor of literature, writing, and new media at Coastal Carolina University in Conway, South Carolina. She and Jennifer Camden are coauthors of a book on transmedia adaptations of nineteenth-century novels, and Kate's scholarship and scholarly reviews have appeared in the *Victorians Institute Journal, Nineteenth-Century Gender Studies, The CEA Critic, ARIEL*, and the edited collection *Straight Writ Queer*. Oestreich is on the Nineteenth Century Studies Association's board and web and publicity committee.

Indu **Ohri** is an English Ph.D. student at the University of Virginia. She is writing her dissertation, *The Cultural Anxieties in Victorian Women's Ghost Stories, 1847–1917*, which examines how the ghosts in women's supernatural fiction reflect various unspeakable social concerns of late–Victorian and early-twentieth-century Britain. Her article examining the ways in which Amelia Edwards's ghost stories offer an ecocritical critique of the destructive effects of Victorian tourism has appeared in the *VIJ Digital Annex* 42.

Carolyn **Oulton** is a professor of Victorian literature and director of the International Centre for Victorian Women Writers at Canterbury Christ Church University. Her books include *Literature and Religion in Mid-Victorian England: From Dickens to Eliot, Romantic Friendship in Victorian Literature, Let the Flowers Go: A Life of Mary Cholmondeley, Below the Fairy City: A Life of Jerome K. Jerome* and *Dickens and the Myth of the Reader*.

Joanne Ella **Parsons** lectures at Bath Spa University. Her Ph.D. thesis is titled "Food and the Male Body: Narratives of Consumption in the Nineteenth-Century Novel." She is co-editor of *The Victorian Male Body* and editor of the *Wilkie Collins Journal*. Her work has also been published in *Nineteenth-Century Contexts*.

Joan **Passey** is a Ph.D. student under the South West and Wales Doctoral Training Partnership between the universities of Exeter and Bristol. She has published work on the sonic Gothic of Ann Radcliffe and Wilkie Collins's dark coastlines.

Christopher **Pittard** is a senior lecturer in English literature at the University of Portsmouth, UK. His publications include the books *Purity and Contamination in Late Victorian Detective Fiction* and *The Cambridge Companion to Sherlock Holmes* (co-edited with Janice M. Allan), and articles in journals including *Studies in the Novel, 19: Interdisciplinary Studies in the Long Nineteenth Century, Women: A Cultural Review, Clues: A Journal of Detection*, and *Victorian Periodicals Review*.

Marjolein **Platjee** is working on a doctoral thesis on representations of the dying and dead body in British Victorian literature and culture at the Amsterdam School for Cultural Analysis at the University of Amsterdam. In her thesis she specifically focuses on popular fiction, such as penny bloods, as well as sensation and detective novels.

Melissa **Purdue** is an associate professor of English at Minnesota State University, Mankato. She has published *New Woman Writers, Authority and the Body* with Stacey Floyd and a critical edition of Rosa Praed's *Fugitive Anne: A Romance of the Unexplored Bush*. Her most recent publications have been on Clemence Housman and Rhoda Broughton. She is also a founding editor/coeditor-in-chief of the journal *Nineteenth-Century Gender Studies*.

Crescent **Rainwater** is a Ph.D. candidate in English at the University of California Los Angeles. She is writing a dissertation titled "Modernist Women and *fin-de-siècle* Culture: Lucas Malet, Netta Syrett, Ada Leverson, Dorothy Richardson, and the Development of the English Novel." In 2010 Crescent completed her master's in gender, sexuality, and culture at University College Dublin.

Lisa C. **Robertson** received her Ph.D. from the University of Warwick in 2016. Her doctoral research examines the literary representation of new forms of domestic architecture in the latter half of the nineteenth century. With Flore Janssen she is editing a collection of essays on the author and activist Margaret Harkness.

Meri-Jane **Rochelson** is a professor emerita of English at Florida International University. She is the author of *A Jew in the Public Arena: The Career of Israel Zangwill* and editor of *Children of the Ghetto: A Study of a Peculiar People*, by Israel Zangwill. She is also editor of a critical edition of Zangwill's *The Melting-Pot*.

Paul Raphael **Rooney** is an early-career researcher of Victorian popular fiction and print culture. He has been an Irish Research Council postdoctoral fellow at Trinity College Dublin and a research assistant at the National University of Ireland, Galway. He has published in *Victorian Periodicals Review, Women's Writing, Publishing History*, and

Victorian Fiction Beyond the Canon. He coedited the collection *Media and Print Consumption in Nineteenth-Century Britain*. His first monograph is *Railway Reading and Late Victorian Literary Series*.

Tracey S. **Rosenberg** earned her Ph.D. from the University of Edinburgh with a dissertation on gender construction and individualism in the work of Mona Caird. She subsequently edited a critical edition of Caird's *The Wing of Azrael*. She teaches on the online M.Sc. in creative writing at the University of Edinburgh, and has published a historical novel and two poetry pamphlets. She lives in Scotland.

Nicholas **Ruddick** is a professor emeritus of English at the University of Regina, where he taught science fiction, late-nineteenth-century literature, and fairy tales, among other courses. He is the editor of the Broadview Edition of Grant Allen's *The Woman Who Did* (2004) and the author or editor of nine other books. His most recent are *The Fire in the Stone: Prehistoric Fiction from Charles Darwin to Jean M. Auel* and *Science Fiction Adapted to Film*.

Anne-Louise **Russell** is an AHRC funded Ph.D. student at Anglia Ruskin University in Cambridge. Her project examines the moment between 1872 and 1876 when four literary magazines were edited by female sensation novelists. She investigates how these author-editors responded to cultural change and legislative events, and how they contributed to agitation for social reform. Her research situates the 1870s revisions to Ellen Wood's *Parkwater* amid contemporary debates about responsibility for the alarming rates of infant mortality among illegitimate children.

Ramit **Samaddar** is an assistant professor of English at Jadavpur University, Kolkata, India, where he received his B.A. (honors), M.A., and M.Phil. degrees in English. He has been awarded the Charles Wallace India Trust Research Grant for his doctoral thesis on Anthony Trollope. His areas of interest are eighteenth- and nineteenth-century literature and culture, travel writing, postcolonial studies, and film criticism. His recent publications include a coauthored essay on Bollywood war films in *A Companion to the War Film*. He is a member of the Trollope Society (UK).

Samuel **Saunders** is a Ph.D. student at Liverpool John Moores University, UK. His thesis explores the role of the Victorian periodical press on the development of crime and detective fiction across the mid– to late–Victorian era, and historicizes these genres alongside the development of law enforcement across Victorian Britain. He has written for *Law, Crime and History* and the *Wilkie Collins Journal*.

Anne **Schwan** is an associate professor and head of humanities and culture at Edinburgh Napier University. She is author of *Convict Voices: Women, Class, and Writing about Prison in Nineteenth-Century England* and co-author of *How to Read Foucault's* Discipline and Punish. Her research ranges from Victorian popular fiction to contemporary television, with a focus on representations of incarcerated women. She is also interested in university-prison engagement.

Mary L. **Shannon** is a senior lecturer in the English and Creative Writing Department at the University of Roehampton, London. Her monograph *Dickens, Reynolds and Mayhew on Wellington Street: The Print Culture of a Victorian Street* won the 2016 Colby prize. She is currently on the board of RSVP and writing about networks of illustrators in early-nineteenth-century London.

Daniel P. **Shea** is an associate professor of English at Austin Peay State University, where he serves as coordinator of the graduate program in English and teaches courses in Victorian literature and culture. He has published on William Morris, Richard Jefferies, Olive Schreiner, H. G. Wells, and Ai Weiwei. He co-edited *Culture on Two Wheels: The Bicycle in Literature and Film* with Jeremy Withers. His research considers rural England and the Victorian agricultural depression.

Suman **Sigroha** teaches English language and literature at the Indian Institute of Technology Mandi, India. Her Ph.D. was on representations, the role of memory, and stereotyping in British literature located in India. She has worked on colonial, imperial and neocolonial aspects focusing on gender, landscape, and more. She has been interested in the popular for some time now and has been researching and teaching its various aspects to graduate and undergraduate students.

Fiona **Snailham** is a Ph.D. candidate at the University of Greenwich, UK. Her thesis aims to re-evaluate the work of Eliza Lynn Linton, investigating the social and textual networks within which she wrote in order to re-establish her reputation as an actor of note in the nineteenth-century literary market. A former high school teacher, she holds B.A.s in law (Oxford) and English (OU), and an M.A. in nineteenth-century literature and culture (Reading).

Tabitha **Sparks** is an associate professor of the nineteenth-century novel at McGill University in Montreal, Canada. Her publications include *The Doctor in the Victorian Novel: Family Practices*, *Victorian Medicine and Popular Culture* (coedited with Louise Penner), a critical edition of Margaret Harkness's *A City Girl*, and a variety of essays and book chapters.

Elizabeth **Steere** researches class, culture, gender, and genre in nineteenth-century literature. She explores these concepts in her book, *The Female Servant and Sensation Fiction: "Kitchen Literature"* and her articles appearing in *Women's Writing, Journal of Neo-Victorian Studies, Victorian Network, GRAAT: Anglophone Studies*, and *Nineteenth-Century Gender Studies*.

Richard **Storer** is a senior lecturer in English at Leeds Trinity University, UK. He has published essays on Hall Caine, Bram Stoker, and other Victorian writers, and is a contributor to the *ODNB*. He is also the author of the volume *F. R. Leavis* (2009) in the Routledge Critical Thinkers series.

About the Contributors

Jessica **Straley** is an associate professor of English at the University of Utah. She is the author of *Evolution and Imagination in Victorian Children's Literature*. Her most recent essay publications include "Oscar Wilde's Fairy Tales and the Evolution of Lying" in *Oscar Wilde and the Cultures of Childhood*, ed. Joseph Bristow.

Laurence **Talairach-Vielmas** is a professor of English at the University of Toulouse Jean Jaurès. She is the author of *Fairy Tales, Natural History and Victorian Culture; Wilkie Collins, Medicine and the Gothic*; and *Moulding the Female Body in Victorian Fairy Tales and Sensation Novels*. She has also edited Mary Elizabeth Braddon's *Thou Art the Man* and *Dead Love Has Chains*.

Antony **Taylor** is a modern British historian working in the field of nineteenth-century popular politics. He has written widely about radical political culture and with reference to platform politics in Britain. His most recent book is *"London's Burning": Pulp Fiction, the Politics of Terrorism and the Destruction of the Capital in British Popular Culture, 1840–2005*.

Emilie **Taylor-Brown** is a postdoctoral research fellow at St. Anne's College, Oxford. She received her Ph.D. in 2016 from the University of Warwick with a thesis titled: "Miasmas, Mosquitoes, and Microscopes: Parasitology and the British Literary Imagination 1885–1935." She has published in literary and scientific journals and her research, as part of the European Research Council funded Diseases of Modern Life project, explores gastrointestinal health in the nineteenth century from an interdisciplinary perspective.

Scott C. **Thompson** is a graduate student in English literature at Temple University in Philadelphia. He specializes in novel studies, realism, and popular literature in the nineteenth century. His current project examines the relationship between realism, sensation, and sympathy in novels by Mary Elizabeth Braddon and George Eliot, tracing the ways in which the authors utilize the genres to engage their readers.

Barbara **Tilley** is a visiting assistant professor in the Writing, Rhetoric, and Discourse Department at DePaul University. She teaches a range of courses, focusing on Sherlock Holmes, social injustices in prison, and death and dying. She has most recently published a critical edition of Emma Frances Brooke's *A Superfluous Woman*. Tilley is working on a critical biography of Brooke's literary works and her life as a socialist in the Fabian Society.

Tom **Ue** was educated at Linacre College, University of Oxford, and at University College London. He is the author of *Gissing, Shakespeare, and the Life of Writing* and *George Gissing* and the editor of George Gissing, *The Private Papers of Henry Ryecroft*. Ue is the Frederick Banting Postdoctoral Fellow in the Department of English at the University of Toronto Scarborough and an honorary research associate at University College London.

Jessica R. V**aldez** is an assistant professor of English at the University of Hong Kong. Her book project, *Re-Forming Nation and Newspaper in the Victorian Novel*, examines the depiction of news and newspapers in nineteenth-century British novels. Other publications include "How to Write Yiddish in English, or Israel Zangwill and Multilingualism in *Children of the Ghetto*," published in *Studies in the Novel* in 2015. She received her Ph.D. from Johns Hopkins University.

Minna **Vuohelainen** is a lecturer in English at City, University of London. Her research focuses on *fin-de-siècle* print culture, Gothic and crime fiction, spatial theory, Richard Marsh, and Thomas Hardy. Her publications include the monograph *Richard Marsh*, the coedited essay collections *Interpreting Primo Levi: Interdisciplinary Perspectives* and *Richard Marsh, Popular Fiction and Literary Culture, 1890–1915: Rereading the fin de siècle*, scholarly articles on Gothic, crime fiction, and print culture, and four critical editions Marsh's fiction.

Tamara S. **Wagner** is an associate professor at Nanyang Technological University, Singapore. Her books include *Victorian Narratives of Failed Emigration: Settlers, Returnees, and Nineteenth-Century Literature in English*, *Financial Speculation in Victorian Fiction*, and *Longing: Narratives of Nostalgia in the British Novel, 1740–1890*. She has also edited collections on *Domestic Fiction in Colonial Australia and New Zealand*, *Victorian Settler Narratives*, and *Antifeminism and the Victorian Novel: Rereading Nineteenth-Century Women Writers*.

Alison S. **Wallace** teaches composition and literature at the United States Military Academy, West Point. She obtained her M.A. degree in English literature and society from the University of Edinburgh in 2015. Her concentration is in the Victorian and Enlightenment periods of British literature, with specific interest in Gothic and horror genres.

Alexis **Weedon** is a professor of publishing at the University of Bedfordshire, UK. She is author of *Victorian Publishing: The Economics of Book Production for the Mass Market*, co-author of *Elinor Glyn as Novelist, Moviemaker, Glamour-Icon and Businesswoman* and editor of *History of the Book in the West*.

Jacquelyn C. **Wenneker** is an instructor in the Los Rios Community College District. Her academic specializations are American nineteenth-century and British Victorian literature. Interests include the trans–Atlantic exchange of literature and culture during the 1800s, women writers, gender representation and social issues, and the novel as an emerging popular genre.

Judith **Wilt** is a professor of English emerita at Boston College, where she taught courses in Victorian literature, women's studies, and popular culture genres for more than thirty years before retiring in 2011. The most recent of her books are *Behind Her Times: Transition England in the Novels of Mary Arnold Ward* and *Women Writers and the Hero of Romance*. She is teaching a course on war stories and writing an essay on Flannery O'Connor.

About the Contributors

Harry **Wood** is a historian working on the cultural history of modern British invasion anxieties. He has taught in the History Department at the University of Liverpool, where he completed his Ph.D. in 2014, and in the Defence Studies Department at King's College London. His previous research has included work on invasion-scare fiction and theater, focusing on authors including H. G. Wells, George Griffith, and William Le Queux.

Erika **Wright** has appointments as a lecturer in the English Department and as a clinical instructor of family medicine at the Keck School of Medicine at the University of Southern California. Her book, *Reading for Health: Medical Narratives and the Nineteenth-Century Novel*, examines the rhetoric of disease prevention and health maintenance in fiction and health manuals. Her new project explores the ethics of professional secrecy in Victorian fiction.

Jude **Wright** is a visiting assistant professor at Loyola University Maryland where he specializes in nineteenth-century British literature. He received his Ph.D. from the University of South Florida in 2013 where he held a Presidential Doctoral Fellowship. His research is centered on Victorian anthropology and its relationship to *fin-de-siècle* literature. He is also working on a critical edition of Arthur Machen's novella *The Great God Pan*.

Bruce **Wyse** is an instructor in the department of English and film studies at Wilfrid Laurier University. His research interests include the representation of mesmerism in nineteenth-century literature, Gothic fiction, the *fin-de-siècle*, and neo–Victorianism. He has published articles on Bulwer-Lytton's *A Strange Story*, his "The Haunted and the Haunters," Conan Doyle's *The Parasite*, Horace Smith's *Mesmerism*, and Du Maurier's *Trilby*, as well as articles on film, television, contemporary drama, and crime fiction.

Emilio **Zampieri** holds a Ph.D. in English literature specializing in the popular fiction of the Victorian *fin de siècle*. His undergraduate thesis analyzed the narrative structure of Bram Stoker's *Dracula*, and his Ph.D. thesis explored social concerns in Guy Boothby's Dr. Nikola series (1895–1901). He takes an interest in the Gothic literature revival of the late nineteenth century and the authorial strategies of Victorian serial fiction.

Index

Ada, the Betrayed, or the Murder at the Old Smithy 3, 142, 206
Adventures of Sherlock Holmes 3–5, 65, 113
Ainsworth, William Harrison 5, 24, 27, 50, 64, 119, 141, 171–172, 179, 184, 241, 243
alcoholism 5–7, 85, 86, 181, 229, 272
Alice's Adventures in Wonderland 7–8, 38–39, 44, 91, 257
All Men Are Liars 8, 249
Allen, Grant 8–9, 10, 51, 65, 76, 143, 159, 188, 210, 238, 247, 267, 269, 270, 271
A.L.O.E. (A Lady of England) 9
amnesia 247
anarchism 9–11, 52, 79, 102, 106, 190–192, 230, 265; see also political violence
anesthesia 11–12, 118, 152, 208
An Angel of Pity 12–13, 147
Anglo-Indian fiction 13–14, 123–126, 132, 134, 234–235; see also India
animals 9, 14–16, 28–29, 46, 62, 79, 125, 129, 131, 132, 149, 157, 175, 180, 240, 256–258, 264; see also vivisection
Anna Lombard 16–17, 61, 203, 212
Anna Marsden's Experiment 17
anti-Semitism 17–19, 93, 131
Arkwright, Richard 19, 73, 195
At Heart a Rake 19

Ballantyne, R.M. 16, 20, 45
Baring-Gould, Sabine 21, 264
Barrie, J.M. 21–22, 39, 57, 61, 74, 84, 157, 179, 221, 245
The Battle of Dorking 22, 40, 102, 126, 208, 210
Belgravia, a London Magazine 9, 22, 32, 37, 40, 50, 105, 113, 131
Beneath the Wave 23, 205
Bennett, Arnold 10, 23, 39, 40, 57, 93, 245, 267
Benson, Edward Frederic 23–24, 76, 112
Bentley's Miscellany 5, 24, 29, 179, 193
Besant, Annie 33, 105, 230

Besant, Walter 9, 24, 43–44, 49, 51, 52, 105, 144, 161, 194, 197–198, 198, 232–233
The Beth Book 25, 100
A Bid for Fortune; or, Dr. Nikola's Vendetta 25, 31
The Big Bow Mystery 25, 277
bigamy 25–27, 31, 49, 114, 125, 147, 155, 159, 199, 202, 205
Black, Clementina 28
Black Beauty 16, 28–29
Blaze de Bury, Marie Pauline Rose 29
The Book of the Thousand Nights and a Night 29–30
Boothby, Guy Newell 25, 30–31, 65, 76, 99, 164–165, 189, 266
Braddon, Mary Elizabeth 6, 11–12, 22–23, 23, 26–27, 31–32, 40, 48, 49, 50, 53, 64, 84, 93, 110, 118, 131–132, 136–138, 155–156, 183, 187, 202, 205, 206, 212, 216, 222, 243, 250, 251, 252, 271, 275
Brontë, Anne 6, 15, 62, 69, 163, 190, 203, 204
Brontë, Charlotte 15, 23, 26, 41, 42, 46, 62, 68, 69, 84, 98, 155, 173, 176, 178, 190, 203, 204, 261
Brontë, Emily 15, 42, 62, 69, 84, 91, 118, 121, 178, 190, 203
Brooke, Emma Frances 33–34
Broughton, Rhoda 34–35, 87–88, 138, 173, 213
Bulwer-Lytton, Edward 15, 31, 35, 54–55, 64, 76, 94, 141, 158, 167, 171–172, 204, 208, 210, 225–226, 228, 247

Caine, Hall [Sir Thomas Henry Hall Caine] 35–36, 76, 110, 250
Caird, Mona 36–37, 212, 267
Cameron, Mrs. H. Lovett 37
Carey, Rosa Nouchette 37, 275
Carmilla 37–38, 139, 183, 203, 255
Carroll, Lewis 6–8, 38–39, 44, 46, 47, 84, 91, 257
Cassell's publications 39, 52, 187, 195, 201, 216
catnach broadsides 39–40, 243
Chatto & Windus 22, 40, 131, 180, 197, 209, 275

Chesney, George Tomkyns 22, 40, 126–127, 208, 210
child abuse 40–42, 43, 163, 177
childhood 7, 20, 21, 25, 35, 38, 40, 41, 42–43, 46, 47, 58, 66, 67, 133, 151, 159, 163, 167, 178–179, 199, 236, 265, 267
Children of the Ghetto: A Study of a Peculiar People 44, 277
children's literature 7–8, 14, 15, 20, 21–22, 23–24, 28–29, 42, 44–47, 59, 67, 68, 83, 84, 92, 132, 133, 146, 167, 179, 198, 205, 207, 218, 219, 252, 272
Cholmondeley, Mary 47
circulating libraries 47–48, 117, 164, 214, 221
A City Girl: A Realistic Story 48, 105, 122, 180–181, 229
Clara Vaughan 48
class(es) 3, 5–7, 10, 16, 17, 18, 21, 22–23, 24, 25, 28, 29, 31, 32, 33, 42, 43, 44, 47, 48–51, 57, 59, 64, 65, 68, 69, 73, 74, 77, 78, 80–83, 85–86, 87, 90, 91, 92, 95, 97, 98, 99, 104–105, 106–108, 110, 118, 119, 133, 136–138, 141, 142, 143, 148, 149, 151, 153, 154, 161, 162–164, 165, 166, 169, 171, 178, 181, 184, 185, 186, 189, 192, 192–194, 197, 200, 201, 202, 204, 205, 208, 211, 214, 219, 220, 221, 222, 225, 226, 227, 229–232, 238, 239, 240, 246–248, 249, 251, 254, 258, 262, 267, 269, 271, 276
Cleeve, Lucas 51, 270
collaboration 5, 24, 51–52, 54, 58, 80, 97, 133, 136, 157, 191, 197, 223
Collins, William Wilkie 15, 26, 27, 31, 39, 40, 47, 48, 49–51, 51–52, 52–54, 62, 64, 67, 87, 90, 98, 107, 109, 112, 118, 121, 125, 148–150, 153, 154, 155–156, 157, 160–161, 202–203, 212, 215, 245, 250, 257–258, 268, 268–269, 271, 275
The Coming Race 15, 35, 54–55, 208, 210, 247
Conan Doyle, Arthur 3–5, 12, 55–56, 64–65, 77, 94, 108, 113, 114, 115, 148, 158, 165, 175, 182, 185,

195, 196, 203, 208, 216, 223, 223–225, 238–239, 241–243, 264
Concerning Isabel Carnaby 57
Corelli, Marie 36, 57–59, 76, 159, 165–166, 202, 208, 221, 233, 240, 243, 272–273
Craik, Dinah Mulock 59, 107, 176–177
cricket 59–61, 114, 195
Crockett, Samuel Rutherford 61
Cross, Victoria 16–17, 61, 203, 212, 270
Crowe, Catherine 61–62, 175, 238 264
The Curse Upon Mitre Square 62–63

The Detections of Miss Cusack 63, 80
detective fiction 9, 35, 57, 63–66, 74, 80, 88, 103, 110, 112, 116, 148, 151, 160, 175, 182, 196, 203, 213, 223, 226, 227, 239, 246, 252, 266, 268, 271
Dickens, Charles 5, 6, 15, 17–18, 24, 25, 35, 41, 42–43, 45, 46, 50–51, 51, 54, 59, 61, 62, 64, 65, 66–67, 67–68, 68–69, 88, 90, 91, 96, 98, 103, 119, 120, 121, 134, 139, 141–142, 153, 155, 157, 158, 159, 163, 172–173, 177–178, 186, 190, 193, 197, 212, 213, 216, 221, 223, 226, 258
Dickens, Mary Angela 67, 68
Diehl, Alice Mangold 68
disease 5–6, 11, 20, 25, 68–70, 100–101, 107, 109, 117, 152, 155, 156, 160, 181–183
Dixon, Ella Hepworth 70, 237
Dr. Phillips: A Maida Vale Idyll 19, 70–71, 92–93, 153
Dora Thorne 71
Dorcas Dene, Detective: Her Adventures 66, 71, 227
Dracula 7, 36, 38, 42, 71, 71–73, 79, 91, 99, 122, 130, 148, 150, 153, 155, 158, 182, 183, 189, 203, 236–237, 240, 253, 255, 259, 264, 272
Driven Home: A Tale of Destiny 19, 73
Dudeney, Mrs. Henry 73
Du Maurier, George 73–74, 253

East Lynne 6, 27, 49, 51, 57, 69, 74, 147, 243, 271
Edwards, Amelia Ann Blandford 74–75, 76, 221
Egerton, George 75–76, 132, 212
Egypt 74, 75, 76–77, 79, 94, 99, 112, 131, 138, 148, 158, 159, 164–165, 181, 189, 237, 266
Eliot, George 15, 41, 59, 62, 68, 69, 79, 118, 121, 141, 153, 163, 165, 173, 177, 182, 190, 208, 213, 261
Ellis, Sarah Stickney 77, 85–86, 229
eugenics 8, 36, 76, 78–80, 129, 150, 274
Eustace, Robert 63, 66, 80

evangelicalism 9, 20–21, 45, 80–83, 113, 144, 160, 217, 219
Everett-Green, Evelyn 83
Ewing, Juliana Horatia 14, 45, 77, 82, 83–85, 177

fairy tales 45–46, 83–85, 167, 227, 237
Family Herald; or Useful Information and Amusement for the Million 85
Family Secrets; or, Hints to Those Who Would Make Home Happy 78, 85–86
Fane, Violet 86–87, 245
fathers/fatherhood 6, 87–88, 205
food 89–91, 92, 96, 259
Fothergill, Jessie 91–92
Four on an Island 92
Frankau, Julia 19–20, 70–71, 92–93

Gaskell, Elizabeth 6, 15, 41, 69, 87, 163, 175, 177, 184, 194, 213, 223
Gerard; or, The World, The Flesh and The Devil 93
Ghosts: Being the Experiences of Flaxman Low 94
Ginx's Baby 94–95
Gissing, George 6, 95–96, 114, 170, 194
gothic fiction 7, 15, 72, 96–100, 129, 139, 142, 144, 149, 158, 164, 189, 203, 213, 223, 240, 258, 264, 268
Grand, Sarah 25, 36, 100–101, 109–110, 110, 167–169, 180, 197, 212, 266
grave robbing 101, 153
Gray, Maxwell 101, 225
The Green Carnation 101–102
Griffith, George 10, 267
Griffiths, Arthur 103
Guy Livingstone; or, Thorough 103

Haggard, H. Rider 104, 107–108, 111, 121–122, 131–132, 135, 140, 143, 158, 165, 188, 203, 208, 210, 216, 217–218, 247, 250, 267
Harkness, Margaret 19, 48, 77, 104–105, 122, 130, 180–181, 229, 231
Harraden, Beatrice 105–106
health 18, 32, 68–70, 90, 106–109, 114, 134
Heart and Science 15, 54, 109, 156, 257
The Heavenly Twins 25, 79, 100, 109–110, 212
Heinemann 110, 209, 229, 237, 244, 251
Henry Dunbar 49, 51, 110, 143, 216
Henty, G.A. 16, 45, 111, 121, 123, 135, 148, 191, 252
Her Father's Name 111–112, 147
Hichens, Robert Smythe 77, 88–89, 101–102, 110, 112, 194
Hocking, Joseph 8, 113, 249
Holmes, Sherlock 3–5, 50, 55–56, 64–65, 108, 113, 114, 116, 130, 148,

161, 175, 195, 203, 208, 216, 217, 223, 239, 241, 243, 247, 266, 201, 203, 206
Hornung, E.W. 39, 113–114, 195, 238–239
Hubback, Catherine 114–115
Hume, Fergusson Wright 64–65, 115, 166, 204–205, 221
Hunt, Violet 116–117
Hurst and Blackett 117
hypnotism 52, 93, 157–159
hysteria 112, 117–119, 153, 155, 156

illustration 7, 24, 39, 40, 46, 55, 79, 106, 119–120, 142, 143, 148, 165, 166, 171, 185, 187, 188, 201, 204, 215, 217, 223, 239, 246, 253, 263
imperial adventure 13, 16, 20, 45, 60, 104, 107, 111, 121–122, 132–133, 140, 148, 203, 254
In Darkest London 19, 105, 122, 131
In Gipsy Tents 123
incest 42, 147, 155
India 9, 13, 14, 22, 30, 40, 45, 51, 53, 60, 61, 65, 100, 110, 121, 123–126, 132, 134–135, 137, 138, 148, 151, 159, 161, 181, 203, 206, 219, 224, 234–235, 241, 264
invasion literature 19, 22, 76, 89, 102, 122, 126–127, 128–129, 140, 148, 164, 182, 191–192, 199–200, 219–220, 247, 259–260, 274–275
The Invasion Network 127–128
The Invasion of 1910 127, 128
Iota 127, 274
The Island of Doctor Moreau 15, 129, 153, 156, 262

Jack the Ripper 19, 25, 62, 116, 129–131, 227
The Jewel of Seven Stars 131, 164, 237
Joseph's Coat 131
Joshua Haggard's Daughter 131–132
The Jungle Book 16, 45, 132, 135, 212

Keynotes 75–76, 109, 132
Kidnapped 132–133, 203, 235
kidnapping 3, 114, 238, 272
Kingsford, Anna 77, 133
Kingsley, Charles 133–134, 145, 149, 179, 207
Kingston, William Henry Giles 134
Kipling, Joseph Rudyard 13, 16, 39, 45, 46, 84, 111, 121, 122, 125, 126, 132, 134–135, 143, 145, 179, 185, 203, 238, 264, 266

Lady Audley's Secret 6, 26–27, 31, 50, 53, 64, 118, 136–138, 143, 155, 156, 202, 243, 251
Lawless, Emily 138
Lee, Vernon 113, 210
Le Fanu, Joseph Sheridan 34, 37–38, 50, 139, 173, 183, 203, 213, 253–254, 255

Index 311

Le Queux, William Tufnell 39, 102, 106, 122, 126, 127, 128–129, 139–140, 191
Linton, Eliza Lynn 51, 105–106, 140–141, 197, 233
Lloyd, Edward 120, 141, 143, 185, 187, 188, 206, 241, 255
Lloyd's Penny Atlas and Weekly Register of Novel Entertainment 142, 143, 187
London Journal; and Weekly Record of Literature Science and Art 39, 143, 166, 187, 188, 198, 216, 217, 228
Longman's Magazine 143–144, 246
The Lost Stradivarius 144
Lucy, the Factory Girl 144
The Ludgate Monthly 65, 144

Machen, Arthur 72, 98, 99, 144–145, 156, 240, 243, 258
Malet, Lucas 118, 145–146, 245, 258
Marryat, Florence 12, 19, 26, 50, 52, 111, 125, 146–147, 158, 212, 264
Marsh, Richard 7, 76, 79, 98, 122, 148, 156, 158, 182, 189, 238, 240
Martin Hewitt, Investigator 31, 65, 113, 148, 161, 266
masculinity 14, 16, 20, 88, 103, 133, 148–150, 156, 195–196, 218, 226, 254, 270, 273
Maugham, William Somerset 110, 150–151
Meade, L.T. 11, 14, 39, 63, 66, 80, 92, 101, 144, 151, 247, 267, 272
medicine 12, 22, 53, 55, 68, 107, 109, 129, 150, 151–153, 157, 160, 183, 211, 234, 239, 262
melodrama 19, 21, 35, 48, 58, 63, 73, 87, 88, 112, 118, 120, 136, 140, 144, 153–154, 185, 187, 189, 197, 202, 206, 213, 226, 227, 228, 231, 232, 239, 241, 245, 272, 275
mental illness 6, 32, 109, 118, 137, 153, 154–156, 215, 269
Mesmerism 12, 54, 66, 93, 109, 117, 148, 157–159, 174, 175, 182, 210, 262
The Mighty Atom 58, 159
Miss Cayley's Adventures 9, 65, 159
Mr. Bazalgette's Agent 157, 159–160
Mona Maclean, Medical Student 153, 160
The Moonstone 50, 53, 64, 121, 125, 160–161, 203, 215
Morrison, Arthur 6, 31, 41, 43, 65, 113, 148, 194, 196, 238, 266
motherhood 33, 36, 38, 51, 114, 118, 162–164, 168, 244, 270, 274
mummies 76, 94, 102, 131, 164–166, 189, 237
murder 3, 6, 12, 18, 19, 20, 23, 25, 26, 31, 42, 48, 49, 50, 58, 62–63, 65, 74, 87, 101, 103, 110, 111, 112, 115, 116, 119, 129–131, 132, 133, 142, 147, 161, 165, 166, 172, 173, 174, 184, 185, 194, 195, 204, 205, 206, 207, 224, 238, 239, 241, 242, 243, 247, 251, 252, 262, 267, 268, 271, 272
The Murder of Delicia 58, 165–166
The Mysteries of London (1844–56) 97, 154, 166, 185, 192, 217, 243, 256
The Mystery of a Hansom Cab 166, 221

Nesbit, Edith 45, 83, 84, 85, 167, 222, 238, 267
The New Monthly Magazine 5, 167, 179, 184, 206
new woman 6, 17, 19, 23, 34, 35, 36, 37, 47, 51, 57, 65, 66, 72, 76, 79, 92, 99, 100, 105, 109, 113, 116, 118, 124, 129, 131, 147, 150, 158, 159, 160, 165, 167–170, 172, 180, 197, 198, 200, 212, 218, 222, 223, 233, 237, 244, 245, 246, 248, 254, 261, 263, 264, 267, 270, 271, 274
Newgate Novels 5, 24, 35, 64, 141, 148, 170–172, 213, 241
Nigel Bartram's Ideal 172
The Night Side of Nature; or, Ghosts and Ghost Seers 61–62, 172–173, 175
Not Wisely, but Too Well 34, 173
The Notting Hill Mystery 64, 173–174

The occult 35, 37, 54, 76, 89, 94, 102, 106, 131, 133, 144, 145, 147, 148, 158, 160, 174–175, 182, 194, 210, 264, 269
Oliphant, Margaret Oliphant Wilson 26, 34, 77, 88, 117, 143, 175–176, 203, 210, 213, 250, 253, 269, 274
Orphans 41, 107, 135, 142, 150, 163, 174, 177–179, 194, 234, 260
Ouida 14, 16, 26, 40, 167, 168, 169, 179, 180, 213, 244, 254–255, 257
Out of Work 48, 105, 122, 180–181, 229

parasite/parasitology 94, 175, 181–184
Parkwater 184
Paul Ferroll 184
Pearson's Magazine 23, 185
penny bloods 3, 185–186, 201, 205, 206, 220, 255–256
penny dreadful 3, 60, 97, 98, 120, 141, 142, 149, 154, 185–186, 213, 220, 240, 241, 258, 259
penny fiction periodicals 39, 49, 85, 143, 186–188, 198, 206
Penny Sunday Times and People's Police Gazette 142, 188–189
Pharos the Egyptian 76, 99, 164, 189, 266
physiognomy 79, 107, 189–190
poverty 6, 20, 25, 55, 62, 69, 91, 97, 98, 104, 116, 122, 130, 136, 148, 161, 180, 192–194, 205, 220, 233, 258, 261
The Purple Cloud 194–195, 220
The Queen Anne's Gate Mystery 19, 195

Raffles stories 50, 113, 114, 195–196, 239
railway bookstalls 196, 220–221, 246, 275
Reade, Charles 12, 26, 27, 32, 153, 155, 197
The Rebel of the Family 141, 197
The Revolt of Man 24, 197–198
Reynolds's Miscellany of romance, general literature, science, and art 39, 166, 187, 198
Rice, James 24, 40, 51
Riddell, Charlotte 41, 147, 198–199, 213, 222
The Riddle of the Sands 122, 126, 199–200
Robert Elsmere 200–201, 202, 260–261
Robin Hood and Little John; or, the Merry Men of Sherwood Forest 201
Robinson, Frederick William 201–202
romance fiction 13, 14, 24, 55, 58, 71, 72, 74, 76, 87, 88, 93, 97, 102, 105, 108, 109, 112, 117, 121, 124, 129, 143, 147, 148, 151, 154, 179, 180, 184, 197, 202–203, 208, 223, 231, 245, 254, 261, 263, 275
Romanies/gypsies 123, 203–205, 272
Russell, Dora 23, 205, 250
Rymer, James Malcolm 3, 97, 120, 141, 142, 186, 198, 205–206, 241, 255–256

St. Martin's Eve 206–207, 271
science 7, 8, 15, 22, 46, 47, 58, 73, 84, 85, 90, 94, 96, 107, 109, 131, 133, 143, 148, 150, 152, 153, 156, 158, 161, 185, 189, 190, 198, 200, 204, 206, 207–208, 236, 245, 256, 257, 258
science fiction 8, 15, 35, 54, 56, 99, 102, 106, 126, 129, 164, 182, 192, 194, 197, 203, 209–211, 220, 223, 234, 239, 245, 246, 262, 266
self-harm 12, 211–212, 243
Sewell, Anna 16, 28–29
Sewell, Elizabeth Missing 217, 219
sensation fiction 6, 11, 20, 22, 23, 25, 26, 31, 32, 34, 35, 37, 40, 41, 42, 48, 49, 53, 54, 57, 58, 61, 62, 64, 65, 67, 68, 74, 75, 81, 83, 84, 87, 88, 98, 99, 103, 107, 109, 110, 118, 127, 138, 139, 142, 143, 147, 148, 149, 151, 153, 154, 155, 172, 173, 179, 184, 191, 196, 197, 199, 201, 202, 205, 206, 211, 212–216, 217, 219, 221, 226, 227, 229, 238, 239, 246, 247, 249, 250, 251, 252, 253, 254, 257, 259, 266, 268, 269, 271, 273, 276
serials/serialization/series 1, 9, 12, 17, 22, 23, 24, 25, 29, 31, 34, 37, 39, 43, 48, 49, 51, 52, 54, 55, 56,

60, 61, 65, 66, 71, 80, 82, 85, 86, 96, 97, 102, 103, 106, 111, 113, 119, 120, 121, 122, 127, 128, 135, 136, 139, 141, 142, 143, 144, 148, 159, 166, 172, 173, 176, 179, 184, 185, 187, 188, 189, 192, 193, 196, 197, 198, 200, 201, 205, 206, 207, 209, 212, 215–217, 219, 223, 228, 229, 230, 231, 232, 234, 235, 237, 238, 239, 241, 248, 250, 251, 252, 253, 254, 258, 263, 264, 265, 266, 267, 268, 269, 271, 273, 275
She 76, 99, 104, 121, 158, 203, 208, 210, 216, 217–218, 267
Sherwood, Mary Martha 4 5, 179, 217, 218–219, 245
Shiel, M.P. 119, 120, 126, 194–195, 219–220, 274–275
shilling shockers 10, 62, 196, 220–221, 239
short stories 3, 8, 11, 19, 29, 31, 35, 36, 47, 52, 54, 55, 56, 58, 59, 61, 62, 65, 67, 68, 73, 75, 75, 77, 80, 85, 92, 95, 101, 105, 106, 111, 112, 113, 114, 116, 125, 129, 132, 134, 138, 143, 144, 145, 146, 148, 151, 157, 158, 159, 164, 170, 177, 179, 182, 185, 188, 192, 194, 198, 201, 203, 209, 210, 212, 220, 221–223, 223, 229, 232, 234, 235, 238, 246, 249, 250, 255, 261, 264, 266, 271
The Sign of Four 4, 55, 65, 113, 125, 203, 208, 223–225
silver fork fiction 35, 225–227
Sims, George Robert 65, 66, 71, 192, 227
Skene, Felicia 227–228
Smythies, Mrs Gordon 85, 228–229
Social Distinction; or, Hearts and Homes 78, 229
socialism 8, 33, 34, 48, 102, 105, 106, 133, 167, 180, 181, 191, 195, 208, 229–232, 244, 246, 261, 262, 265
The Society of Authors 24, 232–233
The Sorrows of Satan 233, 240, 243
Steel, Flora Annie 13, 124, 234–235
Stevenson, Robert Louis 7, 10, 20, 42, 45, 52, 71, 72, 79, 98, 107, 108, 110, 121, 130, 132, 133, 143, 144, 153, 156, 182, 192, 203, 206, 211, 221, 235–236, 239–240, 252, 258, 272, 275
Stoker, Bram 7, 15, 32, 36, 38, 42, 52, 71–73, 76, 79, 91, 98, 108, 122, 130, 131, 139, 148, 150, 153, 155, 158, 164, 182, 183, 189, 203, 208, 236–237, 240, 255, 259, 264, 272
The Story of a Modern Woman 70, 237
The Story of Lilly Dawson 62, 238
Strand Magazine 3, 65, 113, 144, 148, 159, 161, 185, 196, 238–239, 266
Strange Case of Dr. Jekyll and Mr. Hyde 42, 71, 72, 79, 98, 130, 153, 182, 211, 221, 235, 239–240, 258, 272
The String of Pearls 97, 142, 185, 187, 205, 206, 241
A Study in Scarlet 4, 55, 64, 65, 113, 116, 203, 221, 241–243, 266
suicide 7, 12, 23, 66, 109, 111, 173, 174, 189, 205, 233, 239, 255, 258, 267, 270
A Sunless Heart 244
A Superfluous Woman 233, 244
Sutcliff, Halliwell 244–245
Swan Sonnenschein, William 86, 180, 229, 245
Symonds, Emily Morse 6, 245–246
Syrett, Netta 223, 246

technology 22, 58, 85, 117, 120, 126, 127, 175, 191, 209, 246–248, 259, 260, 266
temperance fiction 5, 8, 77, 85, 229, 248–249, 271
Tillotson's Fiction Bureau 23, 180, 205, 250–251
The Time Machine 79, 99, 183, 203, 208, 210, 248, 251, 262
Tinsley Brothers 173, 206, 251–252
The Trail of the Serpent 64, 252
Treasure Island 20, 45, 121, 203, 235, 252–253
Trilby 19, 74, 253
Trollope, Anthony 18, 27, 29, 107, 155, 177, 197, 212, 213, 221, 243
Trollope, Frances 41, 43, 193, 213

Uncle Silas 50, 139, 253–254
Under Two Flags 179, 244, 254–255

vampires 38, 42, 72, 79, 142, 147, 155, 158, 167, 181, 183, 203, 240, 255, 256
Varney the Vampyre; or: the Feast of Blood 97, 98, 99, 139, 142, 206, 220, 255–256

Victorian Popular Fiction Association 256
vivisection 12, 13, 14, 15, 36, 54, 109, 129, 133, 147, 156, 211, 256–258, 267; *see also* animals

The Wages of Sin 118, 258
Wagner, the Wehr-Wolf 97, 220, 258–259, 264
The War of the Worlds 183, 203, 208, 211, 247, 259, 262
Ward, Mrs. Humphry 200–201, 202, 233, 260–261, 276
W.B. Horner and Son 261
Weapons of Mystery 113, 261–262
Wells, Herbert George 8, 9, 15, 40, 57, 71, 79, 99, 102, 126, 129, 153, 156, 157, 167, 183, 185, 188, 203, 208, 209, 210, 211, 229, 238, 247, 248, 251, 258, 259, 260, 262–263, 270
The Were-Wolf 263–264
werewolves 259, 263, 264
Wilde, Oscar 10, 32, 45, 57, 70, 72, 76, 93, 98, 99, 101–102, 108, 112, 144, 155, 182, 183, 192, 195, 237, 240, 264–266, 272
Williamson, Mrs. Harcourt 266, 267–268
Windsor Magazine 31, 65, 161, 189, 196, 266–267
The Wing of Azrael 36, 212, 267
A Woman in Grey 266, 267–268
The Woman in White 49, 51, 52–54, 64, 90, 98, 107, 118, 148, 149, 156, 160, 268–269
The Woman Who Did 8, 51, 267, 269–270
The Woman Who Wouldn't 51, 270–271
Wood, Ellen 6, 12, 26, 27, 31, 49, 57, 69, 74, 87, 147, 163, 184, 206–207, 212, 243, 248, 253
A World of Girls 151, 272
Wormwood 58, 243, 272–273

Yates, Edmund Hodgson 179, 213, 245, 273
A Yellow Aster 129, 274
The Yellow Danger 126, 220, 274–275
yellowbacks 60, 116, 196, 275–276
Yonge, Charlotte Mary 52, 70, 82, 107, 149, 202, 213, 217, 219, 233, 276–277

Zangwill, Israel 110, 201, 277

www.ingramcontent.com/pod-product-compliance
Lightning Source LLC
Chambersburg PA
CBHW081539300426
44116CB00015B/2691